CONTEMPORARY ECONOMICS

D0164882

CONTEMPORARY ECONOMICS

AN APPLICATIONS APPROACH

6TH EDITION

ROBERT J. CARBAUGH

M.E.Sharpe
Armonk, New York
London, England

Copyright © 2011 by M.E. Sharpe, Inc.

All rights reserved. No part of this book may be reproduced in any form
without written permission from the publisher, M.E. Sharpe, Inc.,
80 Business Park Drive, Armonk, New York 10504.

The EuroSlavic and Transroman fonts used to create this work are © 1986–2010
Payne Loving Trust. EuroSlavic and Transroman are available
from Linguist's Software, Inc., www.linguistsoftware.
com, P.O. Box 580, Edmonds, WA 98020-0580 USA, tel (425) 775-1130.

Library of Congress Cataloging-in-Publication Data

Carbaugh, Robert J., 1946–
  Contemporary economics : an applications approach / Robert J. Carbaugh. — 6th ed.
    p. cm.
  ISBN 978-0-7656-2488-8 (pbk. : alk. paper)
  1. Economics—Textbooks. 2 United States—Economic conditions—Textbooks. I. Title.

  HB171.C277 2010
  330—dc22   2010000289

Printed in the United States of America

The paper used in this publication meets the minimum requirements of
American National Standard for Information Sciences
Permanence of Paper for Printed Library Materials,
ANSI Z 39.48-1984.

EB (p)   10   9   8   7   6   5   4   3   2   1

Brief Contents

Contents

PART **2**

The Microeconomy   27

CHAPTER **2**

Market Transactions:
Demand and Supply Analysis   28

CHAPTER **3**

Demand and Supply Applications   55

CHAPTER 4

Production and the Costs of Production   75

CHAPTER **7**

Labor Markets   151

CHAPTER **8**

Government and Markets   173

PART 3

The Macroeconomy   195

CHAPTER 9

The Mixed Economy of the United States   196

CHAPTER **10**

Gross Domestic Product and Economic Growth   221

CHAPTER **11**

The Business Cycle, Unemployment, and Inflation   245

CHAPTER **12**

Macroeconomic Instability: Aggregate Demand and Aggregate Supply   275

CHAPTER 13

Fiscal Policy and the Federal Budget   297

CHAPTER 14

Money and the Banking System   321

CHAPTER **15**

The Federal Reserve and Monetary Policy   345

PART 4

The International Economy   369

CHAPTER 16

The United States and the Global Economy   370

CHAPTER 17

International Finance   391

CHAPTER 18

Economic Systems and Developing Countries   411

Glossary   429

Index   441

NOTE ON ELECTRONIC MATERIALS

Contemporary Economics: An Applications Approach, 6th Edition, is available on the Sharpe eTc electronic textbook center, at www.sharpe-etext.com

Online access to a free Study Guide is available at www.sharpe-student.com (click on text cover).

Online resources for adopting instructors are available at www.sharpe-instructor.com

Preface

As a university instructor, I have enthusiastically taught a one-term survey of economics course for more than 25 years to undergraduate students majoring in business, economics, and other disciplines. Most of the students who take my course are still in their teens and have only a modest awareness of economics. They are interested in learning, but they want to know how economics relates to their daily lives. Learning economic theory, by itself, means little to most students. I sometimes hear students ask, "What good is theory if it doesn't help me get a job or increase my income?"

To make my course come alive for these students, I combine a clear and concise presentation of microeconomic and macroeconomic theory with an abundance of contemporary applications. To illustrate each economic principle, I relate real-world examples taken from current newspapers, magazines, government reports, and economic journals. Also, I show videos to my students that deal with issues such as Social Security reform, the flat-rate tax proposal, and the European Monetary Union. To help my students become informed consumers, I discuss topics such as obtaining mortgages with fixed or variable interest rates and assessing the cost of driving an automobile.

Indeed, combining real-world applications with an exciting and sometimes humorous presentation of economic theory is the main focus of my course. The positive feedback that I have received indicates that I have developed an approach to teaching that makes economics come alive for students.

This pedagogical approach is integrated into my textbook, *Contemporary Economics: An Applications Approach*, 6th edition. The strong sales of the first five editions of this text have convinced me that my approach is meeting the needs of a considerable number of students and faculty. It is with pleasure that I have prepared a sixth edition of this textbook.

MEETING STUDENTS' NEEDS

A challenge faced by instructors of economics survey courses is that many of their students will go on to take courses in the principles of microeconomics and the principles of macroeconomics. To be meaningful for these students, the survey course must provide an introduction to microeconomics and macroeconomics without duplicating the principles courses.

A strength of *Contemporary Economics* is that it addresses such a need. By combining a relatively small number of theoretical tools with an abundance of contemporary applications, my textbook is not an abbreviation of a principles textbook. Rather, it is a distinct survey of economics for economics majors who wish to take an introductory course before moving on to more rigorous courses in microeconomics and macroeconomics and for nonmajors who wish to take only one course in this field.

Contemporary Economics is written mainly for students at 4-year colleges and universities, as well as for students at community colleges. However, this textbook will also be highly attractive to high schools that offer an introductory course in economics.

DISTINGUISHING FEATURES

The distinguishing features of my textbook include a clear and concise presentation of economic theory, global coverage in every chapter, integration of contemporary issues throughout the theoretical presentations, and the inclusion of consumer economics topics.

Presentation of Theory

Presenting economic theory in a clear and easy-to-understand manner is the foundation of this textbook. Students can easily relate to the economic theories because they are presented in terms of realistic examples chosen to appeal to students of all backgrounds and abilities. For example, demand and supply analysis is presented in terms of the market for compact discs, the costs of production in terms of computer printers, perfect competition in terms of the Puget Sound Fishing Co., monopoly in terms of De Beers (the diamond monopoly), and oligopoly in terms of Boeing and Airbus. These contemporary examples are reinforced by additional real-world examples that come from publications such as the *Wall Street Journal, Business Week,* and the *New York Times.*

For example, Chapter 5 discusses why cable television rates are so high. The discussion combines theoretical topics such as barriers to entry, natural monopoly, and potential competition in the pricing of cable television. Because they are familiar with cable television, students can easily identify with its pricing implications.

Students who have read my textbook have commented not only that the presentation is clear and easy to understand, but also that they could remember the specific examples illustrating the theories throughout the textbook. Moreover, all diagrams throughout my textbook use numbers (for example, 10 CDs at a price of $10) on their axes to make the examples familiar and obvious to the student. Many other textbooks use letters on their axes (for example, *OA* units of product *X* at a price of *OY*), which students find remote from their daily lives. Finally, my textbook emphasizes only the economic models that are essential to an introductory understanding of economics: production possibilities analysis, demand and supply for particular markets, production and the costs of production, perfect competition and monopoly, and aggregate demand and supply.

Global Content

No survey of economics textbook can ignore the global economy. *Contemporary Economics* addresses this issue using a two-pronged approach. First, I globalize each chapter so that students will not think of the U.S. economy in isolated terms as they read this textbook.

For example, Chapter 7 discusses whether the outsourcing of jobs by U.S. companies is a threat or an opportunity for American workers. This topic has been publicized in the news media and is familiar to students. Here, they will learn how the U.S. labor market is linked to labor markets in other countries such as India and China.

I also introduce a global component by including separate chapters on international trade, finance, and development. Chapter 16, *The United States and the Global Economy,* discusses the principle of comparative advantage and the effects of free trade and protectionism. Chapter 17, *International Finance,* provides an introduction to the U.S. balance of payments, the foreign exchange market, and the factors that cause fluctuations in the dollar's exchange value. Chapter 18, *Economic Systems and Developing Countries,* discusses alternative economic systems and the role of developing countries in the global economy.

Real-World Applications

Contemporary Economics: An Applications Approach lives up to its name by emphasizing applications and policy questions as often as possible. I have written this textbook for the student who is taking economics for the first time, and I stress the material that students should and do find interesting about the study of our economy. Therefore, I have devoted much attention to applications and policy questions that students hear about in the news and bring from their own lives.

For example, Chapter 9 discusses the future of the U.S. Social Security system. Students learn how its pay-as-you-go system of social security is threatened when the number of workers paying taxes into the system falls relative to the number of beneficiaries. Of particular interest is whether Americans should be allowed to place a portion of their payroll taxes in personal retirement accounts.

Not only are my applications current, but also they show a concern for the diversity among students. As often as possible, I have used examples that are familiar to students: iPod, Microsoft, Northwest Airlines, Wendy's, Ticketmaster, and the like. In particular, here are a few of the many real-world applications that are included in the 6th edition:

- Yankees Slash Prices of Top Tickets to Fill Seats at New Park—Chapter 2

- Oil Prices on a Roller Coaster—Chapter 2

- State Governments Increase Cigarette Tax to Raise Revenue—Chapter 3

- Dell Sells Factories to Slash Costs—Chapter 4

- Acquisition Brews Culture Shock at Anheuser Busch—Chapter 6

- Cap and Trade: Emission Certificates Clears Skies of Acid Rain—Chapter 8

- McDonald's Hustles to Keep Its Burgers Sizzling in Lean Times—Chapter 11

- Social Security COLA: No Increase in Monthly Checks Hard to Swallow for Elderly—Chapter 11

- Is Deflation Good or Bad?—Chapter 12

- Economists Urge Congress to Leave the Fed Alone—Chapter 15

- The Term Auction Facility of the Federal Reserve—Chapter 15

Also, the 6th edition provides extensive coverage of the recession of 2007–2009. Chapter 11 discusses the nature of the recession and how it became global. The response of fiscal policy to the recession is discussed in Chapter 13 and the efforts of the Federal Reserve to stabilize the economy during the recession are discussed in Chapter 15.

Consumer Economics Applications

To help students become informed consumers, *Contemporary Economics* includes applications in consumer economics. Examples include shopping for a mortgage loan, calculating compound interest, identifying electronic codes on a personal check, and shopping for a credit card. I have incorporated these topics into my survey of economics class, and my students find them interesting and beneficial to their lives.

For example, Chapter 4 discusses the costs of driving an automobile. Students learn about the fixed costs and variable costs of driving and how to calculate the cost of driving on a per-mile basis. These concepts provide a nice transition to the costs of production that are discussed later in the chapter.

SUPPLEMENTARY MATERIALS

To help students master the tools of economic analysis, Koushik Ghosh of Central Washington University has prepared an excellent online *Study Guide* (www.mesharpe-student.com and click on the text cover). Each chapter provides a summary of important points and learning objectives, matching review questions, multiple-choice questions, true/false questions, and application exercises.

To assist instructors in the teaching of this textbook, Margaret Brooks of Bridgewater State College has written an online *Instructor's Manual* with test bank. Part I contains learning objectives, lecture hints and ideas, discussion starters, and brief answers to end-of-chapter study questions and problems. Part II contains a comprehensive test bank with multiple-choice, true/false, and essay questions.

ACKNOWLEDGMENTS

This textbook could not have been written and published without the assistance of many individuals. I am pleased to acknowledge those who provided helpful suggestions and often detailed reviews:

- John Olienyk, Colorado State University
- Koushik Ghosh, Central Washington University
- John Adams, Texas A&M International University
- Bruce Pietrykowski, University of Michigan–Dearborn
- Tesa Stegner, Idaho State University
- Clifford Hawley, West Virginia University
- Rolando Santos, Lakeland Community College
- Karin Steffens, Northern Michigan University
- Pam Whalley, Western Washington University
- Margaret Landman, Bridgewater State College
- Barry Kotlove, Edmonds Community College
- R. Edward Chatterton, Lock Haven University
- Dea Ochs, Jesuit College Prep
- Z. Edward O'Relley, North Dakota State University
- Laurence Malone, Hartwick College
- Vicki Rostedt, University of Akron
- Kishore Kulkami, Metropolitan State College
- David Hammes, University of Hawaii at Hilo
- Gary Galles, Pepperdine University

- Bruce Billings, University of Arizona
- Barry Goodwin, North Carolina State University
- Mike Walden, North Carolina State University
- Joseph Samprone, Georgia College and State University
- Robert Grafstein, University of Georgia
- Mark Healy, William Rainey Harper College
- Vani Kotcherlakota, University of Nebraska
- Donald A. Coffin, Indiana University Northwest
- Naga Pulikonda, Indiana University Kokomo
- F. P. Biggs, Principia College
- Ken Harrison, Richard Stockton College of New Jersey
- Donald Bumpass, Sam Houston State College
- Sandra Peart, Baldwin-Wallace College
- Michael Rosen, Milwaukee Area Technical College
- Nicholas Karatjas, Indiana University of Pennsylvania
- Ernest Diedrich, St. John's University
- Arthur Janssen, Emporia State University
- Ralph Gray, De Pauw University
- Maria V. Gamba-Riedel, University of Findlay
- Anthony Patrick O'Brien, Lehigh University
- Charles W. Smith, Lincoln Land Community College
- Paul Comoli, University of Kansas
- Walton Padelford, Union University
- David Gillette, Truman State University

I would also like to thank my colleagues at Central Washington University—Shirley Hood, Tim Dittmer, Koushik Ghosh, David Hedrick, Richard Mack, Tyler Prante, Peter Saunders, Thomas Tenerelli, and Chad Wassell—for their advice and help while I was preparing this manuscript.

It has been a pleasure to work with Lynn Taylor (Executive Editor at M.E. Sharpe, Inc.), who coordinated this project, and her editorial assistant, Erin Coakley, who prepped the manuscript. Thanks are given to Angela Piliouras who orchestrated the production of this book and to Deborah Ring who conducted the copyediting. Thanks are also given to Nancy Connick, the compositor, and to Tony Viggiani, Jim Wright, and Diana McDermott who carried out the marketing. Finally, I am grateful to students and faculty, who commented on the manuscript.

I would appreciate any comments, corrections, or suggestions that faculty or students wish to make so that I can continue to improve this textbook in the years ahead. Please contact me! Thank you for permitting this text to evolve to the sixth edition.

Bob Carbaugh
Department of Economics
Central Washington University
Ellensburg, Washington 98926
Phone: (509) 963-3443
Fax: (509) 963-1992
Email: carbaugh@cwu.edu

About the Author

Known for his excellence in teaching, **Bob Carbaugh** is a professor of economics at Central Washington University. He has been lauded with top teaching awards, including the 1984 Excellence in Teaching award from the University of Wisconsin–Eau Claire and the Distinguished Professor of the University award from Central Washington University in 1993. In 1996, Professor Carbaugh was named Scholar of the Year by the Phi Kappa Phi Honorary Society at Central Washington University. In 2001, he received the Distinguished Professor of the University award for research at Central Washington University. In 2004, he was invited by the directors of the Oxford Round Table to present a lecture, "Trade and Environmental Frictions in the Global Steel Industry," at Oxford University in England.

With a doctorate in economics from Colorado State University, Professor Carbaugh specializes in economic theory and international economics. For more than 30 years, Professor Carbaugh has taught these subjects, as well as managerial economics, money and banking, and introductory and intermediate levels of microeconomics and macroeconomics. His cogent and lively teaching style has made his courses highly popular at Central Washington University.

Professor Carbaugh has published his research in such publications as *Cato Journal*, the *International Review of Economics and Business, Challenge, World Competition: Law and Economic Review*, the *International Trade Journal*, the *Quarterly Journal of Economics and Business*, and the *Journal of Asian Economics*. He has presented papers at the meetings of professional associations, including the Eastern Economics Association, the Midwestern Economics Association, and the Western Economics Association. Professor Carbaugh is also well known for his distinguished textbook *International Economics* (South-Western/Cengage Learning), now in its 13th edition. Professor Carbaugh resides in Ellensburg, Washington.

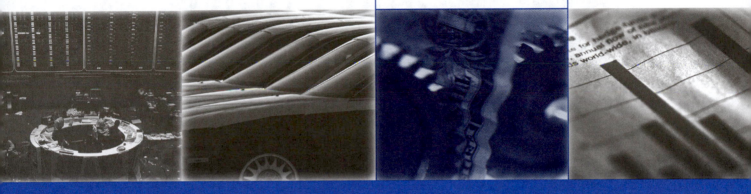

Introduction

Scarcity and Choice

Chapter objectives

After reading this chapter, you should be able to:

1. Discuss the nature of economics and the economic way of thinking.

2. Explain how the concept of scarcity relates to the concept of opportunity cost.

3. Identify the causes of economic growth and decline.

4. Identify the opportunity cost of national security.

5. Describe the purpose and effects of economic sanctions.

economics IN CONTEXT

In the years following World War II, the United States sacrificed in order to equip itself with a national defense that could meet the threat posed by the Soviet Union. Trillions of dollars were spent to produce jet aircraft, tanks, missiles, submarines, and other defense goods. Indeed, the resources of the United States were scarce. The production of more defense goods meant that fewer resources were available for libraries, schools, golf courses, and other civilian goods. Put simply, the United States sacrificed civilian goods to produce more military goods.

Each time the United States developed a new military system, the former Soviet Union would develop a more costly system of its own. Were it not for scarce resources, the Soviets could have produced more civilian goods *and* more military goods. Because of scarcity, however, the Soviets had to produce fewer civilian goods to fulfill the everyday needs of the people. Moreover, the Soviet Union was less efficient at producing goods than the United States and other countries. Civilian goods were thus in short supply

and of poor quality in the Soviet Union, which led to bitter complaints among the people. In 1992, the Soviet Union collapsed under the pressure of its disenchanted citizens. Suddenly, the world appeared to be a calmer and more secure place to live.

That tranquility, however, ended dramatically when terrorists attacked the United States on September 11, 2001, prompting the U.S. military to invade Afghanistan and Iraq. To improve national security, the United States once again increased its expenditures on military goods. However, the production of more military goods meant that fewer resources would be available for the production of civilian goods, such as police and fire protection, hospitals, and highways.

The question of how an economy should use its scarce resources is a main focus of public debate for all societies. In this chapter, we will examine the economic choices that must be made in every society because of scarcity.

WHAT IS ECONOMICS?

Economics means different things to different people. To some, it means making money in stocks, bonds, and real estate. To others, it means understanding how to own and operate a business. To the president of the United States, it may mean developing a new federal budget or formulating plans to reform the welfare system. Although all of these matters are part of economics, the subject has broader dimensions. **Economics** is, first and foremost, the study of *choice* under conditions of *scarcity*. Both individually and as a society, we attempt to choose wisely. We are forced to do so because human and property resources are limited, and it takes resources to produce cell phones, computers, automobiles, CD players, and other goods and services that we desire.

Obtaining the greatest value from resources is the goal of economic choice. At a personal level, we have limited income to spend on the many items we want. For example, we might forgo purchasing a Jeep Grand Cherokee in order to have funds to pay tuition at Northwestern University. Businesses also face alternatives. Should a company use its scarce funds to replace its photocopiers instead of buying new computers? Moreover, the government has to make choices. Should tax dollars be used to purchase additional tanks and missiles, or should these dollars be used to finance the construction of a new highway system?

The field of economics is quite broad. Its reach extends from personal concerns—why does a pound of butter cost more than a pound of margarine?—to issues of national and global importance—will an economic slump in Asia cause the U.S. economy to decline? The field of economics is generally divided into two categories: microeconomics and macroeconomics.

Microeconomics

Microeconomics is the branch of economics that focuses on the choices made by households and firms and the effects those choices have on particular markets. We can use microeconomics to understand how markets work, to make personal or managerial decisions, and to analyze the impact of government policies. Consider these microeconomic questions:

- How would a higher tax on cigarettes affect consumption by teenagers?
- Why do convenience stores often close after several years?
- How would a ban on immigrant workers from Mexico affect U.S. apple growers?
- Should I put my savings in a bank account or invest them in the stock market?
- Will an increase in the federal minimum wage help the working poor?

Macroeconomics

The other branch of economics is macroeconomics. **Macroeconomics** is concerned with the overall performance of the economy. Macroeconomics does not focus on the activities of individual households, firms, or markets; instead, it focuses on the behavior of the economy itself. It deals especially with the determination of total output, the level of employment, and the price level.

We study macroeconomics to learn how the overall economy works and to understand the controversies concerning economic policies. Among the macroeconomic topics that we will examine are the following:

- Why do some economies grow more rapidly than others?
- What causes unemployment and inflation?
- Should the government adopt policies to increase savings and investment?
- Should the government limit the outsourcing of American jobs to foreign nations?
- How does a decrease in interest rates affect the economy?

These two branches—microeconomics and macroeconomics—converge to form the field of modern economics.

THE ECONOMIC WAY OF THINKING

The practice of economics often calls for analysis of complex problems. Although economists may differ in their ideological views, they have developed an "economic way of thinking." This methodology is based on several principles.

Every Choice Has a Cost

Because human and property resources are scarce, individuals and societies must choose how to best use them. Making prudent choices requires trading one thing for another. At the core of economics is the notion that there is no such thing as a "free lunch." A friend may buy your lunch, making it "free" to you, but there still is a cost to someone and, ultimately, to society. This notion expresses the fundamental principle of economics: Every choice involves a cost.

The cost of any choice is the value of the best opportunity that is forgone in making it. For example, you can choose to remain in college or quit college. If you quit, you may find a job at Burger King and earn enough money to buy some Levi's jeans, rent some videos, go golfing and skiing, and hang out with your friends. If you remain in college, you will not be able to afford all of these things now. However, your education will enable you to find a better job later, and then you will be able to afford these and many other items.

People Make Better Choices by Thinking at the Margin

Economists maintain that people make better choices by thinking "at the margin." Making a choice at the margin means deciding to do a little more or a little less of an activity. As a student, you can allocate the next hour to sleeping or studying. In making this decision, you compare the benefit of extra study time to the cost of forgone sleep.

As an example of thinking at the margin, consider how United Airlines decides how much to charge passengers who fly standby. Assume that flying a 300-seat jetliner from Seattle to New York costs the airline $90,000. Therefore, the average cost (per seat) is $300 ($90,000 / 300 = $300). You might conclude that United Airlines should always charge at least $300 per ticket. However, the airline can increase its profits by thinking at the margin. Suppose that a jetliner is going to take off with one empty seat. A standby passenger is waiting at the gate, and he is willing to pay $200 to fly from Seattle to New York. Should United Airlines sell him a ticket at this price? Yes, because the cost of flying one more passenger is negligible. Although the *average* cost of flying a passenger is $300, the *marginal* (extra) cost is only the cost of a can of Sprite, a bag of pretzels, and a chicken sandwich. As long as United Airlines earns revenues that are more than the marginal cost, the addition of an extra passenger is profitable.

Rational Self-Interest

Economics is founded on the assumption of rational self-interest. This means that people act as if they are motivated by self-interest and respond predictably to opportunities for gain. In other words, people try to make the best of any situation. Often, making the best of a situation involves maximizing the value of some quantity. As a student, getting high grades may be an incentive to study hard because they may help you obtain a job interview with a particular employer or get accepted to a prestigious graduate school.

Throughout this text, we will assume that economic incentives underlie the rational decisions that people make. We will assume that a firm's owners want to maximize profit in order to improve their well-being. Also, we will assume that households seek to maximize their satisfaction from consuming goods and services. Because income is limited and goods have prices, we cannot buy all the things we would like to have. Therefore, we should choose an attainable combination of goods that will maximize our satisfaction. Of course, self-interest does not always imply increasing one's wealth, as measured in dollars and cents, or one's satisfaction from goods consumed. In addition to economic motivations, people also have goals pertaining to friendship, love, altruism, creativity, and the like.

Economic Models

Like other sciences, economics uses models. In chemistry, you may have seen a model of an atom—a device with blue, green, and red balls that represent neutrons, electrons, and protons. Architects construct cardboard models of skyscrapers before they are built. Economic models are not built with plastic or cardboard but rather with words, diagrams, and mathematical equations.

Economic **models**, or **theories**, are simplified representations of the real world that we use to help us understand, explain, and predict economic phenomena in the real world. Economic models explain inflation, unemployment, wage rates, exchange rates, and more. For example, an economic model might tell us how the quantity of compact discs (CDs) that consumers purchase will change if sellers raise the price. Other models explain how changes in interest rates in the economy affect investment spending by business. Throughout this textbook, we will use economic models to help us understand contemporary economic issues.

Positive versus Normative Economics

It is important to realize that economics is not always free of value judgments. In thinking about economic questions, we must distinguish questions of fact from questions of fairness.

Positive economics describes the facts of the economy—it deals with the way in which the economy works. Positive economics considers such questions as, why do computer scientists earn more than janitors? What is the economic effect of reducing taxes? Does free trade result in job losses for less-skilled workers? Although these questions are difficult to answer, they can be addressed by economic analysis and empirical evidence.

Normative economics involves value judgments that cannot be tested empirically. Ethical standards and norms of fairness underlie normative economics. For example, should the United States penalize India for violating U.S. patent and copyright laws? Should welfare payments be reduced in order to encourage the unemployed to find income-producing jobs? Should all Americans have equal access to health care? Because these questions involve value judgments instead of facts, there are no right or wrong answers. Both positive and normative economics are important and will be considered throughout this textbook.

Why do economists often appear to give conflicting advice to policy makers? Because economists do not fully understand how the economy operates, they often disagree about actual cause-and-effect relationships. Moreover, economists may have different value judgments—and thus different normative views—about the goals that economic policies should attempt to accomplish.

The first part of this chapter has given us an overview of economics and the economic way of thinking. We will now examine the economic problem of scarcity.

SCARCITY

Whether you are taking just one economics course or majoring in economics, the most important topic you will learn about is **scarcity**. Scarcity means that there are not enough—nor can there ever be enough—goods and services to satisfy the wants and needs of everyone. Consider your own situation: Can you afford the school that you would most prefer to attend or the car that you would most like to own? Do you have sufficient financial resources for all the clothes, computers, concerts, and sporting events that you want? Societies also face a scarcity problem. Money devoted to national defense, for example, is not available for education or food stamps.

The source of the scarcity problem is that people have *limited resources* to satisfy their *unlimited material wants*. Resources, or **factors of production,** are inputs used in the production of goods and services that we want, such as CD players and textbooks. The total quantity of resources that an economy has at any one time determines how much output the economy can produce. The factors of production are classified as follows:

1. **Land.** Land refers to all natural resources—such as raw materials, land, minerals, forests, water, and climate—used in the productive process.

2. **Labor.** This resource includes all physical and mental efforts that people make available for production. The services of professional baseball players, accountants, teachers, and autoworkers all fall under the heading of labor.

3. **Capital.** Capital, or investment goods, refers to goods that are used to produce other goods and services. This includes such things as machinery, tools, computers, computer software, buildings, and roads. Economists do not consider money to be capital because it is not directly used in production.

4. **Entrepreneurship.** This factor of production is a special type of labor. An entrepreneur is a person who organizes, manages, and assembles the other factors of production to produce goods and services. Entrepreneurs seek profit by undertaking risky activities, such as starting a new business, creating a new product, or inventing a new way of accomplishing something. Bill Gates (founder of Microsoft Corp.), Levi Strauss (founder of Levi Strauss Co.), and Henry Ford (founder of Ford Motor Co.) are examples of highly successful entrepreneurs.

economics
IN ACTION

Frederick Smith: Entrepreneur

Frederick Smith, founder of FedEx, is one of America's most successful entrepreneurs. He comes from a family tradition based on transportation. His grandfather was a steamboat captain, and his father established a regional bus company that became the cornerstone of the Greyhound Bus system. Learning to fly as a teenager, Smith worked weekends as a charter pilot while pursuing an economics degree at Yale University in the 1960s.

While flying faculty and other passengers around the country, Smith had an idea that would one day radically change the transportation business. He realized that besides flying people, he often delivered spare parts for firms that could not wait for United Airlines or other carriers to ship essential components to customers. In 1965, Smith formalized his notion of an express delivery service in a term paper that he wrote for an economics course. Although lore has it that Smith received a modest grade of C for his efforts, he recalls doing better.

After serving a tour of duty with the U.S. Marines in Vietnam, Smith began to pursue his ambition. With $4 million in backing from his family and $80 million from other investors, he built the Federal Express Corp. (FedEx)

from scratch in 1971. Its vow: guaranteed 1-day delivery of packages between any two points in the United States.

However, FedEx was no overnight success. The firm drummed up only 7 packages for its first day's run. Therefore, Smith hired additional sales staff to boost sales. Yet deficient volume wasn't the only problem. Until the late 1970s, the U.S. Postal Service was able to use its monopoly power to prevent FedEx from delivering documents. Also, strict airline regulations initially limited FedEx to flying small aircraft instead of larger, more efficient ones. Smith was in such dire need of funds that he traveled to Las Vegas to play the blackjack tables. He sent his $27,000 winnings back to the company.

Smith's perseverance yielded success. By 1980, Americans had come to rely on FedEx's promise to deliver packages by the next day. Although FedEx now has many competitors, it is still the dominant firm, with a 44 percent share of the express delivery market. Its fleet of 650 aircraft and 71,000 trucks transports some 5.5 million packages each day. And all because a college economics major could visualize an opportunity that others couldn't!

Sources: "Frederick Smith: Father of Overnight Delivery Service," Academy of Achievement, February 2005, available at http://www.achievement.org. See also Dean Foust, "No Overnight Success," *Business Week,* September 20, 2004, p. 18; and the home page of Federal Express, available at http://www.fedex.com.

These factors of production have a common characteristic: They are in limited supply. Quantities of mineral deposits, capital equipment, arable land, and labor (time) are available in finite amounts. Because of the scarcity of resources and the limitation this scarcity imposes on productive activity, output is limited.

Limited resources conflict with unlimited wants. Human wants are said to be unlimited because no matter how much people have, they always want more of something. Because not all wants can be fulfilled, individuals must choose which ones to fulfill with limited available resources. In a world of scarcity, every want that is fulfilled results in one or more other wants remaining unfulfilled.

SCARCITY AND OPPORTUNITY COST

The reality of scarcity forces us to make choices that involve giving up one opportunity in order to do or use something else. For example, the cost of going to a Chicago Bulls basketball game includes the value of what is sacrificed to attend. Economists use the term **opportunity cost** to denote the value of the best alternative that is sacrificed. Part of the cost of attending a Bulls game is the price of the ticket. This price represents the other goods and services you could have purchased with that money instead.

In addition, there is the most valuable alternative use of the time devoted to watching the game. Perhaps you could have used this time to study for an upcoming economics exam. Thus, the opportunity cost of attending the game equals the ticket price plus the difference in your test score that the additional study time would have yielded. Let us consider several applications of opportunity cost.

The Opportunity Cost of Attending College

Another example is the opportunity cost of attending college. It is not simply the dollar amount listed in your college catalog. The money you spend on tuition, fees, textbooks, and supplies is only part of the opportunity cost; the income that you could have earned during the years that you are spending in classes is also part of the opportunity cost.

Table 1.1 shows the estimated out-of-pocket costs of a year of college for the average student in 2008–2009. For example, the third column of the table shows the cost for an average in-state resident at a 4-year state college to be $18,326. Of this amount, the student pays $6,585 in tuition and fees, $1,077 in books and supplies, $7,748 for room and board, $1,010 for transportation, and $1,906 in other expenses.

Is the student's opportunity cost for a year of college $18,326? No. Some of this cost must be incurred regardless of whether the student attends college. For example, you would still have to assume room and board expenses—say, by living in an apartment—even if you did not attend college. This cost would not be eliminated even if you lived at home because your family could be renting your room to someone else. The same reasoning applies to transportation and other expenses, at least the portion that you would have assumed if you were not in college. Suppose that these expenses are the same regardless whether you attend college. The opportunity cost of attending college thus consists of tuition and fees ($6,585) and books and supplies ($1,077), which total $7,662.

In addition, the opportunity cost of a year of college includes the amount of forgone income. Assuming that you earn $12 an hour and reduce your work hours by 30 hours a week during the 32 weeks a year that you are in college, the forgone earnings represent a cost of $11,520 ($12 $\times$ 30 hours $\times$ 32 weeks) a year. It should be noted that most students will use their education to generate future earnings that will more than offset this sum. Nevertheless, the $11,520 also represents an opportunity cost of attending college.

The opportunity cost of a year of college thus includes the payments for tuition and fees ($6,585), payments for books and supplies ($1,077), plus the $11,520 of forgone income. This sum totals $19,182. Notice that this amount is greater than the estimated $18,326 of out-of-pocket costs shown in Table 1.1.

Table 1.1   Average Cost of a Year of College, 2008–2009

Type of institution	Two-year public (commuter)	Four-year public (resident)	Four-year private (resident)
Tuition and fees	$ 2,402	$ 6,585	$25,143
Books and supplies	1,036	1,077	1,054
Room and board	7,341	7,748	8,989
Transportation	1,380	1,010	807
Other costs	1,895	1,906	1,397
Total costs	$14,054	$18,326	$37,390

Source: Data from *Trends in College Pricing: 2008–2009*, pp. 1–20, The College Board, available at http://www.collegeboard.com. Based on the College Board's *Annual Survey of Colleges.*

Some students find the opportunity cost of attending college to be even higher. Suppose that you are a talented baseball player or tennis player who could play professionally after graduating high school. The opportunity cost of a year at college could easily exceed $100,000. Tiger Woods, a professional golfer, faced this dilemma after attending Stanford University for 2 years. Upon winning his third straight U.S. Amateur golf title, he chose to turn pro rather than continue his studies at Stanford. He immediately became a multimillionaire, with contracts worth more than $40 million from Nike and Titleist in hand. It is no wonder that talented athletes often consider the opportunity cost of their college education to be too high and thus drop out of school to pursue professional sports.

Opportunity Costs and Choices

Suppose that your student club conducts a fund-raiser, and each club member agrees to spend 8 hours working at a Saturday car wash. A local service station donates its parking area and water, and your club supplies the washcloths and detergent. Club members wave their signs at passing motorists in an attempt to lure business.

After washing several vehicles, the members determine that they can wash 10 compact cars or 5 minivans in an hour's time. In an 8-hour day, then, the club could wash 80 compacts (8 × 10 = 80) or 40 minivans (8 × 5 = 40).

Figure 1.1 illustrates the combinations of compacts and minivans that could be washed in an 8-hour day. Devoting the entire day to washing compacts results in 80 washed cars, shown by point *A* in the figure. Conversely, devoting the entire day to washing minivans results in 40 washed minivans, shown by point *E*. Let us connect these two combinations with line *AE*. Other combinations (*B, C, D*) are attainable on this line. Line *AE* thus shows all the possible combinations of compacts and minivans that could be washed in a day.

Sliding down line *AE*, we see that there is an opportunity cost for washing minivans. For every 10 minivans that the club washes, it must sacrifice the washing of 20 compacts. This implies that

Figure 1.1 | Opportunity Cost and Choice

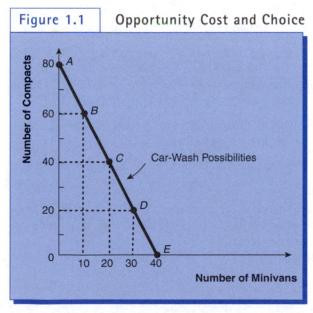

In an 8-hour day, a student club can wash many combinations of minivans and compacts. Line *AE* illustrates these combinations, given the assumption that the entire day is devoted to washing the two types of vehicles. The line is downward sloping, suggesting that there is a trade-off between the number of compacts and the number of minivans that can be washed. Along line *AE*, the opportunity cost of each additional washed minivan is 2 compacts that are not washed.

the opportunity cost for each additional washed minivan equals 2 compacts (20 / 10 = 2) that are not washed. Why does this trade-off occur? Given an 8-hour day, as more hours are devoted to the washing of minivans, fewer hours can be devoted to washing compacts. The 8-hour limitation of our Saturday car wash thus forces the club to make choices concerning how much effort should be devoted to washing compacts or minivans. (Tabular and graphical relationships are discussed in "Exploring Further 1.1" at the end of this chapter.)

CHECK POINT

1. What is economics?

2. Differentiate between microeconomics and macroeconomics.

3. Identify the major principles of the economic way of thinking.

4. How does scarcity force an individual to incur opportunity costs?

5. What opportunity cost do you face in attending college?

THE PRODUCTION POSSIBILITIES CURVE AND OPPORTUNITY COST

Just as scarcity affects the car-wash choices of a student club, it also influences the production choices of a nation. The relationship between the scarcity and choice that an entire nation faces can be illustrated by a **production possibilities curve**. A production possibilities curve illustrates graphically the maximum combinations of two goods that an economy can produce, given its available resources and technology. Several assumptions underlie an economy's production possibilities curve:

1. **Fixed resources.** The quantities of all resources, or factors of production, are held constant. This means that there are no changes in the economy's labor, machinery, and the like. Existing resources can only be transferred from the production of one good to the production of another good.

2. **Fully employed resources.** Everyone who wants a job has one, and all other resources are being used. All resources are producing the maximum output possible.

3. **Technology unchanged.** The existing technology is held fixed, with no new innovations or inventions taking place.

The assumptions of fixed resources and fixed technology imply that we are looking at an economy at a specific point in time or over a very short period. Over a relatively long period, it is possible for resources to change and technological advances to occur.

Figure 1.2 illustrates a hypothetical economy that has the capacity to produce many different combinations of DVD players and computers. If all resources are devoted to computer production, 6 million computers per year can be produced, denoted by point *A* in the figure. If all resources are devoted to DVD player production, 3 million DVD players per year can be produced, denoted by point *D*. Between the extremes of points *A* and *D* are other possible combinations of the two goods, denoted by points *B* and *C*. By connecting these points, we can see the economy's production possibilities curve.

The production possibilities curve in Figure 1.2(*a*) is downward sloping because of the problem of scarcity. Resources of land, labor, capital, and entrepreneurship are limited to particular amounts at

Figure 1.2   Production Possibilities Curve

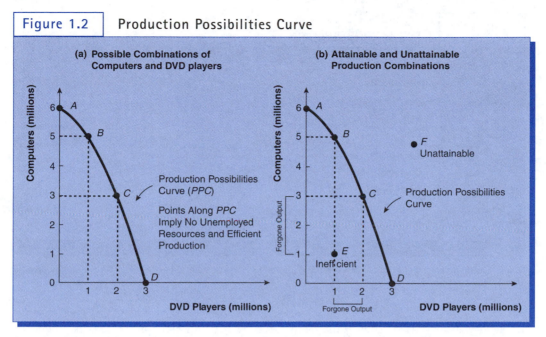

A production possibilities curve illustrates the different combinations of two goods that an economy can produce with full employment, fixed resources, and fixed technology. Points inside the production possibilities curve are economically inefficient, whereas points outside the curve are unattainable given an economy's existing resources and technology.

any one point in time. In a fully employed economy, if more resources are going into the production of DVD players, fewer resources will be left for the production of computers. To produce more DVD players, the cost will be a lower output of computers. The figure thus illustrates a basic truth of economics: All choices have opportunity costs.

Economic Inefficiency

Because all points along a production possibilities curve depict maximum output with given resources and technology, an economy realizes economic **efficiency** when it is operating along the curve. What if an economy does not employ all of its resources at their maximum capacity? For example, during economic downturns, some workers probably cannot find work, and some plants and equipment may become underutilized. In this situation, the economy fails to realize the output potential of its production possibilities curve, and economic **inefficiency** occurs.

In Figure 1.2(*b*), point *E* shows an inefficient output combination for an economy that realizes unemployed labor or other underutilized resources; only 1 million DVD players and 1 million computers are produced. With full employment, the economy can produce a larger output combination—say, 2 million DVD players and 3 million computers, shown by point *C* in the figure. Comparing these two points, we see that unemployment results in forgone output equal to 2 million computers and 1 million DVD players. Generalizing, the effect of unemployment is illustrated graphically by a point *beneath* the production possibilities curve. This point is attainable but not necessarily desirable.

Even if an economy can fully employ all of its resources at their maximum capacity, certain output combinations cannot be realized. In Figure 1.2(*b*), any point outside the economy's production possibilities curve, say, point *F,* is *unattainable* because it lies beyond the economy's current production capabilities. The economy cannot achieve this output combination with its existing resources and

Table 1.2	Capacity Utilization Rates for Major U.S. Industries, 1972–2008 Average	
Total Industry		80.9%
Manufacturing		79.6
Motor vehicles		77.8
Iron and steel		80.6
Aerospace		72.4
Chemicals		85.2
Petroleum		86.7
Mining		87.6
Utilities		86.8

Source: Federal Reserve Board, Statistical Release G.17, *Industrial Production and Capacity Utilization,* available at http://www.federalreserve.gov/.

technology. Scarcity restricts an economy to operating at points along or beneath its production possibilities curve.

Do economies actually operate along their production possibilities curves? Strictly speaking, no. Economies always experience some degree of unemployment and underproduction that causes them to operate beneath their production possibilities curves. A production possibilities curve can thus be viewed as a yardstick against which an economy's production performance can be measured.

To what extent has the United States been able to utilize its industrial capacity? A measure of such utilization is the **capacity utilization rate,** which is the ratio of an industry's production to its capacity. According to this measure, an industry that is operating at full capacity has a 100-percent capacity utilization rate; a rate less than 100 percent implies that at least some plants and equipment are idle.

Table 1.2 illustrates capacity utilization rates for major U.S. industries. We see that from 1972 to 2008 all U.S. industries combined operated at an average capacity utilization rate of 80.9 percent. The average capacity utilization rates for the economy's manufacturing, mining, and utilities sectors during this period equaled 79.6 percent, 87.6 percent, and 86.8 percent, respectively. The table also shows capacity utilization rates for particular U.S. manufacturing industries.

Law of Increasing Opportunity Cost

Figure 1.3 illustrates the production possibilities curve of our hypothetical economy. Notice that the production possibilities curve is bowed outward, or concave. This is because the opportunity cost of DVD players increases as more DVD players are produced. Moving from point A to point B along the curve, the opportunity cost of 1 DVD player is 1 computer; between points B and C, the opportunity cost is 2 computers; and between points C and D, the opportunity cost is 3 computers. These opportunity costs represent what occurs in the real world for most goods: Opportunity costs increase as we produce more of a good. This relationship is known as the **law of increasing opportunity cost**.

But why do opportunity costs generally increase as we produce more of a good? The answer is that *resources are not completely adaptable to alternative uses.* For example, some workers have skills that are more useful for producing DVD players than other workers have. When a company first starts producing DVD players, it employs workers who are most skilled at DVD player production. The most skilled workers are those who can produce DVD players at a lower opportunity cost than others. Yet as the company produces more DVD players, it finds that it has already employed the most skilled workers; thus, going forward, it must employ workers who are less skilled in DVD player

| Figure 1.3 | The Law of Increasing Opportunity Cost |

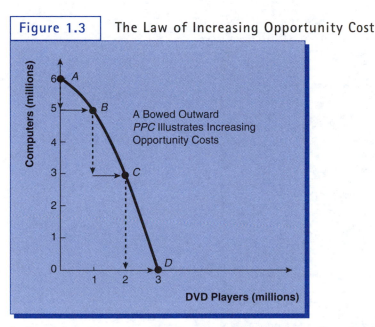

In the real world, most production possibilities curves are bowed outward (concave). This means that, for most goods, the opportunity cost increases as we produce more of them. Increasing opportunity costs occur when resources are not completely adaptable to alternative uses.

production. These workers produce DVD players at a higher opportunity cost. Whereas 2 skilled workers could produce a DVD player in a day, as many as 5 unskilled workers may be required to produce 1 DVD player in the same amount of time. Thus, as more DVD players are produced, the opportunity cost of producing DVD players increases.

ECONOMIC GROWTH

At any particular point in time, an economy cannot operate outside its production possibilities curve. Over time, however, it is possible for an economy to expand its output potential. This occurs through **economic growth**, which refers to the increased productive capabilities of an economy that are made possible by either an increasing resource base or technological advancement.

Economic growth entails an outward shift in an economy's production possibilities curve so that more of all goods can be produced. Figure 1.4 illustrates the significance of an outward shift in a production possibilities curve. Before the occurrence of economic growth, suppose that an economy can produce 2 million DVD players and 3 million computers, shown by point C along curve PPC_0. As a result of growth in the economy's resource base or technological advancement, the production possibilities curve shifts outward to a higher level, PPC_1. Economic growth permits the economy to produce more computers (a movement to point E), more DVD players (a movement to point G), or more of both goods (a movement to point F). Many other previously unattainable combinations also become attainable with economic growth. In short, economic growth allows the economy to produce more of everything! However, growth does not guarantee that the economy will operate at a point along the higher production possibilities curve. The economy might fail to fulfill its expanded possibilities.

One way to increase an economy's production capacity is to gain additional resources. More (or better-trained) workers or more (or improved) plants and equipment can increase a nation's output potential. Worker productivity is also facilitated by investment in infrastructure, such as roads, bridges, airports, and utilities. Another way to achieve economic growth is through research and development of new technologies. Technological development allows more output to be produced

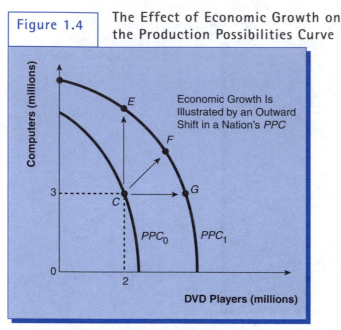

Figure 1.4 The Effect of Economic Growth on the Production Possibilities Curve

Economic growth shifts the production possibilities curve outward and makes it possible to produce more of all goods. Prior to growth in productive capacity, point *C* was on curve PPC_0 and points *E, F,* and *G* were unattainable. After growth, shown by curve PPC_1, points *E, F,* and *G* (and many other previously unattainable combinations) are attainable.

with the same quantity of resources. A faster photocopier, a more smoothly operating assembly line, or a new-generation computer system are examples of technological advances.

Throughout the 20th century, agriculture was a highly productive sector of the U.S. economy. In 1910, the United States had roughly 32 million farmers, constituting 35 percent of the U.S. population; in 2009, there were about 5 million farmers, constituting less than 2 percent of the U.S. population. During this period, total farm output expanded greatly. How could a declining number of farmers produce greater output? The answer is improved technology. Whereas farmers once farmed with negligible capital equipment, today they use modern tractors, computers, pesticides, cell phones, and the like. As a result, more food can be produced by fewer farmers. As farmers left farms, they entered manufacturing and service industries, such as computers, automobiles, aircraft, accounting services, and engineering. Technological advances in farming thus made it possible to produce additional goods in other sectors of the economy. The result was an outward shift in the U.S. production possibilities curve.

ECONOMIC DECLINE

Just as an expanding resource base causes an economy's production possibilities to increase, decreasing resources can likewise reduce an economy's output potential. During World War II, for example, the production possibilities of Europe and Japan decreased. The war disrupted people's lives, and many people did not survive the war. Entire factories, roads, bridges, railway networks, electrical utilities, and other types of capital goods were reduced to rubble. The destructive effects of the war caused the production possibilities curves of Europe and Japan to shift inward.

The physical devastation of Europe and Japan caused by World War II yielded some paradoxical effects for these war-devastated economies. Because a large share of their stock of capital goods was destroyed by the war, these nations had to rebuild their industries from scratch. They did so with the most up-to-date factories and equipment. The result was a substantial increase in labor productivity, which allowed these economies to realize production possibilities exceeding those that had existed before the war. Conversely, nations that had been spared the devastation of the war had their prewar technologies in place and grew slower than those whose stock of capital goods was destroyed and replaced with more modern technology.

For example, the United States was the most powerful steel-producing nation in the world immediately following World War II. The U.S. steel industry came out of the war intact, accounting for nearly half of the world's steel output. Moreover, U.S. firms produced more steel than all of Europe combined and almost 20 times as much as Japan! During the 1950s and 1960s, however, the absence of foreign competition caused U.S. steel companies to become complacent. Instead of investing in new plants, they manufactured steel in outmoded plants using obsolete technologies and paid wages almost twice the average of all other U.S. manufacturing sectors. In contrast, Japan and Europe replaced the steel factories that had been devastated by the war with modern plants that used the most efficient equipment. By the 1970s, the productivity of Japanese and European steel companies was increasing relative to the productivity of U.S. companies, and the competitiveness of U.S. companies dwindled. The threat of foreign competition forced U.S. steel companies to shut down many obsolete factories in the 1980s and replace them with modern plants and equipment.

Natural disasters can also reduce an economy's output potential. For example, in 2005, the states of Alabama, Louisiana, and Mississippi were struck by two major hurricanes (Katrina and Rita) that damaged the productive capacity of the U.S. economy. These hurricanes passed through offshore areas where oil and natural gas platforms are concentrated and then struck onshore areas where petroleum is refined and natural gas is processed. In addition to the tragic loss of life and massive destruction of personal property that they caused, the hurricanes damaged energy equipment and structures—about 28 percent of total U.S. production was shut down. Most of this output loss was the result of the destruction of oil and natural gas operations.[1]

ECONOMIC GROWTH: TRADE-OFFS BETWEEN CURRENT AND FUTURE CONSUMPTION

The production possibilities curve and economic growth can be used to investigate the trade-off between current and future consumption. This trade-off can be illustrated for nations producing consumer goods and capital goods.

Consumer goods are goods such as food, electricity, and clothing that are available for immediate use by households. They do not contribute to future production in the economy. **Capital goods**, such as factories and machines, are used to produce other goods and services in the future. Instead of being consumed today, capital goods are a source of economic growth potential.

A nation that sacrifices current consumption in order to invest in capital goods is forward looking. Rather than getting instant satisfaction from the production of capital goods, the nation increases its capacity to produce consumer goods in the future. This is similar to students attending college. Students devote time to study that could have been spent working, earning income, and therefore engaging in a higher level of consumption. Most students decide to postpone consumption because they expect education to increase their productivity and income, allowing greater consumption in the future.

Figure 1.5 illustrates the production possibilities curves for the United States and Japan. The two axes of each curve are designated as consumer goods (current goods) and capital goods (goods for the future). Assume that the two nations are identical in every respect, except that the U.S. choice along its production possibilities curve strongly favors consumer goods as opposed to capital goods; let this be designated by point A in Figure 1.5(a). Conversely, Japan's choice along its production possibilities curve strongly favors capital goods and is denoted by point A' in Figure 1.5(b).

---

1. "Economic Impact of the 2005 Hurricanes," *Economic Report of the President*, 2006, pp. 26 and 239–240, available at http://www.gpoaccess.gov/eop/index.html.

| Figure 1.5 | Economic Growth in the United States and Japan |

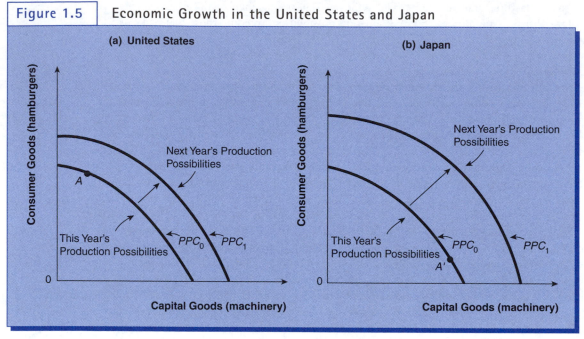

A current choice favoring consumer goods, as made by the United States in (*a*), causes a modest outward shift in the U.S. production possibilities curve. A current choice favoring capital goods, as made by Japan in (*b*), leads to a greater outward shift in the Japanese production possibilities curve. The extra goods made possible by economic growth result in a greater improvement in the living standard in Japan.

The relatively large accumulation of capital goods allows the Japanese economy to grow faster than the U.S. economy. In Figure 1.5, this is illustrated by Japan's production possibilities curve, which shifts farther out to the right than the U.S. curve. Over time, Japan's faster growth rate allows it to produce more consumer goods than the United States. This increase in production, however, requires Japanese households to sacrifice current consumption in exchange for future consumption.

PRODUCTION POSSIBILITIES APPLICATIONS

The production possibilities concept can be applied to national security. Let us consider the application of the production possibilities concept to the terrorist attacks of September 11, 2001, and to the economic sanctions levied by the United States against Iraq in 1990.

Opportunity Cost of National Security

The September 11 terrorist attacks resulted in a tragic loss of life for thousands of innocent Americans. It also jolted America's golden age of prosperity and the promise it held for global growth throughout the 1990s. Because of the threat of terrorism, Americans became increasingly concerned about their safety.

Immediately following the terrorist attacks, businesses and governments made greater efforts to improve their security. For example, Quality Carriers Inc., the country's biggest chemical trucker, rehired the $5,000-a-month night-shift security guard it had previously let go at its tanker-truck terminal in Newark, New Jersey. The company also paid two drivers a total of $1,200 to repark any vehicles loaded with chemicals in plain view and under security lights. For Quality Carriers, achieving extra security required the firm to use more of its resources to protect the company from terrorists, leaving fewer resources available to transport chemicals for its customers. In like manner, security

Figure 1.6	The Opportunity Cost of National Security

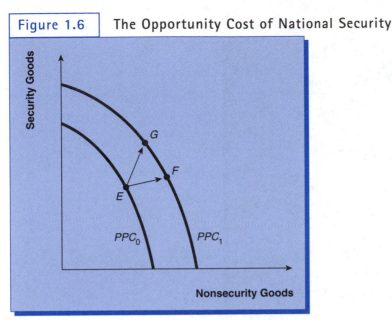

Providing for national security entails an opportunity cost. When we use land, labor, and capital to produce security goods, we sacrifice other things that we could have produced with them.

procedures were beefed up at power plants, communication companies, airports, and government buildings following the September 11 attacks.

Simply put, providing for national security entails an opportunity cost. When we employ labor, capital, and land for security, we sacrifice other things that we could have produced with them. To demonstrate this point, consider Figure 1.6, which depicts hypothetical production possibilities curves for the United States. The vertical axis denotes the annual production of security goods (for example, metal detectors and x-ray monitors), and the horizontal axis denotes the annual production of goods other than security (for example, televisions and autos) that contribute directly to our standard of living. Because of technological progress and growth in the nation's stock of plant and equipment, the production possibilities curve shifts outward, as shown by the movement from curve PPC_0 to curve PPC_1.

Assume that prior to September 11, the United States was located at point E along curve PPC_0. Also assume that in a typical year, economic growth would shift the United States from point E on curve PPC_0 to point F on curve PPC_1. This means that the nation would realize a modest increase in production of security goods, but most of our growth would be used to produce additional quantities of autos, televisions, and other things we enjoy. Because of the September 11 terrorist attacks, however, we move from point E to point G. Notice that although we produce additional quantities of nonsecurity goods, we do not produce *as much* of those goods as we would have if the attacks had not occurred. This limits our economic well-being, as measured by the quantity of nonsecurity goods available for our consumption. Therefore, providing for national security creates an opportunity cost in terms of other goods that we enjoy.

Economic Sanctions and Economic Decline

In our world, nations often disagree with each other's policies. In the 2000s, for example, the United States has disputed the attempt of North Korea and Iran to develop nuclear weapons of mass destruction. Human rights abuses in China have also met strong criticism in the United States in recent years.

Figure 1.7	Effects of Economic Sanctions

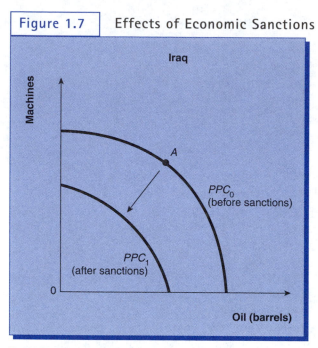

Trade and financial sanctions force the target nation to operate inside its production possibilities curve. Economic sanctions can also result in a leftward (inward) shift in the target nation's production possibilities curve.

Besides the threat of war, are there other ways to convince a foreign government to modify its domestic policies concerning nuclear proliferation, human rights, and so on? One alternative is **economic sanctions**, which are government-imposed limitations, or complete bans, placed on customary trade or financial relations between nations. The nation initiating the sanctions, the imposing nation, hopes to impair the economic capabilities of the recipient target nation. The goal of economic sanctions is to inspire the people of the target nation to force their government to alter its policies. Let us consider the sanctions imposed by the United States on Iraq in 1990.

In 1990, Iraqi president Saddam Hussein ordered his military to cross into Kuwait and occupy the nation. In response to Iraq's aggression, a United Nations (UN) resolution called for economic sanctions to be levied against Iraq. Trade and financial boycotts were imposed by virtually all members of the UN. Under the sanctions program, imposing nations banned exports to Iraq, terminated purchases of Iraqi oil, and suspended investment in, and loans to, Iraq. It was hoped the sanctions would impose sufficient economic pressure on Iraq so that it would exit Kuwait.

Figure 1.7 illustrates the goal of the UN sanctions levied against Iraq. The figure shows the hypothetical production possibilities curve of Iraq for machines and oil. Prior to the imposition of sanctions, suppose that Iraq is able to operate at maximum efficiency, as shown by point A along production possibilities curve PPC_0. Under the sanctions program, the imposing nations' refusal to purchase Iraqi oil leads to idle wells, refineries, and workers in Iraq. The unused production capacity thus forces Iraq to move inside PPC_0. If the imposing nations also target productive inputs, thus curtailing equipment sales to Iraq, the output potential of Iraq would decrease. This is shown by an inward shift of Iraq's production possibilities curve to PPC_1. Economic inefficiencies and reduced production possibilities, both of which are caused by economic sanctions, are thus intended to inflict hardship on the people and government of Iraq.

Although the sanctions did impose hardship on the people of Iraq, Saddam Hussein's grip on power was so strong in the early 1990s that he could not be removed from office or forced to modify his expansionist policies, even though a majority of Iraqi citizens suffered great economic hardship. As a result, President George H. W. Bush concluded that sanctions would not succeed and that military intervention (Operation Desert Storm) was necessary to force Iraq out of Kuwait.

Following the ouster of the Iraqi army from Kuwait in 1991, the UN continued to impose sanctions on Iraq. The sanctions were to be kept in place until Iraq agreed to scrap its nuclear and biological weapons programs. However, Saddam Hussein dug in his heels and refused to make concessions. Therefore, the sanctions program continued until 2003, when the sanctions were lifted following the U.S. and U.K. invasion of Iraq.

The sanctions were devastating for Iraq. Analysts estimate that Iraq's economy shrunk more than two-thirds because of the sanctions. Factories and businesses were shut down, forcing people out of work. Moreover, the people of Iraq suffered from lack of food and medicine because of the sanctions. Indeed, sanctions affected the lives of all Iraqis every moment of the day.

In this chapter, we have examined the economic choices that must be made in every society because of scarcity. The next chapter will consider the role of demand and supply in analyzing market transactions.

CHECK POINT

1. How can we use a production possibilities curve to illustrate opportunity cost for a nation?

2. Concerning economic growth, does it make any difference whether an economy devotes more resources to the production of capital goods as opposed to the production of consumer goods?

3. Identify the opportunity cost of national security.

4. When economic sanctions are placed on a country, how can they affect its production possibilities?

Chapter Summary

1. The source of an economy's scarcity problem is that people have limited resources to satisfy their unlimited material wants.

2. Resources, or factors of production, are inputs used in the production of goods and services. They include land, labor, capital, and entrepreneurship.

3. The reality of scarcity forces us to make choices that involve giving up one opportunity in order to do or use something else. Economists use the term *opportunity cost* to denote the value of the best alternative that is sacrificed.

4. A production possibilities curve illustrates graphically the maximum combinations of two goods that an economy can produce, given its available resources and technology. An economy that is located along its production possibilities curve is operating at maximum efficiency.

5. As we move along an outward-bowed production possibilities curve, opportunity costs increase as more of a good is produced. Increasing opportunity costs occur because resources are not completely adaptable to alternative uses.

6. Economic growth entails an outward shift in an economy's production possibilities curve so that more of all goods can be produced. It is made possible by an increase in an economy's resource base or technological advances.

7. The terrorist attacks of September 11, 2001, forced the United States to beef up its national security. However, the devotion of additional resources to national security entails an opportunity cost in terms of other goods that Americans could consume.

8. Economic sanctions are government-imposed limitations placed on trade and financial relations between nations. The nation initiating the sanctions, the imposing nation, hopes that the economic hardship caused by sanctions will inspire the target nation to alter its political or military policies. Economic sanctions can force a target nation to locate beneath its production possibilities curve and can even cause the target nation's production possibilities curve to shift inward.

Key Terms and Concepts

economics (3)

microeconomics (4)

macroeconomics (4)

models (5)

theories (5)

positive economics (6)

normative economics (6)

scarcity (6)

factors of production (6)

opportunity cost (7)

production possibilities curve (10)

efficiency (11)

inefficiency (11)

capacity utilization rate (12)

law of increasing opportunity cost (12)

economic growth (13)

consumer goods (15)

capital goods (15)

economic sanctions (18)

independent variable (23)

dependent variable (23)

direct relationship (23)

inverse relationship (23)

slope (24)

Self-Test: Multiple-Choice Questions

1. A production possibilities curve that is bowed outward illustrates

   a. increasing opportunity costs.
   b. constant opportunity costs.
   c. decreasing opportunity costs.
   d. zero opportunity costs.

2. The U.S. production possibilities curve will shift outward if

   a. resources are used less efficiently.
   b. unemployment and underproduction are eliminated.
   c. additional resources are discovered in the United States.
   d. Americans' tastes for all goods and services become stronger.

3. Economic sanctions levied against a target country are intended to cause the

   a. country to slide downward along its production possibilities curve.
   b. country to produce under conditions of increasing opportunity cost.

    c. country to move to a point inside its production possibilities curve.
    d. country's production possibilities curve to shift outward.

4. As a subject matter, economics is most concerned with

    a. making money in stocks, bonds, and real estate.
    b. understanding how to own and operate a business.
    c. the study of choice under conditions of scarcity.
    d. the allocation of unlimited resources among limited human wants.

5. The subject of macroeconomics would be most concerned with how

    a. a tax on cigarettes affects consumption by teenagers.
    b. a ban on immigrant workers from Mexico affects U.S. apple growers.
    c. poor growing conditions in Canada affect the price of wheat.
    d. national output and employment respond to changes in government spending.

6. Positive economics is concerned with all of the following questions *except*

    a. Why do engineers earn more than librarians?
    b. Do import tariffs protect the jobs of domestic workers?
    c. Will reducing income taxes cause households to work additional hours?
    d. Should welfare payments be increased to help the poor?

7. The factors of production include all of the following *except*

    a. money.
    b. entrepreneurship.
    c. capital.
    d. labor and land.

8. The United States will move from a point on its production possibilities curve to a point inside the curve if there is a(n)

    a. increase in the unemployment rate.
    b. rise in the level of price inflation.
    c. fall in the productivity of labor.
    d. decline in the birth rate.

9. If the slope of a straight line is –2, then the two variables in the graph are

    a. directly related.
    b. inversely related.
    c. cross-related.
    d. not related.

10. In a graph showing study time and grades in an economic course,

    a. study time and grades are generally considered to be inversely related.
    b. study time is the independent variable and grades are the dependent variable.
    c. the slope of the graph is generally considered to be negative.
    d. the graph generally appears as a downward-sloping straight line.

Answers to Multiple-Choice Questions

1. a   2. c   3. c   4. c   5. d   6. d.   7. a   8. a   9. b   10. b

Study Questions and Problems

1. Suppose that you receive a weekly income of $100, which you spend entirely on pizza and deluxe hamburgers. The price of a pizza is $10, and the price of a hamburger is $5. On a diagram, draw a line that shows your consumption possibilities. What is the opportunity cost of a hamburger? Would the opportunity cost of a hamburger change if the prices of pizza and hamburgers were cut in half? Calculate the opportunity cost of a pizza and a hamburger for each of the following changes:

   a. An increase in the price of pizzas to $20
   b. An increase in the price of hamburgers to $10
   c. A decline in weekly income to $80
   d. A rise in weekly income to $120

2. Table 1.3 shows production possibilities for steel and aluminum.

   a. Plot these production possibilities data on a diagram. On what assumptions is your production possibilities curve based?
   b. What is the opportunity cost of the first ton of steel? Between which points is the opportunity cost of a ton of steel the greatest?
   c. Explain how this curve reflects the law of increasing opportunity cost.
   d. Label a point G inside the curve. Why is this point inefficient? Label a point H outside the curve. Why is this point unattainable?
   e. Why might the production possibilities curve shift inward? Why might it shift outward?

Table 1.3	Production Possibilities Table					
	Production Alternatives					
Product	A	B	C	D	E	F
Steel (tons)	0	1	2	3	4	5
Aluminum (tons)	20	18	15	11	6	0

3. How does each of the following affect the location of an economy's production possibilities curve?

   a. A war leads to casualties for civilian workers.
   b. A new technology permits more oil to be extracted from a well.
   c. The economy's unemployment rate rises from 4 percent to 6 percent of the labor force.
   d. The economy decides to produce more CD players and fewer radios.

4. In the 1990s, civil war erupted in Bosnia. The war led to the destruction of natural resources and capital and caused casualties that decreased the supply of labor for the production of consumer goods and capital goods. Illustrate the impact of the war on Bosnia's production possibilities curve for consumer goods and capital goods.

5. Draw an economy's production possibilities curve for automobiles and airplanes. Assume a technological breakthrough occurs that allows greater productivity for autoworkers but not airplane workers. Draw a new production possibilities curve. Suppose instead that the technological breakthrough allows greater productivity for airplane workers but not autoworkers. Draw a new production possibilities curve.

6.   In response to Iraq's invasion of Kuwait in 1990, the United States and its allies imposed trade and financial sanctions on Iraq. Imports of Iraqi oil were terminated, as were exports of machinery, parts, and the like, to Iraq. Bank loans to Iraq and business investments in Iraq were also curtailed. Illustrate the effects of the economic sanctions on Iraq's production possibilities curve for textiles and oil. Under what conditions would the sanctions have been most likely to cause Iraq to withdraw from Kuwait?

EXPLORING FURTHER 1.1: A PRIMER ON TABLES AND GRAPHS

As you glance at this text, you will notice many tables and graphs. They are included to help you visualize and understand economic relationships. To understand how tables and graphs are constructed, let us consider an example that is familiar to you: the relationship between study time and grades in a college course.

Suppose that we conduct a survey of all students who recently completed an economics course, asking the number of hours they devoted to study each week and their course grade. The resulting information is shown in Table 1.4. According to the table, students who did not study at all received an F in the course. Students who studied 4 hours per week, on average, received a grade of C (2.0), and those who studied 8 hours per week received a grade of A (4.0). In the table, other grades are associated with other amounts of study time.

Let us now use the data in the table to construct Figure 1.8. We want to show visually how course grades change as study time changes. Study time is the determining factor, the **independent variable,** and it is placed on the horizontal axis of the figure. The course grade is the **dependent variable**—it depends on study time—and it is located on the vertical axis.

To plot pairs of study time and grades on a graph, start at the origin, where the axes meet. Count 2 units to the right on the horizontal axis, then count upward 1 unit parallel to the vertical axis, and then mark the spot. We've arrived at the point marked *H,* where 2 hours of study time yield a grade of 1.0 (D). To plot the next pair, we go 2 units to the right from point *H* and then upward 1 unit, arriving at point *I,* where 4 hours of study yield a grade of 2.0 (C). In a similar manner, we can plot all remaining pairs in Table 1.4, as the points *J* and *K.* Once we have plotted all the points describing the relationship between grades and study time, we can connect them with a line (or curve). This line shows how grades are related to the time spent studying. Because the graph is a straight line, we can say that the relationship between study time and grades is *linear.*

The study time–grade line in Figure 1.8(*a*) slopes *upward* to the right, illustrating a **direct** (positive) **relationship** between study time and grades. That is, more hours of study time yield higher grades and fewer hours of study time yield lower grades. Alternatively, if higher grades were associated with less study time, the line in the figure would slope *downward* to the right. Then, we would have an **inverse** (negative) **relationship** because grades and study time would change in opposite directions.

Movements along the Study Time–Grade Line

Referring to Figure 1.8(*a*), what causes movements from one point to another along the fixed study time–grade line? Such movements are caused by a change in the amount of time devoted to studying economics. Increases in study time result in an upward movement along this line, and decreases in study time result in a downward movement.

To illustrate such movements, as study time increases from 4 hours to 6 hours, we slide upward along the study time–grade line from point *I* to point *J,* and the grade point average increases from a 2.0 (C) to a 3.0 (B). Conversely, a decrease in study time from 6 hours to 4 hours would result in

Table 1.4	Studying Pays Off in an Economics Class		
Course Grade	Course Grade Point Average	Hours of Study per Week
F	0.0	0
D	1.0	2
C	2.0	4
B	3.0	6
A	4.0	8

a downward movement along the study time–grade line from point *J* to point *I*, and the grade point average falls from 3.0 to 2.0. Put simply, a change in study time causes us to move along a fixed study time–grade line.

Slope of the Study Time–Grade Line

Inspecting Figure 1.8, you will notice that each time study time increases by 2 hours, course grades increase by one letter grade, or 1.0. For example, when study time increases from 2 hours to 4 hours, the course grade increases from 1.0 (D) to 2.0 (C). Therefore, we conclude that the rate of change in course grades is 1 grade point for every 2-hour increase in study time.

The **slope** of the study time–grade line between any two points, say *I* and *J*, is defined as the vertical distance between the two points (the "rise") divided by the horizontal distance between the two points (the "run"). Between points *I* and *J*, grades increase by 1 grade point on the vertical axis when study time increases by 2 hours on the horizontal axis. Therefore,

$$\text{Slope} = \frac{\text{Vertical change}}{\text{Horizontal change}} = \frac{1}{2} = 0.5$$

Notice that the slope of 0.5 is positive because grades and study time change in the same direction—that is, grades and study time are directly or positively related. The slope of 0.5 indicates that there will be an increase of 1 grade point for every 2-hour increase in study time. Similarly, it tells us that for every 2-hour decrease in study time, there will be a decrease of 1 grade point. Because each 2 hours of additional study result in an improvement of 1 grade point, our graph is a straight line. Put simply, the slope of any straight line remains constant among all points along the line.

Alternatively, if higher grades were associated with less study time, the study time–grade line would slope downward to the right. Therefore, the slope of the line would have a negative value.

Shifts in the Study Time–Grade Line

So far, we have focused on relationships in which grades in an economics course depend on one other variable, study time. However, we recognize that grades are affected by more factors than just study time, such as the grading standard of the instructor, the academic abilities of students, and the availability of tutors for the course. When grades are affected by both study time and some other variable, changes in that other variable generally induce a *shift* in the study time–grade line. This is

Figure 1.8 Study Time–Grade Relationship in an Economics Class

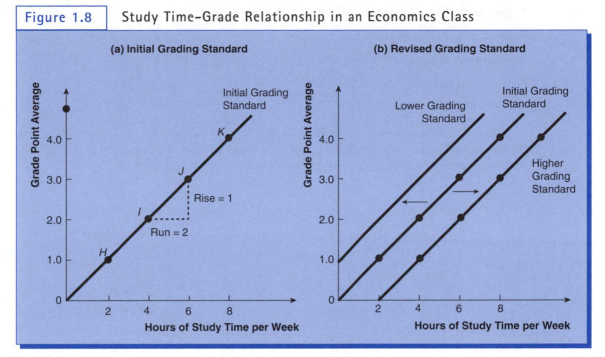

The relationship between study time and grades is depicted in this graph. Study time and grades are directly related because their values change in the same direction, resulting in an upward-sloping line. The slope of this straight line is the ratio of the vertical change to the horizontal change between any two points. When factors other than study time are allowed to change, the graph of the relationship between study time and grades will shift to a new location.

because whenever we draw the line between study time and grades, we are holding constant every other variable that might possibly affect grades.

Suppose that the instructor in the economics course decided to raise her grading standard, making it more difficult to achieve every other grade than an F. To achieve a grade of 2.0 (C), a student would now have to study 6 hours per week instead of only 4 hours, as shown in Figure 1.8(*a*). Whereas students could previously receive a grade of 3.0 (B) by studying 6 hours a week, they now must study 8 hours to get that grade.

Figure 1.8(*b*) illustrates the effect of the higher grade standard. In the figure, we have redrawn the study time–grade line from Figure 1.8(*a*), this time labeling the line *Higher Grading Standard*. Notice that the new line lies to the *right* of the initial line. This means that the underlying relationship between study time and grades has changed: Students now must study a greater amount of time to achieve each grade other than F. Alternatively, if the instructor lowered her grading standard, making it easier to achieve course grades, the study time–grade line would shift to the *left*, as shown by the line labeled *Lower Grading Standard*.

Recall that our study time–grade line may shift in response to factors other than changes in grading standards. For example, if the academic abilities of students increase, they could grasp economic principles in a shorter period of time, and the line would shift to the left. Similarly, greater availability of qualified tutors would cause the line to shift to the left.

This section has used the example of study time and grades in an economics class to illustrate several concepts:

- Independent and dependent variables
- Direct and inverse relationships
- Movement along a line
- Slope of a line
- Shifts in a line

Notice that these concepts also apply to economic relationships, such as supply and demand, investment, and consumption, which you will learn about as you read this text. Familiarize yourself with these concepts and apply them to graphs contained in subsequent chapters.

the
Microeconomy

Market Transactions: Demand and Supply Analysis

Chapter objectives

After reading this chapter, you should be able to:

1. Identify the major factors affecting demand.

2. Identify the major factors affecting supply.

3. Explain how prices and quantities are determined in competitive markets.

4. Explain why prices sometimes decrease and sometimes increase.

5. Predict how prices and quantities will respond to changes in demand or supply.

economics IN CONTEXT

LeBron James isn't the first high schooler to jump to the National Basketball Association (NBA), but he may be the best. A three-time *Mr Ohio* in high school, "King James" was highly promoted in the national media as a future NBA superstar while still a sophomore at St. Vincent - St. Mary's. At just 18, he was selected as the #1 pick in the 2003 NBA draft by the Cleveland Cavaliers and signed a $90 million shoe contract with Nike before his first professional slam dunk. Since that time, James has consistently been selected as an NBA All Star. His basketball IQ hovers at the level of genius, his physical skills are overpowering and off the charts, and despite being one of the league's youngest players, he has displayed the leadership skills of a veteran on a championship level team.

Why do athletes, such as LeBron James and Tiger Woods, earn more than the local telephone operator? Demand and supply. Why does a typical medical doctor earn $150,000 or more per year whereas a primary schoolteacher earns only $35,000? Demand and supply. Why do fresh watermelons cost 20 cents a pound in July and 50 cents a pound in April? You guessed it: Demand and supply. Why did the price of CD players fall from around $800, when they were first introduced in 1983, to less than $200 today? You're right again: Demand and supply. The workings of demand and supply explain many economic questions. Indeed, demand and supply are the most basic and powerful of all the economic tools that you will study in this text.

This chapter will introduce demand and supply analysis of market transactions, which shows how prices are determined by the competition among buyers for goods and services offered by competing sellers. Markets play a key role in addressing the problem of scarcity because they ration the available quantities of goods and services to buyers.

MARKETS

A **market** is a mechanism through which buyers (demanders) and sellers (suppliers) communicate in order to trade goods and services. Markets exist in many forms. The local farmers' market, espresso stand, grocery store, and barber shop are all familiar markets. Pike Place Market in Seattle, Washington, is famous for its fresh fish, fruits, and vegetables. The New York Stock Exchange is a national market in which buyers and sellers of stocks and bonds communicate with each other. At the international level, major banks such as Chase Manhattan Bank and Fuji Bank trade currencies in the foreign currency market. These markets link potential buyers to potential sellers.

This chapter concerns competitive markets in which many sellers compete for sales to many buyers, who are, in turn, competing with one another for available products. In such a market, each seller has a negligible effect on the market price because many other sellers are supplying similar goods. A seller has no motivation to undercut price, and if a seller charges a higher price, buyers will purchase products from other suppliers. Similarly, no single buyer can affect the price because each buyer purchases a negligible quantity. To understand how markets operate, we must first understand the principles of demand and supply.

DEMAND

How many Rolls-Royce automobiles will be bought this year? In explaining buyer behavior, economists emphasize the demand for goods and services. **Demand** is a schedule that shows the amount of a good or service that a buyer is *willing and able* to purchase at each possible price during a particular period. Just because an individual desires a Rolls-Royce, that does not necessarily mean that she has a *demand* for it. She also must be able to pay the $250,000 price, and she must be willing to purchase a Rolls-Royce instead of another vehicle, such as a Mercedes Benz or a BMW.

The amount of a product that is demanded depends on many factors, such as the following:

- Price of the product

- Prices of related products

- Consumer income

- Expectations of future price changes

- Tastes

- Number of consumers

In analyzing the behavior of buyers, we will pay special attention to the relationship between the quantity demanded and the price of a good. To study this relationship, we will hold constant all other factors that affect buyer behavior.

It is helpful to distinguish between *individual demand*, which is the demand of a particular buyer, and *market demand*, which is the sum of the individual demands of all buyers in the market. In most markets, there are many buyers, sometimes thousands or millions. Unless otherwise noted, when we talk about demand, we are referring to market demand.

The Demand Curve and the Law of Demand

Figure 2.1(*a*) shows the market demand schedule for compact discs (CDs). The first column of the table shows possible prices for CDs. The second column shows the quantities of CDs demanded per week at different prices, assuming that all other determinants affecting buyer behavior remain constant. The data in the demand schedule show that when the price of CDs is $25, consumers demand 1,000 CDs per week. At a price of $20, consumers demand 2,000 CDs per week, and so forth.

A market **demand curve** is a graphical representation of a market demand schedule. Figure 2.1(*b*) illustrates the weekly demand curve for CDs by plotting the data from the table. Points on the vertical axis represent price, and points on the horizontal axis represent the quantity demanded.

Notice that the market demand curve slopes downward, reflecting the **law of demand**: Price and quantity demanded are *inversely* or negatively related, assuming that all other factors affecting the quantity demanded remain the same. When the price is higher, the quantity demanded decreases; likewise, when the price is lower, the quantity demanded increases. We call the law of demand a "law" because it can be widely applied to buyer behavior. For example, when Ford finds itself overstocked with automobiles that it wants to get rid of, what does it do? It typically announces a sale, anticipating that a lower price will encourage buyers to purchase additional Ford automobiles.

The pricing of candy provides another example of the law of demand. Mars Inc. once conducted a pricing experiment for its M&Ms candy. Over a 1-year period, the price of a bag of M&Ms was held constant in 150 stores throughout the United States while the content weight of the bag was increased. With price kept constant and content weight increased, the price per ounce decreased. In the stores where the price declined, sales soon increased by 20 percent to 30 percent. As the law of demand would predict, a decrease in the price of M&Ms resulted in an increase in the quantity demanded.

| Figure 2.1 | The Demand Schedule and Demand Curve for CDs |

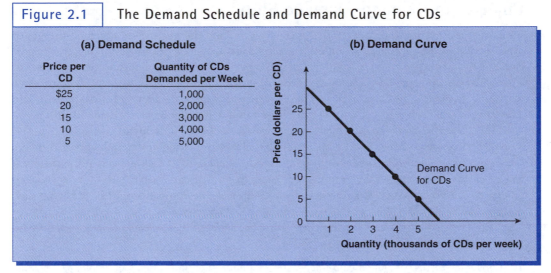

The market demand schedule shows the quantity of CDs demanded at various prices by all consumers. The market demand curve is a graphical representation of the market demand schedule. The market demand curve slopes downward, indicating that as price decreases, the quantity demanded increases. This inverse relationship between the change in the price of a good and the change in quantity demanded is known as the law of demand.

For a particular demand curve, a change in price results in a movement along the demand curve. In Figure 2.1(*b*), if the price of CDs falls from $15 to $10, consumption increases from 3,000 to 4,000 CDs per week. We call the movement along the demand curve—which results from a change in price—a **change in quantity demanded**. Notice that a change in quantity demanded is a movement along a particular demand curve rather than a shift in the demand curve.

What Explains the Law of Demand?

For most products, consumers are willing to buy more units at a lower price than they are at a higher price. This notion of the law of demand appears to be an accurate description of consumer behavior. Economists explain this law in terms of the substitution effect, the income effect, and the law of diminishing marginal utility.

According to the **substitution effect**, when the price of CDs falls—and all other determinants of demand remain the same—the price falls relative to the prices of all other similar goods, such as audio cassette tapes. Consumers have an incentive to substitute the cheaper good, CDs, for audio cassette tapes, which are now relatively more expensive. The lower price of CDs thus results in an increase in the quantity demanded.

The **income effect** also explains the law of demand. According to this principle, a decrease in the price of a CD results in an increase in the purchasing power of consumers' money incomes. As a result, consumers can purchase more CDs with a given amount of money. Generally speaking, a rise in purchasing power provides consumers an incentive to purchase more of a product. In this manner, a lower price of CDs results in an increase in the quantity demanded.

Finally, there is the principle of **diminishing marginal utility** (satisfaction). According to this principle, as a person consumes additional units of a particular good, each additional unit provides less and less additional utility. We can readily see this in the case of CDs. A buyer's desire for a CD when she has none may be very strong; the desire for a second CD is less pronounced, and so on. Therefore, additional CDs are "not worth it" unless the price decreases. This notion underlies the concept of the law of demand.

Changes in Demand: Demand Shifters

Recall that the relationship between the price of a good and the quantity of the good demanded over a period of time also depends on other determinants such as consumer tastes, prices of related goods, consumer expectations, the number of consumers in the market, and consumer income. For a particular demand curve, we assume that these other determinants remain constant. If any of these determinants change, the demand curve will *shift* either outward to the right or backward to the left. Therefore, we call a change in a variable that causes a shift in a demand curve a **demand shifter**. We call a shift in a demand curve caused by a demand shifter a **change in demand**.

Figure 2.2 shows a change in the demand for CDs. Because of changing determinants of demand, if consumers become willing and able to purchase additional CDs at each possible price, the result will be an *increase* in demand. In the figure, we can see that the demand curve shifts to the right, from *Old Demand Curve* to *New Demand Curve*. Conversely, if the determinants of demand change such that consumers are less willing and able to purchase CDs at each possible price, the demand curve for CDs will *decrease*—that is, the demand curve will shift to the *left*. Let us examine how each demand shifter affects the location of the demand curve.

1. **Consumer tastes.** Changing consumer tastes can have important effects on demand. A change in consumer tastes that makes a product more popular will shift the demand curve to the right. For example, as the popularity of Faith Hill (a country music singer) increases, consumers tend to demand more of her CDs. Conversely, if the New York Yankees have a losing season and become less popular with their fans, demand for tickets to their baseball games will shift to the left.

| Figure 2.2 | An Increase in Demand |

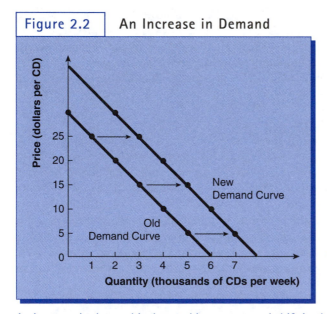

An increase in demand is denoted by an outward shift in the entire demand curve, indicating that more of the product is demanded at each price. An increase in the demand for a product can be caused by

- A favorable change in consumer tastes
- A rise in incomes if the product is a normal good; a fall in incomes if the product is an inferior good
- An increase in the price of a substitute good; a decrease in the price of a complementary good
- Consumer expectations of higher future prices
- A rise in the number of buyers served by the market

economics
IN ACTION

Yankees Slash Prices of Top Tickets to Fill Seats at New Park

The law of demand has many applications, including major league baseball. In 2009 the New York Yankees were proud to open their season in their brand new stadium which replaced their former stadium that was built in 1923. With a capacity of 52,325 seats, the new stadium cost $1.5 billion to construct, making it the second most expensive stadium in the world.

The Yankees dramatically raised ticket prices for the new season, assuming that fans would flock to home games. The Yankees especially thought that New York's business community would be willing to spend a premium for the best sports and entertainment the region had to offer. However, the Yankees were embarrassed after their first home stand of the season when they found that thousands of high-priced seats were unsold. The unsold tickets, some priced as high as $2,500 each, created an odd spectacle at the new park: While the rest of the stadium was packed during the Yankees' home games, many of the best seats closest to the field sat empty. The sight of those empty seats sparked mockery from critics who said the Yankees had badly overreached and ignored their fans who helped build Yankee Stadium with their tax money.

Bowing to the specter of empty seats, the Yankees acknowledged their prices were too steep even by Yankees standards. Therefore, the 25-time world champions slashed their top-end prices to stimulate attendance. For example, tickets going for $2,500 were cut to $1,250 while tickets priced at $1,000 were cut to $650, and so on. So as not to alienate existing season-ticket holders, who had already purchased tickets at premium prices, the Yankees provided them their choice of a refund or a credit. Also, the team doled out complimentary tickets to fill the empty seats behind home plate so visible on TV.

In hindsight, Yankees management realized that their outrageously high ticket prices were out of reach to many of their fans, especially during the weak economy of 2009. Simply put, the initial increase in ticket prices at the beginning of the season resulted in a dramatic decrease in quantity demanded. The result was a marketing problem for a team that traditionally provided the image that it cared about its fans.

Sources: Matthew Futterman and Darren Everson, "Yankees Slash Prices to Fill Costly Seats at New Park," *The Wall Street Journal*, April 29, 2009, pp. B1–B2; and Richard Sandomir, "Yankees Slash the Price of Top Tickets," *The New York Times*, April 28, 2009, available at http://www.nytimes.com/2009/04/29/sports/baseball/29tickets.html.

2. **Number of buyers.** Recall that the market demand is the sum of the individual demands of all consumers in the market. If the number of consumers in the market increases, market demand will shift to the right; a decrease in the number of consumers will cause market demand to shift to the left. In Eugene, Oregon, for example, local merchants are pleased to see student consumers attending the University of Oregon in September. This causes an increase in the demand for their products. When many students return to their homes in other cities over the December holidays, the demand for these products in Eugene decreases.

3. **Consumer income.** College students are well aware that changes in income affect demand. We classify products into two broad categories, depending on how demand for the product responds to changes in income. The demand for normal goods *increases* as income *rises* and *falls* as income *decreases*. Most goods, such as ski trips or new cars, are normal goods. People enjoy these goods and tend to buy more of them as their income rises. In contrast, inferior goods are goods such as public transportation, low-quality clothing, secondhand appliances, less expensive cuts of meat, and low-quality peanut butter. The demand for inferior goods actually *falls* as income *increases;* households will switch away from consuming these inferior goods to consuming normal goods such as new cars and sirloin steak. Conversely, *decreases* in income cause the demand for inferior goods to *increase*.

4. **Prices of related goods.** Changes in the prices of related goods can also affect the demand curve for a particular product. When we draw the demand curve for, say, Pepsi, we assume that the prices of Coke and other colas remain constant. But suppose that we relax this assumption and allow the price of Coke to change. If the price of Coke were to fall suddenly from $5 to $4 per case, there would be an incentive for consumers to switch from Pepsi to Coke. After all, Pepsi and Coke are substitute goods. For **substitute goods**, a *reduction* in the price of one good will *decrease* the demand for the other good; conversely, an *increase* in the price of one good will *increase* the demand for the other good.

A second type of related good is a **complementary good**. Complementary goods "go together" in that they are used in conjunction with each other. Some examples of complementary goods are CD players and CDs, peanut butter and jelly, hamburgers and french fries, cookies and milk, and spaghetti and meat sauce. If the price of CD players falls, we will buy more CD players and, therefore, we will buy more CDs—so the demand for CDs increases. Conversely, an increase in the price of peanut butter results in a decrease in the quantity of peanut butter demanded and thus a decline in the demand for jelly. For complementary goods, a *decrease* in the price of one good will *increase* the demand for the other good; conversely, an *increase* in the price of one good will *decrease* the demand for the other good.

5. **Expected future prices.** The demand for gasoline may change merely because people change their expectations about tomorrow's price of gasoline. When Saddam Hussein ordered the Iraqi army to invade Kuwait in 1990, many people expected that oil supplies would be disrupted because of the war. The anticipated shortage of gasoline—and the resulting price increase—prompted many people to fill their tanks at each opportunity, thus increasing the demand for gasoline. In this manner, changes in consumer expectations can cause the demand curve for a product to change.

Another example of consumer reaction to expected future prices occurred in 2002 when smokers in Oregon purchased cartons of cigarettes by the armload before a 60-cents-per-pack increase in the state tax on cigarettes. The state tax increased from 68 cents to $1.28 after voters approved the tax hike by a two-to-one margin. Following the tax hike, a pack-a-day smoker paid $219 more a year, or $467.20, in taxes for the habit.

CHECK POINT

1. Describe the law of demand and the explanations for the law of demand.

2. Differentiate between a change in quantity demanded and a change in demand, identifying the reason(s) for each. How is each change represented graphically?

3. What factors cause a demand curve to shift? What happens to a demand curve when each of these factors changes?

SUPPLY

The other side of our market model involves the quantities of goods and services that sellers would like to offer to the market. **Supply** is a schedule showing the amounts of a good or service that a firm or household is willing and able to sell at each possible price during a particular period. In economics, *supply* could refer to the number of ice cream bars that a grocery store wants to sell or the number of hours that a worker is willing to spend on the job.

The quantity of a particular good or service that suppliers plan to sell depends on many factors:

- Price of the good
- Prices of resources
- Technology
- Prices of other goods produced
- Expected future prices
- Taxes and subsidies
- Number of suppliers

In analyzing the behavior of suppliers, we will emphasize the relationship between the quantity supplied and the price of a good. Therefore, we will hold constant all other determinants that affect supplier behavior.

It is helpful to distinguish between *individual supply*, which is the supply of a particular seller, and *market supply*, which is the sum of the individual supplies of all sellers in the market. Unless otherwise noted, when we talk about supply, we are referring to market supply.

The Supply Curve and the Law of Supply

Supply shows us the quantities that will be offered for sale at various prices. Supply refers to the schedule that relates price and quantity, and thus it is called a supply schedule or a supply curve. Figure 2.3(*a*) shows the market supply schedule for CDs. The first column of the table shows possible prices for CDs. The second column shows the quantities of CDs supplied per week at different prices, assuming that all of the other determinants of supply remain unchanged. We call this amount the **quantity supplied**. Notice that the quantity supplied refers to a single point on a supply schedule: As the price changes, the quantity supplied changes, but not the entire supply schedule. The data in our supply schedule show that when the price of CDs is $5, producers supply 1,000 CDs per week. At a price of $10, producers supply 2,000 CDs per week, and so forth.

A market **supply curve** is a graphical representation of a market supply schedule. Figure 2.3(*b*) illustrates the weekly supply curve for CDs by plotting the data from the table. Points on the vertical

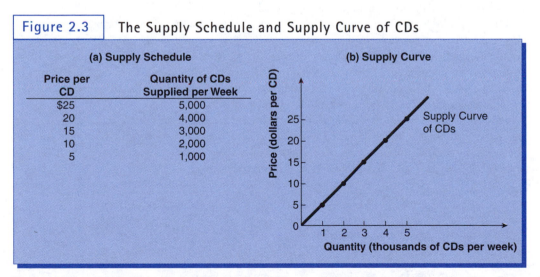

Figure 2.3   The Supply Schedule and Supply Curve of CDs

(a) Supply Schedule

Price per CD	Quantity of CDs Supplied per Week
$25	5,000
20	4,000
15	3,000
10	2,000
5	1,000

(b) Supply Curve

The market supply schedule shows the quantity of CDs supplied at various prices by all sellers. The market supply curve is a graphical representation of the market supply schedule. The market supply curve is upward sloping, indicating that as price increases, the quantity supplied increases. The direct relationship between the change in the price of a product and the change in the quantity supplied is known as the law of supply.

axis show price, and points on the horizontal axis show the quantity supplied. Notice that the data indicate an *upward-sloping* supply curve, which suggests a positive or *direct* relationship between price and quantity supplied. As the price of CDs increases, the quantity supplied increases; as the price decreases, the quantity supplied decreases. We call this relationship the **law of supply**. The law of supply states that, in general, sellers are willing and able to make more of their product available at a higher price than at a lower price, all other determinants of supply being constant.

The tendency for the cost of additional output to increase explains the law of supply—that is, it costs more to produce the second unit of output than the first, more to produce the third than the second, and so on. To produce more CDs, suppose manufacturers have to hire more labor and purchase additional raw materials. If these resources are in relatively short supply, CD manufacturers may have to pay higher prices to obtain them, resulting in higher and higher costs. All other things being constant, CD manufacturers would be induced to produce additional CDs only when the price of CDs rises. As a result, a higher price causes a greater level of output to be supplied to the market.

Oil Firms Squeeze More Crude from Wells

Does the law of supply pertain to oil production? Yes! Major oil firms, such as Shell and ExxonMobil, realize that, as existing oil wells dry up, the continued production of oil will require deeper drilling and more exploration to locate new oil fields. Because these activities add to a producer's costs, they require a higher market price. Unless price rises, a firm cannot realize a net gain (profit) from producing more oil. Consider the following example.

Although there is still plenty of oil left in the ground, most of the supplies that are easy to reach have already been developed; therefore, oil firms must turn to oil deposits that are more expensive to recover. Heavy oils, which can be the consistency of molasses, or even denser, are costlier to bring to the surface than light oils.

From Alaska's North Slope to the Gulf of Mexico, oil producers have invested billions of dollars in *improved oil recovery*—unconventional technology that is designed to extract additional crude oil from existing wells. Conventional drilling methods tap only about 15 percent of a typical well's potential, leaving 85 percent of the oil still locked in the earth. Improved oil recovery techniques increase the amount of oil that can be pulled out of the earth—up to 80 percent of the oil from some reservoirs—thus extending the productive life of fields.

Oil firms have long realized that, by introducing substances deep into underground formations, they can wring more crude oil from existing wells. For example, water forced into crevices in subterranean rocks can flush oil out and, because the oil is lighter, push it up a nearby well. Also, steam injected underground helps thin and loosen trapped oil. Moreover, carbon dioxide and natural gas can be used to flush out stubborn oil. Even gravel and walnut shells are blasted into wells, the idea being to create cracks in adjacent rock and draw more oil into wells.

However, these substances require additional costs. For example, it takes a lot of natural gas to make the steam that is injected into oil wells. The cost of enhanced recovery methods varies widely, though most common methods range between $5 and $10 a barrel. At what price point do energy sources begin to generate some profits? Here are some estimates as of 2008:[1]

- Saudi Arabian oil, $10 (per barrel)
- North Sea oil, $25
- Oil sands with existing facilities, $25
- Venezuelan heavy oil, $25–$30
- Oil sands with net facilities, $50
- Ethanol, $50 and up

---

1. Simmons and Co. International, *Energy Statistics,* available at http://www.simmonsco-intl.com/research_upstream.aspx/.

Crude oil has recently been selling at a high enough price for a long enough time that oil firms could justify the additional costs of improved oil recovery techniques in order to extract every barrel possible. In particular, the high price of oil especially spurred oil production in ultra-heavy oil fields throughout the United States, Canada, and the Middle East.

Changes in Supply: Supply Shifters

Recall that a supply curve refers to the entire relationship between the price of a product and the quantity supplied, when all other determinants of supply remain unchanged. When these other determinants change, the supply curve will *shift* either outward to the right or backward to the left. Therefore, we call a change in a variable that causes a shift a **supply shifter**. A shift in a supply curve induced by a supply shifter is called a **change in supply**.

Figure 2.4 shows the change in the supply of CDs. Because of changing determinants of supply, if producers become willing and able to supply additional CDs at each possible price, the result will be an *increase* in supply. In the figure, we can see that the supply curve shifts to the right, from *Old Supply Curve* to *New Supply Curve*. However, if the determinants of supply change, such that suppliers are less willing and able to supply CDs at each possible price, the supply of CDs will *decrease*—that is, the supply curve will shift to the *left*. Let us examine how each supply shifter affects the location of the supply curve.

1. **Resource prices.** The possible profit at a particular price depends on the prices that a supplier must pay for the resources to produce a good or service. For example, a *decrease* in the prices

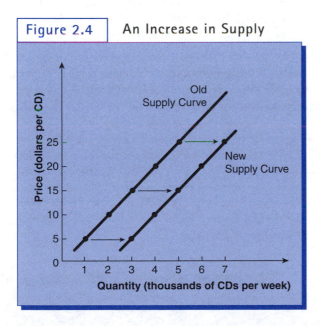

Figure 2.4   An Increase in Supply

An increase in supply is denoted by a rightward shift of the entire supply curve, indicating that more CDs are supplied at each price. An increase in the supply of a good can be caused by

- A decrease in the price of resources used to produce the good
- New technologies that reduce the cost of producing the good
- Expectations of future falling prices, which may cause sellers to increase their current supply to the market
- A decrease in an excise tax on the sale of the good
- An increase in subsidies to producers of the good

of labor and materials used to produce CDs decreases the cost of producing CDs, resulting in a greater profit from selling a particular quantity. This *increases* the supply of CDs. Conversely, increases in resource prices result in falling profitability and a decrease in supply.

2. **Technology.** *Improvements* in technology tend to reduce the amount of resources needed to produce a given level of output, resulting in lower costs of production and increased supply. For example, the development of a new technology by Texas Instruments has reduced the cost of producing calculators and increased their supply.

3. **Prices of other goods.** If a Chrysler assembly line can manufacture either minivans or pickup trucks, the quantity of minivans manufactured depends on the price of trucks, and the quantity of trucks manufactured depends on the price of minivans. Given the price of minivans, a decline in the price of trucks signals to Chrysler that switching to minivans with a higher relative price yields higher profit. The result is an increase in the supply of minivans.

4. **Expected future prices.** Expectations affect the current output of producers. For example, as a result of the 1990 Iraqi invasion of Kuwait, oil companies anticipated that oil prices would increase significantly. Their initial response was to withhold part of their oil from the market so that they could realize larger profits later when oil prices increased. Such a response shifted the supply curve for oil to the left.

5. **Taxes and subsidies.** Certain taxes, such as excise taxes, have the same impact on supply as an increase in the price of resources. The effect of an excise tax placed on the sale of gasoline imposes an additional cost on gas stations, and the supply curve shifts to the left. Conversely, subsidies have the opposite effect. When the state of Washington financed most of the construction cost of a new stadium for the Seattle Seahawks football team, it effectively lowered the cost of Seahawk football games and increased their supply.

6. **Number of suppliers.** Because market supply is the sum of the amounts supplied by all sellers, it depends on the number of sellers in the market. If the number of sellers increases, supply will shift to the right. For example, in 2000 the National Hockey League expanded its membership to include Minneapolis/St. Paul, thus shifting the market supply curve outward to the right.

Flat panel TVs provide an example of change in supply. When flat panel TVs were first introduced in the 1990s, they cost as much as $20,000. By 2009, the price of a 42-inch flat panel TV had fallen to less than $900. The price has decreased due to an increase in supply. Factors that caused the supply of flat panel TVs to increase included improvements in technology that reduced the costs of production, large investments in new manufacturing plants in China, Malaysia, and other Asian countries, and entry of new producers into the market. With an increase in supply came a decrease in price and thus an increase in the quantity demanded of flat panel TVs.

CHECK POINT

1. Describe the law of supply and explain why the supply curve normally slopes upward.

2. Distinguish between a change in quantity supplied and a change in supply, identifying the reason(s) for each.

3. What factors cause a supply curve to shift? What happens to a supply curve when each of these factors changes?

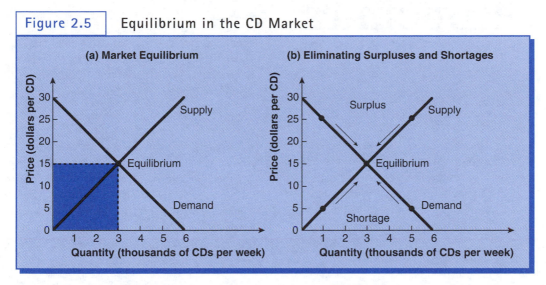

Figure 2.5 | Equilibrium in the CD Market

The demand and supply schedules represent the market for CDs. The intersection of the market supply curve and the market demand curve indicates an equilibrium price of $15 and an equilibrium quantity of 3,000 CDs bought and sold per week. Any price above $15 will result in a weekly surplus of CDs and pressure to push the price downward. Similarly, any price below $15 will result in a weekly shortage of CDs and pressure to push the price upward. By influencing the quantities demanded and supplied, price adjustments promote market equilibrium.

DEMAND, SUPPLY, AND EQUILIBRIUM

Buyers and sellers have different views of a product's price because buyers *pay* the price and sellers *receive* it. Therefore, a higher price is favorable for a seller but is unfavorable for a buyer. As price increases, sellers increase their quantity supplied while buyers decrease their quantity demanded. Through the interaction of demand and supply, we can find a price at which the quantity that buyers want to purchase equals the quantity that sellers will offer for sale.

Market equilibrium occurs when the price of a product adjusts so that the quantity that consumers will purchase at that price is identical to the quantity that suppliers will sell. At the point of market equilibrium, the forces of demand and supply are balanced so that there is no tendency for the market price to change over a given period.

Figure 2.5 combines the demand and supply curves introduced in Figures 2.1 and 2.3.

Referring to Figure 2.5(*a*), notice that the two curves intersect at a price of $15 per CD. At this price, the quantity that buyers want to purchase (3,000 CDs) equals the quantity that sellers wish to offer for sale (3,000 CDs). Therefore, the market for CDs is in equilibrium, implying that the price will not change unless the demand or supply curve shifts. The price at which buyers' intentions are equal to sellers' intentions is called the **equilibrium price**. Notice that the equilibrium price acts to ration CDs so that everyone who wants to purchase the product will find it available, and everyone who wants to sell the product can do so successfully.

If the market does not initially establish an equilibrium price, competition among suppliers to sell the product and competition among buyers to purchase the product will cause the price to move to an equilibrium level. Figure 2.5(*b*) shows the same supply and demand curves we have examined in Figure 2.5(*a*), but this time the initial price is $25 per CD. At this price, we refer to the supply curve and find that suppliers are willing to sell 5,000 CDs per week; referring to the demand curve, we find that buyers are willing to purchase 1,000 CDs per week. The amount by which the quantity supplied exceeds the quantity demanded—4,000 CDs—is called a **surplus**, or excess supply. However, the surplus in the market will not be permanent. To clear the market of their unsold CDs, sellers will

economics
IN ACTION

Rush-Hour Horrors: Congestion Pricing

Traffic jams. Most of us have endured them and perhaps we have even said a few choice words while sitting in them. Longer commutes cost not only time, but money, too. Congestion means reduced fuel efficiency and more wear and tear on vehicles and roads. We build new roads, but we often end up with congestion, as more people choose driving over other modes of transportation. We could build new mass transit systems, but getting people to use existing ones is tough enough. What else can we do?

Economists realize that this dilemma is typical of most economic problems—such as determining how much an acre of land is worth—and thus has a similar solution, namely—market forces. Like acres of land, roads are a scarce resource that our market system effectively divvies up through prices. And prices act to clear away market imbalances between demand and supply.

Congestion occurs when too many drivers want to use the roads, which have fixed capacity, at the same time because their price is too low. Raising the price, which is now essentially zero, would reduce the quantity demanded and better allocate the limited space.

Governments usually provide roads through tax dollars, which are used to pay for their construction and maintenance. Thus, drivers believe they are already paying their way for road and highway usage through gas taxes and licensing fees. What drivers are actually paying for, however, is their direct use of roads. When a person chooses to drive, that person's activity adds an additional car to the traffic flow, which slows the commute cost for all drivers. This additional "cost," which occurs solely because one extra person chooses to drive, is a social cost of driving that is not usually paid for through taxes or fees.

Many economists argue that drivers should be assessed tolls to reduce the amount of rush-hour traffic. Under this system, a person driving during rush hour would have to pay a toll. This would force drivers to decide whether they are willing to pay the price or find an alternative. Electronic metering devices, which read signals from small, prepaid transponders inside cars, are currently available. These devices not only keep traffic moving but can also automatically raise or lower tolls at different times of the day.

In response to the tolls, some drivers might carpool, change their schedules, or commute via mass transit in order to either pay lower tolls or avoid paying them at all. These drivers, now aware of the true cost of their commutes, would alter their habits because this higher cost would be greater than the price they would be willing to pay to drive to work alone during rush hour. In time, then, the real demand for roads and highways would be revealed, promoting better infrastructure decisions and better use of pavement, time, and money.

The use of price rationing for road use has been implemented in Orange County, California, in San Diego, and at all Hudson River crossings between New York and New Jersey. It has also been used in Singapore to reduce rush-hour traffic jams. In conjunction with other measures to control traffic, tolls have helped reduce traffic in central Singapore by 45 percent during peak hours. However, adverse side effects also occurred. For example, just outside the central business district, traffic jams worsened as motorists traveled on roads they could drive on without paying. Other cities using congestion pricing are London (United Kingdom) and Oslo and Bergen (Norway).

reduce the price. The price reduction will result in a decrease in the quantity supplied and an increase in the quantity demanded, thereby eliminating the surplus. The weekly surplus in the CD market will be eliminated when the price falls to $15, the point at which the supply and demand curves intersect.

Just as a price above the equilibrium price results in a surplus, a price below the equilibrium price entails a shortage. Referring to Figure 2.5(*b*), suppose that the initial price is $5 per CD. At this price, we refer to the supply curve and find that sellers are willing to supply 1,000 CDs per week; referring to the demand curve, we find that buyers are willing to purchase 5,000 CDs per week. The amount by which the quantity demanded exceeds the quantity supplied—again, 4,000 CDs—is called a **shortage**, or excess demand. When a shortage occurs, competitive bidding among buyers pushes the price upward. A rising price causes an increase in the quantity supplied and a decrease in quantity demanded until the equilibrium price is restored at $15 per CD.

We have seen how adjustments in price coordinate the decisions of buyers and sellers. If the price rises above the equilibrium level, excess supply will set in motion forces that cause price and quantity to return to their equilibrium levels. If the price falls below the equilibrium level, excess demand will cause price and quantity to return to their equilibrium levels. By regulating the quantities supplied and demanded, adjustments in price serve to promote market equilibrium.

SHIFTS IN DEMAND AND SUPPLY

Market equilibrium is the combination of price and quantity at which the plans of sellers and buyers synchronize. Once a market attains equilibrium, that combination of price and quantity will remain unchanged until a shifter (determinant) of supply or demand changes. A change in a determinant will cause a shift in the supply curve or demand curve; the result will be a change in the equilibrium price and quantity.

Figure 2.6 illustrates the effects of changes in the demand and supply of CDs. In the four cases illustrated, the original equilibrium occurs at the intersection of the market supply curve (S_0) and the market demand curve (D_0). At the equilibrium price of $15 per CD, 3,000 units are demanded and supplied per week.

First, let us consider the effects of a change in demand, assuming that supply is constant. Referring to Figure 2.6(a), suppose that the rising popularity of CDs results in an *increase* in market demand from D_0 to D_1. When demand increases, the price that makes the quantity demanded equal the quantity supplied is $20 per CD. At this price, 4,000 CDs are bought and sold each week. Therefore, an increase in the demand for a product causes both its equilibrium price and equilibrium quantity to increase.

Conversely, suppose that the declining popularity of CDs results in a *decrease* in market demand from D_0 to D_1 as seen in Figure 2.6(b). Because of the decrease in demand, the equilibrium price falls to $10 per CD, and the equilibrium quantity declines to 2,000 CDs per week. Therefore, a decrease in the demand for a product causes both its equilibrium price and equilibrium quantity to fall.

Let us now consider the effects of a change in supply, assuming that demand is constant. Referring to Figure 2.6(c), assume that new cost-saving technologies are introduced in CD manufacturing plants, causing the market supply of CDs to increase from S_0 to S_1. Following the increase in supply, the new equilibrium price is $10 per CD, and the equilibrium quantity is 4,000 units. Therefore, an increase in supply causes the equilibrium price to fall but equilibrium quantity increases.

Finally, suppose that rising wages prompt the market supply of CDs to shift from S_0 to S_1 as in Figure 2.6(d). With the new market supply curve, the equilibrium price is $20 per CD, and the equilibrium quantity is 2,000 units. Therefore, when supply decreases, the equilibrium quantity declines, and the equilibrium price rises.

We can now make the following predictions, all other factors remaining constant:

- When demand increases, both the equilibrium price and the equilibrium quantity increase.

- When demand decreases, both the equilibrium price and the equilibrium quantity decrease.

- When supply increases, the equilibrium price falls and the equilibrium quantity rises.

- When supply decreases, the equilibrium price rises and the equilibrium quantity falls.

| Figure 2.6 | Changes in Demand and Supply: Effects on Price and Quantity |

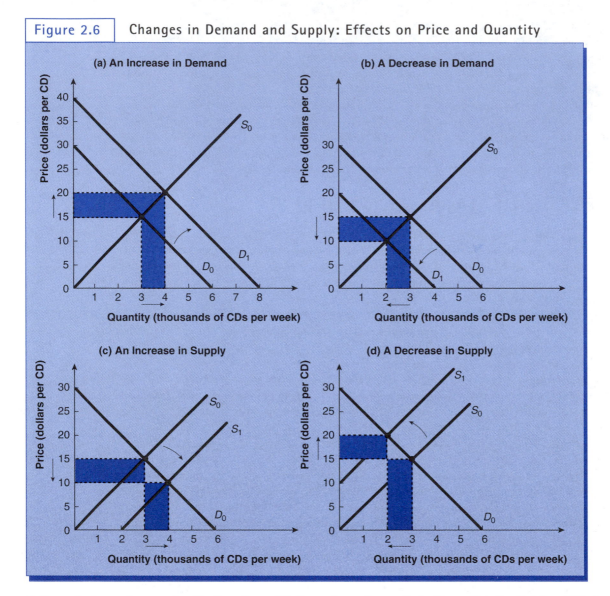

A change in demand or supply will affect the equilibrium price and quantity in the market. Panels (*a*) and (*b*) show the effects of an increase and a decrease in demand, respectively; panels (*c*) and (*d*) show the effects of an increase and a decrease in supply, respectively.

In each of the preceding examples, only one side of the market changed while the other side remained constant. In reality, however, complicated changes involving changes in both demand and supply shifters often occur. For example, both the demand and supply of natural gas might decrease at the same time. Although simultaneous changes in demand and supply are not illustrated in this chapter, try applying your graphing skills to the examples in Table 2.1. See whether you can verify the conclusions of each example.

| Table 2.1 | Impacts of Changes in Demand and Supply | | | |

Change in Demand	Change in Supply	Impact on Equilibrium Price	Impact on Equilibrium Quantity
Decrease	Decrease	Indeterminate*	Decrease
Increase	Increase	Indeterminate*	Increase
Decrease	Increase	Decrease	Indeterminate*
Increase	Decrease	Increase	Indeterminate*

* Indeterminate indicates that the price (quantity) might increase, decrease, or stay the same.

CHECK POINT

1. Explain how the forces of supply and demand push the price toward equilibrium.

2. Draw a diagram that shows how shortages cause the price to rise toward equilibrium and surpluses cause the price to fall toward equilibrium.

3. What happens to the equilibrium price and quantity in a competitive market in each of the following cases: (a) supply increases, (b) supply decreases, (c) demand increases, (d) demand decreases.

CONTEMPORARY APPLICATIONS OF DEMAND AND SUPPLY

Now that we have learned about the effects of changes in demand and supply, let's apply our principles to some real-world situations. Consider the following applications.

Bike Competition Puts the Brakes on Schwinn

The Schwinn Bicycle Co. provides an example of how increasing competition can result in a decrease in demand for a firm's product. Established in Chicago in 1895, the Schwinn Bicycle Co. grew to build bicycles that became the standard of the industry. Although the Great Depression forced most bike companies out of business, Schwinn survived by manufacturing high-quality bikes that were sold by dealers who wanted to promote the brand. Schwinn emphasized constant innovation, adding features to its bikes such as balloon tires, built-in kickstands, head and tail lights, and chrome fenders. By the 1960s, the Schwinn Sting-Ray was viewed as the bike that virtually every child wanted. Celebrities such as Ronald Reagan and Captain Kangaroo were seen on television commercials proclaiming that "Schwinn bikes are the best."

Although Schwinn dominated the U.S. bike industry from the 1940s to the 1960s, the market was changing. Bikers desired something other than heavy, durable bikes which had always been Schwinn's hallmark. Competitors arose such as Trek which produced mountain bikes and Mongoose which built bikes for BMX racing. These firms aggressively marketed their bikes at discounted prices to attract customers away from Schwinn. At the same time, tariffs on imported bikes motivated Americans to buy them from low-cost companies in Taiwan, South Korea, Japan, and eventually China.

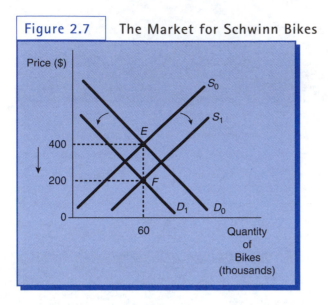

Figure 2.7   The Market for Schwinn Bikes

As competition escalated, Schwinn relocated its production to a plant in Greenville, Mississippi in 1981. Like other U.S. businesses, Schwinn moved its production to the South in order to hire non-union workers at lower wages. Schwinn also acquired components manufactured by low-wage workers in foreign countries. However, production in the Greenville plant was hampered by inefficiency and uneven product quality, and the bikes that it built were no better than the ones imported from abroad. As its losses piled up, Schwinn filed for bankruptcy in 1993.

Eventually Schwinn was bought by the Pacific Cycle Co., which outsourced the manufacturing of Schwinn bikes to low-wage workers in China. Today, most Schwinn bikes are produced in Chinese factories and are sold by Wal-Mart and other discount merchants. And under Pacific's ownership, bikers do pay less for a new Schwinn. It may not be the premier bike that was the old Schwinn, but it sells for about $180, about one-third of the original price in today's dollars.

Analysis.   Referring to Figure 2.7, assume that Schwinn is a typical firm operating in a competitive bike market. Suppose that consumers view the bikes sold by Schwinn and other firms to be substitutes and that the price of a Schwinn bike is $400. As other firms cut the price of their bikes, cyclists demand greater quantities of them. The demand curve for Schwinn bikes thus decreases from D_0 to D_1, resulting in falling sales for Schwinn. To improve its competitiveness, Schwinn decreases its costs by replacing high-wage union workers with non-union workers at lower wages, causing its supply curve to increase from S_0 to S_1. This allows the firm to reduce price and increase sales, although not by enough to avoid bankruptcy.

Rising Health Care Costs Cripple Households

The high costs of health care illustrate another application of demand and supply. Although Americans are living longer, healthier lives, the share of the nation's income that is devoted to health care has been growing rapidly. Growing concern about the rising costs of health care and limited access to insurance has led to the development of many proposals for health care reform.

The costs of health care services are increasing because the market demand curve for health care is rising more rapidly than the market supply curve. Figure 2.8 shows the market for health care services. Assume that the equilibrium price for these services is $200—the point at which the supply curve (S_0) intersects the demand curve (D_0). Suppose that the supply curve of health care services increases to S_1, but the demand curve increases by a larger amount to D_1. Because the increase in

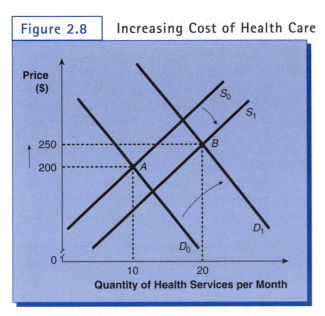

Figure 2.8 | Increasing Cost of Health Care

The increase in the demand curve for health care services is larger than the increase in the supply curve. Because the increase in demand pulls the price of health care up by a larger amount than the increase in supply pushes the price down, the price of health care increases.

demand pulls the price of health care services up by a larger amount than the increase in supply pushes price down, the price of health care services increases to $250. Let us examine further the characteristics that underlie the demand and supply curves of health care.

Demand for Health Care Services. Consumers are generally responsive to changes in the prices of health care services, such as doctors' and hospitals' services. This is because people consider health care to be a necessity rather than a luxury. Economists estimate that a 10-percent increase in the price of medical care tends to decrease the quantity demanded by only 2 percent. This lack of resistance to price changes partly explains why doctors and hospitals have strong incentives to raise prices. In addition, the demand curve for health care has shifted to the right over time, putting upward pressure on price. Here are some of the reasons why the demand for health care services has increased.

- **Rising incomes.** Rising incomes of households in the United States have caused the demand curve for health care services to increase. Economists estimate that per-capita spending on health care increases approximately in proportion to increases in per-capita income.

- **An aging population.** As people age, the demand curve for health care services increases because older people tend to become ill more frequently and remain ill for longer periods.

- **Health insurance.** Because people with health insurance are protected against the full cost of a serious illness or injury, they are likely to go to the doctor more often and choose more complex procedures, thus increasing the demand curve for health care services.

- **Physician incentives.** Because physicians generally know more about health care than their patients, they specify the types and amounts of medical tests and procedures that are consumed. When physicians are paid separately for each service they render, they have an incentive to specify tests and procedures that are not essential. Moreover, because every patient represents a potential source of a malpractice suit, physicians tend to recommend more services than are justified medically in order to protect themselves against malpractice suits.

Supply of Health Care Services. Sluggish increases in the supply of medical services have also contributed to higher prices. For example, the supply of doctors in the United States rose from 435,000 doctors in 1980 to more than 700,000 in 2009, an increase of about 60 percent. However, this increase in supply was more than offset by an increase in demand, and the price of services provided by doctors rose during this period. The sluggish increase in the supply of doctors is attributable to the considerable financial resources and time needed to train doctors as well as barriers that exist to keep human resources out of the medical field. Critics have maintained that the American Medical Association has willingly kept admissions to medical school—and thus the supply of doctors—artificially low in order to give doctors greater ability to increase the price of their services. In recent years, however, these problems have become less serious.

Another cause of rising health care prices is slow productivity growth in the health care industry. Health care is a labor-intensive service, and it is usually harder to increase productivity for services than for goods. For example, how would you noticeably raise the productivity of nurses in the birthing room of a hospital?

Finally, we must consider technology. Technological advancements, such as open-heart surgery and body scanners, increase the quantity and quality of hospital services. The use of new surgical techniques has flourished in recent years. Although improved surgical techniques will likely lengthen the lives of many Americans, they are also costly to develop and administer, thus adding to the cost of health care.

"That's easy," you may have been saying as you read the previous examples, which showed you how to apply the principles of demand and supply to a contemporary issue. Can you conduct economic analysis on your own? As you read the following application, draw supply and demand graphs and use them to explain the effects of changing market conditions. Can you differentiate between the demand shifters and supply shifters in these applications?

Coping with America's Thirst for Oil

Few things generate more attention and anxiety among Americans than the availability and prices of oil and gasoline. Eras of tight supplies and price increases are accompanied by high levels of media attention and consumer questioning about their causes and impacts.

Not only are America's imports of oil larger than the oil consumption of any other country in the world, but also we currently import about 60 percent of our oil, up from 33 percent in the 1970s. This is largely the result of rising demand for oil accompanied by tight domestic supply. For example, the demand for gasoline has soared along with the increase in the number of vehicles on the road, and people are driving them more than ever. Also, we have been buying bigger, heavier cars, minivans, and sport-utility vehicles and getting commensurately lousy gas mileage. Moreover, we insist on driving the highways at 70 to 80 miles per hour, paying a 10-percent to 15-percent penalty in gas mileage over 55 miles per hour.

A decrease in oil imports would offer important benefits for Americans. It would reduce the number of dollars flowing out of the country and help moderate prices in world oil markets. It would also increase our margin of safety when the next accident, such as a Hurricane Katrina, disrupts domestic oil supply. Moreover, it would strengthen our foreign policy by making us less dependent on oil suppliers in the unstable Middle East.

One way of reducing oil imports would be for the United States to increase its supply of oil or substitute energies. This might be accomplished by allowing oil companies to drill offshore or on federal land designated as wilderness in Alaska, where there is a good chance they might find oil. But what happens when the wilderness is destroyed? Who pays for that? Another way of making more oil available is to develop additional plants to refine and process crude oil into usable products such as gasoline and heating oil. However, the building of additional refineries depends on environmental restrictions, as well as the reluctance of oil companies to invest huge sums of money in a refinery that may or may not be needed. Moreover, the United States has developed alternative fuels such as

economics
IN ACTION

Oil Prices on a Roller Coaster

The period 2008-2009 saw extreme volatility in oil prices, with heights of $147 per barrel followed by a sharp decline to less than $40. What accounted for such erratic prices? The principles of supply and demand help explain this situation.

In 2008, tight supply characterized the world oil market. Expansion of supply was limited by delays in investment and shortages of equipment, people, and engineering skills which resulted in costs more than doubling between 2004 and 2008.

As oil prices rose to $100 per barrel, other factors became increasingly important. Expectations of future rising prices triggered a flight to oil and other commodities as a hedge against inflation and political uncertainty in the Middle East. The impact of speculation on rising prices was self-reinforcing, resulting in more speculation and still higher prices. Also, it was widely felt that demand was insensitive to price changes and would remain strong in spite of price increases. Finally, it was thought that oil consumption in developing countries, such as China and India, would continue to grow at a rapid rate. Simply put, strong demand coupled with tight supply set oil prices on their upward surge.

When oil prices skyrocketed to $147 per barrel in 2008, they reached the breaking point and the foundations of price escalation deteriorated. Rapidly increasing oil prices did result in a decrease in the quantity demanded, although it took longer than anticipated. In response to the price of gas rising to more than $4 per gallon, quantity demanded decreased by more than 1 million barrels per day. Also, auto buyers increasingly turned to energy-saving vehicles and businesses looked to ways to achieve energy efficiencies. Then came a global financial crisis that resulted in a severe recession. As the world economy shrank, so did the demand for oil. This reversal resulted in oil prices plunging downward by about $100 per barrel in only 4 months.

A key question for the future is what will happen to the supply of oil. If prices remain low, investments in new oil production capacity will likely be slow. As the world recovers from recession, will the cycle of escalating oil prices again occur?

Source: Daniel Yergin and David Hobbs, "Recession Shock: The Oil Market and the Global Economy," *The Wall Street Journal,* February 10, 2009, p. A7.

biodiesel and ethanol, as well as electric cars, but increasing their production is a lengthy process. Simply put, supply-side policies alone will not easily solve America's oil dependence problem.

Alternatively, the quantity of oil imported would decline if Americans reduced their consumption. The most drastic method of forcing Americans to conserve oil is for the government to implement a system of non-price rationing. During World War II, for example, the U.S. government defined a target consumption level of gasoline (and other products such as meat, sugar, and tires) and gave each household a limited number of nontransferable coupons. For each gallon of gas purchased, the vehicle owner had to pay the government-regulated price and turn in a coupon to the gas station. By printing a limited number of coupons, the government restricted purchases of gasoline. The owner of every registered vehicle received a minimum basic ration of coupons that were good for 4 gallons per week. Additional coupons could be obtained by people, such as doctors and war-plant workers, if they could convince the local rationing board that it was essential for them to drive more. Rationing succeeded in reducing gasoline consumption by about 24 percent during 1942–1944. However, this technique suffered from the stealing and counterfeiting of coupons, the high cost of a government bureaucracy needed to run the program, and the problem of determining how much gasoline should be allotted to a particular consumer's "need." By the end of the war, Americans were generally disenchanted with non-price rationing.

| Table 2.2 | **Excise Taxes and the Retail Price of Gasoline, July 2009 (U.S. dollars per gallon)** |

Country	Retail Price (excluding tax)	Tax	Retail Price (including tax)	Tax as a Percentage of Total Retail Price
Germany	1.57	4.08	5.65	72
United Kingdom	1.31	3.43	4.74	72
France	1.63	3.85	5.48	70
Belgium	1.70	3.80	5.50	69
The Netherlands	1.99	4.39	6.38	69
Italy	1.89	3.67	5.56	66
United States	1.73	0.40	2.13	19

Source: U.S. Department of Energy, Energy Information Administration, available at http://www.eia.doe.gov/. Scroll to "Petroleum," "World Crude Oil Prices," "Prices," "International Petroleum Prices," and "Weekly Retail Gasoline Prices: Selected Countries."

For rationing in the 2000s, why not replace the antiquated coupons of World War II with digitally updated debit cards? This type of rationing is known as **tradeable gasoline rights** (TGRs). Under this system, the gasoline pumps at service stations that now read credit cards and debit cards would be modified to read TGR debit cards as well. A main feature of this system is that gasoline rights are tradeable. People who do not use all of their gas allotment during a month would have excess gasoline rights and could sell them to others experiencing shortfalls. Compared to the rationing approach of World War II, in which gas coupons could be used only by the motorist whom they were assigned to, TGRs provide more flexibility for motorists who need to drive more and thus require additional gas. However, they also require government bureaucrats to mandate the target level of gas consumption and entail a relatively high cost for the government running the system.

Rather than using TGRs to restrict gasoline purchases, why not use a higher gas tax as a rationing tool? As Table 2.2 indicates, European governments assess an excise tax of almost $4 on the sale of a gallon of gas, resulting in gas prices of $5.50, or more, per gallon, whereas the U.S. excise tax (federal plus state tax) is only about 40 cents per gallon. Because a higher excise tax adds to gas stations' costs of doing business, the market supply curve of gas shifts to the left, causing the price to rise and quantity demanded to decline.

The case for a gas tax is supported by the fact that it is relatively easy to collect, its implementation comes at a low cost to the government, and because most Americans drive, few can avoid the tax. However, critics contend that the price of gas would have to increase substantially in order to induce a significant decline in consumption, because most households consider gas a necessity. For example, economists estimate that in order to reduce the consumption of gas in the short run by 20 percent, the price would have to increase by about 100 percent.[2] Such an increase in price would likely be viewed by members of Congress as too burdensome on many Americans, especially the poor. Nevertheless, Europeans maintain that Americans should do their part to conserve gas by dramatically increasing the tax on gas. Europeans point out that they use their cars about 40 percent less than Americans,

2. Dahl, C., and T. Sterner, "Analyzing Gasoline Demand Elasticities: A Survey," *Energy Economics*, Vol. 13, No. 3, 1991, pp. 203–210.

and that their cars are smaller and more energy efficient than the gas guzzling sports-utility vehicles that Americans prefer.

Finally, oil conservation could be fostered by raising the fuel economy standards mandated by the federal government. Analysts estimate that if the gas mileage of new cars had increased by only one mile per gallon each year since 1987, and the mileage of light trucks by a half-mile per gallon, the United States would now be saving 1.3 million barrels of oil each day.[3] However, the idea of increasing fuel economy standards has met resistance from auto producers, who anticipate higher production costs as a result of such a policy.

Indeed, achieving any of these measures involves difficult choices for Americans. This is why forming an energy policy for the United States is very difficult.

In this chapter, we have examined demand and supply analysis of market transactions. The next chapter will broaden our understanding of demand and supply by considering contemporary applications of these principles.

Chapter Summary

1. A market is a mechanism through which buyers and sellers communicate in order to trade goods and services. Through the price system, markets link potential buyers with potential sellers.

2. Demand is a schedule that shows the amount of a good or service that buyers are willing and able to purchase at each possible price during a particular period. A demand curve is a graphical representation of the data that constitute a demand schedule. A movement along a demand curve, resulting from a change in price, is called a change in quantity demanded.

3. According to the law of demand, price and quantity demanded are inversely related, assuming that all other factors affecting the quantity demanded remain the same. Economists explain the law of demand in terms of the substitution effect, the income effect, and the principle of diminishing marginal utility.

4. A demand shifter is a variable that causes a shift in a demand curve. Among the most important demand shifters are consumer tastes, the number of buyers, consumer income, the prices of related goods, and expected future prices. When a demand shifter causes an increase in demand, the demand curve shifts to the right; a decrease in demand causes the demand curve to shift to the left.

5. Supply is a schedule or curve showing the amounts of a good or service that firms or households are willing and able to sell at various prices during a particular period. The quantity supplied refers to a single point on a supply curve. Changes in quantity supplied are caused by changes in the price of the product.

6. According to the law of supply, sellers are willing and able to make more of their product available at a higher price than a lower price, all other determinants of supply being constant. The tendency for the cost of additional output to increase explains the law of supply.

7. A supply shifter is a variable that causes a shift in a supply curve. Among the major supply shifters are resource prices, technology, the prices of other goods, expected future prices, taxes and subsidies, and the number of suppliers. When a supply shifter results in an increase in supply, the supply curve shifts to the right; a decrease in supply shifts the supply curve to the left.

---

3. Natural Resources Defense Council, *Strong, Safe, and Secure: Reducing America's Energy Dependence*, 2005, available at http://www.nrdc.org.

8. In a competitive market, equilibrium occurs when the price of a product adjusts so that the quantity that consumers will purchase at that price is identical to the quantity that suppliers will sell. The price at which buyers' intentions are equal to sellers' intentions is called the equilibrium price. A surplus of a product causes the price to fall to its equilibrium level; a shortage of a product causes the price to rise to its equilibrium level.

9. The following predictions can be made about the demand and supply curves when all other factors remain constant:

   • When demand increases, both the equilibrium price and the equilibrium quantity increase.

   • When demand decreases, both the equilibrium price and the equilibrium quantity decrease.

   • When supply increases, equilibrium price falls and equilibrium quantity rises.

   • When supply decreases, equilibrium price rises and equilibrium quantity falls.

Key Terms and Concepts

market (29)

demand (29)

demand curve (30)

law of demand (30)

change in quantity demanded (31)

substitution effect (31)

income effect (31)

diminishing marginal utility (31)

demand shifter (32)

change in demand (32)

normal good (33)

inferior good (33)

substitute good (34)

complementary good (34)

supply (34)

quantity supplied (35)

supply curve (35)

law of supply (36)

supply shifter (37)

change in supply (37)

market equilibrium (39)

equilibrium price (39)

surplus (39)

shortage (41)

tradeable gasoline rights (TGRs) (48)

Self-Test: Multiple-Choice Questions

1. At the market equilibrium price, the quantity

   a. supplied just equals the quantity demanded.
   b. supplied exceeds the quantity demanded by the maximum amount.
   c. demanded exceeds the quantity supplied by the maximum amount.
   d. supplied and the quantity demanded equal zero.

2. If the price of automobiles increases, it is likely that fewer automobile batteries will be purchased at any given price because automobiles and batteries are

   a. inferior goods.
   b. normal goods.
   c. substitute goods.
   d. complementary goods.

3. Suppose that an increase in their incomes induces consumers to purchase more oranges at any given price. Also suppose that an abundant orange harvest results in a lower price, causing consumers to purchase more oranges. These situations are characterized respectively by a(n)

   a. increase in quantity demanded—decrease in demand.
   b. decrease in quantity demanded—increase in demand.
   c. increase in demand—increase in quantity demanded.
   d. decrease in demand—increase in quantity demanded.

4. A decrease in the price of calculators accompanied by an increase in the quantity sold would result from a(n)

   a. decrease in demand.
   b. increase in demand.
   c. decrease in supply.
   d. increase in supply.

5. An increase in income will

   a. increase the demand for inferior goods and decrease the demand for normal goods.
   b. increase the demand for normal goods and decrease the demand for inferior goods.
   c. increase the demand for inferior goods and leave the demand for normal goods unchanged.
   d. increase the demand for normal goods and leave the demand for inferior goods unchanged.

6. If the market price is below the equilibrium price, the

   a. price will increase, the quantity demanded will increase, and the quantity supplied will decrease.
   b. price will increase, the quantity demanded will decrease, and the quantity supplied will increase.
   c. price will decrease, the quantity demanded will increase, and the quantity supplied will decrease.
   d. price will decrease, the quantity demanded will decrease, and the quantity supplied will increase.

7. The supply curve for gasoline will shift to the right in response to all of the following *except*

   a. an increase in the availability of crude oil used in gasoline production.
   b. seller expectations of the development of gasoline-conserving automobiles.
   c. technological improvements in the production of gasoline.
   d. lower prices of labor and capital used in gasoline production.

8. Over a period of time, suppose that both the price and quantity of grapefruit sold increases. This could be caused by a(n)

   a. increase in the supply of grapefruit.
   b. decrease in the supply of grapefruit.
   c. increase in the demand for grapefruit.
   d. decrease in the demand for grapefruit.

9. As the price of a good increases, consumers tend to switch their purchases toward substitutes and away from this good. This explains why the demand curve for this good

   a. is vertical.
   b. is horizontal.
   c. slopes upward to the left.
   d. slopes downward to the right.

10. A shortage of corn will occur when

   a. the quantity of corn demanded exceeds the quantity supplied.
   b. the quantity of corn supplied exceeds the quantity demanded.
   c. corn production is higher this year than last year.
   d. corn production is lower this year than last year.

Answers to Multiple-Choice Questions

1. a   2. d   3. c   4. d   5. b   6. b   7. b   8. c   9. d   10. a

Study Questions and Problems

1. When personal computers were first introduced in the 1980s, their price exceeded $5,000. Since then, the price has decreased dramatically. Use demand and supply analysis to explain the price reduction of computers. What effect did the price reduction have on the quantity of computers demanded?

2. By the 1970s, postwar baby boomers had reached working age, and it became more acceptable for married women with children to work outside the home. Using demand and supply analysis, explain how the increase in female workers likely affected the equilibrium wage and employment.

3. Suppose a decrease in the demand for the Boeing 777 jetliner results in a sharp decline in the demand for Boeing engineers. Use demand and supply analysis to explain the impact on salaries paid to engineers and on the amount of their labor supplied.

4. In 1994, a severe frost destroyed about 25 percent of Brazil's coffee crop. Using demand and supply analysis, explain the impact of the frost on the price of coffee, and on the quantity of coffee demanded.

5. The tastes of many U.S. consumers have shifted away from beef and toward chicken. Using demand and supply analysis, explain how this change affects the equilibrium price and equilibrium quantity in the markets for chicken and beef.

6. Suppose that the implementation of the North American Free Trade Agreement (NAFTA) permits low-cost shirts, manufactured in Mexico, to enter the shirt market of the United States. Draw a graph showing the likely effects of their entry on the price and quantity of shirts supplied by U.S. firms.

7. Which of the following goods are likely to be classified as normal goods or services?

   a. Snow skiing
   b. Foreign travel
   c. Lima beans
   d. Computers
   e. Used cars

8. Which of the following goods are likely to be classified as substitute goods? Complementary goods?

   a. Cookies and milk
   b. Pizza Hut pizza and Domino's pizza
   c. Automobiles and batteries
   d. E-mail and first-class mail
   e. Wheaties and Cheerios

9. Assume that one of the following events occurs. How will each event affect the quantity demanded or demand curve for gasoline?

   a. The market population decreases
   b. The price of gasoline falls
   c. Buyers' incomes decrease
   d. Buyers expect that the price of gasoline will fall in the future
   e. The price of automobiles increases
   f. The price of gasoline rises

10. Assume that one of the following events occurs. How will each event affect the quantity supplied or supply curve of audio cassettes?

    a. The price of audio cassettes increases
    b. The prices of the resources used to produce audio cassettes increases
    c. Manufacturers expect that the price of audio cassettes will fall in the future
    d. New cost-saving technologies are developed to manufacture audio cassettes
    e. The number of audio cassette manufacturers increases
    f. The price of audio cassettes decreases

11. Construct a market demand curve and market supply curve for computers based on the data in Table 2.3.

    a. What is the equilibrium price and the equilibrium quantity of computers?
    b. Find the price at which there would be a surplus of 40 computers and plot it on your diagram. How would the forces of demand and supply push the price back to equilibrium?
    c. Find the price at which there would be a shortage of 60 computers and plot it on your diagram. How would the forces of demand and supply push the price back to equilibrium?
    d. Suppose that new cost-saving technologies allow manufacturers to supply 20 additional computers at each price. Construct a new supply curve to depict this situation. What is the new equilibrium price of computers and the new equilibrium quantity?
    e. Suppose instead that rising prices for the resources used to produce computers force manufacturers to supply 20 fewer computers at each price. Construct a new supply curve to depict this situation. What is the new equilibrium price of computers and the new equilibrium quantity?
    f. Suppose instead that rising incomes cause buyers to demand 20 additional computers at each price. Construct a new demand curve to depict this situation. What is the new equilibrium price of computers and the new equilibrium quantity?
    g. Suppose instead that worsening preferences cause buyers to demand 20 fewer computers at each price. Construct a new demand curve to depict this situation. What is the new equilibrium price of computers and the new equilibrium quantity?

Table 2.3 Demand and Supply Schedules for Computers

Price	Quantity Demanded per Week	Quantity Supplied per Week
$ 400	90	10
800	80	20
1,200	70	30
1,600	60	40
2,000	50	50
2,400	40	60
2,800	30	70
3,200	20	80

Demand and Supply Applications

Chapter objectives

After reading this chapter, you should be able to:

1. Explain how the quantity demanded responds to a change in price.

2. Describe the manner in which a firm's total revenue is influenced by price changes.

3. Assess the advantages and disadvantages of governmental price ceilings and price supports on individual markets.

4. Evaluate the advantages and disadvantages of governmental price supports for agriculture.

economics IN CONTEXT

Economists have long maintained that "there is no such thing as a free lunch." Even if the lunch is on the house, someone has to pay for the resources used to grow, prepare, and serve the food.

Although the residents of the state of California are among the richest in the nation, for many years, they have demanded cheap electricity, low rents, and free college. To obtain these goods, they have elected government officials who have ignored the laws of demand and supply and kept prices low-- below market equilibrium levels. By 2001, however, Californians were paying the price for this defiance in the form of electricity shortages, which resulted in shut-down businesses and darkened homes.

Government officials in California have traditionally attempted to ensure cheap electricity for state residents by mandating price ceilings on the retail price. Yet in 2001, a robust economy and unseasonably cold weather caused the demand for electricity to rise faster than supply could respond. California's utility companies thus had to purchase power from out-of-state utilities at very high prices and then sell it to consumers at the low, state-controlled prices. Without the price ceiling, the shortage of electricity would have caused power prices to rise until demand and supply came into balance. Businesses and households would have voluntarily responded to the higher prices by reorganizing production, turning down thermostats, and shutting off lights. With the price ceiling, however, shortages prevailed, imposing much hardship on Californians.

The previous chapter introduced demand and supply analysis of market transactions. We learned that competitive markets can guide the allocation of resources to produce the goods and services that people demand. This chapter will broaden our understanding of demand and supply analysis. We will consider how sensitive buyers or sellers really are to a change in price. We will also examine whether a seller's revenue rises or falls following a change in price. Finally, as an application of demand and supply principles, we will analyze the potential effects of governmental price ceilings and price floors on individual markets.

PRICE ELASTICITY OF DEMAND

Suppose that you are the ticket manager for the Los Angeles Lakers, a professional basketball team. You are contemplating an increase in the price of your tickets, and you wonder how your fans will react. According to the law of demand, an increase in price will result in a decrease in quantity demanded. But how much will the quantity demanded fall in response to the price hike? The answer to your question depends on the price elasticity of demand.

The **price elasticity of demand** measures how responsive, or sensitive, buyers are to a change in price. The price elasticity of demand looks at the percentage change in quantity demanded relative to the percentage change in price. The elasticity formula is

$$E_d = \frac{\text{Percentage change in quantity demanded}}{\text{Percentage change in price}}$$

where E_d is the elasticity coefficient.[1]

Suppose that attendance at the Lakers' games decreases by 10 percent when the price of tickets increases by 5 percent. Thus, the price elasticity of demand is 2:

$$E_d = \frac{\text{10-percent change in quantity demanded}}{\text{5-percent change in price}}$$

$$= 2$$

The value of the elasticity coefficient, 2, suggests that game attendance changes 2 percent for each 1-percent change in the price of a ticket.

You may have noticed that instead of 2, the value of E_d should actually be −2. This is because price and quantity demanded are inversely related according to the law of demand. In our example, the increase in ticket prices causes the numerator in the formula to be positive (+10 percent), while the decrease in game attendance causes the denominator to be negative (−5 percent). As a result, E_d will have a negative value. By convention, economists drop the negative sign when calculating the price elasticity of demand, realizing that price and quantity demanded move in opposite directions.

Depending on the response of buyers to a change in price, demand is characterized as elastic, inelastic, or unit elastic.

- **Elastic.** Demand is elastic when the percentage change in quantity demanded is greater than the percentage change in price, meaning that E_d is greater than 1. Example: A 20-percent reduction in the price of Pepsi causes a 30-percent increase in the quantity demanded. Specifically, E_d is 1.5 in this case (30 / 20 = 1.5).

- **Inelastic.** Demand is inelastic when the percentage change in quantity demanded is less than the percentage change in price, meaning that E_d is less than 1. Example: A 30-percent increase in the price of Levi's jeans causes a 10-percent decrease in quantity demanded. Specifically, E_d is 0.33 in this case (10 / 30 = 0.33).

- **Unit elastic.** Demand is unit elastic when the percentage change in quantity demanded equals the percentage change in price, meaning that E_d equals 1.0. Example: An 8-percent decrease in the price of Timex watches causes an 8-percent increase in the quantity demanded (8 / 8 = 1.0).

Table 3.1 reports the estimated price elasticities of demand for selected products. When making such estimates, economists distinguish between a period during which consumers have little time to adjust (the short run) and periods during which consumers have time to fully adjust to a price change (the long run). From the table, we see that the short-run price elasticity of demand for medical care is 0.3, which means that the demand for medical care is inelastic. Our elasticity estimate suggests that if the price of medical care were to change by, say, 10 percent, the quantity demanded would change by 3 percent. The table also shows that in the short run the price elasticity of demand for

---

1. The midpoint formula is used to calculate the elasticity between two points on a demand curve (or supply curve). This formula uses the averages of the two quantities and the two prices under consideration as reference points. According to the midpoint formula, the percentage change in quantity equals the change in the quantity divided by the average of the two quantities; the percentage change in price equals the change in price divided by the average of the two prices. Therefore, the price elasticity of demand equals:

$$E_d = \frac{\text{Change in quantity}}{\text{Sum of quantities / 2}} \div \frac{\text{Change in price}}{\text{Sum of prices / 2}}$$

Table 3.1	Estimated Price Elasticities of Demand		
		Elasticity Coefficient	
Item		Short Run	Long Run
Airline travel		0.1	2.4
Medical care		0.3	0.9
Automobile tires		0.9	1.2
Gasoline		0.2	0.7
Housing		0.3	1.9
Automobiles		1.9	2.2
Movies		0.9	3.7
Natural gas		1.4	2.1

Sources: Robert Archibald and Robert Gillingham, "An Analysis of the Short-Run Consumer Demand for Gasoline Using Household Survey Data," *Review of Economics and Statistics*, November 1980, pp. 622–628; and Hendrik Houthakker and Lester Taylor, *Consumer Demand in the United States* (Cambridge, MA: Harvard University Press, 1970), pp. 56–149.

automobiles is 1.9, suggesting that the demand for automobiles is elastic. Our elasticity estimate implies that a 10-percent change in the price of automobiles would result in a 19-percent change in quantity demanded.

DETERMINANTS OF PRICE ELASTICITY OF DEMAND

As Table 3.1 indicates, the demand for automobiles is elastic, whereas the demand for housing and gasoline is inelastic. What factors account for differences in the price elasticity of demand?

Availability of Substitutes

The demand for a product is more *elastic* if *many* substitutes are available for it. If there are numerous substitutes available for a product, consumers can easily switch their purchases to substitutes when there is a price hike for that product. For example, suppose that the price of Shell gasoline rises. Because there are many substitutes for Shell gasoline, such as Conoco, Arco, and Texaco, motorists will turn to the readily available substitute gasolines as the price of Shell gasoline rises. We would expect the quantity demanded of Shell gasoline to decrease significantly in response to the price hike.

If a good has *few* substitutes, its demand tends to be more *inelastic*. Medical care has no close substitutes, for example. The short-run price elasticity of demand for medical care is estimated to be about 0.3. It is very inelastic.

Many companies hire celebrities to advertise their merchandise. For example, Michael Jordan, a retired basketball star, advertises Nike shoes. What message is he trying to convey? He is suggesting that, for Michael Jordan, Nike shoes are the "only" ones worth having, and all other shoes are clearly inferior. If consumers accept Jordan's message and desire to be like him, they will also feel that there are no good substitutes for Nike shoes. As a result, the demand for Nike shoes will become more inelastic.

Owners of professional basketball teams price their tickets with the elasticity of demand in mind. In 1997, for example, fans encouraged by the Miami Heat's victory in Game 2 of the Eastern Conference play-offs against the New York Knicks were shocked when they lined up to buy tickets for the next home play-off game. The cheap seats at AmericanAirlines Arena, which had gone for $20 in Games 1 and 2 out of the best-of-7 series, jumped unexpectedly to $50 for Game 5. Moreover, the $90 seats jumped to $130. The Heat's management defended the price hikes, arguing that winning Game 5 was a necessity for the future success of the team. The management apparently felt that because Heat fans could not get along without attending Game 5, they would tolerate a price hike. As things turned out, AmericanAirlines Arena was filled to capacity in spite of the higher ticket prices.

Proportion of Income

Most consumers spend a large proportion of their income on automobiles and housing. A 10-percent rise in the prices of these goods would result in price increases of perhaps $2,000 and $15,000, respectively. These price hikes would likely substantially reduce consumers' ability to purchase these goods and significantly decrease the quantity demanded. Therefore, the demand for goods on which a *large* proportion of personal income is spent tends to be quite *elastic*.

On the other hand, a 10-percent rise in the price of a ballpoint pen means a price increase of perhaps 5 cents. This increase represents an insignificant fraction of consumer income and it is unlikely to result in significant decreases in the quantity demanded. The demand for goods on which a *small* fraction of income is spent thus tends to be more *inelastic*.

Time

Suppose that Puget Sound Energy Co. announces an increase in the price of natural gas. How will households in Washington State react? The answer depends partly on how much time we allow for a response. If we consider the household reaction to the price increase by tomorrow, the response will likely be very small. Households have their existing gas-burning furnaces and stoves and cannot significantly reduce their quantity demanded as the price increases.

If we give households a year to react to the price hike, however, their response will be much greater. Some households will switch from furnaces burning natural gas to oil-burning furnaces; others will switch from stoves burning natural gas to electric stoves. In general, demand tends to be more elastic with time because consumers are able to find more substitutes for goods over longer periods. This explains why the short-run elasticity coefficient of natural gas in Table 3.1 is less elastic at 1.4 than the long-run elasticity coefficient of 2.1. The same line of reasoning applies to the other goods shown in Table 3.1.

AIRLINES FAIL TO PASS ON FULL 10-PERCENT TICKET TAX TO PASSENGERS

The concept of price elasticity of demand has many applications. For example, it can help determine how much of an excise tax is borne by the buyer in the form of a higher price. Let us consider the effects of an excise tax levied on the sale of airline tickets.

In 1997, the U.S. government levied a 10-percent excise tax on the sale of domestic airline tickets. American carriers such as Delta and Northwest Airlines attempted to raise ticket prices by the full amount of the tax. Because of market conditions, however, the airlines could raise fares by only 4 percent. As we will see, the price elasticity of demand helps explain this situation.

Assume that the equilibrium price of airline tickets is $500, as shown at point A in Figure 3.1. Now assume the government imposes a 10-percent tax on the sale of tickets, yielding $50 of tax revenue for each ticket sold. Because the tax increases the cost of doing business for the airlines, their supply curve shifts upward by 10 percent, from S_0 to S_1.

Suppose that the demand curve for tickets is perfectly inelastic, denoted by D_0 in Figure 3.1(*a*). Given the extreme situation of perfectly inelastic demand, flying is of such importance to travelers that they will purchase a fixed quantity of tickets at any price. Because travelers are completely

Figure 3.1   10-Percent Tax Imposed on the Sale of Airline Tickets

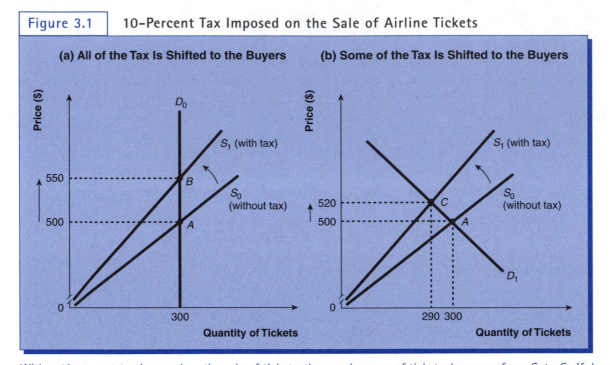

With a 10-percent tax imposed on the sale of tickets, the supply curve of tickets decreases from S_0 to S_1. If demand is perfectly inelastic (D_0), all of the tax will be shifted to buyers. If demand is somewhat elastic (D_1), a portion of the tax will be shifted to buyers, and the remaining portion will be absorbed by the seller. Thus, as the demand curve for tickets becomes more elastic, a smaller portion of the tax is shifted to buyers.

insensitive to price changes, airlines can increase fares from $500 to $550, a 10-percent increase. As a result, airline passengers bear all of the tax in the form of a higher price.

In practice, the quantity demanded for flying decreases as fares increase. This implies that the demand curve for tickets exhibits some price elasticity. This is shown by curve D_1 in Figure 3.1(b). As the supply curve of tickets shifts from S_0 to S_1, following the imposition of the 10-percent tax, the equilibrium price rises $20—from $500 to $520—an amount less than the tax. Thus, the airlines absorb the remainder of the tax. In general, for a specific supply curve, as the *more elastic* the demand curve for a product becomes, the *smaller* the portion of the tax is shifted to buyers.[2]

When the U.S. government imposed a 10-percent tax onto the price of airline tickets, fares fluctuated sharply as carriers tried to add as much of the tax to the price as they could. American Airlines, Delta Air Lines, and others raised fares on most routes by 10 percent after the tax was levied. However, they retreated when Northwest Airlines refused to follow suit. Northwest boosted fares by only 4 percent, an amount that most airlines matched. United Airlines and Continental Airlines went from a 10-percent increase down to a 4-percent hike as events unfolded. A few carriers, such as Southwest Airlines, did not raise fares at all and thus absorbed all of the 10-percent tax.

Northwest reasoned that a full 10-percent increase in fares might drive away more traffic than it was worth. A company spokesperson announced that 4 percent was appropriate to market conditions. Apparently, Northwest felt that because the demand for its tickets was quite elastic it would lose many customers if it raised fares by the full amount of the tax.

---

2. A more complete analysis of the burden of a tax would include the price elasticity of supply of a product. It is left to more advanced texts to discuss this concept.

CHECK POINT

1. What is the price elasticity of demand?

2. How is the price elasticity of demand measured?

3. Differentiate among elastic demand, unit elastic demand, and inelastic demand.

4. Why is demand more elastic for some products and more inelastic for others?

PRICE ELASTICITY OF DEMAND AND TOTAL REVENUE

The price elasticity of demand can also help the managers of a business decide whether or not to change prices in order to increase sales revenues. For example, in 1991, Apple Computer Inc. cut the prices on some models of its Macintosh computers by as much as 50 percent in an attempt to stimulate the quantity demanded. The market reaction to the price reduction was extraordinary. At the end of the year, Apple announced that the sales of its Macintosh computers had increased by 85 percent and that its revenues had skyrocketed. In 1992, Apple again slashed prices, which resulted in rising sales and increased revenues. Clearly, these price reductions benefited Apple.

Determining the impact of a price change on a firm's total revenue is crucial to the analysis of many problems in economics. **Total revenue** (TR) refers to the dollars earned by sellers of a product. It is calculated by multiplying the quantity sold (Q) during a time period by the price (P)

$$TR = P \times Q.$$

For example, suppose that the Dell Computer Corp. charges $3,000 for a computer, and 10,000 computers were sold last month. Total revenue on the sale of computers equals $30 million ($3,000 x 10,000 = $30 million). This amount also equals the total expenditures by consumers over this period.

Suppose that Dell reduces the price of its computers by 10 percent. Although the quantity demanded will increase, will the firm's total revenue rise? The problem in determining the effect of a price change on the total revenue of computers is that a change in price and a change in quantity would move in *opposite* directions. A decrease in price will result in an increase in quantity demanded, and an increase in price will cause the quantity demanded to decrease. However, total revenue is calculated by multiplying price and quantity. It is not clear how Dell's total revenue will react to the opposing forces of price and quantity.

To determine the impact of a price change on Dell's total revenue, we need to know the consumers will respond to the change in price. This response is measured by the price elasticity of demand. Consider the following situations:

- **Elastic demand.** Suppose that the elasticity of demand coefficient for Dell computers is 2. If Dell reduces computer prices by 10 percent, the quantity demanded will increase by 20 percent. Because the percentage increase in the quantity demanded is greater than the percentage decrease in price, the firm's total revenue will rise following the price cut. Conversely, a price increase of 10 percent would result in a 20-percent decrease in the quantity demanded and thus a decline in the firm's total revenue. In general, total revenue will move in the opposite direction of the price change when demand is elastic.

- **Inelastic demand.** Suppose that the elasticity of demand coefficient for Dell computers is 0.5. If Dell slashes computer prices by 10 percent, the quantity demanded will rise by only 5 percent, and total revenue will decrease. Conversely, a 10-percent price hike will cause the quantity demanded to fall by 5 percent, resulting in an increase in total revenue. In general, total revenue will move in the *same* direction of the price change when demand is *inelastic*.

- **Unit elastic demand.** Suppose that the elasticity of demand coefficient for Dell computers is 1.0. If Dell reduces computer prices by 10 percent, quantity demanded will increase by 10 percent, and total revenue will remain unchanged. Likewise, a 10-percent increase in price will leave total revenue unchanged. In general, a change in price will *not* induce a change in total revenue when demand is *unit elastic*.

APPLICATIONS OF PRICE ELASTICITY OF DEMAND AND TOTAL REVENUE

All businesses face the question of what price to charge for their product. The answer is not always obvious. Increasing the price of a product often has the effect of reducing sales as price-sensitive consumers seek alternatives or simply do without. For every product, the extent of that sensitivity is different. Indeed, pricing is a tricky business. It requires a clear understanding of the demand curve and elasticity, as seen in the following examples.

State Governments Increase Cigarette Tax to Raise Revenue

One of the most important excise taxes in the United States is the tax on cigarettes. As of 2009, the federal government levied a tax of $1 a pack while state taxes ranged from 7 cents a pack in South Carolina to $2.58 in New Jersey. Increases in cigarette taxes have been used to discourage smoking and increase tax revenue. From 1990 to 2000, cigarette taxes were raised in 30 states. Although cigarette sales decreased in each state following a tax increase, total cigarette tax revenue increased. That's because the demand for cigarettes tends to be inelastic. Table 3.2 provides examples of the impact of cigarette tax increases on tax revenues.

Colleges Hike Tuition to Offset Cutbacks in State Aid to Higher Education

The recession of 2007–2009 was difficult for higher education as well as many other sectors of the economy. As the economy shrank and tax revenues declined for state legislatures, they decreased their appropriations to colleges. College administrators weighed how far they could push tuition to balance their budgets without driving away students. Administrators noted that if the price of tuition did not increase, revenue shortfalls would trigger substantial layoffs of faculty and staff. This would result in a decline in the number of courses offered to students, which would delay their graduation from college. Does an increase in tuition necessarily result in an increase in total tuition revenue?

| Table 3.2 | State-Level Sales and Cigarette Excise Tax Revenue in Response to Cigarette Excise Tax Increases |

State	Year	Tax Increase (per pack)	New Tax (per pack)	Percentage Decrease in Quantity Transacted	Percentage Increase in Tax Revenue
Arizona	1994	$0.40	$0.58	2.1%	221.6%
Michigan	1994	0.50	0.75	20.8	139.9
California	1999	0.50	0.87	18.9	90.7
Utah	1997	0.25	0.52	20.7	86.2
Oregon	1997	0.30	0.68	8.3	77.0
New York	2000	0.55	1.11	20.2	57.4
Maryland	1999	0.30	0.66	15.3	52.6
Wisconsin	1997	0.15	0.59	6.5	25.8

Source: M. C. Farrelly, C. T. Nimsch, and J. James, *State Cigarette Excise Taxes: Implications for Revenue and Tax Evasion*, RTI International, May 2003.

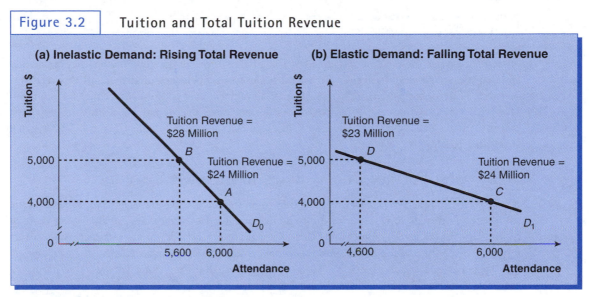

Figure 3.2   Tuition and Total Tuition Revenue

(a) Inelastic Demand: Rising Total Revenue

Tuition Revenue = $28 Million

Tuition Revenue = $24 Million

(b) Elastic Demand: Falling Total Revenue

Tuition Revenue = $23 Million

Tuition Revenue = $24 Million

For the University of Washington, whether a tuition hike will increase total tuition revenue depends on students' elasticity of demand. If demand is inelastic, a tuition increase will result in increased total revenue. But if demand is elastic, an increase in tuition will result in declining total revenue.

Analysis.   Figure 3.2 illustrates the effect of a tuition increase on the total tuition revenue for, say, the University of Washington (UW). Referring to Figure 3.2(*a*), let us consider the effect on total revenue of an increase in tuition from $4,000 to $5,000 per year when demand is inelastic. In this case, the decline in attendance caused by the tuition hike does not offset the increase in tuition revenue per student. The net result is that total tuition revenue increases from $24 million to $28 million when tuition is raised.

But when tuition increases, some students may question whether attending UW is worthwhile. They may switch to a private university or will drop out of school to seek full-time employment. Therefore, a relatively large decrease in attendance may occur following a tuition hike, suggesting that demand is elastic. Referring to the elastic demand curve shown in Figure 3.2(*b*), when tuition increases from $4,000 to $5,000 the decrease in attendance more than offsets the increase in tuition per student. Thus, total revenue decreases from $24 million to $23 million. The attempt to increase total revenue by raising tuition backfires when demand is elastic.

Pittsburgh Pirates Underestimate Fan Reaction: Ticket Price Hike Was Wrong

How should a major league baseball team set a price for its home games? Consider the case of the Pittsburgh Pirates.

In 2002, Pittsburgh Pirates owner Kevin McClatchy, unhappy that the ongoing debate over an unpopular ticket price increase was drawing attention away from his team's success, announced that the price hike had been a mistake. In reaction to fan unrest, which had prompted 40 percent of the team's season ticket holders to cancel their seats in 2002, McClatchy said that season ticket prices would not increase in 2003. McClatchy indicated that the price hike was a decision he regretted, and therefore the Pirates would not increase ticket prices for 2003.

In October 2001, only days after the Pirates ended a 62-100 season that was its worst in 16 years, team management had hiked prices by $1 to $2 per game for thousands of seats in PNC Park. The public displeasure over the price increase drew attention throughout the 2002 season and apparently caught the Pirates by surprise. Four weeks into the season, they rolled back the increase on nearly 4,000 outfield seats and refunded the difference to season ticket holders. That rollback didn't come in time to halt the mass cancellation of season tickets, however, and home attendance dropped about 8,000 seats per game, despite the Pirates' unexpected good start to the season.

Analysis.   When the Pirates contemplated raising ticket prices for the 2002 season, they apparently felt that most fans would continue to attend home games, believing that demand was relatively inelastic. With inelastic demand, a price increase should generate additional revenues for the team. However, widespread outcry against the price hike suggested that demand was much more elastic than the Pirates had estimated. The team's management subsequently cut prices to bolster sagging attendance to support revenues.

U.S. Postal Service Boosts Rates to Increase Revenue

It is no secret that the U.S. Postal Service (USPS) is in need of change. In recent years, it has typically suffered huge deficits in the face of declining demand for first-class mail and increasing costs of running the Postal Service. Alternatives such as e-mail, faxes, and cell phones increasingly substitute for hard-copy letters, reducing the amount of mail handled by the postal service.

To generate additional revenue, the Postal Service increased the price of a first-class stamp from 37 cents to 39 cents in 2006, and from 39 cents to 41 cents in 2007. Rates on other mail services such as priority mail, parcel post, and periodicals were also raised. In 2009, the price of a first-class stamp was increased to 44 cents. Whether the revenue of the postal service would rise or fall depended on the response of users to the rate hikes.

Consider the response of the Bear Creek Corp. of Medford, Oregon.[3] Prior to the rate hikes, the firm sent some 900,000 packages of gourmet cheesecakes, pears, and other specialty items by priority mail, the Postal Service's most economical way to mail packages for delivery in as little as two or three days. Following the rate hikes, however, households could not count on the mail carrier to bring them cinnamon swirls and chocolate truffles. Why? Bear Creek maintained that priority mail was less attractive than its more reliable private-sector competitors—FedEx and United Parcel Service (UPS). Because of the rate hikes, Bear Creek expected its catalog retailers to ship 20 percent fewer priority mail packages. As the manager of Bear Creek stated, "There's a lot of alternatives out there."

Analysis.   The purpose of rate hikes on mail is to increase the revenue of the Postal Service. If there are few substitutes available, the demand for mail tends to be relatively inelastic, and a rate hike results in rising revenue for the postal service. As seen in Table 3.3, the price elasticity of demand for first-class letters and priority mail is estimated to be 0.31 and 0.75, respectively, suggesting that

Table 3.3	Price Elasticity of Demand for Mail Services of the U.S. Postal Service	
	First-class letter	0.31
	Priority mail	0.75
	Express mail	1.49
	Periodicals	0.17
	Parcel post	1.19
	Bound printed matter	0.23
	Media mail	0.14

Source: Postal Rate and Fee Changes, 1997; and testimony of Dr. George Tolley to the U.S. Postal Regulatory Commission, July 1997, Docket No. R97–1, available at http://www.prc.gov. Select "Contents," "Docketed Cases and Matters," "Rate," and then locate the testimony of George Tolley.

---

3. "A Deal No More, Priority Mail Is Prey for Rivals," *The Wall Street Journal*, January 24, 2001, pp. B-1 and B-4.

the demand for these mail services is inelastic. Therefore, we would expect the revenue of the postal service on these services to increase following a rate hike. However, the price elasticity of demand tends to increase with the passage of time. For example, the development of e-mail and other forms of electronic communication to send messages has increased the elasticity of demand for mail and is forcing the Postal Service to reconsider its way of doing business.

CHECK POINT

1. What conclusions can be drawn about the price elasticity of demand when a firm's price and total revenue move in opposite directions? In the same direction? What if total revenue remains unchanged following a change in price?

2. Why did many U.S. colleges rapidly increase tuition in the early 2000s?

3. Why did the Pittsburgh Pirates roll back ticket prices in 2002?

4. What factors explain an increase or decrease in the total revenue of the U.S. Postal Service following a rate increase?

PRICE CEILINGS AND PRICE FLOORS

Having learned about the reaction of consumers to price changes, let us next consider the issue of fairness. Occasionally, government officials feel that the forces of demand and supply result in prices that are unfairly low to sellers or unfairly high to buyers. Government may enact price controls to address these problems. When government imposes a **price ceiling** on a product, it establishes the maximum legal price a seller may charge for that product. Conversely, government may establish a **price floor** to prevent prices from falling below the legally mandated level. Let us analyze the effects of government price controls on individual markets.

Rent Controls Make Housing More Affordable

Rent controls have been used in more than 200 U.S. cities, including New York, Boston, San Francisco, and Washington, DC. The objective is to protect low-income households from escalating rents caused by perceived housing shortages and to make housing more affordable to the poor. By the late 1990s, however, many cities had cut back their rent control measures because of the deescalation of rent inflation and the public's receptiveness to free-market economics applied to housing.

The economic effects of rent controls are illustrated in Figure 3.3. Assume initially that the equilibrium rent for a 2-bedroom apartment in New York City equals $600 per month, shown by the intersection of the market supply curve (S_0) and the market demand curve (D_0). To protect renters from the possibility of escalating rents, suppose that the municipal government passes a rent-control law that freezes the monthly rent at $600. Because the ceiling rate equals the market-equilibrium rate, the ceiling does not affect the market.

Because of the rising population in New York City, suppose that the market demand curve for apartments shifts to D_1. Prices try to rise to $900, the price that would occur in a free market, but are prevented from doing so by the rent ceiling. Renters who already have apartments are protected from the government-placed lid on rent because they pay $600 rather than $900 per month.

Although the rent ceiling protects current renters from rising prices, it results in adverse side effects. Because the $600 ceiling is set below the equilibrium level, families would like to be able to rent 1,000 apartments. However, landlords are willing to supply only 400 apartments at the ceiling price. Thus, when the rent ceiling is set below the free-market equilibrium price, there is a shortage

Figure 3.3 Rent Ceilings and Housing Shortages

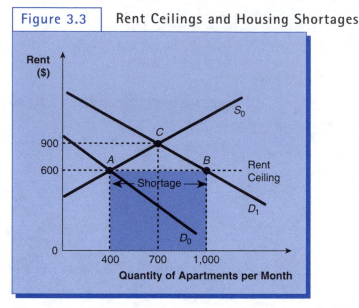

When the equilibrium rent for apartments is equal to or lower than its legal maximum, a rent ceiling has no effect on the market. This occurs when the rent ceiling is $600 and the demand and supply curves for apartments are D_0 and S_0, respectively. When the equilibrium rent rises above its ceiling, the ceiling takes effect and a shortage occurs. This situation occurs when the rent ceiling is $600 and the demand and supply curves are D_1 and S_0, respectively.

of 600 apartments. In 1978, for example, several thousand University of California students could not find housing in Berkeley, following the imposition of rent controls. Many of them slept in the university's gymnasium until suitable housing could be found.

Initially, if the ceiling on rent is not far below the equilibrium price, the adverse effects of rent control may be hardly perceptible. As time passes, however, these effects will grow, yielding the following results:

- **The future supply and quality of rental apartments will diminish.** Because rent ceilings reduce the profitability of apartments for landlords, they serve as a disincentive to the construction of new rental housing. Potential investors in apartments will find it more profitable to invest in shopping malls or office buildings which are not subject to rent controls.

- **Under-the-table markets may develop.** When landlords cannot increase rent, they often adopt other means to collect income. Landlords may require a renter to make under-the-table payments just to get a key ("key money") to the apartment. Other renters may have to purchase the landlord's furniture at outrageous prices in order to obtain an apartment.

- **Discrimination may occur in the rationing of apartments.** Because price no longer serves its rationing role under rent ceilings, landlords may ration available apartments to families according to other criteria such as race or religion.

- **Rent controls will benefit the wealthy.** Because rent controls pertain to units of apartments and are not based on the income of renters, they can benefit the rich. For example, wealthy individuals such as singer Carly Simon and former Mayor Ed Koch have taken advantage of living in New York City, where rent ceilings hold down the cost of apartments.

In spite of these problems, rent controls have their proponents. Supporters argue that eliminating controls wouldn't spur the construction of any low-income rental housing, just more luxury housing.

The low-income people who benefit from the current regulations, they say, would be displaced. Because current renters benefit from rent controls, whereas landlords and future renters suffer, the political lines are clearly drawn in the rent-control debate.

Should Federal Interest–Rate Ceilings Be Imposed on MasterCard and Visa?

Do consumers pay too much interest on their MasterCard and Visa accounts? This has been a topic of much controversy recently.

During the 1960s, the Visa and MasterCard associations developed the infrastructure for a nationwide credit card payment system and convinced merchants to accept their cards. However, state laws limited the amount of interest that could be charged in credit card loans. By the 1970s, banks issuing credit cards were suffering losses as a result of high inflation and high interest rates. They maintained that the interest rate ceilings set by most states were too low to make credit card lending profitable.

In 1978, the U.S. Supreme Court changed the interpretation of law for all types of consumer loans. It ruled that federally chartered banks could charge the highest interest rate allowed in their home state to customers living anywhere in the United States, including states with restrictive ceilings on interest rates. Therefore, major credit card companies began relocating to states with liberal or no ceilings, such as Delaware. They made credit card loans to households in states with restrictive ceilings and charged them the higher interest rates allowed in Delaware.

To hang onto the credit card business, many other states loosened their interest-rate ceilings. In the 1980s, most states capped credit card interest rates at 12 percent to18 percent. By the early 2000s, caps ranged from18 percent to 24 percent, and many states moved in the direction of removing the caps altogether.

Critics of banks that issue credit cards have complained that there is a wide gap between card rates and the interest rates that banks pay for money. They note that banks may pay, for example, 2-percent interest to attract savings deposits and use this money to lend to credit card borrowers at 16-percent interest. As a result, banks can earn large profits on their credit card operations. Such high charges on credit card balances are characterized as excessive and unfair to consumers.

However, banks issuing credit cards argue that the high interest rates reflect the realities of pricing a complex product in a competitive market. Besides interest-rate charges, other pricing decisions include the level of annual fees, the billing cycle to be used, the length of the interest-free grace period, and various service fees. Bankers note that the cost of obtaining deposits to fund credit card operations typically represents less than 40 percent of a bank's overall cost of operating a credit card plan. Other costs, such as various processing and billing expenses and fraud and credit losses, are significant and do not vary with the cost of money.

Another reason that credit-card interest rates are so high is that the demand for credit cards is quite inelastic. That is, people's use of credit cards does not decline very much as interest rates increase. Thus, banks recognize that they do not forego many customers when they increase rates on their current credit card. Why should a bank reduce its interest rate if it realizes that it will not attract many additional customers by doing so?

Consumer groups have called for the federal government to impose a nationwide interest-rate ceiling on credit card accounts. However, a ceiling on interest rates would encourage banks to reduce costs or increase revenues. For example, banks might tighten credit standards for borrowers so as to decrease collection costs, reduce services offered with credit cards such as discounts on transportation and lodging, curtail grace periods for making payments, or increase the annual fee charged to cardholders. Although a federal interest-rate ceiling on credit cards would help consumers in terms of their monthly interest bills, it could impose other burdens on users.

U.S. Farmers Reap High Subsidies from the Government

We have examined the effects of imposing governmental price ceilings on the sale of a product. Let us now consider the effects of price floors.

In 1933, when farmers were suffering from low market prices during the Great Depression, Congress passed the Agricultural Adjustment Act. This act set *price floors* on many agricultural products, such as cotton, milk, wheat, rice, corn, sugar, tobacco, and peanuts, in order to sustain the prices and incomes of farmers. Under this program today, the government guarantees a minimum price above the equilibrium price and agrees to buy any quantity that the farmers are unable to sell at the legal price. The cost of subsidizing American farmers has been enormous. In 2009, for example, the U.S. government spent more than $20 billion on payments to farmers.

Figure 3.4 shows how a price floor works for wheat. With a free and competitive market, the intersection of the market supply curve (S_0) and the market demand curve (D_0) establishes the equilibrium price at $4 per bushel. A total of 9 million bushels of wheat are produced and sold at this price each year, yielding an income of $36 million for farmers.

To support farmers' incomes, suppose that the government sets a price floor of $5 per bushel for wheat. The higher price induces wheat farmers to increase production to 11 million bushels, but consumers demand only 7 million bushels. As a result, there is a surplus of 4 million bushels. To prevent the surplus from causing the price of wheat to fall, the government purchases the surplus and stores it. In this manner, farmers can sell 11 million bushels of wheat at a price of $5 per bushel, thus realizing an income of $55 million. This amount exceeds the income that farmers would earn in a free market.

One result of agricultural price supports is the transfer of money from consumers and taxpayers to farmers. This transfer works in two ways. First, for each bushel of wheat that consumers purchase, they pay a higher price ($5) than they would have paid without a price support ($4). Second, when the government purchases the 4 million bushel surplus at a price of $5 per bushel, it comes at a cost

| Figure 3.4 | Effect of Price Supports for Wheat |

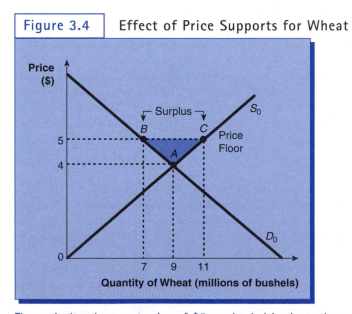

The agricultural support price of $5 per bushel is above the market equilibrium price of $4 per bushel. The support price results in an increase in quantity supplied and a decrease in quantity demanded, causing a surplus of 4 million bushels per year. To prevent the price from falling below the support level, the government purchases the surplus and stores it. The cost to taxpayers of purchasing the surplus is $20 million.

of $20 million to taxpayers. As you can see, when price supports interfere with the operation of a free and competitive market, the result tends to be a misallocation of resources: Households pay higher prices for wheat, as well as higher taxes to subsidize farmers. Moreover, inefficient and high-cost farmers can continue to realize profits when they are subsidized by price supports. These inefficiencies have resulted in political pressure to reduce or eliminate government subsidies to farmers.

Critics have questioned whether the incomes of farmers should be subsidized by other taxpayers. Farmers' incomes tend to be about 35 percent higher than that of the average American household. Also, farmers often earn income from sources other than farming, making them less vulnerable to decreases in the price of farm products. Moreover, although most subsidies go to real farmers who grow crops on their land, sometimes they go to landowners who do not farm at all. Nonfarming recipients of subsidies have included media mogul Ted Turner, Scottie Pippen, a former star basketball player for the Chicago Bulls, and others.

This chapter has broadened our understanding of demand and supply by considering contemporary applications of these principles. The next chapter will consider the role of productivity and the costs of production in influencing business decisions.

CHECK POINT

1. Why does government sometimes impose price controls on individual markets?

2. What are the advantages and disadvantages of a legal price ceiling imposed on the sale of a product? How about a legal price floor?

3. As explained in this chapter, which of the following are price ceilings? Price floors?
   a. Rent controls
   b. Controls on credit card interest rates
   c. Agricultural price controls

Chapter Summary

1. The price elasticity of demand measures how sensitive buyers are to a change in price. Depending on the response of buyers to a change in price, demand is characterized as elastic, inelastic, or unit elastic.

2. Demand tends to be more elastic for some products and less elastic for others. The major determinants of the price elasticity of demand are the availability of substitutes, the proportion of buyer income spent on a product, and the time period under consideration.

3. If a firm's price and total revenue move in opposite directions, demand is elastic. If the firm's price and total revenue move in the same direction, demand is inelastic. If the firm's total revenue does not respond to a change in price, demand is unit elastic.

4. Occasionally, the government will impose price controls on individual markets in which prices are considered unfairly high to buyers or unfairly low to sellers. When the government imposes a price ceiling on a product, it establishes the maximum legal price that a seller may charge for that product. Conversely, the government may establish a price floor to prevent prices from falling below a legally mandated level.

5. Although price controls on individual markets attempt to make prices more "fair" for buyers and sellers, they interfere with the market's allocation of resources. Price ceilings that are set below the equilibrium price level result in market shortages of a product. Price floors that are set above the equilibrium level entail market surpluses.

Key Terms and Concepts

price elasticity of demand (56)

total revenue (61)

elastic demand, inelastic demand,
    unit elastic demand (61)

price ceiling (65)

price floor (65)

rent controls (65)

Self-Test: Multiple-Choice Questions

1. The price elasticity of demand will be greater when

    a. the time period is shorter.
    b. there are fewer substitutes for the good.
    c. the good is considered a necessity rather than a luxury.
    d. the item represents a larger share of consumers' budgets.

2. For which of the following goods is demand likely to be most inelastic?

    a. Medical care.
    b. Sony CD player.
    c. Air travel on United Airlines.
    d. Honda Accord automobile.

3. Suppose that government officials are contemplating a gasoline tax and a tax on energy
    that includes gasoline, natural gas, coal, and electricity. Assuming that the objective is to
    maximize total tax revenue, the gasoline tax will raise

    a. more revenue because the demand for gasoline is more elastic than the demand for energy.
    b. more revenue because the demand for gasoline is less elastic than the demand for energy.
    c. less revenue because the demand for gasoline is more elastic than the demand for energy.
    d. less revenue because the demand for gasoline is less elastic than the demand for energy.

4. If the government imposes a 5-percent tax on airline tickets and air carriers are able to
    increase ticket prices by the full amount of the tax, we would expect the price elasticity of
    demand for airline tickets to be

    a. perfectly elastic.
    b. relatively elastic.
    c. relatively inelastic.
    d. perfectly inelastic.

5. If the government imposes a ceiling on rent charged for private apartments and the ceiling is
    set below the market equilibrium rent, we would expect

    a. a surplus of rental apartments in the immediate future.
    b. an increase in the profits of landlords.
    c. a decrease in housing discrimination against the poor.
    d. some rental apartments to be abandoned or poorly maintained by landlords.

6. If the price elasticity of demand for automobiles is 0.8, a 10-percent increase in the price of
    automobiles would cause the quantity demanded to decline by

    a. 2 percent.
    b. 4 percent.
    c. 8 percent.
    d. 12 percent.

7. Total revenue will increase if price

   a. decreases and the elasticity of demand equals 0.6.
   b. decreases and the elasticity of demand equals 1.0.
   c. increases and the elasticity of demand equals 0.3.
   d. increases and the elasticity of demand equals 2.0.

8. If the state of California levies a tax of 50 cents per pack on the sale of cigarettes in order to increase tax revenues, it will realize the most revenue if the demand for cigarettes is

   a. highly elastic.
   b. somewhat elastic.
   c. highly inelastic.
   d. somewhat inelastic.

9. If the federal government levies a price floor on wheat, it may also have to

   a. produce some of the wheat itself.
   b. purchase the surplus wheat.
   c. initiate programs to reduce demand in the private sector.
   d. initiate programs to increase supply in the private sector.

10. When the supply curve of corn shifts to the right, total revenue will

   a. increase only if demand is relatively elastic.
   b. increase only if demand is relatively inelastic.
   c. decrease only if demand is relatively elastic.
   d. decrease only if demand is perfectly elastic.

Answers to Multiple-Choice Questions

1. d   2. a   3. c   4. d   5. d   6. c   7. c   8. c   9. b   10. a

Study Questions and Problems

1. Suppose that researchers estimate that for every 1-percent change in the price of computers, the quantity demanded will change by 2.5 percent. Describe the price elasticity of demand for computers. What if researchers estimate that the quantity demanded for computers will change by 0.5 percent in response to a 1-percent change in price?

2. Economists estimate the short-run price elasticity of demand for airline travel to be 0.1, 0.3 for housing, 1.5 for glass, and 1.9 for automobiles. What is the meaning of these elasticity coefficients?

3. Why is demand relatively inelastic for medical care and gasoline but relatively elastic for movies and automobiles?

4. An advertisement appears in the *Seattle Times*: "Wanted, two Seahawks tickets for next week's game against the Broncos. Will pay any price. Phone Joe at 271-4597." If Joe really means what he says in his ad, what could you infer about his price elasticity of demand for tickets?

5. How will the following changes in price affect a firm's total revenue?

   a. Price rises and demand is inelastic.
   b. Price falls and demand is elastic.
   c. Price rises and demand is unit elastic.

    d. Price falls and demand is inelastic.
    e. Price rises and demand is elastic.
    f. Price falls and demand is unit elastic.

6. Suppose that the U.S. Postal Service implements an increase in the price of first-class mail in order to generate additional revenue. What can you infer about the price elasticity of demand for first-class mail?

7. Suppose that the Grand Central Movie Theater reduces the price of popcorn by 20 percent, but consumers purchase only 10 percent more of the product. What does this indicate about the price elasticity of demand, and what will happen to total revenue as a result of the price reduction?

8. Assume that the price elasticity of demand for corn is 0.6 and that farmers have a record harvest—corn production is higher than ever. What will happen to the total revenue received by farmers?

9. Suppose that the price elasticity of demand for airline travel is 0.4 in the short run and 2.2 in the long run. If airlines raise the price of tickets, what will happen to their total revenue over these time periods?

10. Assume that the price elasticity of demand for labor is 0.2. If a labor union succeeds in negotiating an 8-percent increase in hourly wages, what effect will this have on its members?

11. Table 3.4 shows the demand schedule and supply schedule for apartments.
    a. Draw the supply curve and demand curve for apartments from the data given in the table. What is the equilibrium rent? What is the quantity of apartments rented?
    b. Suppose that the government imposes a legal rent ceiling at $400 per month. How many apartments will be demanded and supplied? What will be the size of the shortage?
    c. How will landlords likely cope with the rent ceiling?

Table 3.4   Market for Apartments

Rent (monthly)	Quantity Supplied	Quantity Demanded
$700	1,000	200
600	800	400
500	600	600
400	400	800
300	200	1,000

12. Table 3.5 shows the demand schedule and supply schedule for milk. Quantities are in gallons.

Table 3.5   Market for Milk

Price	Quantity Supplied (gallons)	Quantity Demanded (gallons)
$0.50	5,000	9,000
1.00	6,000	8,000
1.50	7,000	7,000
2.00	8,000	6,000
2.50	9,000	5,000

a. Draw the supply curve and demand curve for milk from the data given in the table. What is the equilibrium price? How much milk will be produced and sold? How much revenue will farmers receive from the sale of milk?

b. Suppose that the government imposes a price floor on milk equal to $2 per gallon. How much milk will be produced and purchased? What will be the size of the surplus?

c. If government maintains the floor price by purchasing all the unsold milk from farmers, how much will the government pay? How much revenue will the farmers receive, from consumers and the government, from the sale of milk? What might the government do to dispose of the surplus?

Production and the Costs of Production

Chapter objectives

After reading this chapter, you should be able to:

1. Distinguish between the short run and the long run and between a fixed input and a variable input.

2. Describe how the law of diminishing returns relates to the productivity of a variable input in the short run.

3. Identify the costs of production that a firm realizes in the short run.

4. Explain how economies of scale and diseconomies of scale affect the long-run average total cost curve of a business firm.

5. Distinguish between accounting profit and economic profit.

economics IN CONTEXT

For years, McDonald's has attempted to maximize the output of its existing resources. At every McDonald's restaurant, some workers specialize in taking orders, others prepare food, and others serve customers at the drive-through window operation. Many McDonald's restaurants have installed automated machines to prepare french fries, thus increasing labor productivity. Moreover, McDonald's sophisticated cash registers are user friendly. They merely require an employee to touch a key with a picture of, say, a Big Mac to record the price rather than enter the dollar price of the hamburger on the cash register. This saves time and money for the firm.

Because McDonald's operates in thousands of locations, it can standardize operating procedures and menus, further adding to the company's efficiency. Moreover, McDonald's trains its managers at its Hamburger University, and the firm can spread the cost of its advertising over thousands of individual restaurants. These procedures result in cost savings for the firm.

However, McDonald's does face some problems. Because the firm's menu is standardized across the nation, if customers in some parts of the nation do not like a product, it is generally dropped from the menu despite its popularity elsewhere. McDonald's McRib sandwich, for example, was not popular with some consumers and therefore was dropped from the national menu. Another problem with McDonald's geographically uniform menu is that the ingredients must be available nationwide and cannot be subject to shortages or sharp price fluctuations.

In today's economy, business managers face great pressure to reduce cost while maintaining or improving product quality. Competition has forced firms such as McDonald's, Boeing, Intel, and General Motors to incorporate the latest technologies in order to fulfill these objectives. Moreover, employees of these companies must undergo retraining programs to increase their productivity. It turns out that for most goods and services, cost and output are closely related, implying that the theory of production is intertwined with the theory of cost. In this chapter, we will learn about production and the costs of production.

THE SHORT RUN VERSUS THE LONG RUN

The time frame in which a company plans its operations influences the production techniques that it selects. In general, a firm's production may take place in the short run or the long run. These periods are not defined in terms of days, weeks, or months; rather, they are defined conceptually.

The **short run** is a period during which the quantity of at least one input is fixed and the quantities of other inputs can be varied. A **fixed input** is any resource for which the quantity cannot be varied during the period under consideration. For example, the productive capacity of large machines or the size of a factory cannot easily be changed over a short period. In agriculture and some other businesses, land may be a fixed resource. There are also **variable inputs** whose quantities can be altered in the short run. Typically, the variable inputs of a firm include labor and materials. In response to a change in demand, a firm can employ more or fewer variable inputs, but it cannot alter the capacity of its factory.

The **long run** is a period during which *all* inputs are considered to be *variable* in amount. There are no fixed inputs in the long run. Over the long run, firm managers may contemplate alternatives such as constructing a new factory, modifying an existing factory, installing new equipment, or selling the factory and leaving the business. How long is the long run? That depends on the industry under consideration. For Burger King or Pizza Hut, the long run may be 6 months—the time required to add a new franchise. For General Motors or Ford, it may take several years to construct a new factory.

Table 4.1	Production Function for Chocolate Chip Cookies

1 cup butter or margarine, softened

2 1/4 cups flour

1/2 cup brown sugar

1 cup white sugar

2 eggs

1/2 teaspoon salt

1 teaspoon vanilla

1 teaspoon baking soda

1 package (12 oz.) chocolate chips

Mix butter with white sugar, brown sugar, eggs, and vanilla. In a separate bowl, mix flour, baking soda, and salt. Blend into creamed mixture. Add chocolate chips. Drop by teaspoonsful onto ungreased baking sheets. Bake at 375 degrees for 9 minutes. Makes approximately 6 dozen 2-inch cookies. For variety, add 1 cup of raisins or chopped nuts.

THE PRODUCTION FUNCTION

The transformation of resources into output does not occur haphazardly. When Ford and Toyota produce automobiles, for example, they take many resources (land, labor, capital, and entrepreneurship) and, using a technological production process, transform them into output. **Production** refers to the use of resources to make outputs of goods and services (for example, steel, locomotives, and banking services) available for human wants.

The relationship between physical output and the quantity of resources used in the production process is called a **production function**. For example, a production function might tell us that with one lathe, a machinist can produce a maximum of 20 axles per day. With one lathe and an assistant, a machinist might produce up to 30 axles per day. The production function specifies the *maximum* amount of output that can be produced with a given amount of resources.

The next time you make a batch of chocolate chip cookies, consider that the recipe you are using is an example of a production function. The recipe provides the types and amounts of resources and the processes that are required to produce a particular number of cookies. The resources include the ingredients shown in Table 4.1—brown sugar, white sugar, eggs, butter, and the like—as well as the kitchen equipment and the labor of the cook. The recipe also includes instructions for combining the various resources to produce cookies. Similarly, production functions in industry and agriculture specify the level of output and resources used in the production process.

SHORT-RUN PRODUCTION

To illustrate the production function, consider a simple case with one fixed resource and one variable resource. Figure 4.1 shows the short-run production function of Denver Block Co., a manufacturer of cement blocks used in the construction of buildings. Assume that the essential resources in the production of blocks are capital (a factory that includes a block machine, cement mixer, and forklift) and labor. Also suppose that the factory is already constructed and has a fixed capacity. For simplicity, suppose that the only resource that we can vary is labor, even though in reality the production of cement blocks requires other resources such as water, cement, sand, and gravel. As expected, using more workers with the machinery generally results in more blocks being produced; using fewer workers produces fewer blocks.

| Figure 4.1 | Short-Run Production Function of Denver Block Co. |

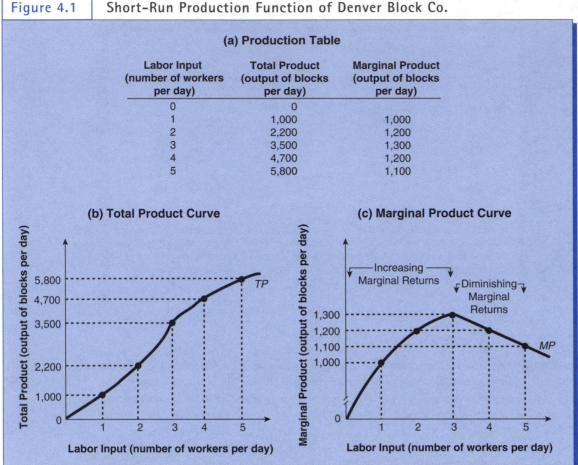

(a) Production Table

Labor Input (number of workers per day)	Total Product (output of blocks per day)	Marginal Product (output of blocks per day)
0	0	
1	1,000	1,000
2	2,200	1,200
3	3,500	1,300
4	4,700	1,200
5	5,800	1,100

(b) Total Product Curve

(c) Marginal Product Curve

The production table shows the maximum number of cement blocks that the firm can produce when it uses one block machine and different amounts of labor. The total product curve and the marginal product curve are based on these data. The law of diminishing returns accounts for the shape of the firm's product curves in the short run.

The purpose of a production function is to tell us how many blocks we can manufacture with varying amounts of labor. Refer to Figure 4.1(*a*) which shows a production function relating the total number of blocks produced (second column) to the amount of labor (first column). Employing zero workers results in no blocks being produced. A single machine operator can produce 1,000 blocks a day; adding a second operator increases output to 2,200 blocks per day, and so on. Figure 4.1(*b*) shows this **total product** (*TP*) schedule graphically.

We are also interested in how many additional blocks can be produced for each additional worker employed. The **marginal product** (*MP*) of labor is equal to the change in output that results from increasing the amount of labor by one unit, holding all other inputs fixed.

$$MP = \Delta \text{ Total product} / \Delta \text{ Labor}$$

where Δ, the Greek letter *delta,* denotes the change in a variable.

The marginal product of labor is calculated in Figure 4.1(*a*). When Denver Block Co. increases labor from zero to one worker, total output rises from zero to 1,000 blocks per day. The marginal product of the first worker is thus 1,000 blocks. Employing a second worker causes total output to rise from 1,000 blocks to 2,200 blocks, and thus the marginal product of the second worker equals

1,200 blocks. Similar calculations generate the remainder of the marginal product of labor. The marginal product curve is illustrated graphically in Figure 4.1(c).

Inspecting the marginal product curve, we see that the marginal productivity of labor rises for a while when the amount of labor used is low. Eventually, however, the marginal productivity of labor decreases. The principle that explains the decline in the marginal product curve is the **law of diminishing marginal returns**: After some point, the marginal product diminishes as additional units of a variable resource are added to a fixed resource.

In Figure 4.1(c), the marginal product of labor increases for the first three workers hired. Beginning with the fourth worker, however, the marginal product declines. Diminishing returns therefore begin with the fourth worker employed in block manufacturing.

It is easy to understand the reasons for the shape of the marginal product curve in Figure 4.1(c). If Denver Block Co. employs just one worker, that person has to perform all of the aspects of block manufacturing: mixing concrete, operating the block machine, and driving the forklift. If the firm hires a second person, the two workers can specialize in different aspects of block manufacturing. Therefore, two workers can produce more than twice as much as one worker. The marginal product of the second worker is thus more than the marginal product of the first worker, and the firm realizes **increasing marginal returns**. As the firm continues to add workers to the machinery, however, some workers may be underutilized because they have little work to do while waiting in line to use the machinery. Because the addition of yet ever more workers continues to increase output, but by successively smaller increments, the firm realizes **diminishing marginal returns**.

Here's a familiar example of the law of diminishing returns. Suppose that the total learning in your survey of economics course depends on the quality of this textbook, your intelligence, the effectiveness of your professor, and the time you devote to study. Assume that the first three variables are fixed, implying that they do not vary throughout the course. Now let us include hours of study time per day over the duration of the course to determine the increased course learning. Will the second hour devoted to studying economics increase learning by as much as the first hour? How about the third hour, and so on? You will probably find that diminishing returns to learning will eventually occur as successively more hours are devoted to studying economics each day. In other words, the marginal product of an additional hour of study will decrease, and eventually become zero.

Improvements in Technology and Work Rules Shift Product Curves Upward

In discussing the general shapes of a firm's product curves, we assumed that the state of technology, quality of human resources, and the amount of capital equipment remained constant as the firm changed its use of a variable resource. But what happens when these factors change? These factors are *shifters* that cause entire product curves to shift upward or downward.

Recall that technology consists of society's pool of knowledge concerning production in industry and agriculture. An important aspect of technology is that it sets restrictions on the amount and types of goods that can be produced from a given amount of resources: A firm cannot produce more than the existing technology will allow. Referring to Figure 4.1, a technological change that increases productivity *shifts* the whole total product curve and the marginal product curve upward. This means that each worker can produce more output so that diminishing returns are delayed to a higher level of output per worker. In this way, technological improvements can thus overcome the adverse effects of the law of diminishing returns. As long as technology improves, diminishing returns can be avoided.

In addition to technological improvements, education, training, and capital investment can also induce upward *shifts* in a firm's total product curve and marginal product curve. For example, increased education results in smarter workers, and vocational training provides specific job skills. Moreover, capital investment relieves strains on production capacity and increases output per worker. This is why economists advocate education, training, investment, and research and development as important factors that increase worker productivity and living standards. Let us consider how improvements in technology and work rules have boosted product curves in the fast food and iron ore industries.

New Technologies Make Drive-Through Lanes Faster. The effect of technological improvements on productivity can be seen in fast-food restaurants such as Wendy's, McDonald's, and Burger King. These firms know that every second represents lost business at their drive-through windows, which account for about 65 percent of their sales revenue. Industry analysts estimate that by increasing drive-through productivity by 10 percent, the average fast-food restaurant can increase its sales by an estimated $55,000 per year.

To beef up speed, fast-food restaurants have implemented new technologies such as windshield transponders that are scanned when the driver passes the menu board; purchases are billed to customers' monthly accounts, thus allowing them to bypass the cash window. Restaurants have also constructed separate kitchens in which meals are prepared for drive-through customers. The griller keeps 25 square burgers sizzling on the grill and, within 5 seconds of a customer's order, puts one on a bun. Once the meat hits the bun, the griller sends it to the sandwich makers, who have no more than 7 seconds to complete each customized creation. To help customers promptly exit the drive-through window, restaurants have developed see-through bags that allow customers to quickly verify that they have received all their items.

A cost of speed, however, can be low morale among workers, who sometimes complain that they cannot keep pace with the fast service goals of the restaurant. Indeed, demanding productivity increases from drive-through workers, who are paid low wages and have high turnover rates, can be tricky. Perhaps you have encountered these problems when you worked for Wendy's, McDonald's, or Burger King.[1]

New Work Rules Bolster Productivity in the Iron Ore Industry. Besides technological improvements, new work rules can boost worker productivity. Consider the case of the U.S. iron ore industry, located in the Midwest. Because iron ore is heavy and costly to transport, producers supply ore only to steel producers located in the Great Lakes region. During the early 1980s, depressed economic conditions in most of the industrial world led to a decline in the demand for steel and thus falling demand for iron ore. Ore producers throughout the world scrambled to find new customers. Despite the huge distance and transportation costs involved, mines in Brazil began shipping iron ore to steel producers in the Chicago area.

The appearance of foreign competition put more competitive pressure on U.S. iron ore producers. To help keep domestic iron mines operating, workers agreed to changes in work rules that would increase labor productivity. In most cases, these changes involved an expansion of the set of tasks that each worker was required to perform. For example, the changes required equipment handlers to perform routine maintenance on their equipment. Before, this maintenance had been the responsibility of repairmen. Also, the new work rules resulted in a flexible assignment of work so that a worker was occasionally required to do tasks assigned to another worker. In both cases, the new work rules led to a better use of each worker's time.

Prior to the changes in work rules, labor productivity in the U.S. iron ore industry was stagnant. However, improvements in work rules contributed to rapid increases in labor productivity. By the late 1980s, the productivity of U.S. iron ore producers had doubled, resulting in upward shifts in the total product curve and the marginal product curve of iron ore firms.[2]

SHORT-RUN PRODUCTION COSTS

If you ask managers about the competitiveness of their firms, their answers are likely to bring up costs. Costs are an extension of the production process. To illustrate, assume that General Motors pays its workers $40 an hour and that 30 hours of labor are required to assemble a vehicle. The cost of

---

1. "An Efficiency Drive: Fast-Food Lanes Are Getting Even Faster," *The Wall Street Journal*, May 18, 2000, p. A-1.
2. Satuajit Chatterjee, "Ores and Scores: Two Cases of How Competition Led to Productivity Miracles," *Business Review*, Federal Reserve Bank of Philadelphia, Quarter 1, 2005, pp. 7–15.

economics
IN ACTION

How Much Does It Cost to Drive?

How much does it cost to drive? Let us apply the notion of economic cost to driving. Some of your driving costs depend on the number of miles driven (gasoline), whereas other costs (vehicle registration) are fixed.

Each year the American Automobile Association (AAA) estimates the costs of driving. Table 4.2 shows AAA

estimates for individuals who purchased selected 2007 automobiles and drove 15,000 miles per year. We see that the cost of driving small sedans averaged 42.1 cents per mile, medium sedans averaged 55.2 cents per mile, and large sedans averaged 65.1 cents per mile.

As you read the table, notice which costs fall under the headings *fixed costs* and *variable costs*. You should be able to apply these concepts to the production costs that are discussed in this chapter.

Table 4.2 The Cost of Driving in 2007

	Small* Sedan	Medium Sedan	Large Sedan
Variable Costs	Costs per Mile (in cents)	Costs per Mile (in cents)	Costs per Mile (in cents)
Gasoline and oil **	9.4	12.3	13.2
Maintenance	4.0	4.7	5.1
Tires	0.5	0.9	0.8
	13.9	17.9	19.1
Variable costs for driving 15,000 miles a year	15,000 miles × 13.9¢	15,000 miles × 17.9¢	15,000 miles × 19.1¢
	$2,085	$2,685	$2,865
Fixed Costs	Cost per Year	Cost per Year	Cost per Year
Insurance	$ 949	$ 907	$ 973
License, registration, taxes	410	562	690
Depreciation	2,332	3,355	4,275
Finance charge***	541	770	963
	$4,232	$5,594	$6,901
Total Cost (yearly)	$6,317	$8,279	$9,766
Cost per Mile****	42.1 cents	55.2 cents	65.1 cents

*Small sedans include Chevrolet Cobalt, Ford Focus, Honda Civic, Nissan Sentra, and Toyota Corolla. Medium sedans include Chevrolet Impala, Ford Fusion, Honda Accord, Nissan Altima, and Toyota Camry. Large sedans include Buick Lucerne, Chrysler 300, Ford Five Hundred, Nissan Maxima, and Toyota Avalon.

**Gasoline costs based on $2.94 per gallon

***10 percent down; loan @ 6% interest for five years

****Total cost / 15,000 miles = Cost per mile

Source: American Automobile Association, *Your Driving Costs*, 2008.

Table 4.3		Hypothetical Short-Run Cost Schedules for HP Printers					
Quantity Produced per Day	Total Fixed Cost	Total Variable Cost	Total Cost	Average Fixed Cost	Average Variable Cost	Average Total Cost	Marginal Cost
0	$50	$ 0	$ 50	$ –	$ –	$ –	$ –
1	50	80	130	50.00	80.00	130.00	80
2	50	150	200	25.00	75.00	100.00	70
3	50	210	260	16.67	70.00	86.67	60
4	50	260	310	12.50	65.00	77.50	50
5	50	320	370	10.00	64.00	74.00	60
6	50	390	440	8.33	65.00	73.33	70
7	50	470	520	7.14	67.14	74.28	80

assembly totals $1,200 per vehicle ($40 × 30 = $1,200). Suppose that improving technology results in a 10-percent increase in labor productivity—only 27 hours of labor are now required to assemble a vehicle. Assembly costs now total $1,080 ($40 × 27 = $1,080) per vehicle. In this manner, higher worker productivity results in lower production costs and thus increased profits for General Motors. Higher productivity would also result in increased wages for General Motors workers if they could capture some of the productivity gains as higher wages.

Total Fixed, Total Variable, and Total Costs

Let us consider the hypothetical costs that Hewlett Packard (HP), a manufacturer of computer printers, realizes in the short run when it employs both fixed inputs and variable inputs.

First, we will consider the fixed costs of HP. **Total fixed cost** is the sum of all costs that do not vary with output. Managers often refer to fixed costs as *overhead costs*. They include such things as the cost of machinery, lease payments on some equipment, rent on a building, property taxes, and interest payments on a loan. The monthly value of HP's fixed inputs represents its monthly fixed cost. We see in column 2 of Table 4.3 that the firm's total fixed costs are $50.

In Figure 4.2(*a*), total fixed cost is shown by the horizontal line at $50. Fixed costs remain constant no matter how many printers are produced.

The production of printers also results in variable costs for HP. **Total variable cost** is the sum of all costs that change as the rate of output varies. They include payments for most labor, materials, storage and warehousing, shipping, electricity, and fuel. As HP produces more printers, more variable inputs are employed, and thus its total variable cost increases. Total variable cost therefore depends on weekly or monthly output. Total variable cost is shown in column 3 of Table 4.3 and it is translated into a total variable cost curve in Figure 4.2(*a*).

The rate at which total variable cost rises as more printers are produced depends on the capacity limitations imposed by fixed inputs. In general, total variable cost rises more slowly at low levels of output and then increases ever more rapidly. This aspect of variable costs is attributable to the principle of diminishing marginal productivity in the short run. As diminishing marginal productivity is encountered, each additional worker adds fewer units to the firm's output, yet the firm pays the same wage to each worker. As a result, total variable costs rise faster and faster.

Total cost represents the sum of the value of all resources used over a given period to manufacture computer printers. Thus, total cost is calculated as the sum of total fixed cost and total variable cost:

$$TC = TFC + TVC$$

| Figure 4.2 | Hypothetical Short-Run Cost Schedules for HP |

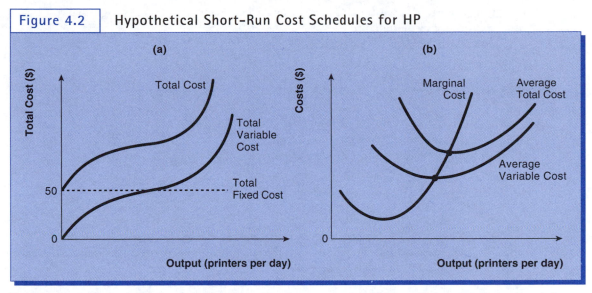

Total cost includes both fixed and variable costs. Fixed costs must be paid even if no output is produced. Average total cost is the sum of average fixed cost and average variable cost. Marginal cost is the addition to total cost resulting from the production of one additional unit of output.

The total cost of HP is shown in column 4 of Table 4.3 and it is translated into a total cost curve in Figure 4.2(*a*). Notice that total fixed cost is represented by the vertical distance between the total cost curve and the total variable cost curve.

Average Costs

Besides caring about total costs, HP managers care about *per-unit*, or *average*, costs. In the calculation of per-unit profit, average cost data are compared against price, which is always stated on a per-unit basis. Average fixed cost, average variable cost, and average total cost make up the per-unit cost schedules of a firm, as shown in columns 5-7 of Table 4.3.

Let us begin with **average fixed cost,** or *AFC*, which is the total fixed cost per unit of output. Average fixed cost equals total fixed cost divided by output (Q), or

$$AFC = TFC / Q$$

Because total fixed cost remains the same no matter how many units are produced, average fixed cost steadily declines as output increases. You can see by inspecting column 5 of Table 4.3 that average fixed cost decreases continually. To keep Figure 4.2(*b*) as uncluttered as possible, the average fixed cost curve is not shown.

Next, we look at **average variable cost,** or *AVC*, which is the total variable cost per unit of output. Average variable cost equals total variable cost divided by output, or

$$AVC = TVC / Q$$

Column 6 of Table 4.3 shows the average variable cost of HP, which we translate into an average variable cost curve in Figure 4.2(*b*). According to this schedule, HP's average variable cost first decreases but eventually begins to increase as the firm produces more printers. Because a typical average variable cost schedule is shaped like the letter *U*, economists refer to this curve as U-shaped.

Finally, **average total cost**, or *ATC*, is the total cost per unit of output. Average total cost equals total cost divided by output, or

$$ATC = TC / Q$$

This can be rewritten as

$$ATC = (TFC / Q + TVC / Q)$$

In other words, average total cost equals average fixed cost plus average variable cost, or

$$ATC = AFC + AVC$$

Column 7 of Table 4.3 shows the average total cost of HP, which we translate into an average total cost curve in Figure 4.2(*b*). Notice that the average total cost curve is U-shaped. Also notice that *ATC* and *AVC* become closer and closer in value as the quantity of printers rises. This is because average fixed cost gets smaller and smaller as output rises.

Marginal Cost

Businesses make decisions "on the margin." When the managers at HP consider a profit-maximization strategy, they are interested in whether the revenue earned from selling an additional printer will more than offset the cost of producing an extra printer. Because marginal means "additional," the managers are interested in marginal cost.

Marginal cost (*MC*) refers to the change in total cost when one more unit of output is produced, or

$$MC = \Delta TC / \Delta Q$$

Marginal cost is easy to calculate: Just measure how much total cost increases as each additional unit of output is produced. Column 8 of Table +.3 shows the marginal cost of HP printers. As the firm increases output from zero printers to one printer, total cost rises from $50 to $130, and thus marginal cost equals $80. Producing a second printer increases total cost from $130 to $200, and thus marginal cost equals $70, and so on. We translate this marginal cost data into a marginal cost curve in Figure 4.2(*b*). Notice that a firm's marginal cost curve is typically U-shaped: As output expands, marginal cost decreases, eventually reaches a minimum, and then increases.

The law of diminishing returns accounts for the U-shaped marginal cost curve. Recall that in the short run, as additional units of labor are added to machinery, the rate at which total output increases initially tends to rise. Assuming that the firm pays the same wage to workers as output expands, as each additional worker adds more to total output than the previous one, the cost of each additional unit of output decreases. This extra cost is the marginal cost. Therefore, as more units are produced, the marginal cost initially falls. This will not occur indefinitely, however. As more labor is applied to machinery, the marginal productivity of labor will eventually diminish. As a result, the marginal cost of production will increase. The U-shaped nature of the marginal cost curve is thus a reflection of diminishing marginal productivity in the production process.[3]

---

3. When you inspect Figure 4.2(*b*), notice the relation of *MC* to *ATC* and *AVC*. *MC* intersects both *ATC* and *AVC* at their minimum points. This will always be the case. So long as the marginal cost of producing one more unit is less than the previous average cost, average cost must decrease. Conversely, average cost must increase so long as the marginal cost of producing one more unit is greater than the previous average cost. Therefore, the *MC* curve intersects the *ATC* and *AVC* curves at their lowest points.

CHECK POINT

1. In general, a firm's production may take place in the short-run or the long-run period. Distinguish between two periods.

2. Distinguish between a firm's total product and its marginal product.

3. As a firm adds more of a variable input to a fixed input in the short run, what happens to the marginal product and the total product? What accounts for this behavior?

4. Classify the following as fixed costs or variable costs per unit of time: wages, rental payments on a factory building, insurance premiums, electricity and water expenses, property taxes, transportation expenses, and advertising expenditures.

5. Why is the marginal cost curve U-shaped?

LONG-RUN PRODUCTION COSTS

So far, we have examined how costs vary in the short run as the rate of output expands for a firm of a given size. In the long run, however, all inputs under the firm's control can be varied: A firm has sufficient time to replace machinery and increase the size of a factory. Because no inputs are fixed in the long run, there are no fixed costs. Therefore, all costs are variable in the long run. In this section, we will examine how altering factory size, and all other inputs, influences the relationship between production and costs in the long run.

A useful way to look at the long run is to regard it as a planning horizon. When operating in today's market, HP must constantly plan and determine its strategy for the long run. For example, even before HP decides to manufacture a new type of computer printer, the firm is in a long-run situation because it can choose from a variety of types and sizes of equipment to manufacture the new printer. Once HP makes this decision, it is in a short-run situation because the type and size of the equipment that it owns are, for the most part, frozen.

The **long-run average total cost curve** (*LRATC*) shows the minimum cost per unit of producing each output level when any desired size of factory can be constructed. Figure 4.3 shows the hypothetical *LRATC* curve of HP. Notice that this curve typically decreases with increases in output up to a certain point, reaches a minimum, and then increases with further increases in output. This U-shaped appearance of the *LRATC* curve is determined by economies of scale and diseconomies of scale, which exist simultaneously at many different levels of output.

Economies of Scale

When a firm realizes **economies of scale**, the *LRATC* curve slopes downward: An increase in scale and production results in a decline in cost per unit. Economies of scale can result from the following factors:

• **Specialization of labor and management.** As a firm becomes larger, it may be able to benefit from greater specialization of labor and management. At Pizza Hut, for example, some workers specialize in taking orders, others make pizza, and others wash dishes.

• **Efficient capital.** Smaller firms may not be able to acquire large, specialized machinery. For example, Wal-Mart employs sophisticated computer systems to track inventories and provide sales information to management.

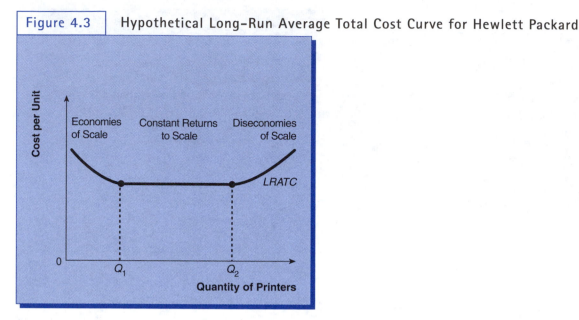

Figure 4.3   Hypothetical Long–Run Average Total Cost Curve for Hewlett Packard

The long-run average total cost curve shows the minimum cost per unit of producing each output level when any desired size of factory can be constructed. The long-run average cost curve above is U-shaped, reflecting economies of scale in the decreasing portion and diseconomies of scale in the increasing portion. The curve also has a flat bottom as a result of an extended stage of constant returns to scale after economies of scale are exhausted.

- **Design and development.** The next time you purchase textbooks, compare the prices of a 2-semester introductory text and a 1-semester advanced text. To your surprise, you may find that the principles text does not cost much more than the advanced text. This is true even if the principles text has 250 more pages and is produced in a multicolor format compared to a black-and-white format for the advanced text. Economies of scale are present in this situation. Publishing introductory and advanced texts requires costs for development and advertising that are approximately the same per page. For introductory texts, these costs are distributed over large levels of output—say, 50,000 copies, compared to only 10,000 copies for an advanced text. This results in a lower cost per copy and a relatively lower price per copy for the introductory text.

Do you know that when you use a prescription drug you are benefiting from the principle of decreasing long-run average cost? For prescription drugs, it costs roughly $350 million to bring a new drug to the market—and that's just for the first pill. Making the second pill costs about a penny. Assuming $350 million in development costs and a 1-cent marginal production cost thereafter, the average total cost falls from $350 million to produce just one pill to $350.01 to make 1 million pills to 4 cents each for sales of 10 billion. Prices fall in inverse proportion to the size of the market, as shown in Table 4.4. This example illustrates that, for pharmaceuticals, demand is not the enemy of price but its friend.

Automatic teller machines (ATMs) provide another example of economies of scale. Located in banks, gas stations, convenience stores, and shopping malls, ATMs dispense cash, accept deposits, and transfer funds between accounts. There are currently about 400,000 ATMs in the United States managing some 11 billion transactions per year. Although buying and installing an ATM is expensive, a single machine is very productive and can perform hundreds of transactions per day. The average cost per transaction declines considerably as the purchase and setup cost is spread over a large volume of transactions. The cost per transaction is estimated to be about one-fourth the cost of a human teller at a bank. As a result, many banks have replaced tellers with lower-cost ATMs.

Table 4.4	Average Total Cost of a Prescription Drug

Quantity of Pills	Average Total Cost
1	$350,000,000.00
100	3,500,000.01
10,000	35,000.01
1,000,000	350.01
100,000,000	3.51
10,000,000,000	0.04

Source: Federal Reserve Bank of Dallas, *The New Paradigm,*1999 Annual Report, p. 20, available at http://www.dallasfed.org.

For example, Gemini Consulting, a management consulting firm, estimates that the average total cost of a transaction is $1.07 for a teller and 27 cents for an ATM. Given these costs, why don't small banks and credit unions lay off their tellers and install ATMs? The reason is scale. To realize the cost advantages of an ATM requires a large number of transactions which small banks and credit unions do not have. Because of their relatively small scale, these financial institutions achieve their least-cost method of serving customers by employing tellers rather than ATMs. Simply put, the least-cost method is not necessarily the one that uses the most advanced technology.

Diseconomies of Scale

Economies of scale are really only half the story. If they were the entire story, the question would then have to be asked why not manufacture automobiles in even larger enterprises? If Ford and General Motors merged, wouldn't they be able to manufacture autos more cheaply and thus realize additional profit per auto than if they produced them separately? Likely not. As a firm gets larger and larger, the opportunities to realize economies of scale are eventually exhausted. As a firm grows, it is likely to encounter **diseconomies of scale**, which cause unit cost to increase and the *LRATC* curve to turn upward.

We can trace diseconomies of scale to the problems of managing large-scale operations. Beyond some scale of operation, the daily production routine becomes removed from the firm's top executives as additional layers of bureaucracy are added to the management team. The paperwork burden grows, and managers must control many business activities—finance, transportation, accounting, sales, research and development, personnel, and so on. The red tape and bureaucratic problems of running a large-scale operation contribute to inefficiencies and increased cost per unit.

Although Ford Motor Co. benefits from economies of scale, its large size also poses problems. For example, during the 1970s, Ford constructed a factory in Flat Rock, Michigan, to manufacture blocks for 8-cylinder engines. Ford followed the principle that large-scale production brings lower costs per unit of output. The firm spent $200 million to build a 4-story factory designed exclusively to manufacture engine blocks in the fastest, most efficient way possible. By 1981, however, Ford had shut down the factory and shifted production to a much older plant in Cleveland. The reason? The Flat Rock plant was too big and inflexible. It had been constructed to make engines at very large volumes, but it could not be converted to produce the 4- and 6-cylinder engines that became popular as gasoline prices rose. In effect, the Flat Rock plant was viewed as an inefficient dinosaur that could not keep pace with the rapidly changing economy.

There may also be an intervening range of output over which a firm realizes **constant returns to scale**. This occurs when a firm's output changes by the same percentage as the change in all inputs. For example, a 20-percent increase in all inputs causes a 20-percent increase in the firm's output.

economics
IN ACTION

From Mass Production to Lean Production

Henry Ford (1863-1947) was a noted pioneer of American industry. In 1903, Ford organized the Ford Motor Co. At first, the company manufactured only expensive automobiles, as its competitors did. However, Ford came from modest, rural roots. He thought that the people who built cars ought to be able to afford one so that they too could go for a spin on a Sunday afternoon. Ford soon began developing a simple, sturdy vehicle that many people of all walks of life could afford. This car became known as the Model T, which appeared in 1908.

Ford maintained that if he paid his factory workers a living wage and produced more cars in less time for less money, everyone would buy them. To make his Model T's affordable, Ford paid his workers $5 a day, double the industry standard. However, he was criticized for his generous pay scale: *The New York Times* dismissed Ford as being "distinctly utopian," and *The Wall Street Journal* accused him of employing "spiritual principles" where they do not belong.

In producing the Model T, Ford realized the importance of economies of mass production. He pioneered assembly-line methods to slash the costs of producing automobiles. In 1908, the Model T sold for $850, which was not cheap in those days. In 1913, Ford installed moving assembly lines in his factories. The frame of the car moved through the plant on a conveyor belt. Workers on each side assembled the car by adding parts that had

been brought to them by other conveyor belts. In 1914, Ford workers could assemble a Model T in little more than 1 1/2 hours. Building the earlier Model T had taken about 12 1/2 hours. The big time savings slashed Ford's production costs. In 1916, the Model T could be sold at a profit for $400, the lowest price of any automobile. Not surprisingly, by 1921, Ford's Model T, which remained largely unchanged for 19 years, had more than 50 percent of the market. It was at this time that Ford made his famous announcement that "any customer can have a car painted any color that he wants so long as it is black." Indeed, standardization, specialization, and mass production were the keys to Ford's low manufacturing costs, and constant price reduction was the key to attracting additional customers.

By the 1970s, however, U.S. auto manufacturers were challenged by lower costs and higher quality products from foreign firms. Japanese manufacturers such as Toyota changed the rules of production from mass production to lean production. Toyota realized that it could not catch up to Ford and General Motors by using traditional mass production methods. Instead, Toyota adopted "lean manufacturing" which places greater emphasis on flexibility and product quality. Instead of mass producing large numbers of identical vehicles, Toyota produces batches of similar vehicles. Toyota's goal is to have parts arrive just as they are needed, and these parts can be used interchangeably in its various models. This has allowed Toyota to manufacture higher-quality vehicles at lower costs and to introduce new models quickly. Toyota's success with lean manufacturing has placed great pressure on American auto firms to improve their manufacturing operations in order to compete in the global auto industry.

As a result, the cost per unit remains constant, and the *LRATC* curve is horizontal. This situation is consistent with many U.S. industries. For example, over an intermediate size range, smaller firms can be as efficient as larger ones in such industries as publishing, shoes, lumber, and apparel.

SHIFTS IN COST CURVES

In discussing the general shapes of a firm's cost curves in both the short run and long run, we assumed that certain other factors—technology, resource prices, and taxes—remained constant as the firm changed its level of output. These factors are *shifters* that cause cost curves to shift upward (downward), suggesting that a given level of output can be produced at a greater (smaller) cost.

- **Technology.** As we have learned, a technological change that increases productivity shifts the total product curve and the marginal product curve upward. Because a better technology allows the same output to be produced with fewer resources, a firm's cost curves *shift downward.* For example, computers and robots reduced the number of labor hours needed to produce automobiles, and printing presses reduced the number of labor hours required to produce books and newspapers, thus resulting in lower costs.

- **Resource prices.** A decrease in the price of resources, such as materials and labor, will reduce the cost of producing each output level. Therefore, a firm's cost curves will *shift downward.* In 1997, for example, the starting price for a personal computer smashed through the $1,000 barrier as manufacturers lowered the prices of chips used to produce personal computers. Lower-priced chips meant that firms such as Dell and Gateway could produce computers at a lower cost, allowing them to slash their computer prices.

- **Taxes.** Taxes are another component of a firm's costs. Suppose that the federal government reduces the excise tax from 25 cents to 20 cents on each gallon of gasoline sold by service stations. This policy lowers the cost of doing business for a service station, which causes the firm's cost curves to *shift downward.*

Foreign Competition Forces Cost Adjustments for U.S. Steelmakers

The U.S. steel industry provides an example of how production costs change in response to competitive pressure. In 1950, the U.S. steel industry was the most powerful in the world, accounting for almost one-half of world steel output. The large U.S. steel companies realized a dominant position of world leadership in plant scale and technology, a position that had gone virtually unchallenged by foreign competitors during the preceding 50 years. Moreover, the United States exported far more steel than it imported.

However, the market dominance of U.S. steelmakers did not last forever. Following World War II, Europe, Japan, and other nations rebuilt their steel industries using the latest technologies. These changes lowered the production costs for foreign steel compared to domestic steel, causing a stream of steel imports to come into the United States during the 1960s and 1970s and a flood of imports during the early 1980s. In 1982, U.S. producers' average total cost per ton of steel was $685 per ton—52 percent higher than that of Japanese producers. This cost differential was largely attributable to the strong U.S. dollar and higher domestic costs of labor and raw materials, which accounted for 25 percent and 45 percent, respectively, of total cost. Moreover, U.S. operating rates were relatively low, resulting in high fixed costs of production for each ton of steel.

Competitive pressure from foreign steel companies encouraged U.S. steelmakers to initiate measures to reduce production costs. Many American steel companies closed obsolete and costly steel mills, coking facilities, and ore mines. They also secured more flexible work rules, offered incentives for efficiency gains to employees, and slashed the ranks of management. Although these adjustments helped to reduce production costs, U.S. steel companies became increasingly burdened by the benefits that had to be paid to legions of retiring steelworkers, which added to production costs. Simply put, although U.S. steelmakers were able to reduce production costs by the 2000s, compared to the early 1980s, production costs remained relatively high by international comparisons, as seen in Table 4.5. Today, China has replaced the United States as the world's largest steelmaker.

COSTS AND PROFIT

An essential characteristic of the cost schedules we have observed is that they include the market value of all the resources used in the production process: land, labor, capital, and entrepreneurship.

Table 4.5	World Steel Cost Comparisons, 2009

Country	Average Cost per Ton
Japan	$634
United States	613
Western Europe	602
China	579
Eastern Europe	557
India	500
Brazil	480
Russia	424
Global average	563

Source: Peter F. Marcus and Karlis M. Kirsis, "World Steel Dynamics," Steel Strategist, 35, September 2009.

economics
IN ACTION

Dell Sells Factories to Slash Costs

The personal computer (PC) business has many rags-to-riches stories. But perhaps none is dramatic as the rise (and decline) of Dell Computer Corporation.

As a 19-year-old student at the University of Texas, in 1984 Michael Dell started a computer company from a dorm room with capital of $1,000 and built it into a $49-billion company with 57,000 employees worldwide. Initially, Dell Computer manufactured PCs in its own factories for a market that was dominated by business customers who bought large quantities of desktop PCs. The company developed an innovative strategy of selling computers directly to customers, only manufacturing them after they were ordered. After a customer placed an order through the Web or over the phone, the company's factories assembled the required components, installed PCs with software, and shipped them in a matter of hours. This system allowed Dell to decrease idle inventory and avoid marketing expenses associated with selling through retail channels. By 1999, Dell overtook Compaq to become the largest seller of PCs in the United States.

Although Dell has been a highly efficient manufacturer of desktop PCs, the firm has not been the low-cost producer of laptops. Years ago, rivals such as Hewlett Packard (HP) and Apple attained cost savings by entering into agreements with other firms to make their laptops; many of these producers are in low-wage countries such as China and Malaysia. Moreover, by the early 2000s, growth had switched to laptops sold to consumers at retail stores such as Office Depot and Best Buy. However, Dell lagged behind its competitors in developing an efficient system to produce laptops. The result was a decrease in Dell's sales and earnings and the company being replaced by HP as world's biggest PC manufacturer.

These adversities have resulted in Dell's selling many of its factories to reduce costs: Rather than producing PCs itself, the company has increasingly contracted with foreign companies to make PCs. In 2008, analysts estimated that Dell could decrease production costs for each computer by 15 percent to 20 percent by relocating manufacturing from the United States to China. It remains to be seen if Dell can decrease its production costs and regain its market leadership.

Sources: Michael Dell, Direct from Dell: Strategies That Revolutionized an Industry (New York: HarperCollins, 2006); Steven Holzner, How Dell Does It (New York: McGraw Hill, 2006); and Justin Scheck, "Dell Plans to Sell Factories in Effort to Cut Costs," The Wall Street Journal, September 5, 2008.

To calculate this cost, we simply identify all the resources used in production, determine their value, and then add things up.

Explicit Costs and Implicit Costs

Economists define the total cost of production as the sum of explicit costs and implicit costs. **Explicit costs** are payments made to others as a cost of running a business. For a local Pizza Hut franchise, explicit costs would include wages paid to labor, the cost of materials and electricity, telephone and advertising expenses, rental charges for the restaurant, health insurance for employees, and the like.

Implicit costs are the costs that represent the value of resources used in production for which no monetary payment is made. For Pizza Hut, implicit costs might include the forgone salary of the restaurant owner who uses her time to run the business. It might also include forgone interest because the owner invests her funds in the firm rather than depositing them into her savings account. If the owner uses her building to house the restaurant, she also sacrifices rent that she could receive from other tenants. With implicit costs, no money changes hands. They represent the imputed value that the firm's resources could command in their best alternative uses.

Accounting Profit and Economic Profit

Consider now what the term **profit** means. Most people think of profit as the difference between the amount of revenues a firm takes in (total revenue) and the amount it spends for wages, materials, electricity, and so on (total cost). If costs are greater than revenues, we call such "negative profits" **losses.** Although this description seems clear enough, accountants and economists have different views concerning the types of costs that should be included in total cost. As a result, they have different notions of profit.

To an accountant, the following formula describes profit:

$$\text{Accounting profit} = \text{Total revenue} - \text{Explicit costs}$$

We know this definition of profit as **accounting profit**. When preparing financial reports, accountants are concerned only with costs that are payable to others, such as wages, materials, and interest.

Besides caring about explicit costs, economists are interested in a firm's implicit costs, such as forgone salary, rent, and interest. **Economic profit** is total revenue minus the sum of explicit and implicit costs:

$$\text{Economic profit} = \text{Total revenue} - (\text{Explicit costs} + \text{Implicit costs})$$

Economists thus subtract the full cost of all resources from revenues in order to obtain a definition of profit.

Because accounting practice does not recognize the implicit costs of owner-supplied inputs, accounting costs, as we've discussed, *underestimate* economic costs. As a result, accounting profits based on accounting costs *overestimate* profits by underestimating costs.

What does zero economic profit imply? In economics, a firm that makes zero economic profit is said to be earning a **normal profit**. It represents the minimum profit necessary to keep a firm in operation. In other words, normal profit occurs when total revenue just covers explicit costs and implicit costs.

Should the owner of a company worry if she has made only a normal profit for the past year? The answer is no. Although a normal profit may appear unattractive, the owner has realized total revenues sufficient to cover both explicit and implicit costs. If, for example, the owner's implicit cost is the forgone salary of $50,000 for managing the business of someone else, then realizing a normal profit suggests that she has done as well as she could have in her next-best line of employment.

This chapter has considered the role of productivity and costs of production in influencing business decisions. In the next chapter, we will learn how a firm goes about maximizing economic profit. We will consider how a firm maximizes profits in a competitive market and also under a monopoly.

CHECK POINT

1. How do economies of scale and diseconomies of scale relate to a firm's long-run average total cost curve?

2. When drawing short- and long-run cost curves, we assume that certain factors remain constant. Identify these factors and their potential effects on a firm's cost curves.

3. Distinguish between explicit costs and implicit costs.

4. Why does the calculation of profit differ for an accountant as opposed to an economist?

5. Why do economists regard normal profit as a cost?

Chapter Summary

1. In general, a firm's production may take place in the short run or the long run. The short run is a period during which the quantity of at least one input is fixed and the quantities of other inputs can be varied. The long run is a period during which all inputs are considered to be variable in amount.

2. The relationship between physical output and the quantity of resources used in the production process is called a production function. A production function shows the maximum amount of output that can be produced with a given amount of resources.

3. According to the law of diminishing marginal returns, as a firm adds more of a variable input to a fixed input, beyond some point the marginal productivity of the variable input diminishes.

4. A firm that produces goods in the short run employs fixed inputs and variable inputs. Fixed costs are payments to fixed inputs, and they do not vary with output. Variable costs are payments to variable inputs, and they increase as output expands.

5. We can describe a firm's costs in terms of a total approach: total fixed cost, total variable cost, and total cost. We can also describe them in terms of a per-unit approach: average fixed cost, average variable cost, and average total cost.

6. Marginal cost refers to the change in total cost when another unit of output is produced. The short-run marginal cost curve is generally U-shaped, reflecting the law of diminishing marginal returns.

7. The long-run average total cost curve shows the minimum cost per unit of producing each output level when any size of factory can be constructed. Economies of scale and diseconomies of scale account for the U-shaped appearance of this cost curve.

8. In discussing the general shapes of a firm's cost curves in the short and long run, we assume that technology, resource prices, and taxes remain constant as the firm changes its level of output. Changes in any of these factors will cause a firm's cost curves to shift upward or downward.

9. Economists define the total costs of production as the sum of explicit costs and implicit costs.

10. According to accounting principles, profit equals total revenue minus explicit costs. Besides caring about explicit costs, economists are interested in a firm's implicit costs. Economic profit thus equals total revenue minus the sum of explicit costs and implicit costs.

11. A firm that makes zero economic profit is said to earn a normal profit. It represents the minimum profit necessary to keep a firm in operation. In other words, the firm earns just enough revenue to cover its explicit costs and implicit costs.

Key Terms and Concepts

short run (76)

fixed input (76)

variable inputs (76)

long run (76)

production (77)

production function (77)

total product (78)

marginal product (78)

law of diminishing marginal returns (79)

increasing marginal returns (79)

diminishing marginal returns (79)

total fixed cost (82)

total variable cost (82)

total cost (82)

average fixed cost (83)

average variable cost (83)

average total cost (84)

marginal cost (84)

long-run average total cost curve (85)

economies of scale (85)

diseconomies of scale (87)

constant returns to scale (87)

explicit costs (91)

implicit costs (91)

profit (91)

losses (91)

accounting profit (91)

economic profit (91)

normal profit (91)

Self-Test: Multiple-Choice Questions

1. The law of diminishing returns suggests that if increasing quantities of labor are applied to a given amount of machinery, the

   a. total product cannot be increased.
   b. total product will decrease.
   c. marginal product must be negative.
   d. marginal product will eventually decrease.

2. When the law of diminishing returns sets in, marginal cost must be

   a. falling at a decreasing rate.
   b. falling at an increasing rate.
   c. constant.
   d. rising.

3. The explicit costs of a firm include all of the following *except*

   a. rent paid for the use of a building.
   b. interest paid for borrowed money.
   c. money payments for the owner's self-employed resources.
   d. payments for the purchase of materials.

4. A firm's short-run production function describes how the

   a. maximum possible output varies as the quantity of labor hired varies in a given factory.
   b. minimum possible output varies as the quantity of labor hired varies in a given factory.
   c. maximum possible output varies as a firm enlarges the size of its factory.
   d. minimum possible output varies as a firm enlarges the size of its factory.

5. For U.S. Steel, the total product curve represents the

   a. maximum amount of steel attainable for each quantity of variable input hired.
   b. minimum amount of steel attainable for each quantity of variable input hired.
   c. lowest cost of producing various amounts of steel.
   d. maximum profit when producing and selling various amounts of steel.

6. Kaiser Aluminum's total product curve will shift upward if the firm

   a. hires additional quantities of labor and materials.
   b. pays lower wages to acquire additional workers.
   c. employs more efficient technologies in aluminum production.
   d. initiates work rules leading to falling productivity of labor.

7. Marginal cost is defined as

   a. total fixed cost plus total variable cost.
   b. total cost divided by the level of output.
   c. the increase in total cost as a firm produces an additional unit of output.
   d. total cost minus total fixed cost.

8. The range over which marginal cost is decreasing is the same range over which

   a. total product is increasing.
   b. marginal product is increasing.
   c. total cost is increasing at an increasing rate.
   d. total cost is decreasing.

9. General Motors will realize diseconomies of scale if an increase in plant size causes

   a. a decrease in long-run average total cost.
   b. an increase in long-run average total cost.
   c. the short-run total product curve to shift upward.
   d. the short-run total product curve to remain constant.

10. For Boeing, technological advances in the production of jetliners will tend to shift the total product and marginal product curves

   a. downward, and total cost and marginal cost curves upward.
   b. upward, and total cost and marginal cost curves downward.
   c. upward, and no change in total cost and marginal cost curves.
   d. downward, and no change in total cost and marginal cost curves.

Answers to Multiple-Choice Questions

1. d   2. d   3. c   4. a   5. a   6. c   7. c   8. b   9. b   10. b

Study Questions and Problems

1. As the manager of a restaurant, you estimate the total product of labor used to cook meals, as shown in Table 4.6. Use these data to calculate the marginal product of labor.
   a. In a diagram, plot the total product and marginal product schedules.
   b. What effect does the law of diminishing marginal returns have on these schedules?
   c. What underlies the law of diminishing marginal returns?

Table 4.6   Productivity Data

Quantity of Labor	Total Product	Marginal Product
0	0	
1	20	
2	45	
3	65	
4	80	
5	90	

2. M. E. Sharpe has maintained data on the labor input and production of economics textbooks, as seen in Table 4.7.
   a. Use these data to calculate the marginal product for each quantity of labor hired. Assume that when no workers are hired, output is zero.
   b. Using two figures, plot the total product curve and the marginal product curve.
   c. Identify the number of workers hired when total product is at a maximum.
   d. At which level of employment does the law of diminishing marginal returns begin?

Table 4.7   The Production of Textbooks

Labor input (workers)	3	5	1	2	4	6	7
Output of texts (total product)	380	600	100	220	520	620	580

3. Hanson Electronics Co. has fixed costs of $2,000 and variable costs as shown in Table 4.8. Complete the table.
   a. In a graph, plot total fixed cost, total variable cost, and total cost. Explain the shapes of these curves in relation to one another.
   b. In another graph, plot average fixed cost, average variable cost, average total cost, and marginal cost. Explain the shapes of these curves in relation to one another.
   c. How does the law of diminishing marginal returns explain the shape of the marginal cost curve?

4. Wassink Instruments has compiled output and cost data, shown in Table 4.9, on its production of microscopes. Use these data to compute total fixed cost, total variable cost, average fixed cost, average variable cost, average total cost, and marginal cost for each output level shown.

Table 4.8   **Cost of Production for Hanson Electronics Co. (dollars)**

Output	Total Variable Cost	Total Cost	Average Fixed Cost	Average Variable Cost	Average Total Cost	Marginal Cost
1	$1,000					
2	1,600					
3	2,000					
4	2,600					
5	3,400					
6	4,800					

Table 4.9   **Cost Data for the Production of Microscopes**

Output	Total Cost
0	$ 400
1	700
2	900
3	1,000
4	1,200
5	1,500
6	1,900

5. Your dry-cleaning firm currently cleans 300 shirts per day. Fixed costs for the firm are $400 per day. Variable costs are $1 per shirt. Calculate the total cost and the average total cost at the existing output level. Calculate the average fixed cost. What price would your firm have to charge in order to realize a normal profit at the current level of output?

6. Your shoe manufacturing company estimates that whenever it triples machinery, labor, and any other inputs in the long run, its output also triples. Assuming that input prices remain constant as your firm expands, construct the firm's long-run average total cost curve.

7. Some people are concerned about the decline of the small family farm and its replacement by large corporate farms. Explain how economies of scale might be a cause of this trend.

8. Increasing student population at the University of Wisconsin results in the nearby Pizza Hut restaurant realizing record sales. It is considering adding a new oven to bake additional pizzas. However, the daytime supervisor recommends simply employing more workers. How should the manager decide which course of action to take?

9. How will rising steel prices affect the average total cost curve and marginal cost curve of ABC Construction Inc., a builder of skyscrapers?

10. The introduction of the personal computer has decreased the number of hours required to type and edit a manuscript. How has this improvement in technology affected the average total cost curve and marginal cost curve of a publishing company?

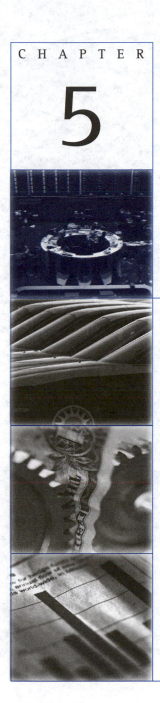

Competition and Monopoly: Virtues and Vices

Chapter objectives

After reading this chapter, you should be able to:

1. Explain the nature and operation of a perfectly competitive firm.

2. Explain how a perfectly competitive firm achieves economic efficiency in the long run.

3. Identify factors that contribute to monopoly.

4. Describe how a monopoly goes about maximizing profits.

5. Assess the advantages and disadvantages of a perfectly competitive firm and a monopoly.

economics IN CONTEXT

The aircraft carrier has been dubbed "97,000 tons of diplomacy." But in the early 2000s, the U.S. Navy was being anything but diplomatic in its sharp criticism of Newport News Shipbuilding Inc. Newport News, whose sprawling shipyard has hugged the St. James River in southern Virginia since it turned out its first tugboat in 1891, has long been the government's only producer of aircraft carriers. Navy officials expressed frustration with the company's failure to deliver promised cost savings.

The situation, Navy officials maintained, highlights what occurs in the absence of healthy competition. As a single producer, Newport News does not have to worry about staying ahead of its rivals to earn profits. Therefore, it lacks an incentive to organize production so as to minimize costs. Excess costs can result from the ineffective supervision of employees, the use of outdated equipment, the payment of large bonuses to management, and the like.

However, the situation cannot be easily remedied because the work that goes into building nuclear-powered warships makes it virtually impossible for a competitor to emerge. A typical carrier takes 5 years to build, stands 20 stories high including its tower, and carries more than 80 heavy fighter jets on a deck that covers 4 1/2 acres. The investment outlay required to construct another shipyard would be mammoth, a fact that discourages others from building a shipyard to compete against Newport News. Indeed, the Navy faced a difficult problem: how to pressure Newport News into making carriers at a reasonable cost when there is no alternative supplier to turn to.

Millions of businesses operate in the U.S. economy; each behaves differently in terms of its control over product price, the types of nonprice policies it uses, and its ability to realize the necessary profit to remain in business over time. Some firms have substantial control over product price, whereas others have little or no price-making ability. Some firms spend millions of dollars on product development or advertising, while others spend only negligible amounts on these activities. Some firms realize large economic profits over the long run while others, no matter how well they are managed, have no such potential.

The degree of competition in a market determines a firm's ability to control the price it charges for its product and its potential to realize continuing economic profits. As we will see, as market competition *increases,* a firm has *less* control over product price and is *less* likely to earn continuing economic profits.

Economists have formulated four market classifications to illustrate different competitive situations: perfect competition, monopolistic competition, oligopoly, and monopoly. With perfect competition, competition is strongest; competition is nonexistent in a pure monopoly. In between are monopolistic competition, which is closer to perfect competition, and oligopoly, which is closer to monopoly.

In this chapter, we will examine the virtues and vices of perfect competition and monopoly. The next chapter will consider monopolistic competition and oligopoly.

PERFECT COMPETITION

Let us begin with **perfect competition**, the most competitive market structure. A perfectly competitive market is characterized by the following:

- **Insignificant barriers to entry or exit.** New firms can enter a market if it appears profitable or exit if they expect losses. For example, lawn maintenance is an easy market to enter. To enter the market, one needs only a lawnmower, an edger, and perhaps an ad in the local newspaper.

- **Many sellers and buyers.** Each firm sells or purchases only a negligible share of the total amount exchanged in the market.

- **A standardized product produced by firms in the industry.** For example, the wheat grown by one farmer is identical to the wheat grown by another farmer. As a result, brand preferences and consumer loyalty are nonexistent.

- **Perfect information.** All sellers and buyers are fully aware of market opportunities. That is, they know everything that relates to buying, producing, and selling the product.

Perfect competition is quite rare in the United States because most markets do not fulfill all of these assumptions. The usefulness of this market structure is that it serves as an important ideal against which real-world markets can be judged. Some markets, however, come close to fulfilling the assumptions of perfect competition and thus provide an approximation that is characterized by ease of entry and exit. Examples include agriculture, the fishing industries, stock markets (such as the New York Stock Exchange), and the foreign exchange market.

The Perfectly Competitive Firm as a Price Taker

In a perfectly competitive market, each seller or buyer is small relative to the size of the market, and so its decision to supply or purchase a particular quantity of a product does not affect the market price. A perfectly competitive firm is called a **price taker** because it has to "take," or accept, the price that is established by the market.

Figure 5.1 illustrates the hypothetical case of Puget Sound Fishing Co., which operates in a perfectly competitive market. In Figure 5.1(*a*) the market price of fish is $7 per pound, as determined by the intersection of the market demand curve and the market supply curve. Once the market price is established, Puget Sound Fishing Co. can sell all the fish it wants to at that price because it supplies an insignificant share of the market output. In Figure 5.1(*b*), the demand curve, as it appears to Puget

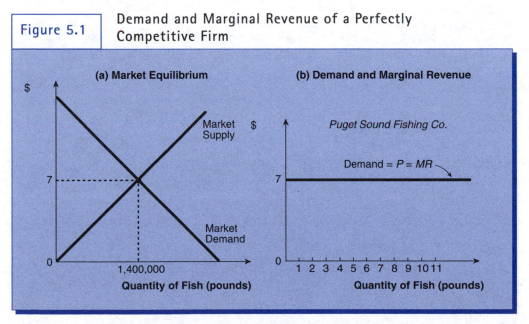

| Figure 5.1 | Demand and Marginal Revenue of a Perfectly Competitive Firm |

As a price taker, Puget Sound Fishing Co. sells additional units of output at a price that is determined by the market. The firm's demand schedule appears horizontal and coincides with its marginal revenue schedule.

Sound Fishing Co., is drawn as a *horizontal* line at the market price. This demand curve is also a *price line* for the firm. Note that the firm's output is much smaller than the market output. For example, hundreds of fishing firms might operate in the market, producing a combined output many times greater than that supplied by Puget Sound Fishing Co.

Why won't Puget Sound Fishing Co. try to raise its price above $7? The reason is that in a perfectly competitive market, many other firms are also selling fish at $7 per pound. If Puget Sound Fishing Co. set its price above $7, it would sell no fish. Conversely, the firm will not set its price below $7 because it can sell all the fish it wants to at the market price; thus, a lower price would decrease its revenue.

economics
IN ACTION

Steve Jobs: A Great Innovator

In market economies, whenever a new opportunity appears, innovators quickly find a way to profit from it. Because innovators are free to pursue their self-interests as they fit, they also profit from ancillary opportunities that are undreamed of by most. Consider the case of Steve Jobs.

The next time you use an iMac computer, listen to an iPod music player, or purchase music online from iTunes, remember the name, Steve Jobs. He is the innovator who brought these technologies to the masses. Born in Los Angeles in 1955, Jobs co-founded Apple Computer in 1976 with Steve Wozniak and became a multimillionaire before the age of 30.

An adopted child, Jobs gained an early appreciation for technology. At the age of 12, Jobs landed an internship at Hewlett Packard Co. There he attended electronics lectures after school and worked during the summer. During his internship, Jobs met Steve Wozniak ("Woz"), an engineering hotshot who had dropped out of the University of California, Berkeley, and had a mania for inventing electronic gadgets.

After dropping out of Reed College in Portland, Oregon, in 1974 Jobs worked as a video game designer at Atari Inc. He attended meetings of Wozniak's computer club and soon convinced Wozniak to help him build a personal computer. Wozniak and Jobs designed a computer in Job's bedroom and they constructed the prototype in his garage.

Encouraged by their efforts, Jobs and Wozniak founded Apple Computer Inc. To raise funds for their start-up, they sold their most valuable possessions: Jobs sold his Volkswagen bus and Wozniak sold his Hewlett Packard scientific calculator, raising $1,300. With that money capital and credit obtained from local electronics suppliers, they established their first production line. Jobs thought up the name of the new company, Apple, in fond memory of a summer he had spent as an orchard worker near Portland.

In 1976, Jobs and Wozniak built their first computer, called the Apple I. They sold it at a price of $666 and earned revenues totaling $774,000. The following year, Jobs and Wozniak put together the Apple II, the first personal computer to hit it big. Though the power of computing previously had been available only to "techies," the Apple II could be delivered to offices, classrooms, and dens. Then came Apple's Macintosh computer in 1984, the first personal computer to feature a mouse, icons, and computer graphics.

Since his early years at Apple, Steve Jobs has continued to develop breakthrough products. In 2001, Jobs rocketed the music business with Apple's iPod music player, and iTunes Music Store in 2003, the first time anyone had convinced all the major record companies to market their songs online. Today, few doubt the innovation and marketing abilities of Steve Jobs.

Sources: Laurie Rozakis and Dick Smolnski, *Steven Jobs: Computer Genius* (Rourke Enterprises, Vero Beach, FL, 1993); and Alan Deutschman, *The Second Coming of Steve Jobs* (New York: Random House, 2001).

For a perfectly competitive firm, **total revenue** (*TR*) is simply the price per unit (*P,* $7 in this example) multiplied by the output level (*Q*), or *TR* = *P* × *Q*. The rate of increase in total revenue is especially important. It represents the increase in total revenue resulting from the sale of another unit of output. We call this rate of increase **marginal revenue** (*MR*). Mathematically, this is expressed as *MR* = Δ *TR* /Δ*Q*.

For Puget Sound Fishing Co., total revenue is zero when no fish are sold. The sale of the first pound of fish increases total revenue from zero to $7 ($7 × 1 = $7), so the marginal revenue is $7. The second pound increases total revenue from $7 to $14, so the marginal revenue is again $7. Marginal revenue is therefore a constant, $7, because total revenue increases by this fixed amount as each additional pound of fish is sold.

What is the relationship between price and marginal revenue for a perfectly competitive firm? In Figure 5.1(*b*), we see that, as a price taker, Puget Sound Fishing Co. sells fish at a constant price of $7 per pound. We also see that the firm's marginal revenue equals $7 for each pound sold. Therefore, in perfect competition, price (*P*) equals marginal revenue, or *P* = *MR*.

PERFECT COMPETITION: PROFIT MAXIMIZATION IN THE SHORT RUN

We have just learned about the demand and revenue schedules of a perfectly competitive firm. The next step is to combine information about the firm's revenues and costs to find the output that will maximize profits in the short run.

Marginal Revenue Equals Marginal Cost Rule

Recall that *MR* represents the addition to total revenue from the sale of another unit of output, and marginal cost (*MC*) represents the addition to total cost of producing another unit of output. If *MR* exceeds *MC,* total revenue will increase more than total cost as output rises. Because total profit is the difference between total revenue and total cost, the production of additional units that add more to total revenue than to total cost will increase total profit. Conversely, if *MC* exceeds *MR,* decreasing output will result in increased total profit. Profit maximization thus occurs at that output where *MR* = *MC*. In economic jargon, this is the **marginal revenue** = **marginal cost rule**: Total profit is maximized when marginal revenue is equal to marginal cost. This rule applies to all firms, whether they operate in perfectly competitive markets, monopolistic markets, oligopolistic markets, or monopolistically competitive markets.

With perfect competition, the *MR* = *MC* rule can be modified. Because price and marginal revenue are identical for a perfectly competitive firm, profit maximization occurs at that output where price equals marginal cost, or *P* = *MC*. This is simply a special case of the *MR* = *MC* rule.

Perhaps you can benefit from the price = marginal cost rule the next time you purchase an automobile. The auto dealer wants to get a price that at least covers all of his costs, including both variable costs and fixed costs. She might, however, be willing to sell you an automobile for only its marginal cost—that is, the wholesale price that he paid for it plus a little labor time for dealer preparation of the vehicle. As long as the price exceeds the marginal cost, the dealer will add to total profit by selling the vehicle. If you are a skilled bargainer, you may be able to buy an auto at a price that is less than the average total cost.

Profit Maximization

Figure 5.2 shows the revenue and cost curves of Puget Sound Fishing Co., which operates in a perfectly competitive market. As expected, the average total cost curve and marginal cost curve are U-shaped. The demand curve is horizontal, which means that price equals marginal revenue at all levels of output.

In Figure 5.2, Puget Sound Fishing Co. maximizes total profits by selling 2,500 pounds of fish, where *MR* = *MC*. The firm's price equals $7 per pound and its total revenue equals $17,500 ($7 ×

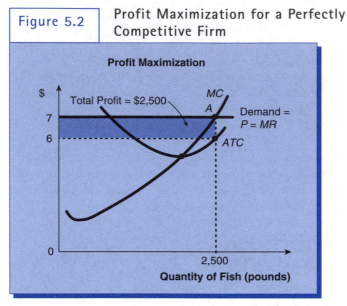

Figure 5.2 | Profit Maximization for a Perfectly Competitive Firm

In the figure, total profit of Puget Sound Fishing Co. is maximized at 2,500 pounds of fish, where marginal cost equals marginal revenue at point A. Total profit ($2,500) equals profit per unit ($1) multiplied by the profit-maximizing output (2,500 units).

2,500 = $17,500). Because the average total cost for 2,500 pounds of fish equals $6 per pound, the total cost for all 2,500 pounds is $15,000 ($6 × 2,500 = $15,000). The firm's total profit is $2,500 ($17,500 − $15,000 = $2,500). This amount is denoted by the shaded area in the figure.

An alternate way to calculate total profit is to multiply *profit per unit* by output. Profit per unit equals price minus average total cost ($P − ATC$). Referring to Figure 5.2, at the profit-maximizing output of 2,500 pounds, the price is $7 and the average total cost is $6. Profit per unit thus equals $1 ($7 − $6 = $1). Multiplying this amount by 2,500 pounds gives us a total profit of $2,500.

Notice that Puget Sound Fishing Co. does not attempt to maximize profit per unit, the point at which price exceeds average total cost by the greatest amount. What matters is *total* profit, not the amount of profit per unit. This is the age-old problem of selling, say, cookies at a school fund-raiser. Perhaps you can maximize profit per unit by selling one box for $5, but you would make more total profit if you sold 100 boxes at a per-unit profit of only 25 cents each. The increase in volume would more than offset the reduction in profit per unit, resulting in a higher total profit. For Puget Sound Fishing Co., total profit is at its maximum when marginal revenue equals marginal cost.

However, Puget Sound Fishing Co. is not guaranteed a profit. For example, a downturn in the economy may cause the firm to realize losses. Loss minimization for a perfectly competitive firm is discussed in "Exploring Further: 5.1" at the end of this chapter.

PERFECT COMPETITION: LONG–RUN ADJUSTMENTS AND ECONOMIC EFFICIENCY

To the owner of a business, profits are obviously desirable and losses are dreadful. From the viewpoint of the overall economy, however, profits and losses play equally important roles in allocating scarce resources efficiently. Although a market economy is often referred to as a profit system, it is really a profit and loss system. Losses are equally important for the efficiency of the economy because they tell businesses what to stop producing. Let us see why this is true.

An important characteristic of perfect competition is the long-run behavior of firms in this market structure. Although the number of firms in a competitive market is fixed in the short run, freedom of entry and exit applies to the long run. Because it is easy to enter into and exit from a market, perfectly competitive firms operate at the *lowest possible cost,* charge the *lowest price* that they can without going out of business, and earn *no economic profit.* These characteristics are ideal from the consumer's perspective.

Let us consider again the case of Puget Sound Fishing Co. Assume that the firm's cost curves are identical to all other firms in the fish market. This assumption allows us to analyze a *typical* or *average* firm, realizing that all other firms are similarly affected by any long-run adjustments that may occur.

Figure 5.3 shows the long-run position of Puget Sound Fishing Co. Notice that the firm produces at point *A,* where its demand curve just touches the lowest point on its long-run average total cost curve. The firm thus produces 500 pounds of fish at $5 per pound. Any other output level would result in a loss for the firm because its demand curve would be below its long-run average total cost curve.

Also notice that point *A* is the *minimum* point on the firm's long-run average total cost curve. This means that the firm produces at the lowest possible cost per unit in the long run. Competition forces the firm to use the least costly—and thus the most economically efficient—production techniques. Efficient production is an important objective for society because the fundamental problem of economics is scarcity; efficiency counteracts the scarcity problem by allowing a greater amount of

Figure 5.3 | Long-Run Adjustments for a Perfectly Competitive Firm

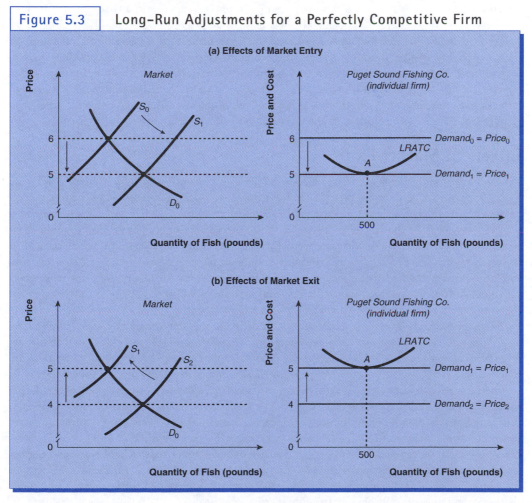

In the long run, competitive price will equal the minimum average total cost of production because short-run profits prompt new firms to enter a competitive industry until those profits have been competed away. Conversely, short-run losses will hasten the exit of firms from the industry until product price barely covers average cost. At the point of long-run equilibrium, price equals minimum average total cost, which allows just a normal profit.

output to be produced with a given amount of resources. What accounts for this long-run position of a perfectly competitive firm? Freedom of entry into and exit from the market is the basis for the position of the average perfectly competitive firm in the long run.

Effects of Market Entry

Let us first consider the effect of entry of sellers into a perfectly competitive market. Referring to Figure 5.3(a), suppose the equilibrium price in the fish market is $6 a pound, shown at the intersection of the market supply curve (S_0) and the market demand curve (D_0). With a market price of $6 per pound, the demand curve of Puget Sound Fishing Co. is located at *Demand*$_1$. The firm realizes an economic profit because its demand curve lies above its long-run average total cost curve. Over time, however, economic profits attract new competitors into the market. The resulting increase in market supply causes a decrease in market price and a decline in economic profits. Entry continues until the market supply reaches S_1, the price falls to $5 per pound, and economic profits fall to zero for Puget Sound Fishing Co. Once economic profits disappear, entry ceases.

The personal computer (PC) industry provides an example of market entry and decreasing prices. When the first PC was introduced by International Business Machines Inc. (IBM) in 1981, there was negligible competition. IBM charged prices as high as $7,000 for a PC and it realized huge economic profits. This attracted other firms, such as Compaq and Dell, to develop PCs that were of the same quality as those produced by IBM. As these firms entered the personal computer market, market supply increased, prices declined, and economic profits decreased for the average firm. Today buyers can purchase a PC that is more than 29 times as powerful as its 1981 ancestor at a price of $400 or less. Note that although IBM does not fulfill all of the assumptions of perfect competition, it illustrates the long-run adjustments that occur in industries with relative freedom of entry.

Effects of Market Exit

Now we will examine the effect when sellers exit a perfectly competitive market. Referring to Figure 5.3(b), suppose the equilibrium price in the fish market is $4 per pound, shown at the intersection of the market supply curve (S_2) and the market demand curve (D_0). At this price, the average firm realizes a loss because the cost of supplying each fish exceeds the price. Lower profits would cause some firms to close their doors and exit the market. This results in a decrease in market supply and an increase in price. The exodus of firms continues until the market supply reaches S_1 and the price rises to $5 per pound, at which point zero economic profits accrue for the remaining firms. Easy entry into and exit from the market thus causes a perfectly competitive firm to operate so that price equals the minimum average total cost, which allows only a normal profit.

Although production under perfect competition occurs in the long run at minimum average total cost, this result does not imply that perfectly competitive firms necessarily are more efficient than firms in other types of market structures. However, it does mean that, given the technology available to the firm, economic forces in perfect competition require producers to minimize the per-unit cost of production.

International Harvester Inc. was a firm that provided an example of the effects of market exit during the 1980s. For decades, International Harvester was famous as a manufacturer of farm equipment such as tractors and combines. As International Harvester encountered strong competition from other firms, however, it realized declining revenues and economic losses. By the mid-1980s, International Harvester exited the farm equipment market. Today it manufactures trucks, school buses, and engines under the name of Navistar International Corporation. Note that although International Harvester did not fulfill all of the assumptions of perfect competition, it illustrated the long-run adjustments that occur in industries with relative freedom of exit.

Will Online Music Start-ups Be Singing the Blues?

We have learned that when new firms enter a competitive market, the price decreases and the economic profit of each existing firm falls. Although the online music business that we will consider does not fulfill all of the assumptions of perfect competition, it illustrates the long-run adjustments that occur in industries with relative freedom of entry and exit.

The author of this text once asked his economics principles students whether they downloaded music from the Internet. The students laughed and virtually everyone raised his or her hand. Indeed, bootlegged services, such as LimeWire, through which songs can be grabbed for free, threaten the livelihood of performers and music companies such as BMG, EMI, and Sony Music. That's why the music industry has filed lawsuits against these services and their participants. To the music industry, the sharing of music files is tantamount to stealing.

During the early 2000s, the music and technology industries cast about for a legal Internet music service that would rival the bootlegged services. However, the early services were generally considered to be inadequate. They all required monthly fees, and they stressed "streaming" music, which users can listen to, but can't download. Use of their songs expired if monthly fees were not paid. Playback of songs was usually restricted to one or two computers, and the songs often could not be used on portable music players. The ability to burn songs to CDs was either very limited or it required a per-burn payment on top of the service's monthly fee.

In 2003, however, Apple Computer launched the first really useful and legal Internet music service, the iTunes Music Store. The iTunes Store had a simple rule. Each song costs 99 cents—no strings attached and no subscription required. You can purchase as many or as few songs as you like. Once you purchase a song, it's yours to keep. You can copy it to as many as three computers. Also you can copy each song to an unlimited number of portable music players and burn each song to an unlimited number of home-made CDs. For each 99-cent song that Apple's iTunes Store sold, the music companies received a licensing royalty of 65 cents to 70 cents. The iTunes Store also had to come up with another dime or so to pay for bandwidth, servers, and the staff to run them. Apple originally targeted Mac computer users, but it soon rolled out a Windows version of its iTunes Store.

By 2009, Apple's Music Store commanded about 75 percent of the online-song market, with a catalog of over 10 million songs. However, analysts questioned how long iTunes Store would be able to remain on the cutting edge. If it figured out how to make money by selling music on the Internet, rivals would eventually follow. In the past few years, Amazon, Microsoft Corporation, Sony Corp., and Yahoo have entered the online music market and swayed all major labels to sign on with them. They were also faster than iTunes Store to offer more songs without copy protection. This competitive pressure has resulted in iTunes Store's cutting prices and improving product quality in order to protect its market share. In 2009, iTunes Store revised its pricing policy by making songs available at one of three price points: 69 cents, 99 cents, and $1.29, with many more songs priced at 69 cents than $1.29; most albums were priced at $9.99. Also, songs purchased from iTunes Store could be copied or moved to multiple computers. It remains to be seen whether competition will force the iTunes Store to start singing the blues.

CHECK POINT

1. Identify the assumptions of a perfectly competitive market.

2. Why is a perfectly competitive firm a price taker?

3. How does a firm determine its profit-maximizing output?

4. Why does a perfectly competitive firm produce at the lowest point on its average total cost curve in the long run? Why does the firm realize zero economic profits in the long run?

MONOPOLY

If you attend a college in a small town, you might find that you can obtain textbooks from only one store. The same is often true of your college or university cafeteria. The firm that sells food in your school cafeteria is usually granted an exclusive franchise to do so by your college or university. Moreover, if you have visited a national park or a ski resort and had lunch at one of its restaurants, you were probably purchasing food from a firm granted an exclusive franchise. As we shall learn, when a firm does not face competition, it can charge a higher price and produce output of lesser quality than if there were more competition in the market. Let us consider markets in which competition is severely restricted by barriers to entry, a situation that is known as *monopoly.*

A **monopoly** is a market structure that is characterized by a single supplier of a good or service for which there is no close substitute. With monopoly, the firm (the monopolist) and the industry are one and the same. For many years, the suppliers of local electricity, natural gas, water, and phone service were examples of local monopolies; however, competition has increased in these industries during the past two decades.

Do you know that every time you pay for an item with paper currency, say, a dollar bill, you are using a product that comes from a near monopoly? Since 1879, virtually all of the paper purchased by the U.S. Treasury Department's Bureau of Engraving and Printing has come from one supplier: Crane & Co., Inc., of Dalton, Massachusetts. The U.S. reliance on a single source for currency paper is not unique; most other industrial nations also rely on a single domestic supplier for their currency paper.

How does a firm become a monopoly? The first requirement is to produce a good or service that has *no close substitutes.* If a good has close substitutes, even though one firm may produce it, the firm faces competition from other firms that produce the substitute goods. Note, however, that technological change and innovation can create new products and thus weaken a monopoly's control of the market. For example, the development of e-mail and fax machines has eroded the U.S. Postal Service's monopoly on first-class letter mail. Also, the development of satellite dishes has diminished the monopoly of local cable television firms. Furthermore, technological advances in telecommunications, such as cellular telephones, have eroded the telephone monopoly on local telephone calls.

BARRIERS TO ENTRY

Another characteristic of monopoly is the existence of barriers that make it difficult or impossible for new firms to enter an industry. **Barriers to entry** are impediments created by the government or by the firm or firms already in the market that protect an established firm from potential competition.

In the airline industry, established firms benefit from several barriers to entry. First, restricted access to takeoff and landing slots at many large airports has greatly deterred entry of competing airlines. These slots are allocated by federal legislation aimed at limiting the number of takeoffs and landings during peak traffic periods. Also, new entrants often have limited access to airport facilities such as gates, ticket counters, and baggage handling and storage. Furthermore, established airlines often enact aggressive price-cutting policies to discourage new competitors from entering the market. Research has shown that major airports dominated by only a few airlines tend to have higher airfares than those having intense competition among airlines. Passengers flying at dominated airports typically pay about 40 percent more than do their counterparts flying at airports where airline competition is strong.[1]

Legal Barriers

Many legal barriers are created by government policy. *Patents,* for example, help prevent entry by giving an inventor (for example, Microsoft) the exclusive right to produce a particular good (Windows

---

1. U.S. General Accounting Office, *Aviation Competition: Challenges in Enhancing Competition in Dominated Markets,* March 13, 2001.

computer software) for a specified period. *Copyrights* refer to exclusive rights granted to a composer or author of an artistic, musical, literary, or dramatic work. *Licenses* regulate entry into particular occupations such as medicine, law, and architecture. Finally, *public franchises* give a holder the sole legal right to supply a good or service. The U.S. Postal Service, for example, has the exclusive right to deliver first-class letter mail. Another example of a public franchise can be found on our freeways, where particular companies are awarded the sole right to sell food and gasoline.

Taxicabs provide an example of legal barriers that shut out competition. In New York City, the government restricts the number of taxicabs to one cab for every 600 people. As a result, about 13,000 yellow cabs service the city. To operate a taxi, one must obtain a license and place an official medallion on the taxi's hood as proof of legality. Licenses are auctioned off to the highest bidder. Although taxi drivers often complain about the unpleasant task of working more than 60 hours per week, encountering robbers, and arguing with impolite customers, they are willing to pay more than $200,000 for a license. Why? Restricting competition decreases the supply of taxis, drives up fares, and allows the remaining taxis to expand their market share. The increased profits realized by cab drivers come at the expense of travelers and excluded competitors. Operating taxis in New York City is lucrative, and drivers have no difficulty selling their licenses when they decide to leave the business.

Control over Essential Inputs

Sole control over the entire supply of raw materials and other inputs is another way to prevent potential competitors from entering an industry. From the early 1900s until the end of World War II, Alcoa (Aluminum Co. of America) monopolized the U.S. aluminum industry through its ownership of most of the bauxite mines in the world (bauxite is used to manufacture aluminum). Likewise, the International Nickel Co. of Canada once owned nearly all of the world's nickel. In professional sports, it is virtually impossible to compete with the National Hockey League, the National Football League, and the National Basketball Association. Why? These teams have contracts with the best players and leases with the best arenas and stadiums. Moreover, Nintendo weakened its rivals by prohibiting game developers from designing games for anyone else, and Topps Chewing Gum established a 14-year monopoly on baseball cards by signing players to exclusive contracts.

Economies of Scale

Economies of scale can also cause monopoly. A **natural monopoly** occurs when one firm can supply a product to the entire market at a lower cost per unit than could be achieved by two or more firms each supplying only some of it. The monopolist can drive average total cost down by taking advantage of economies of scale over the entire range of market demand.

Figure 5.4 illustrates the hypothetical case of Northern States Power Co., a natural monopoly that supplies electricity to the residents of St. Cloud, Minnesota. Suppose the market demand for electricity equals 5 million kilowatt-hours (kWh). Given the firm's average total cost curve, *ATC*, we observe economies of scale—that is, decreasing average total cost—throughout the relevant range of production. As a single producer, Northern States Power Co. can service the entire St. Cloud market at a cost of 7 cents per kWh, resulting in a total cost of $350,000 ($0.07 × 5 million kWh = $350,000).

Instead of having a monopoly serve the St. Cloud market, suppose that the market is divided evenly among five competing firms. Assume that each firm realizes a cost curve shown by *ATC*. With each firm producing 1 million kWh, unit cost equals 11 cents. The total cost for each firm thus equals $110,000 ($0.11 × 1 million kWh = $110,000), resulting in a total cost for the market of $550,000.

Comparing the cost of serving the St. Cloud market for Northern States Power Co. and the five competing firms, we conclude that, with economies of scale, the lowest cost of servicing the market occurs under monopoly. Northern States Power Co. can provide 5 million kWh of electricity at a cost of $350,000, whereas the cost of the five competing firms is $550,000 for the same level of service.

Figure 5.4   Economies of Scale and Natural Monopoly

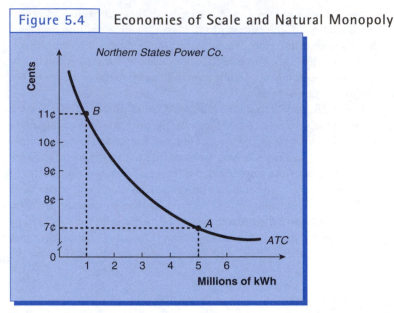

Because of economies of scale, average total cost may decrease over the entire range of market output. In this situation, one firm can serve consumers at a lower cost than two or more firms. This describes a natural monopoly.

Clearly, economies of scale serve as a barrier to entry that protects Northern States Power Co. from competition, assuming that the firm is the first to operate in the market.

Many public utilities, such as natural gas, water, electric, cable television, and local telephone companies, have traditionally been considered to be natural monopolies. The government grants an exclusive franchise to these firms in a geographic area. With economies of scale, the firms are able to drive down average costs by producing large amounts of output. The government then regulates the monopolies to ensure that the cost savings are passed on to the public in the form of lower prices.

CABLE TELEVISION: WHY RATES ARE SO HIGH

Recall that the existence of a monopoly requires barriers to entry, whether they are technological, legal, or some other type. The owners of cable television companies have often benefited from legal barriers in the form of a monopoly franchise to serve a particular community. The head of the Justice Department's Antitrust Division has referred to the cable industry as "one of the most persistent monopolies in the American economy."[2]

The owners of cable systems have traditionally justified their monopoly status on the grounds that cable television is a natural monopoly, much like the utilities. The central issue is one of high fixed costs. What would be the payback for a competitor to build an additional cable plant in a city? The infrastructural costs of wires and other technology are enormous. Therefore, many communities decided that having more than one cable system was inefficient. Most cable television companies were thus granted a monopoly franchise over the market they served. Therefore, few consumers anywhere have a choice of cable television providers.

However, critics challenge the view that cable is naturally monopolistic by noting that technological developments allow companies to provide cable programming without the need for stringing or

2. Statement of Joel Klein, Assistant Attorney General, May 12, 1998, announcing a U.S. Justice Department suit to block Primestar Inc. from acquiring direct broadcast satellite assets of Newscorp and MCI.

laying cable throughout a city. These technologies include direct broadcast satellite, wireless cable, and the use of common carrier lines. Also, local telephone companies could easily provide cable to consumers in their jurisdictions.

Potential competitors face another barrier to entry: getting quality programming. The way cable works is that an operator must obtain programming from network suppliers such as ESPN, TNT, and the Discovery Channel. These programs make up the essential ingredients of cable service, without which it would be nearly impossible to sell cable television. According to industry analysts, programmers are often reluctant to sell to competitive cable operators either because the programmers are owned outright by established cable-system operators or because the established operators use their market power to convince programmers not to sell to would-be competitors. Without such programming, competitors are at a serious disadvantage.

Although cable television companies have realized considerable monopoly power, competition from substitute providers has emerged. By the early 2000s, satellite television and phone companies were beginning to cut into the market share of cable television firms. With growing numbers of people switching to satellite television, cable companies came under pressure to hold down rates. Several of the nation's largest cable companies introduced cheaper packages that were intended to compete more effectively with attractive offers from satellite companies. Other cable companies that did not cut price offered more services, such as free movies and video clips, as a way to attract customers.

By 2008, however, the growth spurt for satellite-television broadcasters was dimming amid a resurgent cable industry and changes in what consumers want from their television providers. Cable television companies such as Cablevision Systems Corp. and Time Warner began to attract customers by providing video, telephone, and high-speed Internet services in a competitively priced bundle. Technology differences preclude satellite providers from offering phone service and restrained their ability to offer high-speed Internet access. It remains to be seen how competition in the television broadcasting business will evolve.

DE BEERS: THE "GIFT OF LOVE"

The diamond industry provides another example of how barriers to entry can break down over time. Let us consider the case of De Beers.

Throughout much of the 1900s, De Beers Consolidated Mines of South Africa was one of the world's most famous monopolies. Although De Beers mines accounted for approximately 15 percent of the world's diamond production, the firm monopolized the sale of diamonds by purchasing for resale a large share of the diamonds produced by other mines throughout the world. De Beers was thus able to sell more than 80 percent of the world's diamonds to a select group of manufacturers and dealers.

De Beers controls the price of diamonds in order to maximize its profits. This was accomplished by limiting the sale of diamonds to an amount that would yield prices that exceed the cost of production. In good times, De Beers's profits surpassed 60 percent of revenues.

When the demand for diamonds decreased and prices fell, De Beers reduced sales to maintain price. The firm also advertised on television and in magazines to bolster demand. You may have seen some of these ads which promote the giving of diamonds for engagements, anniversaries, and other occasions as a "gift of love" and "diamonds are forever." Conversely, when the demand for diamonds strengthened, De Beers increased sales by delving into its inventory of diamonds and selling them on the market.

To defend its monopoly position, De Beers attempted to prevent competing firms from selling diamonds. De Beers maintains an inventory of diamonds that could be dumped on the market to reduce prices and thus drive competing sellers out of business. In the early 1980s, for example, Zaire attempted to sell diamonds independently of De Beers. As a result, De Beers flooded the market with diamonds, causing the price of diamonds to decrease. Zaire thus stopped competing against De Beers and sold its diamonds to De Beers for resale on the world market.

At the turn of the century, however, several events were occurring that weakened the monopoly power of De Beers. New diamond discoveries in Angola and Canada resulted in an increasing flow of diamonds onto the market outside De Beers's control. Although Russia was part of the De Beers consortium, this poor nation ignored the dictates of De Beers and sold substantial quantities of diamonds on the world market. Also, Australian diamond producer Argyle decided to pull out of the De Beers consortium. Moreover, the recent discovery of diamonds in Siberia have led to additional production, which has further undermined the monopoly power of De Beers. By 2000, De Beers directly controlled only about 40 percent of the world diamond production.

In 2001, De Beers gave up on its efforts to control the world supply of diamonds. It declared that it would alter its structure from a diamond consortium to a company selling high-quality diamonds under the De Beers label. Therefore, it would decrease its stockpile of diamonds and adopt a policy of increasing overall demand for diamonds through sales promotion. With its large share of the diamond market and ability to control its own production levels, De Beers will have a substantial impact on the price of diamonds in the years ahead. However, the De Beers monopoly has turned out to be impermanent. Competition has finally come to the diamond business.

PROFIT MAXIMIZATION FOR A MONOPOLY

In the previous section, we learned that De Beers has earned substantial profits by controlling most of the world's diamond production. Let us now consider how a monopolist goes about achieving a combination of price and output that yields maximum profits.

Price and Marginal Revenue

A perfectly competitive firm is a *price taker* that is at the mercy of the market in which it operates. The firm faces a horizontal demand curve for its product at a price that is established by market demand and supply. Because each additional unit of the firm's output sold adds a constant amount (price) to total revenue, its marginal revenue is constant and equals product price.

In contrast, a monopolist is a *price maker* which can decide its own product price. Why? A monopolist is the sole producer of the product that it sells, and thus its output decisions necessarily affect product price. The firm's price will rise only if output falls; conversely, output will rise only if the price falls. A monopolist, unlike a perfectly competitive firm, faces a downward-sloping demand schedule. Note that a monopolist is not completely immune from market forces in deciding price and output. Although a monopolist can charge any price it wishes, it knows that at higher prices, less output will be sold. Therefore, a monopoly faces a downward-sloping demand curve instead of a perfectly horizontal demand curve.

Table 5.1 shows the demand and revenue conditions for De Beers, which is assumed to be a monopoly in the sale of diamonds. Referring to columns 1 and 2 of the table, as De Beers reduces the price of diamonds, the quantity demanded increases. For example, De Beers can choose a price of $3,600 and count on customers demanding 1 diamond, or it can reduce the price to $3,200 and sell 2 diamonds.[3] Figure 5.5 translates this information into graphical form. The figure shows a downward-sloping demand curve for De Beers.

Column 3 of Table 5.1 shows De Beers's total revenue, which is calculated by multiplying the market price by the quantity of diamonds ($TR = P \times Q$). Changes in both price and quantity demanded thus result in changes in the firm's total revenue. For example, if the price of diamonds

---

3. In reality, De Beers sells many thousands of diamonds in a year. To keep our example as simple as possible, we assume that it sells only small quantities of diamonds.

| Table 5.1 | Demand and Revenue Schedules for De Beers as a Monopolist |

Quantity of Diamonds	Price ($)	Total Revenue ($)	Marginal Revenue ($)
0	$4,000	$ 0	
			$3,600
1	3,600	3,600	
			2,800
2	3,200	6,400	
			2,000
3	2,800	8,400	
			1,200
4	2,400	9,600	
			400
5	2,000	10,000	
			−400
6	1,600	9,600	

| Figure 5.5 | Profit Maximization for a Monopolist |

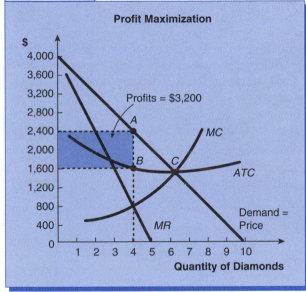

The figure shows how De Beers can maximize profits by producing 4 diamonds, the output corresponding to the intersection of its marginal revenue and marginal cost curves. At this output, price ($2,400) exceeds average total cost ($1,600), and profit per unit equals the difference ($800). The firm's total profits ($3,200) are calculated by multiplying the profit per unit by the profit-maximizing output.

falls from $3,600 to $3,200 per diamond, thus resulting in an increase in quantity demanded from 1 diamond to 2 diamonds, total revenue would rise from $3,600 to $6,400.

Column 4 of Table 5.1 shows the marginal revenue schedule of De Beers. Recall that marginal revenue is the addition to total revenue when another unit of output is sold. In the table, as De Beers increases sales from, say, 1 diamond to 2 diamonds, total revenue rises from $3,600 to $6,400.

economics
IN ACTION

Would Vouchers Improve the U.S. Education System?

Vouchers don't work. Smaller class size and proven academic programs do, and they are doable tomorrow. Given a choice between serving ideology and maybe helping a relative handful of children—at the expense of the rest—or responding to the legitimate demands of the vast majority of Americans and serving the needs of all children, the choice is clear. Let's do what's right and what works.

~American Federation of Teachers

Competition and the profit motive must be reintroduced into education so that teachers and school administrators will once again have a powerful incentive to meet the needs of the children and parents they serve.

~Andrew Coulson, Scholar at the Washington, D.C.–based Education Policy Institute

For decades, many frustrated parents have challenged one of America's near-monopolies, public education. Concerned about the poor quality of the U.S. elementary and secondary education system, evidenced by high numbers of school dropouts and declining

reading and math skills, they ask whether it is fair to tax families, compel their children's attendance at schools, and then give them no choice between teaching methods, religious or secular education, and other matters. The question is, how can we make our educational system more productive?

One method would be to reform the structure of elementary and high school education by giving parents vouchers (a stipulated amount of money) to spend on their children's education. This would enable children to attend the public or private school of their choice. The program would operate like this: Suppose that the cost of education at a public school is $5,000 per student. For each school-age child, parents would receive a voucher redeemable for $5,000 toward education. If a family decided to send the child to a public school, it would turn in the voucher and be assessed no additional charges. The family could also decide to send the child to a different school, either public or private, and use the voucher to pay for the cost of schooling there. For example, assume that the cost of educating a student at a private school is $6,000 per year. The family would turn in its voucher there and pay $1,000 to the school. The school would turn in the voucher to the government and receive $5,000.

Proponents maintain that the competition attributable to vouchers, innovative uses of computers and the Internet would offer new paths to learning. New methods of teaching would replace the old, and costs

The marginal revenue of the second diamond is thus $2,800 ($6,400−$3,600 = $2,800). Like all marginal measurements, marginal revenue is plotted midway between the quantities. Note that as De Beers lowers the price to sell additional diamonds, its marginal revenue on each additional unit sold is less than the price. Translating this information into the graphical representation of Figure 5.5, the monopolist's marginal revenue schedule is downward-sloping and lies beneath its demand curve.

Maximizing Profits

Although De Beers cannot dictate how many diamonds people will demand at different prices, it can select a particular price and quantity combination that will result in maximum profits. How does the firm find this combination? According to the profit-maximizing rule, as discussed earlier in this chapter, a firm will maximize total profit by selling that output where marginal revenue equals marginal cost.

would go down just as surely as quality would go up. This happened, for example, when parcel and message delivery services were opened up to competition, when the telephone monopoly was dismembered, when air travel was deregulated, and when Japanese competition forced the U.S. automobile industry to change its ways. Government schools would have to meet the competition or close up shop.

The teachers' unions that control the government school monopoly today would not relish that competition. However, proponents of vouchers contend that the potential winners are far more numerous. Students would benefit from an improvement in the quality of their education. Good teachers would benefit from a wider market for their services. Existing private schools would be in a far better competitive position and could use the additional funds to further improve the education they provide.

The voucher proposal is contested by public schools, which see it as a threat to the pay and job security of their faculties. Moreover, they fear that a voucher system would be ineffective at improving quality, especially in communities with less-educated parents, who would be less able to make informed decisions and be less effective at influencing school policies than would more highly educated parents. Finally, any voucher system must solve the practical problem of the extraordinary funding and programming required to educate special-needs children at the schools their parents choose.

Researchers at the National Bureau of Economic Research have examined the effects of vouchers on student achievement. For the time period 1996–1999, they compared the state exam scores of students attending Milwaukee public schools that were part of a voucher system to the scores of students attending other Wisconsin public schools that were not part of a voucher program. They found that math scores increased by about 7 percentile points per year for Milwaukee students, whereas math scores of other students increased by 4 percentile points per year. They also found that social studies scores in Milwaukee schools rose by 4.2 percentile points per year, whereas social studies scores in other schools rose by only 1.5 percentile points per year. The researchers came to similar conclusions when they adjusted the achievement scores to reflect differences in tax dollars being spent on students in more- and less-wealthy school districts. The researchers concluded that competition from vouchers tends to yield strong, positive effects on student achievement. Note that this study was based only on the State of Wisconsin. It remains to be seen whether other studies will yield the same results for the nation as a whole. Indeed, the debate over vouchers will continue as we look for ways to improve the quality of education.

Source: Satyajit Chatterjee, "Ores and Scores: Two Cases of How Competition Led to Productivity Miracles," *Business Review,* Federal Reserve Bank of Philadelphia, First Quarter 2005, pp. 7–15.

Figure 5.5 shows hypothetical revenue and cost schedules of De Beers. The firm would maximize total profit by selling 4 diamonds, that output at which marginal revenue equals marginal cost. Having determined its profit-maximizing output, De Beers must now decide what price to charge for diamonds. To set product price, De Beers uses its demand curve and finds the highest price at which it can sell the profit-maximizing output. In De Beers's situation, the highest price at which it can sell 4 diamonds is $2,400 per diamond, shown by point *A* in Figure 5.5. Multiplying price ($2,400) by output (4), we calculate De Beers's total revenue to be $9,600. At the profit-maximizing output, the firm's average total cost is $1,600. Multiplying this amount by four units, we calculate total cost to be $6,400. The firm's total profit thus equals $3,200, found by subtracting total cost ($6,400) from total revenue ($9,600).

There is another method for computing total profits. First, subtract average total cost ($1,600) from product price ($2,400), which gives profit per unit ($800). Then multiply this amount by the profit-maximizing output (4) to compute total profit ($3,200).

Notice that De Beers does not charge the highest possible price for diamonds. Because De Beers is a price maker, it could have charged a price higher than $2,400 and sell fewer than 4 diamonds. However, any price higher than $2,400 does not correspond to the intersection of the firm's marginal revenue and marginal cost curves, which establishes the profit-maximizing output.

The fact that De Beers has a monopoly does not guarantee profits. Decreasing demand for diamonds can result in losses for the firm, as discussed in "Exploring Further 5.1" at the end of this chapter.

Continuing Monopoly Profits

Recall that with perfect competition, economic profits are unattainable in the long run. Because of low barriers to entry, the existence of economic profits will induce firms to enter a competitive industry until those profits have been competed away.

Sizable economic profits, however, *can* persist under monopoly—if the monopolist is protected by barriers to entry. With blockaded entry, a monopolist can charge the price that will maximize its short-run profit and still attract no rivals. The attainment of long-run economic profits is thus possible under monopoly. Remember, however, that barriers to entry are rarely complete and thus detract from the ability of a firm to realize persistently high profits. As technologies change and new products are developed, the monopolies of today will evolve into firms operating in the competitive industries of tomorrow. For example, throughout the 1960s and 1970s, Boeing accounted for more than two-thirds of the noncommunist world's production of jetliners. Because of the rise of Europe's Airbus during the 1980s, by 2000 Boeing's market share had declined to about 50 percent.

THE CASE AGAINST MONOPOLY

From what we have seen so far, monopoly isn't *all* bad. At times, a monopoly can fully take advantage of the economies of scale that occur under natural monopolies. Moreover, some innovative firms, such as IBM and Xerox, once had monopolies simply because each was the first to enter its industry. Why, then, do people often dislike monopoly?

Imagine an industry that is made up of many identical competitive firms. Suppose that a single firm buys out all of the individual firms and creates a monopoly. Given identical cost conditions, a monopolist is likely to charge a *higher* price and earn *higher* profits than a competitive industry, which harms consumers. The monopolist attains excess profits by consciously *restricting* output and increasing price above the competitive level. The output restriction comes at the expense of society, which would have preferred additional output and thus additional resources devoted to the production of the good.

Figure 5.5 shows the effect of restricted output for De Beers as a monopoly. In the figure, we see that De Beers maximizes profits by producing four units of output, at which point marginal revenue equals marginal cost. At this output, the firm's average total cost is at point B. However, average total cost is at a minimum at point C. By restricting output, De Beers fails to operate at the lowest point on its average total cost curve. In contrast, firms in a competitive industry operate at the minimum point on their average total cost curves.

A monopolist also lacks the incentive to organize production so as to reduce cost. Recall that competition serves as a major source of disciplinary pressure on firms, which hold down costs in order to survive. But a monopolist is insulated from the rigors of competition by barriers to entry and thus does not have to produce at minimum average total cost or use inputs in the most efficient manner irrespective of the rate of output. Excess costs can be the result of the ineffective supervision of employees, the payment of large bonuses to management, the provision of company perks such as jet planes and vacation lodges, and the like.

Moreover, high-quality service is not always a characteristic of monopoly. Have you ever been frustrated trying to force, with both hands, a letter into a drive-by mailbox that is completely filled with other letters? (This author has.) Have you ever been annoyed with the local cable TV company or telephone company—the only ones in town—because of its agonizingly slow repair service? The phrase "The customer is always right" does not necessarily apply when barriers to entry protect a firm from the discipline of competition.

Monopoly may also promote inequality in the distribution of income. To the extent that a monopolist charges a higher price than a competitive firm with identical costs, the monopolist levies a "tax" on consumers that goes into economic profits. These profits, however, are not uniformly distributed among members of society because corporate stock tends to be largely owned by the wealthy. The distribution of income is thus altered in favor of the wealthy.

Finally, government grants of monopoly, such as exclusive franchises to serve a market, encourage firms to waste resources in the attempt to secure and maintain them. Indeed, business executives often spend vast sums on political contributions and the hiring of lobbyists to convince government officials that their firm should become or remain a legal monopoly. From the perspective of economic efficiency, such expenditures are wasteful because they do not contribute to increased output.

Keep in mind, however, that monopoly may have some advantages. Recall that with natural monopoly, economies of scale are best fulfilled when one firm produces the entire market output. Also, a monopolist can eliminate certain types of duplication that are unavoidable for several small, independent firms—for example, a few large machines may replace the many small pieces of equipment used by competitive firms, or one purchasing agent may do a job that formerly required many buyers.

Monopolies have an advantage in pursuing research and development activities, which can result in new products, improving technologies, and decreased unit cost. The vast resources (profits) of monopolies can finance expensive research and development programs. Moreover, because monopolies are sheltered from competition, they do not have to be preoccupied with day-to-day decisions regarding costs and revenues. Instead, they can take the longer view that is necessary for successful research and development.

However, the research and development argument does not consider monopoly *incentives*. Just because a monopoly has the potential to conduct research and development does not necessarily mean that it will. Instead, a monopoly may prefer to rely on existing products and technologies and earn sizable profits merely because of its monopoly power. The firm may conclude that research and development is not essential for its survival. In contrast, a competitive firm cannot continue to earn profits unless it stays ahead of its rivals; this pressure results in incentives to produce better products at a lower cost.

CHECK POINT

1. Identify the major barriers to entry that foster monopoly.

2. Compare the price-making ability of a monopoly with that of a perfectly competitive firm.

3. Discuss the strategy of profit maximization for a monopoly.

4. Evaluate the cases for and against monopoly.

THE U.S. POSTAL SERVICE AS A LEGAL MONOPOLY

Although monopoly is relatively uncommon, it can occur when the government grants a firm a legal monopoly to provide a service. Consider the case of the U.S. Postal Service (USPS).

To shield the Postal Service from competition, the federal government provides it with an exclusive franchise on the delivery of first-class letter mail. Competing firms also cannot deliver addressed circulars, advertisements, solicitations, mass mailings, or other third-class mail. Moreover, no firm except the Postal Service can place anything in the mailbox of a home or business, even if the owner consents. As of 2009, about 80 percent of the Postal Service's business was protected from competition.

The Postal Service has a tremendous amount of power. It can create postal regulations governing its competitors and it can effectively set its own monopoly rates. Although these rates must be approved by the federal government's Postal Regulatory Commission, a unanimous vote of the Postal Service governors can overrule the commission and set rates that the Postal Service wants.

As a legal monopoly, the Postal Service is mandated to operate on a businesslike basis without the benefit of government subsidies. Unlike private carriers such as FedEx, the Postal Service has a certain financial advantage: It does not have to pay taxes to the government or dividends to shareholders. However, the Postal Service is required to function as a public enterprise and provide mail service to all communities, not just those that are profitable to serve.

Proponents of the Postal Service's legal monopoly justify it on several grounds. A legal monopoly for the delivery of letter mail is necessary to ensure that the Postal Service has sufficient revenues to carry out its public service mandates, including regular mail delivery service (typically 6 days a week) to all communities. Without restrictions on private delivery, "cream skimming" by private competitors in the most profitable postal markets would undermine the Postal Service's ability to provide universal service at reasonable, uniform rates to patrons in all areas, however remote. Moreover, as a single provider, the Postal Service can operate at a lower cost to the nation than multiple suppliers can. This is because mail delivery fits the economic model of a natural monopoly—unit cost per delivery decreases as mail volumes increase.

Critics, however, maintain that the government-mandated postal monopoly has produced some economic problems. Because the Postal Service does not face the threat of competition, it lacks incentives to control costs and maintain high quality. Instead, the Postal Service can overpay its postal employees in salaries, perks, and benefits while reducing work obligations for each employee. For example, Postal Service employees earn wages about 25 percent to 30 percent more than employees of private-sector mail firms. Also, the Postal Service does not put pressure on workers to maximize effort, reduce waste and costs, and produce the best service for consumers, as do organizations that face competition every day. Moreover, the Postal Service is slow to adopt cost-saving or quality-enhancing innovations because it need not be concerned about competitors adopting such innovations first. The Postal Service has also suffered from delivery delays, actual losses (accidental and purposeful) of mail, and excessive increases in postal rates. Simply put, it is easier for the Postal Service to raise rates than to do the hard work of cutting costs, including standing firm against unreasonable union demands.

Also, the USPS has never been a hallmark of efficiency. If the cost of a postage stamp had increased at merely the rate of inflation since 1950, when a stamp cost two cents, in 2010 you could send a first-class letter for about 30 cents. Instead, the cost increased to 44 cents. These higher prices have corresponded to worsening service. The USPS used to deliver mail twice a day in urban areas. Now, it is considering stopping Saturday service to decrease costs.

Critics also question whether the Postal Service is a natural monopoly, as it alleges. When we think of a natural monopoly, we think of large fixed costs, such as those involved in laying electricity lines in a city. However, labor costs account for more than 80 percent of the Postal Service's total costs, compared with only 56 percent at United Parcel Service and 42 percent at FedEx, while its capital costs are modest. It is hard to comprehend such a labor-intensive industry characterized by large economies of scale. In practice, it is the Postal Service's status as a legal monopoly—rather than a natural monopoly—that has kept it in business.

Although the Postal Service is a legal monopoly in the delivery of first-class and third-class mail, competition for mail delivery services has grown substantially since the 1970s. Private firms deliver urgent (overnight) mail, 2-day and 3-day letters and parcels, and unaddressed advertising circulars and periodicals. Together, these groups compete on a local, national, and international basis for portions of markets previously served only by the Postal Service.

In letter mail, the Postal Service faces increasing competition from fax machines, e-mail, and electronic bills, statements, and remittances which give us the opportunity to send and receive messages within minutes. Home shopping television channels, toll-free telephone numbers, and interactive television allow us to order tickets, clothing, and merchandise with the push of a button. Even checks are not always sent in the mail anymore; often, they are sent and deposited electronically. These technological advances have reduced the Postal Service's share of the communications market, resulting in falling revenues. From 2000 to 2010, postal mail volume decreased by almost 20 percent, and the average household receives one-third fewer letters.

Critics of the USPS, however, maintain that additional efforts are needed to promote competition in mail delivery. The most overdue reform is to remove the USPS's monopoly on first-class mail and bulk mail, according to critics. Also, critics have called for the **privatization** of the USPS. One approach to privatization would be to auction the USPS to an owner who would operate it on a for-profit basis. It is argued that the resulting cost savings and quality improvements would promote reasonable prices for consumers. In the years ahead, the market share of the USPS will continue to erode as competition from the Internet and private express companies continues.

The argument has been made for more than 200 years that the postal monopoly is needed to "bind the nation together." Perhaps that was true at one time. But today the Internet delivers to the most remote parts of the country at one-one-hundredth the cost of snail mail. It remains to be seen whether the USPS will lose its monopoly on first-class mail and bulk mail and whether it will be privatized.

REDUCING MONOPOLY POWER: GENERIC DRUGS COMPETE AGAINST BRAND-NAME DRUGS

Not only have barriers to entry broken down in the delivery of mail, but also they have broken down in the prescription drug industry. Our monopoly model predicts that when barriers to entry break down and competition appears, the result is declining price, rising output, and increasing efficiency. Consider the case in which generic drugs come into the market to compete against brand-name drugs.

For decades, the U.S. government has established competing policy goals regarding the pricing of prescription drugs. On one hand, it desires to ensure that brand-name drug companies have sufficient incentives to invest in the research and development of innovative drugs. To achieve this goal, a drug company is given patent protection for 14 years from the time of the patent approval by the Food and Drug Administration, thus providing the firm a temporary monopoly for its product.[4] During this period, the firm can charge a price for its brand-name drug that covers its costs of discovery and development, allowing the firm to earn an economic profit. Thus, the firm has an incentive to invent new products that benefit consumers. Without patents, many new drugs would be easily and quickly duplicated by other firms, preventing the innovator from obtaining enough reward to justify its investment. Examples of brand-name, patented drugs include Paxil (for depression) and Lipitor (for high cholesterol).

On the other hand, the government wants to discourage the firm from charging excessively high prices for their brand-name drugs. To meet this goal, it allows generic drugs to compete against brand-name drugs. A generic drug is a copy that is identical to the brand-name drug in active ingredients, dosage, and performance. Because generic drugs are copies rather than original formulations, they

---

4. Patents do not grant total monopoly power to drug companies. Often, several chemicals can be developed that use the same basic mechanisms to treat a disease. Because a patent applies to a specific chemical or production process, different firms can end up patenting similar, competing drugs based on the same innovative principle. Also, drug therapies often compete with nondrug therapies.

are not patentable. Also, generic drugs are usually sold under their chemical name rather than under a brand name. For example, the generic version of Paxil is paroxetine and atorvastatin is the generic equivalent of Lipitor. When the patent expires on the brand-name drug, generic producers enter the market as competitors.

In general, generic drugs are less expensive than brand-name drugs because generic firms do not have the development costs that the producer of a new brand-name drug has. Currently, about half of all prescriptions in the United States are filled with generic drugs. Researchers have found that, on average, drug prices decrease by 40 percent or more when generic drugs compete against brand-name drugs. This saves consumers an estimated $8 billion to $10 billion a year at retail pharmacies. Even greater sums are saved when hospitals use generics.[5]

Moreover, producers of generic drugs tend to compete intensely with each other on the basis of price, partly because they sell identical products. Although the list prices of brand-name drugs do not usually decrease after generic competitors enter the market, some brand-name producers offer discounts and rebates to some purchasers, and those discounts tend to be larger when generic versions of the drug are available. Moreover, competition from generic firms has prompted brand-name firms to produce copies of their own drugs, which they then sell under generic names at reduced prices in order to capture a share of that market. Simply put, the performance of the prescription drug industry is consistent with the competitive model: When competition is introduced into a market, price declines, output rises, and efficiency improves.

In this chapter, we have learned how a firm maximizes profits in a competitive market and also under monopoly. The next chapter will consider how firms behave in the imperfectly competitive markets of monopolistic competition and oligopoly.

CHECK POINT

1. What is the justification for granting the Central Office Supply System or the U.S. Government Printing Office an exclusive franchise to be the sole supplier of goods and services to government agencies?

2. Why does the U.S. Postal Service have a legal monopoly on the delivery of first-class letter mail? Explain why critics of the U.S. Postal Service argue that privatization of mail delivery would result in a more efficient allocation of resources for the nation. Do you agree?

Chapter Summary

1. A perfectly competitive market is characterized by many sellers and buyers, firms that produce a standardized product, perfect information among buyers and sellers, and easy entry into and exit from a market.

2. Because a perfectly competitive firm supplies a negligible share of the market output, it has to "take" or accept the price that is determined in the market.

---

5. U.S. Congressional Budget Office, *How Increased Competition from Generic Drugs Has Affected Prices and Returns in the Pharmaceutical Industry,* July 1998; and U.S. Government Accountability Office, *Prescription Drugs: Price Trends for Frequently Used Brand and Generic Drugs from 2000 to 2004,* August 2005.

3. Given favorable demand conditions, a firm will maximize total profit by selling that output at where marginal revenue equals marginal cost.

4. If total revenue exceeds total variable cost, a firm will minimize short-run losses by producing output where $MR = MC$ rather than shutting down. As a result, losses are less than the fixed-cost losses that would be realized if the firm shut down.

5. Because of easy entry into and exit from a market, perfectly competitive firms operate at the lowest possible cost, charge the lowest price they can without going out of business, and earn no economic profit. These characteristics are ideal for the consumer.

6. Barriers to entry are impediments, created by the government or by the firm or firms already in the market, that protect an established firm from potential competition. The major barriers to entry are legal barriers, control over essential resources, and economies of scale.

7. A monopoly differs from a perfectly competitive firm in that the monopoly's demand curve and marginal revenue curve are downward-sloping rather than horizontal. Like a perfectly competitive firm, a monopolist will maximize total profit by operating at that output where marginal revenue equals marginal cost.

8. Given identical costs, a monopolist will find it profitable to produce a smaller output and charge a higher price than a perfectly competitive firm. Moreover, a profit-maximizing monopoly will not operate at the minimum point on its average total cost curve in the long run. However, economies of scale may make lower average total cost more attainable for a monopoly than for a competitive firm. Moreover, a monopolist generally has greater financial resources for research and development programs than a competitive firm, making it possible for the monopolist to achieve a lower cost per unit.

Key Terms and Concepts

perfect competition (98)

price taker (99)

total revenue (101)

marginal revenue (101)

marginal revenue = marginal cost rule (101)

monopoly (106)

barriers to entry (106)

natural monopoly (107)

privatization (117)

shut-down rule (124)

Self-Test: Multiple-Choice Questions

1. The U.S. Postal Service has a monopoly as a result of its exclusive government franchise on the delivery of

   a. small packages.
   b. large packages.
   c. express mail.
   d. first-class letter mail.

2. A perfectly competitive market has all of the following characteristics *except*

   a. freedom of entry into and exit from the market.
   b. firms in the market producing differentiated products.
   c. a large number of sellers and buyers.
   d. perfect information among buyers and sellers.

3. Barriers to entry into a market include all of the following *except*

   a. exclusive government franchises granted to producers of a good.
   b. demand curves that are highly elastic.
   c. large advertising budgets required to promote a new product.
   d. sole control over the supply of raw materials.

4. A perfectly competitive firm will maximize total profits by

   a. producing all the output it can at any particular price.
   b. setting price so that total revenue is at a maximum.
   c. setting price so that marginal revenue equals marginal cost.
   d. setting price so that price exceeds average total cost by the greatest amount.

5. A perfectly competitive firm

   a. can realize an economic profit in the short run, but not in the long run.
   b. can realize an economic profit in the long run, but not in the short run.
   c. will always realize an economic profit, irrespective of revenue and cost conditions.
   d. will never realize an economic profit, no matter how large the firm's revenues.

6. In a perfectly competitive market, if firms realize economic profits in the short run

   a. new firms will enter the market in the long run, forcing down price and profits.
   b. firms will attempt to reduce output so as to further increase price and profits.
   c. weaker firms will exit the market before price begins to decline.
   d. increased entry of new firms will shift the market supply curve to the left.

7. Which industry best meets the assumptions of perfect competition?

   a. Automobiles.
   b. Commercial aircraft.
   c. Steel.
   d. Agriculture.

8. If in the short run, price falls below minimum average variable cost, Hodges Electric Co.

   a. should produce that output where marginal revenue equals marginal cost.
   b. should shut down and produce no output.
   c. will realize a loss but should continue to produce in the short run.
   d. will realize a profit in the short run but not in the long run.

9. Which of the following is *not* a characteristic of a pure monopoly?

   a. A demand curve that is highly sensitive to changes in price.
   b. Barriers preventing the entry of other firms into the market.
   c. Products for which there are no close substitutes.
   d. An industry consisting of one seller.

10. If the electricity market is a natural monopoly, production by a single firm is preferable to several smaller firms because

   a. profits are maximized.
   b. marginal revenue is maximized.
   c. average total cost is minimized.
   d. price is maximized.

Answers to Multiple-Choice Questions

1. d   2. b   3. b   4. c   5. a   6. a   7. d   8. b   9. a   10. c

Study Questions and Problems

1. Suppose that a perfectly competitive firm sells 300 batteries at $10 each. At this output, the firm's total variable cost is $1,800 and its total fixed cost is $600. Calculate the firm's profit per unit and total profit from this information.

2. Eddy's Pizza Parlor receives $15 per pizza and sells 100 pizzas to maximize profits. Assuming that the firm's variable cost is $8 per pizza and total fixed costs are $500, what is the profit per unit on a pizza at the profit-maximizing level of output? What is the firm's total profit?

3. Suppose that a monopolist can sell 9 diamonds at $500 each. To sell 10 diamonds, the firm must reduce the price to $475. Calculate the marginal revenue of the tenth diamond.

4. Assume that a monopolist finds that at existing output and price levels, marginal revenue is $20 and marginal cost is $15. The firm would maximize profits or minimize losses by _____ price and _____ output.

5. Table 5.2 shows the revenue and cost conditions for Johnson Electronics Inc.

   a. Graph the information contained in the table.
   b. In what market structure does this firm operate? Why?
   c. What level of output will maximize the firm's total profit? What price will be charged?
   d. Compute the firm's maximum total profit.

Table 5.2   Revenue and Cost Conditions for Johnson Electronics Inc.

Output	P = MR	ATC	MC
10	$ 10	$20.80	
20	10	12.40	$ 4.00
30	10	9.92	5.00
40	10	9.00	6.20
50	10	8.80	8.00
60	10	9.00	10.00
70	10	9.56	13.00
80	10	10.50	17.00

6. Table 5.3 shows the revenue and cost data for Charette Technologies Co.

   a. Graph the information contained in the table.
   b. In what market structure does this firm operate? Why?
   c. What level of output will maximize the firm's total profit?
   d. Compute the firm's maximum total profit.

7. Table 5.4 shows the short-run revenue and cost data for a television manufacturer that sells in a perfectly competitive market.

Table 5.3   Revenue and Cost Data for Charette Technologies Co.

Output	Price	MR	ATC	MC
0	$35.00			
1	32.00	$32.00	$48.00	$48.00
2	29.00	26.00	30.00	12.00
3	26.00	20.00	23.34	10.00
4	23.00	14.00	21.00	14.00
5	20.00	8.00	20.00	16.00

Table 5.4   Cost Data for a Perfectly Competitive Firm

Quantity of Televisions	AFC	AVC	ATC	MC
1	$600	$200	$800	$200
2	300	150	450	100
3	200	140	340	120
4	150	146	296	160
5	120	160	280	220
6	100	180	280	280
7	86	206	292	360
8	76	238	312	460
9	66	276	342	580
10	60	320	380	720

a. Graph the information contained in the table.
b. Assuming that the market price is $280 per television, determine the firm's profit-maximizing output and total profit.
c. Assuming that the market price is $580 per television, determine the firm's profit-maximizing output and total profit.
d. Assuming that the market price is $160 per television, will the firm continue to produce or should it shut down? Why? What if the market price is $120 per television?

8. Figure 5.6 shows the short-run cost conditions faced by a perfectly competitive firm.

a. If the product price equals $35 per unit, the firm would maximize profits or minimize losses by producing and selling _____ units of output. At this level of output, the firm's total revenue equals _____ , total cost equals_____, and total profit (loss) equals _____.

b. If the product price equals $20 per unit, the firm would maximize profit or minimize losses by producing and selling _____ units of output. At this level of output, the firm's total revenue equals _____, total cost equals _____, and total profit (loss) equals _____. Why would the firm prefer to continue to produce rather than shut down?

c. If the product price equals $10 per unit, the firm would maximize profits or minimize losses by producing and selling _____ units of output. Why?

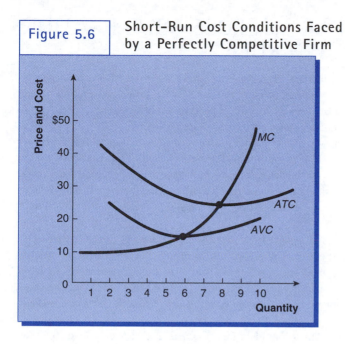

Figure 5.6

Short–Run Cost Conditions Faced by a Perfectly Competitive Firm

9. Figure 5.7 shows the demand and cost conditions faced by a monopolist.

   a.   To maximize profits or minimize losses, the firm should produce and sell _____ units of output and charge a price of _____ per unit.

   b.   At the profit-maximizing (loss-minimizing) level of output, the firm's average total cost equals _____ and profit (loss) per unit equals _____.

   c.   At the profit-maximizing (loss-minimizing) level of output, the firm's total revenue equals _____, total cost equals _____, and total profits (losses) equal _____.

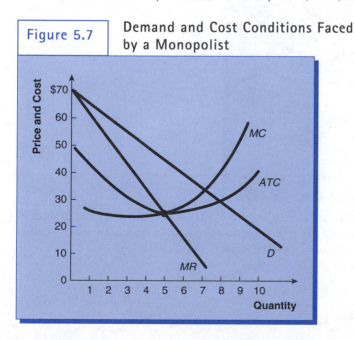

Figure 5.7

Demand and Cost Conditions Faced by a Monopolist

EXPLORING FURTHER 5.1: LOSS MINIMIZATION AND THE SHUT-DOWN RULE

Suppose that a temporary decrease in demand depresses the price of product below the average total cost curve of a firm. Faced with losses at all levels of output, how will the firm respond to this situation? It could temporarily produce at a loss or shut down production until the price rises. Let us first apply this situation to Puget Sound Fishing Co., a perfectly competitive firm.

If Puget Sound Fishing Co. shuts down, not only does it earn zero revenue, but also it must still pay any interest on borrowed money, insurance premiums, license fees, and other fixed costs that it incurs even when output is zero. Simply put, if a firm shuts down, its losses equal its total fixed costs. If, however, the firm stays in operation, it earns revenue that can be applied first to its total variable costs (wages) and then to its total fixed costs. Which situation will result in the smallest loss for Puget Sound Fishing Co.?

The following **shut-down rule** serves as a guide for a firm that realizes losses in the short run: If *total revenue exceeds total variable cost,* the firm should continue to produce because all of its variable costs and some of its fixed costs can be paid out of revenue. If the firm shuts down, all of the fixed costs must be paid out of the owner's pocket. By producing output where *MR* = *MC,* the firm's loss will be *less* than its total fixed cost. Conversely, a firm should shut down if total variable cost exceeds total revenue.

Referring to Figure 5.8, assume that Puget Sound Fishing Co. has a total fixed cost of $3,728[6] and that the price of fish is $4 per pound. Because the price lies below the firm's average total cost curve, all levels of output result in losses. Which output should the firm choose? The logic of the *MR* = *MC* rule, as discussed previously, applies in this situation. At 1,600 pounds of fish, corresponding to the intersection of the firm's marginal revenue and marginal cost curves, the firm's revenues total

Figure 5.8	Loss Minimization for a Perfectly Competitive Firm

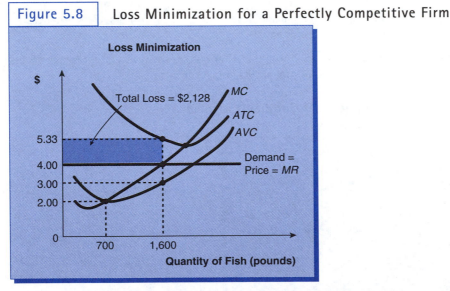

Because average total cost always exceeds price, the firm suffers a loss at every level of output. The firm could minimize short-run losses by continuing to operate as long as price at least covers average variable cost, as some of this revenue can be applied to fixed costs.

---

6. Total fixed cost can be calculated from the data in Figure 5.8. First, compute average fixed cost at some level of output—say 1,600 pounds of fish; the difference between the average total cost ($5.33) and average variable cost ($3) gives the average fixed cost ($2.33). Next, multiply $2.33 times 1,600 pounds of fish which gives a total fixed cost of $3,728.

$6,400 ($4 × 1,600 = $6,400). Moreover, average total cost equals $5.33 per pound at this output, resulting in total costs of $8,528 ($5.33 × 1,600 = $8,528). Puget Sound Fishing Co. thus loses $2,128, the difference between total revenue and total cost. Conversely, the firm would lose $3,728 in fixed costs if it shut down.

According to the shut-down rule, Puget Sound Fishing Co. should continue to operate because total revenue exceeds total variable cost. Referring to Figure 5.8, because the firm's average variable cost is $3 at 1,600 units of output, total variable cost equals $4,800 ($3 × 1,600 = $4,800). Because total revenue ($6,400) exceeds total variable cost ($4,800), the difference ($1,600) can be used to pay off some of the firm's fixed costs. The firm thus loses a smaller amount ($2,128) by producing than by shutting down ($3,728). Keep in mind, however, that a firm cannot stay in operation when it is continually losing money; over the long run, it must at least break even.

Besides applying to a perfectly competitive firm, the shut-down rule applies to other market structures including monopoly, monopolistic competition, and oligopoly (discussed in the next chapter). For example, suppose that a temporary decrease in demand depresses the price of a product below the average total cost curve of a monopolist. If the firm can charge a price that exceeds average variable cost, it will minimize short-run losses by producing a level of output where $MR = MC$ rather than shutting down.

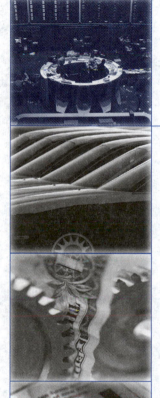

Imperfect Competition

Chapter objectives

After reading this chapter, you should be able to:

1. Distinguish between monopolistic competition and oligopoly.

2. Identify the goals and effects of advertising.

3. Explain how a seller successfully practices price discrimination.

4. Discuss the major theories of oligopolistic behavior.

5. Distinguish between a horizontal merger, a vertical merger, and a conglomerate merger.

6. Explain how the threat of potential competition encourages firms to produce high-quality products and sell them at reasonable prices to consumers.

economics IN CONTEXT

In U.S. history classes that you have taken in the past, you have learned that in 1620 the Pilgrims sailed on the *Mayflower* and landed at Plymouth Rock. What you may not have learned is that the Pilgrims had intended to sail to Virginia, not Massachusetts. What caused them to modify their route? One voyager noted in his diary that the ship's food and drink were in short supply—especially beer. Simply put, the voyage was cut short because the Pilgrims were running out of beer! Although historians may argue about the effect on U.S. history of the beer supply on the *Mayflower*, there is no doubt that beer production has become a major industry.

From the 1930s to the 2000s, the beer industry underwent a dramatic shakeup. Although beer sales doubled during this period, the number of breweries declined by more than 90 percent, from 404 to 29 breweries. Along with the decrease in the number of breweries came an increasing market share for the largest breweries. Today, the top five companies account for almost 90 percent of the U.S. market. These companies include Anheuser-Busch, Miller, Coors, Stroh's, and Heineken. Competition in the U.S. market from foreign producers has never been a strong force in the beer industry, compared with that in markets such as steel, automobiles, and consumer electronics. Indeed, the concentration of sales by the top brewers has enhanced their market power.

The beer industry does not fit into the abstract world of perfect competition, in which each firm is a price taker and realizes zero economic profits in the long run. Nor does it pertain to the stable world of monopoly, where a seller can earn persistent economic profits as a result of barriers that shut potential competitors out of the market. Rather, the beer industry belongs in the world of imperfect competition, which lies between the polar cases of perfect competition and monopoly.

Imperfect competition exists when more than one seller competes for sales with many other sellers, each of which has some price-making ability. Individual sellers in the market can influence the price of their product by controlling its availability to buyers or by differentiating their product by either brand or quality. For example, loyal customers of Pepsi are willing to pay higher prices than they would for Safeway Cola, and buyers of Advil pay higher prices than they would for Kmart nonaspirin.

Imperfectly competitive markets fall into two broad categories. Monopolistic competition is a market structure in which a large number of firms compete with each other by offering similar but slightly different products. Monopolistic competition thus involves a considerable amount of competition and a small dose of monopoly power. The other market structure is oligopoly, in which a small number of firms compete with each other. Oligopoly is characterized by more monopoly power and less competition.

CONCENTRATION RATIOS

Economists use **concentration ratios** to measure how close an industry comes to the extremes of competition and monopoly. A concentration ratio is the percentage of an industry's sales that are accounted for by the four largest firms in that particular industry, and range from zero to 100 percent. A low-concentration ratio suggests a high degree of competition: The four largest firms account for a small portion of industry output and therefore compete with many other firms in the industry. On the other hand, a high concentration ratio implies an absence of competition. In the extreme case of monopoly, the concentration ratio is 100 percent—the largest firm accounts for the entire industry output.

The top four concentration ratios can give us a rough idea of whether an industry is monopolistically competitive or oligopolistic. When the four largest firms control 40 percent or more of industry

Table 6.1	Top-Four Concentration Ratios for Selected U.S. Manufacturing Industries*

Low-Concentration Industries (monopolistically competitive)		High-Concentration Industries (oligopolistic)	
Industry	Ratio	Industry	Ratio
Machine shops	2%	Cigarettes	95%
Retail bakeries	4	Breweries	91
Metal stamping	8	Electric lamps	89
Printing	10	Small arms	83
Ready-mix concrete	11	Breakfast cereals	78
Chemicals	14	Computers	76
Sawmills	15	Office machinery	75
Curtains and drapes	16	Tires	73
Jewelry	16	Chocolate	69
Plastic pipe	19	Cookies and crackers	67

* Measured by the value of shipments in 2002.

Source: U.S. Department of Commerce, Census Bureau, *Concentration Ratios,* May 2006, available at http://www.census.gov.

output, the industry is generally regarded as oligopolistic. By this standard, approximately one-half of all the industries in the United States are oligopolies. When the four largest firms control less than 40 percent of industry output, the industry approximates monopolistic competition or perfect competition, depending on how low the concentration ratio is.

Table 6.1 shows the top-four concentration ratios for selected U.S. manufacturing industries. Column 1 of the table shows examples of low-concentration industries that are characteristic of the market structure of monopolistic competition. Column 2 shows high-concentration industries that are characteristic of oligopoly.

Be wary, however, of relying on concentration ratios alone to identify industry concentration. Most importantly, they do not take into account foreign competition and competition from substitute domestic products. For example, the U.S. automobile industry is highly concentrated. Yet it still faces significant competition from foreign manufacturers. Because concentration ratios consider only U.S. sales by U.S. firms, they overstate the monopoly power of U.S. auto companies.

For example, increased foreign competition has caused U.S. firms to lose their control of the American automobile market. During the 1960s, General Motors (GM) sold half of the new cars purchased by Americans, and together, the "Big Three" U.S. automakers —GM, Ford, and Chrysler —accounted for more than 90 percent of sales. At this time, GM was the industry's dominant firm and price leader. From the 1970s to the 2000s, however, GM's market share dwindled; by 2009, it was about 20 percent of the domestic market, as shown in Table 6.2. The decline of GM was accompanied by growing Japanese competition in the U.S. market, especially from Toyota. Despite heavy U.S. import restrictions in the early 1980s, Japanese firms continued to penetrate the American market, and by 2009 they accounted for more than one-third of all U.S. auto sales.

U.S. companies have been forced to design more technologically advanced and fuel-efficient automobiles so as to match the features offered by the Japanese automakers. Pricing their vehicles competitively has required U.S. automakers to cut overhead expenses, limit wage increases, and increase output per worker. Indeed, Japanese competition has improved the quality of the autos sold to American buyers and decreased the ability of the U.S. Big Three to tacitly increase prices.

Table 6.2	U.S. Automobile Market: Market Shares: January 2009

Manufacturer	Percentage Share of U.S. Market
General Motors	19.6
Toyota	17.9
Ford	13.9
Honda	10.8
Chrysler	9.4
Nissan	8.2
Volkswagen	2.7
BMW	2.2
Other	15.3

Source: Ward's AutoInfoBank, available at http://www.wards.com.

MONOPOLISTIC COMPETITION

The market structure that is closest to perfect competition is **monopolistic competition**. This market structure is based on a large number of firms, each having a relatively small share of the total market. Although monopolistic competition typically does not involve hundreds, or thousands, of firms, as in perfect competition, it does involve a relatively large number of firms, say, 30 or more. With a high degree of market competition, firms do not consider the reactions of their rivals when forming their product price and output policies. Moreover, the ability to cooperate so as to reduce competition is all but impossible given the large number of sellers in the market. Monopolistic competition also assumes that there is relative freedom of entry into the market and exit from the market.

Monopolistic competition differs from perfect competition in one important aspect: It assumes that the product of each firm is not a perfect substitute for the product of competing firms. **Product differentiation** is thus a fundamental characteristic of monopolistic competition. This gives each firm some power to control the price of its product. For example, people who believe that Nike shoes are more comfortable than other athletic shoes may be willing to pay a higher price for Nikes. Similarly, people who like the look and feel of Levi's jeans will be willing to pay more for them than for other jeans. Even with product differentiation, however, a monopolistically competitive firm does not have unlimited control over price. Because many other firms produce similar goods and services, a firm that increases price too much risks losing many of its customers.

Similar to the demand curve for a monopoly, the demand curve for a monopolistically competitive firm is downward sloping. If a firm increases its price, it will lose some—but not all—of its sales. Conversely, price reductions result in increased sales. Because a monopolistically competitive firm faces competition from substitute goods sold by rivals, its demand curve is more sensitive to price changes (more elastic) than the demand curve for a monopoly, which does not face competition from close substitutes. This implies that if a monopolistically competitive firm raises the price of its product, it will lose a relatively large amount of sales to competitors.

Monopolistic competition can be found in industries in which a large number of small retailing firms compete with each other. Restaurants compete in monopolistically competitive markets. In most towns, there are many restaurants, each offering slightly different meals. Each restaurant has

---

| Figure 6.1 | Market Outcomes under Monopolistic Competition |

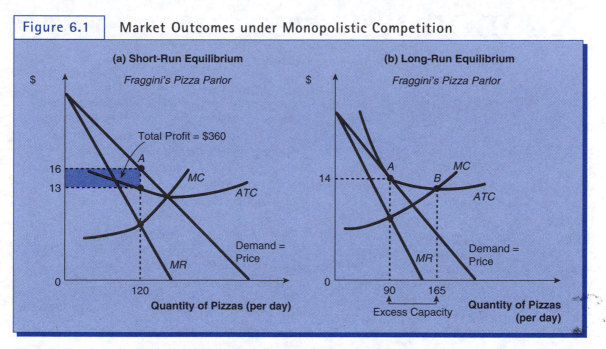

Given favorable demand conditions, a monopolistically competitive firm can maximize total profit in the short run by operating at that output where marginal revenue equals marginal cost. Over the long run, the existence of profits in a monopolistically competitive industry will attract new firms. With entry, the demand curve and marginal revenue of a typical firm decreases, eventually resulting in zero economic profit for the firm. The firm does not increase production to the output where average total cost is at its lowest point because it would lose money by doing so.

many competitors, including other restaurants, fast-food outlets, and frozen-food cases at local grocery stores. Other examples of monopolistic competition are supermarkets, gasoline service stations, accounting and law firms, parlors and barbershops, auto repair shops, video rental stores, book publishers, and shoe stores.

Profit Maximization in the Short Run

Figure 6.1 shows the hypothetical revenue and cost schedules for Fraggini's Pizza Parlor, a typical firm in the local pizza business. Fraggini's competes with Domino's, Godfather's, Pizza Hut, and many other firms in a market that has relative freedom of entry and exit. Notice that Fraggini's demand curve is downward sloping, which suggests that Fraggini's product is sufficiently superior to some of its customers that a price above those of its competitors will not reduce sales to zero, at least over a small range of prices. As a result, Fraggini's marginal revenue curve is downward sloping and lies beneath the demand schedule. To sell more pizzas, Fraggini's must reduce its price, and thus the marginal revenue from additional units will be less than the price.

Refer to Figure 6.1(a). Given the marginal revenue curve, MR, and the marginal cost curve, MC, Fraggini's will maximize total profit by selling 120 pizzas per day, the output where marginal revenue equals marginal cost. Fraggini's demand curve indicates that the firm must charge a price of $16 per pizza to sell this quantity. Looking at the firm's average total cost curve, we see that Fraggini's cost per unit is $13 at the profit-maximizing output. Fraggini's thus earns a profit of $3 per pizza, or a total daily profit of $360 ($3 × 120 = $360). Assuming that Fraggini's is open every day, this amounts to yearly profits of $131,400.

economics
IN ACTION

Concentration Keeps the Beer Industry Foaming

According to anthropologists, our ancient ancestors may not have been lured out of their caves by a thirst for knowledge, but by a thirst for beer. When people learned to ferment grain into beer thousands of years ago, it became one of their most important sources of nutrition. Beer gave people protein that unfermented grain couldn't supply. Besides, it tasted a whole lot better than the unfermented grain did. But in order to have a steady supply of beer, it was necessary to have a steady supply of beer ingredients. People had to give up their nomadic ways, settle down, and begin farming. Once they did, civilization was just a stone's throw away.

Today, beer is big business in the United States. The annual retail value of the brewing industry's products is currently more than $50 billion. Surveys show that approximately 90 million American men and women drink the "beverage of moderation." To meet the great demand for beer, American breweries annually produce 69 billion 12-ounce bottles and cans of malt beverages.

The brewing industry has experienced a significant transformation since the 1940s, when more than 400 independent brewing companies were spread throughout the country. Whereas the four largest brewers sold only 16 percent of the nation's beer in 1946, the top four brewers today (InBev Anheuser-Busch, Miller, Coors, and Pabst) currently sell 90 percent of the nation's domestically produced beer. InBev Anheuser-Busch, with its trademark Clydesdales and lavish Super Bowl ads, controls nearly half of all U.S. beer sales. Competition from foreign producers has never been as strong a force in the beer industry as it has been in markets such as automobiles and consumer electronics. However, the amount of beer imported into the United States has been increasing and provides an important source of competition to the premium brands. Indeed, breweries operate in an oligopolistic market.

What led to the evolution of the beer industry from low concentration to high concentration? On the supply side of the market, technological advances have increased the speed of bottling and canning lines. Today, a modern production line can produce 1,100 bottles or 2,000 cans of beer per minute. Also,

The Long Run: Normal Profit and Excess Capacity

Seeing the handsome economic profit earned by Fraggini's, competitors will be interested in entering the pizza business. Suppose that firms enter the market and sell similar but not identical pizzas. With entry, the available supply of substitute pizzas increases. For Fraggini's, this results in a decrease in its demand and marginal revenue curves, a decline in the price at which it sells pizza, and a reduction in profits. Entry continues until Fraggini's economic profits are competed away. We conclude that because of easy entry, monopolistically competitive firms tend to earn only a *normal profit* in the long run.

Figure 6.1(*b*) illustrates the market position of Fraggini's in the long run. At the output where marginal revenue equals marginal cost, 90 pizzas, the average total cost curve is tangent to the demand curve. Because the price ($14) just covers the average total cost ($14), Fraggini's economic profit is zero. At any smaller or larger output, the average total cost curve would be above the demand curve, causing Fraggini's to operate at a loss.

Although the long-run equilibrium position of Fraggini's produces zero economic profit, the firm produces *less* than the output at which it would minimize average total cost. The difference between the output corresponding to minimum average total cost and the output produced by a monopolistically competitive firm in the long run is called **excess capacity**. Referring to Figure 6.1(*b*), Fraggini's long-run equilibrium output equals 90 pizzas per day. However, the firm's average total cost would be at a minimum if the firm sold 165 pizzas per day. Therefore, Fraggini's excess daily capacity is 75 pizzas.

automated brewing and warehousing permit large brewers to decrease labor costs. Moreover, plant construction costs per barrel are about one-third less for a 4.5 million-barrel plant than for a 1.5 million-barrel plant. Simply put, efficiencies in production appear to be a significant barrier to entry in the beer industry.

Changes on the demand side of the market have also fostered concentration. First, consumer tastes have switched from the stronger-flavored beers of the small brewers to the light products of the larger brewers. Indeed, Bud Light and Miller Light are popular brands in today's market. Second, the consumption of beer has moved away from taverns and into homes. The significance of this change is that taverns were usually supplied with kegs from local brewers; however, the acceptance of aluminum cans for home consumption made it possible for large distant brewers to compete with the local brewers.

Consumer tests have confirmed that many beer drinkers cannot distinguish among brands of beer. To increase sales, then, brewers vigorously advertise. Brewers that sell national brands, such as InBev Anheuser-Busch and Miller, realize substantial cost advantages over brewers such as Pabst that have many regional brands such as Rainier and Schmidt's. The reason is that national television advertising is less costly per viewer than local advertising.

Although mergers have taken place in the brewing industry, they have not been a major driver of the increasing concentration. Mergers generally have represented the termination of a small, inefficient brewer that salvaged some portion of its worth by selling out to another brewer. The acquiring brewer thus gained no market power, but it might have gained access to an improved distributional network or a new market. Dominant brewers, such as InBev Anheuser-Busch and Coors, have generally expanded by vigorously advertising their main brands and by creating new brands instead of acquiring other brewers. This has sustained product differentiation as a significant barrier to entry.

A smaller brewer, producing premium beer and marketing it so as to keep transportation costs low, can survive in today's market by finding a special niche for itself. This appears to be the status of Jacob Leinenkuegel Brewing Co. of Chippewa Falls, Wisconsin. However, such cases are rare. In brewing, large capital-intensive plants are necessary to exploit economies of scale to survive.

Sources: Kenneth Elzinga, "Beer," in Walter Adams and James Brock, eds., *The Structure of American Industry* (Upper Saddle River, NJ: Prentice Hall, 2001), pp. 85-113. See also Philip Van Munching, *Beer Blast* (New York: Random House, 1997) and Douglas Greer, "Beer: Causes of Structural Change," in Larry Duetsch, ed., *Industry Studies* (New York: M.E. Sharpe, 1998), pp. 28-64.

Excess capacity implies that monopolistically competitive markets are crowded, with each firm using an underutilized plant. In other words, there tend to be too many pizza parlors or gasoline service stations at the corner than those required for maximum efficiency. Underutilized plants result in rising costs and higher prices for the consumer. Notice, however, that an advantage of monopolistic competition is product differentiation, which allows consumers to choose from a wide range of types, style, brands, and quality variants of a product. If excess capacity is the price we pay for differentiated products and increased consumer choice, is it too high a price?

DESPITE COMPETITION FROM STARBUCKS, MOST INDEPENDENT COFFEEHOUSES SURVIVE

The model of monopolistic competition can be applied to a variety of markets. Let us consider coffeehouses.[1] In1998, the owners of the Broadway Café, a coffeehouse in Kansas City, Missouri, were shocked to learn that Starbucks Corp. was about to open a shop in the same city block. Despite

1. "At Starbucks, a Blend of Coffee and Music Creates a Potent Mix," *The Wall Street Journal,* July 19, 2005, pp. A1 and A11; and "Despite the Jitters, Most Coffeehouses Survive Starbucks," *The Wall Street Journal,* September 24, 2002, pp. A1 and A11.

concerns that it would be wiped out by the coffee giant, the Broadway Café continued to thrive following the entry of Starbucks.

Some people feel that Starbucks crushes the independent coffeehouses—encroaching on their turf, stealing their patrons, and bankrupting their owners. However, most independents across the country have continued to operate—not just in spite of Starbucks, but maybe because of it. In Kansas City, for example, many of the coffeehouses that were in business before Starbucks arrived in 1998, were still operating in 2009. Moreover, other independents opened, increasing their numbers well beyond the 25 stores that Starbucks had in the market. Like the Broadway Café, many of the independents were located within a few steps of a Starbucks shop.

Many coffeehouses have found proximity to Starbucks to be an advantage. For example, a small Seattle chain called Tully's Coffee Corp. deliberately places its stores near a Starbucks outlet. Why? Analysts maintain that Starbucks increases the overall market and attract new customers to gourmet coffee shops who then patronize the independent cafe next door.

However, critics of Starbucks often compare it with Wal-Mart Stores. But Starbucks doesn't enjoy the advantages that have made Wal-Mart the curse of numerous Main Street retailers—lower prices, wider selection, and longer hours. The Starbucks menu isn't cheaper or broader than the independents', and the chain's hours are often shorter. This may be why independents still dominate the industry.

A major reason for the success of independent coffeehouses is product differentiation: They are less like restaurants and more like neighborhood taverns, a concept that chains do not threaten. Customers often come alone to an independent café in search of conversation and friendship. There they are served by familiar employees, sit in an intimate room with upholstered chairs and antique tables, and enjoy poetry readings, jazz performances, and films. Moreover, the emergence of Starbucks has inspired independents to upgrade their cafes and broaden their menus.

Many independents are probably not as profitable as Starbucks shops. The size of its gourmet coffee orders means that Starbucks receives purchasing discounts that fatten its profit margins. But the profit margins on gourmet coffee drinks are so high that independent cafes can prosper even without volume purchasing discounts. That's especially true for coffeehouses that roast their own coffee beans because of the plunging prices of raw beans.

ADVERTISING

Product differentiation is the hallmark of many imperfectly competitive firms. Such firms often engage in **advertising** either to make buyers aware of the unique features of their products or convince buyers that their product really is different from those of their competitors, or both. Advertising constantly surrounds us—in magazines and newspapers and on radio, television, and billboards. In 2007, about $280 billion was spent on advertising in the United States, as shown in Table 6.3.

Many imperfectly competitive markets are characterized by brand names and continual product development and improvement as well as product promotion. For example, the brand name Prestone has become a synonym for antifreeze, while Pennzoil is synonymous with motor oil. As a result of the acceptance of these brands by consumers, the manufacturers of Prestone and Pennzoil charge significantly higher prices for their products than those charged for competing brands. Indeed, the market value of product brands can amount to billions of dollars.

The objective of nearly all advertising is to increase the demand for a firm's product. Consider the Coca-Cola Co., which engages in extensive advertising. By persuading consumers that Coke really is better than Pepsi and other rivals, Coca-Cola can expect to increase the amount of soda that it can sell at each price. In Figure 6.2(*a*), this is shown by a rightward shift in the firm's demand curve. Without advertising, the Coca-Cola Co. sells 6 million cases at a price of $5 per case, denoted by point *A* on

Table 6.3	Advertising Expenditures by Medium, 2007

Medium	Expenditures
Television	$ 71.4 billion
Direct mail	60.2
Newspapers	42.1
Radio	19.2
Yellow pages	14.3
Magazines	13.7
Other	58.7
Total	$279.6 billion

Source: U.S. Department of Commerce, Bureau of the Census, *Statistical Abstract of the United States*, 2008, Table 1239.

demand curve D_0. As a result of persuasive advertising, the firm's demand curve may shift to D_1. At the $5 price, the firm can now sell 10 million cases.

Besides increasing the demand curve of Coke, persuasive advertising can make demand less sensitive to price changes (less elastic). By successfully generating brand loyalty through advertising, Coca-Cola Co. convinces consumers that there exist fewer substitutes for its product. By allowing the firm to charge higher prices with a smaller loss of sales, advertising enhances the price-making ability of the Coca-Cola Co. Profits rise when advertising increases the firm's revenue more than the cost of advertising.[2]

Persuasive advertising also affects the long-run average total cost of Coke, as shown in Figure 6.2(*b*). Without advertising, the Coca-Cola Co.'s average total cost curve is denoted by ATC_0. At a price of $5, the firm sells, say, 6 million cases of Coke. The firm's unit cost is $3 per case, shown by point *A*. To increase its market share, suppose the Coca-Cola Co. decides to advertise. The advertising expenditures result in an upward shift in the firm's cost curve to ATC_1. Through successful advertising, suppose Coke's sales increase to, say, 10 million cases. By producing additional cases of Coke, the firm can take advantage of economies of scale that decrease unit cost to $2, shown by point *B*. The reduction in unit cost, made possible by economies of large-scale production, more than outweighs the increase in unit cost, resulting from advertising. Thus, consumers can purchase Coke at a lower price with advertising than they would without.

On the other hand, what if PepsiCo, Inc., initiates an advertising campaign that offsets the demand-increasing effects of Coke's advertising campaign. In this case, the market share of each firm remains unchanged as the result of advertising. For the Coca-Cola Co., advertising results in an increase in its cost curve from ATC_0 to ATC_1. Because the firm's sales remain at 6 million cases, however, unit cost rises to $5 per case (point *C*). The consumer thus faces a higher price because of advertising. Critics of advertising argue that this is the typical case rather than the reduction in unit cost from point *A* to point *B*. Instead, advertising expenditures could be used for hospitals, education, or other useful products that might better improve the well-being of society.

---

2. However, not all advertising is persuasive. Sometimes, advertising can be informative. Advertising is judged to be informative when it provides trustworthy information about the quality and price of a good or service or the location of suppliers. Such advertising results in greater price elasticity of demand and less price-making ability for firms.

Figure 6.2 | The Effect of Advertising on Demand and Average Total Costs

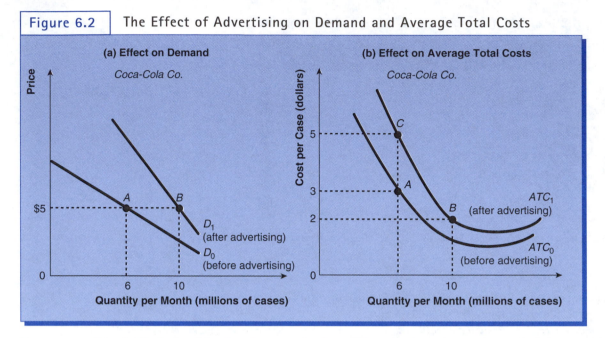

The purpose of nearly all of advertising is to increase the demand for a firm's product and to make it less sensitive to price changes (less elastic). As a result, the firm's market share increases, as does its price-making ability. By fostering an increase in market share and production, advertising can help the firm more fully realize economies of scale and decreasing unit costs.

PRICE DISCRIMINATION

We have learned that imperfectly competitive firms seek to determine the price that will maximize their total profits. Sometimes, the firm may charge more than one price for a particular good. For example, golf courses often charge senior citizens a lower price than other adults to play a round of golf. Movie theaters often give discounts to students to see a movie. In these cases, the firm charges different prices to different customers for what is essentially the same product or service. These practices are known as **price discrimination**—that is, charging some customers a lower price than others for an identical good even though there is no difference in the cost to the firm for supplying these consumers.

To engage in price discrimination, a seller must have price-making ability and thus operate in an imperfectly competitive market. It also must prevent significant resales of products from the lower-priced to the higher-priced market. If buyers can resell a product, price discrimination is unlikely to succeed. Finally, the seller must divide its customers into groups each having a different willingness and ability to pay. Price-sensitive buyers (those with *more elastic* demand schedules) will pay a *lower* price than buyers who are not as sensitive to price (those with less-elastic demand schedules).

Airline carriers provide an example of price discrimination. Consider a recent United Airlines flight from its hub at O'Hare International Airport in Chicago to Los Angeles. If any of the passengers had compared notes, they would have found that they had paid 27 different fares. One paid nothing, using frequent flyer miles; another who bought a first-class ticket on the day of departure paid $1,249; and one who bought a coach ticket on the day of travel paid $108. In general, the people who bought their tickets earlier paid less, but not always.

Although this pricing strategy may seem chaotic, its purpose is to squeeze as many dollars as possible out of each seat and mile flown. That means trying to project just how many tickets to sell at a discount without running out of seats for the business traveler, who usually books at the last minute and therefore pays full fare. According to the airlines, "You don't want to sell a seat to a guy for $79 when he's willing to pay $450."

Airlines use price discrimination to maximize their revenues. For airline travel, the key distinction among travelers is between leisure travel and business travel. Leisure travelers have relatively elastic demand because they can plan ahead and are flexible in their schedules. To encourage these price-sensitive customers to fly on their planes, airlines will charge them relatively low prices and, of course, do so in a manner that prevents them from reselling their tickets to less-price-sensitive passengers. Business passengers, however, have less-elastic demand because they often must travel on short notice, do not stay over weekends, and are insensitive to ticket fares. As a result, airlines charge higher fares to business travelers, who are a primary source of airline profits. To preserve their fare structures, airlines generally make their tickets nontransferrable. Otherwise, vacationers might purchase tickets when they are cheap and resell them to other travelers closer to departure, when fares are much higher. Or vacationers might purchase cheap tickets and sell them to business travelers who would normally have to pay a higher fare for a ticket. Such behavior would create competition for the airlines in the high-price segment of the market and undermine their price discrimination policy. Travelers can fly at a later date on their unused tickets by applying the value of the ticket to an alternate trip after subtracting change fees which can run as high as $150 on a domestic flight and $250 on international flights. But most airlines require the new ticket to be in the original passenger's name. Industry analysts estimate that about 2 percent to 3 percent of all tickets expire unused. In 2009, that translated into about $2 billion worth of tickets thrown away.

Colleges also use price discrimination. In 1995, for example, Johns Hopkins University began offering aid according to the student's price elasticity of demand for attending the university.[3] Johns Hopkins wanted to attract academically gifted students who would major in humanities but might attend other universities. These students had relatively elastic demand curves for education at Johns Hopkins, given the availability of substitute universities. By granting them an extra $3,000 in aid, the university was able to increase enrollment in that group by 20 percent. However, Johns Hopkins did not worry about losing prospective pre-med students, whose demand curves for education at Johns Hopkins were relatively inelastic. Because most of these students were already hooked on its pre-med program, a price increase would not knock many out. Johns Hopkins cut this group's aid by $1,000 per student and still increased net revenue. Today, this pricing strategy is being tried out at colleges and universities all over the nation. Perhaps your relatively elastic demand for the college you are attending contributed to your receiving a scholarship.

CHECK POINT

1. Identify the characteristics of an imperfectly competitive market structure.

2. How do concentration ratios attempt to measure how closely an industry comes to the extremes of competition and monopoly?

3. Explain how monopolistic competition involves a considerable amount of competition and a small dose of monopoly power.

4. How does a firm successfully practice price discrimination?

3. "Colleges Manipulate Financial-Aid Offers Shortchanging Many," *The Wall Street Journal*, April 1, 1996, pp. A1 and A11.

OLIGOPOLY

Oligopoly is another form of imperfect competition. In oligopoly, a small number of firms compete with each other, and each firm has significant price-making ability. Oligopoly embodies a range of market situations. It includes a situation in which two or three firms dominate an entire market, as well as a situation in which seven or eight firms share, say, 75 percent of the market (while a competitive fringe of remaining firms accounts for the remainder). Oligopoly also includes firms that produce standardized products as well as differentiated products. The steel and pharmaceutical industries are generally regarded as oligopolistic. The quantity sold by an oligopolist depends not only on that firm's product price but also on the other firms' prices and quantities sold. Therefore, each firm must consider the impact of its own actions on the actions of other firms.

To understand the interaction between prices and sales, consider the following example. Suppose that you operate one of three grocery stores in a small town. If you reduce your prices and your rivals do not reduce theirs, your sales will increase, but the sales of your two rivals will decrease. In this situation, your rivals are likely to cut their prices as well. If they reduce prices, your sales and profits will decline. So before deciding to decrease your prices, you attempt to predict how your rivals will react, and you try to estimate the impact of those reactions on your profit.

Why are some industries dominated by a few firms? We can provide some partial answers here:

- **Barriers to entry.** Oligopolistic industries may be fostered by barriers to entry such as product differentiation and advertising, patents, and the control and ownership of key resources. Historical control of raw materials explains the dominance of Alcoa (Aluminum Co. of America) in the aluminum industry. The high costs of obtaining needed plant and equipment may also deter entry. The aircraft and cigarette industries are characterized by high investment requirements.

- **Economies of scale.** With economies of scale, a firm's average total cost declines as output expands. Smaller firms in this situation tend to be inefficient because their average total costs will be greater than those realized by a larger firm. With economies of scale, a firm may be able to drive its smaller rivals out of the market and prevent potential competitors from entering the market. Economies of scale are noticeable in the cement and rubber industries.

- **Mergers.** Another reason that oligopoly occurs is that firms combine under a single ownership or control, a practice known as **merger**. The merged firm is larger, and therefore it may realize economies of scale as output expands and usually has a greater ability to control the market price of its product. In the beer industry, for example, giants such as Inbev Anheuser–Busch and Miller have grown through the acquisition of competing breweries.

RIVALRY IN THE SOFT DRINK INDUSTRY

Concerning oligopoly, one may get the impression that because there are only a few sellers in the market, there is little, if any, rivalry among them. In reality, firms often fight for market share through vigorous price competition, product promotion, and improvements in product quality. Let us consider the rivalry between the Coca-Cola Co. and PepsiCo, Inc. in the U.S. soft drink industry.

Historically, the Coca-Cola Co. has dominated the soft drink industry. Sales and profits have generally risen ever since Coke was first introduced to the market. Prior to the 1950s, no second-place firm was even worth considering. Consumers generally regarded Pepsi, Coke's closest competitor, to be an inferior drink.

During the 1950s, PepsiCo embarked on a strategy to increase its market share. The company improved the taste of its soft drink by using less sugar in its formula and establishing uniform control over local bottlers, who previously added varying amounts of carbonated water to the syrup so that Pepsi's taste varied throughout different regions of the country. It also offered consumers a 12-ounce bottle that sold for the same price as Coke's famous 6 1/2–ounce bottle. To enhance its image, PepsiCo adopted advertising campaigns featuring young women and men drinking Pepsi in high-income surroundings. The campaigns featured Pepsi as "the light refreshment," implying indirectly that Coke was "heavy." PepsiCo also adopted promotional efforts to increase sales in grocery markets where Coke was comparatively weak. Moreover, Pepsi attacked Coke in the vending machine and cold-bottle segments of the market by offering financing to local bottlers who were willing to buy and install Pepsi vending machines.

As Pepsi's market share increased, the Coca-Cola Co. launched retaliatory advertising campaigns. Using slogans such as "The really refreshed" and "No wonder Coke refreshes best," these campaigns picked up Coke's sales. In return, PepsiCo initiated two new advertising campaigns —"Be sociable" and "Think young." These campaigns especially caught on with teenagers, who account for the highest per-capita consumption of soft drinks. The youth theme suggested that Coke was an old-fashioned drink. The Coca-Cola Co. countered with its new advertising theme of "Things go better with Coke."

By 1980, the Coca-Cola Co. decided that it needed to compete more directly with Pepsi, which had a sweeter flavor than Coke. The firm developed a new formula for its soft drink and called it "New Coke." In spite of heavy advertising, public acceptance of New Coke was at best lukewarm and, at worst, disastrous. Several months after its introduction, the Coca-Cola Co. was forced to bring back "Classic Coke," which was based on the original formula used by Coke. It is estimated that the fiasco cost the firm's shareholders up to $500 million.

As of 2009 Coke and Pepsi continued to dominate the soft drink market. It remains to be seen how their competitive struggle will play out.

GAME THEORY AND OLIGOPOLY BEHAVIOR

A basic feature of oligopoly is that firms must weigh the impacts of their decisions on other firms and anticipate how those other firms will react. Basically, the behavior of an oligopoly can be viewed as a high-stakes game in which the goal is to earn economic profits by outguessing your competitors. In the real world, Boeing and Airbus have been rivals in the commercial jetliner market, as have Coca-Cola and PepsiCo, Inc. in the soft drink market; InBev Anheuser-Busch, Miller, and Coors in the beer market; Ford, General Motors, and Chrysler in the auto market; and General Mills, Post, and Kellogg's in the breakfast cereal market. These firms tend to form their price policies based on the price policies of their rivals.

We can gain important insights into oligopolistic markets by examining a method of analysis called game theory. **Game theory** examines oligopolistic behavior by examining a series of strategies and payoffs among rival firms. A strategy is a course of action, say, to charge a high price or a low price—and the payoff is the economic profit that results from that strategy.

Consider a hypothetical market with two competing airline firms, American and United, whose goals are to increase their economic profits by price changes. Each firm makes its pricing decisions independently, without knowing in advance what its rival will do. Figure 6.3 shows the profit-payoff matrix for these firms. Each cell in the matrix shows the yearly profit that each of the two firms can expect to earn depending on its own pricing strategy and that of its rival. The top portion in each cell shows the profit of United, and the bottom portion shows American's profit.

Competitive Oligopoly and Low Prices

As shown in Figure 6.3, the option that is available to each firm is to charge either a high price or a low price, and the payoff matrix shows the profit that each firm can expect to earn, given its own pricing choice and that of its competitor. For example, if both firms charge high prices (cell *A*), each

Figure 6.3   Game Theory and Oligopoly Behavior

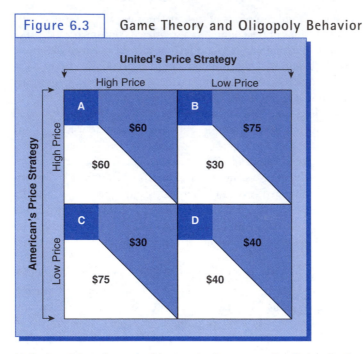

United and American would earn the largest profits if they both selected a high-price strategy. If they behave independently, either firm might realize higher profits by selecting a low-price strategy against its rival's high-price strategy. However, such rivalry tends to cause both firms to gravitate to a low-price strategy.

will earn a profit of $60 million. Instead, suppose that United charges a low price and American charges a high price (cell *B*). United will then attract customers from its rival and earn a profit of $75 million; American will earn a modest profit of $30 million. Conversely, if American charges a low price and United charges a high price, American will earn a profit of $75 million, while United will earn a profit of only $30 million.

As the payoff matrix shows, each firm will realize additional profits if both firms charge a high price. However, the maximum payoff for any particular firm will be achieved when its rival charges a high price while it alone charges a low price, thereby attracting customers from its rival. The minimum payoff for a particular firm will be achieved when it charges a high price while its rival charges a low one, because then it will lose many sales to its rival.

The outcome of this game yields a tendency toward a low-price strategy for competitive oligopoly. If United or American charges a low price, it is doing the best that it can do, given the behavior of the other firm. Thus, once United and American reach cell *D* in the figure, neither firm will desire to alter its price. The market thus gravitates toward a low-price strategy for each firm. Simply put, fear of what the rival firm will do is what causes each firm to offer a low price. The low price is good for consumers, but it is not good for the firms, which realize a profit of only $40 million rather than the $60 million that each would have earned if both had charged high prices (cell *A*).

Cooperative Behavior and Cheating

How can United and American avoid the modest profits associated with cell *D?* The answer is to cooperate with each other and decide how to set prices. For example, the managers of the two firms might strike an agreement that each will charge a high price. This action will cause the firms to locate at cell *A* in the figure, where each earns profits of $60 million instead of $40 million.

Although cooperative behavior can increase the profits of each firm, the profits are not at a maximum. Therefore, each firm may be enticed to cheat on this pricing agreement and charge a low price while its rival maintains a high price. For example, if United agrees to charge a high price, but secretly charges a low price, the outcome will move from cell *A* to cell *B*, where United earns a profit of $75 million. Similarly, if only American cheats, the outcome will move from cell *A* to cell *C*, and the firm will earn a profit of $75 million. Therefore, there is a tendency for cooperative price-fixing agreements to break down.

AIRBUS AND BOEING RIVAL FOR SUPREMACY IN THE JETLINER INDUSTRY

The commercial jetliner industry provides an example of oligopolistic rivalry. Consider the competitive battle between Boeing and Airbus.

Although the Europeans developed the first commercial jetliner in the 1950s, Boeing and other U.S. manufacturers learned from the Europeans' mistakes and leapfrogged ahead. European manufacturers were concerned that competition from the Americans would wipe out their weak and divided aviation industry. Hence, the European governments exercised the only option they felt was available to them: pooling their resources to establish a company that could compete against the Americans. This led to the formation of the Airbus Co. in 1969.

When Airbus was first created, analysts generally doubted whether it could compete against Boeing which enjoyed a virtual monopoly in the sale of jetliners. Maintaining that they were nurturing an "infant industry," the governments of Europe granted subsidies to Airbus. By the 1980s, Airbus had become a strong competitor against Boeing, and by the early 2000s it accounted for about half of the world jetliner market. However, production delays, cost overruns, and political infighting were plaguing Airbus by 2006.

As Airbus has grown, manufacturers in the United States have increasingly complained that the company's success is primarily the result of unfair subsidies from the European governments. U.S. officials argue that these subsidies place Boeing at a competitive disadvantage. Airbus receives loans for the development of new aircraft that are made at below-market interest rates and can amount to 70 percent to 90 percent of an aircraft's development cost. Rather than repaying the loans according to a prescribed timetable as would occur in a competitive market, Airbus is allowed to repay them as it delivers an aircraft. Also, Airbus can avoid repaying its loans in full if sales of aircraft that are being financed fall short of forecasts. Although Airbus says that has never occurred, Boeing contends that Airbus has less business risk, making it easier to obtain financing. The United States maintains that these subsidies allow Airbus to set unrealistically low prices, offer concessions and attractive financing terms to airlines, and write off development costs.

Airbus defends its subsidies on the grounds that they prevent the United States from holding a worldwide monopoly in commercial jetliners. In the absence of Airbus, European airlines would have to rely exclusively on Boeing as a supplier. Fears of dependence and the loss of autonomy in an area that is on the cutting edge of technology motivate European governments to subsidize Airbus.

Airbus also argues that Boeing benefits from government assistance. For example, governmental research organizations support aeronautics and propulsion research that is shared with Boeing. Support for commercial jetliner innovation also comes from military-sponsored research and military procurement. Research financed by the armed services yields indirect but important technological spillovers to the commercial jetliner industry, most notably in aircraft engines and aircraft design. Boeing also receives tax breaks from the state of Washington, which houses sizable Boeing production facilities. Moreover, the Japanese government helps Boeing by providing loans to Japanese subcontractors that manufacture wings for Boeing aircraft.

economics
IN ACTION

Is Wal-Mart Good for America?

Given Wal-Mart's presence around the country, it would be surprising to find someone who has not shopped at a Wal-Mart store or does not recognize the name "Wal-Mart." Today, Wal-Mart is widely recognized as one of the most powerful companies in U.S. business history. Although the company has been praised as a model of economic efficiency, Wal-Mart has also been condemned as a bad bargain. Is Wal-Mart good for America?

Let us begin by looking at Samuel Walton, the founder of Wal-Mart, and the factors that contributed to his company's success. Born in Kingfisher, Oklahoma, Samuel Walton (1918-1992) stumbled into retailing. He first learned how to compete playing high school football and basketball. As a student at the University of Missouri, Walton waited tables, managed newspaper routes, and worked as a lifeguard. After earning an undergraduate degree in economics in 1940, he contemplated pursuing an MBA degree, but he could not afford it. So he accepted an offer to be a management trainee with J. C. Penney Co.

When discount retailing emerged in the 1960s, Walton became a wealthy man, operating some 15 variety stores in Arkansas, Oklahoma, and Missouri. They were traditional small-town stores that charged relatively high price markups. As a student of retailing, Walton saw that discount stores had great potential. Walton opened his first Wal-Mart Discount City in Rogers, Arkansas, in 1962. That same year, rivals K-Mart and Target got their start. Discount retailing had entered the American way of life.

Once committed to discount retailing, Walton developed a business model that he held to for the rest of his life: to remove costs from the merchandising system wherever they existed—in retail stores, in the manufacturers' profit margins, and with the wholesalers —all with the goal of driving prices down. His stores also provided a wide assortment of good quality merchandise, guaranteed satisfaction on all purchases, friendly and knowledgeable service, and free parking.

Using that model, Walton slashed his profit margins to the bone, making it necessary for Wal-Mart to increase sales at a rapid pace. It did, and Walton hit the road to open stores wherever he saw profitability. He would buzz towns in his low-flying airplane, surveying the lay of the land. When he had calibrated the proper intersection between a few small towns, he would purchase a piece of farmland there and open another Wal-Mart store.

To Walton's great delight, Wal-Mart became the world's number one retailer, surpassing the profitability of its competitors such as Sears and K-Mart. Walton's extraordinary leadership skills inspired hundreds of thousands of employees to believe in Wal-Mart's success, and many rode the firm's stock to wealth. Walton's cost-cutting techniques have been emulated by Home Depot, Barnes & Noble, and other retailers.

However, not everyone admires Wal-Mart's business success. Critics maintain that as a result of Wal-Mart's fanatical efforts to cut costs, the company has become hostile to labor unions, violated child labor laws, paid low wages, refused to pay workers for some of their work, discriminated against women, and hastened the shift of production jobs overseas. Moreover, because Wal-Mart does not pay sufficient wages, American taxpayers are forced to pick up the tab in the form of payments for health care and other social services. Simply put, critics conclude that the costs of Wal-Mart's low prices are too high.

Source: Sam Walton and John Huey, *Sam Walton. Made in America: My Story* (New York: Doubleday, 1993); Daniel Gross, *Forbes Greatest Business Stories of All Time* (New York: John Wiley & Sons, 1996); and *Everyday Low Wages: The Hidden Price We All Pay for Wal-Mart*, Democratic Staff of the House Committee on Education and the Workforce, February 16, 2004.

In 2005, Boeing and Airbus filed suits at the World Trade Organization (WTO) which contended that each company was receiving illegal subsidies from the governments of Europe and the United States. In 2010, the WTO made a finding that Airbus did receive illegal subsidies from European governments. This finding was to be followed by another WTO finding concerning Airbus's contention that Boeing received illegal support from the U.S. government. At the writing of this text in 2010, it remains to be seen how renewed tensions between Boeing and Airbus will be resolved.

COLLUSION AND CARTELS

Recall that game theory considers the possibility that oligopolistic firms may form collusive agreements with each other rather than behave as competitors. Let us further examine how oligopolies form collusive agreements, known as cartels.

A **cartel** is a formal organization of firms that attempts to act as if there were only one firm in the industry (monopoly). The purpose of a cartel is to reduce output and increase the price in order to increase the joint profits of its members.

A widely known cartel is the **Organization of Petroleum Exporting Countries (OPEC)**, a group of nations that sells oil on the world market. Although OPEC has generally disavowed the term *cartel*, its organization consists of a secretariat, a conference of ministers, a board of governors, and an economic commission. The countries that belong to OPEC are generally located in the Middle East and include Saudi Arabia, Iran, Kuwait, Qatar, and so on. OPEC has assigned production controls among its members in an attempt to make oil scarce, thus supporting prices higher than would exist under more competitive conditions.

After operating in obscurity throughout the 1960s, OPEC captured control of oil pricing in 1972–1974 when the price of oil rose from $3 to $12 per barrel. Triggered by the Islamic Revolution in Iran in 1979, oil prices skyrocketed to more than $35 per barrel in 1981. During this era, OPEC's success at increasing oil prices was largely attributable to strong consumer demand for oil and insensitivity to price increases (inelastic demand). Moreover, OPEC accounted for half of the world's oil production and about two-thirds of the world's oil reserves throughout this era.

By the mid-1980s, however, OPEC had fallen into disarray as a result of increased competition from non-OPEC nations (the former Soviet Union, Mexico, United Kingdom), conservation among the oil-importing nations, and falling oil demand caused by a downturn in the world economy. By 1986, the price of oil had tumbled to $10 per barrel, hammering industry profits and stock prices. The industry had little choice but to cut oil exploration and production budgets. By the early 2000s, the world demand for oil had rebounded. With oil inventories being low, prices shot to more than $140 per barrel in 2008, thus enhancing profits of the OPEC nations. As the world economy fell into recession and the demand for oil declined, the price of oil decreased to under $50 per barrel in 2009.

Although a cartel attempts to maximize the profits of its members, several obstacles may limit its success. Recall from our discussion of game theory, that once a cartel is established, incentives arise for individual member producers to leave the cartel and operate independently. If a single producer were to price below the common cartel price, this would attract additional sales to that producer, at the expense of other members, possibly increasing its profits above what they would be under the cartel. However, if other cartel members follow suit and reduce their prices, all firms will receive both lower prices and profits than they enjoyed under the cartel arrangement. Because of the incentive for individual members to leave the cartel and establish prices independently, the life span of most cartels is short.

Besides the problem of cheating, other obstacles to forming and maintaining a cartel can arise. Among the obstacles that cartels face are the following:

- **Number of sellers.** Generally speaking, the larger the number of sellers, the more difficult it is to coordinate price and output policies among cartel members.

- **Cost and demand differences.** When cartel members' costs and demands differ greatly, it is more difficult to assign production controls and agree on price.

- **Potential competition.** The increased profits that occur under a cartel may attract new competitors, thus restricting the cartel's control of the market.

Table 6.4	Selected Mergers in the United States		
Firm Acquired	**Acquiring Firm**		**Year**
Lexar Media	Micron Technology		2006
Arroyo Video Systems	Cisco Systems		2006
Compaq	Hewlett Packard		2002
AOL (America Online)	Time Warner		2000
McDonnell Douglas	Boeing		1997
Warner Communications	Time		1989
RCA	General Electric		1986
Marathon Oil	USX (U.S. Steel)		1981

- **Economic downturn.** As market sales dwindle in a weakening economy, profits decline, thus undermining the success of a cartel.

- **Government policy.** In the United States, cartels are illegal. Business executives who are found guilty of engaging in collusion can be fined and sent to jail. This does not mean that firms do not engage in collusion. However, it is usually done secretly and is difficult to prove.

MERGERS AND OLIGOPOLY

Mergers can promote the development of oligopolistic market structures. A merger is the combination of the assets of two firms to form a single new firm. By combining their assets, the acquiring firm and the acquired firm hope to become more profitable than they were before the merger. Table 6.4 gives examples of mergers between U.S. firms.

Three are three types of mergers: A **horizontal merger** occurs when one firm combines with another firm that sells similar products in the same market. The merger of Jones & Laughlin Steel and Republic Steel to form LTV Steel is an example of a horizontal merger. A **vertical merger** is a merger between firms that are in the same industry, but at different stages in the production process. For example, Bridgestone (tires) has acquired rubber plantations in Indonesia and Malaysia, and the Campbell's Soup Co. has acquired mushroom farms throughout the United States. Finally, a **conglomerate merger** brings together two firms producing in different industries. The merger of Greyhound (bus service) and Armour and Co. (meat products) is an example of a conglomerate merger.

Of these three types of mergers, the federal government looks most carefully at proposed horizontal mergers. The reason is that horizontal mergers can unite firms that formerly competed against one another, thus reducing competition and increasing the monopoly power of the newly formed firm. But mergers can also contribute to cost savings and other efficiencies. For example, the newly formed firm might (1) add to industry output and promote additional competition, (2) enter markets that neither merging firm could have entered individually, or (3) realize cost reductions that would have been unavailable if each merging firm had performed the same function separately. Such cost reductions could be the result of economies of scale, integration of production facilities, plant specialization, and lower transportation costs. In deciding whether a horizontal merger should be approved, the federal government weighs the benefits of increased efficiencies versus the costs of increased monopoly power.[4]

---

4. Federal Trade Commission, *Revision to the Horizontal Merger Guidelines* (Washington, DC: U.S. Government Printing Office, April 8, 1997).

economics
IN ACTION

Acquisition Brews Culture Shock at InBev Anheuser-Busch

Although mergers and acquisitions may improve a firm's profitability through cost cutting and revenue increases, many of them fail to produce any benefit for the company's shareholders and some actually destroy value. Up to the point in a transaction where papers are signed, a business combination is mostly financial —valuing assets, determining price, and so on. When the ink is dry, this financially driven deal becomes a human transaction filled with emotion, trauma, and survival behavior. In the case of international mergers and acquisitions, the complexity of these processes are often compounded by the difference in national cultures. People living and working in different countries react to the same situations or events in very different manners. Consider the acquisition of Anheuser-Busch by InBev in the beer industry.

Anheuser-Busch is a company that is familiar to many American college students. Headquartered in St. Louis, Missouri, it is the largest brewing company in the United States with about a 50-percent share of beer sales. Anheuser-Busch's best known beers include brands such as Budweiser, Michelob, and Natural Light and Ice. Another famous brewery is InBev, the second largest brewery company in the world. Headquartered in Leuven, Belgium, InBev operates in some 30 countries across the Americas, Europe, and Asia Pacific. Its most notable brands include Stella Artois and Beck's.

In 2008 InBev acquired Anheuser-Busch for $52 billion and the combined company was renamed InBev Anheuser-Busch. The combination of these firms is intended to create a diversified, global company to achieve profitability in terms of both cost savings and revenue. Given the complementary nature of the two companies, cost savings are expected to be realized by sharing best business practices and economies of scale, and rationalizing overlapping corporate functions. Also, there are potential revenue opportunities through

expansion of Budweiser on a global scale. InBev has been the top brewer in 10 markets where Budweiser has a limited presence, and has a superior footprint in 9 markets where Budweiser was already present. Also, Budweiser is a strong and growing national brand in China, and InBev's business in southeastern China will be enhanced by Anheuser-Busch's strength in northeastern China. Simply put, the business combination is intended to provide an unparalleled global distribution network and the application of best business practices across the new organization.

In spite of these intentions, InBev's acquisition of Anheuser-Busch has resulted in unease for American workers. Following the signing of the acquisition papers, it took about 6 months for InBev to turn a family-led company that spared little expense into one that stresses cost cutting and profit margins. The new owner slashed jobs, modified the compensation system, and eliminated perks that had made Anheuser-Busch workers the envy of others in St. Louis. Managers accustomed to flying on company planes or first class on commercial planes had to fly coach. Free tickets to St. Louis Cardinal baseball games became scarce. The company also announced that in the future it will pay salaried workers 80–100 percent of the market rate for comparable jobs, and any increases above that will require special justification and approval. Moreover, InBev informed NBC that it will spend about 50 percent less on its Olympic advertising package which included the 2010 Winter Games in Vancouver and the 2012 Summer Games in London. InBev justified the cost-cutting measures by stating that the leaner the business, the more money it will have at the end of the year to share.

However, analysts question how employees of Anheuser-Busch will react to the change in corporate culture. Will the loss of company perks and the change in compensation policy weaken worker commitments to the job at hand? Will key employees look for jobs in other companies, thus strengthening the competition? These are among the unanswered questions at the writing of this text: It is not clear how the new corporate culture being developed by InBev will pan out.

CHECK POINT

1. Oligopoly involves a considerable dose of monopoly and a small dose of competition. Explain.

2. How does game theory illustrate the mutual interdependence of firms in oligopoly?

3. Why are cartels difficult to form and operate?

4. Distinguish between a horizontal merger, a vertical merger, and a conglomerate merger.

5. Why do government regulators especially scrutinize proposed horizontal mergers?

Chapter Summary

1. Imperfect competition exists when more than one seller competes for sales with many other sellers, each of which has some price-making ability. Imperfect competition comprises the market structures of monopolistic competition and oligopoly.

2. Economists use concentration ratios to measure how closely an industry comes to the extremes of competition and monopoly. A low concentration ratio suggests a high degree of competition, and a high concentration ratio implies a low degree of competition.

3. Monopolistic competition is characterized by a large number of sellers, each having a relatively small share of the total market, relative freedom of entry into and exit from the market, and product differentiation among sellers. Although monopolistically competitive firms tend to earn zero economic profits in the long run, they suffer from the problem of excess capacity.

4. The goal of persuasive advertising is to shift a firm's demand curve to the right and make it less sensitive to price changes. Advertising results in an upward shift in a firm's cost curve. However, the economies of large-scale production made possible by increased sales volume because of advertising may lead to lower unit costs than would occur without advertising.

5. Price discrimination is the practice of charging some customers a lower price than others for an identical good or service, even though there is no difference in the cost to the firm for supplying these consumers. A firm that practices price discrimination will charge a lower price to buyers with more elastic demand and a higher price to buyers with less elastic demand.

6. In oligopoly, a small number of firms compete with each other, and each firm has significant price-making ability. Oligopolistic markets are characterized by high barriers to entry, economies of scale, and mergers. Because uncertainty about the interaction of competing firms in oligopoly makes it virtually impossible to formulate a single theory of oligopoly behavior, a number of different theories exist. However, game theory can be used to illustrate the mutual interdependence of firms in oligopolistic markets.

7. Rather than engage in cutthroat competition, oligopolies may decide to collude and form a cartel. The purpose of a cartel is to restrict output and drive up price, thus maximizing the joint profits of its members.

8. Oligopolies are characterized by horizontal mergers, vertical mergers, and conglomerate mergers. Of these three types of mergers, government regulators monitor proposed horizontal mergers most closely. The reason is that horizontal mergers can unite firms that formerly competed against one another, which may increase the monopoly power of the newly formed firm.

Key Terms and Concepts

imperfect competition (128)

concentration ratios (128)

monopolistic competition (130)

product differentiation (130)

excess capacity (132)

advertising (134)

price discrimination (136)

oligopoly (138)

merger (138)

game theory (139)

cartel (143)

Organization of Petroleum Exporting Countries (OPEC) (143)

horizontal merger (144)

vertical merger (144)

conglomerate merger (144)

Self-Test: Multiple-Choice Questions

1. Retail gasoline stations provide an example of

   a. perfect competition.
   b. pure monopoly.
   c. oligopoly.
   d. monopolistic competition.

2. Which of the following is a characteristic of monopolistic competition or oligopoly, but not perfect competition?

   a. Profit-maximizing behavior according to the $MR = MC$ rule.
   b. Negligible barriers to entry into a market.
   c. Relatively large number of firms in the industry.
   d. Product differentiation.

3. All of the following are characteristic of oligopolies *except*

   a. mergers that facilitate growth.
   b. mutual interdependence.
   c. advertising and nonprice competition.
   d. price-taking behavior among firms.

4. The operation of a cartel tends to be inhibited by

   a. economic downturn and cheating by members of the cartel.
   b. a small number of sellers in the market.
   c. relatively inelastic demand schedules.
   d. highly similar demand and cost conditions among members of the cartel.

5. Successful advertising by Pizza Hut will shift its demand curve

   a. to the right, making it more elastic.
   b. to the right, making it more inelastic.
   c. to the left, making it more elastic.
   d. to the left, making it more inelastic.

6. Which of the following industries is best represented by oligopoly?

   a. Farming and commercial fishing.
   b. Gasoline retailing.
   c. Commercial jetliners.
   d. Fast-food restaurants.

7. By practicing successful price discrimination, Liberty Theater will charge

   a. a relatively higher price to customers with more elastic demand curves.
   b. a relatively higher price to customers with less elastic demand curves.
   c. a relatively lower price to customers with more inelastic demand curves.
   d. the same price to all customers regardless of their elasticities of demand.

8. If the Coca-Cola Co. and PepsiCo Inc. agree to divide the market for soft drinks and fix prices, which factor will limit the effectiveness of their agreement?

   a. The relatively large size of these firms in the soft drink industry.
   b. The substantial economies of scale realized by these firms.
   c. The degree to which large profits would attract entry of a new firm into the soft drink industry.
   d. The ease of monitoring the advertising strategies and product innovation by these firms.

9. Neither perfectly competitive firms nor monopolistically competitive firms can realize economic profits in the long run because

   a. substantial barriers to entry prevent established firms from realizing profits.
   b. the firms tend to encounter diseconomies of scale in the long run.
   c. free entry and competitive pricing cause prices to decline to the level of production costs.
   d. price-sensitive buyers force sellers to charge prices that just cover their average variable costs.

10. The merger of Jones & Laughlin Steel and Republic Steel to form LTV Steel is an example of a(n)

   a. integrative merger.
   b. conglomerate merger.
   c. horizontal merger.
   d. vertical merger.

Answers to Multiple-Choice Questions

   1. d.   2. d   3. d   4. a   5. b   6. c   7. b   8. c   9. c   10. c

Study Questions and Problems

1. What is the meaning of a top-four concentration ratio of 20 percent? 85 percent?

2. Suppose that Don's Texaco is a typical gas station in a monopolistically competitive market. Draw a diagram showing the market position of the firm in the long run. Will the firm encounter the problem of excess capacity? Why or why not?

3. Figure 6.4 shows the short-run position of Hal's Electronics, a typical firm selling radios in a monopolistically competitive market.
   a. Hal's profit-maximizing output, price, and total revenue will be_____, _____, and _____.
   b. At the profit-maximizing output, Hal's average total cost and total cost will be_____ and _____.
   c. Hal will earn an economic profit of_____.
   d. Attracted by short-run economic profits, suppose that firms enter this industry. In the long run, what will be the effect on Hal's demand curve, marginal revenue curve, and economic profits?

4. Draw a diagram that shows how persuasive advertising affects a firm's demand curve and average total cost curve. Under what conditions will advertising result in lower cost per unit? How would you modify your diagram if advertising were assumed to be informative rather than persuasive?

| Figure 6.4 | Short-Run Position of a Monopolistically Competitive Firm |

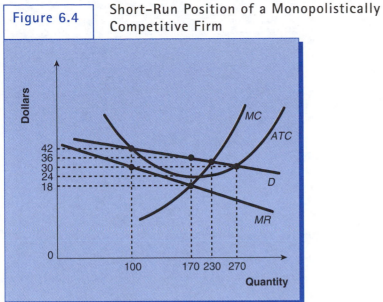

5. Suppose that Northwest Airlines practices price discrimination in the sale of tickets to business travelers and tourists. Discuss how price discrimination can result in higher revenues and profits for the firm than those that would occur in the absence of price discrimination.

6. Assume that Nike and Reebok are the only sellers of athletic shoes in the United States. They are contemplating how much to charge for similar basketball shoes. The only two choices are a high price and a low price. Table 6.5 shows the payoff matrix for these firms, with profits stated in millions of dollars per year.

   a.   Use the payoff matrix to discuss the interdependence that characterizes these firms.
   b.   In the absence of cooperative behavior, what will be the likely pricing strategy for each firm?
   c.   Why might cooperative behavior be beneficial for these firms? Why might there be an incentive to cheat on a price-fixing agreement?

7. Why do oligopolists have the incentive to fix prices? What are the obstacles to successful collusion?

| Table 6.5 | Hypothetical Profit–Payoff Matrix for Nike and Reebok |

		Nike	
		High Price	Low Price
Reebok	High price	Nike = $600 Reebok = $600	Nike = $750 Reebok = $150
	Low price	Nike = $150 Reebok = $750	Nike = $150 Reebok = $150

CHAPTER 7

Labor Markets

Chapter objectives

After reading this chapter, you should be able to:

1. Explain how a firm determines the quantity of workers demanded.

2. Explain why even if U.S. wages are higher than foreign wages, U.S. labor can still be competitive if it is more productive than foreign labor.

3. Identify the advantages and disadvantages of a minimum wage law that raises the wage rate above the market equilibrium level.

4. Describe the methods that unions employ to increase the wages of their members and the factors that give a union strength.

5. Explain why domestic workers are often fearful of international trade and liberal immigration policies.

economics IN CONTEXT

In 2009, Theresa Johnson was treated like royalty. She was flown around the country on all-expense-paid trips to Los Angeles, Phoenix, St. Louis, and Miami and was wined and dined at the finest restaurants. Such benefits used to accrue to individuals applying for high-profile professions such as computer engineering and consulting. But 28-year-old Theresa Johnson was part of a group of job seekers, students with Ph.D.s in accounting, who wanted to teach college students.

Traditionally, the job search for these assistant professors was a long battle that resulted in modest pay and an ill-equipped office. At the turn of the century, however, an increase in the number of students desiring to learn about accounting and a scarcity of Ph.D.s in accounting resulted in job seekers being treated like big shots. Accounting graduates were receiving lucrative packages in 2009, with many colleges offering salaries in excess of $120,000. What explains the high salaries of Ph.D.s in accounting?

In this chapter, we will learn about the theory of wage determination. In particular, we will learn why some workers receive higher wages than others and what methods workers can use to increase their wages without losing their jobs. Table 7.1 shows the annual earnings for workers in selected occupations in 2007.

LABOR MARKET EQUILIBRIUM

Like other markets in the economy, labor markets are influenced by the forces of demand and supply. In labor markets, households are the sellers and business firms are the primary buyers. We call the price of labor the wage rate.

We can analyze a labor market and the factors that determine the wage rate and quantity in that market by using the model of demand and supply. Figure 7.1 (page 154) refers to the market for apple pickers in Mt. Pleasant, Michigan. In the figure, the market demand curve for apple pickers is labeled D_0. Notice that the demand for apple pickers exists because there is a demand for the apples that apple pickers help to produce. The demand for apple pickers is therefore a **derived demand:** It is derived from the demand of consumers for apples. An increase in the demand for apples will inspire growers to plant additional apple trees and hire more apple pickers; thus the demand for apple pickers will increase. Conversely, a decrease in the demand for apples results in a reduced demand for apple pickers.

We would expect that apple growers would be willing to hire more apple pickers at lower wages than at higher wages. There are two reasons why fewer apple pickers will be demanded as their wages rise: (1) Producers will switch to substitute resources, such as machinery; and (2) consumers will purchase fewer apples as they become more expensive because of the higher wages being paid to apple pickers, suggesting that fewer apple pickers will be needed to produce apples. "Exploring Further 7.1" at the end of this chapter further discusses the factors underlying the demand for labor.

Figure 7.1 also shows the market supply curve of apple pickers, labeled S_0. As wages rise, other things remaining the same, additional workers will be drawn into the labor force, thus increasing the quantity supplied.

Referring to Figure 7.1(*a*), the point of intersection of the labor demand and labor supply curves determines the equilibrium wage and employment level: 1,000 workers are hired at a wage of $500

Table 7.1	Annual Earnings for Selected Occupations, 2007

Occupation	Average Annual Earnings
Family practice physician	$156,080
Associate actuary	109,167
Lawyer	94,930
Economist	94,098
High school principal	92,965
Accountant	54,630
Librarian	51,160
Mail carrier	45,300

Source: U.S. Department of Labor, Bureau of Labor Statistics, *Occupational Outlook Handbook,* 2008–2009, available at http://stats.bls.gov.

per week. Any wage above $500 per week would result in a surplus of apple pickers and eventually decrease the wage to $500. Any wage below $500 per week would cause a shortage of apple pickers and impose upward pressure on the wage.

In any labor market, certain changes can occur that will result in increases or decreases in the labor supply curve or the labor demand curve. When these changes take place, the equilibrium wage rate and quantity of workers demanded are affected.

Referring to Figure 7.1(*b*), suppose that the number of teenagers in the population rises, resulting in more workers available to pick apples. Therefore, the supply curve of labor shifts to the right, to S_1. As supply increases, the equilibrium wage falls from $500 per week to $400 per week, and the number of apple pickers employed increases from 1,000 to 1,200.

Let's now consider the effect of a change in the demand curve for labor. Referring to Figure 7.1(*c*), suppose that the market demand for apples increases. Because the demand for apple pickers is derived from the demand for apples, the demand for apple pickers shifts to the right—say, to D_1—in the figure. As demand increases, the equilibrium wage rate rises from $500 per week to $600 per week, and the number of workers employed rises from 1,000 to 1,200.

We will next apply the theory of labor markets to some contemporary labor issues—the minimum wage law, labor unions, outsourcing, and immigration.

CHECK POINT

1. Explain how the demand for labor is derived from the product that labor helps produce.

2. How is equilibrium determined in the labor market?

3. What factors cause the market demand curve for labor or the supply curve of labor to increase or decrease?

4. What effect does an increase in the market supply curve of labor have on the wage rate and the quantity of labor demanded? How about an increase in the market demand curve for labor?

Figure 7.1 | Market for Apple Pickers

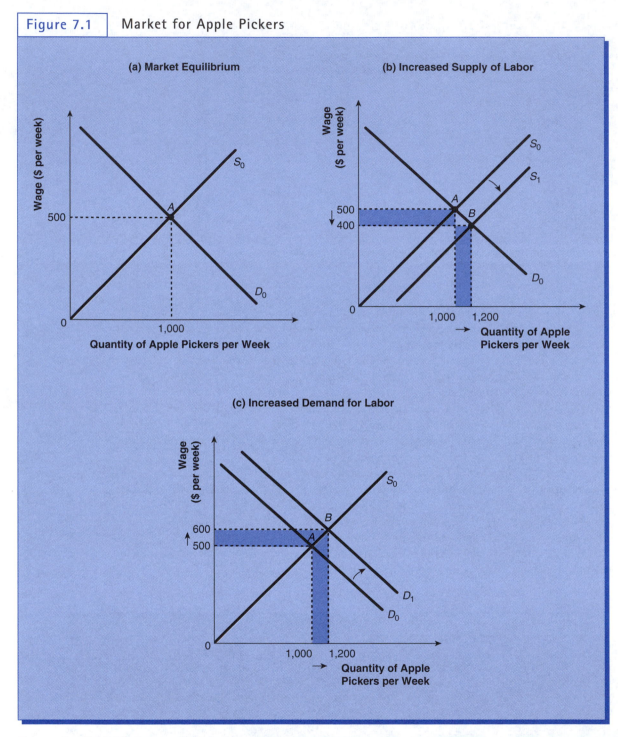

(a) Market Equilibrium

(b) Increased Supply of Labor

(c) Increased Demand for Labor

The market demand curve for labor is downward-sloping, showing that a lower wage results in an increase in the quantity of labor demanded. The market supply for labor is upward-sloping, implying that higher wages cause the quantity supplied of labor to increase. The point of intersection between the labor demand and labor supply curves determines the equilibrium wage and employment level. An increase in the market supply of labor results in a fall in the wage rate and an increase in the amount of labor employed. An increase in the market demand for labor causes a rise in the wage rate and an increase in the amount of labor employed.

DO MINIMUM WAGE LAWS HELP WORKERS?

To help the working poor during the Great Depression, in 1938 Congress passed *The Fair Labor Standards Act*. This law established a federal **minimum wage**, the smallest amount of money per hour that an employer can legally pay a worker. Congress set the first federal minimum wage at 25 cents per hour, and periodically increased it to $6.55 per hour by 2008. However, some workers are not covered by this legislation and earn less than the minimum wage. These people primarily work in the leisure and hospitality industry. Also, many people who work in food preparation, such as waiters, earn less than the minimum wage because of the "tip-credit law," which allows employers to pay workers less per hour if they meet minimum-wage standards based on tips.

In addition to the federal legislation, about 40 states have passed their own minimum wage laws. In any state where the minimum wage exceeds the federal minimum wage, the employee is entitled to receive the higher wage. Table 7.2 provides examples of states with the highest minimum wages.

To government officials, raising the minimum wage is an attractive method of reducing poverty because it does not require an increase in government welfare payments or an accompanying tax increase. Proponents maintain that a national standard for wages is essential to restore wages to the barest minimum and to prevent any further cuts below it. However, opponents note that by increasing the minimum wage, the government doesn't guarantee jobs. It guarantees only that those who get jobs will be paid at least that minimum wage. By requiring this, critics argue, the government destroys jobs.

To understand the arguments for and against the minimum wage, consider Figure 7.2. It illustrates the competitive market for low-skill workers, a group whose equilibrium wage rate is likely to be below the minimum wage. Suppose that the equilibrium wage equals $4 per hour, shown at the intersection of the market supply curve (S_0) and the market demand curve (D_0). At the equilibrium wage, workers supply 8 million hours of labor per week, and businesses demand 8 million hours of labor per week.

Suppose that the federal government imposes a minimum wage of $6 per hour—a rate that is higher than the market equilibrium wage. What are the effects of this wage floor? First, consider the impact of the wage hike on the quantity of labor demanded. Recall that a profit-maximizing employer will hire

| Table 7.2 | Highest State Minimum Wage Rates, 2009 |

State	Minimum Wage (dollars per hour)
Washington	$8.55
Oregon	8.40
Connecticut	8.25
Vermont	8.06
California	8.00
New Mexico	7.50
Ohio	7.30
North Carolina	7.25
Alaska	7.15
Federal	6.55

Source: U.S. Department of Labor, *Minimum Wage Laws in the States*, January 1, 2009, available at http://www.dol.gov/esa/minwage/america.htm/.

| Figure 7.2 | Effects of a Minimum Wage |

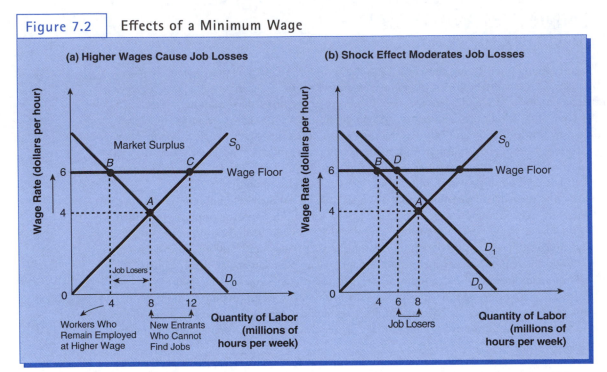

By raising the wage rate above the market equilibrium wage, a minimum wage increases the quantity of labor supplied but decreases the quantity of labor demanded. Some workers realize higher wages, but others remain or become unemployed. If a wage hike causes the marginal productivity of labor to increase, the demand for labor will increase and unemployment will decline.

a worker only if the value of the output the worker produces is greater than the wage. Assuming that a legislated increase in the price of labor does not increase workers' productivity, the quantity of labor demanded will decrease in response to a wage increase. In Figure 7.2(a), as the wage rises from $4 to $6 per hour, the quantity of labor hours demanded falls from 8 million hours to 4 million hours. Put simply, raise the wage, and workers are priced above the value they can add. An excessive price for labor yields a reduced quantity of workers demanded—the least-productive ones will lose their jobs.

In Figure 7.2(a), also notice what happens on the supply side. The rise in wages from $4 to $6 per hour attracts people into the labor market. As a result, the quantity of labor supplied rises from 8 million hours to 12 million hours per week. Everybody prefers one of those higher paying jobs. At the minimum wage of $6 per hour, there is a *surplus* of labor equal to 8 million hours per week (12 million − 4 million = 8 million). In other words, there are 8 million hours of labor that people wish to provide at the minimum wage, but are unable to provide. With more job seekers than jobs, *unemployment* results.

The minimum wage benefits workers who are fortunate enough to find work at a wage level that exceeds the market equilibrium wage. However, it harms many workers, including teenagers and young adults, who seek employment at the higher wage, but cannot find jobs. Critics maintain that the minimum wage law says to the potential worker, "Unless you can find a job paying at least the minimum wage, you may not accept employment." For those who lose their jobs because of the minimum wage, it is hard to understand why they would think such a law is a good idea.

The minimum wage tends to have its greatest impact on unskilled workers, especially teenagers. Because teenagers are often the least experienced and least skilled members of the labor force, their market equilibrium wage is low. Teenagers, chiefly minorities, are therefore the most likely to lose jobs as a result of increases in the minimum wage.

Chris Dussin, owner of the Old Spaghetti Factory in Portland, Oregon, provides an example of the effects of increasing the minimum wage. He felt that he could only raise prices so much before he would start chasing customers away, even in a prosperous economy. In 2002, Oregon increased its minimum wage from $6 to $7.50 per hour. From 2002 to 2006, costs at Dussin's three Oregon restaurants increased by $300,000, more than the increase in revenues. Mr. Dussin saw his bottom line eroding and his profit margin decreasing to only 2 percent to 3 percent of sales. Although he was able to increase prices on some items, he had to decrease the number of hostesses and increase the number of tables assigned to each server. Moreover, higher labor costs forced him to abandon plans to open an Old Spaghetti Factory in Bend, Oregon. However, he opened another restaurant in Boise, Idaho, which had a minimum wage of $5.15 and, unlike Oregon, allowed employers to pay less to workers who collect tips.[1]

Numerous studies have sought to quantify the effects of raising the minimum wage on employment. The debate focuses on how sensitive, or elastic, the demand for labor is in response to changes in the wage rate. The preponderance of empirical evidence suggests that increases in the minimum wage do result in decreases in employment, but this effect is likely to be small. On average, studies estimate the elasticity of labor demand to be 0.2. This means that a 10-percent increase in the minimum wage would result in a 2-percent decrease in employment.[2]

However, some economists argue that increasing the minimum wage may yield some benefits to employers that can potentially offset the rise in labor costs. For example, higher wages might reduce worker turnover and thus lower training costs. Also, workers may be motivated by increased wages to become more productive. Moreover, higher wages may shock firms into upgrading their technology, improving their management, and using labor more efficiently. These benefits would likely cause the demand for labor to shift to the right, thus lessening the employment-reducing effects that a higher minimum wage might cause. This so-called **shock effect** is illustrated in Figure 7.2(*b*) where we assume that the minimum wage leads to an increase in the demand for labor, from D_0 to D_1. The increase in the demand for labor moderates some of the unemployment that otherwise would have occurred; the quantity of labor demanded declines by only 2 million hours per week rather than by 4 million hours.

Such a shock effect occurred in 1914 when Ford Motor Co. offered to double the wages of its employees from $2.50 to $5 per day.[3] At that time, the prevailing wage in manufacturing was only $2 to $3 per day. The offer to increase wages was motivated by the high rates of absenteeism and turnover that occurred among workers at Ford's factories. Ford apparently hoped that an increase in wages would improve the morale of workers and encourage them to work harder in order to keep their high-paying jobs. As a result, Ford believed that labor productivity would increase. Immediately following the wage hike, more than 10,000 workers applied for employment with Ford. According to analysts, Ford's tactic was successful. Employees remained on the job and worked harder, resulting in labor productivity gains exceeding 50 percent.

ARE WORKERS BETTER OFF WITH LABOR UNIONS?

Throughout this chapter, we have assumed that individual workers actively compete in the sale of their services. In some markets, workers form **unions** in order to sell their services collectively. Unions exist because workers realize that acting together provides them with more bargaining power

---

1. "Weighing Minimum Wage Hikes," *The Wall Street Journal*, November 3, 2006, p. A-4.
2. Alice Sasser, *The Potential Economic Impact of Increasing the Minimum Wage in Massachusetts*, Federal Reserve Bank of Boston, NEPPC Research Report Series, No. 06–1, January 2006.
3. Daniel Raff and Lawrence Summers, "Did Henry Ford Pay Efficiency Wages?" *Journal of Labor Economics*, October 1987, pp. S57–S86.

Table 7.3	Percent of Wage and Salary Workers Belonging to Unions, 2007

Salary Worker	Wage and Salary Workers
Agriculture	1.5%
Mining	9.3
Construction	13.9
Manufacturing	11.3
Transportation and utilities	22.1
Financial activities	2.0
Professional and business people	2.4
Education and health services	8.8
Government	35.9
All workers	12.1

Source: U.S. Department of Commerce, Bureau of the Census, *Statistical Abstract of the United States*, 2009 (Washington, DC: U.S. Government Printing Office), Table 643.

than they would have if they acted individually—putting them at the mercy of their employers. You are probably familiar with unions such as the United Auto Workers, the United Steel Workers, and the Teamsters.

In 1970, about 25 percent of the U.S. labor force belonged to unions. Only about 12 percent are members as of 2007, as seen in Table 7.3. With the declining role of manufacturing jobs in the workforce, continued union success hinges on penetrating the service sector. That's very difficult to organize. Service workers tend to work in many different locations, and many jobs in the service sector are transient.

The chief aim of a labor union is to improve the wages, hours, working conditions, and job security of its members. Unions act on behalf of workers to bargain with employers on matters relating to employment, a process known as **collective bargaining**. This process allows one negotiator to act as the workers' agent rather than having each worker negotiate his own labor contract.

Most disagreements between labor and management involve wages, hours, or other conditions of employment. If labor and management cannot settle their differences, they may receive outside help called **mediation**. If the two parties still cannot agree, they may submit to a process known as **arbitration**. A person called an arbitrator listens to both sides of a dispute and makes a decision that is binding on both sides. **Strikes** may also occur when workers feel that stopping work is the best way to pressure their employer into granting their demands. Before a union calls a strike, it must put the question to a vote by its members. Generally, a strike cannot be called unless a majority of the voting members support it.

Increasing Union Wages

Indeed, economic researchers estimate that, on average, union workers earn about 15 percent more than nonunion workers. To increase the wages of their members, unions use several strategies: (1) increase the demand for labor; (2) restrict the supply of labor; or (3) impose an above-equilibrium wage floor on the market. Let us consider each of these strategies.

Increase the Demand for Labor. From the perspective of a labor union, the most preferable technique for increasing wages is to increase the demand for labor. As seen in Figure 7.3(*a*), an

Figure 7.3 | Unions' Methods of Increasing Wages

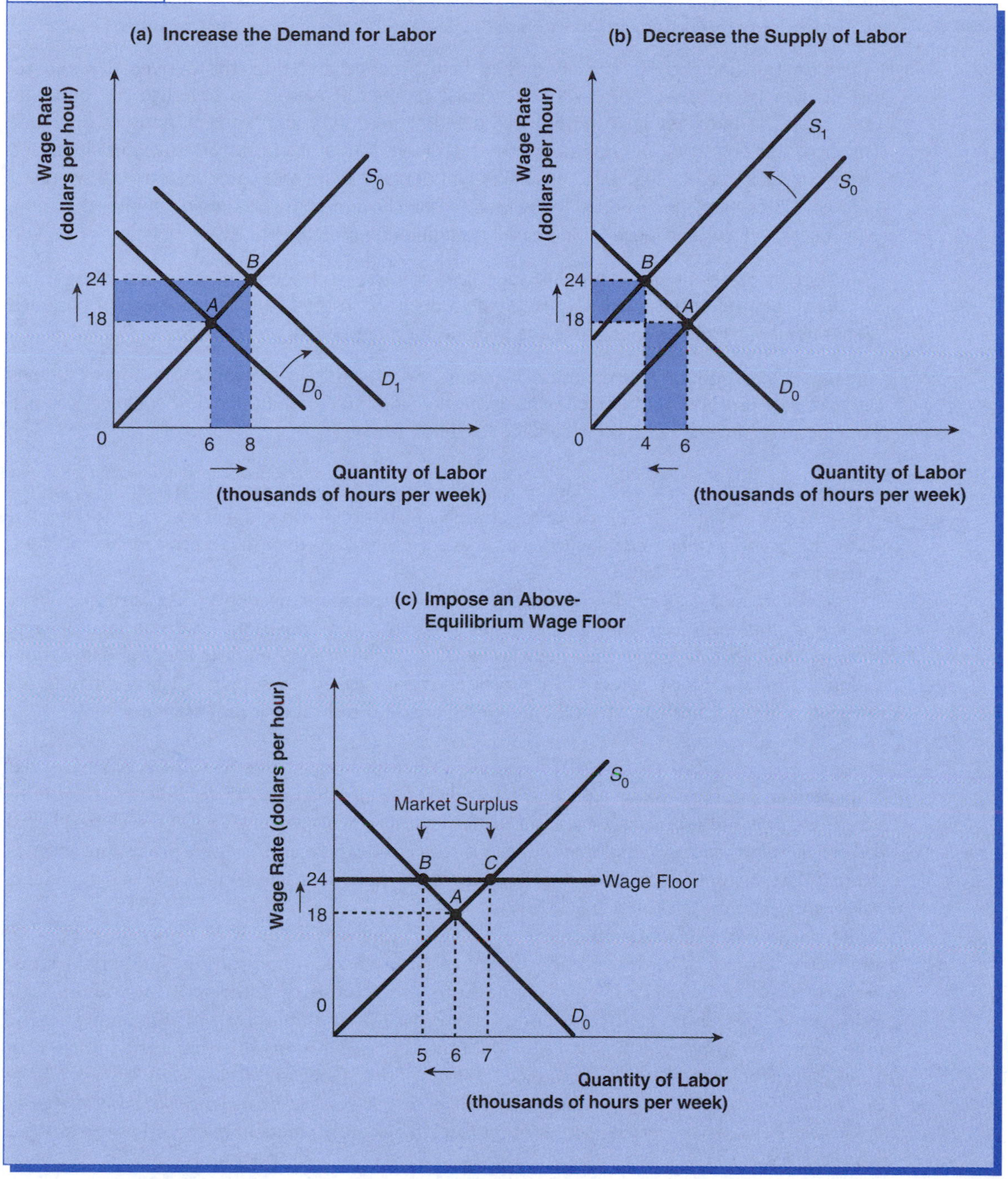

(a) Increase the Demand for Labor

Wage Rate (dollars per hour)

S_0

24
18

B
A

D_0 D_1

0   6 8

Quantity of Labor
(thousands of hours per week)

(b) Decrease the Supply of Labor

Wage Rate (dollars per hour)

S_1 S_0

24
18

B
A

D_0

0   4 6

Quantity of Labor
(thousands of hours per week)

(c) Impose an Above-Equilibrium Wage Floor

Wage Rate (dollars per hour)

Market Surplus

S_0

B   C
A

24 ─────────────── Wage Floor
18

0
D_0

5 6 7

Quantity of Labor
(thousands of hours per week)

From the perspective of a union, the most preferable method of increasing wages is to increase the demand for labor. An increase in the demand for labor causes an increase in both the wage rate and the quantity of labor demanded. Another way to increase wages is to restrict the supply of labor. Workers who keep their jobs receive higher incomes, but fewer workers are employed. A successful industrial union will impose an above-equilibrium wage floor on the market for its members. Although the wage hike will increase the incomes of those members having jobs, some members may be priced out of the market.

increase in the demand for labor causes an increase in both the wage rate and the quantity of labor demanded. Employment and incomes thus rise for union members, a most favorable outcome.

Unions adopt several strategies to increase the demand for the labor of their members:

- **Increase the demand for the good they help produce and thus the derived demand for their own labor services.** One way to increase product demand is to advertise and persuade the public to purchase only those goods manufactured by union workers. Another approach might be to pressure Congress to impose restrictive tariffs or quotas on, say, steel imported from South Korea, so that U.S. consumers will demand more steel produced by U.S. workers. Moreover, teachers' unions often lobby for increased government spending on public education, and aerospace workers push for increased spending on national defense.

- **Support increases in the minimum wage laws to increase the cost of unskilled labor.** A rise in the wage rate of unskilled labor results in a decrease in the quantity demanded of unskilled labor demanded and an increase in the demand for more skilled, union workers.

- **Increase the productivity of union members.** By establishing grievance procedures, unions may reduce turnover and promote stability in the workforce—conditions that enhance workers' productivity, thus increasing the demand for union workers.

Decrease the Supply of Labor. Another way of promoting wage increases is to restrict the supply of labor. As seen in Figure 7.3(*b*), a decreased supply of labor results in a higher wage rate, although it reduces the quantity of labor demanded. Those workers who keep their jobs receive higher incomes, but fewer workers are employed.

Craft unions, such as bricklayers and electricians, often adopt restrictive membership policies such as high initiation fees, long apprenticeship programs, and limitations on union membership. *Professional associations,* such as the American Bar Association or the American Medical Association, are similar to craft unions in terms of their restrictive impact on the supply of labor. Entry into a profession is limited through certification requirements and control over professional schools.

Impose an Above-Equilibrium Wage Floor. Rather than organizing the workers of a particular occupation, an *industrial union* represents all workers in a specific industry, regardless of their skills or craft. Examples of industrial unions are the United Auto Workers (UAW) and the United Postal Workers. Similarly, public employee unions represent the workers in a given profession, such as teaching. The National Education Association, for example, is a powerful union that represents teachers throughout the United States.

The purpose of an industrial union or a public employee union is to bring all workers in an industry into a union, thus putting them in a strong bargaining position. Industrial unions must also organize workers at most of the firms in an industry. Otherwise, nonunion firms might gain a cost advantage by paying lower wages to their employees and thus undersell the union-organized firms. In practice, industrial unions may fail to organize an entire industry. In automobiles, for example, the UAW has organized Ford, General Motors, and Chrysler—the "Big Three" of the U.S. auto industry—as well as several foreign firms with assembly plants in the United States. However, workers at other foreign assembly plants have chosen not to affiliate with the UAW.

Figure 7.3(*c*) shows the impact of the UAW on the market for autoworkers. The competitive wage and employment levels are $18 per hour and 6,000 hours of labor demanded per week, respectively, as seen at point *A* in the figure. Suppose that the UAW organizes the U.S. Big Three auto companies and bargains for a wage rate of $24 per hour. The bargained wage rate has the effect of imposing an above-equilibrium wage floor imposed on the labor market. Although the wage hike results in increased incomes for those workers who remain employed, the quantity of labor demanded falls from 6,000 hours to 5,000 hours per week. The push for higher wages thus prices some workers out of a job. Generally, unions adhere to the policy of "last hired, first fired." Workers with the least amount of seniority are the first ones to lose their jobs. Also, the higher wage increases the quantity supplied of labor to 7,000 hours per week, resulting in a surplus of labor equal to 2,000 hours per week.

What Gives a Union Strength?

Not all unions are able to increase the wages of their members. What factors allow unions to obtain large wage increases while suffering only modest reductions in employment?

If nonunion workers are good substitutes for union workers, an employer may turn to these substitutes and reduce its demand for union labor as it becomes more costly. Higher union wages will therefore price union workers out of the market, resulting in a sharp decline in their employment. For this reason, unions lobby against liberal immigration policies and the importation of goods produced by foreign workers. Unions have also attempted to obtain contracts with a **union shop** provision. This provision requires that all employees join the recognized union within a specified length of time (usually 30 days) after their employment with the firm begins. Each state has the option to accept or reject union shops.

Besides substituting nonunion for union labor, firms may substitute other factors of production for union workers as their wages are pushed upward. For example, General Motors may automate some production operations, replacing people with robots. When machines are good substitutes for labor, the bargaining power of labor declines.

The strength of a union also depends on the number of substitutes that are available for the product that its members help produce. For example, during the 1980s the U.S. trucking industry was deregulated in an attempt to foster additional competition and the more efficient use of resources. Unionized firms in the trucking industry therefore began to compete with nonunion firms having lower labor costs. The labor-cost advantage allowed many nonunion trucking firms to slash prices in order to win a larger share of the market. The result was a decline in the market share of unionized trucking firms and a loss of more than 100,000 jobs for Teamsters' members. The sharp decline in employment eventually led the union to agree to a 30-percent cutback in wages and fringe benefits in an attempt to save jobs.

The experience of the U.S. auto industry illustrates how nonunion workers can threaten the employment levels and wage structures of union workers. For decades, the UAW has represented workers at the U.S. Big Three—Ford, GM, and Chrysler—whose factories are located in the northern states where the UAW is strong. Being an effective bargainer, for decades the UAW pushed its members' wages above the levels of the average American manufacturing worker. By the 1980s, however, nonunion Japanese companies had established automobile assembly plants in the southern part of the United States, where unions are not strong. Lower wages combined with more efficient workers have given the Japanese a labor-cost advantage in the production of automobiles. This has allowed them to capture an increasing share of the U.S. auto market, causing fewer sales for the U.S. Big Three and job losses for UAW members. As the number of nonunion workers in the auto industry grows, the UAW's power to set wages and working conditions is weakened.

CHECK POINT

1. Explain why an increase in the minimum wage may be beneficial to some workers but harmful to others.

2. How might an increase in labor productivity offset the adverse effects of a higher minimum wage?

3. Identify the methods that labor unions use to increase the wages of their members. Which method is most preferable to a union?

4. What factors underlie the ability of a union to increase the wages of its members?

OUTSOURCING OF JOBS: THREAT OR OPPORTUNITY FOR U.S. WORKERS?

In recent discussions about jobs, attention has focused on international trade and terms such as "outsourcing" The concern is that a free-trade environment allows good jobs to drain from the U.S. economy, sending them to China, India, and other countries where workers command much lower salaries. In the extreme, some would like to see restraints on trade to protect those jobs and halt the globalization trend. Let us consider the nature and effects of outsourcing.

In its broadest sense, **outsourcing** is simply the contracting out of functions that once were done in-house, a longtime practice. When a car manufacturer in Michigan buys brake pads from an intermediate supplier in Ohio rather than producing them in-house, that's outsourcing. When a company replaces its cleaning and cafeteria workers with an outside contractor that performs the same services more cheaply, that's outsourcing. Clearly, outsourcing can result in job losses if the outside supplier is more efficient and uses fewer workers.

Instead of turning to domestic providers, firms may decide to purchase a good or service from an overseas provider because of lower costs. Outsourcing, too, has a long history in U.S. manufacturing; for example, firms in Mexico supply seat covers and wiper blades to Detroit automakers. What is new about outsourcing is its effect on workers in the service sector who never expected to see foreign competition for their jobs—data managers, computer programmers, medical transcribers, and the like.[4]

What Prevents U.S. Jobs from Being Outsourced Abroad?

In today's global economy, job security is a vital concern for many workers. Indeed, many Americans fear that U.S. companies will relocate production to Mexico, Malaysia, Singapore, or other developing countries where wages are much lower than in the United States. Thus, U.S. workers will be displaced by, say, Mexican workers.

Although this concern is real, can we be sure that jobs will flow to countries with low wages? Suppose that you are the manager of El Paso Radio Co., a firm located in the United States. Wouldn't you want to locate your assembly plant in Mexico, where labor is cheaper? The answer is that firms are interested in more than just the wages that they must pay to workers. They are also interested in the marginal product of labor in different nations.

For example, suppose that a typical radio assembler in the United States earns $9 per hour and a radio assembler in Mexico earns $4 per hour. Also assume that the marginal product of the U.S. assembler is 18 radios per hour and that the marginal product of the Mexican assembler is 4 radios per hour. Therefore, we have higher productivity in the United States but lower wages in Mexico. Where will the El Paso Radio Co. locate its assembly plant?

It will locate its plant in the United States because more radios are produced per every dollar paid to labor than in Mexico. To illustrate, with a marginal product of 18 radios and a wage rate of $9 per hour, the U.S. worker assembles 2 radios per every dollar that he is paid (18 / 9 = 2). In contrast, with a marginal product of 4 radios and a wage rate of $4 per hour, the Mexican worker assembles 1 radio for every dollar that she is paid (4 / 4 = 1). Because the firm receives more output for every dollar spent on assemblers in the United States than in Mexico, the firm will find it less costly—and hence more profitable—to hire U.S. workers rather than Mexican workers. The conclusion is that even if U.S. wages are higher than Mexican wages, if U.S. labor is more productive than Mexican labor, U.S. labor can still be competitive.

---

4. Robert Parry, "Globalization: Threat or Opportunity for the U.S. Economy?" *Economic Letter*, Federal Reserve Bank of San Francisco, May 21, 2004, pp. 1–3.

The Effects of Outsourcing

Proponents of outsourcing emphasize how it can help increase productivity growth in the United States. For example, technologies such as computers and the Internet have made the U.S. service sector a candidate for outsourcing on a global scale. High-tech companies such as IBM can easily outsource software programming to India, and American medical centers are relying on Indian doctors to process data.

Proponents of outsourcing maintain that it can create a win-win situation for the global economy. Obviously, outsourcing benefits the recipient country, say, India. Some of its people work for, say, a subsidiary of Delta Air Lines of the United States and make telephone reservations for Delta's travelers. Moreover, incomes increase for Indian vendors supplying goods and services to the subsidiary, and the Indian government receives additional tax revenue. The United States also benefits from outsourcing in several ways:

- **Reduced costs and increased competitiveness for Delta,** which hires low-wage workers in India to make airline reservations. Whereas in the United States many of the outsourced jobs are viewed as relatively undesirable or of low prestige, in India they are often considered attractive. Thus, Indian workers may be highly motivated to outproduce their counterparts in the United States. Higher productivity of Indian workers leads to falling unit costs for Delta.

- **New exports.** As business expands, Delta's Indian subsidiary may purchase additional goods from the United States, such as computers and telecommunications equipment. These purchases result in increased earnings for U.S. companies such as Dell and AT&T and additional jobs for American workers.

Simply put, proponents of outsourcing contend that if U.S. companies cannot locate work abroad they will become less competitive in the global economy as their competitors reduce costs by outsourcing. This will weaken the U.S. economy and threaten more American jobs. They also note that job losses tend to be temporary and that the creation of new industries and new products in the United States will result in more lucrative jobs for Americans. As long as the U.S. workforce retains its high level of skills and remains flexible as companies improve their productivity, high-value jobs will not disappear in the United States.

Critics, however, note that if outsourcing were a limited practice driven by domestic scarcity of a few specific skills, the United States might benefit from outsourcing. However, outsourcing is a problem because many U.S. jobs in manufacturing and service industries can be transferred abroad. The higher the wages paid to Americans, the greater the incentive to outsource work to China or India, where enormous excess supplies of labor guarantee relatively low wages for years to come. Faith that new industries and occupations will arise to replace the lost ones is troublesome, because the same incentive will encourage replacement industries to be outsourced as well.

Of course, the benefits of outsourcing to the United States do not eliminate the burden on Americans who lose their jobs or find lower-wage ones because of foreign outsourcing. This is why American labor unions often lobby Congress to prevent outsourcing and several U.S. states have considered legislation to severely restrict their governments from contracting with companies that move jobs to low-wage developing countries. Indeed, getting the American public to accept outsourcing will likely require giving workers a safety net in the form of income assistance and training to qualify for the jobs being created in the United States. Education is the bedrock of the U.S. edge in productivity and technology is the key to producing workers with the flexibility to learn new skills as markets evolve.

DO LIBERAL IMMIGRATION LAWS HARM AMERICAN WORKERS?

Besides the outsourcing of jobs, immigration is a controversial issue for American workers. Historically, the United States has been a favorite target for international migration. Because of the vast inflow of migrants, the United States has been described as the "melting pot" of the world. Migrants are motivated by better economic opportunities and by noneconomic factors such as politics, war, and religion.

Although the migration of foreign workers into the United States can enhance the nation's productivity, many Americans prefer restrictions on immigration. They argue that open immigration tends to reduce their employment opportunities and wages. For example, responding to higher wages, low-skilled Mexican workers may migrate to the United States. This leads to a reduction in the Mexican labor supply and an increase in the U.S. labor supply. Wage rates fall in the United States while they rise in Mexico, which has an equalizing effect. In particular, U.S. labor unions tend to support restrictions on immigration because competition from foreign workers reduces their members' jobs and wages.

No substantial restrictions were placed on immigration into the United States until the passage of the Quota Law of 1921. This law set quotas on the number of immigrants based upon the country of origin. The Quota Law primarily restricted immigration from eastern and southern Europe. The Immigration and Nationality Act Amendments of 1965 eliminated the country-specific quota system and instead established a limit on the total number of immigrants allowed into the United States. Under this act, preferential treatment is given to those who immigrate for the purpose of family reunification. Those possessing exceptional skills are also given priority. No limit, however, is placed upon the number of political refugees allowed to immigrate into the United States. Not all immigrants, of course, enter the country through legal channels. Individuals often enter on student or tourist visas and begin working in violation of their visa status. Other individuals enter the country illegally without a valid U.S. visa. The Immigration Reform and Control Act of 1986 addressed the issue of illegal immigration by imposing substantial fines on employers that hire illegal immigrants.

The Illegal Immigration Reform and Immigrant Responsibility Act of 1996 imposed several new restrictions on immigration. Host families can now accept immigrants only if the host family's income is at least 125 percent of the poverty level. This act also requires that the Immigration and Naturalization Service maintain stricter records of entry and exit by nonresident aliens.

However, even the less-skilled immigrants contribute to our economy and our lives by working in jobs most Americans do not want, such as cleaning offices, cooking in restaurants, and ringing up purchases in the grocery store. They also buy homes, clothes, and groceries. The wonderful cultural diversity brought to the United States by immigrants has become secondary to their willingness to work hard and become part of today's America.

Moreover the infusion of foreigners into the United States does not include only people with minimal skills and education. The United States also reaps a bonanza of highly educated newcomers who enhance the competitiveness of its firms. America's high-tech industries, from biotechnology to semiconductors, depend on immigrant scientists, engineers, and entrepreneurs to remain competitive. In Silicon Valley, the jewel of U.S. high-tech centers, much of the workforce is foreign born. With their bilingual skills, family ties, and knowledge of how things are done overseas, immigrants also contribute to the export of made-in-the-USA goods and services. Moreover, they help revitalize America by establishing new businesses and generating jobs, profits, and taxes to pay for social services. These benefits must be weighed against the economic disruptions caused by the infusion of less-educated and less-capable people into the nation.

This chapter has examined the market for labor and the determination of wages. The next chapter will consider the role of government in the market economy.

economics
IN ACTION

Does Immigration Result in Lower Wages for Americans?

Has the immigration of foreign workers into the United States significantly decreased the wages of Americans? According to economists at the National Bureau of Economic Research, the wage effect of immigration is quite small. They investigated the wage effect of Mexican-origin immigrants into the United States during 1980–2000, and found that in the short run, immigration reduced the average wage of competing U.S. workers by 3 percent. For workers who dropped out of high school, the average wage fell by 8 percent. The economists also found that over the long run, the wage of the average competing American worker was not significantly affected by immigration, but the wage of high school dropouts still decreased by 5 percent. The results of the researchers' findings are summarized in Table 7.4.

These findings support the view that immigration has had only a small negative effect on the pay of America's least skilled workers. The implication of these findings is that if Congress desires to decrease wage inequality, establishing strict borders around the United States is a highly questionable way of going about it.

Table 7.4	Labor Markets Work: Wage Change Due to Immigration Influx, 1980–2000	
	Percentage Wage Change	
Labor Category	**Short Run**	**Long Run**
All workers	−3.3%	0.1%
High school dropouts	−8.2	−4.8
High school graduates	−2.2	1.1
Some college	−2.6	0.8
College graduates	−3.8	−0.5

Source: George Borjas and Lawrence Katz, *The Evolution of the Mexican-Born Workforce in the United States.* National Bureau of Economic Research, Cambridge, MA, 2005.

CHECK POINT

1. What methods do labor unions use to improve the economic well-being of their members?

2. What factors underlie the strength of a labor union?

3. Does outsourcing benefit American workers? Why are some workers fearful of outsourcing?

4. Although the United States has been described as the "melting pot" of the world, many Americans are fearful of liberal immigration policies. Why?

Chapter Summary

1. As in other markets, the forces of demand and supply underlie labor markets. The point of intersection of the labor demand and labor supply curves determines the equilibrium wage and level of employment. The demand for labor is derived from the demand for the product that labor helps produce.

2. In a competitive market, a firm will maximize profits by hiring workers up to the point at which the value of the marginal product of labor equals the wage rate. Moreover, the value of the marginal product curve of labor constitutes a firm's demand curve for labor.

3. Even if U.S. wages are higher than Mexican wages, if U.S. labor is more productive than Mexican labor, U.S. labor can still be competitive.

4. An increase in the market supply curve of labor causes the equilibrium wage to decrease and the quantity of labor demanded to increase. As the market demand curve for labor increases, both the equilibrium wage and the quantity of labor supplied increase.

5. To help the working poor, in 1938 Congress established a federal minimum wage, the smallest amount of money per hour that an employer may legally pay a worker. The minimum wage benefits workers who can find work at a wage level that exceeds the market equilibrium wage. However, it harms workers who seek employment at the higher wage, but cannot find jobs. To the extent that a higher wage causes labor to become more productive, the demand for labor increases, thus offsetting the unemployment effects caused by the minimum wage.

6. Labor unions use several strategies to increase the wages of their members: increase the demand for labor, restrict the supply of labor, and impose an above-equilibrium wage floor on the market. The ability of a union to increase the wages of its members is threatened by nonunion labor, by other factors of production (machinery) that may be substituted for labor, by the availability of good substitutes for the product that members help produce, and by a high labor share of production costs.

7. In the discussion about jobs, much attention has focused on outsourcing. The concern is that a free-trade environment allows good jobs to drain from the U.S. economy, sending them to China, India, and other countries where workers command much lower salaries.

8. Although the migration of foreign workers into the United States can enhance the nation's productivity, many Americans prefer restrictions on immigration. They argue that open immigration tends to reduce their employment opportunities and wages.

Key Terms and Concepts

derived demand (152)

minimum wage (155)

shock effect (157)

unions (157)

collective bargaining (158)

mediation (158)

arbitration (158)

strikes (158)

union shop (161)

outsourcing (162)

marginal product of labor (170)

value of the marginal product of labor (171)

demand curve for labor (171)

Self-Test: Multiple-Choice Questions

1. The ability of the United Steel Workers' union to increase the wages of its members is enhanced by a(n)
   a. decrease in the demand for steel by U.S. auto companies.
   b. decrease in tariffs on steel imported by the United States.
   c. elastic demand for the labor of U.S. steelworkers.
   d. inelastic demand for the labor of U.S. steelworkers.

2. By increasing the wages of their members, unions tend to
   a. cause employers to seek substitutes for union labor.
   b. increase the wages of nonunion workers.
   c. increase the productivity of all workers.
   d. shift the demand for labor to the right.

3. If the demand for labor in the United States is inelastic, the migration of workers from Mexico to the United States will
   a. decrease the total amount of wage earnings received by U.S. workers.
   b. increase the total amount of wage earnings received by U.S. workers.
   c. leave unchanged the total amount of wage earnings received by U.S. workers.
   d. cause the demand curve for U.S. workers to shift to the right.

4. In a competitive labor market, the demand curve for labor is the curve showing the
   a. value of the marginal product of labor.
   b. marginal physical product of labor.
   c. value of the total product of labor.
   d. total physical product of labor.

5. A rightward shift in the supply curve of labor would be caused by
   a. a reduction in the value of the marginal product of labor.
   b. lower available wages in other industries.
   c. quotas placed on the number of immigrants who can enter the country.
   d. a decrease in the total physical product of labor.

6. As an industrial union, the United Auto Workers would be most successful in improving the wages, jobs, and working conditions of its members if it could
   a. shift the supply curve of autoworkers to the right.
   b. unionize all the firms in the auto industry.
   c. initiate policies that cause the demand for autos to decrease.
   d. collect membership dues from all of its workers.

7. If the federal government imposes a minimum wage that is above the market equilibrium wage, we can expect a
   a. decrease in the wage costs of employers.
   b. decrease in the number of workers that participate in the labor market.
   c. shortage of labor.
   d. surplus of labor.

8. With a competitive market for aerospace workers, a reduction in the price of jetliners will result in
   a. lower employment and a lower wage.
   b. lower employment and a higher wage.

c. higher employment and a higher wage.
d. higher employment and a lower wage.

9. Assume that a union shop provision applies to the market for electricians. If the electricians' union reduced the supply of its members, all of the following will occur *except*

a. wages of union electricians will increase.
b. employment of union electricians will decrease.
c. the cost of construction projects will increase.
d. the demand for nonunion electricians will decrease.

10. Proponents of higher minimum wage laws maintain that they will

a. inspire workers to become more productive, thus increasing the demand for labor.
b. increase the mobility of workers among occupations that are subject to the minimum wage.
c. result in shortages of workers, which impose extra upward pressure on wages.
d. make less-skilled workers less desirable for part-time employment.

Answers to Multiple-Choice Questions

1. d   2. a   3. a   4. a   5. b   6. b   7. d   8. a   9. d   10. a

Study Questions and Problems

1. Draw a figure showing how the intersection of the market demand curve for labor and the market supply curve of labor determines the equilibrium wage rate and employment level. How are the equilibrium wage rate and employment level affected by

a. an increase (decrease) in the market supply curve of labor?
b. an increase (decrease) in the market demand curve for labor?

2. Explain how U.S. labor can be competitive with Mexican labor, even if U.S. wage rates are higher than Mexican wage rates.

3. Table 7.5 pertains to the hiring decision of Youngquist Strawberry Co., which hires workers and supplies strawberries in competitive markets.

Table 7.5   Labor Data for Youngquist Strawberry Co.

Labor Input (workers per week)	Total Product (boxes of berries per week)	Marginal Product of Labor (boxes of berries per week)	Product Price	Value of the Marginal Product of Labor
0	0			
1	100		$8	$
2	190		8	
3	270		8	
4	340		8	
5	400		8	
6	450		8	

a. Complete the remaining columns of the table.
b. In a figure, draw the firm's demand curve for labor.
c. If the wage rate is $560 per week, how many workers will the firm hire? What if the wage rate is $400 per week?

4. Table 7.6 shows the market for less-skilled workers.

a. In a figure, plot the market demand curve for labor and the market supply curve of labor. Find the equilibrium wage rate and the level of employment.
b. Suppose that the government enacts a minimum wage of $6 per hour. How much labor will be supplied and demanded at this wage rate? Will the level of employment be higher or lower than the employment level that exists in the absence of a minimum wage? By how much?
c. Suppose that the minimum wage inspires workers to become more productive. Draw a new demand curve for labor that results in the same level of employment as that which occurs in the absence of a minimum wage.

Table 7.6   **Market for Less-Skilled Labor**

Wage Rate (dollars per hour)	Quantity of Labor Supplied (thousands of hours)	Quantity of Labor Demanded (thousands of hours)
$1.00	10	70
2.00	20	60
3.00	30	50
4.00	40	40
5.00	50	30
6.00	60	20
7.00	70	10

5. In a figure, draw the market supply curve of labor and the market demand curve of labor. What techniques do labor unions use to raise their members' wages? Assuming these techniques succeed in raising wages, what effect do they have on the quantity of labor demanded? Show the effects graphically. Which technique is most favorable for a union?

6. What factors underlie the extent to which the UAW will, or will not, increase its demand for higher wages?

7. In a figure, draw the market supply curve and the market demand curve of autoworkers. Assume that the UAW organizes U.S. auto firms. In your figure, show the effects of the following situations:

a. The UAW imposes an above-equilibrium wage floor on the market for autoworkers.
b. Japanese firms export additional autos to the United States, which causes a decrease in the demand for domestic autos and also a decrease in demand for members of the UAW. Concerning jobs and wages, what options does the UAW have to minimize the adverse effects of the decreased demand for its members? What is the limitation of each option?

8. Explain verbally, and show graphically, why domestic workers may be apprehensive about liberal immigration policies.

EXPLORING FURTHER 7.1: A FIRM'S HIRING DECISION

Concerning a firm's demand curve for labor, consider how the Mt. Pleasant Apple Co., a typical apple producer, chooses the quantity of workers demanded. Suppose that the firm sells apples in a competitive market and thus cannot affect the price it gets for the sale of apples. Also assume that the firm hires workers in a competitive market and therefore has no influence on the wages it pays to apple pickers. Finally, assume that the firm is a profit maximizer—that is, it cares only about the difference between the total revenue obtained from the sale of apples minus the total cost of producing them.

When hiring apple pickers, Mt. Pleasant Apple Co. must know how much workers contribute to its output. Figure 7.4 gives a numerical example. Referring to Figure 7.4(a), the first column of the table shows the number of apple pickers. The second column shows the amount of apples harvested each week by the workers. The firm's production data suggest that one worker can harvest 90 boxes of apples per week, two workers can harvest 170 boxes, and so on. The third column in the table gives the **marginal product of labor**, the *additional* output from hiring each worker. When the firm increases the number of workers from, say, one to two, the amount of apples harvested rises from 90

Figure 7.4	Mt. Pleasant Apple Co.'s Demand Schedule for Labor

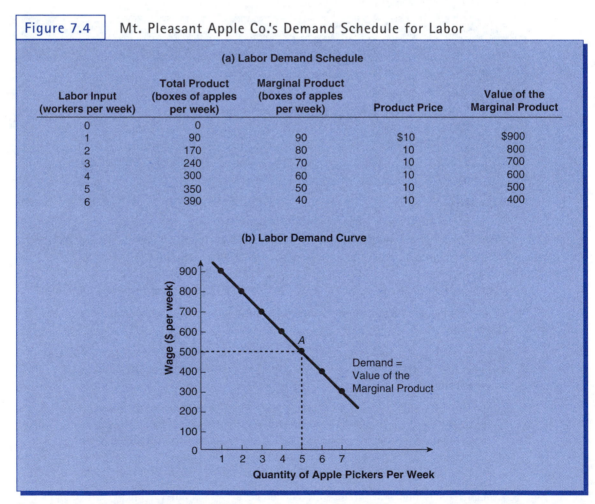

(a) Labor Demand Schedule

Labor Input (workers per week)	Total Product (boxes of apples per week)	Marginal Product (boxes of apples per week)	Product Price	Value of the Marginal Product
0	0			
1	90	90	$10	$900
2	170	80	10	800
3	240	70	10	700
4	300	60	10	600
5	350	50	10	500
6	390	40	10	400

(b) Labor Demand Curve

Demand = Value of the Marginal Product

A firm's demand schedule for labor is based on its value of marginal product schedule, which decreases as extra workers are employed.

boxes to 170 boxes. The marginal product of the second worker is thus 80 boxes (170 − 90 = 80). Similarly, the marginal product of the third worker is 70 boxes of apples (240 − 170 = 70), and so on. Consistent with the law of diminishing returns (discussed in Chapter 4), the marginal product decreases as the firm hires more workers. In this example, diminishing marginal productivity sets in with the first worker hired.

Besides needing to know about the amount of apples harvested by each additional worker, the Mt. Pleasant Apple Co. needs to know each worker's contribution to revenue. The **value of the marginal product of labor** is the increase in revenue that results from hiring an additional worker. In other words, the value of the marginal product is the dollar value of a worker's contribution to production.

We calculate the value of the marginal product by multiplying the marginal product of a worker by the price of apples. Referring to Figure 7.4(*a*), suppose that the price of apples is $10 per box. The value of the first worker's product equals $900, found by multiplying his marginal product by the price of apples (90 x $10 = $900). Similarly, the value of the second worker's productivity is $800 (80 x $10 = $800). The value of the marginal product schedule of labor is illustrated graphically in Figure 7.4(*b*).

How many workers should the Mt. Pleasant Apple Co. hire? The firm will hire additional labor as long as doing so adds more to revenue than to cost—that is, as long as the value of the marginal product is greater than the wage rate. The firm will stop hiring labor only when the two are equal. Suppose that the market wage is $500 per week. In this case, the first worker is profitable because the dollar value of his output ($900) is greater than the cost of hiring the worker ($500). Hiring the second worker, the third worker, and the fourth worker is also profitable because the dollar value of their additional outputs exceeds the wage rate. Hiring stops with the fifth worker because the value of her marginal product equals the wage rate. After the fifth worker, additional hiring is unprofitable. For example, the value of the sixth worker's marginal product is $400, but the wage rate is $500. Mt. Pleasant Apple Co. thus maximizes profits by hiring five workers. The conclusion is that a firm will hire workers up to the point at which the value of the marginal product of labor equals the wage rate.

The value of the marginal product of labor curve constitutes the firm's **demand curve for labor**. Recall that a labor demand curve shows the number of workers that the firm is willing to hire at each possible wage rate that might exist. The firm makes its hiring decision by selecting the quantity of labor at which the value of the marginal product of labor equals the prevailing wage. Therefore, when the wage rates and the amounts of labor that the firm is willing to hire at each rate are plotted in a graph, we have the firm's demand curve for labor.

Government and Markets

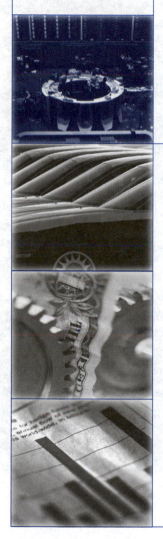

Chapter objectives

After reading this chapter, you should be able to:

1. Explain why markets sometimes fail to allocate resources efficiently.

2. Describe the nature and operation of antitrust policy.

3. Assess the advantages and disadvantages of economic regulation versus social regulation.

4. Explain why public utilities, such as electricity and cable television, have traditionally been provided an exclusive franchise to serve a local community.

5. Identify the factors that contribute to the failure of the market system.

economics IN CONTEXT

For decades, individuals have made tape recordings of live musical performances or musical performances sold on records, tapes, or CDs. These recordings were often copied and traded with friends and other collectors. However, taped copies were of a lower quality than the original, thus reducing the possibility for widespread copying of music files as an alternative to purchasing music from recording companies. By the late1990s, however, technological improvements made it possible to record music files from the Internet. As a result, musical recordings could be compressed into compact files that could be played back at near-CD quality.

In 1999, Shawn Fanning, a freshman at Northwestern University, introduced the Napster program and music service. Using the Internet, Napster allowed users to swap music files with other users of this service. Napster provided the software that users need to locate and download music files and maintained a central directory containing the addresses of computers that contained such files.

However, a significant share of the music traded through Napster involved illegal transfers of copyrighted music. In 2000, the Recording Industry of America initiated a lawsuit against Napster, claiming that the service was engaged in copyright violation. According to the music industry, Napster had no rights to its recordings and therefore was preventing the music industry from making money on its recordings. However, Napster argued that its

service allowed new musicians to distribute music to a wide audience at virtually no cost. Napster also argued that the existing system of music distribution provided the recording companies with a monopoly control over the distribution of a given artist's music. This resulted in high prices and profits for these companies, but only limited rewards to most musicians. Moreover, Napster contended it was difficult for new artists to break into the market under the existing system.

Agreeing with the music industry, the court ruled against Napster, shutting down the free distribution service that it provided. In spite of the Napster trial, the online distribution of music has become a low-cost alternative to the existing system of selling music on CDs and cassette tapes. The recording industry faces the challenge of developing a business model that will allow it to take advantage of the low-cost distribution mechanism provided by the Internet while remaining profitable. Apple Computer's iTunes Music Store, launched in 2003 (see Chapter 5), has become a viable business model.

In this chapter, we will examine the role of government in the market economy. As we will see, in some cases unregulated markets may not provide the best answers to the fundamental economic questions of society. Whenever that occurs, government intervention is needed to temper the market's operation and to make it conform to the interests of society.

MARKET FAILURE

The U.S. economy relies mainly on the market system to determine what goods and services are produced, in what quantities, and at what prices. Americans have generally accepted the market system as the most effective way of allocating resources to meet the needs and wants of households and families. The market system provides firms with strong incentives to produce the goods that consumers want at the lowest possible cost and to find innovative ways of meeting consumer demands. Firms that efficiently produce the goods that consumers desire will prosper; others will be driven out of business, and the resources they employ will be reallocated to more highly valued uses. The interaction among many producers and many consumers results in the production and consumption of an ideal quantity of each good. Markets are also flexible and accommodate change well. Changes in technology and consumer demands are quickly registered in the market, rearranging the types, prices, and quantities of goods and services that are offered for sale. The quest for profits encourages firms to develop new products and cheaper ways of producing existing products.

Some markets, however, fail to allocate resources efficiently—a situation called **market failure**. When a monopoly serves a market, for example, it makes output artificially scarce and sets the price higher than would occur in a more competitive market in order to maximize profits. In other markets, some people who are affected by the production or consumption of a good are not able to influence those choices. For example, a steel mill may ignore the pollution problems that it creates, or a toy manufacturer may not provide full information about the risks of using its product—information that consumers may need to make the best decision. Such market failures provide a legitimate reason for governments to consider intervening in the private sector through such means as regulation. Sources of market failure include the following:

- Monopoly power

- Spillovers or externalities

- Public goods

- Inadequate information

- Economic inequality

Let us consider the nature of these problems and then see why government intervention is desirable in each situation.

MONOPOLY POWER

Although competition generally results in the most efficient use of a nation's resources, an individual firm would prefer to conduct business in an environment that is more akin to monopoly. If allowed, some competing firms may attempt to create a monopoly environment by colluding with rivals, merging with rivals, or driving rivals out of business.

As we have learned, a monopoly tends to produce much less desirable outcomes than a competitive market. Given the same costs, a monopoly maximizes profit by selling a smaller output and charging a higher price than would a competitive market. Also, substantial barriers to entry may shelter a monopoly from the pressure of competition, meaning that the monopoly's costs are above their lowest possible level. The lack of competition also suggests that there is no external pressure for advancements in technology in monopoly. Simply put, monopoly results in market failure because the monopoly uses too few resources in order to produce goods at an artificially higher price.

Antitrust Policy

What can the government do to counteract monopoly power? One approach is to adopt a rigorous antitrust policy. **Antitrust policy** is the attempt to foster a market structure that will lead to increased competition and curb anticompetitive behavior that harms consumers. Antitrust laws are designed to prevent unfair business practices that restrain trade, such as price-fixing conspiracies, corporate mergers that are likely to reduce the competitive vigor of particular markets, and predatory acts that are designed to achieve or maintain monopoly power.

By the late 1800s, large corporations had begun to dominate many U.S. industries, including oil, railroads, and banking. These firms were run by the so-called robber barons, who attempted to drive competitors out of business, monopolize markets, and gouge consumers. They realized their monopoly power by forming *trusts,* the 19th-century name given to cartels and other business agreements intended to restrain competition. In the oil industry, for example, Standard Oil of New Jersey acquired small, competing firms and eventually accounted for 90 percent of sales in the domestic market. In tobacco, American Tobacco controlled up to 90 percent of the market for tobacco products.

Concern about the growing monopoly power of these firms prompted the federal government to intervene in the private-sector economy in order to prevent the acquisition and exercise of monopoly power and to encourage competition in the marketplace. These efforts culminated in the passage of the **Sherman Act of 1890,** the cornerstone of federal antitrust law. This act prohibits contracts and conspiracies in the restraint of trade as well as monopolization and the threat of monopolization of an industry. For example, conspiracies such as collusive agreements among competing sellers to fix prices and control markets are outlawed. Firms that are found in violation of the Sherman Act may be broken up, and the parties responsible for illegal conduct can be fined and imprisoned. Moreover, the parties harmed by illegal monopoly behavior can sue for three times the amount of monetary injury inflicted upon them.

Although the Sherman Act attempted to provide a solid foundation for government action against business monopolies, its vague language allowed the courts wide latitude in interpreting its meaning. The **Clayton Act of 1914** was enacted to make explicit the intent of the Sherman Act. The Clayton Act outlaws price discrimination, certain types of mergers, and tying (exclusive) contracts between a supplier and a buyer that substantially lessen competition. It also prohibits interlocking boards of directors among competing companies.

The U.S. Department of Justice and the Federal Trade Commission enforce the antitrust laws. The Justice Department is exclusively responsible for enforcing the Sherman Act and, with the Federal Trade Commission, it is responsible for enforcing the Clayton Act. The majority of antitrust cases initiated by these agencies are settled by an agreement between the government and the defendant. This saves the federal government time and money.

Microsoft provides an example of a firm that has violated the antitrust laws. In 1998 the U.S. Department of Justice filed antitrust charges against Microsoft under the Sherman Act. The government maintained that Microsoft engaged in anticompetitive tactics intended to maintain its monopoly in its Windows line of operating systems for personal computers. Microsoft refuted the accusations, maintaining that its success was due to its superior product innovations and legal business behavior. It also noted that its 95-percent share of the software market was temporary due to rapid improvements in technology that would occur in the near future. In 2000 the court ruled that Microsoft was guilty, not because of its dominant market position, but because it used illegal methods of preserving its monopoly power. Among these practices were contracts that Microsoft forced commercial users of its operating system to sign that penalized them for promoting operating systems that competed with Microsoft's product. The final court ruling prevented Microsoft from retaliating against any firm that developed, sold, or used operating systems that competed with Microsoft's Windows system. Also, Microsoft had to pay more than $1 billion in fines to the government and payouts to firms that were adversely affected by its illegal business practices.

ECONOMIC REGULATION AND DEREGULATION

Is the best approach to improving the performance of markets the vigorous enforcement of the antitrust laws? Or should we consider more extreme intervention in the marketplace? If market forces fail to establish prices that are equal to the cost of production, why not enact direct government regulation and mandate that prices be set this way?

Besides using antitrust laws to regulate business behavior, the federal government can enact **economic regulation** to control the prices, wages, conditions of entry, standards of service, or other important economic characteristics of particular industries. Industries that have been subject to economic regulation have included airlines, trucking, railroads, banking, communications, and energy.

Industries were originally made subject to economic regulation for many and varied reasons. For example, the natural monopoly enjoyed by industries with large economies of scale made meaningful competition impossible. In other instances, fear of "destructive competition" provided the primary rationale for regulation. Extending the scope of service was yet another aim behind government intervention.

By the late 1970s, however, the tide of opinion was turning against economic regulation. It became obvious that the growth of the economy and technological progress had eroded many former natural monopolies, converted nascent industries into mature ones, and created conditions conducive to reliable competitive services. Because the existing economic regulations were applicable to outdated economic conditions, it was time for a change.

Recognizing the problems of economic regulation, in the late 1970s the federal government initiated steps to dismantle regulations in several industries in which the existing regulations had outlived their usefulness—airlines, trucking, railroads, energy, telecommunications, and banking. The purpose of such **deregulation** was to increase price competition and provide incentives for companies to introduce new products and services. Economic research has shown that by making markets work better, deregulation has led to technical and operating innovations that have been accompanied by price reductions for consumers.

Public–Utility Regulation

Economic regulation involves the regulation of public utilities such as electricity, gas pipelines, telephones, and cable television. Rather than promoting competition in these industries through the use of antitrust laws, the U.S. government has traditionally allowed public utilities to operate as private monopolies subject to government regulation of price and output policies. Some nations have tried government ownership as an alternative; but with few exceptions, these have proved to be less effective than private ownership and regulation.

Usually, the reason that governments resort to regulating a monopoly rather than promoting competition through antitrust policy is that the industry in question is believed to be a *natural monopoly*—an industry in which product demand can be supplied most efficiently by a single firm. In such cases, the judgment may be made that competition is not workable and that the market is best served by a single monopoly firm that can fully exploit the advantage of economies of scale, but would be prevented from exercising monopoly power over customers by price regulation.

Figure 8.1 shows the hypothetical cost and revenue curves for Dallas Power and Light Co., which is assumed to be a natural monopolist in the electricity industry. As an unregulated monopolist, Dallas Power and Light Co. would maximize profits by applying the familiar $MR = MC$ rule. Referring to Figure 8.1(*a*), the firm's price and output of electricity would thus be 10 cents per kilowatt-hour (kWh) and 6 million kWh, respectively. Because price exceeds average total cost at 6 million kWh, the firm realizes an economic profit.

Suppose that the legislature decides to impose public-utility regulation on Dallas Power and Light Co. In addition to overseeing service and entry into and exit from the industry, public-utility regulation determines the price of the monopolist. Legislatures have traditionally allowed regulated firms to receive a **fair-return price**—that is, the firm can charge a price that is just high enough to cover its average total cost. In our example, Dallas Power and Light Co. will set its price at the point where its demand curve intersects its average total cost curve; the fair-return price is thus 7 cents per kWh. Recall that average total costs include a "normal" or "fair" profit. Although fair-return regulation eliminates the excess profit for Dallas Power and Light Co., it allows the firm to earn a fair profit for its stockholders.

But what type of costs should be included in the average total cost of Dallas Power and Light Co.? When economists construct average total cost curves such as the one in Figure 8.1(*b*), and conclude

Figure 8.1 | Public–Utility Regulation of Natural Monopoly

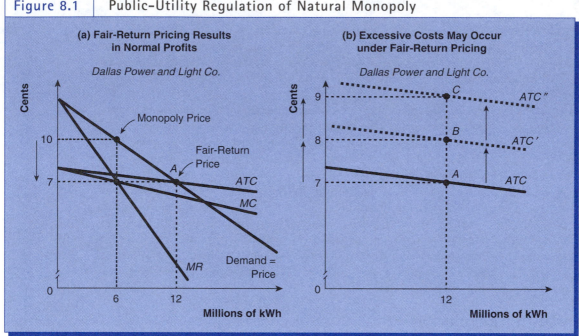

As an unregulated monopolist, Dallas Power and Light Co. would maximize profits by charging 10 cents per kilowatt-hour (kWh) of electricity. Public-utility commissioners would typically require the firm to charge a price of 7 cents, the fair-return price. Although this eliminates excess profit, the firm can still earn a normal profit for its stockholders. Critics of fair-return pricing contend that it reduces incentives for public utilities to innovate or to contain costs because the firm realizes essentially the same profit regardless of its efforts.

that, for 12 million kWh of electricity, it costs 7 cents per unit to provide electricity, they are referring to only the least possible cost. It is possible to produce 12 million kWh at 8 cents or 9 cents—as shown by points *B* and *C* in the figure.

Cost curves are drawn as they are because we usually assume that profit-seeking firms will use the most efficient methods available. In situations in which public-utility regulators set rates that cover average total cost, however, the incentive to hold costs down may not be very great. What is to prevent the managers from awarding themselves large salaries and forcing the customers to foot the bill? Should the utility be allowed to charge prices that cover obviously foolish expenditures such as the purchase of fuel from one supplier at a price twice as high as other suppliers? In short, fair-return regulation tends to reduce the incentives for public utilities to innovate or to contain costs, because the firm realizes essentially the same profits regardless of its efforts.

Although the regulation of public utilities can result in economic inefficiency, so can deregulation as seen in the case of California's electricity market.[1] For decades, government officials in California regulated the price and output policies of electric utilities. However, critics maintained that because the utilities could easily pass on costs to customers, they lacked incentives to produce electricity cheaply. Paying 50 percent more for power than their counterparts in other states, California businesses pushed for the deregulation of electric utilities as a way of providing market incentives to reduce cost. In 1996, California restructured its electricity industry, allowing consumers to obtain power from out-of-area (often out-of-state) suppliers. As a result, many local utilities sold their power

1. "Power Struggle," *Fedgazette*, Federal Reserve Bank of Minneapolis, January 2001, pp. 1–3.

generation plants, purchased power on the wholesale market from other suppliers, and resold it to their retail customers. By breaking the power-generation monopoly of local utilities, state officials anticipated decreases in electricity costs.

However, California's policy had a major flaw: It resulted in only *partial* deregulation rather than the complete deregulation of electric utilities. Although state officials tried to provide consumers with access to cheap electricity by freezing the retail price, the wholesale price was not regulated; it varied according to changing conditions in the national market. When rising electricity costs pushed the wholesale price above the frozen retail price, many California utilities suffered losses. Simply put, California's partial deregulation of electricity was not generally viewed as a success.

Peak-Load Pricing: Buying Power by the Hour

Another aspect of public-utility pricing involves peak-load pricing. For decades, power economists have recognized that consumers do not have an incentive to conserve electricity at times when they should conserve. To promote the conservation of electricity, many utilities have enacted a variable pricing system called **peak-load pricing** or time-of-use pricing. To understand how peak-load pricing works, let us first consider the costs of producing electricity.

Producing electricity entails fixed costs and variable costs. Fixed costs mainly consist of the costs of electric power generators, the costs of the plants that house them, and the costs of transmission lines. These costs do not vary with changes in electricity production. Variable costs include the costs of labor, coal, natural gas, and diesel fuel. As more power is produced, more of these inputs are needed to operate the generators.

For a typical utility, fixed costs are very high relative to total costs in electricity production. Also, power plants generally operate most of the time with a large amount of excess capacity. Therefore, customers who buy power during the peak periods cause electric companies to incur very high costs—the cost of constructing and operating generators that are used only during the peak period and that stay idle at other times.

Moreover, the variable costs of producing electricity change substantially throughout the day. During the night, the demand for electricity is smallest, and the variable costs of producing electricity are lowest because the utility uses very efficient plants that operate 24 hours a day. These plants use coal or nuclear fuel to boil water to turn the electrical turbines, which take a long time to rev up. As demand climbs, say around midafternoon on a summer afternoon, additional plants—which are more expensive to operate—are called into operation to supply power for people's air conditioners. These "peak-load" plants usually use gas turbines that run on exhaust gases instead of boiling water. Although they can be brought online almost instantly, they use expensive fuels (diesel and natural gas). The variable costs of providing peak service are thus greater than those of providing off-peak service.

Apparently, those who purchase electricity during the middle of the night should pay a lower price per kWh than those who purchase electricity during the afternoon. But often, they do not. Most of us pay a constant price per kWh regardless of whether we use expensive hours or cheap ones. Thus, we have no reason to conserve power during hours of high demand. Peak-load pricing changes all of this.

With peak-load pricing, prices reflect the difference in the cost of providing electricity during peak hours and off-peak hours. Therefore, consumers are charged more for electricity during peak demand periods when it costs more to provide power. The higher price encourages consumers to switch part of their usage to the cheaper off-peak periods. The shift in demand is achieved in several ways. For example, people may purchase timers that operate air conditioners, water heaters, and space heaters only during off-peak periods. Similarly, they may avoid using washing machines, clothes dryers, and dishwashers during peak periods. The effect of such consumption shifts is that a utility can serve its customers with much smaller generating capacity.

The state of Wisconsin provides an example of peak-load pricing for electricity. In 2009, Wisconsin households had the option of purchasing all of the electricity they needed during a week at a fixed price of 10 cents per kWh hour. They could also choose electricity under a peak-load option. From Monday through Friday, the price of electricity purchased during the off-peak period (8 P.M. to 8 A.M.) was 5 cents per kWh; a price of 19 cents per kWh was charged for purchases during the peak period (8 A.M.to 8 P.M.). The off-peak price was also applied to weekend consumption of electricity. The large differential between the peak and off-peak prices provided considerable motivation for households to shift consumption to the off-peak times of the day.

CHECK POINT

1. How does monopoly power contribute to market failure?

2. How do the Sherman and Clayton Acts attempt to combat monopoly power?

3. Why have public utilities traditionally been granted an exclusive franchise to serve a local community? Identify the problems of public-utility regulation.

4. How does peak-load pricing attempt to spread the available power around throughout the day?

SPILLOVER EFFECTS

We have learned that monopoly power can result in market failure. Another source of market failure involves what economists refer to as spillover effects.

A **spillover,** or **externality**, is a cost or benefit imposed on people other than the producers and consumers of a good or service. For example, if a smelter pollutes the air or water, and neither the firm nor its customers pay for the harm that pollution causes, the pollution becomes a **spillover cost** for society. In some cases, however, spillovers can be desirable. For example, the development of laser technology has had beneficial effects far beyond whatever gains its developers captured, improving products in industries as diverse as medicine and telecommunications. Laser technology is an example of a **spillover benefit**.

How does the market system fail when the production of a good or service entails spillover effects? When the production of some good results in spillover *costs, too much* of it is produced and resources are *overallocated* to its use. Conversely, *underproduction* and *underallocation* of resources arise from spillover *benefits*. Let us show these conclusions graphically.

Spillover Costs

How can spillover costs cause failure in a market for chemicals? Referring to Figure 8.2, the market demand curve for chemicals is shown by D_0 and S_0 denotes the market supply curve. Notice that the market supply curve includes the firms' private marginal costs of producing chemicals, such as labor and material costs. In equilibrium, 900 pounds of chemicals are sold at a price of $80.

Now suppose that the production of chemicals results in toxic wastes. If firms can dump these wastes into the waterways and thus pass their pollution costs on to the public, their private marginal costs of producing chemicals are lower. Referring to Figure 8.2, market supply curve S_0 includes only the firms' private marginal costs of producing chemicals. Therefore, it lies too far to the right of a supply curve that includes all costs (both private costs and spillover costs of pollution). This means that the equilibrium output, 900 pounds, exceeds the optimal output of 700 pounds. Simply put, the market supply curve does not reflect all of the costs resulting from the production of chemicals.

| Figure 8.2 | Correcting for Market Failure: Spillover Costs |

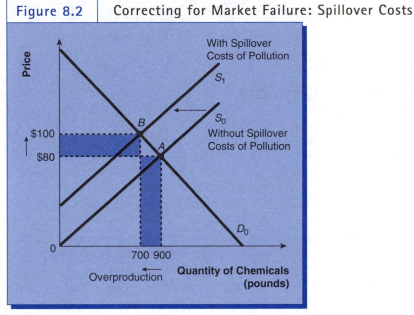

In the case of pollution, market failure occurs when firms fail to account for spillover costs. As a result, too much output is produced at too low a price. To correct this market failure, the government could require firms to install pollution-abatement equipment or pay a tax on pollution.

Therefore, the market produces too many chemicals and thus overallocates resources to their production.

How can the government force the market to decrease its pollution? The approach that has dominated public policy in the United States to date involves **command-and-control regulations** that impose restrictions on the amount of the polluting activity that can occur, as well as stipulate how the goal will be fulfilled. Clean air and water laws restrict the amount of pollutants that firms can place into the air, rivers, and lakes. Moreover, toxic-waste legislation specifies special procedures and dump sites for the disposal of contaminated solvents and soils.

By mandating that chemical firms be responsible for pollution abatement, such laws increase the firms' private marginal cost of production. In Figure 8.2, the market supply curve thus shifts from S_0 to S_1. The price of chemicals rises from $80 to $100, and the equilibrium output falls from 900 pounds to 700 pounds. In this manner, the overallocation of resources to chemical production is corrected.

Another way to reduce spillover costs is to establish **incentive-based regulations**, which set an environmental objective but are flexible because producers can find different ways to achieve the objective. Companies that are unable to fulfill the objective pay penalties in the form of taxes, but they are not rewarded for exceeding the objective. For example, the government may levy an excise tax on the production of chemicals in order to encourage firms to reduce pollution. Facing this tax, firms must decide whether to pay it or expend additional funds to develop new methods to reduce pollution. In either case, the tax will increase the private marginal cost of producing chemicals, again shifting the market supply curve from S_0 to S_1 in Figure 8.2. Any tax revenue resulting from the regulations could be used to compensate those harmed by the pollution.

Economists generally favor incentive-based regulations over command-and-control regulations. The main problem with command-and-control regulations is that regulators lack the detailed knowledge of individual production facilities and processes and of alternative production and abatement methods that would be necessary to implement an efficient regulatory program through command and control. It can also be costly to monitor and enforce the regulations. However, incentive-based regulations make it profitable for firms to develop the most efficient techniques to reduce pollution.

Cap and Trade Emission Certificates Clear Skies of Acid Rain

The trading of pollution certificates provides an example of incentive-based regulations on the environment. As part of a science project, sixth-grade students at Glens Falls Middle School in New York removed 330 tons of sulfur dioxide from the air. Conducting bake sales, raffles, and auctions over a 3-year period, they raised $25,000 to purchase 330 pollution certificates through the acid-rain-emissions trading program of the U.S. Environmental Protection Agency (EPA). Each certificate allows the owner to emit 1 ton of sulfur dioxide into the air. Public utilities trade the certificates—some purchase them to comply with air-quality regulations, whereas others sell them for a profit. However, the sixth-graders decided to keep these certificates so that the air would be that much cleaner.

Known as a **cap and trade system**, the trading of pollution certificates is a market-oriented solution to the problem of pollution. Under this system, the EPA sets a cap on the total amount of the pollutant it will allow in the air. This amount is divided into units. The EPA then issues a limited number of certificates, each certificate giving the holder—say, an electric utility—the right to produce a unit of pollution. Such certificates are sold by the EPA at auction. The certificates are tradable, so firms that find ways to emit less pollution than they are entitled to can sell some of their certificates to others. The EPA auction and the private resale market thus establish a price on the use of the environment. The more pollution a user engages in, the more certificates it must buy, thus raising its costs of production. Because consumers will buy less of the product that becomes more costly, the polluter has an incentive to use cleaner technologies in place. The program does not tell power producers how to reduce pollution; rather, they are free to choose the most cost-effective method for achieving reductions. Simply put, the cap and trade system promotes conservation by increasing the price of goods whose production harms the environment.

By giving polluters a financial incentive to reduce pollution in the least expensive possible way, emissions trading decreases the costs of environmental protection. Firms with high pollution-control costs can buy permits from firms with low pollution-control costs. Thus, firms find it profitable to reduce their emissions and sell their surplus permits. Therefore, greater responsibility for reducing pollution is allocated to those firms that can do so at the least expense. Moreover, conservation groups also have a direct method of affecting the environment. They can buy and hold some of the pollution certificates, thereby directly reducing the amount of pollution allowed and increasing the cost of pollution.

Emissions trading encourages firms to hunt for the most cost-efficient ways to reduce pollution. For Milwaukee-based Wisconsin Electric Power Co., the 1995 EPA limit meant that it had to reduce sulfur-dioxide emissions from its five power plants by about 30,000 tons. The company calculated that it could remove 20,000 tons relatively cheaply by switching to low-sulfur coal. Removing the remaining 10,000 tons would be difficult. The firm would have to purchase two $130 million machines called "scrubbers." Because other electric utility companies had decreased their emissions well below the EPA's limit, the market was flooded with cheap pollution certificates. Wisconsin Electric Power Co. then bought 10,000 certificates, resulting in cost savings of more than $100 million.

During President Barack Obama's first term in office, he proposed that a cap and trade system be widely used throughout the United States to reduce pollution. At the writing of this text, it remains to be seen if this system will be adopted.

| Figure 8.3 | Correcting for Market Failure: Spillover Benefits |

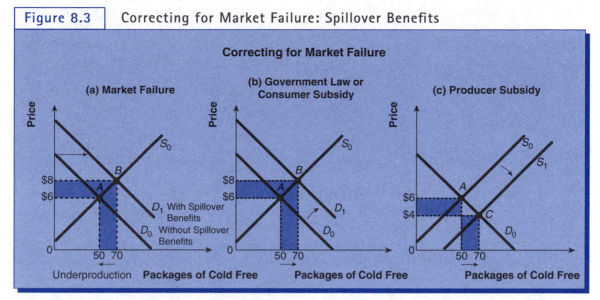

With spillover benefits, market failure occurs because the market demand curve does not reflect the spillover benefits of a good. As a result, the good is underproduced and underconsumed. The government could correct this market failure by requiring consumers to purchase additional units of the product, granting subsidies to consumers to finance purchases of the product, or subsidizing producers so that they could supply additional units of the product at a lower price.

Spillover Benefits

Recall that in the case of spillover costs, the market supply curve understates the total costs associated with the production of a good. Now we will see that the market demand curve understates the total benefits associated with the purchase and consumption of a good that entails spillover benefits.

Assume that a new drug, called "Cold Free," is developed; this drug cures the common cold. In Figure 8.3(a), the market demand curve, D_0, shows the price that private individuals would be willing to pay for Cold Free to receive the benefits of having fewer colds. The market supply curve, S_0, shows the quantity of Cold Free that is offered for sale at different prices. At equilibrium point A, 50 packages of Cold Free are sold at a price of $6.

Because of spillover benefits, however, this equilibrium point fails to achieve an optimum allocation of resources. Why? When buyers take Cold Free, other people who do not purchase the drug also benefit because the virus is less likely to spread. For society in general, taking Cold Free results in a healthier population, yielding widespread output and income benefits. The market demand curve, D_1, represents the private benefits from using Cold Free plus the extra, or spillover, benefits accruing to society in general. With market demand curve D_1, the optimal equilibrium at point B is established, shown by the intersection of D_1 and S_0. We conclude that with spillover benefits, the actual equilibrium output, 50 packages, is less than the optimal output, 70 packages. The market fails by not producing enough Cold Free and thus underallocating resources to its production.

How could the government prevent market failure in this instance? One approach would be for the government to require all citizens to purchase and use Cold Free each year. In Figure 8.3(b), such a policy would shift the market demand curve to the right, from D_0 to D_1. This explains why all children must receive diphtheria, tetanus, pertussis, polio, and other vaccines before entering primary school. Another solution would be for the government to provide subsidies to individuals to help them pay for the cost of Cold Free, again shifting the market demand curve to the right.

Alternatively, the government might grant subsidies to the producers of Cold Free. Such a subsidy would lower the producers' cost of production so that the market supply curve would increase from S_0 to S_1 in Figure 8.3(c). Producers could thus offer more Cold Free to consumers at a lower price.

In practice, subsidies are granted for a number of activities that yield spillover benefits. Education, for example, receives large subsidies. Students in public schools, from kindergarten through high school, receive an education that is virtually free. Moreover, the cost of a student's education at a state college or university is only partially paid for by student tuition and fees—the remainder comes from government tax dollars. The government also provides subsidies for public television and mass transit and medical programs, as well as for the construction of stadiums for professional sports. Are these subsidies justified?

SHOULD GOVERNMENT SUBSIDIZE PROFESSIONAL SPORTS?

Are large governmental subsidies of new sports stadiums a good investment for cities? Many professional sports teams have insisted that the local community grant subsidies to them if they are to operate in the community. For example, government funds are often used to finance a substantial portion of the construction or renovation of a sports stadium. Because all of the major sports leagues (baseball, football, basketball, and hockey) tightly control both the creation of new franchises and the relocation of teams, cities' demand for teams far exceeds the supply. Hence, the price that cities must pay to acquire teams has gone up. Table 8.1 provides examples of publicly financed sports stadiums and arenas.

Often, subsidies are justified on the grounds that attracting or retaining sports teams more than offsets itself in increased local tax revenue by creating new jobs and more spending. Also, local officials often view a downtown stadium project as an important part of the revitalization of the central city's urban core. Advocates of this approach point to Coors Field in Denver and Camden Yards in Baltimore as models of how stadium-based development can work.

However, researchers at the Brookings Institution have found that the promised stadium-driven booms generally turn out to be disappointments. At best, they have a tiny, and sometimes even a negative, impact on local employment. Whatever good may be achieved is more than canceled out by the cost of taxes levied to subsidize them. Looking at personal income trends in 37 cities over 26 years, Brookings found that sports stadiums actually reduce per-capita income in their hometowns.

Why? Subsidies for sports stadiums mean that taxes must rise or that local governments must reduce other spending. Those funds could have been used to dredge a harbor, fund education, or provide more police, all of which would make the economy more productive and produce more local spending than a stadium. Also, subsidized stadiums use taxpayer money to generate more wealth for owners and players, who do not tend to spend a large portion of their income in the local area. Meanwhile, the new facility siphons money away from other local establishments. When more people fill the seats in an expanded stadium, fewer dollars are spent on other entertainment, such as bowling, golf, or theater.[2]

Yet proponents of subsidies contend that the critics miss a basic issue: Professional sports teams add to residents' quality of life in cities that host teams. People may obtain benefits from having a local sports team even if they never go to a game. They root for local athletes, look forward to reading about their success or failure in the newspaper, and share in the citywide joy when the home team

2. Melvin Burstein and Arthur Rolnick, "Congress Should End the Economic War for Sports and Other Businesses," *The Region*, Federal Reserve Bank of Minneapolis, June 1996; Roger Noll and Andrew Zimbalist, eds., *Sports, Jobs, and Taxes: The Economic Impact of Sports Teams and Stadiums*, The Brookings Institution, Washington, DC, 1997; Raymond Keating, *Sports Pork: The Costly Relationship Between Major League Sports and Government*, Cato Institute, Washington, DC, 1999; Dennis Coates and Brad Humphreys, "The Stadium Gambit and Local Economic Development," *Regulation*, Vol. 23, No. 2, 2000; and Rodney Fort, *Sports Economics* (Upper Saddle River, NJ: Prentice Hall, 2003).

| Table 8.1 | Publicly Financed Sports Stadiums and Arenas | | |

City	Sport	Cost (millions)	Percentage of Public Funds
Cincinnati	Baseball	$334	91%
Pittsburgh	Baseball	262	85
San Antonio	Basketball	175	84
Milwaukee	Baseball	394	77
Denver	Football	400	75
Seattle	Baseball	517	72
Pittsburgh	Football	252	70
Seattle	Football	420	70

Source: Street and Smith's *SportsBusiness Journal,* March 27, 2000; May 8, 2000; and July 17, 2000.

wins a championship. If people benefit from having a pro sports franchise in their community, they are presumably willing to pay for it—if not directly through the purchase of tickets, then indirectly through higher taxes. Thus, residents should think of a pro sports team in the same way they think of a new art museum or new symphony hall that receives public subsidies.

Simply put, subsidy proponents maintain that professional sports yield spillover benefits that are similar to quality-of-life benefits such as clean air and scenic views. If the value of these spillover benefits is large enough, they alone might justify the subsidies that local taxpayers grant to teams. However, measuring these spillover benefits is difficult and subject to criticism.[3]

SOCIAL REGULATION

We have learned that government implements economic regulation by setting standards for prices, wages, conditions of entry, and standards of service in particular industries. Since World War II, the government has assumed an ever-increasing role in regulating the *quality of life* for society. **Social regulation** is intended to correct a variety of undesirable side effects in a market economy that relate to health, safety, and the environment—effects that markets, left to themselves, often ignore. Markets do not respond well to these problems, primarily because only a small fraction of the benefits gained from lessening these problems accrues to those who produce the side effects. Incentives to take action or to collect information leading to health, safety, and environmental improvements are thus lacking in the private business sector.

Whereas economic regulation governs the conditions of doing business in a particular industry, social regulation addresses the conditions under which goods are produced in a variety of industries. Social regulation applies to a particular issue (such as environmental quality) and affects the behavior of firms in many industries (such as automobiles, steel, or chemicals). Consider the following examples of social regulation:

- The Environmental Protection Agency regulates the amount of pollutants that firms can discharge into the air, lakes, and rivers.

- The Consumer Product Safety Commission removes dangerous products from the marketplace. It can also establish standards for product safety, such as controls that automatically shut off the engine of a lawnmower when the operator lets go of the handle.

3. Gerald Carlino and Edward Coulson, "Should Cities Be Ready for Some Football? Assessing the Social Benefits of Hosting an NFL Team," *Business Review,* Federal Reserve Bank of Philadelphia, Quarter 2, 2004, pp. 7–17.

- The National Highway Transportation Safety Administration requires that automobiles be equipped with seat belts and brake lights.

- The Food and Drug Administration approves the sale of both prescription and nonprescription drugs.

- The Occupational Safety and Health Administration establishes standards that are intended to decrease workers' exposure to injury and to health risks, such as those associated with asbestos.

As with other types of government regulation, not everyone agrees on the merits of social regulation. Some people claim that compliance with social regulations results in higher operating costs for the firms striving to meet them. These higher costs are similar to a tax. Suppose that the imposition of health and safety regulations increases a firm's costs by $10 per unit. The firm's supply curve therefore shifts upward by that amount, which results in higher prices and a decrease in output. Like other taxing situations, the consumer absorbs part of the regulatory tax in the form of a higher price, while a firm's revenues are reduced by the remainder of the tax.

Proponents of social regulation, however, contend that although the costs are high, the benefits are even higher. They may claim, for example, that government regulations on asbestos lead to 2,000 fewer people dying from cancer each year; highway fatalities would be 30 percent higher in the absence of auto safety features required by regulation; and that mandated child-proof lids result in 85 percent fewer child deaths caused by the accidental swallowing of poisonous substances. Although social regulation results in higher consumer prices, is this too much of a burden when compared to an improved quality of life for society?

Although social regulation based on a careful balancing of costs and benefits can sometimes improve market performance, policymakers often ignore the fact that the government is an imperfect regulator. Critics of social regulation, for example, claim that regulators often lack accurate information about an industry and cannot always predict the effects of specific regulations. Although the decision to regulate may be well intentioned, the regulations themselves can have adverse and unintended consequences.

Do Corporate Fuel Economy Standards Promote Fuel Conservation?

The U.S. government's fuel-economy standards for automobile manufacturers provide an example of the problems of social regulation. The Arab oil embargo of 1973–1974 and the consequent tripling of the price of crude oil brought into sharp focus the fuel inefficiency of U.S. automobiles. New car fleet fuel economy had decreased from 14.8 miles per gallon (mpg) in 1967 to 12.9 mpg in 1974. In search of ways to reduce the U.S. dependence on imported oil, automobiles were an obvious target. It was apparent that decreasing U.S. reliance on imported oil would be very difficult without imposing a large price increase on gasoline to promote conservation or increase the efficiency of the automobile fleet in use.

In 1975, the U.S. government enacted standards for **corporate average fuel economy (CAFÉ)** that apply to all cars and light trucks sold in the United States. The standards are based on the average fuel efficiency of vehicles sold by all manufacturers. For model year 2007, the standard is 27.5 mpg for passenger cars and 22.2 mpg for light trucks. Manufacturers whose average fuel economy falls below this standard are subject to fines. However, manufacturers are allowed to earn CAFÉ credits in any year in which they exceed the fuel-economy requirements, which they may use to offset deficiencies in other years.

Proponents of CAFÉ maintain that high fuel-economy standards are necessary to conserve gasoline. They argue that without governmental regulation, auto companies lack the incentive to carry out the costly research and development activities that are necessary to produce fuel-efficient vehicles. By mandating a system of fuel requirements, CAFÉ helps the United States conserve gasoline, reduce its dependence on foreign oil, decrease air pollution, and combat global warming.

However, CAFÉ is subject to criticism. According to auto companies such as Ford and General Motors, the costs of meeting the CAFÉ standards are very high and will push them toward bankruptcy if the standards are raised in the future. This is because producers would face higher manufacturing costs from adopting new fuel-saving technologies in their vehicles. U.S. auto companies also note that it costs them more to produce fuel-efficient autos than it costs their foreign competitors, whose fleets are already filled with lighter, more efficient vehicles.

Critics also contend that auto companies tend to use the least expensive method to meet the higher fuel-economy standards by decreasing vehicle weight which makes autos less safe in accidents. Moreover, CAFÉ has not really increased the total miles per gallon of all vehicles. Although CAFÉ has succeeded in increasing gasoline mileage on the fleet of passenger cars, it has induced individuals who prefer larger and heavier vehicles to shift their purchases to sports utility vehicles which are allowed to have lower gasoline efficiency under CAFÉ standards. Furthermore, by reducing the cost of operating a vehicle, higher CAFÉ standards tend to encourage people to drive more, thus increasing congestion.

Thus, critics question the extent to which CAFÉ has promoted gasoline conservation. They contend that what did stimulate improvements in fuel efficiency have been stimulated by intense competition from high-mileage imports such as Hondas and Toyotas rather than CAFÉ standards. Indeed, the effect of CAFÉ on the conservation of gasoline is a controversial issue.

One way of reforming CAFÉ would involve a market-oriented solution to boost fuel economy. Auto manufacturers would be allowed to trade fuel-economy credits, similar to the trading of emission certificates discussed earlier in this chapter. Under a credit-trading system, firms that exceeded one of the CAFÉ standards would generate credits that they could sell to firms falling below that standard. The selling and buying of credits would be voluntary. Such a policy would allow manufacturers to concentrate production in their area of cost competitiveness, whether it be small, fuel-efficient vehicles or large, inefficient ones. This would allow firms to choose the means of complying with CAFÉ standards that is least expensive for them, resulting in aggregate cost savings.

PUBLIC GOODS

So far, we have analyzed market failure in terms of monopoly power and spillover effects. Another source of market failure is public goods. Let us consider the nature of private goods and public goods and see why the latter contribute to market failure.

Private goods, which are produced through the market system, are *divisible* in that they come in units that are small enough to be purchased by individual consumers. For example, we can go to McDonald's and buy one (or several) Big Macs and a small, medium, or large Coke. Private goods are also subject to the *exclusion principle,* the notion that only those who have the ability to pay can purchase the good, whereas those who do not possess the ability to pay are excluded from consumption. Moreover, the *principle of rival consumption* applies to private goods. When I eat a Big Mac, you cannot eat the same one. Thus, you and I are rivals for that hamburger. In general, the market system works well in producing private goods in accordance with the needs of consumers.

An entire class of goods is not considered private goods and thus is not provided by the market system. These are called **public goods** and include things such as national defense, highways, lighthouses, and air-traffic control. These goods are *indivisible* because they cannot be produced and sold very easily in small units. For example, you cannot go down to the local store and purchase $10 worth of national defense. Moreover, the exclusion principle does not pertain to public goods. For example, all households are protected by national defense even if they don't have the money to pay for it. Finally, more people can use public goods at no extra cost. Once money has been spent to construct a lighthouse, the benefit you receive does not lessen the amount of protection received by anyone else.

The reason the market system fails to supply public goods efficiently is that the exclusion principle does not apply. Consider the snow removal system of Buffalo, New York. Such a system is justified if the benefits of improved transportation exceed the costs of buying and operating snowplows, dump trucks, and the like. However, the benefit received by each individual motorist would not justify the cost of such a large and indivisible product. Once the snowplows clean the streets, there is no practical method of excluding certain motorists from their benefits. As a result, why should any motorist voluntarily pay for benefits received from clean streets? Clean streets are available for everyone, and a motorist cannot be excluded from driving on them if he decides not to pay.

Economists call this the **free-rider problem,** because it is impossible to exclude you from the consumption of a public good. Whether or not you pay for it, you still consume it. Of course, if everyone behaved in this manner, no money would be spent on public goods, and entrepreneurs would have no incentive to supply them to the market. We conclude that the market system fails by *underproducing* public goods!

Because of the free-rider problem, citizens still look to government to provide public goods through the use of tax financing. Of course, there is no guarantee that public goods, such as national defense and pollution control, will be provided in optimal amounts.

INADEQUATE INFORMATION

Another source of market failure is inadequate information, a less visible type of market failure than monopoly power, externalities, and public goods. This inefficiency occurs when either sellers or buyers have incomplete or inaccurate information about the price, quality, or another aspect of a good or service. Without adequate information, markets may give false signals, incentives may get distorted, and sometimes markets may simply not exist. In such cases, government may decide to step in to correct the market failure.

Lack of information often arises in the sale of used cars. The sellers of used cars know the flaws of their cars, whereas buyers often do not. Because the owners of the worst cars are more likely to sell them than the owners of the best cars, car buyers may be fearful of purchasing a "lemon." Therefore, many people refuse to purchase cars in the used-car market.

Let us examine market failure by considering how inadequate information about sellers and their goods can disrupt the operation of the gasoline market. Suppose there were no government inspection of gas pumps, no system of weights and measures established by law, and no laws against false advertising. Each gas station could announce that its gas has a minimum octane rating of 87 when in actuality it is only 80. Moreover, the gas station could calibrate its pumps to show that they are pumping, say, 10 gallons of gas, when in fact they are pumping only 9 gallons. In this situation, the cost to the motorist of obtaining reliable information would be very high. Each motorist would have to purchase samples of gas from various stations and have them analyzed to determine the level of octane. Motorists would also have to pump gas into, say, 5-gallon containers to make sure that a station's pump is calibrated correctly. Because of the high costs of obtaining information about the seller, many motorists might prefer to opt out of this chaotic market. More realistically, government might step in to correct the failure of the market. It could pass legislation against false advertising, hire inspectors to check the accuracy of pumps, and establish a system of weights and measures.

Inadequate information about sellers disrupts the efficient operation of a market, but so can inadequate information about buyers. In the labor market, an employer has several economic incentives to provide a safe workplace. A safe workplace fosters higher worker productivity by reducing job accidents, thus decreasing the costs of training new workers. It also entails lower insurance premiums for a firm that, by law, must provide insurance against job injuries. These factors would reduce a firm's costs and thus increase its profit. Conversely, providing safe equipment and protective gear results in additional costs, which reduce the firm's profit. When deciding how much safety to provide, a firm must consider the extra benefits and extra costs associated with a safe workplace.

In a competitive market, if workers have complete information about the workplace safety of firms, they will be reluctant to work for those firms with unsafe workplaces. The supply of labor to those firms will decrease, forcing the firms to increase their wages in order to attract additional labor. The increased wages reduce the firm's profits and give it an extra incentive to provide a safe workplace.

Instead, suppose that workers are unaware of the safety at various workplaces. Because of inadequate knowledge, the employer will not have to pay higher wages in order to attract additional workers. The incentive of the employer to eliminate safety hazards is diminished, and society does not receive the desirable amount of workplace safety. Indeed, market failure can impose hardships on workers.

How can government intervene to correct the problem of inadequate information in the labor market? It can require that firms give information to workers about known workplace dangers and it can mandate standards of workplace safety that are enforced by inspection and fines. The government can also give information to workers about the workplace safety records of firms.

ECONOMIC INEQUALITY

As we have learned, monopoly power, spillover effects, public goods, and inadequate information all cause market failure. When these phenomena occur, the market system fails to produce the optimal mix of output for society. Besides being concerned about what goods to produce, we also care about whom output is produced for. Does the market system result in a distribution of output that is fair to all members of society?

In a market economy, output is disproportionately distributed to people with the most income. Although this may be efficient, it is not necessarily equitable. Persons who are disabled or elderly, for example, may not be able to earn as much income as young, healthy individuals. However, they are still considered "worthy" of receiving goods and services.

In some situations, society may desire to modify the way in which the market system distributes goods. Rather than relying exclusively on the individual's ability to pay for these goods, society provides income transfers. Such transfers are payments from the government to households and firms for which no goods or services are currently rendered. Transfer payments include payments such as unemployment compensation, food stamps, Temporary Assistance for Needy Families, Medicare, and business subsidies. They are intended to supplement the income of those for whom the market system provides too little. Recipients of transfer payments can therefore obtain a greater share of the nation's output.

To finance the costs of its transfer payment programs, the government enacts graduated taxes on households and businesses and channels these funds to the needy. Through this system of taxation and transfer payments, income is redistributed from the wealthier to the less wealthy.

This chapter has discussed the role of government in the market economy. The next chapter will broaden our understanding of government by considering the mixed economy of the United States.

CHECK POINT

1. Explain how the market system fails to allocate resources efficiently when the production of some good entails spillover costs or spillover benefits. What can the government do to correct for market failure in these situations?

2. What is the purpose of social regulation? Identify some government agencies that are involved in social regulation. Why

are people sometimes critical of social regulators?

3. How does the market system fail to allocate resources efficiently in the case of public goods? How about when society experiences economic inequality?

4. How does inadequate information cause market failure?

Chapter Summary

1. In some cases, unregulated markets may not provide the best answers to the fundamental economic questions of society. Whenever that occurs, government intervention is needed to temper the market's operation and to make it conform to the interests of society.

2. Some markets fail to allocate resources efficiently, a situation called market failure. The main sources of market failure are monopoly power, spillovers or externalities, public goods, inadequate information, and economic inequality.

3. Antitrust policy is the attempt to curb anticompetitive behavior and to foster a market environment that will lead to increased competition. The Sherman Act of 1890 and the Clayton Act of 1914 are the foundations of federal antitrust policy.

4. Besides using antitrust laws to regulate business behavior, the federal government sometimes enacts economic regulation to control the prices, wages, conditions of entry, and standards of service of an industry. Industries that have been subject to economic regulation have included airlines, trucking, railroads, banking, communications, and energy. By the late 1970s, however, it was generally agreed that many economic regulations were no longer suited to prevailing economic conditions. As a result, the federal government initiated steps to dismantle many economic regulations, a process known as deregulation.

5. Public utilities have traditionally been subject to economic regulation on the grounds that they are natural monopolies. In return for being granted an exclusive franchise to serve a local market, the utility is subject to price regulation according to the fair-return principle. Although fair-return pricing allows a utility to realize a price that covers its average total cost, it does not provide an incentive for a utility to minimize its costs.

6. A spillover is a cost or benefit that is imposed on people other than the producers and consumers of a good or service. When the production of some good results in spillover costs, too much of it is produced, and resources are overallocated to its use. Conversely, underproduction and underallocation of resources arise from spillover benefits.

7. Social regulation attempts to correct a variety of undesirable side effects in a market economy that relate to health, safety, and the environment—effects that markets, left to themselves, often ignore. Federal government agencies involved in social regulation include the Environmental Protection Agency, the Consumer Product Safety Commission, the Food and Drug Administration, and the Occupational Safety and Health Administration.

8. Public goods, such as national defense, are indivisible and are not subject to the exclusion principle. As a result, the market system fails to supply public goods efficiently.

9. Without adequate information, markets may give false signals, incentives may get distorted, and sometimes markets may simply not exist. In such cases, government may decide to step in to correct the market failure.

10. Because an unregulated market may fail to provide a fair distribution of income and output for society, government modifies the distribution of income through taxation and transfer payment programs.

Key Terms and Concepts

market failure (175)

antitrust policy (175)

Sherman Act of 1890 (176)

Clayton Act of 1914 (176)

economic regulation (176)

deregulation (177)

fair-return price (177)

peak-load pricing (179)

spillover (180)

externality (180)

spillover cost (180)

spillover benefit (180)

cap and trade system (182)

command-and-control regulations (181)

incentive-based regulations (181)

social regulation (185)

corporate average fuel economy
  (CAFÉ) (186)

private goods (187)

public goods (187)

free-rider problem (188)

Self-Test: Multiple-Choice Questions

1. The attempt to curb anticompetitive behavior that harms consumers and foster a market structure that will lead to increased competition is called

   a.   social regulation.
   b.   economic regulation.
   c.   antitrust policy.
   d.   command-and-control regulation.

2. The Clayton Act does *not* outlaw

   a.   profit maximization according to the *MR* = *MC* rule.
   b.   tying (exclusive) contracts between a seller and a buyer.
   c.   mergers that substantially lessen competition.
   d.   price discrimination that is not justified by cost differences.

3. Which of the following has been used to control the prices, conditions of entry, and standards of service for industries such as airlines, trucking, and railroads?

   a.   Fair-return regulation.
   b.   Economic regulation.
   c.   Social regulation.
   d.   Command-and-control regulation.

4. With spillover benefits, the market fails because the demand curve does not reflect all of the benefits of a good. Therefore, all of the following are true *except*

   a.   the good is underproduced and underconsumed.
   b.   the good is overproduced and overconsumed.
   c.   government could correct the market failure by granting subsidies to consumers to finance the purchase of the good.
   d.   government could correct the market failure by subsidizing producers so that they can supply more of a product.

5. Sources of market failure include all of the following *except*

   a.   monopoly power.
   b.   spillovers or externalities.
   c.   inadequate information.
   d.   private goods.

6. Concerning electric utilities, peak-load pricing is considered to be a method of

    a. allowing utilities to earn exorbitant rates of return on invested capital.
    b. encouraging electricity consumption during the peak periods of the day.
    c. more evenly distributing the demand for electricity throughout the day.
    d. conserving power by charging lower rates to big industrial buyers.

7. Usually, the reason that governments resort to regulating a monopoly, rather than promoting competition through antitrust policy, is that the industry in question is believed to be

    a. perfectly competitive.
    b. monopolistically competitive.
    c. a pure monopoly.
    d. a natural monopoly.

8. Suppose that market failure occurs when Kaiser Aluminum Co. does not take into account spillover costs. Thus, the firm produces

    a. too much aluminum and charges too high a price.
    b. too much aluminum and charges too low a price.
    c. too little aluminum and charges too high a price.
    d. too little aluminum and charges too low a price.

9. Economists generally maintain that the least costly method of decreasing pollution in, say, the steel industry is to

    a. require all steel companies to reduce their pollution by the same percentage.
    b. require steel companies with the greatest profits to decrease pollution the most.
    c. require all steel companies with the lowest profits to exit the market.
    d. provide incentives for companies that can decrease pollution at the lowest cost to make relatively large reductions.

10. If the government adopts command-and-control regulations to reduce acid rain

    a. a tax will be imposed on factories for each unit of pollutants emitted.
    b. a lump-sum tax will be imposed on polluters irrespective of the extent that they pollute.
    c. restrictions will be imposed on the amount of pollutants emitted by a factory.
    d. subsidies will be granted to firms to help them finance the cost of pollution.

Answers to Multiple-Choice Questions

1. c   2. a   3. b   4. b   5. d   6. c   7. d   8. b   9. d   10. c

Study Questions and Problems

1. Table 8.2 shows hypothetical demand and cost data for New England Power and Light Co., a monopolist that sells electricity in Massachusetts.

    a. Draw a figure that illustrates the firm's demand curve, marginal revenue curve, marginal cost curve, and average total cost curve.
    b. As an unregulated monopolist, the firm would maximize economic profits by producing _____ units of electricity and selling them at a price of $_____. The firm's total revenue equals $_____, total cost equals $_____, and total profit equals $_____.
    c. Suppose that the legislature imposes public-utility regulations on the firm and sets the price of electricity according to the fair-return principle. Such regulations result in the

Table 8.2	Hypothetical Demand and Cost Data for New England Power and Light Co.				

Quantity of Electricity	Price	Marginal Revenue	Average Total Cost	Marginal Cost
0	$52.50			
1	48.00	$48.00	$72.00	$72.00
2	43.50	39.00	45.00	18.00
3	39.00	30.00	35.00	15.00
4	34.50	21.00	31.50	21.00
5	30.00	12.00	30.00	24.00
6	25.50	3.00	29.25	25.50

firm producing _____ units of electricity and selling them at a price of $_____. The firm's total revenue equals $_____, total cost equals $_____, and total profit equals $_____.

d. Why might fair-return regulation result in inefficiencies for the firm?

2. Under what conditions do unregulated markets fail to allocate resources efficiently?

3. How do the antitrust laws attempt to combat the problem of monopoly power?

4. By the late 1970s, many economic regulations were being removed in industries such as trucking, airlines, and communications. Comment on the advantages and disadvantages of such deregulation.

5. By the 1990s, deregulation was spreading to the electricity and cable television industries. Explain why this occurred.

6. Why does the government regulate markets that generate spillover costs and spillover benefits?

7. Compare and contrast social regulation versus economic regulation. Give examples of each.

8. Why does the market system provide goods such as Pepsi-Cola, while the government provides goods such as highways and lighthouses?

9. How does the government attempt to correct the failure of markets resulting from economic inequality?

The Mixed Economy of the United States

Chapter objectives

After reading this chapter, you should be able to:

1. Distinguish between the functional distribution of income and the personal distribution of income and identify the sources of income inequality.

2. Identify the major sources of revenue and expenditures of the federal government and of state and local governments.

3. Evaluate proposals for reforming the Social Security system.

4. Assess the strengths and weaknesses of the U.S. tax system.

5. Identify the merits of a flat-rate income tax, a value-added tax, and a national sales tax.

the
Macroeconomy

economics IN CONTEXT

At the turn of the century, the nation's economy was performing at peak levels. The number of workers employed was at an all-time high, the unemployment rate was at a 30-year low, and inflation-adjusted wages were increasing after years of stagnation. Single women with children, immigrants, and minorities, whose economic status had not improved in decades, were experiencing progress. Besides spreading the benefits of economic growth more widely, the robust economy generated other benefits. It contributed to a decrease in welfare caseloads, allowing the government to focus more resources on designing and implementing welfare reform. Moreover, low unemployment and, in particular, a rise in average wages contributed to a reduction in crime.

By 2008, the economy was headed into a pronounced downturn. As consumers and business owners became increasingly pessimistic about their future incomes, they cut their expenditures in order to "save for a rainy day." Such withdrawals of cash from the economy pulled it down even further. Therefore, President Barack Obama cut household and business taxes and increased government spending in 2009 to help prop up the economy. According to Obama, the private sector of the economy needed the help of the government to reduce the hardship caused by the economic downturn. This topic will be discussed further in subsequent chapters.

In previous chapters, we have emphasized the private sector of the economy, which includes households and businesses. By adding the role of government to our discussion, we will now examine the **mixed economy**. In the mixed economy of the United States, the private sector consists of the millions of households and businesses in the nation. The public sector in the United States comprises the federal, state, and local governments. These two sectors illustrate a few pertinent factors concerning our mixed economy.

HOUSEHOLDS AS INCOME RECEIVERS

Everyone knows that there are many rich and many poor people in our society. The **distribution of income** is the way income is divided among members of society. It reflects the manner in which people share in the rewards from the production of goods and services. Income distribution can be analyzed in two ways.

The **functional distribution of income** refers to the shares of a nation's income that accrue to the *factors of production*—land, labor, capital, and entrepreneurship—as rent, wages, interest, and profits. Here, income is shared by the factors of production according to the functions they perform. Table 9.1 illustrates the functional distribution of income for the United States in 2007. Notice that the largest source of the nation's income accrued to labor as wages and salaries.

How do *individual households* share the nation's income? This issue is addressed by the **personal distribution of income,** as seen in Table 9.1. The table indicates the share of before-tax annual money income received by *quintiles*—that is, each one-fifth of families, ranked from lowest to highest. In 2006, for example, the poorest 20 percent of all families received 3.4 percent of total money income; if income were equally distributed, these families would have received 20 percent of the total. Conversely, the richest 20 percent of families received 50.6 percent of total money

Table 9.1	Distribution of Income in the United States

Functional Distribution of Income, 2007	
Wages and salaries	72%
Interest	5
Proprietor income	9
Corporate profit	13
Rents	1
	100%

Personal Distribution of Income, 2006	
Lowest 20 percent	3.4%
Second 20 percent	8.6
Middle 20 percent	14.5
Fourth 20 percent	22.9
Top 20 percent	50.6
	100.0%

Source: U.S. Department of Commerce, *Statistical Abstract of the United States, 2009* (Washington, DC: U.S. Government Printing Office), Table 675; and *Economic Report of the President*, 2009 (Washington, DC: U.S. Government Printing Office), Table B-29.

income. The richest one-fifth of all families thus received over 14 times more of the before-tax money income as the poorest quintile. Note, however, that the distribution of income is not the same as the distribution of wealth. A complete account of a family's wealth would also include things such as bank savings deposits, houses, land, cars, pensions, Social Security, and stocks and bonds. Moreover, human skills can be thought of as a type of wealth.

SOURCES OF INCOME INEQUALITY

Concerning the personal distribution of income, income inequality decreased significantly between the 1930s and 1950. Since 1970, however, income inequality has increased. Why do some people earn more income than others? The most important determinants of income differences are age, differences in productive resources, investment in human capital, inheritance, and discrimination.

Age is a determinant of income because, generally, with age comes more education, more training, and more experience. Income is usually lower when people start working at age 18; it rises to a peak at around age 45 to 50, then gradually decreases as people approach retirement age. When individuals begin working at a young age, they usually have little work-related experience and earn less than older workers with more experience. As workers become older, they develop additional work skills, become more productive, work longer hours, and develop seniority, and thus they earn a higher income. At the age of 45 to 50, the productivity of workers usually peaks. As workers reach retirement age, the number of hours they work usually declines, along with their stamina and strength. These factors detract from the income-earning ability of older workers.

Other determinants of income are the quantity and quality of resources that an individual possesses. In a market economy, those who use their human and physical resources to produce many things that are highly valued by others have high incomes. For example, Shaquille O'Neal, the star basketball player of the Miami Heat, earns millions of dollars by leading his team to victory. The connection between personal reward and productivity provides individuals with a strong incentive to use their resources efficiently and to figure out better ways of doing things.

People are not born with equal amounts of talent or intelligence. However, inherited differences can be magnified or offset by acquired skills. Sharpening one's productive talents or acquiring new skills is called investment in **human capital.** People invest in their education, training, and health care for self-improvement that leads to higher productivity and higher income. If you invest in yourself by going to college instead of going to work after high school and earning more income today, you will likely be rewarded in the future with a more interesting job or a better paying job, or both.

Inheritance also affects income. It is not unusual for people to inherit cash, stocks, bonds, homes, or land that generates profit, interest, or rental income. Such gifts represent the benefits of someone else's labor or investments rather than the benefits of one's own labor or investments.

Finally, discriminatory labor markets can influence income. Economic discrimination occurs whenever female or minority workers who have the same education, training, abilities, and experience as white male workers earn lower wages or receive less access to jobs or promotion. African Americans and other minorities have historically encountered discrimination in the acquisition of human capital. For example, the amount and quality of schooling offered to black Americans has often been inferior to that offered to whites. Moreover, many women maintain that they have been forced to accept low-paying jobs as secretaries, janitors, or food service workers because other jobs were closed to them. In some cases, occupations predominantly held by women offer low pay despite the fact that similarly skilled, predominantly male occupations pay much higher incomes.

HOUSEHOLDS AS SPENDERS

Besides receiving income, householders are also spenders. Part of household income flows into consumption expenditures, while the rest is used to pay taxes or goes into savings.

Table 9.2 illustrates the disposition of household income in 2007. The table shows that 86 percent of household income was used for consumption expenditures. Consumer purchases include durable goods, such as computers and automobiles; nondurable goods, such as food and clothing; and services, such as the work done by doctors and lawyers for consumers. The U.S. economy is service oriented, with more than half of household consumption expenditures paying for services in 2007.

Besides spending money as consumers, households allocate a portion of their income for taxes, of which the federal personal income tax is the most important component. As seen in Table 9.2, 13 percent of household income was used to pay taxes in 2007.

Table 9.2	Disposition of Household Income, 2007		
		Amount	Percentage of Total
Personal consumption expenditures		$9,710.2 billion	86%
Durable goods		1,082.8	10
Nondurable goods		2,833.0	25
Services		5,794.4	51
Personal taxes		1,492.8	13
Personal savings		57.4	1
		$11,260.4 billion	100%

Source: Economic Report of the President, 2009, Tables B-16 and B-30.

The amount of household income that is not used for consumption expenditures or to pay taxes is saved. In 2007, the household saving rate was 1 percent of household income, as seen in Table 9.2. Household savings are put into bank accounts, stocks and bonds, insurance policies, and the like. The motivation to save is usually driven by a desire to create a nest egg for unforeseen adversities, education for children, or retirement. People also save for speculation. For example, an individual might purchase stock in IBM with the hope of selling it in the future at a higher price, thus realizing a handsome profit.

THE BUSINESS SECTOR

Business is the second component of an economy's private sector. A business is an organization that is established to produce and sell goods and services. In the United States, there are more than 24 million businesses. Many are small firms, such as local gas stations or grocery stores. Others are large firms such as automobile and computer manufacturers.

A business firm can be organized in one of three ways: as a sole proprietorship, a partnership, or a corporation. The structure that is chosen determines how the owners share the risks and liabilities of the firm and how they participate in decision making. Table 9.3 shows the distribution of these three business types in the United States. Although sole proprietorships are numerically dominant, corporations account for the largest share of total sales.

A **sole proprietorship** is a firm that is owned and operated by one individual. These establishments are typically small, such as a local espresso stand or pizza business. A sole proprietorship is relatively easy to organize and operate, and its owner is not responsible or answerable to anyone. The size of a sole proprietorship, however, is limited by the proprietor's wealth and credit standing, as well as by business profits. The greatest disadvantage of a sole proprietorship is the proprietor's unlimited liability—that is, the personal assets of the owner are subject to use for payment of business debt. Almost everything that a proprietor owns, such as an automobile or a home, may be sold to pay the firm's debts if it fails or is held liable for damages in a lawsuit.

A **partnership** is an extension of the sole proprietorship. Rather than being owned by one individual, a partnership has two or more owners who pool their financial resources and business skills. Many doctors, for example, form partnerships. This allows them to share office expenses and reduces the need to be on call 24 hours a day, 7 days a week. Lawyers and accountants also tend to organize partnerships. In a partnership, each partner has unlimited liability. One partner's poor business decisions may impose significant losses on the other partners, a problem that sole proprietors need not worry about. Also, decision making is usually more cumbersome in a partnership than in a sole proprietorship because there are more people involved in making decisions. Moreover, a partnership is usually terminated when one partner dies or voluntarily withdraws from the business.

Table 9.3	U.S. Business Firms, 2005			
Form of Business	Number of Firms (millions)		Business Receipts (billions)	
	Number	Percent	Dollars	Percent
Sole proprietorship	21.5	72%	$1,223	4%
Partnership	2.8	9	3,719	13
Corporation	5.7	19	24,060	83
Total	30.0	100%	$29,002	100%

Source: U.S. Commerce Department, Bureau of the Census, *2009 Statistical Abstract of the United States* (Washington, D.C.: U.S. Government Printing Office), Table 724.

A **corporation** is a "legal person" that conducts business just as an individual does. Corporations can produce and sell output, make contracts, pay fines, and sue and be sued. General Motors, IBM, Boeing, and Microsoft are examples of corporations that have become household names.

Corporations are owned by stockholders, who receive profits in the form of dividends. Large corporations, such as General Electric, may have hundreds of thousands of stockholders; however, some smaller corporations have only a few stockholders. The stockholders vote, according to the amount of stock they own, for a board of directors. The board, in turn, appoints officers to run the corporation according to the guidelines established by the board.

One advantage for the stockholders of a corporation is limited liability. When a corporation declares bankruptcy, a stockholder can lose only the money used to purchase the firm's stock. Moreover, corporations can obtain funds by selling shares of stock or by borrowing money. Corporations borrow by issuing bonds to investors or by obtaining loans directly from banks and other financial institutions. In contrast, sole proprietorships and partnerships can only obtain outside funding through loans. Finally, corporations are efficient at transferring ownership. When a stockholder of a corporation wishes to give up her ownership rights, she can sell her stock to other investors.

However, corporations also have several drawbacks. The first is the double taxation of income. The profits of a corporation are first subject to corporate income taxes. Then, if any of the after-tax profits are distributed to stockholders as dividends, those payments are taxed as personal income. Corporate profits are thus taxed twice under our current tax system; the profits of sole proprietorships and partnerships are taxed only once as personal income.

Corporations can also suffer from the problem of separation of ownership and control. The stockholders of a corporation often have little to do with its actual operation. Instead, officers, who may own little or no corporate stock, manage the firm. The objective of the stockholders is to maximize the dividends they receive from their stock ownership in the firm. Unless the officers receive compensation in corporate stock, their motivation may differ from that of stockholders. For example, officers may reward themselves with extravagant salaries or lavish offices, neither of which is necessary for the efficient operation of the company. Such luxuries increase the cost of doing business and decrease the dividends of stockholders.

CHECK POINT

1. Distinguish between the functional distribution of income and the personal distribution of income.

2. Identify the determinants of an individual's income and how income is spent.

3. Describe the advantages and disadvantages of the three legal forms of business organization.

GOVERNMENT IN THE MIXED ECONOMY

The activities of government have a major influence on our lives. In a mixed economy, the government provides an appropriate legal and social framework, promotes competition, alters the distribution of income by taxing income away from some people and giving it to others, provides public goods such as national defense, encourages businesses to produce goods entailing spillover benefits (such as public television), discourages companies from polluting the environment, and initiates policies to promote price stability and high employment for the nation. These functions require government expenditures that are financed through the taxes paid by households and businesses.

Government expenditures, or outlays, consist of purchases and transfer payments made by the federal, state, and local governments. **Government purchases** are expenditures on goods and services. They include such items as street lighting, sewage systems, city playgrounds, national parks, county roads, police cars, fire trucks, tanks, computers, and jet planes. Governments also purchase the labor services of engineers, teachers, accountants, and lawyers to produce goods ranging from highway construction to college education. When a government purchases goods and services, fewer resources are available to produce goods and services used in the private sector.

Government expenditures also include **transfer payments,** which are payments of income from taxpayers to individuals who make no contribution to current output for these payments. Transfer payments thus provide a *safety net* of income security for the poor and needy. The major governmental transfer payment programs include the following:

- **Unemployment compensation** provides temporary income support for unemployed workers. The amount an unemployed worker receives each week and the number of weeks an unemployed worker is allowed to receive benefits vary among the states.

- **Food stamps** are given to the poor, elderly, and disabled so that they can acquire nutritionally adequate products. Recipients receive a quantity of stamps each month; these stamps are redeemable for goods at most grocery stores.

- **Supplemental Security Income** payments are made to the disabled, blind, and elderly who are unable to work.

- **Temporary Assistance for Needy Families** provides payments to surviving spouses with small children and also to single-parent families. These families are usually headed by women who cannot work because they must care for their young children.

- **Medicaid** provides health care payments to low-income families and to the blind, elderly, and disabled.

- **Housing and energy subsidies** are granted to low-income families to help them afford the cost of a dwelling.

- **Agricultural assistance** to farmers consists of subsidies and grants such as minimum price supports and low-interest-rate loans to farmers who have difficulty in obtaining credit elsewhere. Such assistance attempts to stabilize farm incomes and thus provides consumers with a stable supply of food.

The United States has devised a system of taxes and transfer payments to alter the distribution of income in favor of the poor—in other words, economically advantaged "Peter" is taxed to help economically disadvantaged "Paul." Critics of the system, however, maintain that many transfer payments are doled out without concern for need. Moreover, the welfare system has historically contained powerful disincentives against work and personal responsibility, thus promoting continued welfare.

In 1996, the Personal Responsibility and Work Opportunity Reconciliation Act was passed by Congress and signed into law by President Bill Clinton. The act established the principle that individuals and families are not automatically entitled to government support just because they are poor. Specifically, the law established a "workfare" requirement, stipulating that recipients must give up most of their welfare benefits unless the family head begins to work within 2 years. Families can collect welfare more than once, but lifetime benefits are limited to 5 years. The law also decentralized welfare policy through federal lump-sum grants to state governments, which are free to operate their own welfare programs. Moreover, the law tightened welfare payments to immigrants who are noncitizen legal aliens. The reforms were intended to force welfare parents to get even modest jobs, thereby providing new hope and motivation for their children. Indeed, the pros and cons of workfare have been widely debated, and it will be many years before the long-run effects on the efficiency and coverage of welfare systems can be known.

SOCIAL SECURITY

The major sources of growth in transfer payments have been the Social Security and Medicare programs.

Social Security is the largest retirement and disability program in the United States. Social Security was created in 1935 as a means of providing income security upon retirement to people who would not otherwise have that form of security. As of 2006, the Social Security system provided cash benefits to more than 50 million retired and disabled workers and to their dependents and survivors.

In 1965, the federal government added a health insurance program, **Medicare**, to the Social Security system. Its objective is to reduce the financial burden of illness on the elderly. Medicare covers physician fees, hospitalization, outpatient care, and skilled nursing care at home. As of 2009, Medicare provided health insurance to more than 42 million people.

Social Security is a *pay-as-you-go* system that is financed by payroll taxes. In 2009, workers paid a flat-rate tax of 6.2 percent for Old-Age, Survivors, and Disability Insurance on their wages up to $106,800, with an equal match by their employers. In addition, employees and employers each paid a 1.45-percent tax on all wages to finance Medicare. Social Security taxes flow into the U.S. Treasury, and each program's share is credited to separate trust funds—one for retirement and survivors, another for disability, and two others for Medicare. Social Security and Medicare contributions are mandatory for most wage earners, whether they like it or not.

Contrary to popular belief, the Social Security trust funds do not themselves hold money to pay benefits. They are simply accounts that are located at the U.S. Treasury. These balances, like those of a bank account or a government savings bond, represent a promise (IOU) from the government. It pledges to obtain resources in the future, equal to the value of the trust-fund accounts, if funds are needed to pay Social Security benefits. Any surplus of taxes in the Social Security system is used to purchase U.S. Treasury securities. The federal government then uses these funds as part of its operating cash, which is used to pay for the many functions of government, such as national defense and unemployment compensation benefits.

For more than 3 decades after Social Security was created, the system's income routinely exceeded its payout, and its trust funds grew. Beginning in the 1970s, however, the trust funds started to decline. This was largely the result of benefit increases. Not only was the number of beneficiaries growing, but benefits were being periodically adjusted to keep pace with inflation. By the 1980s, Social Security benefits were automatically increased annually to reflect inflation. These **cost-of-living adjustments,** or **COLAs,** also contributed to revenue shortfalls.

Another concern regarding Social Security is that the number of workers paying into Social Security has declined relative to the number of Social Security beneficiaries. An aging post–World War II baby boom generation, falling birth rates, and increasing life expectancies have all contributed to this decline. In 1945, for each worker collecting benefits, there were 46 workers paying payroll taxes. By 1996, there were only 3 workers for every beneficiary. Estimates suggest that there will be only 2.4 workers for every beneficiary by 2050. The bottom line is that, in the future, there will be relatively fewer people of working age to support a growing elderly population. Simply put, the declining ratio of young to old foretells serious solvency problems for Social Security. Economists estimate that the Social Security system's trust funds will be depleted in 2042, at which time only 73 percent of its benefits will be payable with incoming receipts. Consider a man who was born in 2000 and earns the average income over his working life. He will be promised $290,900 in today's dollars—but the system will only have the resources to pay him $211,700.

From the 1940s to the 1980s, Social Security recipients received a good deal for the taxes they paid to support the system. Most recipients received more than the value of the taxes they paid. However, because Social Security tax rates have increased over the years and the eligibility age for full benefits has risen, it is becoming increasingly apparent that Social Security will not be such a good deal for many future recipients. Workers who earned average wages and retired at age 65 in 1980 recovered the value of the retirement portion of the combined employee and employer shares of their payroll taxes plus interest in 2.8 years. For their counterparts retiring at age 65 in 1996, it took 14 years. For those retiring in 2025, it will take a projected 23 years.

Concerns about Social Security's financing problems and survival have led to proposals to reform the system. One option that has been proposed is to increase the Social Security tax rates paid by current employees. However, wage earners may resist future increases. Because Social Security is a pay-as-you-go system, not a penny of the tax goes into the accounts of those who make the contributions. To these workers, Social Security may be viewed as a program that offers little in return. Instead of raising the payroll taxes of current wage earners, why not decrease the benefits of the elderly? Consider these options:

- **Adopt means testing.** Social Security recipients must qualify on the basis of financial need, similar to other welfare programs such as food stamps and Medicaid. Elderly people who are wealthy could easily forego Social Security benefits.

- **Remove the income cap.** As of 2009, workers are paid Social Security taxes only on wages up to $106,800 per year. Thus, those who earn millions a year pay the same tax as a worker who earns only $106,800 a year. Removing the income cap would create more tax revenue without further taxing strained paychecks.

- **Raise the retirement age.** Congress did so, but under current law, the retirement age won't rise from 65 to 67 until 2027. A revised law should phase in this change at an earlier date. By 2020, the retirement age should be 70 or higher, reflecting the increased life expectancy of future generations.

- **Decrease the COLA.** Social Security benefits are increased annually to reflect inflation. Benefit levels are adjusted each year according to the change in average U.S. wages. Over the long term, wages have outpaced consumer prices by roughly 1 percent a year, causing Social Security benefits to be too large. The formula could be changed so that benefits keep pace with prices instead of wages.

- **Fully tax Social Security benefits.** Rather than taxing Social Security benefits only partially, treat them as ordinary income subject to full taxation.

None of these options is politically popular with senior citizens. Many of them lived through the Depression and World War II, and they believe the wolf is always at the door. Their generation took care of their parents and frequently lived with and supported them in extended families. Why shouldn't the next generation do the same? Given the voting power of the AARP (formerly the American Association of Retired Persons), it is not difficult to see why the president and Congress have been reluctant to cut Social Security benefits.

However, critics see Social Security as an anachronism, built on Depression-era concerns about high unemployment and widespread dependency among the aged. They see the prospect of reform today as an opportunity to modernize the way society saves for retirement. Believing that government-run, pay-as-you-go systems are unsustainable in aging societies, they prefer a system that would let workers acquire wealth by investing for their own retirement rather than the current system, which must impost tax hikes on future workers to meet promised benefits.

Should Social Security Be Privatized?

In his second inaugural address, in 2005, President George W. Bush proposed that workers under 55 be allowed to divert 4 percentage points of their 12.4 percent annual Social Security payroll tax to personal retirement investment accounts. This approach would allow participants to take advantage of the superior growth prospects offered by the stock market. Today, the promised benefits of Social Security work out to about a 2-percent annual return on payroll taxes. The same funds invested in a balanced portfolio of stocks might earn a greater amount.

Private investment accounts have several advantages. They would allow retirement plans to be tailored to individual needs and preferences. Individuals who can bear more risk, perhaps because they own their houses outright, might prefer to hold retirement portfolios that are more heavily weighted with stocks. Private accounts would also allow healthy persons who like their jobs to work past the usual retirement age without having to sacrifice a part of their retirement incomes. Simply put, private accounts would allow individuals to save for retirement with their preferred mix of stocks and securities, and they would also choose their own best time to retire.

However, critics of private investment accounts argue that the funds going into them would be removed from the social insurance system. Therefore, they would no longer be available to pool risk and transfer income between high- and low-wage workers, between families with and without children, and between the able and the disabled during retirement. Rather than offering a guaranteed government benefit, Social Security payments to individual workers would depend on asset values, interest rates, and investment strategies, as well as lifetime earnings.

Critics also note that adding private accounts to Social Security doesn't absolve us of the promises still outstanding to retirees. Maintaining existing benefits would entail just as high a cost to a privatized Social Security system as would the current system. For example, suppose a privatized program places 4 percent of your Social Security tax in a private investment account. The rest continues to pay current beneficiaries, except that now there is less revenue to cover the same bill. The money has to come from somewhere, so taxes must be increased, money borrowed, or benefits cut.

Finally, there is the cost of changing the existing Social Security system. If workers shift, say, 4 percentage points of payroll tax to their individual retirement accounts, the government would have to find other money to pay benefits to current retirees. The transition cost over the next decade could easily total $1 trillion to $2 trillion. To come up with the money, the government would have to either raise taxes or borrow money. At the time this textbook was written, it remained to be seen how our Social Security system will be reformed.

GOVERNMENT FINANCE

We now compare the expenditures and receipts of the federal, state, and local units of government. Indeed, the preparation of the federal government's annual budget is a complicated process, as seen in Figure 9.1.

Table 9.4 gives a breakdown of the federal budget for fiscal year 2008. It may be surprising that the largest component of federal spending was not national defense. Instead, it was *income transfer programs* such as Social Security, Medicare, and public assistance to the poor and disabled. These items made up 50 percent of federal expenditures in 2008. The next largest expenditure in that year was *national defense,* which accounted for 21 percent of federal spending.

Another category of federal expenditures is *interest on the public debt.* In the past, the federal government often incurred a budget deficit, which is the amount by which expenditures exceed tax revenues. The national or *public debt* is the total accumulation of the federal government's combined deficits over many years. To finance its debt, the federal government sells securities (U.S. savings bonds) to investors. When a security matures, investors are paid its face value plus the accumulated interest. Federal expenditures for interest on the public debt stood at 8 percent of government expenditures in 2008. As the government uses more tax dollars to pay for interest

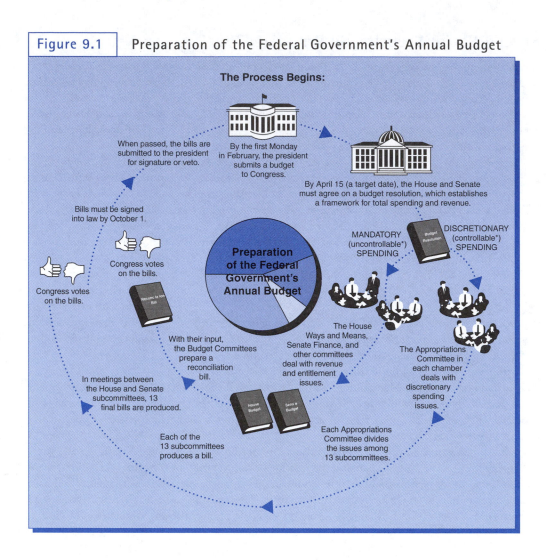

Figure 9.1   Preparation of the Federal Government's Annual Budget

on the public debt, fewer tax dollars are available for public education, police and fire protection, and other governmental programs.

Where does the federal government obtain its funds? Table 9.4 gives a breakdown of federal government receipts in fiscal year 2008. We see that the largest share of revenue came from the *personal income tax* (45 percent), which is paid by households, sole proprietorships, and partnerships. This was followed by *Social Security* contributions, or payroll taxes (37 percent). The federal government also levied *corporate income taxes* on corporate profits (12 percent) and consumption taxes taking the form of excise taxes or sales taxes on goods such as gasoline, tobacco, and alcohol (4 percent). Other miscellaneous taxes consisted of death and gift taxes, customs duties, and licenses.

The expenditures and receipts of government vary among the different government units. Referring to Table 9.4, we see that state and local governments allocated 34 percent of their expenditures to *public education* in 2006. *Public welfare* was the second most important expenditure of state and local government (18 percent), followed by expenditures on highways (6 percent). On the revenue side, state and local governments relied primarily on *sales and excise taxes* (19 percent) and *property taxes* (16 percent) in 2006. Personal income taxes accounted for only 12 percent of state and local revenues. This is unlike the federal government, which relies primarily on the personal income tax as its main revenue source. Besides collecting tax revenues, state and local governments receive grants from the federal government, which amounted to 21 percent of state and local receipts in 2006.

| Table 9.4 | Government Receipts and Expenditures (percentage of total) |

Federal Government, 2008

Receipts		Expenditures	
Personal income taxes	45%	Social Security, Medicare, income security	50%
Social Security, Medicare, retirement taxes	37	National defense	21
Corporate income taxes	12	Net interest on the public debt	8
Excise taxes	4	Health	9
Other	2	Other	12
	100%		100%

State and Local Government, 2006

Receipts		Expenditures	
Sales and excise taxes	19%	Education	34%
Revenue from the federal government	21	Public welfare	18
Property tax	16	Highways	6
Personal income tax	12	Other	42
Corporate income tax	2		100%
Other	30		
	100%		

Source: Economic Report of the President, 2009, Tables B-80 and B-86..

How does the tax burden of the United States compare with that of other countries? Table 9.5 presents total tax receipts at all levels of government as a share of gross domestic output for eight countries in 2006. This measure relates the size of the tax burden in each nation to its economic output, and it is equivalent to an average tax rate for the nation as a whole. As can be seen in the table, the United States had an average tax rate of 28 percent of domestic output. Sweden topped the list with an average tax rate of 49 percent. By international standards, U.S. citizens have a lighter tax burden than many other people living in the industrialized world.

| Table 9.5 | Total Tax Receipts as a Percentage of Gross Domestic Output, 2006 |

Nation	Average Tax Rate
Sweden	49%
Norway	45
France	44
United Kingdom	38
Canada	34
United States	28
Japan	28
South Korea	26

Source: Organization for Economic Cooperation and Development, *Revenue Statistics,* 2008, available at http://www.oecd.org.

TAXATION PRINCIPLES: BENEFITS RECEIVED VERSUS ABILITY TO PAY

Much of the public debate regarding taxation, as reported in the press, concerns the issue of equity. Are taxes fair? People are generally more likely to comply voluntarily with tax policies if they believe that the policies are reasonable and equitable. A fair tax system is usually regarded as one that is based on people's ability to pay taxes, although some contend that taxes should instead be based on how much people benefit from public expenditures.

According to the **benefits-received principle** of taxation, taxes should be paid in proportion to the benefits that taxpayers derive from public expenditures. Just as people pay private dollars in proportion to their consumption of private goods, such as food and clothing, an individual's taxes should be related to his or her use of public goods, such as parks or roads. From this viewpoint, the ideal tax would be a *user charge,* like those that would be established if business firms provided public goods.

The *gasoline tax,* for example, is consistent with the benefits-received principle. Gas taxes are used to finance the construction and maintenance of roads and other transportation systems. The number of gallons of gas that an individual buys is an indicator of the amount of transportation services used; the larger the number of gallons bought, the greater the tax paid. Also, *taxes on airline tickets* are used to finance air-traffic control, airport operations, and airport security. Frequent fliers obtain greater benefits from the airline transportation system and thus pay higher taxes to fund its operation. Moreover, if the construction of a new bridge is financed by *tolls* on the bridge, this payment method follows the benefits-received principle because drivers pay for the bridge only if they use it.

Difficulties arise, however, when we attempt to apply the benefits-received principle to many important categories of government spending, such as national defense, police and fire protection, and public education. How could we calculate the benefit that particular individuals get from these goods and the amount of tax they should have to pay? We cannot make such a calculation! Moreover, it is even more difficult to apply the benefits-received principle to programs that redistribute national income. For example, it would not make sense to force unemployed workers, who receive unemployment compensation, to pay all the taxes to finance their welfare benefits. Although there are many situations in which the benefits-received principle applies, it has historically played a minor role in the development of the U.S. tax system.

The **ability-to-pay principle** sharply contrasts with the benefits-received principle. Ability-to-pay taxation is founded on the notion that people with greater income and wealth should be taxed at a higher rate because their ability to pay is presumably greater. Most people would find it reasonable for Bill Gates, the founder of Microsoft Corp. and one of the wealthiest people in the United States, to pay more taxes than those with modest income; he should also pay a higher proportion of his income in taxes! As we will see in the next section, progressive income taxation incorporates the ability-to-pay concept.

A limitation of the ability-to-pay principle is that there is no precise way to calculate one's fair ability to pay taxes. How much higher should the tax rate be for those with higher incomes? The answer seems to be based on guesswork and on the government's need for revenue.

PROGRESSIVE, REGRESSIVE, AND PROPORTIONAL TAXES

Recall that governments raise revenues from a variety of taxes, such as income taxes, property taxes, Social Security taxes, and sales taxes. These taxes fit into one of three types of taxation systems: *proportional* taxation, *progressive* taxation, and *regressive* taxation. Taxes are proportional if they take a constant fraction of income as income rises; progressive if they take a larger fraction of income as income rises; and regressive if they take a smaller fraction of income as income rises.

Table 9.6	Progressive, Proportional, and Regressive Taxes				
		Total Income	Taxes Due	Total Average Tax Rate	Marginal Tax Rate	
Progressive Tax	$ 0	$ 0	—	—	In a progressive tax system, the average tax rate and the marginal tax rate rise as income increases.
	100	5	5%	5%	
	200	20	10	15	
	300	45	15	25	
Regressive Tax	$ 0	$ 0	—	—	In a regressive tax system, the average tax rate and the marginal tax rate fall as income increases.
	100	30	30%	30%	
	200	50	25	20	
	300	60	20	10	
Proportional Tax	$ 0	$ 0	—	—	In a proportional tax system, the average tax rate and the marginal tax rate remain the same as income increases.
	100	10	10%	10%	
	200	20	10	10	
	300	30	10	10	

Table 9.6 shows the average tax rate and marginal tax rate under these tax systems. Column 1 shows different levels of total income earned by an individual. Column 2 shows the total taxes due at various levels of income. Column 3 shows the **average tax rate,** which is equal to total taxes due divided by total income:

$$\text{Average tax rate} = \frac{\text{Total taxes due}}{\text{Total income}}$$

Column 4 shows the **marginal tax rate,** which is the fraction of additional income paid in taxes:

$$\text{Marginal tax rate} = \frac{\text{Change in taxes due}}{\text{Change in income}}$$

Let us first calculate the average tax rate under a *progressive* tax system. Referring to the upper portion of Table 9.6, at an income of $100, the average tax rate is 5 percent ($5/$100 = 0.05); at an income of $200, the average tax rate is 10 percent ($20/$200 = 0.10); at an income of $300, the average tax rate is 15 percent ($45/$300 = 0.15). As these figures show, this tax system is progressive because the average tax rate increases as income rises.

Now we will compute the marginal tax rate under a progressive tax system. Referring to Table 9.6, as income increases in the first bracket from $0 to $100, taxes due rise from $0 to $5. The marginal tax rate of the first bracket thus equals 5 percent ($5/$100 = 0.05). Moving to the second bracket, as income rises from $100 to $200, taxes due increase from $5 to $20, and the marginal tax rate equals 15 percent ($15/$100 = 0.15). As income increases by another $100, taxes due rise by $25, and the marginal tax rate equals 25 percent. Our current tax system is progressive because the marginal tax rate increases as an individual moves to higher brackets of income. We conclude that in a progressive tax system, both the average tax rate and the marginal tax rate rise as income increases. Progressive taxation is thus consistent with the ability-to-pay principle of taxation.

Next, we consider a *regressive* tax. With regressive taxation, a smaller fraction of income is taken in taxes as income increases. Refer to the regressive tax shown in Table 9.6. As income increases, taxes due also rise. The tax is regressive, however, because the average tax rate and the marginal tax rate fall as income increases. A regressive tax thus imposes a relatively larger burden on the poor than on the rich and thus contradicts the ability-to-pay principle of taxation.

Finally, there is the *proportional* tax, also called a *flat-rate* tax. Proportional taxation means that as an individual's income rises, taxes due rise by the same fraction. Refer to the proportional tax shown in Table 9.6. As income rises, the average tax rate is 10 percent for each tax bracket, and the marginal tax rate turns out to be 10 percent as well.

What is the relationship between a proportional tax and the ability-to-pay principle of taxation? Consider a 20-percent tax that collects $2,000 from Joe Smith, who earns $10,000 a year, and $20,000 from Helen Miller, who earns $100,000 a year. Although each individual pays an identical tax rate of 20 percent, the tax imposes a greater burden on Joe than on Helen. After paying the tax, Joe has little income left to buy groceries for his family; Helen, however, can live comfortably after paying her tax. One could argue that Helen is not paying a fair share of her income in taxes according to the ability-to-pay principle.

THE U.S. TAX STRUCTURE

Let us now try to understand the principles on which the U.S. tax system is constructed. What can be said about the progressivity, regressivity, or proportionality of the major taxes in the United States?

Federal Personal Income Tax

The most important tax in the U.S. economy is the federal personal income tax. All U.S. citizens, resident aliens, and most others who earn income in the United States are required to pay federal taxes on all **taxable income.** Taxable income is gross income minus exemptions, deductions, and credits:

Gross Income (wages, salaries, tips, bonuses, and so on)

- **Exemptions** (an allowance for each household member)
- **Deductions** (home mortgage interest payments, business expenses, charitable contributions, medical expenses, and certain state and local taxes)
- **Credits** (child care, elderly and disabled, low-income allowance)

Taxable Income

Table 9.7 shows the federal income tax rates for a single taxpayer in 2009. The federal income tax is *progressive* because the average tax rate and the marginal tax rate increase as an individual moves into higher brackets of taxable income. Table 9.8 shows the share of federal income taxes paid by various income groups in 2006. These figures are also consistent with the progressive impact of the federal

| Table 9.7 | Federal Income Tax Rates for a Single Taxpayer, 2009 |

Tax Bracket		Taxes Due*	Average Tax Rate	Marginal Tax Rate
Over	Up to			
$ 0	$ 8,350	$ 835	10%	10%
8,350	33,950	4,675	14	15
33,950	82,250	16,750	20	25
82,250	171,550	41,754	24	28
171,550	372,950	108,216	29	33
372,960 and over				35

*Computed according to the top of the six taxable income brackets.

Source: Internal Revenue Service, *2009 Tax Rate Schedules,* available at http://www.irs.gov.

Table 9.8	Percentage of Federal Personal Income Tax Paid by Income Groups, 2006	
Percentile (ranked by adjusted gross income)	**Percentage of Federal Personal Income Tax Paid**	
Top 1%	40%	
Top 5	60	
Top 10	71	
Top 25	86	
Top 50	97	
Bottom 50	3	

Source: *Top 1 Percent of Tax Filers Pay Highest Share in Decade*, Joint Economic Committee, October 29, 2008, available at http://www.house.gov/jec.

income tax. For example, the top 1 percent of tax filers paid 40 percent of federal taxes, while the top 10 percent of tax filers paid 71 percent. These data must be kept in mind when evaluating proposals to revise the tax system. Simply put, the tax shares already paid by various income groups largely determine the distributional outcomes of most major tax proposals, not the tax rate structure of the legislation itself.

Federal Corporate Income Tax

After a corporation has determined its annual income and met all of its expenses, it must pay part of its income to the federal government. The corporate income tax is essentially a *proportional* tax, with a flat rate of 35 percent for almost all corporations.

Social Security Tax

As of 2009, the Social Security tax was imposed on an individual's wage income up to $106,800. The Social Security tax (excluding Medicare) equaled 12.4 percent, split evenly between employee and employer (6.2 percent each).

The Social Security tax is largely a proportional tax because it taxes a fixed percentage of wage earnings. It does have some regressive features, however, because the tax rate is higher on low wages than on high wages. For example, in 2009, a worker's Social Security tax rate was 6.2 percent, applied to the first $106,800 of wage income. A worker earning exactly $106,800 would pay a Social Security tax of $6,621.60 ($0.062 \times \$106,800 = \$6,621.60$). However, a worker who earns twice as much, $213,600, would also pay a Social Security tax of $6,621.60, resulting in a tax rate of only 3.1 percent ($\$6,621.60 / \$213,600 = 0.031$). We conclude that the Social Security tax becomes regressive once wage income exceeds $213,600.

The regressivity of the Social Security tax is magnified by the inclusion of nonwage income such as dividends and interest, which tend to be received more by higher income individuals. In the previous example, suppose our worker with wage income of $213,600 also received dividends of $100,000, so that his total income was $313,600. The Social Security tax would then amount to only 2 percent ($\$6,621.60 / \$313,600 = 0.02$) of total income.

Sales, Excise, and Property Taxes

States obtain most of their revenues from general sales taxes on goods and services. In addition, states usually add their own excise taxes to the federal excise taxes on gasoline, liquor, and cigarettes. As for local governments, most of their revenues come from property taxes.

Sales taxes are regressive because lower-income families generally spend a larger fraction of their income to purchase consumption items that are subject to sales and excise taxes. Higher-income families, however, generally save a portion of their income and thus devote a smaller fraction of their income to consumption goods that are subject to sales and excise taxes.

Assume, for example, that the state of Wisconsin imposes an 8-percent sales tax on all purchases. The Miller family earned $30,000 during the past year, while the Jefferson family earned $100,000. The Millers, with a $30,000 income, spend their entire income on food and other necessities, whereas the Jeffersons, with a $100,000 income, spend $40,000 on food and other necessities and save the remainder. Because each family pays an 8-percent sales tax, the lower-income Millers pay taxes of $2,400 (0.08 × $30,000 = $2,400), which is about 1/12 of their income. The higher-income Jeffersons, however, pay taxes of $3,200 (0.08 × $40,000 = $3,200), which is about 3/100 of their income. Although the wealthier Jeffersons pay more taxes than the poorer Millers, the sales tax is regressive because the Jeffersons' average tax rate is lower than that of the Millers.

Excise taxes, such as those on cigarettes, are also *regressive.* Cigarettes are widely recognized as an inferior good—that is, consumption decreases as income increases. Individuals with lower incomes thus tend to spend more on cigarettes than those with higher incomes. The cigarette taxes paid by low-income people account for a larger fraction of their incomes than the taxes paid by high-income people.

Property taxes are levied mainly on real estate—buildings and land. Each locality establishes an annual tax rate that is applied to the assessed value of property. Economists generally agree that property taxes on real estate are *regressive,* for the same reasons that sales taxes are regressive: As a fraction of income, property taxes are higher for the poor than the wealthy because the poor must spend a larger share of their income on housing.

Overall U.S. Tax System

As we have seen, the federal tax system (especially the personal income tax) is somewhat progressive. However, state and local governments rely mainly on sales, excise, and property taxes, which are regressive. Most economists argue that when federal, state, and local taxes are combined, the overall effect is roughly *proportional.* The overall tax system itself does not significantly affect the distribution of the nation's income because the rich and poor alike pay roughly the same fraction of their income as taxes.

Although the U.S. tax system does not substantially redistribute income from the rich to the poor, the U.S. system of transfer payments does decrease income inequality. Transfer payments to the poorest fifth of American families are almost four times as much as their combined incomes. The U.S. transfer payment system is therefore more progressive than the U.S. tax system by itself.

CHECK POINT

1. Distinguish between government expenditures and transfer payments.

2. Identify the major sources of revenues and expenditures of the federal government, as well as state and local governments.

3. Which of the following taxes is consistent with the ability-to-pay principle, and which is consistent with the benefits-received principle: federal income tax, gasoline tax, tolls used to finance the construction of a bridge.

4. Define a proportional tax, a progressive tax, and a regressive tax. Classify the major federal taxes, as well as state and local taxes, according to these tax systems.

SHOULD THE U.S. TAX SYSTEM BE REFORMED?

Because the distribution of income in the United States is quite unequal, many people look to the federal income tax to redistribute income. Recall that the federal income tax is designed to be *progressive,* bearing down harder on the rich than on the poor. It fulfills this objective by defining five brackets of taxable income and taxing each at progressively higher rates ranging from 15 percent to 39.6 percent.

In reality, however, federal tax burdens are not so progressively distributed. Legal tax rates pertain only to taxable income. Much income is nontaxable because of tax loopholes established by Congress. Tax loopholes include exemptions, deductions, and credits, as previously discussed.

Suppose that Helen Smith earns a salary of $50,000. She is unmarried with no children, lives in a rented apartment, has no retirement plan, and doesn't benefit from any tax shelters. Helen puts all of her savings into a certificate of deposit (CD) at a local bank. In this situation, she cannot take advantage of any tax loopholes. When determining her taxable income, Helen benefits from only the personal exemption ($2,000). This decreases her taxable income to $48,000 and leads to a tax bill of $10,400.

Now suppose that Helen alters her financial position. She borrows money from a savings and loan institution to purchase a house, sets up an individual retirement account (retirement plan) at her bank, and donates money to her church. Helen still earns $50,000, but she now has several tax loopholes.

Helen again uses the personal exemption of $2,000, which decreases her taxable income to $48,000. From this amount, she can also deduct the interest payments on her home mortgage ($8,000), contributions to her individual retirement account ($2,000), and charitable contributions ($1,000). Helen's taxable income now totals $37,000, which results in a tax bill of $7,300. By taking advantage of these loopholes, Helen can decrease her average tax rate from 21 percent ($10,400/$50,000 = 0.21) to 15 percent ($7,300/$50,000 = 0.15). In short, the many exemptions, deductions, and credits permitted by the Internal Revenue Service *decrease the progressivity* of the federal income tax system.

Critics of the federal income tax system maintain that it is unfair and inefficient. They contend that the federal income tax favors the rich, who are able to shelter much of their income by using tax loopholes. Is it fair that some wealthy individuals pay little or no taxes? Second, critics argue that the federal income tax system is costly for taxpayers, who must keep records and fill out tax forms. Given the complexity of the federal regulations, an estimated 40 percent of all taxpayers pay for professional help devoted to legal tax avoidance. Such costs could be avoided with a simpler tax system. Third, it is maintained that progressive tax rates discourage saving and investment, which promote economic growth. Finally, the tax system violates the principle that people with the same income pay the same taxes. Depending on the composition of a particular taxpayer's household, Americans with identical incomes may pay wildly different taxes.

These concerns have prompted proposals for reforming the federal tax system. Any reasonable reform would reduce loopholes, lower rates, and abolish the tax bias against saving and investment. The result would be a simpler system that is easy for taxpayers to figure out and one that is transparent, so that the cost of government services would be readily visible. Three of the most widely discussed reforms that have been proposed are the flat-rate income tax, the value-added tax, and the national sales tax.

Flat-Rate Income Tax

In its purest form, a **flat-rate income tax** system would junk the existing array of five different tax rates on personal income and replace them with a single tax rate. In addition, all exemptions, deductions, and credits would be abolished. By eliminating tax loopholes, all income, regardless of its source, would be taxed at the same rate, ending complaints that many taxpayers, especially the rich, are able to shelter much of their income by using tax loopholes. A flat-tax system would be designed to generate the same revenue as the current progressive income tax. It is estimated that a flat tax of about 20 percent would yield identical revenue.

| Figure 9.2 | Replacing the Progressive Income Tax with a Flat-Rate Tax |

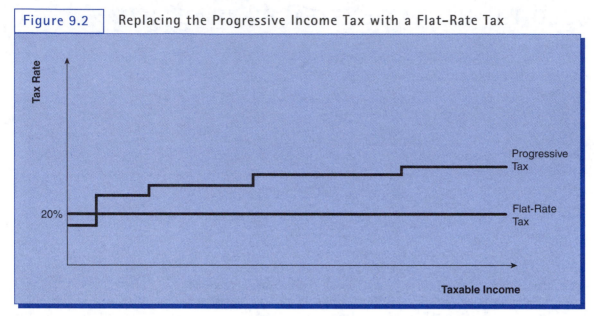

Replacing the progressive income tax with a flat-rate tax of 20 percent would decrease the tax burden of higher-income individuals while increasing the tax burden of the poor and lower-middle class. The poor could be protected by giving them some tax loopholes, such as a standard deduction and personal exemptions for dependents.

As seen in Figure 9.2, replacing the progressive income tax with a flat-rate tax would have a dramatic impact on the distribution of the U.S. tax burden. Holding tax revenue constant, a flat-rate tax would reduce the tax burden on higher-income individuals while increasing the burden on the poor and lower-middle class. Because such an income redistribution is widely perceived as unfair, the proposals for a flat tax include some tax loopholes to protect the poor.

Proponents of a flat tax contend that it would simplify the tax system and thus reduce the cost of keeping records and filling out tax forms. The gains in simplicity would be immense: Families and businesses could file their returns on forms the size of postcards. The numbers entered on these forms would be clear and easy to calculate. Opportunities for cheating would be minimized.

In spite of the advantages of a flat-rate income tax, several difficulties remain. One problem is the costly transition that it would involve. Individuals and corporations have made major decisions and investments designed to maximize income based on certain deductions and tax rates under the current tax structure. Thus, the introduction of a flat tax and the elimination of tax loopholes would alter long-standing tax rules sharply. A flat tax would also alter the distribution of income and wealth by increasing taxes on some income groups and decreasing taxes on others. The elimination of all deductions likely would encounter opposition from special interest groups representing churches, schools, state and local governments, housing industries, and the elderly who benefit from tax deductions.

A less extreme reform of the federal tax system would be to close tax loopholes while retaining the current progressive income tax. Advocates of this reform argue that there are plenty of loopholes that don't make economic sense. Tax breaks for second homes and lavish deductions for business expenses, for example, could be eliminated in order to cut taxes on working families. Nobody likes taxes. But if we are to have public services, doesn't it make sense to pay for them by taxing wealthy people at higher rates than the middle and working class?

Value-Added Tax

The U.S. government taxes it citizens mostly on the income they earn rather than on what they spend on consumption. However, many economists argue that this policy creates disincentives to

Table 9.9	Taxes on Goods and Services as a Share of Total Tax Revenues, 2006	

Country	Taxes on Goods and Services (percentage of total tax revenue)
Germany	29.4%
Canada	24.4
Japan	29.1
United Kingdom	29.1
Italy	26.0
France	24.9
United States	16.5

Source: U.S. Department of Commerce, Bureau of the Census, *Statistical Abstract of the United States*, 2009, Table 1317.

earn income. A household who earns income and then invests that income for the future pays taxes twice: first on the original amount and next on any income earned from the investments. Therefore, a system that taxes households on their income rather than consumption provides them an incentive to spend their income today rather than to save and invest for the future. Yet, economists recognize that Americans need to save more for education expenses and retirement and investment is a source of economic growth. This underlies the rationale for a system that taxes consumption rather than a system that taxes income.

A **value-added tax (VAT)** is proposed by some as a substitute for current federal taxes: it would tax consumption instead of taxing income. A VAT operates like a retail sales tax, except that it is collected from businesses at the various *stages of production* of goods and services. For a loaf of bread, for example, the VAT would be collected from the farmer for wheat production, from the miller for flour production, from the baker at the cooking stage, and from the grocer at the retail sale stage. A VAT thus amounts to a *national sales tax* on consumer goods, that is, a consumption tax.

Many European nations, such as Sweden and Germany, currently use the VAT as a source of revenue. This is reflected in Table 9.9, which illustrates taxes on goods and services as a fraction of total tax revenues for selected nations. By the time the VAT reaches the final consumer, it averages around 20 percent in Europe.

Proponents of VAT argue that Americans need to increase savings and investment and that VAT would help fulfill this objective. Also, a VAT would make tax avoidance extremely difficult. This is because tax-paying businesses leave a paper trail, which reduces the potential for tax evasion. However, the United States has not implemented a VAT for several reasons. Because the VAT is largely hidden, final customers may be unaware of the VAT included in the price of a product. Voters may thus underestimate their true tax burden and thus support additional spending made possible by the expansion of tax revenues. Other objections are that the VAT generally has high administrative costs and that it is a regressive tax that takes a larger share of poor people's incomes than it takes from the rich.

National Sales Tax

Another alternative to the current federal income tax is a **national sales tax.** This system would entail a federal consumption tax collected at the retail level by businesses. Used items would not be taxed. The national sales tax would equal a set percentage of the retail price of taxable goods and services. Retail businesses would collect the tax from individuals and remit the tax revenues to the federal government.

Proponents argue that a national sales tax is a fair and simple alternative to the current federal income tax. The national sales tax is a voluntary consumption tax in which the more you buy, the more you pay in taxes; the less you buy, the less you pay in taxes. Also, this system would collect taxes from everyone living in the United States, including aliens, illegal aliens, and the underground cash economy and thus add billions to the nation's treasury. To make sure that a national sales tax would not bear down excessively on low-income families, who spend almost every penny they earn on subsistence items, tax rebates would be provided for poverty-level expenditures. Moreover, as a tax on consumption rather than a tax on income, a national sales tax would better promote saving and investment than the current federal income tax.

However, critics maintain that the rates would be crushing if a national sales tax were established to generate the same amount of revenue that is generated under the current federal income tax. The national sales tax rate could be as much as 50 percent—or more—and out of proportion with any existing state sales tax. The temptation to evade the national sales tax would thus become overwhelming, according to critics.

This chapter has examined the mixed economy of the United States. The next chapter will focus on how productivity influences the U.S. economy by considering its gross domestic product.

CHECK POINT

1. Do tax loopholes make the federal income tax more or less progressive? Why?

2. Why do critics of the current federal income tax system maintain that it is unfair and inefficient?

3. How does a flat-rate income tax differ from a progressive income tax?

4. Explain why a value-added tax is essentially a national sales tax.

Chapter Summary

1. The way income is divided among members of society is known as the distribution of income. There are two approaches to analyzing income distribution. The functional distribution of income refers to the shares of a nation's income that accrue to land, labor, capital, and entrepreneurship as rent, wages, interest, and profits. The personal distribution of income refers to the shares of income received by poor, middle-income, and wealthy families.

2. Household income flows into consumption expenditures, taxes, and savings. The United States has a service-oriented economy, with more than half of household consumption expenditures used to pay for services.

3. A business firm can be organized in one of three ways: as a sole proprietorship, a partnership, or a corporation. Although sole proprietorships are numerically dominant in the United States, corporations account for the largest share of total business sales.

4. Government expenditures include federal, state, and local government purchases of goods and services, as well as transfer payments. Transfer payments have been the main source of growth in government expenditures in the past four decades.

5. Social Security is the largest retirement and disability program in the United States. It is a pay-as-you-go system that is financed by payroll taxes levied on employees and their employers. Social Security is mandatory for most workers, who must belong whether they like it or not. Social Security's financial problems largely stem from liberal benefit increases and a declining number of workers paying into Social Security compared to an increasing number of beneficiaries.

6. For the U.S. government, the personal income tax is the major source of revenue. Income transfer programs—such as Social Security and Medicare—are the major expenditures. State and local governments rely primarily on sales taxes, excise taxes, and property taxes to raise revenues. Education is their major expenditure.

7. The U.S. tax system is founded on the benefits-received and ability-to-pay principles. Taxes fit into one of three types of systems: proportional taxation, progressive taxation, and regressive taxation. The federal tax system is somewhat progressive, whereas state and local tax systems tend to be regressive.

8. Tax loopholes—including exemptions, deductions, and credits—decrease the progressivity of the federal income tax. Critics of the federal income tax contend that it favors the rich, who can shelter much of their income by using tax loopholes. Proposed reforms of the federal tax system include the flat-rate income tax, the value-added tax, and the national sales tax.

Key Terms and Concepts

mixed economy (197)	Social Security (203)
distribution of income (197)	Medicare (203)
functional distribution of income (197)	cost-of-living adjustment (COLA) (203)
personal distribution of income (197)	benefits-received principle (208)
human capital (199)	ability-to-pay principle (208)
sole proprietorship (200)	average tax rate (209)
partnership (200)	marginal tax rate (209)
corporation (201)	taxable income (210)
government expenditures (202)	flat-rate income tax (213)
government purchases (202)	value-added tax (VAT) (215)
transfer payments (202)	national sales tax (215)

Self-Test: Multiple-Choice Questions

1. The U.S. Social Security system

    a. is essentially a pay-as-you-go system that is financed by payroll taxes.
    b. is a welfare system that is financed by personal income taxes.
    c. requires all workers to have personal investment accounts with the system.
    d. earns a profit that is turned over to state and local governments.

2. The functional distribution of income shows how

    a. income is divided among land, labor, capital, and entrepreneurship.
    b. income is divided among low-, middle-, and high-income groups in society.
    c. households divide their income among consumption, savings, and taxes.
    d. households divide their income among durable goods, nondurable goods, and services.

3. The Social Security tax is

    a. proportional at low incomes and progressive at high incomes.
    b. proportional at low incomes and regressive at high incomes.

    c. regressive at low incomes and progressive at high incomes.

    d. progressive at low incomes and regressive at high incomes.

4. For a value-added tax, all of the following are true *except* that it is

    a. essentially a national sales tax on consumer goods and services.

    b. used more widely in the United States than in Europe.

    c. collected at various stages of production of goods and services.

    d. a tax on consumption rather than a tax on saving.

5. All of the following taxes tend to be regressive *except*

    a. sales taxes of state governments.

    b. excise taxes of state governments.

    c. property taxes of local governments.

    d. income tax of the federal government.

6. The Personal Responsibility and Work Opportunity Reconciliation Act of 1996

    a. terminated all federal welfare assistance to the needy.

    b. reduced federal payments by 10 percent to all recipients.

    c. limited the time that households can receive welfare.

    d. increased welfare payments to immigrants.

7. In its purest form, a _____ would eliminate all exemptions, deductions, and credits so that a person's gross income would equal taxable income.

    a. value-added tax

    b. consumption tax

    c. flat-rate tax

    d. regressive income tax

8. The ability-to-pay principle is most evident in

    a. tolls used to finance the construction and operation of a bridge.

    b. taxes on airline tickets that are used to finance airport security.

    c. gasoline taxes that are used to finance the construction and maintenance of roads.

    d. the progressive income tax of the federal government.

9. The largest source of revenue of the federal government is the

    a. corporate income tax.

    b. Social Security tax.

    c. sales tax.

    d. personal income tax.

10. For state and local governments, the largest sources of revenue are

    a. sales taxes and property taxes, respectively.

    b. excise taxes and license fees, respectively.

    c. personal income taxes and property taxes, respectively.

    d. corporate income taxes and excise taxes, respectively.

Answers to Multiple-Choice Questions

1. a   2. a   3. b   4. b   5. d   6. c   7. c   8. d   9. d   10. a

Study Questions and Problems

1. Compare the advantages and disadvantages of a sole proprietorship, a partnership, and a corporation.

2. Distinguish between the benefits-received principle of taxation and the ability-to-pay principle of taxation. Which principle is more evident in the U.S. tax system?

3. Describe the progressivity, proportionality, or regressivity of the major taxes of the federal government and of state and local governments.

4. The U.S. tax system alone is more progressive than the U.S. system of taxes and transfer payments combined. Do you agree with this statement?

5. Table 9.10 gives four levels of taxable income and the taxes to be paid at each of the income levels.

   a. Calculate the average tax rate and the marginal tax rate at each level of taxable income.
   b. Indicate whether the tax is progressive, proportional, or regressive.

Table 9.10 | **Hypothetical Tax Data**

Total Taxable income	Total Taxes Paid	Average Tax Rate (%)	Marginal Tax Rate (%)
$10,000	$3,500		
20,000	6,000		
30,000	7,500		
40,000	8,000		

6. Assume that the state of California levies an 8-percent sales tax on all consumption expenditures. Consumption expenditures for four income levels are illustrated in Table 9.11.

   a. Calculate the sales tax paid at the four income levels.
   b. Calculate the average tax rate at these incomes.
   c. If income were used as the tax base, the sales tax would be classified as a _____ tax.

Table 9.11 | **Hypothetical Sales Tax Data**

Income	Consumption Expenditures	Sales Tax Paid	Average Tax Rate (%)
$10,000	$10,000	$	
11,000	10,800		
12,000	11,600		
13,000	12,400		

7. Would the proposed flat-rate income tax, value-added tax, or national sales tax lead to a more fair and efficient tax system than the current federal income tax?

Gross Domestic Product and Economic Growth

Chapter objectives

After reading this chapter, you should be able to:

1. Discuss the nature of gross domestic product and explain how it is calculated.

2. Distinguish between nominal gross domestic product and real gross domestic product.

3. Describe the factors that underlie a nation's rate of economic growth in the long run.

4. Discuss the policies that a government might enact to speed up economic growth.

5. Distinguish between traditional growth theory and new growth theory.

economics IN CONTEXT

Has the growth in technological innovation affected the economy as a whole? Yes, by increasing the productivity of the economy. Labor productivity in manufacturing, retail and wholesale trade, finance, business services, and other sectors of the economy has risen as a result of technological advances, improved organizational practices, and increased global competition. As we have learned, a more efficient economy can produce more output with a given amount of resources.

The changes witnessed in the steel industry exemplify these changes in production processes and management practices. The fundamental processes of steelmaking remain much as they always were: melting raw material, forming it into an intermediate product, and shaping and treating that product to create the final goods. But a number of technological advances—many incorporating computer technology to measure, monitor, and control these processes—have affected almost every step in the production of steel.

As recently as 1990, steelmaking involved extensive manual control and setup and relied heavily on operators' experience, observation, and intuition to control the process. Computer processing of data from sensors, using innovative software, has improved the ability to control the process, allowing faster, more efficient operation.

For example, the availability of computing power to quickly process data has enabled steelmakers to reduce both energy consumption and wear and tear on equipment. The setup for casting molten steel into an intermediate product has changed from a process in which several operators would "walk the line," setting the controls for every motor and pump, to one in which a single operator uses an automatic control system that synchronizes and sets the equipment. The rolling process now incorporates sensors that constantly inspect the steel for deviations from the desired shape, allowing operators to make corrections before material is wasted. Operators can remotely control the speed and clearance of the rolls using computer-controlled motors to correct problems as they occur.

The result of this computer integration into steelmaking has been a significant improvement in steelmaking performance. Together with other technological changes, such as larger furnaces and improvements in casting practices, as well as the closing of older, inefficient plants, the new technologies have contributed to higher product quality and productivity. Steelmakers today require fewer than 4 worker-hours to produce a ton of steel, down from 6 worker-hours in 1990. The best-performing mills can produce a ton of steel in less than 1 worker-hour.

In this chapter, we will learn how productivity influences the performance of not only a particular industry but also the economy as a whole. Just as a doctor gives a physical exam to determine how well a patient is, economists use statistics to get a quantitative measure of the economy's performance. This chapter will introduce the broadest measure of the total output of an economy—that is, gross domestic product—and discuss the factors that determine the long-run growth rate of an economy.

MEASURING AN ECONOMY'S OUTPUT

The output of an economy includes millions of different goods. We could tabulate how much of each product an economy produced in a given year: 3,600,224 houses, 2,436,789 radios, 40,987,345 apples, and so forth. Although such data may be useful for some purposes, they don't accurately measure an economy's output. Suppose that next year, the output of houses falls by 4 percent, the output of radios falls by 8 percent, and the output of apples rises by 2 percent. Has total output increased or decreased? By how much?

We need a single statistic to measure the output of an economy. But how do we add up all the houses, radios, apples, and millions of other goods produced in an economy? To make such a calculation, we compute what is known as **gross domestic product**, or **GDP**.

GROSS DOMESTIC PRODUCT

What exactly is GDP? GDP is the *market value of all final goods and services produced within a country in a given year*. All of the words in this definition are important.

- **"GDP is the market value"**
  You have likely heard the expression "You can't compare apples and oranges." However, GDP makes just such a comparison. GDP combines the different types of goods and services that an economy produced into a single measure of economic activity. To do this, it uses the total "market value" of the economy's output. Total market value means that we take the quantities of goods produced, multiply them by their respective prices, and add up the totals. For example, if an economy produced 200 apples at $0.20 an apple and 400 oranges at $0.15 an orange, the market value of these goods would be:

$$(200 \times \$0.20) + (400 \times \$0.15) = \$100$$

  Adding the market value of all goods and services gives the total market value, or GDP. The reason we multiply the quantity of goods by their respective prices is that we cannot simply add the number of apples and the number of oranges. Using prices permits us to express everything in a common standard of value, in this case dollars.

- **"of all final goods and services"**
  GDP is a comprehensive measure of a nation's output. It measures the market value of not only apples and oranges but also many other goods, such as jetliners, calculators, and clothing. GDP also comprises intangible services, such as banking, engineering, medical, and legal services. When you purchase a video of your favorite rock concert, you are purchasing a good, and the purchase is part of GDP. When you go to a football game, you are buying a service, and the ticket price is also part of GDP.

  Note that only "final" goods and services are included in GDP. Many goods and services are purchased for use as inputs in the production of other goods. For example, McDonald's buys ground beef to make Big Macs. If we counted the value of the ground beef and the value of the Big Mac, we would be counting the ground beef twice, thereby overstating the value of the production. Final goods, therefore, are finished goods and services that are produced for the end consumer.

- **"produced"**
  GDP measures the current production of an economy. Many financial transactions take place, but they do not directly generate current output, and so they must be excluded from GDP. These transactions include transfer payments such as welfare and Social Security payments that the government makes to individuals. They also include a college student's yearly subsidy from his family to finance his college education. Moreover, purchases and sales of stocks and bonds are not part of GDP because they do not represent the production of new goods and services.

- **"within a country"**
  GDP includes the value of production within the boundaries of a country. When a Mexican citizen works temporarily in the United States, her production is part of U.S. GDP. When General

Motors owns an assembly plant in Canada, the autos produced at that plant are part of Canada's GDP rather than U.S. GDP.

- **"in a given year"**
  Because GDP is expressed as a rate of current production, goods produced in previous years are not included in this year's GDP. If you sell your 2006 Honda Accord to a relative, this transaction would not be included in this year's GDP because no current production has occurred.

CHECK POINT

1. How do economists define gross domestic product (GDP)?

2. What is the significance of the following definitional characteristics of GDP?

   a. Market value
   b. Final goods and services
   c. Produced within a country
   d. In a given year

THE COMPONENTS OF GDP

The GDP of an economy can be calculated by totaling the expenditures on goods and services produced during the current year. National income accountants refer to this method of calculating GDP as the **expenditure approach**. When GDP is derived by the expenditure approach, its four components are (1) personal consumption expenditures, (2) gross private domestic investment, (3) government purchases of goods and services, and (4) net exports to foreigners.[1] Table 10.1 shows the components of GDP for the United States in 2008. Let us examine each of these components.

Personal consumption expenditures (C) are purchases of final goods and services by households and individuals. Some items are durable goods, such as refrigerators, that last for a number of years. Nondurable goods are items that consumers use soon after purchase, such as gasoline and food. Services include intangible items such as the services of mechanics and engineers. For the United States, personal consumption expenditures typically account for two-thirds or more of GDP.

Gross private domestic investment (I), commonly known as gross investment, consists of all private-sector spending on investment. Gross investment includes the purchase of capital equipment and structures, such as an IBM assembly plant, as well as purchases of new homes by households, a type of capital good. Moreover, gross investment includes changes in business inventories during the year. When General Motors' automobile inventories increase from one year to the next, they are added to investment. Increases in business inventories represent goods produced during the current year that have not yet been sold to buyers in the market. Conversely, decreases in business inventories during the year are counted as negative investment.

Government purchases of goods and services (G) include spending on final output by federal, state, and local governments. Each tank, filing cabinet, calculator, and desk purchased by government is part of the government purchases portion of GDP. Also included is the entire payroll of all

---

1. GDP can also be derived by the *income approach*. This approach calculates GDP by adding together the income payments to the resource suppliers and the other costs of producing those goods and services.

Table 10.1	Gross Domestic Product, 2008 (billions of dollars)	

Component	Amount	Percentage of Total
Personal consumption expenditures:	10,058	71
Durable goods	1,023	
Nondurable goods	2,965	
Services	6,070	
Gross private domestic investment:	1,994	14
Fixed investment (plant, equipment)	2,040	
Business inventories	−46	
Government purchases of goods and services:	2,882	20
Federal	1,072	
State and local	1,810	
Net exports of goods and services:	−669	−5
Exports	1,859	
Imports	−2,528	
Gross domestic product	$14,265	100%

Source: Bureau of Economic Analysis, *Gross Domestic Product 2008*, available at http://www.bea.gov.

governments, representing the purchases of labor services by governments. Recall that government purchases exclude transfer payments, such as welfare and Social Security payments, because they do not represent newly produced goods.

Net exports $(X - M)$ comprise the last component of GDP. Sales of a country's goods and services to foreigners during a particular time period represent its exports (X). For the United States, exports include the sale of an IBM computer to a Mexican buyer or the purchase of a ticket to Disneyland by a tourist from Germany. Purchases of foreign-produced goods and services by a country's residents constitute its imports (M). U.S. imports include the purchase of an Airbus jetliner by United Airlines, or a stay in a Toronto motel by the New York Yankees baseball team. Subtracting imports from exports yields net exports.

As shown in Table 10.1, in 2008, foreign buyers purchased $1,859 billion of goods and services from the United States. That same year, Americans purchased $2,528 billion of goods and services from foreign countries. The difference between these two figures, −$669 billion, represents the net exports of the United States in 2008. Net exports were *negative* because imports exceeded exports. Conversely, net exports would be positive if exports exceeded imports. In the past 3 decades, U.S. net exports have consistently been negative.

A Formula for GDP

GDP is the sum of purchases in the four sectors of the economy. Therefore, we can write the following equation for GDP:

$$GDP = C + I + G + (X - M)$$

Applying this formula to 2008, the U.S. GDP equaled $14,265 billion.

$$\$14,265 = \$10,058 + \$1,994 + \$2,882 - \$669$$

economics
IN ACTION

Why Are Some Countries Rich and Others Poor?

There are great discrepancies in living standards throughout the world, as Table 10.2 makes clear. If we ask a simple question, such as "Why are some economies rich and others poor?" we get a simple answer: Rich economies have greater resources per capita—that is, they have more human capital (skills) and physical capital (machinery) and better technology. But this answer only begs another question: "Why do some economies have high levels of capital and technology, whereas others do not?"

A nation's choice of institutions greatly influences its wealth and development. What separates the economic "haves" from the "have-nots" is whether an economy's institutions, especially its public institutions, facilitate or confiscate the production of wealth.

What elements must a government put in place to allow an economy to take full advantage of the possible gains from trade? Economists note that a well-functioning economy requires a foundation of enforceable property rights, generally accepted accounting principles, sound financial institutions, a stable currency, and the like.

Table 10.2	Comparisons of Living Standards throughout the World, 2007
Country	Gross National Income per Person*
Luxembourg	$63,590
United States	45,850
Canada	35,310
Japan	34,600
Russian Federation	14,400
Mexico	12,580
Ethiopia	780
Sierra Leone	660

* Measured at purchasing power parity.
Source: World Bank, World Development Indicators Database, available at http://www.worldbank.org/data/. Scroll to Data and Quick Reference Tables.

Throughout the world, there are great disparities in these institutions, which tends to promote differences in living standards. A key question is how a government can create the sort of environment in which people find it worthwhile to accumulate human and physical capital and carry out technological development, thus creating economic prosperity.

This equation is a key element in analyzing macroeconomic problems and formulating macroeconomic policy. When economists analyze the economy at large, they apply this equation to predict the behavior of the major sectors of the economy: households, business, government, and foreign commerce.

What GDP Does Not Measure

GDP is our best single measure of the value of output produced by an economy. Yet it is not a perfect measure; it has several flaws in construction. First, GDP ignores transactions that do not take place in organized markets. If you grow your own vegetables, repair your car, paint your house, clean your apartment, or perform similar productive household activities, your labor services add nothing to GDP because no market transaction is involved. Such nonmarket productive activities are sizable—10 percent or more of total GDP.

GDP also ignores the **underground economy,** in which unreported barter and cash transactions take place outside recorded market channels. For example, owners of flea markets may make "under the table" cash transactions with their customers. The underground economy also includes transactions involving illegal goods and services, such as prostitution, gambling, and drugs. These illegal goods and services are final products that are not part of GDP. Estimates of the value of the transactions that take place in the underground economy are as high as one-third of GDP.

GDP does not value changes in the environment that arise through the production of output. Pollution and other aspects of industrial activity impose costs on society. However, these costs are not subtracted from the market value of final goods when GDP is calculated. For example, suppose that a chemical firm produces $1 million worth of output but pollutes the water and decreases its value by $2 million. Rather than indicating a loss to society, GDP will show a $1 million increase.

GDP also excludes leisure, a good that is valuable to each of us. Suppose that Canada achieves a $25,000 per-capita GDP with an average workweek of 35 hours. Germany might achieve an identical per-capita GDP with a 40-hour workweek. With regard to economic well-being, Canada is better off because it generates additional leisure time while producing the same output per person. However, GDP does not account for this fact.

Another problem of using GDP as a measure of well-being is that it does not show how much output is available per person. For example, suppose that Nigeria and Kuwait have the same GDP—say, $40 billion. Kuwait has a population of 2 million people, and Nigeria has a population of 124 million people. This suggests that people in Kuwait have more than 60 times as many goods per person. In Kuwait, the $40 billion GDP must be divided among 2 million people, resulting in $20,000 worth of GDP per person ($40 billion/2 million = $20,000). In Nigeria, however, there is just $323 worth of GDP per person ($40 billion/124 million = $323). The people in Kuwait, on average, are better off than the people in Nigeria, even though the total value of GDP is the same for both nations.

The distribution of goods among different people in a nation also poses a problem for GDP. If most of a nation's GDP is consumed by a very small fraction of the people, there will be few rich people and many poor people. If a nation's GDP is more evenly distributed, however, the number of poor people will be smaller and the middle class will be larger. GDP is blind as to whether a small fraction of the citizenry consumes most of the nation's GDP or consumption is evenly divided.

Finally, GDP does not reflect the quality and kinds of goods that make up a nation's output. Today, new cars are safer and more fuel efficient than the automobiles of 30 years ago. Dental procedures are usually less painful than they were 20 years ago. Moreover, the efficiency of the workplace has improved as a result of new products such as personal computers, scanners, fax machines, and the Internet. In short, GDP is a *quantitative* rather than a *qualitative* indicator of the output of goods and services.

In spite of these limitations, GDP is a reasonable estimate of the rate of output in the economy. GDP was never intended to be a complete measure of economic well-being or the happiness of a nation's residents.

REAL GDP VERSUS NOMINAL GDP

We often want to compare GDP figures from year to year. Many people think that we are economically better off if GDP increases from one year to the next. However, we must exercise caution when making such a comparison.

So far, we have expressed GDP in terms of the prices existing in the year in which the goods and services were produced. Such an expression gives what is known as **nominal GDP,** or current-dollar GDP. To make comparisons over time when prices are changing, we must adjust nominal GDP so that it reflects only changes in output and not changes in prices. **Real GDP,** or constant-dollar GDP, is nominal GDP adjusted to eliminate changes in prices. It measures actual (real) production and shows how actual production—rather than the prices of what is produced—has changed. Real GDP is thus superior to nominal GDP for assessing the performance of the economy, especially rates of economic growth.

Suppose, for example, that in 2009, a computer cost $2,000. The identical computer in 2010 cost $2,200. When the computer was counted as part of GDP in 2010, each computer added $200 more to GDP than it did in 2009. Even if the same number of computers were sold in 2010, GDP would have increased in 2010. The actual amount of goods available in the economy would not have increased, but the dollar value would have risen. The increase in the GDP would thus be the result of a rise in prices rather than an increase in output. When using GDP to assess growth, we must realize that part of the growth that we observe may be the result of rising prices.

In order to convert nominal GDP to real GDP, it is necessary to have a measure of price changes over the years. Economists use a **price index** to adjust GDP figures so that the figures show only changes in actual output. The broadest price index used to calculate real GDP is called the **GDP deflator**.[2] It equals the ratio of the cost of buying all final goods and services in the current year to the cost of buying the identical goods at base-year prices. The GDP deflator is a weighted average of the prices of all final goods and services produced in an economy: consumer goods, business investment, government purchases of goods and services, and net exports. It is a weighted average because the various goods and services are not of equal importance. In the base year, the GDP deflator has a value of 100. Currently, the base year for the GDP deflator is 2000.

Now let's calculate real GDP, or the GDP adjusted for price changes. To do so, we value the current-year output at the base-year prices. Thus, we divide the nominal GDP for a given year by the GDP deflator for that year and then multiply that answer by 100.

$$\text{Real GDP for a given year} = \frac{\text{Nominal GDP for a given year}}{\text{GDP deflator for that year}} \times 100$$

Table 10.3 shows the nominal GDP, real GDP, and GDP deflator for the United States during the 1990–2008 period. Let us first calculate real GDP in 2000, the base year. To calculate real GDP, we divide nominal GDP in 2000 ($9,817 billion) by the GDP deflator in 2000 (100) and multiply that answer by 100, as follows:

Table 10.3   Nominal GDP, Real GDP, and GDP Deflator, 1990–2008

Year	Nominal GDP ($billion)	Real GDP ($billion)	GDP Deflator (2000 = 100)
1990	5,803	7,113	81.6
1992	6,338	7,337	86.4
1994	7,072	7,836	90.3
1996	7,817	8,329	93.9
1998	8,747	9,067	96.5
2000	9,817	9,817	100.0
2002	10,487	10,075	104.1
2004	11,728	10,837	108.2
2006	13,178	11,295	116.7
2008	14,265	11,654	122.4

Source: Bureau of Economic Analysis, *Gross Domestic Product 2008,* available at http://www.bea.gov.

---

2. In more technical jargon, the GDP deflator is known as the *GDP chain price index.* This index is a moving average of a price level's "deflator" index, calculated by a complex chain-weighted geometric series.

$$\text{Real GDP} = \frac{\$9{,}817 \text{ billion}}{100.0} \times 100 = \$9{,}817 \text{ billion}$$

Real GDP in 2000 was $9,817 billion, the same as nominal GDP in that year. In the base year, real GDP will always equal nominal GDP.

Now we will calculate real GDP in 2008. To compute real GDP, we divide nominal GDP in 2008 ($14,265 billion) by the GDP deflator in 2008 (122.4) and multiply that answer by 100. Therefore,

$$\text{Real GDP} = \frac{\$14{,}265 \text{ billion}}{\$122.4} \times 100 = \$11{,}654 \text{ billion}$$

From 2000 to 2008, nominal GDP increased from $9,817 billion to $14,265 billion. However, the GDP deflator increased from 100.0 to 122.4 over this period, which suggests a 22.4 percent increase in prices. To calculate real GDP in 2008, therefore, we must subtract the increase in prices that occurred from 2000 to 2008. As a result, real GDP increased from $9,817 billion to only $11,654 billion over this period. This example clearly illustrates the usefulness of real GDP as a measure of economic growth. It is apparent that real GDP grew between 2000 and 2008, but not by as much as the growth in nominal GDP suggested.

CHECK POINT

1. How do economists calculate GDP according to the expenditure approach?

2. What are the major weaknesses of GDP as an indicator of economic well-being?

3. Distinguish between nominal GDP and real GDP. Which measure of GDP is superior for assessing the performance of the economy, especially rates of economic growth?

LONG-RUN ECONOMIC GROWTH

In the past 25 years, we have seen the development of many new products, such as personal computers, cell phones, and fax machines. Indeed, new products are a reflection of our economic progress. Over time, we produce not only more goods and services but also new and better goods and services. As a result, our material standard of living increases.

A nation realizes **economic growth** when it increases its full production level of output over time. Recall from Chapter 1 that economic growth can be expressed in terms of the production possibilities model. When economic growth occurs, a nation's production possibilities curve shifts outward, or to the right. Economic growth is a *long-run* objective that can be achieved over a period of time.

Although economic growth suggests an increase in full production output over time, it is more accurately defined as a rise in full production output *per person* over time. Suppose that output rises by 10 percent over time, but population grows at 12 percent over the same period. As a result, output per person would decrease. Even with more goods and services available, the average person would be worse off.

The Rate of Economic Growth

Let us now calculate the rate of growth in an economy. The **rate of economic growth** is the percentage change in the level of economic activity from one year to the next. Typically, analysts look at the rate of growth in an economy's real GDP.

economics
IN ACTION

Productivity Gains: Working Smarter, Not Harder

Compare America today with earlier times, and one fact stands out: We live better. Give most of the credit to productivity. Through it, we get more goods and services from each bit of work. Through it, we secure economic progress and earn bigger paychecks. We've taken plenty of our added productivity as material gains—more cars, bigger and better-equipped houses, sophisticated computers, and the like. Also, we work less. Over the past few generations, the typical worker has gone from a 6-day workweek with little vacation to an average of 34 hours per workweek plus 3 weeks off. Indeed, the power of productivity has made the United States a rich nation. Consider these examples of productivity gains:

- With ATMs, electronic fund transfers, and the Internet, banks can handle more transactions using fewer tellers and support staff. Output per hour in commercial banking has doubled since 1970.

- Electronic telephone switches have taken over much of the nation's long-distance and toll-call traffic. Calls per operator have risen from 17 per day in 1950 to about 2,100 today.

- Dr Pepper/Seven-Up Bottling Group Inc. grew more productive by using huge machines that fill and package 800 bottles or 1,500 cans per minute, almost double the previous generation.

Day in and day out, markets encourage companies to push for greater output per hour. Do the job faster. Reduce inputs. Improve quality. Trim a few cents off the cost of production. The relentless march of productivity comes in myriad ways, limited only by technology and human ingenuity.

Indeed, as productivity reorganizes the economy, it changes how we use our innate skills and talents in the workplace. Each generation of inventions produces tools to take on more of the tasks once done by human beings. Americans adjust by taking jobs that put our other talents to work. Over time, our work moves up a hierarchy of human talents, focusing on new tasks that require higher-order skills, ones that machinery can't do as well. By redefining the way we work, the economy creates a new and more productive mix of technology and human talents. For example, workers once used muscle power to dig with picks and shovels. Over time, ever-larger digging and loading machines have allowed a single operator to do what once required legions of laborers.

This serves as a lesson for today's college students. Americans who want to prepare for the better jobs of the future will concentrate on developing skills that allow them to ascend the hierarchy of human talents. A college education is a window of opportunity that can help you improve your productivity.

Source: Federal Reserve Bank of Dallas, A *Better Way: Productivity and Reorganization in the American Economy,* 2003 Annual Report, pp. 3–23, available at http://www.dallasfed.org.

The rate of economic growth is simply the change in real GDP between two periods, divided by real GDP in the first period. To illustrate, suppose that in year 1, real GDP is $1,000, and in year 2, real GDP is $1,100. Hence, the rate of growth between years 1 and 2 would be:

$$\text{Rate of growth} = \frac{\text{Year 2 real GDP} - \text{Year 1 real GDP}}{\text{Year 1 real GDP}}$$

$$= \frac{\$1,100 - \$1,000}{\$1,000}$$

$$= 0.1$$

Thus, the rate of growth for the economy between years 1 and 2 would be 10 percent.

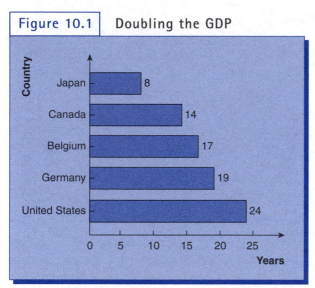

Figure 10.1   Doubling the GDP

The figure shows how many years it took for GDP to double, starting in 1960, for selected nations.

Source: Angus Maddison, *Dynamic Forces in Capitalist Development* (New York: Oxford University Press, 1991).

A useful rule of thumb can help us appreciate the power of growth rates. Suppose that you know the constant rate of growth of real GDP, but you want to know the number of years it will take for the level of real GDP to double. The answer is given by the **rule of 70**:

$$\text{Years to double} = \frac{70}{\text{Percentage growth rate}}$$

As an example, suppose that real GDP grew at 3 percent a year. Thus, it would take about 23 years for the real GDP to double $\left(\frac{70}{3} = 23\frac{1}{3}\right)$.

How fast can the U.S. economy grow on a sustainable basis? Most mainstream analysts believe that real GDP can grow about 2.5 percent per year. However, some analysts assert that much more rapid growth, possibly as much as 5 percent per year, may be sustainable. The answer to this question has profound implications for the future well-being of the American people. If the mainstream view is correct, real output will double only every 28 years or so according to the rule of 70. But if the alternative view is correct, real output could double every 14 years. Figure 10.1 shows how long it took for several nations to double their output beginning in 1960.

WHAT DETERMINES ECONOMIC GROWTH?

The output level of an economy is determined by the level of inputs (land, labor, capital, and entrepreneurship) used and the production methods employed to convert the inputs into goods and services. Output can only be increased through additional inputs or more efficient use of the available inputs. How fast we can increase inputs is limited, however: Land is essentially fixed. Population growth and participation rates determine the size of the labor force.

In less-developed economies, such as Mexico or China, a large fraction of inputs are underutilized, and the level of capital is usually low. These economies can grow rapidly by increasing inputs and/or increasing production efficiency—for example, by moving toward state-of-the-art technology and raising the level of education. A developed economy, such as that of the United States or Germany, which is starting from a higher level of input use and efficiency, has more difficulty sustaining high rates of economic growth. Innovation and improvements in existing technology are the keys to increased growth rates.

In the final analysis, the keys to long-run economic growth are the incentives that induce individuals to work and firms to invest in production technology, within the limits imposed by demographics and the rate of technological advancement. Let us consider the major determinants of economic growth.

Natural Resources

The first pillar of economic growth is natural resources, which are gifts of nature that are usable in the production process. Resources such as mineral deposits, land, forests, and rivers come under this classification. Some natural resources, such as oil, are nonrenewable. Because it takes nature thousands of years to produce oil, there is a limited supply. When a barrel of oil is extracted from a well, it is impossible to produce more. Other natural resources, such as forests, are renewable. When we cut down a tree, we can replace it by planting a seedling in the ground to be harvested in the years ahead.

Although countries rely on natural resources as productive inputs, a domestic supply of natural resources is not crucial for an economy to produce goods and services. For example, Japan is a highly productive and wealthy nation, even though it has few natural resources. International trade allows Japan to be a productive nation. Japan imports natural resources, such as iron ore and oil, and transforms them into steel, automobiles, electronics, and other manufactured goods to be exported to nations that have abundant natural resources.

You may wonder whether natural resources present a limit to growth. If the world has a fixed supply of nonrenewable resources, how can production, population, and standards of living continue to increase in the years ahead? Won't the supplies of resources eventually dry up, thus halting economic growth and causing living standards to decrease?

Although such arguments are appealing, most economists are optimistic about the economy's capacity to grow. They contend that technological progress provides alternatives to the scarcity of resources. Comparing our current economy to that of years ago, we see many ways in which resources are better utilized. More productive oil rigs have increased the amount of oil harvested from wells. Modern automobiles have more efficient engines that allow them to run on less gasoline. New houses are better insulated and require less energy to cool or heat them. The recycling of oil, aluminum, tin, plastic, glass, cardboard, and paper permits the conservation of resources. Technological progress has also allowed us to substitute abundant resources for scarce resources. For example, plastic has replaced tin as an input used to manufacture food containers, and telephone calls often travel over fiber-optic cables that are made from sand. In short, technological progress has contributed to the more efficient use of crucial resources.

Physical Capital

The second pillar of economic growth is physical capital, which enables workers to produce more goods and services. No matter how educated workers are, they still need computers, machinery, and other equipment to produce goods and services. Capital investment is thus a key determinant of both productivity and growth. For example, when workers build a house, they use saws, hammers, electric drills, and other tools. Additional investment provides workers with more and better tools.

Productivity increases through capital investment have often involved exploiting economies of large-scale production. Industries such as electricity generation, food processing, and beverages are cases in point. In the beverage industry, for example, high-speed canning lines have raised productivity, but their contribution has been made possible in part by the development of large markets. To operate efficiently, these lines must produce nearly 500 million cans per year!

Of course, investment is not a free gift of nature; an opportunity cost is involved. When additional resources are used to produce equipment and manufacturing plants, fewer resources are available for the production of current-consumption goods, such as hamburgers. However, those who save and invest will be able to produce more in the future.

Besides the economy's private sector, government is also a source of physical capital for the economy. Historically, investment in public capital such as roads, bridges, airports, and utilities has made a significant contribution to the nation's productivity growth. Such public capital is called **infrastructure**.

Human Capital

A third pillar of economic growth is **human capital:** the knowledge, experience, and skills of the workforce. As the economy has changed, the demands imposed on the brainpower of the American workforce have increased enormously. Increases in the hourly output of the average worker can reflect an improvement in the characteristics that allow workers to accomplish the same tasks in less time, adapt to changing situations with greater flexibility, and become engineers of change themselves.

The importance of human capital can be seen in the shipbuilding that took place during World War II. Between 1941 and 1944, U.S. shipyards produced more than 2,500 units of a cargo ship, known as the Liberty Ship, to a standardized design. In 1941, it required 1.2 million labor-hours to construct a ship. By 1943, it required only 500,000. Thousands of workers learned from experience and attained human capital, more than doubling their productivity in two years.

Providing individuals with formal education is one way to increase their human capital, thus contributing to aggregate productivity growth. Estimates suggest that investment in U.S. education boosted U.S. labor productivity about 0.3 percentage point per year, on average, between 1963 and 1995. Another way of increasing human capital is training workers on the job. Research has found that companies that offer more training enjoy higher rates of productivity growth.

The returns to education, measured by the difference in incomes between college and high school graduates, have risen sharply in the past 20 years. Today, the average college graduate can expect to earn between 5 percent and 15 percent more than the average high school graduate. Much of this difference probably reflects the increasing importance of computer skills in the workplace. Moreover, the payoff from formal training, including apprenticeships, can be quite substantial: A year of training typically provides returns of a similar magnitude to those offered by a year of formal schooling. Perhaps it would be worthwhile if you obtained a summer internship with a local employer.

Productivity

A fourth pillar of growth is **productivity.** Economists think of productivity as a ratio that measures the quantity of output produced relative to the amount of work required to produce it. Mathematically, it appears as follows:

$$\text{Productivity} = \frac{\text{Total output}}{\text{Hours worked}}$$

An increase in productivity occurs when total output increases faster than the amount of work required to produce it. For example, an increase in the quantity of output with no increase in hours worked would result in an increase in productivity.[3]

Rearranging the terms can help illustrate the significance of productivity for economic growth:

$$\text{Total output} = \text{Productivity} \times \text{Hours worked}$$

---

3. The most popular measure of productivity for the U.S. economy is average labor productivity. Labor productivity is measured in terms of average output per hour. It is a ratio of the quantity of output to the hours of work done. The quantity of output is based on real GDP, as discussed in this chapter.

| Table 10.4 | Annual Rates of Growth in U.S. Labor Productivity and Real Compensation per Hour in the Business Sector, 1960–2007 |

Time Period (average)	Labor Productivity Growth Rate (%)	Real Compensation per Hour Growth Rate (%)
1960s	3.2	2.9
1970s	1.8	1.3
1980s	1.2	0.2
1990s	1.9	1.2
2000–2007 (avg.)	2.6	1.5

Source: Economic Report of the President, 2009, p. 343, available at http://www.gpoaccess.gov.

This shows that total output depends on both work and productivity. Any increase in total output must come from an increase in either hours worked or productivity.

As seen in Table 10.4, U.S. productivity growth has been erratic. During the 1960s, productivity grew by 3.2 percent per year. But during the next three decades, productivity growth fell to less than 2 percent per year, only to improve at the turn of the century. Higher rates of productivity growth permit rising real compensation for labor, as this table illustrates.

What factors contribute to changes in productivity? Clearly, technological advancement has much to do with productivity gains. During the past century, the development of power-driven machines such as tractors, improvements in transportation such as railroads and airlines, and the growing stock of computers have increased the productivity of workers.

Obviously, technological advancement requires invention—that is, the discovery of a new process or product. Yet it also encompasses innovation, the successful introduction and adoption of a new process or product. Henry Ford did not invent the automobile; instead, he was an innovator who pioneered assembly-line production techniques that allowed workers to produce more automobiles in an hour's time, resulting in falling costs for each automobile produced.

Improving the productivity of the economy is not just a matter of improving technology. How the economy is organized plays an important role in creating incentives for firms to use their capital and labor as efficiently as possible. If the market economy is to deliver on its promise of growth and prosperity, markets have to be competitive, for it is competition that motivates firms to be efficient and innovative. Firms, however, often find it easier to increase profits by reducing competition than by improving efficiency in response to competition. Monopolies and oligopolies not only can charge inefficiently high prices and restrict output but also may have a diminished drive to innovate.

Another source of increasing productivity in the economy is reorganization resulting from international trade. As competition forces producers to seek comparative advantage in the marketplace, resources shift to their best uses, creating a more efficient deployment of labor in the economy. As the economy reorganizes to produce more, it also lowers prices relative to wages, so our paychecks buy more. Indeed, international trade can be every bit as powerful as technology in making us productive. Trade's productivity gains provide a strong justification for open markets. Economists widely agree that enormous benefits are lost when countries bow to their producers' narrow interests and enact protectionist measures that block imports or raise their prices.

Economists at Harvard University and the Federal Reserve Bank of New York have examined the sources of U.S. productivity growth during the 1990s. They analyzed three classic sources of productivity growth: capital investment, labor quality, and technological progress. They found

economics
IN ACTION

Intel's Microprocessor and the Computer Revolution

The computer revolution of the late twentieth century is often cited as a source of economic growth. Indeed, increased computing power has raised the productivity of households, business, and government.

What spurred the computer revolution was the development of the microprocessor by Intel Corp. A microprocessor is a tiny electronic device that serves as an engine for computation. It consists of millions of transistors attached to a silicon chip as small as a fingernail. The microprocessor is often called a "computer on a chip."

Intel's first microprocessor was produced in 1971 for use in handheld calculators. The chip contained 2,300 transistors and was capable of executing 60,000 operations a second.

These calculators were very expensive, and few people could afford them. However, advanced manufacturing techniques soon decreased the cost of manufacturing microprocessors. The low cost, small size, and modest power requirements of microprocessors soon led to their use in hundreds of other products besides calculators. These products included microwave ovens, digital watches, telephones, sewing machines, and video games. Microprocessors also made possible the computerization of store checkout lines, bank records, gasoline pumps, medical instruments, and many other products that made the economy more productive. By

the early 1980s, the microprocessor made possible the development of the personal computer.

Intel saw great potential for its technological breakthrough. If a bundle of transistors could be made to fit on a silicon chip, ways could be found to double the capacity of a single chip, and then redouble it. Intel's goal has been to double the power of memory chips about every 2 years. Early microprocessors could execute up to 100,000 instructions per second. Today, microprocessors carry out more than 7 billion instructions per second.

Because Intel was the first firm to produce microprocessors, initially, it could charge a premium price that resulted in large profit margins. By the 1980s, however, firms such as Motorola and Texas Instruments, as well as Japanese companies, had developed their own microprocessors. Silicon chips thus became a commodity, with many different companies manufacturing them. This resulted in lower chip prices and falling profits for Intel.

The advent of competition has forced Intel to operate as if it were a research institution. The firm plows much of its profit into product development to stay ahead of the competition. Like a jogger running on an accelerating treadmill, Intel has to run faster just to maintain its position, and even faster just to stay ahead of its competitors.

_____

Sources: Tim Jackson, *Inside Intel: Andy Grove and the Rise of the World's Most Powerful Chip Company* (New York: Dutton, 1997); Andrew Grove, *Only the Paranoid Survive: How to Exploit the Crisis Points That Challenge Every Company and Career* (New York: Currency Doubleday, 1996); and T. R. Reid, *The Chip: How Two Americans Invented the Microchip and Launched a Revolution* (New York: Random House, 1985).

that major gains came from technological progress. Breaking down productivity even further, they found that 44 percent of the gains from technological progress were directly related to productivity gains in the information technology sector—including computers, software, and communications equipment.[4]

_____

4. Dale W. Jorgenson and Keven J. Stiroh, *Raising the Speed Limit: U.S. Economic Growth in the Information Age*, May 1, 2000, available at http://www.economics.harvard.edu/faculty/jorgenson/papers/dj_ks5.pdf.

The Significance of Technological Innovation

We have learned how technological gains result in increased productivity. Over the long run, economic progress in advanced countries such as the United States hinges largely on technological progress. Each of the great industrial revolutions of the past was founded on innovation. The late 1800s and early 1900s, for example, witnessed the invention and general use of electricity, the radio, the telephone, the internal combustion engine, the automobile, the factory assembly line, and the airplane. The surge of innovation that took place in the late 20th century was powered by the microprocessor, which gave rise to information technology and rapid growth in productivity.

Growth without technological advancement winds up becoming sluggish. If an economy continues to produce the same goods even with modest improvements, the result is stagnation. Without technological breakthroughs, the strategy of improving and refining existing production methods runs into diminishing returns and eventually fizzles out. Simply put, it's the jump to a new technology, such as computers or perhaps solar power, that radically improves people's lives.

If the pace of technological advance dwindles, there will be less need for college-educated workers. Jobs will be routinized, and companies will replace expensive college-educated workers with cheaper workers with associate degrees or even less education. Companies will also have greater incentives to outsource routine jobs to foreign workers, whose wages are a fraction of domestic workers. Advances in technology create better-paying jobs that require analytical reasoning, imagination, creativity, and people skills.

Economists often quote an old saying: "There is no such thing as a free lunch." The notion is that you generally get what you pay for. However, technological gains provide an exception to the free-lunch concept, furnishing a stimulus to growth and higher living standards. Simply put, rising productivity makes it easier to pay for things such as Social Security, better education, and other goods that improve the quality of our lives.[5]

The Role of Government

Without a doubt, the future rate of increase in an economy's productive capacity will largely be determined by the decisions of millions of individual businesses and households in the private sector of the economy. In addition, government can help promote the growth of an economy. Let us consider government policies that might speed up economic growth.

- **Boosting productivity by increasing domestic saving.**   Historically, nations that have saved the most have also invested the most, and investment is strongly correlated with productivity. To stimulate national saving, government could reduce its spending, thus freeing resources to be used for investment. Government could also induce the private sector to save more by providing tax incentives.

- **Improving the skills of the workforce.**   To help workers invest in skill acquisition, the government could adopt policies to promote lifelong learning. By funding basic education and by setting high standards in basic skills such as mathematics, science, and language, the government could improve the nation's production capabilities.

- **Stimulating research and development.**   Increasing investment in research and development is one way to promote technological innovation and productivity growth. Since the 1800s, the U.S. government has sponsored research on agricultural practices and advised farmers on how

---

5. Michael J. Mandel, *Rational Exuberance: Silencing the Enemies of Growth and Why the Future Is Better Than You Think* (New York: HarperCollins, 2004).

best to manage their land. The government has also supported aerospace research through NASA and the U.S. Air Force and has provided tax breaks for firms practicing research and development.

- **Working to reduce trade barriers.** Economists have found that a country can raise its growth rate by increasing its openness to international trade, the education of its people, and its supply of telecommunications infrastructure. The impact on growth can be as much as 4 percentage points for a country that progresses from significantly below the average to significantly above the average on all of these indicators.[6] As a result, economists generally argue for the reduction of trade barriers and the opening of markets to global competition.

- **Improving the efficiency of regulation.** In many cases, an improvement in government regulation can simultaneously promote the more effective attainment of policy objectives and increase the efficiency of the economy. For example, a traditional approach to the problem of reducing pollution from the air might entail mandatory investment in costly new pollution-reduction equipment by all polluters. Instead, a system that is based on tradable emissions certificates (see Chapter 8) can achieve the same results while encouraging the efficient allocation of pollution reduction among polluters.

CHECK POINT

1. Describe the concept of long-run economic growth. How do economists measure the rate of economic growth?

2. Of what significance is the "rule of 70" for economic growth?

3. Identify the major determinants of economic growth.

4. What policies might government enact to speed up economic growth?

THEORIES OF ECONOMIC GROWTH

The traditional theory of economic growth has its origins in the writings of Adam Smith, who wrote *The Wealth of Nations* in 1776.[7] According to Smith, larger markets encourage individuals to specialize in different parts of the production process and coordinate their labor. In turn, specialization is the chief engine of increased productivity. It fosters productivity gains by allowing workers to save time that would be lost in shifting from one type of work to another. In Smith's view, the inventive activity that improves production techniques is a by-product of specialization because, as a worker concentrates attention on one activity, time-saving inventions often come to mind. Simply put, Smith's principles of economic growth emphasize two resources—labor and capital. Technology is discussed, but only in a superficial manner.

---

6. World Bank, *World Development Report* (Washington, DC: World Bank, 1999), p. 23.
7. Adam Smith, *The Wealth of Nations* (New York: Modern Library, 1937).

In the early 1900s, economists began formulating a different theory of economic growth. Considering technological progress to be within the scope of economic theory, they began to view innovation and creativity as economic activities. This perspective on economics found its foremost advocates in a Harvard professor named Joseph Schumpeter in 1942 and professor Paul Romer of Stanford University in the 1980s.[8]

Schumpeter constructed a theory of economic growth in which technological innovation is the prime source of growth in a modern economy and profits are the fuel. He argued that what is most important about a capitalist market system is precisely that it rewards change by allowing those who create new products and processes to capture some of the benefits of their creations in the form of monopoly profits. They provide entrepreneurs with the means to (1) fund creative activities in response to perceived opportunities; (2) override the natural conservatism of other parties who must cooperate with the new product's launch, as well as the opposition of those whose markets may be harmed by the new products; and (3) widen and deepen their sales networks so that new products can be quickly made known to a large number of customers. Competition, if too vigorous, would deny these rewards to creators and instead pass them on to consumers, in which case firms would have scant reason to create new products.

The drive to temporarily capture monopoly profits promotes, in Schumpeter's words, **creative destruction,** as old technologies, goods, and livelihoods are replaced by new ones. Thus, whereas Smith saw monopoly profits as an indication of economic inefficiency, Schumpeter saw them as evidence of valuable entrepreneurial activity in a healthy, dynamic economy. Indeed, in Schumpeter's view, new technologies and products are so valuable to consumers that governments of countries should encourage entrepreneurs by granting temporary monopolies over innovations and inventions.

Although technological innovation tends to benefit consumers, why are the forces opposing it so strong? One factor limiting technological innovation is that it puts existing products at risk. An example is the personal computer, whose power and speed have been rising at rapid rates for more than 20 years. In the competition to supply components of the personal computer, such as modems and memory, any firm that wants to play the game has to invest in creating newer, faster, and smaller versions of the component. To earn profits and to justify this investment and its uncertainties, the resulting innovation must leapfrog the competition by creating a new generation. The first firm to market with the new generation can often grab the bulk of the market and, with it, almost all the profits to be had. Of course, this typically wipes out the profitability of the previous generation and sets the stage for the next leapfrogger, who will then destroy the profits of the current leader.

Also, being creative is inherently risky. You don't know what will work until you try it. Although successful new products may earn immense returns, others inevitably fail and create losses for their creators and supporters. An example of a product that was expected to fare well in the marketplace but did not was the Betamax, which looked like a technology winner to most experts when videocassette recorders were invented in the late 1970s. Beta was competing with VHS, and insiders knew that Sony had the opportunity to develop either Beta or VHS and chose Beta as the superior technology. But the corporations developing VHS were able to more rapidly lengthen videocassette playback times. Consumers who did adopt Beta eventually found that they had to switch to VHS, as Sony was forced to abandon the system as a result of the greater availability of prerecorded videocassettes on VHS. Simply put, when consumers choose one system, its rivals may suffer irreversible setbacks, as the Beta system did. Moreover, VHS was being replaced by DVD systems by 2000.

---

8. Joseph Schumpeter, *Capitalism, Socialism, and Democracy* (New York: Harper, 1942); and Paul Romer, "Economic Growth," in David R. Henderson, ed., *The Fortune Encyclopedia* (New York: Warner Books, 1993).

IS ECONOMIC GROWTH DESIRABLE?

Our analysis of economic growth in this chapter makes it appear to be beneficial. Is it?

The main justification for economic growth is that it allows a nation to realize rising material abundance and increased standards of living. Expanding output and rising incomes allow households to purchase additional medical care, education, recreation and travel, and higher-quality consumer goods. Growth is also an avenue for supporting more of the arts, including theater, music, and drama. The high living standard that growth permits increases our leisure and provides additional time for self-fulfillment.

Growth also helps generate more resources for national defense, police and fire protection, care of the disabled and sick, and improvements in our nation's infrastructure, such as roads and communications. In today's world, the additional jobs made possible by economic growth may be the only achievable method for decreasing poverty, given society's reluctance to increase the amount of national income that it shares with the poor.

Although economic growth may provide benefits, it can also entail costs. Some individuals maintain that additional economic growth results in more pollution, more crowded cities, excessive emphasis on materialism, and psychological problems that result in suicide and drug use. They contend that the country would be better off with less growth rather than more. What's wrong with a slower and more peaceful life?

Antigrowth advocates also contend that economic growth has not solved society's problems, such as poverty, discrimination, and homelessness. According to the antigrowth view, poverty in the United States is largely attributable to the distribution of the nation's income rather than the growth of production and income. To alleviate poverty, society must be willing to adopt policies to redistribute income and wealth in favor of the poor rather than making investments in new technologies more profitable for the rich.

Another concern is the relationship between economic growth and the availability of resources. Recall that many people argue that continued increases in population and the size of the economy will cause us to run out of scarce resources. At some point, the time will come when there is no more clean air and pure water, no more natural resources, and no more open space in which to live comfortably. As a result, the nation's living standard will decline. These people contend that we must reduce the rate of economic growth and conserve our scarce resources.

Others argue that economic growth does not cause these problems. They maintain that growth brings about many favorable things, such as higher real income, less poverty, and greater economic security. Moreover, if the government would strictly enforce environmental laws, pollution would not be a major problem. Finally, we are not running out of natural resources. If and when the scarcity of resources becomes a barrier to growth, the rising relative prices of these resources will force households to conserve them and develop alternative resources. As you can see, there are no simple answers to the question of the optimal rate of economic growth.

This chapter has considered the U.S. economy's gross domestic product and the role of economic growth. The next chapter will examine the impacts of the business cycle, unemployment, and inflation on the economy.

CHECK POINT

1. Distinguish between the traditional theory of economic growth and new growth theory.

2. Describe the principle of creative destruction. Why are the forces opposing creativity so strong?

3. Identify some of the disadvantages of economic growth.

Chapter Summary

1. Economists have developed a single statistic to measure the output of an economy. This statistic is known as gross domestic product, or GDP. GDP is the market value of all final goods and services produced within a country in a given year.

2. The GDP of an economy can be calculated by totaling the expenditures on goods and services produced during the current year. When GDP is derived by the expenditure approach, it has four components: personal consumption expenditures, gross private domestic investment, government purchases of goods and services, and net exports to foreigners. For the United States, personal consumption expenditures are the largest component of GDP, typically accounting for two-thirds or more of GDP.

3. Although GDP is our best single measure of the value of the output produced by an economy, it is not a perfect measure of economic well-being. For example, GDP ignores transactions that do not take place in organized markets. GDP also ignores the underground economy, as well as changes in the environment that arise through the production of output. Furthermore, GDP does not account for leisure, nor does it show how much output is available per person. Finally, GDP does not reflect the quality and kinds of goods that compose a nation's output.

4. Nominal GDP, or current-dollar GDP, is expressed in terms of the prices existing in the year in which goods and services were produced. Real GDP, or constant-dollar GDP, is nominal GDP adjusted to eliminate changes in prices. It measures actual (real) production and shows how actual production—rather than the prices of what is produced—has changed. Real GDP is superior to nominal GDP for assessing rates of economic growth.

5. An economy realizes economic growth when it increases its full production level of output over time. The rate of economic growth is the percentage change in the level of economic activity from one year to the next. Typically, analysts look at the rate of growth in an economy's real GDP.

6. The keys to long-run economic growth are the incentives that induce individuals to work and firms to invest in production technology, within the limits imposed by demographics and the rate of technological advancement. The major determinants of economic growth are natural resources, physical capital, human capital, and economic efficiency. Government may enact policies to foster economic growth, such as boosting productivity by increasing domestic saving, stimulating research and development, working to reduce trade barriers; and improving the efficiency of regulation. Governments may also target and subsidize specific industries that might be especially important for technological progress.

7. According to the traditional theory of economic growth pioneered by Adam Smith, economic efficiency is spurred by perfect competition. Traditional growth theory emphasizes two resources—labor and capital. Technological progress is viewed as being outside the scope of economic theory, and thus something that we accept as a given.

8. According to the new growth theory pioneered by Joseph Schumpeter, technological progress is within the scope of economic theory, and creativity is an economic activity. According to Schumpeter, ideas and creativity are the prime sources of growth in a modern economy and profits are the fuel. The drive to capture monopoly profits promotes creative destruction, as old goods and livelihoods are replaced by new ones. Thus, whereas Adam Smith saw monopoly profits as an indication of economic inefficiency, Schumpeter saw them as evidence of valuable entrepreneurial activity in a healthy, dynamic economy.

9. Although economic growth may provide benefits for a nation, it can also entail costs. Critics maintain that additional economic growth promotes more pollution, more crowded cities, excessive emphasis on materialism, and psychological problems that result in suicide and drug use. Economic growth may also cause the depletion of scarce resources, eventually resulting in a decline in the nation's standard of living. However, proponents argue that economic growth does not cause these problems; rather, it fosters higher real income, less poverty, and greater economic security.

Key Terms and Concepts

gross domestic product (GDP) (223)

expenditure approach (224)

personal consumption expenditures (224)

gross private domestic investment (224)

government purchases of goods and services (224)

net exports (225)

underground economy (226)

nominal GDP (227)

real GDP (227)

price index (228)

GDP deflator (228)

economic growth (229)

rate of economic growth (229)

rule of 70 (231)

infrastructure (233)

human capital (233)

productivity (233)

creative destruction (238)

Self-Test: Multiple-Choice Questions

1. Economists measure nominal GDP in _____ prices and real GDP in _____ prices.

   a. domestic, foreign
   b. final, intermediate
   c. current-year, base-year
   d. base-year, current-year

2. GDP is calculated as the sum of

   a. transfer payments, interest, rents, and profits.
   b. personal consumption, gross investment, government purchases, and net exports.
   c. wages and salaries, unemployment compensation benefits, and gross investment.
   d. intermediate goods and final goods.

3. Real GDP best measures the

   a. market value of all intermediate goods.
   b. level of real output.
   c. standard of living of domestic households.
   d. level of society's welfare.

4. Suppose that in 2002, the nominal GDP was $1 trillion and the price index was 100; in 2006, the nominal GDP was $1,200 and the price index was 110. On the basis of this information, we can say that real GDP equaled

   a. $1 trillion in 2002 and $1.091 trillion in 2006.
   b. $1 trillion in 2002 and $2.010 trillion in 2006.

c. $1 trillion in 2002 and $991 billion in 2006.
d. $1 trillion in 2002 and $889 billion in 2006.

5. In GDP accounts, all of the following are final products *except*

   a. a tank bought by the U.S. Department of Defense.
   b. a computer bought by Stanford University.
   c. steel bought by General Motors.
   d. a refrigerator bought by Memorial Hospital.

6. GDP is the sum of the market value of

   a. final goods and services.
   b. intermediate goods and services.
   c. industrial production and business services.
   d. normal goods and services.

7. According to the "rule of 70," if real GDP grows at 4 percent per year, it will take about
   _____ for the real GDP to double.

   a. 10 years
   b. 14 years
   c. 18 years
   d. 22 years

8. The major determinants of economic growth include all of the following *except*

   a. tastes and preferences of households.
   b. natural resources.
   c. physical capital.
   d. technological advancement.

9. If investors purchased $200 million of Microsoft stock on the New York Stock Exchange, this
   would

   a. be included in GDP as gross investment.
   b. be included in GDP as domestic investment.
   c. be included in GDP as retail services.
   d. not be included in GDP.

10. According to Adam Smith's economic growth theory,

    a. the model of pure monopoly spurs economic efficiency.
    b. economic growth is primarily the result of creativity and new ideas.
    c. technological progress is something that we accept as a given.
    d. smaller markets encourage firms to specialize and reduce costs.

11. The new growth theory pioneered by Joseph Schumpeter maintains that

    a. monopoly profits are an indication of economic inefficiency.
    b. ideas and creativity are the prime sources of growth in a modern economy.
    c. a highly competitive economy best enhances long-run economic growth.
    d. creative destruction leads to declines in output and economic activity.

Answers to Multiple-Choice Questions

1. c   2. b   3. b   4. a   5. c   6. a.   7. c   8. a   9. d   10. c   11. b

Study Questions and Problems

1. Which of the following are included in calculating this year's GDP?

   a. Interest received on a security of the U.S. government
   b. The purchase of a new automobile
   c. The services of a gardener in weeding her garden
   d. The purchase of a life insurance policy
   e. The money received by John when he sells his computer to Mary
   f. The purchases of new office equipment by the U.S. government
   g. Unemployment compensation benefits received by a former autoworker
   h. A new apartment building built by a construction firm
   i. Travel by people in Canada to the United States to visit Disneyland

2. Table 10.5 shows hypothetical GDP data for the United States. On the basis of this information, calculate GDP.

3. Table 10.6 shows the nominal GDP and the GDP deflator for the United States for selected years. On the basis of this information, calculate real GDP.

4. Assume that the average workweek declines by 20 percent because U.S. citizens decide to take life a little easier. How will this affect GDP for the United States? How will it affect the welfare of the United States?

Table 10.5	Gross Domestic Product Data ($ billion)
Government purchases of goods and services	360
Compensation of employees	210
U.S. imports of goods and services	40
Interest and dividend income	23
Personal consumption expenditures	720
Social security earnings	13
Gross private domestic investment	77
Household saving	12
U.S. exports of goods and services	28
Household taxes	45

Table 10.6   Calculation of Real Gross Domestic Product

Year	Nominal GDP ($ billion)	GDP Deflator	Real GDP (billions)
2000	6,139	93.6	
2001	6,079	97.3	
2002	6,244	100.0	
2003	6,386	102.6	
2004	6,609	105.0	

5. Assume that the United States produces only radios and calculators. In 2001, it produced 100 radios at a price of $25 and 50 calculators at a price of $30. In 2005, the United States produced 120 radios at a price of $30 and 60 calculators at a price of $35. Calculate the nominal GDP for each year.

6. Why do economists prefer to compare real GDP figures for different years instead of nominal GDP figures?

7. If real GDP is $8,880 billion and nominal GDP is $9,988 billion, what does the GDP deflator equal?

8. Suppose that GDP for a given year equals $9,650 billion. What does this mean?

9. Why would removing a barrier to trade, such as a tariff, result in more rapid economic growth?

10. Explain how higher saving can promote a faster rate of economic growth.

CHAPTER 11

The Business Cycle, Unemployment, and Inflation

Chapter objectives

After reading this chapter, you should be able to:

1. Discuss the four phases of the business cycle.

2. Explain what the unemployment rate means and how it is calculated.

3. Identify the types of unemployment and their costs on the economy.

4. Discuss the importance of the consumer price index as a measure of inflation.

5. Identify who benefits from and who is hurt by inflation.

6. Describe the causes of inflation.

economics IN CONTEXT

In the late 1990s, computer makers were boosting already-robust sales by marketing elegant new hardware designs and faster processors. By the early 2000s, however, things had become ugly in the personal computer (PC) market: The PC market witnessed a brutal price war in which dealers rapidly slashed retail prices and provided generous rebates and lots of freebies. Dell Computer Corp., which initiated the price battle, tossed in a free printer, free delivery, and free Internet access to customers who purchased a PC through its Web site.

Although that was good for customers, computer makers winced as the intensifying competition sliced into profits. Compaq Computer Corp., the world's largest PC maker, downsized its operations and laid off workers in order to compensate for the new price reductions. Other computer makers slashed jobs and warned investors of reduced sales. The focal point of the industry's problems was a dramatic slowdown in revenue growth. Fears of recession hurt sales as consumers and many companies held onto their computers longer. PC producers announced that if

demand continued to decline and PC prices fell, the resulting squeeze could trigger a wave of consolidation among the biggest PC makers, as seen in the merger between Hewlett Packard and Compaq in 2002.

Indeed, the history of U.S. capitalism is marked by recurrent periods of boom and bust. Sometimes business conditions are robust, with plenty of job vacancies, factories working near maximum capacity, and strong profits. The 1990s was a period of sustained economic expansion for the United States. At other times, goods are unsold and pile up as excess inventories, jobs become scarce, and profits are low. Sometimes a downturn is mild; at times, like the Great Depression of the 1930s, a downturn is prolonged and traumatic.

In this chapter, we will explore the nature and effects of macroeconomic instability. We will begin with an overview of the business cycle—the recurrent periods of recession and expansion that characterize our economy. Then we will examine the nature and causes of unemployment and inflation.

THE BUSINESS CYCLE

In an ideal economy, real gross domestic product (GDP) would increase over time at a smooth and steady pace. Moreover, the price level would remain constant or increase slowly. However, economic history shows that the economy never grows in a smooth and steady pattern. Instead, it is interrupted by periods of economic instability, as shown in Figure 11.1.

The economy may realize several years of expansion and prosperity. Then national output declines, profits and real incomes decrease, and the unemployment rate increases to uncomfortably high levels as many workers lose their jobs. Eventually, the economic contraction vanishes and recovery begins. The recovery may be slow or fast. It may be partial, or it may be so strong that it results in a new era of prosperity. Or it may be characterized by escalating inflation, soon to be followed by another downturn. The upward and downward movements in output, employment, and inflation form the **business cycle** that characterizes all market economies.

Phases of the Business Cycle

The term *business cycle* refers to recurrent ups and downs in the level of economic activity over several years. Although business cycles may vary in intensity and duration, we can divide each into four phases, as shown in Figure 11.2.

Figure 11.1   Historical Business Fluctuations in the United States

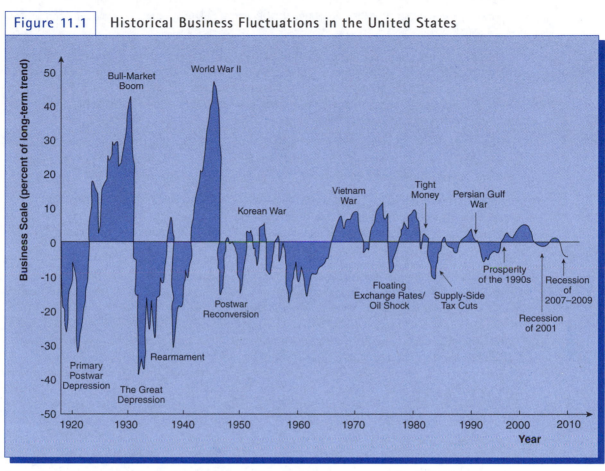

Source: *Economic Report of the President,* various years, available at http://www.gpoaccess.gov/eop/index.html.

Figure 11.2   The Business Cycle

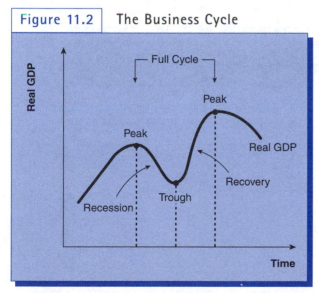

Over time, real GDP fluctuates around an overall upward trend. Such fluctuations are called the business cycle.

- **Peak.** At the **peak** of a business cycle, real GDP is at its highest point. Employment and profits are usually strong.

- **Recession.** A **recession** is a period of significant decline in total output, income, employment, and trade that usually lasts from 6 months to a year and is marked by widespread contraction in many sectors in the economy. A recession begins at a peak and ends at a trough. For example, the U.S. economy began a recession after it peaked in late 2007. The recession continued throughout 2008 and 2009 at the writing of this book.

- **Trough.** The low point of real GDP, just before it begins to turn upward, is called the **trough** of a business cycle. At the trough, unemployment and idle productive capacity are at their highest levels relative to the previous recession. The trough may be short-lived or quite long.

- **Recovery.** **Recovery** is an upturn in the business cycle during which real GDP rises. During the recovery or expansion phase of the business cycle, industrial output expands, profits usually increase, and employment moves toward full employment. The economic expansion of 1991–2001 was the longest on record in the United States.

Note that business-cycle patterns are erratic. Business cycles are like mountain ranges with different valleys and hills. Some valleys are deep and long, as in the Great Depression; others are shallow and narrow, as in the recession of 2001. We measure an entire business cycle from peak to peak. Usually, business cycles average 4 to 5 years, although a few have been longer and some shorter. Since World War II, the average U.S. expansion has lasted about 3 1/2 years; the average recession has lasted about 10 months, as shown in Table 11.1. During these recessions, U.S. real GDP fell by an average of 2.5 percent.

Despite these ups and downs, the U.S. economy has grown significantly over the long run, so the growth during expansions has more than offset the declines during recessions. Output has increased over the long run because of increases in the amount and quality of resources, better technology, and improvements in methods of production.

Although no two business cycles are alike, they do have similar characteristics. When the economy enters a period of recession, we can usually expect the following: First, consumer expenditures decrease abruptly while business inventories of steel, automobiles, and other durable goods rise unexpectedly. As businesses react by curtailing production, real GDP declines. Soon thereafter, business investment

Table 11.1   Post-World War II Recessions in the United States

Period	Duration (months)	Decline in Real GDP (percent)
1949	11	−2.0
1953–1954	10	−3.7
1957–1958	8	−3.9
1960–1961	10	−1.6
1969–1970	11	−1.1
1973–1975	16	−4.9
1980	6	−2.4
1981–1982	16	−3.4
1990–1991	8	−1.8
2001	8	−0.5
2007, Dec.–?*		
Average	10	−2.5

Source: From National Bureau of Economic Research, available at http://www.nber.org. Select "Data," then scroll to "Business Cycle Dates."

* Data not available at the writing of this text.

in plants and equipment falls. Second, the demand for labor decreases. This is first seen in a reduction in the average workweek, followed by layoffs and increased unemployment. Third, as output falls, the demand for materials, services, and labor decreases, which may result in a decline in prices or a slowdown in the rate of price increases. Finally, business profits decline during recessions. In anticipation of this, stock prices generally drop as investors become pessimistic about the decline in business activity. Moreover, because the demand for credit decreases, interest rates usually also decline during recessions. Simply put, a recession is a period of declining output and not just a period of slower economic growth.

Identifying the dates of beginnings and ends of recessions requires time. This is because analysts must look at a variety of economic data, such as industrial production and retail sales, to determine turning points in the economy. Compiling such data takes some time which means they are only available after the events they describe. Also, because it takes time to discern changes in trends given the usual month-to-month volatility in economic data, it takes some time before analysts can agree that a recession began at a certain date. It can be a year or more after the fact that analysts announce the date of the beginning of a recession.

What is the difference between a recession and a depression? Analysts describe a recession as a decrease in real GDP for at least two consecutive quarters. A **depression** is a very deep and prolonged recession. Because no subsequent recession has approached the severity of the Great Depression, the term *depression* is often used to refer to the long and pronounced recession of the 1930s. How severe was the Great Depression for the United States? During that slump, the unemployment rate skyrocketed to 25 percent and industrial output fell by more than 40 percent over a 3-year period, hampering business activity for more than a decade.

economics
IN ACTION

Firms Slash Wages to Preserve Jobs

During the recession of 2007-2009, pay cuts, instead of layoffs, increasingly were used by many firms as a method of decreasing labor costs as demand weakened. For example, union members at the Boston Globe accepted an 8.3 percent pay cut, among other concessions, in order to save the paper from bankruptcy, and thus preserve their jobs.

As unemployment increased during the recession, many workers had few choices, or little bargaining power, but to continue to accept the lower wages. This especially occurred in banking, autos, retailing, and other industries that were hit hard by the economic slump.

Besides large companies announcing pay cuts, state and local governments also trimmed wages or forced workers to take unpaid furloughs.

Many companies reacted against decreased wages as much as their workers did. Pay cuts can be demoralizing, and low morale can result in decreases in worker productivity, which is an indirect way of increasing costs. Moreover, valued employees may decide to bolt for greener pastures.

Pay cuts also have implications for the unemployment rate as a measure of hardship. If enough firms use pay cuts to avoid layoffs in the future, then the unemployment rate will tend to lose its reliability as to how workers fare during an economic downturn.

Source: "More Firms Cut Pay to Save Jobs," *The Wall Street Journal*, June 9, 2009, p. A4.

In summary, business cycles have three main characteristics:

- Fluctuations in the economy are irregular and unpredictable. Sometimes recessions are close together, as seen in the recessions of 1980 and 1981–1982; sometimes economic expansions continue for many years, such as the expansion of 1991–2001.

- Most macroeconomic variables that measure some aspect of production, income, or spending fluctuate together throughout the business cycle. When real GDP decreases during a recession, so do national income, business profits, household expenditures, investment spending, industrial production, auto sales, retail sales, and the like.

- Fluctuations in the economy's output of goods and services correspond strongly to changes in the rate of unemployment. When real GDP decreases, unemployment rises, and vice versa.

Theories of the Business Cycle

Over the years, economists have debated the sources of the business cycle. What causes the economy to turn downward or upward?

Many economists believe that a change in total spending (demand) is the immediate determinant of domestic output and employment. Recall that total spending in the economy includes expenditures for final goods by households, businesses, government, and foreign buyers.

Why do changes in total spending explain fluctuations in economic activity? If total spending decreases, businesses may find it unprofitable to produce the existing level of output. As they decrease production, they employ less land, labor, and capital. Thus, reductions in total spending result in decreases in national output, employment, and incomes. These decreases, in turn, can cause a recession in the economy. Conversely, an increase in total spending results in a rise in national output, employment, and incomes. These increases, in turn, promote economic expansion.

Business cycles may also be caused by changes in the supply side of the market. For example, the development of a new technology might result in new investment spending, thus causing an economic expansion. Conversely, a decrease in the availability of natural resources could cause an increase in the costs of production, resulting in a recession. Also, shocks may foster recession. Although the September 11 terrorist attacks did not cause recession in the U.S. economy in 2001 (the recession actually began in March of that year), they were clearly a factor that deepened the downward spiral of economic activity.

As we continue our study of macroeconomics, we will learn more about the causes of business cycles. Using aggregate demand and aggregate supply curves, we will learn why changes occur in national output, employment, income, and the price level.

Do Economic Expansions Die of Old Age?

One question that has intrigued economists is whether each economic expansion contains the seeds of its own destruction. Is it true that the longer an expansion lasts, the more likely it is to end in the next quarter or the next year? Studies find no compelling evidence that expansions possess an inherent tendency to die of old age. Instead, they appear to fall victim to specific events related to economic disturbances or government policies.

For example, the Iraqi invasion of Kuwait, which caused oil prices to double in the fall of 1990, contributed to the decline in economic activity during the recession of 1990–1991. American consumers, having suffered through the oil shocks of 1973–1974 and 1979, anticipated negative repercussions on the U.S. economy, and consumer confidence declined sharply and consumption fell, resulting in a decline in total spending.

The economic downturn of 2007 provides another example of cyclical slowdown. During the last few months of 2007, the U.S. economy began to encounter weakness in the financial sector that it could not shake off. Those financial shocks combined with other factors—record high commodity prices, natural disasters, and continued weakness in the housing market—caused the economy to contract. Despite rapid economic stimulus programs of the U.S. government, the economy entered into recession at the end of 2007. The magnitude of the downturn required unprecedented policy responses to reduce the extent of the damage to the economy.

CHECK POINT

1. Identify the four phases of the business cycle.

2. What factors cause the economy to turn upward or downward?

3. Do economic expansions die of old age?

UNEMPLOYMENT

One reason we want to avoid recessions and depressions is that they cause hardship among individuals. During a recession, not only does real GDP decline, but also fewer people are able to find jobs. Economists define the **unemployed** as individuals who do not have jobs but are actively seeking work.

Besides imposing costs on individuals, unemployment generates a cost for the economy as a whole because it produces fewer goods and services. When the economy does not provide enough jobs to employ everyone who is seeking work, the productivity of that unemployed labor is foregone. This lost output, combined with the hardship that unemployment imposes on individuals and their families, is the real cost of unemployment.

Measuring Unemployment

The unemployment rate is a closely watched measure of an economy's health. How is the unemployment rate calculated, and what does it mean?

Every month, the U.S. Bureau of Labor Statistics conducts a random, nationwide survey of about 60,000 households to gather information on labor market activities. The survey divides the adult (16 years old and over) population into three categories:

- Those who have jobs are classified as employed.

- Those who don't have jobs but are looking for them and are available for work are classified as unemployed.

- Those who don't have jobs and are not looking for work are not classified as members of the labor force.

The **unemployment rate** is the number of people who are unemployed divided by the labor force (the number of people holding or seeking jobs).

$$\text{Unemployment rate} = \frac{\text{Number of persons unemployed}}{\text{Number of persons in the labor force}}$$

In February 2009, the unemployment rate was 8.1 percent:

$$\text{Unemployment rate} = \frac{12,467,000}{154,214,000} = 8.1 \text{ percent}$$

Although the Bureau of Labor Statistics takes great care in calculating the unemployment rate, it suffers from several shortcomings. Part-time employment represents one problem. Although some part-time workers work less than a full week because they want to, others do so only because they cannot find a suitable full-time job. Nevertheless, a worker who has been cut back to part-time work is still counted as employed, even if that worker would prefer to work full time. During a recession, workers may find their work hours reduced from 40 hours to 30 hours a week because of slack demand for the product their employer produces. Because the statistics don't measure the "underemployment" of these workers, they tend to *underestimate* the actual extent of unemployment in the economy.

Unemployment statistics also suffer from the problem of discouraged workers. A **discouraged worker** is a person who is out of work, would like to work, and is available for work but has stopped looking for work because of lack of success in finding a job. Discouraged workers are not considered part of the labor force because they are not actively seeking employment. As a result, we do not count them as unemployed. Because the official unemployment rate does not include discouraged workers, the actual degree of unemployment in the economy tends to be underestimated.

Although the overall unemployment rate in February 2009 was 8.1 percent, the burdens of unemployment were not equally distributed. As seen in Table 11.2, unemployment rates tend to vary considerably among different groups in society. In particular, unemployment rates among blacks have roughly been double that of whites. This may be the result of the concentration of blacks in less-skilled occupations or in the inner city, where job opportunities are negligible and there is discrimination in employment and education. Moreover, teenagers tend to have much higher unemployment rates than adults. This is largely because teenagers have relatively modest job skills, have little geographic mobility, and more frequently leave their jobs than adults.

Three Kinds of Unemployment

Not everyone who is unemployed is unemployed for the same reason. Unemployment is classified into three types based on its causes. As you will see, some kinds of unemployment may not be as important as others.

Table 11.2   The Burdens of Unemployment in February 2009

Unemployment Rates by Demographic Characteristics (percent)	
All workers	8.1
Adult men	8.1
Adult women	6.7
Teenagers	21.6
White	7.3
Black or African American	13.4
Hispanic or Latino ethnicity	10.9

Source: Bureau of Labor Statistics, *The Employment Situation: February 2009,* available at http://www.bls.gov/news/.

Some people are unemployed because they cannot currently find work that matches their qualifications. For example, think of college students majoring in accounting or computer science. When they finish school, they will look for jobs that match their skills, but finding such jobs may take time. Yet the students will likely find jobs soon because their skills are marketable. This unemployment is temporary. Economists refer to this type of unemployment as frictional unemployment. **Frictional unemployment** is the unemployment that arises from normal labor turnover—that is, when people are "between jobs." Frictional unemployment is not of much concern when dealing with the national unemployment problem.

However, not all unemployment is short-lived. **Structural unemployment** is unemployment that occurs when individuals' skills do not match what employers require or when job seekers are geographically separated from job opportunities. Substantial structural unemployment is often found alongside job vacancies because the unemployed lack the skills required for newly created jobs. For example, there may be vacancies for electrical engineers, while truck drivers are unemployed. Moreover, there may be worker shortages in the Southwestern states that are undergoing economic growth and unemployment in states that are suffering economic contraction, as in the Midwest during the era of weak demand for U.S. automobiles in the 1980s. Because both skill and location problems are usually of long duration, structural unemployment is perhaps the most serious type of unemployment.

Cyclical unemployment is the fluctuating unemployment that coincides with the business cycle. Cyclical unemployment is a repeating short-run problem. The amount of cyclical unemployment increases when the economy goes into a slump and decreases when the economy goes into an expansion. A steelworker who is laid off because the economy enters a recession and is rehired several months later when the upswing occurs experiences cyclical unemployment. Government policy makers are especially interested in decreasing both the frequency and extent of this type of unemployment by reducing the frequency and extent of the recessions that account for it. The government also attempts to lessen the impact of recessions by providing unemployment compensation for those who are temporarily laid off.

Mitigating the Costs of Unemployment

The U.S. government has many policies and programs at its disposal to reduce the costs that unemployment imposes on some workers. The main policy instrument used to address the immediate needs of workers who lose their jobs is the unemployment insurance system. Other policies, such as mandatory advance notice of layoffs, may provide short-run benefits as well. Still other policies, such as education and training programs, attempt to improve the longer-term fortunes of those hurt by unemployment.

Unemployment insurance was established in the United States as part of the Social Security Act of 1935. This system helps support consumer spending during periods of job loss and provides economic security to workers through income maintenance. Another benefit of the unemployment insurance system is that it provides individuals with the financial resources to prolong their job search until they receive an offer that is appropriate to their skills. Although the federal government maintains control over the broad design of the unemployment insurance system, individual states have considerable autonomy in tailoring the program's features within their jurisdictions.

Unemployment insurance provides weekly benefits to workers who have been laid off or who have lost their jobs for reasons other than misconduct or a labor dispute. Only workers with a sufficiently long employment history—usually 6 months of significant employment—are eligible. Benefits are a fraction of the average weekly earnings on the job that was lost, up to a maximum dollar amount, paid up to 26 weeks in most states. This fraction is typically between 50 percent and 70 percent. Benefits are financed, in most states, by a payroll tax levied on firms.

Although the unemployment insurance system has benefited millions of workers over the years, these benefits do not come without costs. Many economists contend that higher unemployment benefits lead to longer unemployment spells. Providing benefits to unemployed workers reduces their incentive to search intensively for a new job. Research suggests that a 10-percentage-point increase in unemployment benefits results in an additional 1 week to 1.5 weeks of unemployment, when an average insured unemployment spell lasts roughly 15 weeks. Job finding rates also increase somewhat as the exhaustion of benefits approaches.[1]

What Is Full Employment?

Indeed, a high-employment economy provides benefits for society. But what do economists mean by full employment? Does full employment mean zero unemployment?

Recall that total unemployment in an economy consists of frictional, structural, and cyclical unemployment. We call the level of unemployment at which there is no cyclical unemployment the **natural rate of unemployment**. In other words, the natural rate of unemployment is the sum of frictional and structural unemployment, which economists consider essentially unavoidable. The natural rate of unemployment is economists' notion of **full employment**. Therefore, we define full employment as something less than 100-percent employment of the labor force.

In the United States today, most economists estimate that the natural rate of unemployment is between 4 percent and 6 percent. In 2000, the U.S. economy realized an unemployment rate of 4 percent, suggesting that there was little, if any, slack in the economy. Put simply, the economy was at "full employment" for all practical purposes.

Note that the natural rate of unemployment can vary over time. Changes in the natural rate of unemployment occur in response to shifting demographics of the labor force or changes in society's customs and laws. In the early 1990s, for example, structural unemployment increased as a result of corporate downsizing and decreases in defense spending. These changes increased the natural rate of unemployment. However, the aging of the workforce in the 2000s will likely decrease the amount of frictional unemployment because older workers are less likely to quit their jobs than younger workers. This will cause the natural rate of unemployment to decrease. Not only can the natural rate of unemployment change over time, but also it tends to differ among countries. In Europe, for example, estimates of the natural rate of unemployment put it between 7 percent and 10 percent.

The Recession of 2007–2009

In 2007–2009, much of the industrialized world fell into a deep recession. It was triggered by the disruptions in U.S. financial markets that began in 2007 and worsened to the point that the U.S. economy was in crisis in 2008. U.S. financial markets were disrupted by substantial declines in housing prices, rising default rates on residential mortgages, and a resulting sharp decline in the value of mortgages. These assets were held by banks and other financial institutions which play a vital role in the functioning of financial markets. Hundreds of billions of dollars in losses on these mortgages undermined the financial institutions that originated and invested in them.

The use of borrowed funds by these institutions made them vulnerable to large mortgage losses. Some financial institutions failed, such as Wachovia and Washington Mutual, and others were on the verge of failure. The remaining institutions pulled back from lending to each other, and the interest rates that they charged each other on a dwindling number of loans increased to unprecedented levels. This placed enormous stress on financial markets. Credit was frozen, and confidence in the financial system eroded.

Government also contributed to the financial crisis by pressuring banks to serve poor borrowers and poor regions of the country. This resulted in mortgages being made to many households who were unable to repay their loans. Also, poorly designed regulations resulted in banks not having sufficient safety cushions (capital) during periods of economic decline. Moreover, history shows that financial crisis tends to occur when money is plentiful and inexpensive: Cheap money encourages

---

1. *Economic Report of the President*, 1997, p. 159, available at http://www.gpoaccess.gov/eop/index.html.

excessive debt and risk taking. During the early 2000s, funds swept into the United States from high-saving countries such as China. Moreover, the Federal Reserve adopted a policy of providing abundant money to the U.S. economy. Simply put, there was much blame to share concerning the origins of the financial crisis.

As default rates for American households rose, lenders became increasingly reluctant to make any but the least risky loans. Many banks tightened standards on mortgages and consumer debt. Therefore, consumers found it increasingly difficult to finance purchases of "big ticket" items such as automobiles and houses. As the crisis continued, consumption spending declined and the economy slumped.

The financial crisis also affected businesses through several channels. Banks tightened lending standards for business loans, forcing businesses to reduce their expenditures on their ongoing operations, investments in equipment, and the like. As U.S. consumer demand weakened, many businesses became less willing to make investments to expand production. Businesses also faced weaker demand abroad as the financial crisis worsened the outlook for global economic growth. Because of these factors, business confidence declined and layoffs of workers increased. By 2008, the U.S. economy was falling into a severe recession.

The economic crisis soon spread to many other countries who saw their financial systems under stress, economic activity declining, and unemployment rising. The economic downturn was massive in scale and far-reaching in scope. This resulted in the U.S. government, and governments of other countries, taking many new and drastic actions to limit further damage to their economies. While many different responses were undertaken by different governments, all of the responses were designed to preserve the stability of financial institutions, increase the liquidity in financial markets, and provide fiscal stimulus to economies. These topics will be discussed in subsequent chapters of this book.

Bursting of Housing Bubble Triggers Recession

The bursting of the housing bubble in 2006–2007 led to a wave of housing foreclosures that triggered the recession of 2007–2009. How did this occur?

From 2000 to 2006, housing prices in many major U.S. cities increased much faster than overall inflation as measured by the consumer price index. While the CPI increased about 13 percent during this period, home prices in cities such as Los Angeles, San Francisco, and Miami almost tripled. The increase in home prices was fueled by a limited supply of homes caused by a shortage of buildable land: Environmental regulations, beaches, oceans, mountains, and the like restricted the land that was available for residential homebuilding in these cities. Strong demand for homes, supported by population growth and rising incomes of home buyers, also contributed to price increases.

Many economists felt that the increase in housing prices gave rise to a housing bubble. This can occur when the price of homes significantly increases above their fundamental values that are based on household incomes and other measures of affordability. Homes become overvalued when their prices rise beyond the abilities of households to pay for them.

Housing bubbles are founded on the expectation of increased prices which causes people to purchase houses. When you think that the price of a house is going to increase, you have the incentive to buy now, which only adds to the demand for the house and thus reinforces the increase in price. You think that you can sell the house later at a higher price and thus realize a gain.

What adds to the bubble is borrowed money. If you must make a 20-percent down payment on a $300,000 house ($60,000) you can borrow the remainder, or $240,000. If you have to make a down payment of only 5 percent on this house, you can borrow $285,000. The smaller down payment allows you to borrow more money to buy the house and provides you with the ability to pay a higher price. Low interest rates also add to the bubble because they allow more buyers to enter the market.

Aided by cash flows pouring into the United States from countries like China and a low-interest rate policy of the Federal Reserve, the mortgage market accelerated after the recession of 2001. Higher housing prices meant that borrowers could refinance their homes with even larger loans

economics
IN ACTION

McDonald's Hustles to Keep Its Burgers Sizzling in Lean Times

The recession of 2007–2009 imposed economic hardship on many firms and workers. However, one firm that was able to perform relatively well during this era was McDonald's. This is because many Americans flocked to the fast-food giant as an inexpensive substitute for sit-down meals. Similarly, Wal-Mart's sales remained buoyant as households were attracted to the discounter's merchandise.

However, business was not so good for McDonald's in other parts of the world, such as Europe and Asia, where about two-thirds of its revenues come from. Besides a worsening global economy which flattened its sales, McDonald's suffered from a strengthening (appreciating) U.S. dollar that made its burgers, french fries, and shakes more expensive for foreign customers. Also soaring commodity costs were putting intense pressure on McDonald's. Restaurant outlets complained that the high cost of beef, cheese, buns, and other ingredients, combined with a rising minimum wage and high energy costs, were softening their profits.

How did McDonald's attempt to buoy its sales and profits during such lean times? By focusing on improving restaurant operations, lowering prices, and slashing costs. To reduce operating costs, McDonald's removed gas-guzzling automobiles from the firm's fleet and held meetings at the company's Hamburger University in suburban Chicago rather than at exotic and expensive locations. The firm also convinced media firms to negotiate decreased advertising rates for McDonald's products, and ceased constructing new restaurants in markets that showed economic weakness. Moreover, McDonald's increased investments in highly profitable coffee drinks that competed with

Starbucks, and improved drive-through windows that increased sales and productivity.

Many of these adjustments actually began in 2003 when McDonald's revised its operating strategy to rebound from lethargic sales. It halted ambitious expansion of restaurants and instead emphasized improvements in its food, service, atmosphere, and marketing. The result was a more comprehensive menu that included items ranging from low-cost salads to a Southern-style chicken biscuit served at breakfast, and restaurants equipped with flat-screen televisions sets and comfortable leather seats for customers. These activities helped McDonald's feed an additional 2 million customers a day.

As the recession of 2008–2009 intensified, McDonald's increasingly encouraged restaurant managers across the world to more closely scrutinize labor, food, and utility costs. Moreover, the food giant gave its restaurant managers more freedom to price items in line with changing demand conditions. During previous eras of inflation, restaurant managers simply increased the price of large burgers by a dime and the price of small burgers, drinks, and french fries by a nickel. By 2008, one restaurant manager might increase the price of a milk shake by 4 cents while another decreased it by 5 cents. In particular, the firm shied away from increasing prices, and thus losing customers, at outlets in economically depressed areas of the country.

Simply put, the strategy used by McDonald's to cope with the global recession was to cut costs and promote lower-priced items perceived as a good value. At the same time, franchise owners would have to tolerate lower profit margins until the economy improved.

Sources: "McDonald's: Capitalizing on the Downturn with an Even Greater Presence," *Food Business Review*, January 28, 2009, p. 1; "Should You Be Buying McDonald's in This Recession?" *The Dynamic Wealth Report*, January 28, 2009, p. 1; and "McDonald's Seeks Way to Keep Sizzling," *The Wall Street Journal*, March 10, 2008, pp. A1 and A11.

when their houses increased in value. Buyers were also unlikely to default because they could sell their house to pay off the loan. Also, many banks had lax lending standards that required negligible down payments on houses, thus allowing many buyers into the market. These factors added to the demand for homes, which caused prices to increase. Simply put, the housing bubble was the result of too much money chasing too few houses, causing houses to become overvalued.

Home prices increased rapidly until they became unsustainable relative to household incomes. When that occurred in 2006–2007, the bubble burst and housing prices crashed. Many homeowners found that their mortgage debt was higher than the value of their houses and they could not pay back their mortgages. They walked away from their homes and turned the keys back to the banks who now held assets of decreasing value. As the survival of many banks was threatened, they restricted the supply of loans to businesses and households, which pushed the economy into recession.

Inflexible Labor Markets Cost Jobs

We have learned how the business cycle can affect a country's unemployment rate. As the economy dips into recession, business profits decrease, as does the demand for workers. This causes the unemployment rate to rise.

Another determinant of the unemployment rate is the degree of flexibility in a country's labor market. Countries with highly regulated and inflexible labor markets tend to have higher rates of unemployment and lower per-capita income, as seen in Figure 11.3. Although laws that hinder the dismissal of workers may sound appealing at first, such policies impede workers' ability to compete. When companies face onerous labor regulations, they can't adjust quickly to new opportunities in the marketplace. They are often wary of hiring new workers, who will be difficult to shed if optimistic sales expectations turn sour.

Many economists argue that, compared to the United States, inflexible labor markets cause the natural rate of unemployment to be higher in Europe. Let us consider some labor practices that affect these countries' rates of unemployment.

Europe   Europe's approach to labor markets has generally been to protect workers, especially low-skilled workers, which keeps their wages relatively high and penalizes firms for firing them. Europe was the birthplace of the welfare state, and countries such as the Netherlands, France, and Sweden have legislated generous welfare benefits and unemployment insurance. This allows people a longer duration of time to conduct a job search, thus increasing the natural rate of unemployment. Moreover, companies pay high employment taxes to help the welfare state. This adds to the cost of hiring labor, which decreases the quantity demanded.

Another factor affecting unemployment is unionization. The unionized portion of Europe's labor force is two to three times larger than that of the United States. To the degree that strong unions in Europe force wages above market-equilibrium levels and decrease wage flexibility, they increase the natural rate of unemployment. Moreover, many European governments maintain minimum wages that are at or above equilibrium wage rates in some industries and occupations. This results in wage inflexibility and a higher natural rate of unemployment.

Besides adding to the cost of hiring labor, many European nations, hoping to thwart job losses, have saddled companies with burdensome rules on when and how they can dismiss workers. The red tape and reproach involved in cutting jobs makes firms wary of hiring new workers in the first place. With few new opportunities opening up, workers cling to existing jobs. As a result, too many of Europe's labor resources remain frozen, and companies cannot respond quickly and aggressively to changes in the market. Europe may have managed to save a few existing jobs, but at a high cost in economic performance.

Companies, such as Caterpillar, that conduct business in Europe are aware of the problems of inflexible labor markets. Even though Europe has high-skilled, well-trained, and educated workers, companies say the shorter work hours result in additional costs that reduce their competitiveness in a global economy. Simply put, an engineer who works only 35 hours is not worth it for Volkswagen. As a result, many companies are reluctant to hire European workers, even if demand is strong. Instead, they establish manufacturing subsidiaries in other parts of the world where labor markets are more flexible and workers are less expensive to hire. Inflexible labor markets also help explain why Europe hasn't become as attractive a home for foreign investment as the United States.

For example, in 2004 Mercedes-Benz threatened its German autoworkers that if they did not agree to lower pay and more hours of work, the firm would move production to the Czech Republic or Poland

Figure 11.3 | Labor Market Flexibility Contributes to Higher Per-Capita Incomes

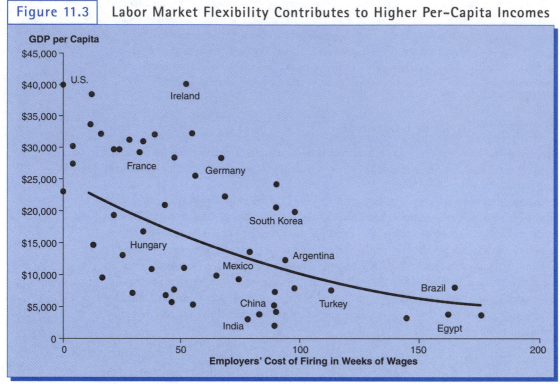

Highly globalized nations tend to allow greater freedom in the hiring and firing of workers. Increased labor mobility helps make these economies more productive and dynamic, resulting in higher per-capita incomes.

Source: Federal Reserve Bank of Dallas, *Racing to the Top: How Global Competition Disciplines Public Policy,* 2005 Annual Report, p. 12, available at http://www.dallasfed.org.

where workers earn less than a third the average wage in Germany. Yes, German workers were more productive. But workers in Eastern and Central Europe, with the help of state-of-the-art plants, were becoming more productive, too.

As a result, some labor leaders in Europe have begun to make concessions in hopes of saving jobs. The change could revolutionize labor relations in Europe, fostering a trend toward more flexible labor rules and weaker unions. That would enhance Europe's competitiveness, which has dwindled because of high labor costs and an opposition to reforms, but could also increase social tension as workers encounter the possibility of losing jobs, taking lower pay, and working longer hours.

United States.   In contrast, the United States has done a better job of achieving job growth and maintaining relatively low unemployment rates. Compared to Europe, policies in the United States are more laissez-faire and leave labor market arrangements to employers and employees. The United States has relatively weak unions, a relatively low minimum wage, and substantial competition for low-skilled jobs from foreign workers and immigrants. As a result, labor has a weaker bargaining position in the United States, making it easier and cheaper for American firms to hire workers. Also, there are less generous unemployment and welfare benefits in the United States, which makes welfare even less attractive compared to work. Job security for U.S. workers has also been threatened by company downsizing. These practices make labor markets more flexible in the United States than in Europe.

We can understand the differences between the labor markets of these countries in terms of Figure 11.4. Europe's more rigid labor market is shown in Figure 11.4(*a*), while the more flexible U.S. labor market is shown in Figure 11.4(*b*). The labor market equilibrium is shown by point *A* in the figures, where the equilibrium wage is $24 per hour. Suppose that the demand for labor declines in each

| Figure 11.4 | Rigid Wages Can Result in Involuntary Unemployment |

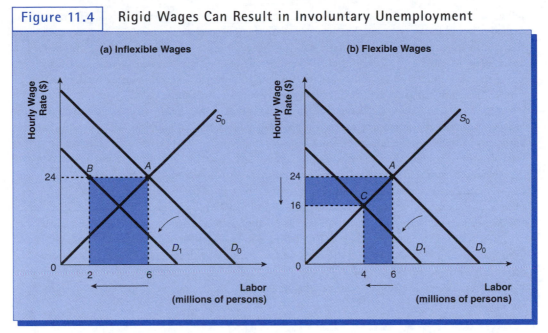

During a business recession, market rigidities may prevent wages from decreasing, resulting in involuntary unemployment. In a flexible labor market, wages decrease during a recession. The wage reduction clears the market of involuntary unemployment. Many believe that Europe's labor market is more rigid, whereas the U.S. labor market is more flexible.

market because of a business recession. The market rigidities of Europe prevent wages from declining to the new equilibrium at point *C*, resulting in a relatively large decrease in the quantity of labor demanded at point *B*, from 6 million persons to 2 million persons. In the more flexible U.S. market, however, wages fall during the recession. Although the quantity of labor demanded declines from 6 million persons to 4 million persons during the slump, it does not decrease as much as in Europe. Put simply, the rigidity of Europe's labor market causes a relatively large decline in the quantity of labor demanded and involuntary unemployment.

THE PRODUCTIVITY–JOBS CONNECTION

In 2005, the *Washington Post* ran a story explaining that, a quarter-century ago, General Motors needed about 500,000 workers to turn out 5 million automobiles a year. By the early 2000s, however, improvements in productivity allowed the company to employ only a quarter of those workers to produce the same number of cars. Does this mean that strong productivity growth necessitates job losses?

Productivity is simply the amount of output for a given quantity of labor. Thus, increases in productivity must reflect either an increase in output for a fixed amount of employment or a decrease in the amount of labor required to produce a fixed amount of output. Of course, both the amount of labor and output could change at once.

Any economist will tell you that faster productivity growth leads to higher real wages and improved living standards. Yet if higher productivity allows firms to shed workers, how can it raise wages and living standards? If productivity does lead to improved wages and living standards, why do workers often feel that productivity growth leaves them behind? To answer these questions, we must consider the short- and long-run effects of changes in productivity.

Concerning the short run, if firms see the demand for their products rising, they will respond by expanding production. If labor productivity remains unchanged, they will need to hire more workers in order to increase production. But if labor productivity is increasing, then it has the potential to reduce employment growth because firms can satisfy demand using fewer workers. Likewise, if the overall demand in the economy has not expanded, then an increase in labor productivity could lead to a fall in unemployment in the short run. In this case, faster productivity growth might lead to an increase in job losses without a corresponding increase in job creation in new and expanding industries. Eventually, employment catches up to the increased levels of output made possible by productivity growth. However, the problem can remain for some time.

In the long run, however, income and employment depend not on demand but instead on supply factors, including the economy's stock of capital, labor force, and technology. Whereas the short-run perspective emphasizes the impact of productivity on the number of workers needed to produce a *given* level of output, the long-run perspective emphasizes that an increase in labor productivity *increases* potential output. It does so directly by allowing more output to be produced with the same level of employment, but it also increases employment because it decreases the cost of labor to firms.[2] As new technological innovations boost productivity, new industries arise and new jobs are created. The increased demand for labor tends to boost wages as firms compete to hire additional workers and raises total employment.

There is little debate among economists about the long-run effect of productivity on employment: Faster productivity growth should translate into an increase in the overall demand for labor in the economy. This, in turn, will lead real wages to rise, just as an increase in the demand for a typical good or service acts to bid its price up. Figure 11.5 shows the relationship between productivity

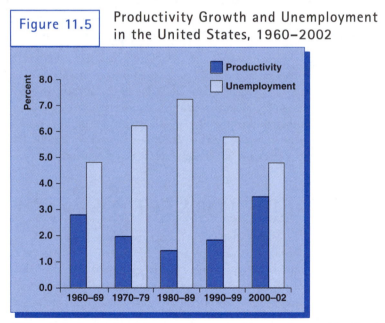

| Figure 11.5 | Productivity Growth and Unemployment in the United States, 1960–2002 |

Although faster productivity growth may reduce employment in the short run, it promotes higher employment and wages in the long run.

Source: Economic Report of the President, 2006, available at http://www.gpoaccess.gov/eop/index.html.

_____

2. For firms, the relevant cost of labor is not measured simply by the wages and benefits paid to the workers. Rather, it is measured by the costs of these wages and benefits *relative* to the output the workers are able to produce. Just as a rise in wages will increase labor costs if worker productivity remains constant, a rise in labor productivity will lower the cost of labor at a given level of wages and benefits. If higher productivity makes labor less costly, firms will find it profitable to expand employment.

growth and the unemployment rate. It suggests that although faster productivity growth may reduce employment in the short run, it promotes employment in the long run. However, this process can be costly and painful for the workers whose skills are no longer in demand.[3]

CHECK POINT

1. What is meant by the unemployment rate, and how is it calculated?

2. Economists classify unemployment according to its causes. Explain.

3. What is meant by full employment, and how is it measured?

4. What factors explain unemployment rate differences in the United States and Europe?

INFLATION

Since the end of World War II, the United States has experienced almost continuous inflation. We can define **inflation** as a sustained or continuous rise in the general price level. We should note several things about this definition. First, inflation refers to the movement in the *general* level of prices. However, some individual prices may fall. During the 1990s, for example, the prices of computers fell, while the prices of many other goods increased. During an inflationary period, rising prices outweigh falling prices, causing the average level of prices to increase. Second, the rise in the price level must be substantial and continue over a period longer than a day, week, or month.

When there is inflation, the purchasing power of a given amount of money decreases. Table 11.3 shows what would happen to the real value of $10,000, from January 1, 2000, to January 1, 2010, at different rates of inflation. At 2 percent inflation, $10,000 would purchase only $8,200 of goods in 2010. At 10 percent inflation, that same $10,000 would be worth only $3,860.

Table 11.3   Impact of Inflation on the Real Value of $10,000, 2000–2010

Year	Annual Inflation Rate				
	2%	4%	6%	8%	10%
2000	$10,000	$10,000	$10,000	$10,000	$10,000
2002	9,610	9,250	8,900	8,570	8,260
2004	9,240	8,550	7,920	7,350	6,830
2006	8,880	7,900	7,050	6,300	5,640
2008	8,530	7,310	6,270	5,400	4,670
2010	8,200	6,760	5,580	4,630	3,860

3. Carl Walsh, "The Productivity and Jobs Connection: The Long and the Short Run of It," *Economic Letter,* Federal Reserve Bank of San Francisco, July 16, 2004, available at http://www.frbsf.org; and Mark Schweitzer and Saeed Zaman, "Are We Engineering Ourselves out of Manufacturing Jobs?" *Economic Commentary,* Federal Reserve Bank of Cleveland, January 1, 2006, available at http://www.clevelandfed.org.

The average price level may decrease or increase. We refer to a continuing decline in the average price level as **deflation.** It occurs when price reductions on some goods and services outweigh price increases on all others. The last deflation in the United States occurred during the Great Depression of the 1930s.

Measuring Inflation: The Consumer Price Index

The most frequently cited indicator of inflation is the **consumer price index (CPI).** The CPI is calculated by the Bureau of Labor Statistics by sampling thousands of households and businesses. When a news report says that the "cost of living" rose by, say, 3 percent, it is usually referring to the CPI.

To construct the CPI, the Bureau of Labor Statistics selects a "market basket" of about 400 goods and services that are assumed to be most crucial to the spending of the typical American consumer. Then it assigns weights to those goods and services according to past patterns of consumer expenditures. The major groups of product categories, examples of these categories, and their weights are summarized as follows:

- Housing (rent equivalent of primary residence, fuel oil, bedroom furniture), 40%
- Food and beverages (breakfast cereal, milk, chicken, wine, full service meals), 16%
- Transportation (new vehicles, airline fares, gasoline, motor vehicle insurance), 13%
- Education and communication (college tuition, postage, telephone services), 6%
- Medical care (prescription drugs, physicians, services, eyeglasses), 5%
- Apparel (men's shirts, women's dresses, jewelry), 4%
- Other goods and services (haircuts, funeral expenses), 16%

Every month, government data collectors visit or call thousands of retail stores, service establishments, rental units, and doctors' offices, all over the United States, to obtain information on the prices of the thousands of items used to track and measure price changes in the CPI. These collectors record the prices of about 80,000 items each month in order to compute the current cost of the market basket. Because buying patterns change, the market basket is revised about once each decade. Therefore, the CPI measures inflation as experienced by consumers in their day-to-day living expenses.

The Bureau of Labor Statistics arbitrarily sets the average value of the goods and services in the market basket for some base period (currently 1982–1984 = 100). Referring to Table 11.4, we see that the CPI was 215.2 in 2008. This means that prices in 2008 were about 115.2 percent *higher* than prices in the base period. A typical bundle of goods and services worth $1,000 in the base period would have cost $2,152 in 2008 ($1,000 $\times$ 2.152 = $2,152).

Once we have the CPI for selected years, we can calculate the rate of inflation between years. We use the following formula:

$$\text{Rate of inflation} = \frac{\text{CPI}_{\text{Given year}} - \text{CPI}_{\text{Previous year}}}{\text{CPI}_{\text{Previous year}}} \times 100$$

For example, suppose that we wanted to compute the rate of inflation between 2007 and 2008. Referring to Table 11.4, we see that the CPI equaled 207.3 in 2007 and 215.2 in 2008. The rate of inflation between the two years thus equals 3.8 percent, calculated as follows:

$$\text{Rate of inflation} = \frac{215.2 - 207.3}{207.3} \times 100 = 3.8 \text{ percent}$$

The CPI can be used to calculate how prices have changed over the years. Let's say you have $10 to purchase goods and services today (year 2008). How much money would you have needed in 1950 to buy the same amount of goods and services? Given

1. The CPI for 1950 = 24.1

2. The CPI for 2008 = 215.2

Table 11.4	Consumer Price Index and Rate of Inflation for Selected Years (1982–1984 = 100)		
	Year	CPI	Yearly Percentage Change in CPI (annual rate of inflation)
	2000	172.2	3.4
	2001	177.1	2.8
	2002	179.9	1.6
	2003	184.0	2.3
	2004	188.9	2.7
	2005	195.3	3.4
	2006	201.6	3.2
	2007	207.3	2.8
	2008	215.2	3.8

Source: Data from *Economic Report of the President*, 2009.

Use the following formula to compute the calculation:

$$1950\ \text{Price} = 2008\ \text{Price} \times \frac{1950\ \text{CPI}}{2008\ \text{CPI}}$$

$$= \$10.00 \times \frac{24.1}{215.2}$$

$$= \$1.12$$

You would have needed $1.12 in 1950 to buy the same amount of goods and services in 2008.

The CPI is the principal source of information concerning trends in consumer prices and inflation in the United States. The CPI is used as the basis for making cost-of-living adjustments to the wages paid to millions of union workers, payments to Social Security recipients and retirees of the federal government and military, and entitlement programs such as food stamps and school lunches. Also, many banks link the interest rates they charge on mortgages, automobile loans, and personal loans to the CPI. Moreover, individual income tax brackets and personal exemptions are adjusted upward to account for the rate of inflation. Finally, the Federal Reserve bases its monetary policy on the rate of inflation as measured by the CPI.

Although the CPI is used as a measure of the cost of living for a typical urban family, it is really an imperfect measure. One weakness of the CPI is that people's buying patterns change, so the change in what people actually spend on "living" deviates from measured increases in, say, bacon and eggs. As some prices rise, people switch to cheaper goods. Thus, the CPI overstates the actual cost of living.

Another problem with the CPI is that its fixed market basket fails to keep pace with the development of better products, such as computers offering greater memory and faster speeds. The price of a new computer may be higher, but its capabilities may be much better than those of an older model. Part of a price increase may reflect higher quality rather than simply a higher price for the same product. To the extent that product quality improves, the CPI overstates the rate of inflation.

Finally, the CPI ignores price discounting. New types of discount stores, such as OfficeMax, Costco, Home Depot, and Wal-Mart, have gained an increased share of the market by offering lower prices than their competitors. Again, the CPI overstates the rate of inflation. For these reasons, most economists maintain that the CPI overstates inflation, but there is no consensus about the amount of overstatement.

Besides the CPI, there are other price indexes that are used to measure price changes in the economy. The producer price index (PPI), formerly called the wholesale price index, tracks the average change

economics
IN ACTION

Social Security COLA: No Increase in Monthly Checks Hard to Swallow for Elderly

Employment contracts, pension benefits, and government entitlements are sometimes tied to a cost-of-living index, generally the Consumer Price Index (CPI). A cost-of-living allowance (COLA) makes adjustments in incomes, usually annually, based on changes in the cost-of-living index. Consider the case of Social Security.

In 2009, the trustees who oversee Social Security projected that recipients would not receive an increase in monthly checks in the year ahead, the first time in a generation that payments would not rise. The reason? Throughout 2009, inflation was negative as measured by the CPI, largely because energy prices were below 2008 levels. Therefore, there would be no automatic cost-of-living increases that were tied to inflation. That hasn't happened since automatic increases were adopted in 1975.

By law, Social Security benefits cannot go down. However, monthly payments would drop for millions of older people in the Medicare prescription drug program because the premiums, which often are deducted from Social Security payments, were scheduled to go up slightly.

Advocates for sticking by Social Security rules maintained that with negative inflation, Social Security checks would have greater buying power, and thus there is no need to increase the monthly checks. They also noted that Social Security recipients received one-time $250 payments in 2009 as part of the government's economic stimulus program. Although retirees may have perceived that they are being hurt because there was no COLA, in fact they are not getting hurt, according to the advocates.

However, the AARP argued that older people still faced higher prices because they spend a disproportionate amount of their income on health care, where costs increase faster than inflation as measured by the CPI. Many also suffered from decreasing home values and shrinking stock portfolios just as they were relying on those assets for income. Therefore, the AARP contended that higher monthly checks for the retired were justified under Social Security even though the CPI did not indicate inflation.

Source: "Stick by Social Security Rules: No Inflation, No Cost of Living Increase," *Yakima Herald-Republic*, August 27, 2009, p. 4-A; and "Millions Face Shrinking Social Security Payments," AARP *Bulletin Today*, August 23, 2009.

in prices over time of domestically produced and consumed goods. The index comprises prices for both consumer goods and capital equipment, but excludes prices for services. A primary use of the PPI is to deflate revenue streams in order to measure real growth in output. The other widely used price measure is the GDP deflator, as discussed in Chapter 10. It is a measure of the level of prices of all new, domestically produced, final goods and services in an economy. The GDP deflator is a gauge of the cost of goods purchased by U.S. households, government, and industry and thus serves as an indicator of domestically generated inflation.

WHO BENEFITS FROM AND WHO IS HURT BY INFLATION?

Why are economists concerned about inflation? As we will see, inflation can greatly affect the national standard of living. It can also influence economic behavior and lead to significant impacts on the operation of the economy.

Inflation and the Purchasing Power of Income

No matter what the inflation rate is, it is interesting to know whether you are beating inflation or whether inflation is beating you. In other words, has your nominal income increased by a smaller percentage, the same percentage, or a greater percentage than the inflation rate?

To answer this question, we must adjust nominal income for changes in the price level. **Nominal income** is the actual number of dollars of income received during a year. **Real income** is the actual number of dollars received (nominal income) adjusted for any change in price. Real income, therefore, measures your real purchasing power—that is, the amount of goods and services that can be purchased with your nominal income. Real income is computed as follows:

$$\text{Real income} = \frac{(\text{Nominal income})}{\text{CPI}} \times 100$$

This formula can help us determine whether we are beating inflation.

For example, assume that Emily's nominal income rises from $50,000 in 2007 to $56,000 in 2008, an increase of 12 percent. Also suppose the CPI rises from 207.3 in 2007 to 215.2 in 2008, an increase of 3.8 percent. Because Emily's nominal income rose by a greater percentage than the inflation rate, she has more than kept up with inflation. In other words, her real income rose from 2007 to 2008. Using the preceding formula, we can calculate her real income, stated in terms of the base year, for the two years, as follows:

$$\text{Real income}_{2007} = (\$50,000/207.3) \times 100 = \$24,120$$

$$\text{Real Income}_{2008} = (\$56,000/215.0) \times 100 = \$26,022$$

Emily's real income rose from $24,120 in 2007 to $26,022 in 2008.

The preceding example illustrates how inflation affects real purchasing power. Conclusion: If your nominal income increases by a greater percentage than the inflation rate, then your purchasing power rises. But if the inflation rate rises faster than your nominal income, then your purchasing power falls.

Concerning the purchasing power of income, have you ever wondered what a Big Mac costs throughout the world? Every year, *The Economist* publishes the so-called Big Mac Index, as shown in Table 11.5. For example, the cheapest burger on the chart is sold in South Africa, at $1.66, compared with an average American price of $3.54. American tourists traveling to South Africa would find Big Macs a good buy.

Redistribution of Wealth from Lenders to Borrowers

What is the impact of inflation on lenders and borrowers? To the extent that inflation is unanticipated, it creates winners and losers among these groups. If inflation is higher than anticipated, the winners are those who agreed to borrow money at an interest rate that did not reflect the higher inflation. The losers are those who agreed to lend money at that interest rate. In other words, unanticipated inflation benefits people who are in debt because the purchasing power of their dollars will decrease over the life of the loan. Borrowers thus pay back principal and interest using dollars that are less valuable than they were when they incurred the loan. As a result, unanticipated inflation results in a decrease in purchasing power for lenders.

The federal government is another debtor that has benefited from unanticipated inflation. Historically, the federal government has financed its budget deficits by borrowing from the public through the sales of Treasury bills and other securities. Unanticipated inflation has allowed the federal government to pay off its loans using dollars that have less purchasing power than the dollars it

Table 11.5	The Price of a Big Mac, 2009		
Country		Big Mac Price (in local currency)	(in dollars)
Norway		40.00 kroner	$5.79
Switzerland		6.50 francs	5.60
Denmark		29.50 kroner	5.07
United States		3.54 dollars	3.54
Brazil		8.02 reals	3.45
Mexico		33.00 pesos	2.30
Russia		62.00 rubles	1.73
South Africa		16.95 rand	1.66

Source: Data from "Big Mac Index," The Economist, February 4, 2009, available at http://www.economist.com.

originally borrowed. Therefore, unanticipated inflation decreases the real burden of the public debt to the federal government.

Indeed, unanticipated inflation may cause a redistribution of wealth from lenders to borrowers. However, if inflation is steady and predictable, many people may correctly anticipate its effects on the purchasing power of money and thus can avoid the decline in real income that inflation causes. For example, if the lending officer at Wells Fargo Bank correctly anticipates inflation, she can avoid the unwanted impact on her bank's real income by attaching an inflation premium to the nominal interest rate she charges for new auto or real estate loans. The additional nominal interest rate compensates the bank for the loss in the purchasing power of money attributable to inflation.

Inflation and Real Interest Rates

Inflation may also hurt savers and investors. For example, suppose that you have a 2-year certificate of deposit that yields 6 percent per year. If inflation is 10 percent per year, you will lose on your savings each year. Although you will receive interest payments of 6 percent, they will not keep pace with 10 percent inflation. The result will be a decline in your purchasing power.

The interest rate that the bank pays is called the **nominal interest rate,** and the interest rate that is adjusted for inflation is called the **real interest rate.** The relationship between the nominal interest rate and the real interest rate is given by the following formula:

Real interest rate = Nominal interest rate − Inflation rate

The real interest rate is the difference between the nominal interest rate and the inflation rate. Although the nominal interest rate is always positive, the real interest rate can be positive or negative. When the real interest rate is negative, savers and lenders are hurt because interest does not keep pace with inflation. Table 11.6 shows the real and nominal interest rates for the United States from 2003 to 2008.

Because inflation threatens people's financial well-being by reducing the purchasing power of their money, they take great pains to find investments for which returns exceed the inflation rate, such as stocks, bonds, and many other financial instruments. When returns are corrected for inflation, however, investors sometimes see negative numbers.

Table 11.6	Nominal and Real Interest Rates, 2003–2008 (%)		
	Nominal Interest Rate*	Inflation Rate	Real Interest Rate
2003	1.0	2.3	−1.3
2004	1.4	2.7	−1.3
2005	3.2	3.4	−0.2
2006	4.7	3.2	1.5
2007	4.4	2.8	1.6
2008	1.4	3.8	−2.4

* 3-month Treasury bills.
Source: Federal Reserve, *Statistical Releases*, available at http://www.federalreserve.gov.

In 1996, the U.S. government made financial history by announcing its intention to issue the first U.S. securities indexed to the rate of inflation. Dubbed *Treasury inflation-protection securities* (TIPS), the indexed securities were first sold in 1997. Now, U.S. investors can purchase a financial instrument that provides a guaranteed hedge against the loss of purchasing power that accompanies increases in the CPI.

Inflation and Taxpayers

Inflation hurts taxpayers because it pushes up tax bills without any explicit changes in the tax laws. The reason: Part of our country's tax system is based on nominal income instead of real income.

We will first consider the federal income tax system that existed before 1985. During this era, the progressive structure of the individual income tax ensured that as incomes rose during a time of inflation, the average rate of tax paid by most taxpayers went up. In other words, tax bills didn't just rise as fast as inflation—they actually rose faster.

To illustrate, suppose that the average price level rises by 10 percent from year 1 to year 2. Suppose also that Alice has a cost-of-living provision in her labor contract that causes her nominal wages to increase by 10 percent from year 1 to year 2. On the surface, it appears that she broke even with inflation. Yet this does not account for the fact that a 10-percent rise in nominal income will push Alice into a higher tax bracket with a higher tax rate. Although Alice's nominal income keeps pace with inflation, her real income falls because she pays a higher tax rate as a result of inflation. Alice's real income is redistributed to the government and, ultimately, to those who benefit from government spending. Notice that Alice's tax rate increases without any congressional action to increase taxes. Critics refer to this situation as *taxation without representation*.

To prevent the redistribution of real income through the federal personal income tax system, in 1985, the U.S. government indexed the federal personal income tax. Each year, tax brackets and personal exemptions are corrected to reflect the rate of inflation. Therefore, households are pushed into a higher tax bracket only if their real incomes increase, not by inflation alone.

Home Ownership as a Hedge against Inflation

One potential hedge against inflation is home ownership. As you complete your college education and enter the workforce, you may decide that buying a house is a good investment instead of paying rent year after year to live in a dwelling that will never be yours. Table 11.7 shows the median costs and financial terms for buying a new house in 2008.

If you decide to buy a house, you must consider what you can afford to buy and how much you can borrow. Most mortgage lenders require you to have at least 10 percent of the purchase price

Table 11.7   The Costs of Buying a New Home

Mortgage on Average New Home, 2008		Interest Rate on Mortgage			
		Loan	7.00%	7.50%	8.00%
Terms		$100,000	$665	$699	$734
Purchase price	$353,500	150,000	998	1,049	1,101
Amount of loan	253,400	200,000	1,331	1,398	1,468
Loan-to-price ratio	71.7%	250,000	1,663	1,748	1,834
Maturity	28.6 years	300,000	1,996	2,098	2,201
Fees and charges (percentage of loan amount)	1.1%	400,000	2,661	2,797	2,935
		500,000	3,326	3,496	3,669
Interest rate	5.93%	600,000	3,991	4,195	4,403

Use this chart to estimate your monthly principal and interest payments based on your mortgage loan amount and interest rate.
Source: Federal Reserve Board, *Statistical Supplement to the Federal Reserve Bulletin,* August 2008, available at http://www.federalreserve.gov/pubs/supplement/

as a down payment, plus enough cash on hand for closing costs. Closing costs include filing fees, mortgage and real estate taxes, attorneys' fees, and points. A point is an up-front interest charge paid to the lender. A point equals 1 percent of the mortgage amount; paying 2 to 3 points is typical. If you borrow $100,000 for a mortgage, for example, you may pay $3,000 as a service fee (points) for the loan.

Lenders generally assume that you can afford to spend 28 percent of your total income on your mortgage, property taxes, and homeowner's insurance. Even if you meet this requirement, you still may be rejected if your mortgage expenses and other regular debt payments (student and auto loans) are more than 36 percent of your total income.

If you borrow from a mortgage lender, you will have the option of a fixed-rate mortgage or an adjustable-rate mortgage (ARM). The best choice for you depends on your available cash, how frequently you move, and, most important of all, whether you think interest rates will rise or fall.

Fixed-rate or *conventional* mortgages have been around since the 1930s. The total interest and monthly payments are set at the closing. You repay the principal and interest in equal (usually monthly) installments over a 15-, 20-, or 30-year period. You will always know how much you will pay and for how long. Even if interest rates increase, your monthly mortgage will not go up. However, you won't benefit if interest rates fall.[4]

ARMs were introduced in the 1980s to help more borrowers qualify for mortgages and to protect lenders by letting them pass along higher interest costs to borrowers. An ARM has a variable interest rate that changes on a regular basis—say, once a year—to reflect fluctuations in the cost of borrowing. Lenders tie the variable interest rate to another interest rate, such as the rate on 1-year U.S. Treasury securities. As the rate on Treasury securities fluctuates, so does the rate on your mortgage, as well as your monthly mortgage payment.

---

4. If interest rates decline, are you stuck with your fixed-rate loan for, say, the next 25 years? No. You may want to refinance your fixed-rate loan to get a lower rate. This will reduce your monthly payment and the overall cost of the mortgage. However, refinancing usually requires you to again bear the closing costs on a mortgage. Refinancing a mortgage requires an application and credit check, new survey, title search and insurance, an appraisal and inspection, and attorneys. Thus, refinancing may force you to pay sizable closing costs and up-front fees again, even if your mortgage is only several years old. Although every situation is different, the general rule is that it pays to refinance if you can obtain an interest rate at least 2 percentage points lower than you're currently paying.

Compared to fixed-rate mortgages, ARMs are usually offered at lower initial rates and with lower closing costs. Also, the interest rate on an ARM will decrease if other interest rates decline. Keep in mind, however, that you will have to pay more interest if the rate on your ARM rises. ARMs have limits, or caps, on the amount of interest that can be charged over the life of a contract.

EFFECTS OF SEVERE INFLATION

During periods of severe inflation, when the annual rate of inflation is 10 percent or higher, economic behavior may change. Many people feel discouraged because their income cannot keep up with rising prices. They cannot plan for future expenses because they do not know how much their money will buy later.

Some consumers fight the effects of inflation by purchasing more than usual during an inflationary period. Many consumers borrow money or use credit for large expenses instead of purchasing later, when prices will probably have risen even further. Moreover, some consumers may barter their services, do their own home repairs, or make their own clothing.

Some people attempt to protect themselves against inflation by investing in items that quickly increase in value. Such items include gold bars, rare stamps, gold and silver coins, diamonds, and art objects. Many people purchase real estate during inflationary periods because the value of land and buildings tends to increase rapidly at such times.

Some businesses may prosper during periods of inflation. They include discount stores, credit card agencies, and agencies that collect overdue debts. Businesses that lease items such as large appliances and automobiles, which many people cannot afford to purchase, also thrive at these times.

It is possible for a country to experience **hyperinflation**, a rapid and uncontrolled inflation that destroys its economy. For example, hyperinflation caused the collapse of the German economy after World War I ended in 1918. The German government printed large amounts of currency to finance itself after the war. Therefore, prices in Germany increased more than 1 trillion percent from August 1922 to December 1923. In 1923, $1 in U.S. currency was worth more than 4 trillion marks! Many Germans took to burning their paper money because it was a cheaper source of fuel than firewood.

The hyperinflation left a traumatic impression on the German economy. Business owners discovered the impossibility of rational economic planning. Profits declined as employees demanded frequent increases in wages. Workers were often paid daily and sometimes 2 and 3 times a day, so that they could purchase goods in the morning before the inevitable afternoon increase in prices. Workers became demoralized and were reluctant to work as their money became worthless or virtually worthless. Also, patrons at restaurants found that they had to pay more for their meals than was listed on the menu when they ordered. Also, speculation became rampant, which disrupted production. The result was a 600 percent increase in unemployment between September 1 and December 15, 1923. As the hyperinflation intensified, people could not find goods on the shelves of retailers. Indeed, hyperinflation crushed the middle class of Germany and left an imprint on the country that affects its governmental policy to this day.

CAUSES OF INFLATION

Recall that inflation is an increase in the general level of prices and that prices are the result of the interaction of buyers' demand and sellers' supply decisions. Therefore, forces taking place on the buyers' side of the market or the sellers' side of the market may cause inflation. Inflation originating from upward pressure on the buyers' side of the market is called **demand-pull inflation.** Inflation caused by upward pressure on the sellers' side of the market is termed **cost-push inflation.**

The most familiar type of inflation is demand-pull inflation, which occurs when buyers' demands to purchase goods and services outrun sellers' capacities to supply them, thus forcing up prices on the goods and services that are available. Businesses cannot respond to this excess demand because all available resources are fully employed. Demand-pull inflation is often described as a situation in which "too much money chases too few goods."

However, some economists argue that inflation is caused on the sellers' side of the market. When businesses raise their prices in response to cost increases, the result is cost-push inflation. Workers then may demand higher wages to keep up with rising prices, and a wage-price spiral occurs. If wages and prices rise but production does not, the supply of goods and services cannot meet the demand for those items.

CHECK POINT

1. What is meant by inflation, and how is it measured?

2. Who is helped or hurt by inflation?

3. What are the sources of inflation?

Chapter Summary

Cost-push inflation also occurs if a limited number of businesses controls the supply of certain products. The increase in oil prices during the 1970s provides a good example. During this period, the Organization of Petroleum Exporting Countries limited the supply of oil in order to drive up prices and thus earn higher profits. Because oil is a resource that is used to make other goods, the cost of those items also rose, resulting in cost-push inflation.

This chapter has considered the impacts of the business cycle, unemployment, and inflation on the economy. In the next chapter, we will use aggregate demand curves and aggregate supply curves to analyze the causes of macroeconomic instability.

1. The business cycle refers to recurrent ups and downs in the level of economic activity over several years. Although business cycles may vary in intensity and duration, we can divide each into four phases: peak, recession, trough, and recovery.

2. When real GDP decreases for at least two consecutive quarters, we say that the economy is in a recession. A depression is a very deep and prolonged recession. Because no subsequent recession has approached the severity of the Great Depression, the term *depression* is often used to refer to the slump of the 1930s.

3. Many economists believe that a change in total spending is the immediate determinant of domestic output and employment. However, other economists maintain that business cycles are caused by changes in the supply side of the market, such as the development of better technologies or decreases in natural resources.

4. The unemployment rate is the number of people who are unemployed divided by the number of people in the labor force. Although economists take great care in calculating the unemployment rate, it suffers from problems involving the measurement of part-time employment and discouraged workers.

5. Not everyone who is unemployed is unemployed for the same reason. In describing labor markets, economists refer to frictional unemployment, cyclical unemployment, and structural unemployment. To mitigate the costs of unemployment, government has many programs, such as education and training programs and unemployment insurance.

6. Economists call the level of unemployment at which there is no cyclical unemployment the natural rate of unemployment. The natural rate of unemployment is the sum of frictional and structural unemployment, and it is the economist's notion of full employment. Most economists estimate the natural rate of unemployment to be between 4 percent and 6 percent of the labor force.

7. Inflation is a sustained or continuous rise in the general price level; deflation is a continuing decline in the average price level. The most frequently cited indicator of inflation is the consumer price index.

8. Inflation results in a decrease in the purchasing power of a fixed amount of income, a redistribution of wealth from creditors to debtors, declining real interest rates on savings, and higher tax revenues for the government.

9. Inflation may be caused by forces taking place on the buyers' side of the market or the sellers' side of the market. Inflation originating from upward pressure on the buyers' side of the market is called demand-pull inflation. Conversely, cost-push inflation is caused by upward pressure on the sellers' side of the market.

Key Terms and Concepts

business cycle (246)	natural rate of unemployment (254)
peak (248)	full employment (254)
recession (248)	inflation (261)
trough (248)	deflation (262)
recovery (248)	consumer price index (CPI) (262)
depression (249)	nominal income (265)
unemployed (251)	real income (265)
unemployment rate (251)	nominal interest rate (266)
discouraged worker (252)	real interest rate (266)
frictional unemployment (253)	hyperinflation (269)
structural unemployment (253)	demand-pull inflation (269)
cyclical unemployment (253)	cost-push inflation (269)
unemployment insurance (253)	

Self-Test: Multiple-Choice Questions

1. The turning point of the business cycle is the

   a. peak.
   b. recession.
   c. depression.
   d. recovery.

2. If the consumer price index increases by 5 percent and Helen Osborne's nominal income increases by 3 percent, her real income will

   a. increase by 8 percent.
   b. increase by 2 percent.
   c. decrease by 2 percent.
   d. decrease by 8 percent.

3. Although all segments of the economy feel the business cycle, it tends to affect _____ industries the most.

   a. durable goods
   b. nondurable goods
   c. business services
   d. consumer services

4. The unemployment rate is the percentage of the

   a. labor force that is unemployed.
   b. total population that is unemployed.
   c. labor force that has been fired or laid off.
   d. total population that has been fired or laid off.

5. Upon graduation from college, John Smith begins his job search. Two months later, Hewlett Packard hires him as a systems analyst. During this period, John Smith encounters

   a. structural unemployment.
   b. cyclical unemployment.
   c. frictional unemployment.
   d. seasonal unemployment.

6. The natural rate of unemployment, which is the economist's notion of full employment, is the sum of

   a. frictional unemployment and structural unemployment.
   b. frictional unemployment and cyclical unemployment.
   c. structural unemployment and cyclical unemployment.
   d. none of the above.

7. Compared to the United States, Europe has experienced a higher unemployment rate in recent years. Which of the following is *not* a plausible reason for this discrepancy?

   a. Relatively high wages in the nonunion sectors of the European economy.
   b. Relatively high wages in the union-controlled sectors of the European economy.
   c. Relatively high minimum wage laws in Europe.
   d. Relatively low welfare benefits in Europe.

8. The most frequently cited indicator of inflation in the United States is the

   a. wholesale price index.
   b. business price index.
   c. consumer price index.
   d. producer price index.

9. Assume that you have $10 to purchase goods and services in 2004. The consumer price index in 1960 equaled 24.1, and the consumer price index in 2004 equaled 160.5. You would have needed _____ in 1960 to buy the same amount of goods and services.

   a. $1
   b. $1.25
   c. $1.50
   d. $1.75

10. Assume that in 1950, it cost 25 cents to go to a baseball game. The consumer price index equaled 24.1 in 1950, and the consumer price index equaled 160.5 in 2006. What would attending a baseball game in 2006 be worth in 2006 dollars?

   a. $1.27
   b. $1.41
   c. $1.53
   d. $1.67

Answers to Multiple-Choice Questions

1. a   2. c   3. a   4. a   5. c   6. a   7. d   8. c   9. c   10. d

Study Questions and Problems

1. Suppose that the Bureau of Labor Statistics announces that of all adult Americans, 129 million are employed, 7 million are unemployed, 3 million are not in the labor force, and 2 million are part-time workers looking for full-time jobs. What is the unemployment rate?

2. Discuss how the following individuals would be affected by inflation of 9 percent per year:

   a. A student who heavily is indebted with loans.
   b. A retired nurse who is receiving a fixed pension.
   c. An individual who has a savings account that pays an interest rate of 4 percent a year.
   d. An autoworker who has a cost-of-living adjustment included in his labor contract.

3. If the consumer price index was 155 last year and is 160 this year, what was this year's rate of inflation?

4. How can you realize an increase in nominal income and a decrease in real income at the same time?

5. Suppose that the interest rate on your passbook savings account is 4 percent per year, and this year's inflation rate is 5 percent. Are you better off or worse off as a saver?

6. Assume that the consumer price index equaled 50 in 1960 and 150 in 1990. Suppose that you had $60 in 1990 to purchase goods and services. How much money would you have needed in 1960 to buy the same amount of goods and services?

7. In 1914, Henry Ford paid his employees $5 a day. If the consumer price index was 11 in 1914 and 161 in 1997, how much is the Ford paycheck worth in 1997 dollars?

8. In Table 11.8, compute the inflation rate for 2001, 2002, and 2003. Also compute the real wage in each year.

Table 11.8   Inflation and Real Wages

Year	CPI	Inflation Rate	Nominal Wage	Real Wage
2000	100		$12.00	
2001	106		14.00	
2002	110		15.00	
2003	112		15.50	

9. In Table 11.9, compute the real interest rate for 2001, 2002, and 2003. Assume that the CPI refers to the price level at the end of each year.

Table 11.9	Nominal and Real Interest Rates

Year	Inflation Rate (%)	Nominal Interest Rate (%)	Real Interest Wage
2001	6	8	
2002	3	3	
2003	5	4	

10. How can hyperinflation result in depression?

CHAPTER 12

Macroeconomic Instability: Aggregate Demand and Aggregate Supply

Chapter Objectives

After reading this chapter, you should be able to:

1. Explain why the classical economists felt that the economy would automatically move to full employment and why John Maynard Keynes argued that the market economy is inherently unstable.

2. Develop a macroeconomic model of aggregate demand and aggregate supply to understand how prices and output are determined in the short run.

3. Use the model of aggregate demand and aggregate supply to analyze the origins of recession and inflation.

4. Distinguish between demand-pull inflation and cost-push inflation.

5. Identify policies that the government might use to counteract recession or inflation.

economics IN CONTEXT

For American consumers in the late 1990s, it couldn't get much better: Unemployment was down and real wages were growing. With higher incomes, consumers went on a spending spree.

Consider Mary Ann Turnquist, a typical American consumer. In 1999, she and her husband Fred purchased a 4-bedroom home for $398,000 in Boulder, Colorado. Then they spent $3,500 in cash on a new bedroom set and $7,000 on new kitchen and laundry appliances. The couple, she a clerk in the state court and he a truck mechanic, were not concerned about their job security or paying off their mortgage. With a strong economy in 1999, they had every right to feel secure. So did most Americans.

Indeed, consumers had plenty of cash to spend, which supported their spending sprees. For example, steady pay increases prompted Pam Miller of Pittsburgh to buy a new Ford Taurus to replace her Mercury Sable. Nothing was wrong with the 5-year-old vehicle, but Pam said that having extra cash gave her an itch for new wheels.

Paychecks went a lot further at the turn of the century, thanks to a low inflation rate that was reinforced by cheap imports from Asia as a result of its economic crisis. Also, low mortgage rates allowed more families to own homes. Furthermore, consumer installment debt as a percentage of take-home pay had declined, giving consumers more freedom to take out home-equity loans to use for computers, college tuition, and vacation. Finally, the stock market's "bull run" continued to increase household wealth.

However, the economy's dependence on consumers did have its risks. A sudden shock, such as a big decrease in stock prices, could cause consumers to feel less wealthy and snap shut their pocketbooks, leaving businesses with too much inventory and too many workers. Another risk was that all of the consumer buying could become too much of a good thing. Excess spending could result in an overheated economy, in which more competition for workers could push labor costs above gains in productivity, resulting in inflation. If that trend continued and businesses started increasing prices, the Federal Reserve might slam on the monetary brakes, perhaps pushing the economy into recession.

Indeed, the growth performance of the U.S. economy has been uneven. In most years, the output of goods and services rises as a result of increases in the capital stock, increases in the labor force, and advances in technological knowledge. In some years, however, economic growth does not take place. Firms find themselves unable to sell the goods and services that they have produced, so they shut down factories and lay off workers. As a result, the economy's real gross domestic product (GDP) declines.

The central focus of macroeconomics is what causes short-run fluctuations in economic activity and what, if anything, the government can do to promote full employment without inflation. To answer these questions, we need a model of the macroeconomy. Most economists use the model of aggregate demand and aggregate supply. In this chapter, we will develop aggregate demand and aggregate supply curves that will help us analyze the problems of recession and inflation.

THE STABILITY OF THE MACROECONOMY

The stability of the macroeconomy is of concern to households, businesses, and government. Let us examine the classical and Keynesian views concerning this topic.

The Classical View

Prior to the Great Depression of the 1930s, a group of economists known as the **classical economists** dominated economic thinking. According to classical economists, the market economy automatically adjusts to ensure the full employment of its resources. Although an economic downturn might force producers to decrease their output and lay off workers, the downturn would be short-lived. Because the classical economists believed economic downturns to be temporary, they argued that the government should not interfere in economic affairs.

The optimism of the classical economists was founded on the assumption of freely flexible wages and flexible prices. If some workers become unemployed during an economic slump, they argued, they will make themselves attractive to employers by offering their services at lower wages. With falling wages, firms will find it more profitable to hire workers. As a result, the downward adjustment in wages will guarantee that everyone who wants a job can find one.

Flexible prices also help eliminate economic downturns, according to the classical economists. During a recession, firms realize a decrease in demand for products. To clear the market of excess supply, they are willing to accept price reductions. If prices decline enough, all of the output produced can be sold. Therefore, workers need not be laid off because of declining consumer demand.

The classical economists also contended that the economy would never suffer from a level of spending that would be inadequate to purchase the full-employment level of output. This contention was based on **Say's Law,** attributed to the 19th-century economist Jean-Baptiste Say. According to Say's Law, "supply creates its own demand." Whatever is produced (supplied) will create the income necessary to purchase that production. Say's Law thus suggests that there will always be enough spending to buy the full-employment output. Thus, overproduction is an impossibility according to classical economists. Simply put, the classical model attempted to explain the long-run behavior of the economy in terms of powerful forces that drive the economy to full employment.

The Great Depression

Although the classical economists advocated the impossibility of long-run unemployment, the Great Depression was a stunning blow to their theory. The depression was a global economic downturn that lasted for more than a decade. It was the worst and longest period of low business activity and high unemployment in modern times. It even caused some nations to change their leader and type of government.[1]

The Great Depression began in October 1929, when stock values in the United States declined sharply. Thousands of stockholders lost huge amounts of money, and many went bankrupt. Factories, banks, and stores shut down, leaving millions of people jobless and penniless. Many Americans had to depend on charity or the government for food and other basic necessities. The Great Depression affected almost every nation. It ended after nations increased their output of war goods at the beginning of World War II. The rising level of production provided jobs and put large sums of money back into circulation.

The depression was caused by several factors. During the 1920s, many bank failures, together with low incomes among farmers and factory workers, set the stage for the depression. Farmers were hit hard by slumping prices of agricultural goods. Although industrial production rose dramatically in the 1920s, the incomes of factory workers rose far more slowly. Thus, these workers could not purchase products as fast as industry produced them. Most economists agree that the stock market crash of 1929 triggered the depression. The crash was the result of rampant speculation, which prompted people to buy stocks in the hopes of making larger profits following future price increases.

---

1. John Kenneth Galbraith, *The Great Crash, 1929* (New York: Houghton Mifflin, 1979); and Robert Stobel, "The Great Depression," in *World Book Encyclopedia* (Chicago, 1988), pp. 363–367.

When stock values decreased dramatically in 1929, many investors panicked and sold huge amounts of stock at a loss.

In 1925, about 3 percent of the nation's workers were unemployed. The unemployment rate rose to 9 percent in 1930 and 25 percent in 1933. Many Americans who maintained or found jobs had to absorb wage reductions. In 1932, wage cuts averaged about 18 percent. Many people, including college graduates, felt lucky to find any job. In 1932, the New York City Police Department estimated that 8,000 people over age 17 sold pencils or shined shoes for a living. A popular song of the 1930s, "Brother, Can You Spare a Dime?," symbolized the despair of Americans.

Herbert Hoover was the president when the depression began. He thought that business, if left alone to operate without government regulation, would correct the economic downturn. He vetoed several bills intended to combat the depression because he believed they provided the federal government with too much power. Instead, he felt that it was the states' responsibility to provide assistance to the poor. Because most Americans thought that Hoover had performed inadequately in combating the depression, they elected Franklin D. Roosevelt as president in 1932.

Roosevelt thought the federal government had a major responsibility to combat the Great Depression. He called Congress into special session to enact legislation to help the needy. Roosevelt called his program the New Deal. The new laws gave states money for the poor and provided jobs in the construction of such public projects as highways, parks, schools, bridges, and dams. The federal government also fostered recovery by spending large amounts of money and increased trade by lowering tariffs on imported goods, in return for which other nations agreed to lower tariffs on the products they purchased from the United States. Congress also created agencies to supervise banks, prevent unfair labor practices, and protect investors from purchasing unsafe stocks and bonds. In 1935, Congress passed the Social Security Act to provide money for retired and unemployed people. Although the New Deal did not end the depression, it did provide economic relief and renewed the confidence of Americans in the federal government.

The Great Depression altered the opinions of many Americans toward business and the federal government. Before the depression, most people considered bankers and business executives the nation's leaders. After the stock market crashed and these leaders could not promote prosperity, many Americans lost confidence in them. They thought that the government, not business, had the responsibility of stabilizing the economy. The stage was set for John Maynard Keynes, and his emphasis on an activist government, to influence economic thinking and policy making.

The Keynesian View

In 1936, in the midst of the Great Depression, British economist **John Maynard Keynes** formed a theory that provided an explanation for prolonged depressed conditions.[2] According to Keynes and his followers, the market economy is inherently unstable, and the Great Depression was no accident: Adverse shocks that occur in one sector of the economy can quickly affect other sectors, causing reductions in total output and employment. Although the classical economists might have been able to explain the economy's operation in the long run, the long run could be a very long time in arriving, according to Keynes. Keynes thus developed a macroeconomic model focused on the causes of economic fluctuations in the short run.

Keynes's main disagreement with the classical economists was that prices and wages, he believed, are not sufficiently flexible to guarantee the full employment of resources. According to Keynes, prices and wages are rather inflexible, or "sticky," in a downward direction. Even when demand is weak, Keynes argued, powerful labor unions and large businesses will resist wage and price reductions. Therefore, output and employment fall during economic downturns.

The essence of Keynesian economics is simple: The level of economic activity depends on the total spending of consumers, businesses, and government. If business expectations are pessimistic,

2. John Maynard Keynes, *The General Theory of Employment, Interest, and Money* (New York: Harcourt, Brace, 1936).

investment spending will be reduced, resulting in a series of decreases in total spending. If this should occur, the economy can move into a depression and remain there.

Because the market economy is unstable, Keynes argued that an activist government must intervene to protect jobs and income. To avoid a depression, Keynes recommended that government increase spending, promote lower interest rates, and make more money available for loans. These actions, he maintained, would encourage investment and consumption spending, resulting in a greater increase in national output, employment, and income. Simply put, Keynes was a champion of the modern mixed economy, in which government increases its spending during downturns to increase the overall level of demand and thus employment.

Keynes's ideas altered the thinking of many economists and became increasingly accepted in colleges and government agencies in the 1940s and 1950s. By the 1960s, most of the economics profession had adopted his theory. Macroeconomics became Keynesian economics, and the classical model was subsequently eliminated from most economics textbooks.

However, a counterrevolution to Keynesian economics emerged during the 1970s and 1980s. Today, many economists who find classical theory inadequate in explaining economic fluctuations in the short run find it useful in explaining long-run economic trends. The policy prescriptions of Keynesian economics will be discussed further in Chapters 13 and 15.

CHECK POINT

1. Why did the classical economists maintain that the market economy would automatically ensure the full employment of its resources?

2. According to John Maynard Keynes, the market economy is inherently unstable and the Great Depression was no accident. Explain.

3. What is the proper role for government in the economy according to the classical economists? According to John Maynard Keynes?

AGGREGATE DEMAND AND AGGREGATE SUPPLY

In the tradition of Keynes, let us develop a model of aggregate demand and aggregate supply that we can use to understand how output and prices are determined in the short run.

Just as we analyze an individual market with a market demand curve and a market supply curve, we analyze fluctuations in the economy as a whole using a model of aggregate demand and aggregate supply. This model is shown in Figure 12.1. On the vertical axis is the average price level in the economy, measured by the consumer price index. On the horizontal axis is the total quantity of goods and services. Because we are adding together many different kinds of products, their dollar value is used to represent quantity in Figure 12.1. To keep out the effects of inflation, this quantity is given in *real* terms—that is, real GDP.

In Figure 12.1, the **aggregate demand curve** shows the total demand of all people for all final goods and services produced in an economy. The **aggregate supply curve** is the total supply of all final goods and services in an economy. The economy is in equilibrium when aggregate demand equals aggregate supply. This is where the two lines cross in Figure 12.1 at point *A*. To understand the nature of macroeconomic equilibrium, let us examine the forces that shape the aggregate demand and aggregate supply curves.

Figure 12.1   Macroeconomic Equilibrium

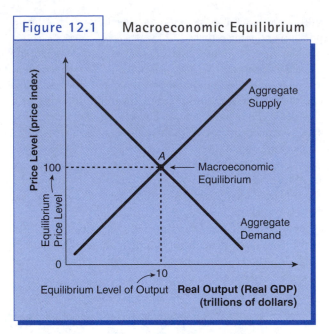

The economy is in equilibrium when aggregate demand equals aggregate supply (point *A*). This intersection determines the equilibrium price level and output for the economy.

AGGREGATE DEMAND

The aggregate demand curve shows the total amount of final goods and services (real GDP) that buyers will purchase at alternative price levels during a given year. Recall that the total amount of final goods and services can be divided into the amounts spent for consumption, investment, government purchases, and net exports. The **aggregate quantity demanded** is the quantity of final output that buyers will purchase at a given price level.

As seen in Figure 12.1, the aggregate demand curve may look like a market demand curve, but it's really different. Instead of showing the relationship between the price and quantity demanded of a single good—say, motorcycles—the aggregate demand curve describes the relationship between the price level and the aggregate quantity of all final goods and services demanded in the economy.

Movements along the Aggregate Demand Curve

Referring to Figure 12.1, notice that the aggregate demand curve is downward sloping. As the price level *falls,* other things being equal, the total amount of final goods and services purchased *rises.* What explains this relationship?

The price level is a determinant of the amount of money demanded. As the price level declines, households need to hold less money to purchase the goods and services they desire. Households thus try to decrease their holdings of money by lending it out as the price level falls. For example, a household might place its excess money in an interest-bearing savings account at a bank. The increased supply of savings drives interest rates downward, thereby encouraging borrowing by households that wish to invest in new housing or by businesses that want to invest in new plant and equipment. Put simply, a lower price level decreases interest rates, which results in additional spending on investment goods and thus increases the aggregate quantity of goods and services demanded.[3]

---

3. This explanation of the downward-sloping aggregate demand curve is known as the interest-rate effect. Other explanations include the so-called real wealth effect and the foreign-trade effect, which can be found in more advanced textbooks on macroeconomics.

The downward slope of the aggregate demand curve suggests that, other things being equal, a decrease in the price level increases the aggregate quantity of goods and services demanded. Movements along the aggregate demand curve are thus caused by a change in the price level of the economy.

Shifts in the Aggregate Demand Curve

So far, we have found that changes in the price level induce changes in the level of spending by consumers, businesses, government, and foreigners. However, the spending patterns of these sectors are affected by factors other than the price level. If one or more of these other factors change, the aggregate demand curve shifts.

A change in aggregate demand is shown by a rightward or leftward shift in the aggregate demand curve. An *increase* in aggregate demand is represented by a *rightward* shift in the aggregate demand curve. When aggregate demand increases, a greater quantity of goods and services is demanded at each alternative price. Conversely, a *decrease* in aggregate demand is denoted by a *leftward* shift of the aggregate demand curve.

There are many possible events that can shift the aggregate demand curve. Here are a few examples:

- Because of expectations of a future economic recession, U.S. business firms do not think they can sell all of their current output. Therefore, they decrease their purchases of machines and equipment, shifting the aggregate demand curve to the left.

- Economic weakness in Japan slows its economic growth, thereby depressing demand for U.S. exports of beef, lumber, and chemicals. As a result, the aggregate demand curve for the United States shifts to the left.

- Because of political tensions in the Middle East, Congress decides to increase purchases of new weapons systems. As the overall quantity of goods purchased increases, the aggregate demand curve shifts to the right.

- With the prices of stocks and homes rising, household wealth increases. Thus, households suddenly become less concerned about saving for retirement and increase their current consumption. Because the quantity of goods and services demanded increases at each alternative price level, the aggregate demand curve shifts to the right. Economists estimate that a $1 increase in household wealth boosts the level of consumption by about 3 cents to 5 cents.[4]

THE MULTIPLIER EFFECT

According to Keynesian economics, if an increase in demand occurs in the economy, then the final effect on national output will be much greater. In other words, there will be a multiple expansion of output. How does this happen?

Suppose that the U.S. government purchases additional uniforms for members of the military. When clothing production increases, the demand for the textiles used in that production also rises. Increasing textile production then strengthens the demand for fibers, aiding the chemical manufacturer, cotton farmer, and sheep rancher alike. And when those producers are also able to sell their goods, the providers of production equipment, parts, fuel, and seed are able to sell theirs. Moreover, commercial support services also feel the prosperity: software specialists, engineers, architects, bankers, insurance companies, truckers, railroaders, utilities, and construction workers. With U.S. factories in operation, countless small businesses then prosper: car dealerships, dry cleaners, barbershops, and restaurants, among many local services. Simply put, an increase in one part of the economy moves throughout its length and breadth, aiding owners, workers, suppliers, distributors, communities, states, and ultimately the whole nation. In other words, an improvement in economic activity in one sector

4. *Economic Report of the President*, 2003, p. 31, available at http://www.gpoaccess.gov/eop/index.html.

of the economy multiplies as it flows through the economy. But these forces also operate in reverse: A decline in one sector of the economy results in a magnified contractionary effect on the overall economy. Economists call this the **multiplier effect.**

To understand the multiplier effect, imagine someone throwing a rock into a pond: There is an initial splash (the increased spending on military uniforms), then additional ripples as the recipients of the initial money spend it, and so on, until the ripples decline in strength as they reach the bank.

The multiplier effect recognizes that all economies experience fluctuations in aggregate demand caused by autonomous changes in spending on consumption, investment, government purchases, and net exports.[5] For example, a rise in aggregate demand of $100 million gives rise to further increases through the impact of higher incomes on consumer spending. This results in, say, a $300 million increase in national output. The **multiplier** is the ratio of the change in national output to the change in aggregate demand; in this example, the multiplier equals 3 (300/100 = 3). It indicates the extent to which the change in aggregate demand is "multiplied" into changes in larger output. The mechanics of the multiplier effect are discussed in "Exploring Further 12.1" at the end of this chapter.

The multiplier effect is of great importance to economic policy makers. To combat a weak economy, policy makers may inject a stimulus by increasing government expenditures. Such a policy results in an increase in aggregate demand, which can lead to a magnified increase in the economy's output, employment, and income. Indeed, the multiplier effect is an integral part of economic policy making, as discussed in the next chapter.

AGGREGATE SUPPLY

Now let's turn to the aggregate supply curve. The aggregate supply curve shows the relationship between the level of prices and the amount of final goods and services (real GDP) that will be produced by the economy in a given year. The **aggregate quantity supplied** is the quantity of final output that will be supplied by producers at a particular price level. Figure 12.2 shows the economy's aggregate supply curve. When drawing the aggregate supply curve, we assume that all resource prices and the availability of resources in the economy are constant. We also assume that the level of technology remains fixed during the current period.

Movements along the Aggregate Supply Curve

Referring to Figure 12.2, notice that the aggregate supply curve has three segments: a horizontal range at price level 105, a positively sloped range from price level 105 to price level 110, and a vertical range at price level 110 and above.

Along the horizontal segment of the aggregate supply curve, the economy is assumed to be in recession. Notice that the full-employment level of real output is at $14 trillion, far beyond the output level of the horizontal region of the aggregate supply curve. Recall that during a deep recession or depression, there is much excess capacity and many unemployed resources in the economy. Therefore, producers are willing to sell additional output at current prices, and workers are willing to work extra hours at current wages. Because excess capacity places no upward pressure on prices and wages, changes in aggregate demand cause changes in real output—but no change in the price level—along the horizontal segment of the aggregate supply curve.

Throughout the positively sloped region of the aggregate supply curve, higher price levels provide an incentive for companies to produce and sell additional real output, while lower price levels decrease real output. Therefore, the relationship between the price level and the amount of output that firms offer for sale is positive or direct. Consequently, as the price level rises from 105 to 110, firms find it

---

5. An autonomous variable is one that is assumed not to depend on the state of the economy—that is, it does not change when the economy changes.

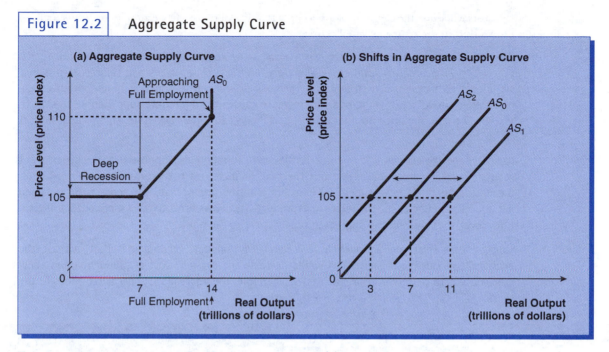

Figure 12.2   Aggregate Supply Curve

The aggregate supply curve has three distinct segments: (1) a horizontal region in which the economy is in deep recession or depression, (2) an upward-sloping region in which the economy approaches full employment, and (3) a vertical region in which the economy is at full employment. An increase (decrease) in aggregate supply is denoted by a rightward (leftward) shift in the aggregate supply curve.

profitable to increase real output from $7 trillion to $14 trillion. As companies increase production, they hire additional workers, which causes the unemployment rate to decline.

However, there is a physical limit to the amount of output that can be produced in a given year. Once the economy reaches its full-employment output level—$14 trillion in this illustration—the aggregate supply curve becomes vertical. At that point, it is impossible to hire the labor and other resources needed to expand output further. Any rise in the price level will not call forth extra output because the economy is already operating at maximum capacity. Individual companies may attempt to increase output by offering higher wages to attract workers from other companies. This will raise production costs and ultimately prices. However, the extra workers and output that one company gains will be foregone by other companies that lose workers. Therefore, despite the increase in wage rates and price level, real output will not expand when the economy is at full employment.

Shifts in the Aggregate Supply Curve

The aggregate supply curve shows the quantity of goods and services that companies produce and sell at alternative price levels. However, the amount that firms will produce does not depend on the price level alone. Many events can induce shifts in the aggregate supply curve.

A change in aggregate supply is shown by a rightward or leftward shift in the aggregate supply curve. Referring to Figure 12.2(*b*), an *increase* in aggregate supply is represented by a *rightward* shift in the aggregate supply curve. When aggregate supply increases, a greater quantity of output is supplied at each possible price. Conversely, a *decrease* in aggregate supply is represented by a *leftward* shift in the aggregate supply curve.

Recall that the aggregate supply curve is drawn under the assumption that the level of all resource prices, the availability and quality of resources, and technology are fixed. A change in one or more of these factors will cause the aggregate supply curve to shift. Here are a few examples of events that can result in a shift in the aggregate supply curve.

- Wages and salaries are the largest expense for many companies, typically accounting for 70 percent to 75 percent of total costs. Therefore, an increase in wages and salaries results in a significant cost increase. With unit costs rising, a firm cannot produce as much output at any given price. Therefore, a wage or salary increase causes the aggregate supply curve to shift to the left. A rise in the price of other resources will also cause the aggregate supply curve to shift to the left.

- To encourage the economy to increase its stock of capital goods, suppose that the government reduces taxes for businesses. Because the tax cut increases the profitability of investment, businesses purchase new, superior equipment, causing productivity to increase. By reducing per-unit production costs, the increase in productivity allows firms to offer more output at each price level, thus shifting the aggregate supply curve to the right.

- Suppose that entrepreneurs such as Bill Gates develop new technologies that increase the economy's productive capacity. This would decrease the per-unit cost of production and allow more output to be produced at each price. Therefore, the aggregate supply curve shifts to the right.

CHECK POINT

1. What factors account for the inverse relationship between the aggregate quantity demanded and the price level? What events might cause the aggregate demand curve to shift to the right or to the left?

2. What is the multiplier effect? What accounts for the size of the multiplier?

3. Why does the aggregate supply curve have a horizontal region, an upward-sloping region, and a vertical region? What events might cause the aggregate supply curve to shift to the right or to the left?

THE ORIGINS OF RECESSION

Now that we have introduced the model of aggregate demand and aggregate supply, we have the tools we need to analyze short-term fluctuations in economic activity. We will first apply the aggregate demand and aggregate supply model to the problem of recession, and then to inflation.

Decreases in Aggregate Demand

Referring to Figure 12.3(a), assume that the economy is in equilibrium at point A, where the price level is 100 and real output is $12 trillion. Suppose that, for some reason, a wave of pessimism hits the U.S. economy. The source might be an economic crisis in East Asia, a war abroad, or a crash in the stock market. Because of this disturbance, many Americans lose confidence in the future and modify their behavior. Households curtail their purchases of dishwashers and furniture, and companies postpone purchases of new equipment and machinery.

How does this wave of pessimism affect the economy? Such an event decreases the aggregate demand for goods and services. This means that at any given price level, households and companies now desire to purchase a smaller quantity of goods and services. As aggregate demand shifts leftward from AD_0 to AD_1 in Figure 12.3(a), the economy moves to equilibrium at point B, where real output

Figure 12.3	The Origins of Recession

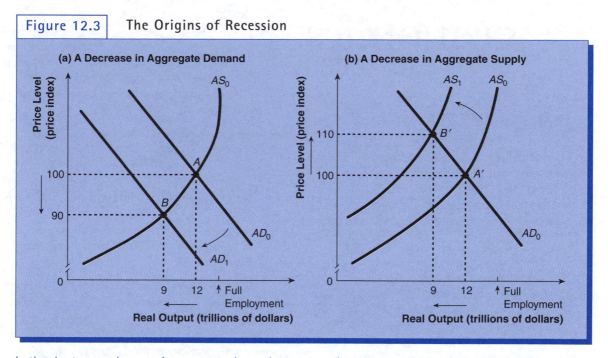

In the short run, a decrease in aggregate demand may cause the economy to move into recession. Government policy makers might attempt to offset the recession by increasing government spending in order to increase aggregate demand. A recession may also be caused by some event—say, rising oil prices—that leads to a decrease in aggregate supply. For a given aggregate demand curve, a decrease in aggregate supply can also cause stagflation—a combination of recession and inflation.

falls to $9 trillion and the price level declines to 90. As real output decreases, companies lay off workers and unemployment rises. The decrease in real output suggests that the economy moves into a contraction because of the reduction in aggregate demand. Therefore, the pessimism that triggered the reduction in aggregate demand is, to some degree, self-fulfilling: Pessimism about the future results in declining economic activity.

What should policy makers do when they are confronted with such a recession? According to Keynes, policy makers should increase government spending or make more money available for loans. These actions would shift the aggregate demand curve to the right, thus causing an increase in output, employment, and income in the economy.

The recession of 2001 provides an example of a demand shock that plagued the U.S. economy. Before 2001, companies eagerly invested in the equipment necessary to develop new technologies, including the Internet. New businesses were established to sell electronics, books, clothing, and prescription drugs via the Internet. They needed office space, capital equipment, and warehouses, which resulted in increased investment spending. By 2001, however, this investment had caught up with the needs of the market, and the level of investment began to decline. The terrorist attacks of September 11, 2001, contributed to the falling investment. The uncertainty and fear that gripped Americans after the attacks caused investment in jet airliners, hotels, and other goods to decrease. Although consumption spending continued to increase, partly because of a 10-year cut in income taxes that was implemented in June 2001, the decrease in investment more than offset the increase in consumption spending. This resulted in a decrease in the aggregate demand curve. As the negative multiplier effect kicked in, real GDP and employment declined, and the economy fell into recession. The recession lasted from March to November 2001. Chapters 13 and 15 will discuss the role of fiscal policy and monetary policy in counteracting this recession.

economics
IN ACTION

Is Deflation Good or Bad?

During the Great Depression, the general price level in the United States fell 25 percent from 1929 to 1933. As prices declined, so did employment. By the time prices reached bottom, a quarter of the labor force was out of work. Not surprisingly, the United States emerged from the Great Depression with much anxiety regarding falling prices.

Deflation is a sustained decrease in the general level of prices. It occurs when the annual inflation rate falls below zero percent, meaning a negative inflation rate. This should not be confused with disinflation, a slowdown in the inflation rate—for example, the inflation rate declines from 5 percent to 4 percent.

It would not be uncommon for prices to decrease in a particular sector because of rising productivity, falling costs, or weak demand relative to the wider economy. For example, although the overall price level of the U.S. economy increased about 34 percent during 1998–2008, the price of computers over the same period fell nearly 76 percent due to steadily falling production costs. Such declines are rarely a problem for the overall economy, and do not constitute deflation. Deflation occurs when price decreases are so widespread and sustained that they cause a broad-based price index such as the Consumer Price Index to steadily decrease for more than one or two quarters.

Whether deflation is on balance good or bad depends on whether the force generating the falling price level is increasing aggregate supply or decreasing aggregate demand. Both forces exert downward pressure on the price level but have opposite effects on the level of economic activity. For example, the U.S. deflation in the late 1800s occurred because aggregate supply was increasing faster than aggregate demand, exerting downward pressure on the price level but also causing output and employment to increase. Such positive supply-side shocks typically emanate from technological innovation, rising productivity, or trade liberalization.

Conversely, the U.S. deflation during the Great Depression and Japan's deflation during the 1990s occurred because of decreasing aggregate demand, exerting downward pressure on the price level, but also decreasing output and employment. Such a negative demand shock could be caused by a severe economic downturn, the bursting of an asset price bubble in the housing or stock market, or overly tight macroeconomic policies.

There are several ways in which deflation from a negative demand shock contributes to economic downturn. First, falling prices cause consumers to postpone purchases in the hope of experiencing even lower prices in the future, thus causing decreases in output and employment. Also, decreasing prices increase the burden of debt because borrowers are now forced to repay their loans with dollars that now have greater purchasing power. Capital investment, purchases of new homes, and other types of spending decline which worsens the economic downturn. Moreover, if product prices decline more rapidly than wages, profit margins decrease which causes firms to reduce production and employment.

During the economic downturn of 2007–2009, policy makers attempted to offset the negative effects of a deflation caused by a negative demand shock. The tools that were used included an expansionary fiscal policy (increased government spending and reduced taxes) and an expansionary monetary policy (increased money supply and reductions in interest rates), as discussed in subsequent chapters in this text.

Sources: Craig Elwell, *Deflation: Economic Significance, Current Risk, and Policy Responses,* Congressional Research Service, Washington, D.C., April 14, 2009; and Ben Bernanke, *Deflation: Making Sure It Doesn't Happen Here,* Remarks Before the National Economists Club, Washington, D.C., November 21, 2002.

Decreases in Aggregate Supply

Just as a decrease in aggregate demand can force the economy into recession, so can a decrease in aggregate supply. Referring to Figure 12.3(*b*), assume that the economy is in equilibrium at point *A'*, where the price level is 100 and real output is $12 trillion. Now suppose that firms realize an increase in production costs. It might result from an increase in the level of wages that is not matched by productivity increases or from an increase in the price of a key resource such as oil.

What is the macroeconomic effect of such an increase in production costs? At any given price level, firms will be willing to offer a smaller quantity of goods to the market. Therefore, as Figure 12.3(*b*) shows, the aggregate supply curve shifts to the left, from AS_0 to AS_1. The decrease in aggregate supply moves the economy from its initial equilibrium at point *A'* to a new equilibrium at point *B'*. The real output of the economy decreases from $12 trillion to $9 trillion, and the price level rises from 100 to 110. The decline in aggregate supply is especially detrimental because it results in falling output, increased unemployment, and rising prices. Such an event is called **stagflation**—that is, recession (stagnation) with inflation.

The recession of 1990–1991 provides an example of a supply shock that burdened the U.S. economy. In 1990, Saddam Hussein and his Iraqi army invaded Kuwait, a major oil producer. Within 6 hours, Iraq had occupied the entire country. Although the United States and its allies were able to oust the Iraqi army from Kuwait, during the conflict, the oil produced by both Kuwait and Iraq was taken off the world market. The decrease in the supply of oil caused oil prices to spike from $14 to $27 per barrel. Consistent with the prediction of the model of aggregate demand and aggregate supply, rising oil prices caused the aggregate supply curve to decrease, while the aggregate demand curve remained relatively constant. This resulted in a 1.5 percent decrease in real GDP during the first quarter of 1991 and a rise in the unemployment rate. Also, the consumer price index increased more rapidly as the recession gripped the nation.

THE ORIGINS OF INFLATION REVISITED

We will now apply the model of aggregate demand and aggregate supply to the types of inflation introduced in the previous chapter: demand-pull inflation and cost-push inflation.

Demand-Pull Inflation

Recall that *demand-pull inflation* is an increase in the average price level caused by an excess of total spending—that is, aggregate demand. The expression "too many dollars chasing too few goods" is often used to describe this type of inflation. "Too many dollars" suggests that the total spending in the economy is excessive. "Too few goods" suggests that the total supply of goods in the economy is too low relative to demand.

When firms cannot supply all the goods and services demanded by buyers, they respond by increasing prices. The average price level is thus pulled up by the total spending of buyers. A general increase in the availability of money and credit in the economy is a common cause of demand-pull inflation.

The degree to which an increase in aggregate demand pulls up the price level depends on how close the economy is to the level of real output that corresponds to full employment. Suppose that there is considerable unused capacity in the economy and significant unemployment during the year. Such a situation puts downward pressure on the prices charged by companies and on workers' wages. In this situation, the main effect of an increase in aggregate demand will be a rise in real output, with little or no upward pressure on the price level.

Now suppose instead that factories and offices are operating around the clock, and there is little, if any, slack capacity or unemployment. In this situation, the main effect of a rise in aggregate demand will be an increase in the price level; there will be little, if any, impact on real output. As seen in Figure 12.4(*a*), an increase in aggregate demand from AD_0 to AD_1 will pull up the price level from 105 to

Figure 12.4 | The Origins of Inflation

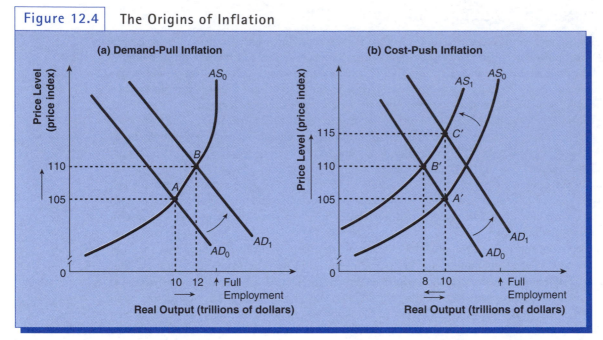

When buyers' demands for goods and services exceed sellers' capacities to supply them, prices are forced up on the goods and services that are available, and demand-pull inflation occurs. Demand-pull inflation tends to occur when the economy is close to or at full employment. When price increases are caused by pressure from the sellers' side of the market, cost-push inflation occurs. Cost-push inflation can be caused by the bargaining power of resource owners, limited availability of resources, declining productivity, or chance events.

110, a considerable increase. The price-level increase that is associated with the rise in aggregate demand indicates demand-pull inflation because the shift in aggregate demand pulls up the price level. To generate continuous demand-pull inflation, the aggregate demand curve would have to keep shifting out along a given aggregate supply curve.

What should policy makers do when they are confronted with demand-pull inflation? To reduce inflation, policy makers must decrease the growth in aggregate demand by, for example, reducing the growth rate of the money supply or decreasing government spending. As aggregate supply grows over time, slower growth in aggregate demand will reduce the inflation rate.

However, a policy that reduces aggregate demand is not without problems. Although decreasing the growth rate of aggregate demand reduces the inflation rate, it is likely to be accompanied by a rise in unemployment in the short run because of companies' contractual obligations to pay higher wages. Such contracts were presumably signed when it seemed that inflation would accelerate. As inflation decreases, firms will see that the prices of their goods will rise less rapidly, if at all. Therefore, firms may have to lay off workers so as to fulfill their contractual obligations to those workers still employed. Such layoffs cause the unemployment rate to increase.

Increases in unemployment often accompany decreases in inflation. During the late 1970s, inflation accelerated in the United States, reaching a level of 13.5 percent in 1980. To reduce inflation, the Federal Reserve (see Chapter 15) sharply decreased the growth rate of the money supply in 1981. This policy reduced the growth rate of aggregate demand and resulted in a dramatic decline in the inflation rate. By 1983, the inflation rate was only 3.2 percent. However, the unemployment rate rose from 7.6 percent in 1981 to 9.6 percent in 1983, causing much hardship for many households. If the Federal Reserve had not pursued its anti-inflation policy in 1981, the inflation rate likely would

economics
IN ACTION

Productivity Growth Dampens Inflation

During the late 1990s, economists struggled to apply traditional economic models to what was happening in the United States. Growth was robust, stocks were soaring, and job markets were tightening—yet inflation was negligible. Quarter after quarter, the pattern held. And try as they did, economists couldn't explain it using the old rules.

Instead, they considered a new view: The United States was in the midst of a technology-driven boom related to computers, the Internet, electronic commerce, and inventory management systems. This boom allowed the economy to grow faster than was once thought possible without igniting growth-inhibiting wage or price increases. Indeed, unemployment stood at a 29-year low, the economic expansion was robust, and the money supply was growing rapidly. But with inflation in check, these indicators could no longer be interpreted in the same manner.

The key to the new thinking was the belief that productivity growth, which had languished at 1 percent during the 1970s and 1980s, had taken a long-term leap to 2 percent or more as companies used technology to become more efficient. Economists pondered whether the adoption of productivity-enhancing technology had changed the way the economy operates. The possibilities of a long-term productivity rate of 2 percent were enormous for policy makers. It meant that they could live with stronger growth without fearing resurgent inflation.

By 2001, however, the U.S. economy had returned to traditional economic principles. A sizable decline in investment spending caused aggregate demand to decrease, and the economy slumped into recession in March 2001. The recession was prolonged by declining private spending associated with the terrorist attacks of September 11, 2001. By 2002, the recession was over, and economic expansion followed.

Analysis

Traditional theory suggests that the relationship between the economy's price level and real output is such that as production increases, the price level increases more rapidly as full employment is approached. Figure 12.5 shows this relationship. Given aggregate supply curve AS_0, as aggregate demand increases from AD_0 to AD_1, the price level rises from 100 to 105. However, suppose that the increase in aggregate demand is accompanied by an increase in productivity. This results in a decrease in per-unit production cost and an increase in the aggregate supply curve from AS_0 to AS_1. Therefore, the price index decreases from 105 to 101 in the figure. Real output increases and the price level remains virtually unchanged as aggregate demand and aggregate supply increase. Simply put, productivity growth is a moderating influence on the economy's inflation rate.

 Figure 12.5   **Productivity Growth as a Cure for Inflation**

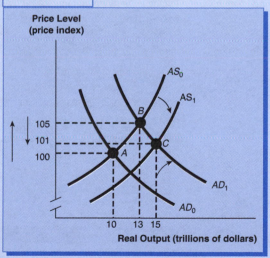

have continued to accelerate. This would have required an even tougher anti-inflation policy, which would have caused more unemployment than occurred during 1981–1983.

Cost-Push Inflation

Although economists widely agree that inflation can be caused by demand-pull forces, some economists argue that inflation can also result from events on the supply side of the market. Recall that *cost-push inflation* arises from events that increase the cost of production at each price level. Two events that result in cost-push inflation are increases in wages and increases in the prices of nonlabor inputs, such as energy and raw materials. With an increase in the costs of production, the aggregate supply curve shifts to the left, while the aggregate demand curve remains unchanged. A decrease in aggregate supply usually leads not only to a higher price level but also to a falling level of output, a combination that is identified in Figure 12.4(*b*) as *stagflation*.

We can show the nature of cost-push inflation in Figure 12.4(*b*). The economy is initially assumed to be located at point A', where the price level is 105 and real output equals $10 trillion. Suppose that workers are able to secure increases in wages that exceed gains in productivity. As wages and unit production costs rise, the aggregate supply curve shifts leftward from AS_0 to AS_1. The price level therefore increases from 105 to 110, as shown by point B' in the figure.

Cost-push inflation creates a dilemma for government policy makers. If aggregate demand remains unchanged at AD_0 in Figure 12.4(*b*), real output will fall from $10 trillion to $8 trillion because of the leftward shift in aggregate supply, resulting in a new equilibrium at point B'. The government may attempt to offset the decline in real output by enacting policies to increase aggregate demand, say, to AD_1. Such a policy, however, would further intensify inflation by raising the price level from 110 to 115 (point C'). Therefore cost-push inflation forces policy makers to choose between stable prices and high levels of aggregate output and employment.

CHECK POINT

1. Use the model of aggregate demand and aggregate supply to explain the origins of recession.

2. What do economists mean by stagflation, and why is it a problem for economic policy makers?

3. Use the model of aggregate demand and aggregate supply to explain the origins of inflation.

4. If the government enacts policies to counteract demand-pull inflation, adverse side-effects may ensue. Explain.

5. Why does cost-push inflation create a dilemma for economic policy makers?

Chapter Summary

1. The growth performance of the U.S. economy has been uneven. Although the output of goods and services rises in most years, in some years economic growth does not occur. The central focus of macroeconomics is what causes short-run fluctuations in economic activity and what, if anything, the government can do to promote full employment without inflation.

2. Prior to the Great Depression of the 1930s, the classical economists dominated economic thinking. According to the classical economists, the market economy automatically ensures

the full employment of all of its resources. The optimism of classical economists was largely based on the assumption of freely flexible wages and prices.

3. During the 1930s, John Maynard Keynes formed a theory that provided an explanation for the Great Depression. According to Keynes, the level of economic activity depends on the total spending of the economy. If business expectations are pessimistic, investment spending will be reduced, resulting in a series of decreases in total spending. If this should occur, the economy can move into a depression and remain there. Because the market economy is inherently unstable, Keynes argued that government must intervene to protect jobs and income.

4. The model of aggregate demand and aggregate supply can be used to show how output and prices are determined in the short run. An economy is in equilibrium when aggregate demand equals aggregate supply.

5. The aggregate demand curve shows the total amount of real output that buyers will purchase at alternative price levels during a given year. Movements along an aggregate demand curve are caused by changes in the price level of the economy. Shifts in the aggregate demand curve are caused by changes in nonprice factors that affect household consumption expenditures, business investment, government expenditures, and net exports of goods and services.

6. According to the multiplier effect, a change in any one of the components of aggregate demand (consumption, investment, government spending, or net exports) will have a magnified impact on national output and income. The size of the multiplier depends on the spending and saving habits of consumers and businesses.

7. The aggregate supply curve shows the relationship between the level of prices and amount of real output that will be produced by the economy in a given year. The aggregate supply curve is horizontal when the economy is in deep recession or depression, upward sloping when the economy approaches full employment, and vertical when the economy achieves full employment. Changes in factors such as resource prices, resource availability, and the level of technology will cause the aggregate supply curve to shift.

8. The model of aggregate demand and aggregate supply can be applied to the problems of recession and inflation. According to this model, decreases in aggregate demand or aggregate supply can push the economy into recession; inflation may be the result of increases in aggregate demand or decreases in aggregate supply. An economy experiences "stagflation" when there is both recession and inflation.

Key Terms and Concepts

classical economists (277)

Say's Law (277)

John Maynard Keynes (278)

aggregate demand curve (279)

aggregate supply curve (279)

aggregate quantity demanded (280)

multiplier effect (282)

multiplier (282)

aggregate quantity supplied (282)

stagflation (287)

marginal propensity to consume (295)

marginal propensity to save (295)

Self-Test: Multiple-Choice Questions

1. According to Say's Law,

    a. demand creates its own supply.
    b. supply creates its own demand.
    c. prices are inflexible in a downward direction.
    d. prices are inflexible in an upward direction.

2. According to the classical economists,
    a. the market economy automatically ensures the full employment of its resources.
    b. economic downturns are usually permanent, and therefore the government needs to intervene in economic affairs.
    c. inadequate consumer demand often causes workers to become permanently laid off.
    d. inflexible prices of commodities help sustain the buying power of households, which promotes maximum consumption and full employment.

3. In the Keynesian macroeconomic model,
    a. the market economy is inherently unstable and unemployment is no accident.
    b. the labor market will always be in equilibrium at full employment.
    c. flexible prices guarantee that the overproduction of goods will not occur.
    d. active government intervention cannot move the economy toward full employment.

4. The aggregate demand curve will shift to the left if
    a. households become more optimistic about their future income.
    b. government expenditures on roads, dams, and bridges increase.
    c. businesses invest more in plant and equipment.
    d. the government increases personal income taxes.

5. If the cost of resources declines, the
    a. aggregate supply curve will shift to the left.
    b. aggregate supply curve will shift to the right.
    c. aggregate demand curve will shift to the left.
    d. aggregate demand curve will shift to the right.

6. Given an upward-sloping aggregate supply curve, an increase in aggregate demand results in a(n)
    a. decrease in the price level and a decrease in the level of output.
    b. increase in the price level and an increase in the level of output.
    c. decrease in the price level and an increase in the level of output.
    d. increase in the price level and a decrease in the level of output.

7. According to the _____, if government increases demand in the economy, then the final effect on national output will be much greater.
    a. multiplier effect
    b. foreign-trade effect
    c. interest-rate effect
    d. real balances effect

8. The marginal propensity to save
    a. is the fraction of income that people desire to save.
    b. is the fraction of additional income that people desire to save.
    c. equals 1 plus the marginal propensity to consume.
    d. equals the marginal propensity to consume minus 1.

9. If the marginal propensity to consume equals 0.9, then an increase in income will cause consumption to increase by
   a. 9 times the increase in income.
   b. 10 times the increase in income.
   c. nine-tenths of the increase in income.
   d. one-tenth of the increase in income.

10. Assume that the economy has idle resources and a constant price level. If the marginal propensity to consume is 0.8, the multiplier equals
   a. 4.
   b. 5.
   c. 8.
   d. 10.

Answers to Multiple-Choice Questions

1. b   2. a   3. a   4. d   5. b   6. b   7. a   8. b   9. c   10. b

Study Questions and Problems

1. According to the classical economists, flexible prices and flexible wages guarantee that all output produced can be sold and everyone who wants a job can find one. Explain. Why did John Maynard Keynes believe that prices and wages are not sufficiently flexible to guarantee the full employment of resources?

2. What explains the inverse relationship between the aggregate quantity demanded and the price level?

3. What accounts for the shape of the aggregate supply curve?

4. Explain whether each of the following events would increase, decrease, or have no effect on the short-run aggregate demand curve:

   a. A decrease in the U.S. price level makes American goods more attractive to foreign buyers.
   b. Households decide to consume a larger share of their income.
   c. Worsening profit expectations cause firms to decrease their expenditures on new machinery and equipment.
   d. As the price level declines, the purchasing power of currency increases, and thus Americans increase their purchases of computers and office equipment.
   e. Because of decreasing political tensions in North Korea, the U.S. Congress reduces purchases of jet fighters and tanks.
   f. Economic expansion in Europe results in an increase in the European demand for Boeing jetliners.
   g. Fearing a future economic downturn, households decide to save a larger fraction of their income.

5. Suppose that the marginal propensity to consume in the economy is 0.75. Assuming that prices are constant, what effect would a $50 million increase in investment spending have on the equilibrium real GDP?

6. Suppose that the marginal propensity to save in the economy is 0.1. Assuming that prices are constant, what effect would a $20 million decrease in net exports have on the equilibrium real GDP?

Table 12.1	Aggregate Demand and Aggregate Supply Data	
Real Domestic Output Demanded (billions)	Price Level (price index)	Real Domestic Output Supplied (billions)
$ 6,000	130	$16,000
8,000	120	16,000
10,000	110	14,000
12,000	100	12,000
14,000	90	10,000
16,000	90	8,000

7. Explain whether the following events would increase, decrease, or have no effect on the short-run aggregate supply curve:

   a. A tornado damages factories in Wisconsin and Minnesota.
   b. Because of expectations of a booming economy, auto companies invest in more efficient machinery and equipment.
   c. New technologies result in declining prices of crude oil.
   d. The United Steel Workers union wins a large increase in wages from domestic steel companies.
   e. Workers participate in retraining programs that enhance their productivity.

8. Table 12.1 shows the short-run aggregate supply and aggregate demand schedules for a hypothetical economy.

   a. What are the economy's equilibrium price and quantity of real output?
   b. The full-employment segment of the economy's aggregate supply schedule is associated with what level of real output?
   c. If the economy is in the horizontal segment of its aggregate supply schedule, what will be the impact of an increase in aggregate demand?
   d. Given the initial data in the table, suppose that the quantity of real output supplied rises by $4,000 at each price level. What will be the new equilibrium price level and real output?

9. Why is an increase in aggregate supply "doubly beneficial" and a decrease in aggregate supply "doubly detrimental"?

10. Use the model of aggregate demand and aggregate supply to explain the differences between demand-pull inflation and cost-push inflation.

EXPLORING FURTHER 12.1: THE NATURE AND OPERATION OF THE MULTIPLIER EFFECT

According to the multiplier effect, an autonomous change in aggregate demand will have a magnified effect on the economy's income and output. Why is there a multiplier effect for the economy? The basic idea is quite simple, as seen in Table 12.2. Suppose that General Electric constructs a factory in your town at a cost of $100 million. Also suppose that people spend 80 percent of their additional income and save 20 percent. According to the table, the increase in investment of $100 million,

Table 12.2	The Multiplier Process		
Spending Rounds	Increased Income and Output	Increased Consumption (spend 80%)	Increased Saving (save 20%)
Original increase in investment	$100.0	$80.0	$20.0
Second round	80.0	64.0	16.0
Third round	64.0	51.2	12.8
Fourth round	51.2	41.0	11.2
	etc.	etc.	etc.
	$500.0	$400.0	$100.0

when spent, becomes income of $100 million for the owners of the construction firm and for the workers who build the factory. Suppose that these people save 20 percent of their additional income, or $20 million, and use the rest, $80 million, to purchase new Ford automobiles. The $80 million becomes income to the owners of Ford Motor Co. and its workers. These people, in turn, spend 80 percent of the $80 million ($64 million) on food and save the remaining $16 million. This results in $64 million in income for food producers. This process of receiving income and then respending the money, which generates income for others, continues until the original amount of money ($100 million) is all held in savings by the various individuals. At that point, no more income can be created. Through this process, the initial investment of $100 million results in an increase of $500 million in income and output. Therefore, in this example, the multiplier has a value of 5.

The multiplier effect also works in reverse. Suppose that consumers become more thrifty and reduce their consumption spending. According to the multiplier effect, national output and income will decline by an amount greater than the initial decrease in consumption spending.

Calculating the Value of the Multiplier

As you examine Table 12.2, notice that the size of the multiplier depends on the spending and saving patterns of individuals and businesses in the economy. In the jargon of economists, the multiplier depends on the marginal propensity to consume and the marginal propensity to save.

The **marginal propensity to consume** (*MPC*) is the fraction of additional income that people spend. Referring to Table 12.2, we assume that people spend 80 percent of their additional income. This means that the *MPC* = 0.8. Similarly, the **marginal propensity to save** (*MPS*) is the fraction of additional income that is saved. Referring to the table, we assume that people save 20 percent of their additional income. Thus, the *MPS* = 0.2. Notice that *MPS* and *MPC* always add up to 1 because all of the consumer income that is not spent on goods and services must be saved.

The formula for the multiplier is as follows:

$$Multiplier = 1/(1 - MPC)$$

To illustrate this formula, if *MPC* = 0.8, then the multiplier is 1/(1 − 0.8), or 5.

Because *MPC* + *MPS* = 1, it follows that *MPS* = (1 − *MPC*). Therefore, we can restate the multiplier formula as:

$$Multiplier = 1/MPS$$

To illustrate this formula, if $MPS = 0.2$, the multiplier is $1/0.2 = 5$.

If aggregate demand changes, equilibrium income and output will change by the amount of the change in aggregate demand times the multiplier. This process can be summarized as follows:

$$\Delta \text{ Aggregate demand} \times \text{Multiplier} = \Delta \text{ Equilibrium income}$$

For example, if investment spending rises by \$100 million and the multiplier is 5, equilibrium output and income will rise by \$500 million (\$100 million $\times$ 5 = \$500 million).

Graphical Illustration of the Multiplier Effect

Figure 12.6 shows the full multiplier effect of a \$100 million increase in investment spending.

The direct effect of the increase in investment spending will be a \$100 million increase (a rightward shift) in the aggregate demand curve, from AD_0 to AD_1. Moreover, aggregate demand gets an additional boost from the additional consumption that occurs as people receive income and then respend it. This causes aggregate demand to increase by \$400 million (another rightward shift), from AD_1 to AD_2. In all, the \$100 million increase in investment spending shifts aggregate demand from AD_0 to AD_2, causing national output to increase by \$500 million.

For the full multiplier effect to occur, there must be some idle resources in the economy and a constant price level, as shown in Figure 12.6. If an increase in aggregate demand occurs when the economy is already at or close to full employment, consumers and others will bid up prices by attempting to purchase more output than the economy is capable of producing. This results in inflation, suggesting an increasing price level that offsets the multiplier effect. Therefore, without idle resources and a constant price level, the multiplier effect is impeded. Simply put, price-level increases weaken the multiplier.

Figure 12.6 | The Multiplier in Action

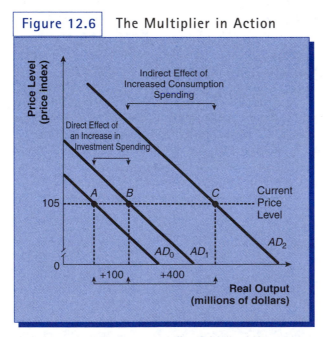

An increase in investment spending initially shifts aggregate demand to the right, from AD_0 to AD_1. Aggregate demand gets an extra boost from the additional consumption that occurs as people receive income and respend it. Because of the multiplier effect, aggregate demand increases from AD_1 to AD_2.

Fiscal Policy and the Federal Budget

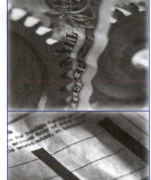

Chapter objectives

After reading this chapter, you should be able to:

1. Discuss the operation of fiscal policy and the problems it encounters.

2. Explain how discretionary fiscal policy attempts to combat the problems of recession and inflation.

3. Describe how automatic stabilizers help cushion an economy during a recession.

4. Evaluate the strengths and weaknesses of supply-side fiscal policy.

5. Identify the potential effects of the federal debt.

economics IN CONTEXT

Once upon a time, tax cuts commanded almost universal support among economists as the desired method of combating recessions. When Congress passed the Kennedy-Johnson tax cuts in 1964, such enthusiasm was at its peak. As time passed, however, changes in taxes and spending gradually lost favor to changes in interest rates by the Federal Reserve.

As the U.S. economy slowed in 2001, companies such as Hewlett Packard, Nortel, and Cisco argued that the high-tech economy was so bad that they could not foresee profits for that year. Moreover, job losses would likely occur for thousands of Americans. As a result, they lobbied for a fiscal boost in the form of a tax cut. In response to the weakening economy, President George W. Bush assaulted the conventional wisdom by implementing a reduction in taxes in 2002. The United States needed a tax cut, he argued, because the federal government was pulling too much money out of the private economy, creating a drag on U.S. growth. Another tax cut followed in 2003.

Those who believe that the economy is inherently unstable often urge the government to intervene to protect jobs and income. The government can help stabilize the economy through its use of spending and tax policies, as discussed in this chapter.

Before we proceed to government stabilization policies, recall that the federal budget consists of two components: government expenditures and tax revenues or receipts. When government spending exceeds tax revenues in a given year, a budget deficit occurs. When the budget is in deficit, the federal government must borrow funds by issuing securities such as Treasury bills, notes, and bonds. If tax revenues exceed government spending, a budget surplus exists. When the federal government incurs a budget surplus, it can use the excess revenues to pay off some of its debt. Finally, when government spending equals tax revenues, we have a balanced budget.

FISCAL POLICY

Recall from Chapter 12 that John Maynard Keynes believed the Great Depression had been caused by insufficient aggregate demand. Because he thought that prices and wages are inflexible in a downward direction, Keynes maintained that the classical economists' optimism that the economy would move automatically and quickly to full employment was incorrect. To Keynes and his followers, an activist government must increase aggregate demand in order to protect jobs and income. In other words, expansionary fiscal policy initiated by the federal government is the way to stabilize the economy.

Fiscal policy is the use of government expenditures and taxes to promote particular macroeconomic goals, such as full employment, stable prices, and economic growth. Government expenditures consist of purchases of goods and services, such as the procurement of jet aircraft from Boeing, and transfer payments, such as unemployment compensation and food stamps. In the United States, Congress and the president set fiscal policy; therefore, it reflects a collective decision-making process. Table 13.1 shows recent examples of U.S. fiscal policies.

Fiscal policies may be expansionary or contractionary. An *expansionary fiscal policy* increases real output, employment, and income. Such a policy can be used to move the economy out of recession. A *contractionary fiscal policy* decreases real output, employment, and income. It can be used to combat inflation.

Table 13.1	Examples of U.S. Fiscal Policies

Year	Economic Problem	Policy
1964	Recession	With the economy in a slump, Presidents Kennedy and Johnson enact permanent tax cuts for individuals and corporations. The top tax rate for individuals is cut from 91 percent to 70 percent.
1968	Inflation	To dampen inflationary pressures, President Johnson orders a temporary tax increase. This one-time surcharge of 10 percent is added to individual income tax liabilities.
1969	Inflation	Facing an overheated economy, President Nixon orders reductions in government expenditures.
1975	Recession	Fearing a recession caused by the oil-price hikes of OPEC, President Ford orders a temporary tax reduction of 10 percent. The tax cut is enacted immediately by Congress.
1981	Recession	In response to a sluggish economy, President Reagan calls for a sharp cut in individual income taxes and an increase in defense spending. The top tax rate for individuals is cut from 70 percent to 28 percent.
1992	Recession	President Bush orders a reduction in withholding rates in order to raise take-home pay in 1992 and to increase consumption.
1993	Recession	In response to unacceptably high levels of unemployment, President Clinton calls for a $16 billion jobs program consisting of government expenditures and tax reductions intended to increase investment. The measure is turned down by Congress.
2007–9	Recession	Presidents Bush and Obama convince Congress to cut taxes and adopt massive increases in government spending.

Fiscal policies are used to alter the economy's aggregate demand curve and aggregate supply curve so as to promote full employment and stable prices. Let us analyze both possibilities, beginning with the use of fiscal policy to shift the aggregate demand curve.

FISCAL POLICY AND AGGREGATE DEMAND

Let us pick up where we left off in Chapter 12 by discussing the use of **discretionary fiscal policy,** as Keynes urged, to help stabilize the economy. Discretionary fiscal policy is the deliberate use of changes in government expenditures and taxation to affect aggregate demand and to influence the economy's performance in the short run, when its capacity to produce is fixed. Recall that aggregate demand has four components: consumption, investment, government spending, and net exports. In the short run, fiscal policy affects the economy's business cycle by combating recession or inflation.

Combating Recession

Referring to Figure 13.1, suppose that the economy suffers from recession at equilibrium point *A,* where the aggregate demand curve intersects the aggregate supply curve. In equilibrium, the level of

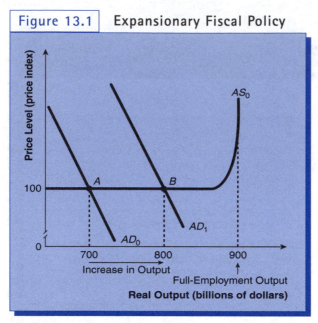

Figure 13.1   Expansionary Fiscal Policy

If the government wants to expand the economy, it can do so by increasing government spending or by lowering taxes. Either policy will shift the aggregate demand curve to the right, resulting in an increase in real output and an increase in prices as the economy approaches full employment.

output is $700 billion, below the full-employment output of $900 billion. Here, the economy can be improved by following Keynesian economics and shifting the aggregate demand curve to the right—say, from AD_0 to AD_1. By doing so, the economy's output increases from $700 billion to $800 billion. Notice that the price level remains constant given the abundance of idle resources in the economy.

How can the government increase aggregate demand? It has three fiscal policy options: (1) increase government spending, (2) cut taxes, or (3) combine the two in some manner. If the federal budget is initially balanced, fiscal policy should move toward a *budget deficit* (government spending in excess of tax revenues) in order to combat recession.

Increase Government Spending.   The simplest method would be to increase government spending. If government were to step up its purchases of jet planes, highways, and other goods, the increased spending would add directly to aggregate demand. According to the multiplier effect discussed in Chapter 12, aggregate demand would rise by more than just the added government spending.

If the government purchases, say, $25 billion of jet aircraft from Boeing, this sets the multiplier process in motion. The initial effect of the increased demand from the government is to stimulate employment and profits at Boeing. As Boeing workers realize fatter paychecks and the firm's owners realize higher dividends, they respond by increasing their own spending on autos, appliances, and the like. Therefore, government purchases from Boeing increase the demand for the products of many other companies, such as Ford, Whirlpool, and General Electric. Therefore, these firms hire more workers and realize higher profits. Higher earnings and profits lead to increased consumer spending once again, and so on. Each round of added spending increases aggregate demand a little more. When all of these effects are combined, the total impact on the quantity of goods and services demanded can be much larger than the initial stimulus from increased government expenditures. Referring to Figure 13.1, government purchases of $25 billion increase aggregate demand by $100 billion. See "Exploring Further 13.1" at the end of this chapter for additional information about fiscal policy and the multiplier effect.

Since the days of President Franklin D. Roosevelt, the federal government has implemented public-works projects to combat downturns in the economy and to create jobs. During the Great Depression of the 1930s, Roosevelt established the *Works Project Administration* (WPA). The WPA provided jobs building highways, streets, dams, bridges, schools, courthouses, parks, and other projects that were intended to have long-range value. It also created work for artists, writers, actors, and musicians. The WPA employed an average of 2 million workers annually between 1935 and 1941. Roosevelt also established the *Civilian Conservation Corps* (CCC) from 1933 until 1942. The CCC gave work and training to 2 1/2 million young people. It achieved great success with its programs for flood control, forestry, and soil. These government projects cost a great deal of money—much more than the government was collecting in taxes. The deficit was made up partly by raising taxes and partly by borrowing. As a result, the national debt rose higher than ever before.

In recent years, the federal government has provided public-works spending for mass transit, highways, and other transportation projects. When President George H. W. Bush signed a $151 billion transportation bill in 1991, he declared that the effect would be "jobs building roads, jobs building bridges, and jobs building railways."

Besides providing long-term public-works projects, the federal government has enacted public-employment projects. The notion underlying these programs is clear: If the economy suffers from high unemployment, why not create jobs directly? Public-employment projects are intended to hire unemployed workers for a limited period in public jobs, after which time those workers can take jobs in the economy's private sector. During the 1970s, for example, the *Comprehensive Employment and Training Act* provided public-service jobs for more than 700,000 hard-core unemployed and young people. These workers did everything from working in theaters and museums to raking leaves.

Decrease Taxes.   Other than increasing spending, is there any other way the government could cause aggregate demand to increase? Another expansionary fiscal policy intended to increase aggregate demand is for the government to reduce taxes.

Lowering *taxes on personal income* increases the amount of take-home pay that people have. If take-home pay goes up, we can expect households to save more and consume more than they did prior to the tax reduction. The initial consumption spending induced by the tax cut sets the multiplier process in motion. The new consumer spending creates additional income for owners of firms and workers, who then use the additional income to increase their own consumption. This results in a cumulative increase in aggregate demand that exceeds the initial increase in consumption. Put simply, the multiplier effect makes tax reductions a powerful tool of fiscal policy.[1]

A reduction in the *tax rate on corporate profits* also tends to stimulate aggregate demand. After a tax reduction, firms have additional funds to spend on new machinery and equipment. They may also distribute more money to shareholders who, in turn, may spend at least a portion of it.

Another type of tax cut for businesses is an *investment tax credit*. Such a policy allows a company to decrease its tax liability by a fraction of the investment that it initiates during a particular period. Suppose that the investment tax credit is 10 percent. If Microsoft purchases $10 million worth of new equipment

---

1. However, the multiplier effect for a change in taxes is smaller than the effect for an equivalent change in government spending. For example, assume that the economy's marginal propensity to consume (*MPC*) is 0.75, which suggests that the expenditures multiplier is 4: multiplier = $1 / (1 - MPC) = 1 / (1 - 0.75) = 4$.

Suppose that the federal government cuts personal income taxes by $25 billion. With more spendable income, households will increase consumption spending by $18.75 billion ($25 billion × 0.75 = $18.75 billion) and save $6.25 billion. If the economy's prices remain constant, aggregate demand will increase by $75 billion as a result of the multiplier effect (4 × $18.75 billion = $75 billion).

Instead, suppose that the government increases spending by $25 billion. According to the multiplier effect, aggregate demand will increase by $100 billion (4 × $25 billion = $100 billion) as a result of the increased government spending.

Comparing these examples, we see that the increase in government spending results in a larger increase in aggregate demand, and thus real output, than the decrease in personal income taxes. This is because part of the tax reduction increases saving rather than consumption.

Table 13.2	Discretionary Fiscal Policies	
Economic Problem:	Recession	Inflation
Solution:	Expansionary fiscal policy	Contractionary fiscal policy
	1. Increase government spending	1. Decrease government spending
	2. Decrease taxes	2. Increase taxes

during a year, its tax liability will fall by $1 million for that year. The purpose of an investment tax credit is to make investment more profitable and thus to promote additional private-sector investment. As a result, aggregate demand rises, causing an increase in real output, employment, and income. The investment tax credit was used during the 1960s as a way to stimulate the sluggish economy.

As seen in Table 13.2, spending increases and tax reductions are expansionary fiscal policies. The levels of both government spending and taxation affect output and employment in the short run through their influence on the demand for goods and services in the economy. Simply put, the purpose of an expansionary fiscal policy is to provide short-term stimulus to the economy by generating enough demand to engage more of the economy's existing productive capacity. But which fiscal policy is most effective?

The goal of an expansionary fiscal policy is to increase spending, and fiscal policies can differ in the extent to which they induce spending. Whereas a fiscal stimulus delivered through a direct increase in government expenditures has a relatively straightforward effect, a fiscal stimulus delivered through a personal tax cut tends to have a more muted effect on the economy because only part of it will be spent. The smaller the share spent, the smaller the stimulus. It is also possible that consumers who feel uncertain about the future will not spend a tax cut. Therefore, a tax reduction must be somewhat larger than an increase in government expenditures if it is to yield an equal amount of stimulus to the economy.

Combating Inflation

The preceding example showed how expansionary fiscal policy moves an economy closer to full employment. Suppose, however, that aggregate demand exceeds the economy's capacity to produce, resulting in demand-pull inflation. In this case, a contractionary or restrictive fiscal policy may help control it.

Referring to Figure 13.2, suppose that a stock market boom boosts household wealth. This causes the aggregate demand curve to shift to the right, from AD_0 to AD_1, so that the economy operates at point B on the full-employment range of the aggregate supply curve, AS_0. The increase in aggregate demand raises the price level from 110 to 120. However, we want stable prices. If the government desires to combat this inflation, it may adopt a contractionary fiscal policy to reduce aggregate demand. The cost of doing so could be a lower level of real output and a higher rate of unemployment.

To decrease aggregate demand, the government has three fiscal options: (1) cut government spending, (2) increase taxes, or (3) combine the two in some manner. When the economy encounters demand-pull inflation, fiscal policy should move toward a *budget surplus* (tax revenues in excess of government spending).

FISCAL POLICY IN ACTION

Although the basic elements of Keynesian fiscal policy were developed during the Great Depression, it took many years before these principles were accepted by politicians. In particular, they feared the consequences of the large budget deficits that might result from an increase in government spending or a decrease in taxes.

Figure 13.2 | **Contractionary Fiscal Policy**

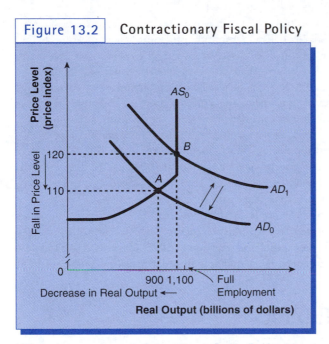

If the government wants to combat inflation, it can do so by decreasing government spending or by increasing taxes. Either policy will shift the aggregate demand curve to the left. Although inflation may decline as a result of a contractionary fiscal policy, real output may fall and unemployment may rise.

By the early 1960s, Keynesian fiscal policy had become accepted as one of the country's main weapons for combating recession and inflation. When President John F. Kennedy entered office, the unemployment rate stood at 6.7 percent. However, analysts estimated that the unemployment rate at full employment was about 4 percent. Also, they noted that the federal deficit in 1961 was negligible, less than 1 percent of gross domestic product (GDP). As a result, President Kennedy proposed substantial tax cuts to boost the economy out of its slump.

In 1962, the government enacted legislation that provided for a 7-percent tax credit on investment in new equipment and machinery, thereby strengthening the incentives for businesses to invest. In 1964, the government provided permanent tax reductions for individuals and corporations. Following the tax cuts, the economy grew rapidly, and unemployment declined from 5.2 percent in 1964 to 4.5 percent in 1965.

During this period, another expansionary force developed: the Vietnam War buildup. The escalation of the Vietnam War between 1965 and 1967 resulted in a 40-percent rise in government spending on national defense. War-related expenditures increased government spending a further 15 percent in 1968. As military spending increased, unemployment declined. By 1969, the unemployment rate had dropped to 3.5 percent, and analysts began to worry that the economy was overheating and inflationary pressures would ensue.

To dampen the inflationary momentum, Congress enacted a temporary, 1-year tax surcharge of 10 percent so that consumption spending would decrease. However, the surcharge did not cause consumer spending to fall as much as analysts had forecasted. Because the tax increase was temporary, households were only marginally affected and thus continued to engage in consumption spending. As a result, inflation rose from 1.9 percent in 1965 to 5.6 percent in 1970. Put simply, the temporary tax surcharge had little, if any, effectiveness in combating inflation.

During the 1970s, there were many changes in government spending and taxes but no major fiscal policy initiatives. The 1980s, however, ushered in a new fiscal era. In 1981, Congress enacted the fiscal policy of President Ronald Reagan, which called for sharp tax reductions, a large increase in defense spending, and a few reductions in civilian expenditure programs. These measures helped nudge the economy out of the deep recession of 1981–1982 and into a rapid expansion of the economy. However, the Reagan fiscal policy led to a sharp rise in the government's budget deficit.

When President Bill Clinton entered office in 1993, he faced a major dilemma: The government's deficits remained high, but the economy was stagnating and the level of unemployment was unacceptably high. Should the president confront the deficit by reducing government spending and raising taxes, which would suggest a contractionary fiscal policy? Or should the president worry that a contractionary fiscal policy might throw the economy into a major slump? In the end, the president decided that the budget deficit was the main priority. The Budget Act of 1993 enacted fiscal measures that reduced the deficit by about $150 billion over the next 5 years. As it turned out, the economy did not slump. Instead, it continued on an expansionary path throughout the 1990s.

By 2001, the economy was weakening. As a result, President George W. Bush signed into law a sweeping $1.35 trillion tax cut to bolster the economy. This was followed by another tax cut in 2003. President Bush again signed a tax cut into law during the recession of 2007–2009. This was followed by President Barack Obama's increases in government spending in order to stimulate the economy (see box essay).

AUTOMATIC STABILIZERS

Recall that discretionary fiscal policy entails an alteration in spending and taxes by the government to promote full employment, stable prices, and economic growth. "Discretionary" implies that changes in government spending programs and tax rates are made at the option of Congress and the White House.

Unlike discretionary fiscal policy, **automatic stabilizers** are changes in government spending and tax revenues that occur automatically as the economy fluctuates. The automatic stabilizers prevent aggregate demand from decreasing too much in bad times and rising too much in good times, thus stabilizing the economy. It is important to note that automatic stabilizers operate silently in the background and do their job without requiring explicit policy changes by Congress or the White House. Economists estimate that automatic stabilizers can offset about 8 percent of an economic shock to GDP.[2]

The most important automatic stabilizer is the tax system. The personal income tax depends on the earnings of households; the corporate income tax depends on companies' profits; and the Social Security tax depends on workers' wages. When the economy goes into recession, income, profits, and wages all decline, which results in a decrease in tax collections for the government. This automatic decline in tax revenues bolsters aggregate demand and reduces the severity of the recession.

Government transfer payments also serve as an automatic stabilizer. When the economy goes into recession and workers are laid off, they become eligible for unemployment insurance benefits, food stamps, and other welfare benefits. This automatic increase in transfer payments supports consumption spending and aggregate demand, which helps offset the decline in economic activity. The automatic stabilizers in the U.S. economy are not strong enough to eliminate recessions completely; however, they provide a cushion for the economy as it goes into a slump.

During times of economic prosperity, tax collections automatically rise and transfer payments automatically decline. The increase in tax collections and the decrease in transfer payments slow the growth of aggregate demand, thus controlling the upward pressure on the price level when the economy is expanding. In this manner, automatic stabilizers help prevent an economy from overheating.

The recession of 1973–1975 provides an example of how automatic stabilizers work.[3] During that slump, real GDP contracted by 4.9 percent, and the unemployment rate jumped from 4.9 percent to

---

2. Alan J. Auerback and Daniel Feenberg, "The Significance of Federal Taxes as Automatic Stabilizers," National Bureau of Economic Research, Working Paper No. 7662, April 2000, available at http://www.nber.org.

3. The recession of 1973–1975 provides a good example of the impact of automatic stabilizers because government spending programs and tax rates were largely unchanged during this period.

economics
IN ACTION

Presidents Bush and Obama Implement Fiscal Stimulus Programs to Combat Recession

Following 6 consecutive years of expansion, the U.S. economy peaked in December 2007, beginning a recession that continued throughout 2008 and 2009. Policy makers moved quickly in 2008 to address the economic downturn. Although the Federal Reserve cut its key interest rate to help stimulate the economy, it was felt that monetary policy alone would not provide sufficient stimulus. Past expansionary monetary policy had decreased interest rates to under 1 percent, thus limiting the ability of the Federal Reserve to further cut interest rates.

In February 2008, Congress passed and President George Bush signed the Economic Stimulus Act. It was designed to provide temporary (one-time) tax rebates to those lower- and middle-income individuals and households who would immediately spend it. About $113 billion was dispensed, which amounted to about 0.8 percent of GDP. Under this act, the Treasury mailed checks ranging between $300 and $600 to taxpayers filing as individuals. Individuals who earned $3,000 (the minimum under the act) received a $300 check; those who earned between $3,000 and $75,000 received a check for up to $600. The act also authorized businesses to deduct 50 percent of the cost of investment equipment installed during 2008 from their 2008 taxes.

The Bush administration hoped that the tax rebates would burn such a hole in people's pockets that they would not be able to resist spending it, therefore adding to aggregate demand. However, this optimism appeared to be unwarranted. It turned out that only 10-20 percent of the tax rebate dollars were spent: Most of the money went into household saving or for paying down past debt such as credit card bills, neither of which directly expanded the economy. Simply put, the spike in household income caused by the tax rebate added only about $20 billion to consumer spending, a amount that was insufficient to induce significant economic expansion. However, the price of the tax rebate program was that the federal government would need to either cut spending or increase taxes in the years ahead to pay for the tax cut. This experience supports the view of critics that temporary tax rebates are not an effective way to stimulate the economy.

According to many economists, the Bush tax rebate was ineffective because it only provided a temporary increase to households' current incomes, rather than a permanent increase in income. However, households base their consumption expenditures on permanent income, which refers to expected future income, instead of on their current income. For example, a computer engineering student may have a low income while in college, but a high expected future income after graduation. Therefore, the student might borrow against this high expected future income to finance her education and other consumption, rather than not being able to attend college. By basing consumption spending on permanent income, a household can smooth out expenditures over a period of years, rather than having to adjust expenditures to each fluctuation in current income. One-time tax rebates, such as those used by President Bush in 2008, increase consumers' current income, but not their permanent income. Only a permanent reduction in taxes increases consumers' permanent income. Therefore, the Bush tax rebate likely stimulated consumption spending less than would a permanent tax cut. However, getting Congress to agree to a permanent decrease in taxes is very difficult, and this is perhaps why Bush opted for a temporary tax rebate.

When Barack Obama became president in 2009, he inherited an economy that was falling deeper into recession. Obama noted that decreases in consumption spending and investment spending continued to drag the economy downward. Thus, a massive increase in government spending was necessary to stimulate the economy, similar to the policy recommendations of J. M. Keynes during the Great Depression of the 1930s. In February of 2009, the U.S. Congress passed and Obama signed into law a fiscal stimulus program of $789 billion, the most expansive unleashing of the government's fiscal firepower in the face of a recession since World War II. The program included $507 billion in spending programs and $282 billion in tax relief. The intent of the program was to boost short-run aggregate demand: If more goods and services are being bought, whether cement for a new highway or groceries paid for with a household tax cut, there is less chance that decreasing demand will result in companies laying off workers, resulting in greater declines in demand and a deeper downturn.

The Obama fiscal stimulus program was controversial. Critics were concerned that the program would result in huge government budget deficits which would require much higher taxes in the future. They also contended that the best way for fiscal policy to encourage economic expansion is to permanently decrease marginal tax rates which encourage additional work, saving, and investment, all of which increase productivity. At the writing of this text, the extent to which Obama's fiscal stimulus program results in an expanding economy remains to be seen.

_____

Source: John Taylor, "Why Permanent Tax Cuts Are the Best Stimulus," *The Wall Street Journal*, November 25, 2008.

Table 13.3	Automatic Stabilizers during the Recession of 1973–1975			
	Year	Unemployment Rate	Percentage Change in Personal Income Tax Collections	Percentage Change in Transfer Payments
	1974	5.6%	14.2%	11.8%
Trough of the recession	----1975	8.5	3.9	29.1--
	1976	7.1	7.6	17.0
	1977	7.1	21.3	8.3

Source: Economic Report of the President, 1990.

8.5 percent. As seen in Table 13.3, the personal income tax and transfer payments played stabilizing roles during this period. As the economy fell toward its trough, which occurred in 1975, tax collections grew at a diminishing rate, while transfer payments grew at an increasing rate. These factors helped offset the economic downturn. As the economy rebounded in 1976 and 1977, tax collections grew faster and transfer payments grew slower, thus imposing a constraint on inflationary pressures.

CHECK POINT

1. What are the tools of fiscal policy?

2. How does discretionary fiscal policy attempt to combat recession? How about inflation?

3. What impact does an expansionary fiscal policy have on the budget of the federal government? How about a contractionary fiscal policy?

4. How do automatic stabilizers help cushion the economy during a recession? What are some examples of automatic stabilizers?

PROBLEMS OF FISCAL POLICY

Although Keynesian economists generally view fiscal policy as effective at combating recession and inflation, others are concerned about the shortcomings of fiscal policy. Let us examine some of these concerns.

Timing Lags

In theory, Congress and the president should work together to enact timely and effective fiscal policies. In practice, however, it takes months and often years for fiscal policies to be enacted and to have an impact on the economy. In particular, three timing lags constrain the operation of fiscal policy:

• **Recognition lag.** The recognition lag refers to the time between the beginning of inflation or recession and the recognition that it is actually occurring. For example, if the economy goes into a slump in March, the decline may not be apparent for 3 or 4 months. Once policy makers become aware of a problem in the economy, they rarely enact policies immediately. Instead, they want to be sure that the problem is more than a short-term disturbance.

- **Administrative lag.** The way Congress operates makes it difficult to get quick action on fiscal policy. Much debate occurs before fiscal policy can change. This process can take months.

- **Operational lag.** Once enacted, a fiscal policy measure takes time to be put into operation. Although changes in tax rates can be implemented quickly, increased spending for public-works programs requires construction firms to submit bids for the work, negotiate contracts, and so on.

Most postwar recessions in the United States have been short, lasting just under 11 months on average. By the time a fiscal program begins to boost business and consumer demand—that is, once policy makers recognize that economic growth has slowed, propose a fiscal package, debate it, pass it, and send it to the president for his signature—the economy is already likely to be recovering. For this reason, discretionary fiscal policy in the United Sates is generally viewed as too unwieldy for dealing with the mild recessions experienced in recent decades.

For example, evidence appeared in late 2000 that the U.S. economy was slowing. Congress did pass a tax cut in 2001, but this had been part of President George W. Bush's legislative agenda before any hint of an economic slowdown. It took Congress until March 2002 to pass the Economic Recovery Act to provide further stimulus to the economy. Simply put, many economists are skeptical of fiscal policy as a stabilization tool, particularly through the mechanism of tax cuts. Because of lags in decision making and administrative lags in getting tax cuts to individuals, a fiscal stimulus enacted through a tax cut can be poorly timed.

Crowding-Out Effect

Another potential problem of expansionary fiscal policies is the **crowding-out effect.** With crowding out, private spending (consumption spending or investment) falls as a result of increased government expenditures and subsequent budget deficits. The source of the decline in private spending is higher interest rates generated by budget deficits.

For example, suppose that the government enacts an expansionary fiscal policy—say, an increase in defense spending. The policy must be financed either by increased taxes or by borrowing funds to finance the enlarged federal deficit. If the government borrows funds to finance the deficit, the total demand for funds will increase as the government competes with the private sector to borrow the available supply of funds. The additional government borrowing thus increases the demand for funds and pushes up interest rates. Because of higher interest rates, businesses will delay or cancel purchases of machinery and equipment, residential housing construction will be postponed, and consumers will refrain from buying interest-sensitive goods, such as major appliances and automobiles. Therefore, the higher interest rates caused by government borrowing squeeze out private-sector borrowing. Thus, crowding out reduces the effectiveness of an expansionary fiscal policy.

Although economists see the logic of the crowding-out argument, they also recognize that government deficits don't necessarily squeeze out private spending. During recessions, the main problem is that people are not spending all of their available funds. Typically, consumers are saving more than businesses intend to invest. Such a shortage of spending is the main motivation for increased government spending. In this recessionary situation, deficit-financed government spending doesn't crowd out private spending. Moreover, when open international investment markets allow countries to draw on each other's savings, increases in one country's deficits may be offset by savings pulled into that country from abroad, with barely changed interest rates. This has been the situation for the United States, which has increasingly financed its deficits by borrowing funds from the Chinese, Japanese, and other global investors.

FISCAL POLICY AND AGGREGATE SUPPLY: LONG-RUN GROWTH

We have seen that by influencing the aggregate demand curve, fiscal policy has short-run effects on the business cycle, when the economy's capacity to produce is fixed. Fiscal policy can also alter the economy's productive capacity in the long run through its effect on aggregate supply. This expansion in real output—this economic growth—depends on the quantity of labor, the quantity of capital, and the state of technology. Taxes can affect all three of these factors, thereby influencing the quantity of real output supplied.

Supply-Side Effects of Changes in Taxes

When Congress alters tax rates, it affects people's incentives to earn income by working, saving, and investing, which, in turn, alters the economy's productive capacity in the long run. From a supply-side perspective, the *marginal tax rate* is of crucial importance. Recall that the marginal tax rate is the fraction of additional income paid in taxes. A decrease in marginal tax rates increases the rewards stemming from extra work, saving, and investment and therefore tends to encourage these activities.[4]

According to advocates of supply-side economics, a policy that reduces marginal tax rates will increase the economy's capacity to produce because individuals will work harder and longer, save more, and invest more. As a result, the total supplies of labor and capital in the economy increase, causing the aggregate supply curve to shift to the right and real output to increase. Although supply-side incentives are essential for economic growth in the long run, they do not directly address the current problem of the economy's short-term inability to use its existing capacity to produce goods and services.

Figure 13.3 shows possible effects of fiscal policy on aggregate supply. Referring to Figure 13.3(*a*), if an expansionary fiscal policy can shift the economy's aggregate supply curve from AS_0 to AS_1, prices will decline and output will expand. Policy makers will have succeeded in reducing inflation, raising real output, and lowering unemployment at the same time. Hence, the trade-off between unemployment and inflation will have been defeated. This is the objective of supply-side policies.

Although proponents consider supply-side policies a painless remedy for our economic problems, critics consider it wishful thinking. Their first objection is that supply-side policies are too optimistic. The hoped-for favorable impacts of a tax cut on incentives to work, save, and invest may not be nearly as large as supply-side advocates maintain. Just because cutting tax rates increases the return on work does not mean that people will actually work more. As they realize an increase in after-tax wages, people may work less, not more. The reason is that, with higher after-tax wages, an individual may be able to work fewer hours while still maintaining or even improving his standard of living. Similarly, if cutting tax rates increases the return on savings, people may find their savings objectives more easily fulfilled and respond by saving less. As a result, the aggregate supply curve may shift to the right by only a modest amount in response to a tax cut. Thus, supply-side policies may cause, at most, only a small increase in real output.

Second, supply-side advocates underestimate the effects of tax cuts on aggregate demand. If personal taxes are reduced, individuals may work more, but they will surely spend more, thus shifting

---

4. Although lower tax rates can result in a more prosperous economy, not all taxes are created equal for the purposes of promoting growth. According to economists at the U.S. Treasury Department, reductions in dividends and capital-gains taxes are especially effective at promoting investment and thus growth. Conversely, tax cuts from the 10-percent bracket, child credit, and marriage-penalty relief put money in people's pockets when, during a recession, the economy needs a short-run boost in aggregate demand. However, these tax reductions have relatively small effects on long-run growth. See the U.S. Department of the Treasury, *A Dynamic Analysis of Permanent Extension of the President's Tax Relief*, July 25, 2006, available at http://www.treasury.gov.

Figure 13.3	Supply-Side Fiscal Policy

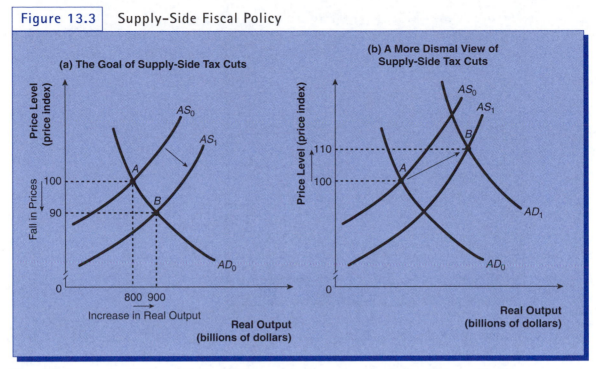

The goal of a supply-side tax cut is to shift the aggregate supply curve to the right, resulting in a lower price level and increased real output. The tax cut, however, also shifts the aggregate demand curve to the right. If the increase in aggregate demand more than offsets the increase in aggregate supply, the result will be a higher price level.

the aggregate demand curve to the right. The demand-side effects of tax reductions are likely to be much larger than the supply-side effects, especially in the short run.

The implications of these two concerns are shown in Figure 13.3(b). In response to a tax cut, there may be a small rightward shift in the aggregate supply curve, reflecting the first concern, and a large rightward shift in the aggregate demand curve, reflecting the second concern. As a result, the economy's equilibrium moves from point A to point B following a decrease in taxes. Prices thus rise as output increases. This situation contradicts the view that supply-side economics is a painless remedy for our economic problems. According to critics, supply-side policies should not be considered a substitute for short-run stabilization policy. It is best suited to promoting economic growth in the long run.

Do Tax Cuts Cause Tax Revenues to Rise (Fall)?

If income tax rates are cut, will tax revenues rise or fall? Most people think that the answer is obvious: Declining tax rates will result in lower tax revenues. Supply-side advocate Arthur Laffer, however, maintains that this may not be true.

To illustrate how tax rates influence tax revenues, we will use a simple device, the **Laffer curve,** named after Arthur Laffer. The Laffer curve shows the relationship between the income tax rate that a government imposes and the total tax revenues that the government collects. The amount of revenue that the government collects depends on both the tax rate and the level of taxable income:

Tax revenues = Tax rate × Taxable income

| **Figure 13.4** | **The Laffer Curve** |

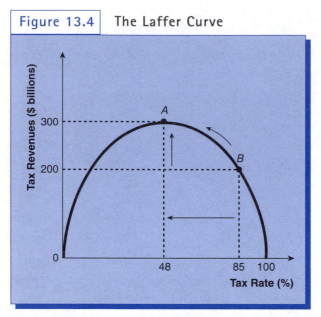

The Laffer curve is a graphical illustration of the relationship between tax rates and the total tax revenues raised by taxation. According to the Laffer curve, if tax rates are high enough it may be possible to increase tax revenues by cutting those tax rates.

The essence of the Laffer curve is that high tax rates may cause tax revenues to decline. Taxable income falls when tax rates are too high because people are discouraged from working, saving, and investing—taxable income decreases, which results in falling tax revenues.

Figure 13.4 illustrates the Laffer curve. On the vertical axis are hypothetical tax revenues, measured in billions of dollars per year. On the horizontal axis are hypothetical tax rates from 0 to 100 percent. There are two tax rates at which no tax revenues will be collected: 0 and 100 percent. Obviously, no tax revenues will be collected if the tax rate is 0. If the tax rate is 100 percent, the incentive to earn income disappears, and tax revenues are again 0. As the tax rate rises above 0, total revenues will rise until, at some tax rate, they finally begin to fall toward 0. This occurs when the high tax rate discourages so many people from seeking work that employment declines, the result being a smaller tax amount of taxable income. If the decrease in taxable income exceeds the increase in the tax rate, total tax revenues will fall.

In Figure 13.4, the maximum amount of tax revenues collected is $300 billion per year, generated by a tax rate of 48 percent. After this point, a rise in tax rates actually decreases total tax revenues. For example, at a tax rate of 85 percent, revenues will fall from a maximum of $300 billion to $200 billion. Put simply, the Laffer curve provides a reminder to the White House and Congress that increases in tax rates may be counterproductive, causing a decline in economic activity, as well as a decrease in total tax revenues.

Such thinking provided the intellectual underpinnings of the economic policies of the Reagan administration (1981–1989). During his administration, President Ronald Reagan dramatically cut the personal income tax rate in order to foster increased economic activity, and perhaps to increase tax revenues. The Reagan tax cut lowered the top tax rate from 70 percent to 28 percent. Subsequent history, however, has failed to confirm that the Reagan tax cuts resulted in higher total tax revenues. When Reagan reduced taxes, the result was falling tax revenues. Revenues from personal income taxes (per person, adjusted for inflation) declined by 9 percent from 1980 to 1984, even though average income (per person, adjusted for inflation) increased by 4 percent during this period. Because the tax cut could not generate enough revenues to finance government spending, the government ran large budget deficits during the Reagan administration.

THE FEDERAL DEFICIT AND FEDERAL DEBT

Recall that the main mechanism of fiscal policy is the federal government's budget. As we have learned, changes in federal taxes or spending are tools for shifting the aggregate demand curve and the aggregate supply curve. The use of the federal budget to stabilize the economy suggests that the budget will often be *unbalanced*. To combat recession, the federal government must increase spending or reduce taxes, giving rise to a budget deficit. Conversely, counteracting inflation means decreasing government spending or increasing taxes, resulting in a budget surplus. From the viewpoint of economic stabilization, budget deficits and surpluses are a common feature of fiscal policy.

The **federal deficit** (surplus) is the difference between total federal spending and revenues in a *given year,* as seen in Figure 13.5. To cover this gap, the government borrows from the public. Each yearly deficit adds to the amount of debt held by the public. Referring to the figure, we see that the federal government's budget has generally been in deficit. Also, the term **federal debt** represents the cumulative amount of outstanding borrowing from the public over the nation's history. It has been rising because of the persistent federal deficits that have occurred on an annual basis.

The main measure of the U.S. federal debt is the *debt held by the public.* This is the measure most commonly used because it reflects how much of the nation's wealth is absorbed by the federal government to finance its obligations and thus best represents the current impact of past federal borrowing on the economy. As seen in Table 13.4, the federal debt held by the public was about $5,421 trillion in 2008. In contrast, the federal debt was only $43 billion in 1940.

The amount of a borrower's debt by itself is not a particularly good indicator of the debt's burden. If size were the only thing that mattered, a wealthy individual with a large mortgage would be judged to have a greater debt burden than a person of modest means with a smaller mortgage. In order words,

| Figure 13.5 | Deficits and Surpluses of the U.S. Government, 1981–2008 |

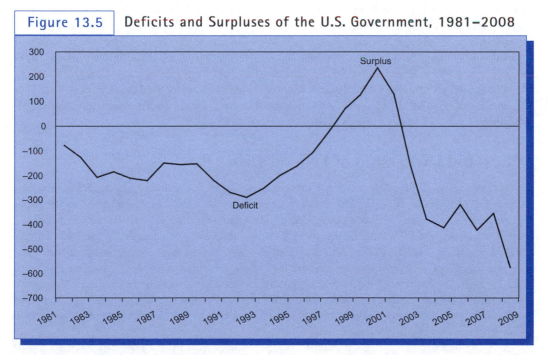

Source: *Economic Report of the President,* 2009, p. 377.

Table 13.4	Federal Debt Held by the Public	

Year	Federal Debt (billions)	Federal Debt as a Percentage of GDP
1940	$ 43	44%
1945	236	106
1955	227	57
1965	261	38
1975	395	25
1985	1,500	36
1995	3,603	49
2000	3,410	35
2005	4,592	37
2008	5,421	38

Source: Economic Report of the President, 2009, p. 377.

a borrower's income and wealth are also important in assessing the burden of debt. Therefore, to get a better sense of the burden represented by the federal debt, debt should be viewed in relation to the nation's income. A commonly used measure of national income is GDP. Comparing the debt to GDP provides a better indicator of the debt burden than the debt's dollar value because it captures the capacity of the economy to sustain the debt.

As of 2008, the federal debt equaled 38 percent of GDP. Although this level is high by historical standards, it is not as high as the debt levels of many other nations, where debt may equal 60 percent of GDP or more. In the past, the debt–GDP measure of the United States has only risen substantially as a result of wars and recessions. The peak period in U.S. history occurred immediately after World War II, when, as a result of wartime borrowing, the federal debt was 106 percent of GDP, meaning that it exceeded the annual output of the economy. After the war, spurred by economic growth and inflation, this measure fell dramatically over the next three decades to a postwar low of 24 percent in 1974. Since the mid-1970s, the debt–GDP ratio has generally crept upward.

The federal government is not the only borrower that has increased its debt since the 1980s. The borrowing of individuals, businesses, and state and local governments have all risen significantly during this period, but not as much as the federal debt.

Sales and Ownership of Federal Debt

How does the federal government borrow? The federal government borrows by issuing securities, mostly through the U.S. Treasury Department. Most of the securities that constitute the debt held by the public are marketable, meaning that once the government issues them, they can be resold by whoever owns them. These marketable securities consist of Treasury bills, notes, and bonds with a variety of maturities ranging from 3 months to 30 years. The mix of outstanding securities changes regularly as new debt is issued.

The mix of securities is important because it can have a significant impact on interest payments. For example, a long-term Treasury bond typically carries a higher interest rate than a short-term Treasury bill because of investors' perception that longer-term securities are subject to greater risks, such as higher inflation in the future. However, long-term bonds offer the certainty of knowing what your payments will be over a longer period.

Who lends to the federal government? The federal debt held by the public is owed to a wide variety of investors. In 2008, 50 percent of the federal debt was owned by the U.S. Treasury and other federal agencies including the Federal Reserve, 24 percent by private domestic investors, and 26 percent by foreign investors.

A Treasury security can be purchased by anyone. Although debt ownership is concentrated among businesses and other institutions, many small investors also own debt securities. For example, anyone who owns a U.S. savings bond holds a portion of the federal debt. Furthermore, many pension funds own debt securities, so small investors are also represented indirectly through these holdings.

The United States benefits from foreign purchases of government securities because, as foreign investors fill part of our borrowing needs, more domestic savings are available for private investment, and interest rates are lower than they otherwise would be. However, to service this foreign-owned debt, the U.S. government must send interest payments abroad, which adds to the income of citizens of other countries rather than to that of U.S. citizens.

U.S. FISCAL POLICY: DOES THE FEDERAL DEBT CHEAT FUTURE GENERATIONS?

As the U.S. financial system and economy faltered during 2007–2009, the U.S. government initiated massive increases in spending to stabilize the economy, resulting in unprecedented government deficits. Many feel that the current generation of Americans is being unfair to future generations through runaway government debt. What are the economic consequences of government debt?

Many believe that borrowing is appropriate under certain circumstances. For example, some believe that the automatic increases in federal borrowing that occur during recessions help the economy by maintaining income and spending levels. Wartime borrowing is also widely considered to be beneficial because it allows the government to increase defense spending without enacting large tax increases that could be disruptive to the economy. Moreover, federal borrowing may also be appropriate for investment spending, such as building roads, training workers, or conducting scientific research. If an investment is well chosen, it can ultimately boost worker productivity and economic growth in the long term, producing a larger economy from which to pay the interest on borrowed funds.

However, if federal borrowing is not used for any of the purposes mentioned earlier, many believe that the costs outweigh the benefits. In this case, the benefits of any increased federal spending are likely to be more concentrated in the short term, while the costs tend to occur mainly in the long term. This timing difference can have important implications for different generations. The impact of today's increased borrowing will be felt by tomorrow's workers and taxpayers, who may not fully share in the benefits of the additional spending made possible by the borrowing. To the extent that deficits reduce national investment, the economy's stock of capital decreases which reduces labor productivity, the economy's production of goods and services, and real wages. Therefore, when the government increases its debt, future generations are born into an economy with lower incomes. Moreover, when the government's debts and accumulated interest come due, future generations will face the difficult decision of paying increased taxes, enjoying less government spending, or both to free up resources to pay off the debt and accumulated interest.

Federal borrowing can reduce the funds that are available for private investment and put upward pressure on interest rates. Because the federal government competes with private investors for scarce capital, federal borrowing can reduce the amount that is available for other investors. Government borrowing can be large enough to affect the overall level of interest rates, making borrowing more expensive for individuals and families who take out loans for homes, cars, and college.

Since the 1970s, the large amounts of federal borrowing have been particularly troublesome because private saving has been declining as a share of the U.S. economy. These two trends have had a significant impact on the economy: Federal deficits are eating up a larger portion of a shrinking pool of private savings, sharply reducing the amount of saving that is available for private investment. However, part of the decline in national saving has been offset by increased borrowing from foreign investors.

How does borrowing affect the federal budget? Although borrowing allows the government to provide more services today than it could otherwise afford, the cost is borne tomorrow in the form of interest payments. To make these payments while avoiding larger deficits, the government has to forego spending money on other national priorities. It also means less money is available for unexpected needs.

SHOULD THERE BE A BALANCED-BUDGET AMENDMENT?

Although federal budget surpluses briefly appeared at the end of the 1990s, skeptics are concerned that the U.S. government has a bias toward overspending. Therefore, they call for Congress to enact laws to force the federal government to eliminate its deficit. In the United States, 49 states have balanced-budget requirements. Why not require the federal government to achieve what most states require for their own governments?

One approach would be to enact a constitutional amendment to balance the budget. The rule most commonly proposed includes several provisions. Each year, the president would submit a balanced budget to Congress in which tax revenues match expenditures. Congress would then work on the budget. A budget deficit could be approved only by 60 percent of the members of Congress on a roll-call vote, name by name. In the event of war or national emergency, the balanced-budget requirement could be suspended.

Proponents of the balanced-budget amendment note that Congress lacks the willpower to exercise fiscal restraint. Although, in principle, it might make sense to have a deficit when the economy enters a downturn, the reality is that the budget has often been in deficit irrespective of underlying economic conditions. Only the power of a constitutional rule could permanently make the government live within its means over the long haul.

However, critics of this rule argue that it could make recessions more frequent and severe. A balanced-budget requirement would make recessions longer and more painful, first by eliminating the automatic stabilizers that protect people during downturns, and second, by instead requiring measures to cut spending or increase taxes during slowdowns when the economy is already suffering from a lack of demand.

Critics of the balanced-budget amendment also maintain that even if it were enacted, Congress would figure out ways to escape its restrictive provisions. For example, Congress might use mechanisms such as "off-budget" expenditures and unrealistic budget projections to avoid the amendment's discipline.

This chapter has discussed fiscal policy as a possible solution to macroeconomic instability. The next chapter will consider the roles of money and the economy's banking system.

CHECK POINT

1. Identify the major shortcomings of fiscal policy.

2. Why do proponents of supply-side fiscal policy consider it a painless remedy for our economic problems?

3. The federal debt entails both benefits and costs for the economy. Explain.

4. Identify advantages and disadvantages of a balanced-budget amendment for the federal government.

Chapter Summary

1. Fiscal policy is the use of government expenditures and taxes to promote particular macroeconomic goals, such as full employment, stable prices, and economic growth. In the United States, fiscal policy is conducted by Congress and the president. An expansionary fiscal

policy attempts to nudge the economy out of a recession, whereas a contractionary fiscal policy attempts to combat inflation.

2. Discretionary fiscal policy is the deliberate use of changes in government expenditures and taxation to affect aggregate demand and to influence the economy's performance in the short run. To combat recession, the government can cut taxes and/or increase expenditures in order to boost aggregate demand. The government can combat inflation by increasing taxes and/or cutting expenditures, thus decreasing aggregate demand.

3. Automatic stabilizers are changes in government spending and tax revenues that occur automatically as the economy fluctuates. Automatic stabilizers prevent aggregate demand from decreasing too much in bad times and rising too much in good times, thus moderating fluctuations in economic activity. Automatic stabilizers include the personal income tax, the corporate income tax, and transfer payments such as unemployment insurance benefits, food stamps, and other welfare benefits.

4. Although Keynesian economists generally view fiscal policy as effective at combating recession and inflation, others are concerned about its shortcomings. Among the problems of discretionary fiscal policy are timing lags, inflationary bias, the crowding-out effect, and the foreign-trade effect.

5. Besides having potential effects on aggregate demand, fiscal policy can also influence the level of economic activity through its effect on aggregate supply. According to supply-side fiscal policy, a reduction in marginal tax rates will cause productivity to increase because individuals will work harder and longer, save more, and invest more. Therefore, the aggregate supply curve will shift to the right, which leads to higher real output.

6. During the early 1980s, supply-side economists argued that a cut in tax rates would enhance incentives to work, save, and invest, thus promoting an increase in economic activity and national income. In theory, the enlarged income would cause total tax revenues to rise even though tax rates would be lower. However, the evidence from the 1980s does not support this outcome.

7. The federal deficit is the difference between total federal spending and tax revenues received in a given year. The federal debt represents the cumulative amount of outstanding borrowing from the public over the nation's history. The federal government borrows by issuing securities, mostly through the U.S. Treasury Department.

8. Federal borrowing entails both benefits and costs. Many believe that federal borrowing is beneficial when it helps the economy by supporting income and spending levels, when it is used to increase defense spending, and when it helps finance investment spending on roads, dams, bridges, and the like. Critics of federal borrowing fear that it will slow the growth in living standards for future generations and reduce private consumption and investment expenditures. As a result, critics prefer laws that would force the federal government to refrain from deficit spending.

Key Terms and Concepts

fiscal policy (298)

discretionary fiscal policy (299)

automatic stabilizers (304)

recognition lag (306)

administrative lag (307)

operational lag (307)

crowding-out effect (307)

Laffer curve (309)

federal deficit (311)

federal debt (311)

Self-Test: Multiple-Choice Questions

1. _____ refers to the use of government expenditures, transfer payments, and taxes to promote full employment, stable prices, and economic growth.

   a. industrial policy
   b. commercial policy
   c. monetary policy
   d. fiscal policy

2. Assume that the economy has idle resources and a constant price level. Also suppose taxes are constant and the marginal propensity to consume is 0.75. If government expenditures increase by $10 billion, real GDP will

   a. increase by 10 billion.
   b. increase by 20 billion.
   c. increase by 30 billion.
   d. increase by 40 billion.

3. When tax receipts fall short of government expenditures, government must

   a. increase transfer payments.
   b. increase tax rates.
   c. reduce its spending.
   d. borrow funds.

4. Crowding out tends to occur when government

   a. restricts certain types of business investments.
   b. increases personal income tax rates.
   c. finances a deficit by printing new money.
   d. finances a deficit by borrowing.

5. The creation of public debt is burdensome for the economy for all of the following reasons *except*

   a. it results in crowding out.
   b. it is held largely by domestic investors instead of foreigners.
   c. it reduces the supply of capital goods.
   d. it creates inflation.

6. Countercyclical fiscal policy can best be exemplified by

   a. an increase in government spending and an increase in tax rates during recessions.
   b. an increase in government spending and a decrease in tax rates during recessions.
   c. a decrease in government spending and an increase in tax rates during recessions.
   d. a decrease in government spending and a decrease in tax rates during recessions.

7. Automatic stabilizers include all of the following *except*

   a. national defense spending.
   b. welfare payments such as food stamps.
   c. unemployment compensation payments.
   d. the federal income tax.

8. Suppose that the economy's aggregate demand is $400 billion below its full-employment output. If the marginal propensity to consume is 0.8, how much would government

expenditures have to increase in order to push aggregate demand to the full-employment output?

a. $40 billion
b. $60 billion
c. $80 billion
d. $100 billion

9. During the Great Depression of the 1930s, President Herbert Hoover initiated a fiscal policy that resulted in a balanced budget instead of a budget deficit. According to Keynesian economics, a balanced budget is inappropriate during a depression because it

a. results in more inflation for the economy.
b. causes declines in economic activity, thus increasing unemployment.
c. contributes to only minor gains in economic activity and employment.
d. decreases personal saving more than business investment.

10. Countercyclical fiscal policy suggests that government should combat recession by

a. running a budget surplus, thus increasing aggregate demand.
b. running a budget surplus, thus decreasing aggregate demand.
c. running a budget deficit, thus increasing aggregate demand.
d. running a budget deficit, thus decreasing aggregate demand.

Answers to Multiple-Choice Questions

1. d   2. d   3. d   4. d   5. b   6. b   7. a   8. c   9. b   10. c

Study Questions and Problems

1. Explain how each of the following fiscal policies would affect aggregate demand.

   a. The government increases its expenditures on highways and bridges by $10 billion.
   b. Personal income tax rates are increased by 10 percent across the board.
   c. Expenditures on the food-stamp program are increased by 15 percent in order to help the poor.
   d. The government slashes national defense expenditures as peace spreads throughout the world.

2. In each of the following situations, explain whether discretionary fiscal policy is expansionary or contractionary.

   a. The government increases tax rates for households and corporations.
   b. The government increases funding for unemployment insurance benefits.
   c. The government approves funding for highway improvements in the Pacific Northwest.
   d. The government's budget shows a deficit because of increased expenditures.

3. Tax reductions tend to affect both aggregate demand and aggregate supply. Does it matter which is affected more? Use the model of aggregate demand and aggregate supply to explain your answer.

4. Some economists argue in favor of using discretionary fiscal policy to combat recession and inflation, whereas some argue against it. Discuss the advantages and disadvantages of using discretionary fiscal policy to stabilize the economy.

Table 13.5	Hypothetical Tax Data for the United States

Tax Rate (percent)	Tax Revenues (billions of dollars)
0	0
10	90
15	150
20	180
25	150
30	90
35	0

5. Explain how changes in government spending and taxes can have a multiplier effect on aggregate demand and real output.

6. The following questions are based on Table 13.5.

   a. What 2 points indicate 0 tax revenues? How can this occur?
   b. What tax rate results in maximum tax revenues for the government?
   c. Suppose that the economy imposes a tax rate of 25 percent, yielding tax revenues of $150 billion. What will happen to tax revenues if the tax rate rises to 30 percent? Why might this occur?
   d. Suppose that the economy imposes a tax rate of 10 percent, yielding tax revenues of $90 billion. What will happen to tax revenues if the tax rate rises to 15 percent? Why might this occur?

7. Using the model of aggregate demand and aggregate supply, describe the destabilizing effects of fiscal policy if a constitutional amendment mandating an annually balanced budget were enacted.

8. Keynesian economists emphasize the effects of fiscal policy on aggregate demand, whereas supply-side economists focus on the effects on aggregate supply. Discuss the process by which a tax reduction might result in an increase in real output and employment according to these two approaches. If tax reductions are beneficial for the economy, why doesn't the government slash taxes to 0?

9. Why is crowding out an important issue in the debate over the merits of discretionary fiscal policy? Is crowding out equally likely to occur during all phases of the business cycle?

10. If the government today decides that aggregate demand is deficient and causing a recession, what is it likely to do? What if the government decides that aggregate demand is excessive and causing inflation?

11. Expansionary fiscal policy can combat recessions, but it usually results in a cost in terms of higher inflation. This dilemma has sparked interest in "supply-side" tax cuts that are intended to stimulate aggregate supply. Use the model of aggregate demand and aggregate supply to explain the purpose of supply-side economics. Identify the problems associated with supply-side tax cuts.

12. Assume that the economy's marginal propensity to consume is 0.8. To combat a recession, suppose that the federal government increases its expenditures by $50 billion. If prices remain constant, what impact will this policy have on the economy's aggregate demand and real output? Instead, suppose that prices increase as the economy's aggregate demand increases. What effect would this have on your answer?

13. Assume that the economy's marginal propensity to consume is 0.67. To combat a recession, suppose that the federal government is considering whether to reduce personal income taxes by $40 billion or to increase government expenditures by $40 billion. Assuming a constant price level for the economy, what effect would each of these policies have on aggregate demand and real output? Which policy is more expansionary? Why?

EXPLORING FURTHER 13.1: FISCAL POLICY AND THE MULTIPLIER

Recall from Chapter 12 that the formula for the multiplier is $1 / (1 - MPC)$, where MPC is the economy's marginal propensity to consume. If $MPC = 0.75$, the value of the multiplier is 4: $1 / (1 - 0.75) = 4$. In our example of an expansionary fiscal policy, we assume that government purchases increase by $25 billion. Given a multiplier of 4, the aggregate demand curve will shift to the right by 4 times the distance of the initial $25 billion increase in government purchases. Indeed, the multiplier makes government spending a very powerful policy tool for stimulating output and production.

To illustrate this multiplier effect, refer to Figure 13.6. The direct effect of the increase in government purchases is to shift the aggregate demand curve to the right by $25 billion, from AD_0 to AD_2. According to the multiplier process, the indirect effect of increased consumption spending is shown by a rightward shift in aggregate demand by an additional $75 billion, from AD_2 to AD_1. Altogether, the $25 billion increase in government purchases results in a $100 billion increase in aggregate demand, shown by the shift from AD_0 to AD_1. This fourfold increase in aggregate demand is due to the multiplier effect.

Notice that this particular increase in aggregate demand takes place within the horizontal region of the aggregate supply curve, where the economy's price level is constant. Thus, real output will increase by the full amount of the multiplier. Moreover, unemployment will decline as firms employ workers who were laid off during the recession.

| Figure 13.6 | Fiscal Policy and the Multiplier Effect |

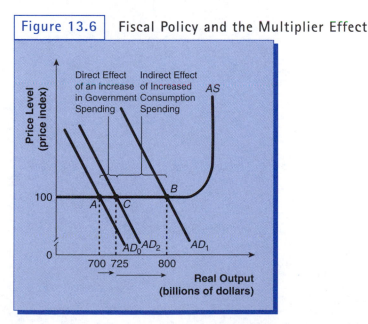

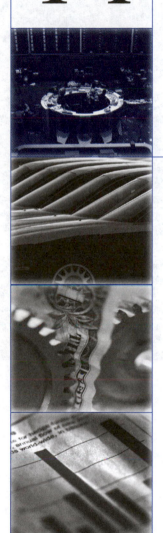

Money and the Banking System

Chapter objectives

After reading this chapter, you should be able to:

1. Define money and identify the functions of money.

2. Describe the collection process that a check goes through.

3. Describe the major depository institutions in our economy.

4. Explain how banks attempt to make a profit for their stockholders.

5. Discuss the process by which money is created in the banking system.

6. Identify the purposes of the Federal Deposit Insurance Corporation.

economics IN CONTEXT

In 2000, the U.S. Mint issued its eighth dollar coin. The Golden Dollar coin, as it is known, bears the image of Sacagawea, the only woman on the Lewis and Clark expedition. Proponents of the dollar coin point out that its widespread use would result in considerable savings for the government. On average, coins have a projected life of 30 years, compared with about 18 months for a dollar bill. Although dollar bills cost about 4 cents to produce, compared to 13 cents for the dollar coin, the relatively short life of dollar bills makes them more expensive in the long run.

Dollar coins, however, have never been widely adopted for day-to-day transactions in the United States. One explanation is simply that people find coins inconvenient compared to paper currency. Accordingly, dollar coins would replace notes only if the public had no choice. Despite a $45 million ad campaign, approximately half the new coins remained in the vaults of the Federal Reserve Banks and the U.S. Mint a year after the coin was first introduced. The other half was "in circulation." However, many of these coins were apparently being hoarded, as few of them were observed in day-to-day transactions.

According to the adage, money makes the world go around. As far back as 300 B.C.E., Aristotle maintained that everything must be assessed in money because this allows people to exchange their services and so makes society possible. Indeed, money is an integral part of our everyday life.

In this chapter, we will examine money and the role that it plays in the economy. We will focus on the nature of money, the operation of our banking system, and the process by which money is created.

Throughout this chapter, we will refer to the Federal Reserve System, which is the *central banking system* of the United States. The Federal Reserve supplies banks[1] with currency, operates a nationwide clearing mechanism for checks, serves as a lender of last resort for troubled banks, supervises and examines member banks for safety and soundness, provides checking accounts for the U.S. Treasury, issues and redeems government securities, and conducts monetary policy for the nation. We will discuss the nature and operations of the Federal Reserve System more fully in the next chapter.

THE MEANING OF MONEY

When you go to Pizza Hut to purchase a dinner, you obtain something of value—a pizza and a soft drink. To pay for these items, you might hand the waiter some cash or a personal check. The restaurant is happy to accept either of these pieces of paper, which, in themselves, are worthless. Nevertheless, they are considered money.

We begin with a simple question: What is **money?** Money is the set of assets in the economy that people use regularly to purchase goods and services from others. Gold and silver were once the most common forms of money. But today, money consists primarily of paper bills, coins made of various metals, and checking account deposits.

---

1. The U.S. economy has an array of banks, including commercial banks, savings and loan associations, mutual savings banks, and credit unions. We call these *depository institutions:* They accept deposits from people and provide checking accounts that are part of the money supply.

Each country has its own system of money. In the United States, for example, the basic unit of money is the U.S. dollar. Canada uses the Canadian dollar, Mexico uses the peso, Japan uses the yen, and so on. We call the money in use in a country its **currency**.

Money has three functions in the economy: It is a medium of exchange, a unit of account, and a store of value. These functions distinguish money from other assets such as stocks, bonds, and real estate.

Medium of Exchange

First, money is a **medium of exchange:** It is something that people are willing to accept in payment for goods and services. In the United States, a penny, a dime, a quarter, and a $1 bill are media of exchange because people are willing to accept these items in payment, realizing that they can be used for other purchases. The transfer of money from the buyer to the seller allows the transaction to occur.

Without a medium of exchange, people would have to trade their goods and services directly for other goods and services. For example, if you wanted a motorcycle, you would have to find a motorcycle owner willing to trade. Suppose that the motorcycle owner wanted a computer in exchange for the motorcycle, and you did not own a computer. You would then have to find something that the owner of a computer wanted and trade it for a computer to give to the owner of the motorcycle.

Such trading, called *barter,* is inefficient because you could spend days running around looking for someone who has what you want and wants what you have. Also, some items, such as animals, simply are not divisible, and deals must be struck at uneven rates of exchange. Finally, barter restricts productive capacities. As societies become more sophisticated and produce a greater range of goods, the exchange process becomes too complicated for barter alone. However, a medium of exchange, or money, removes the problems of barter. Wants need not coincide because everyone is willing to accept money in return for goods and services.

Unit of Account

A second function of money is that it serves as a **unit of account.** People state the prices of goods and services in terms of money. In the United States, people use dollars to specify prices. When you go shopping, you might observe that a pair of pants costs $40 and a 12-pack of Pepsi costs $4. The unit-of-account function of money allows us to compare the relative values of goods. If a pair of pants costs $40 and a 12-pack of Pepsi costs $4, then one pair of pants equals ten 12-packs of Pepsi ($40 / $4 = 10). Put simply, people use money to specify price, just as they use kilometers to measure distance or hours to express time.

Store of Value

A third function of money is that it provides a **store of value.** People can save money and then use it to make purchases in the future. Of course, money is not the only store of value in the economy. Other stores of value include gold, real estate, paintings, jewels, or even baseball cards. However, money has the advantage that it can be used immediately to meet financial obligations.

The store-of-value function of money helps us appreciate how severe and prolonged inflation can weaken an economy. With inflation, the ability of money to serve as a store of value deteriorates. Thus, people may be unwilling to save money if they expect that its future purchasing power will erode because of increasing prices. Moreover, borrowing money for productive investment may be hampered if lenders expect that the repaid loans will have less purchasing power.

Any object or substance that serves as a medium of exchange, a unit of account, and a store of value is considered money. To be convenient, however, money should have several other characteristics. It should be portable so that people can carry enough money to purchase what they need. It should come in pieces of standard value so that it does not have to be weighed or measured every time it is used. It should be durable and hold up over time. Finally, it should be divisible into smaller units so that people can make small purchases and receive change.

Are Credit Cards Money?

Most people think of credit cards, such as MasterCard and Visa, as "plastic money." After all, credit cards serve as a convenient form of financing transactions.

Are credit cards money? Not at all! MasterCard may be accepted as readily as money, but the reason merchants honor these cards is that they expect to be paid by the financial institution that issued the card. Eventually, you must pay your bill by writing a check to the financial institution that gave you the card. Yet, without an adequate amount of funds in your checking account, MasterCard would soon discover that the credit receipt that it received with your signature on it is virtually worthless. Put simply, if you use your MasterCard to make a purchase, you obtain a short-term loan from the financial institution that issued the card. Credit cards are thus a method of postponing payment for a brief period.

Often, credit cards are more convenient than writing checks or making payments in cash. People who have credit cards can pay many of their bills at once at the end of the month, instead of sporadically as they make purchases. Therefore, people who have credit cards tend to hold less cash on average than people who do not have credit cards. Thus, the increased use of credit cards may decrease the amount of money that people desire to hold.

SHOPPING FOR A CREDIT CARD

This year, you may receive invitations to get a credit card. Card companies mail billions of unsolicited credit offers to U.S. households during a year and make tens of millions of telephone calls to sell their cards. Today, some large issuers, such as First USA Bank, which has 12 million cards in circulation, are banks in name only. Credit cards are their primary business. The business can be highly profitable as long as cardholders stay in debt. Today, the typical U.S. adult has a credit card account with a balance of more than $1,800. Table 14.1 provides a comparison of selected bank credit cards.

Credit associations such as Visa and MasterCard sign up banks that offer cards to consumers; firms such as Discover and American Express offer cards directly to consumers. How does the amount on your charge slip end up on your monthly statement, and how does it get paid along the way?

| Table 14.1 | How Bank Credit Cards Compare, July 2008 |

Card Issuer	Annual Percentage Rate	Type of Interest Rate	Grace Period (days)	Annual Fee ($)
Adirondack Trust Co. (Visa)	15.0	Fixed	25	15
Capital One Bank (Visa)	19.6	Variable	25	None
First National Bank of St. Louis (MasterCard)	17.4	Fixed	25	None
Home Federal Bank of Tennessee (Visa)	12.8	Fixed	25	15
Valley National Bank (MasterCard)	16.8	Fixed	25	None

Source: Federal Reserve Board, *Survey of Credit Card Plans*, July 31, 2008, available at http://www.federalreserve.gov. This survey is updated every 6 months.

Suppose that you go to Wal-Mart and purchase a CD player with your Visa card. The cashier runs the card through an electronic approval machine to see whether the card is valid and whether you have enough credit to make the purchase. You sign the receipt, which becomes your agreement to repay. Within 5 business days, Wal-Mart sends the receipt to Visa, which serves as a clearinghouse for all sales receipts. Visa contacts Wal-Mart's bank, which pays the store the sales price minus a fee, which is generally around 3 percent, depending on the store's monthly sales volume and other considerations. Merchants can't increase prices to consumers to cover the bank's fees, but they can offer discounts to customers who pay by cash or check. Then, Visa clears the receipt from its books by charging the bank that issued the card. Your bank immediately pays Wal-Mart's bank the entire amount. Your bank then mails you a statement for the full amount of the purchase and any other purchases you made during the period.

No credit card will fulfill all of the needs and usage patterns of every consumer. You'll have to do some homework if you want to take advantage of the best available terms. For example, in the disclosure provided by the credit card issuer, a key credit term to consider is the *annual percentage rate* (APR). A low APR can make a big difference if you often carry a balance from month to month. Unfortunately, credit card issuers with low APRs (around 10 percent) are very particular about whom they extend credit to; they may turn down people with sizable credit card debts—the very folks who would benefit the most from a lower rate.

Equally important is the *grace period*—the time between when you make purchases and when you have to pay to avoid finance charges. Also remember that if you exceed your credit line, the bank may charge an *over-limit fee* of, say, $15. If your minimum payment is overdue, there is often a *late payment fee* as well. Moreover, most banks also charge *cash advance fees* for money that is withdrawn from an automatic teller with your credit card. Don't forget that you begin paying interest on cash advances immediately—there is no grace period.

How can you get a better rate on your credit card? It might sound crazy, but experts say consumers should just ask for one. Past experience and consumer studies show that credit card issuers are often willing to negotiate with their best customers in order to keep them from switching to a rival. As a word of caution, if you call a bank and say that you've gotten a better credit card offer elsewhere, be prepared for the issuer to call your bluff. The wisest use of a credit card, by far, is to pay off your debt every month and avoid high interest costs. Consider making it your top financial priority.

CHECK POINT

1. What is money?

2. Identify the functions of money.

3. Why are credit cards not considered a form of money?

4. As a consumer, what factors should you weigh when comparing credit cards?

THE U.S. MONEY SUPPLY

Money is anything that people agree to accept in exchange for the things they sell or the work they do. Gold and silver were once the most common types of money. Today, however, money consists mainly of currency and checking account deposits. Let us first examine the currency of the United States.

U.S. currency consists of coins and paper money. Under federal law, only the Federal Reserve System can issue paper currency, and only the U.S. Treasury can issue coins. The Federal Reserve issues paper currency called *Federal Reserve notes*. All U.S. currency carries the nation's official motto, "In God We Trust."

Coins

Coins come in six denominations: pennies (1 cent), nickels (5 cents), dimes (10 cents), quarters (25 cents), half-dollars (50 cents), and $1.

The U.S. Mint—with satellites in Philadelphia, Denver, West Point, and San Francisco—produces coins for circulation. All U.S. coins typically bear a mint mark showing which mint produced them. Coins minted in Philadelphia bear a *P* or no mint mark; those minted in Denver, a *D;* in San Francisco, an *S,* and in West Point, a *W.* All of the U.S. coins currently minted portray past U.S. presidents. All U.S. coins now issued bear the motto "In God We Trust" in a form similar to that used on other nations' money.

All coins are made from alloys (mixtures of metals). Pennies are copper-coated zinc alloyed with less than 3 percent copper. Nickels are a mixture of copper and nickel. Dimes, quarters, half-dollars, and dollars consist of three layers of metal. The core is pure copper, and the outer layers are an alloy of copper and nickel. Federal law requires that coins be dated with the year that they were made. Coins also must bear the word *liberty* and the Latin motto *e pluribus unum,* meaning "out of many, one." This motto refers to the formation of the United States from the original 13 colonies.

When producing coins, the U.S. Mint rolls ingots of metal alloys into flat sheets of proper thickness. Blanks are punched from the metal sheets, and the good blanks are sorted from the scrap. After being softened and washed, blanks are put into a machine that gives them a raised edge. Blanks are then weighed and inspected before stamping. The front and back are stamped simultaneously at pressures exceeding 40 tons. Finally, the coins are weighed, counted, and shipped to the Federal Reserve Banks for distribution.

Why do coins have ridges? When coins were made of gold and silver, cheating was a common occurrence. People would shave the edges of their coins before spending them, eventually collecting enough shavings to use as money. Milled edges, the ridges, were devised to discourage these cheaters. Today, gold and silver are no longer used to make coins, but the style still remains. Placing ridges on coins also helps visually impaired people recognize certain denominations. For example, the ridges on a dime distinguish it from a penny, which has a smooth edge.

Paper Money

Federal Reserve notes make up all the paper money issued in the United States today.[2] They come in seven denominations: $1, $2, $5, $10, $20, $50, and $100. The notes are issued by the 12 Federal Reserve Banks in the Federal Reserve System. Each note has a letter, number, and seal identifying the bank that issued it. Moreover, each note bears the words *Federal Reserve Note* and a green Treasury seal. It costs about 4 cents to produce a Federal Reserve note.

The Bureau of Engraving and Printing in Washington, D.C., is responsible for designing and printing our paper currency. There is also a satellite production facility in Fort Worth, Texas. All notes bear the words *Washington, D.C.,* below the upper-right serial number on the face of the note. Notes printed in Fort Worth also show the letters *FW* immediately to the left of the plate serial number in the lower-right corner of the note's face.

New paper money is shipped to the 12 Federal Reserve Banks, which pay it out to commercial banks, savings and loan associations, and other depository institutions. Customers of these

---

2. The other small part of paper currency consists of *U.S. notes,* which are still in circulation but are no longer issued. These notes, which were issued in the denomination of $100, are the descendants of Civil War *greenbacks.*

institutions withdraw cash as they need it. Once people spend their money at grocery stores, department stores, and so on, the money is redeposited in depository institutions. As notes wear out or become dirty or damaged, depository institutions redeposit them at the 12 Federal Reserve Banks.

Money wears out from handling, and it is sometimes accidentally damaged or destroyed. The average life of a $1 bill, for example, is about 18 months. For a $5 bill, the average life is 15 months; for a $20 bill, 2 years. The $10 bill has about the same life as a $1 bill. The larger bills, $50s and $100s, last longer than the smaller denominations because they don't circulate as often. A $50 bill usually lasts 5 years, and a $100, 8 1/2 years.

Banks send old, worn, torn, or soiled notes to a Federal Reserve Bank to be exchanged for new bills. The Federal Reserve Banks sort the money they receive from commercial banks to determine if it is "fit" or "unfit." Fit (reusable) money is stored in their vaults until it goes out again through the commercial banking system. The Federal Reserve Banks destroy worn-out paper money in shredding machines and burn the shredded paper into a mulch; they return damaged and worn coins to the U.S. Treasury.

Paper money that is mutilated or partially destroyed may be redeemable at full face value. Any badly soiled, dirtied, defaced, disintegrated, limp, torn, or worn-out currency that is clearly more than half the original note can be exchanged at a commercial bank, which processes the note through a Federal Reserve Bank. More seriously damaged notes, those with not clearly more than half the original surface, or those requiring special examination to determine their value, must be sent to the U.S. Treasury for redemption.

Checking Accounts

In the U.S. economy, the supply of money includes more than dollar bills and coins. Many people choose to pay for goods using a check instead of currency. The "money balances" that you have in your checking account can be used to purchase goods and services and to pay debts, or they can be retained for future use. Because checking accounts perform the same functions as currency, we must include checking account balances in our notion of money.

With a checking account, you use checks to withdraw money from the account in which you have deposited it. Therefore, you have quick, convenient, and, if needed, frequent access to your money. Typically, you can make deposits into a checking account as often as you choose. Many institutions allow you to withdraw or deposit funds at an automated teller machine (ATM) and to pay for purchases at stores using your ATM card.

Some checking accounts pay interest; others do not. A regular checking account, frequently called a **demand deposit account,** does not pay interest. The money in the account is available to the account holder "on demand" by writing a check, making a withdrawal, or transferring funds. Another type of checking account is a **negotiable order of withdrawal (NOW) account,** which does pay interest but typically requires a larger minimum balance. Credit unions offer accounts that are similar to checking accounts at other depository institutions but have different names. Credit union members have share draft accounts rather than checking accounts.

Institutions may impose fees on checking accounts, in addition to the charge for the checks you order. Fees vary among institutions. Some institutions charge a maintenance or flat monthly fee regardless of the balance in your account. Other institutions charge a monthly fee if the balance in your account drops below a certain amount. Some charge a fee for every transaction, such as for each check you write or for each withdrawal you make at an ATM. Many institutions impose a combination of these fees.

Although a checking account that pays interest may appear more attractive than one that does not, it is important to look at fees for both types of accounts. Often, checking accounts that pay interest charge higher fees than regular checking accounts, so you could end up paying more in fees than you earn in interest.

economics
IN ACTION

The Dollar Bill

Have you ever stopped to examine the features of the dollar bill, as shown in Figure 14.1? It's more than a piece of paper printed with green and black ink. Take a look at a dollar bill—it probably is a Federal Reserve note. To the left of the portrait of George Washington is a seal of the Federal Reserve Bank that issued the note. The seal bears the name and the code letter of that bank. Which Federal Reserve Bank issued your currency? To the right of the portrait is the Treasury seal, which is printed over the face of each note. The dollar bill also contains the signatures of the treasurer of the United States and the secretary of the Treasury, as well as the expression "legal tender for all debts, public and private."

A serial number appears in the upper-right and lower-left corners of a dollar bill. No two dollar bills have the same serial number. Counterfeiters are often caught when they make batches of a bill bearing the same serial number. Businesses and banks may have lists of dollar bills with certain serial numbers that are known to be counterfeit.

The Great Seal of the United States, adopted in 1782, appears on the back of a dollar bill. The face of the seal,

on the right-hand side of the bill, shows the American bald eagle with wings and claws outstretched. Above the eagle's head is a "glory," or burst of light, containing 13 stars. The number 13 represents the original 13 colonies. The eagle's right claw holds an olive branch with 13 leaves, representing peace, and the left, a bundle of 13 arrows, symbolizing war. The eagle's head is turned toward the olive branch, indicating a desire for peace. The shield (with 13 stripes) covering the eagle's breast symbolizes a united nation. The top of the shield represents Congress; the head of the eagle, the executive branch; and the nine tail feathers, the Supreme Court. A ribbon held in the eagle's beak bears the Latin motto e *pluribus unum* (13 letters), which means "out of many, one."

The back of the Great Seal, on the left-hand side of the dollar bill, depicts a pyramid, a symbol of material strength and endurance. The pyramid is unfinished, symbolizing the nation's striving toward growth and perfection. Above the pyramid, a glory, with an eye inside a triangle, represents the benevolent gaze of God, placing the spiritual above the material. At the top edge is the 13-letter Latin motto *annuit coeptis*, meaning "He has favored our undertakings." The base of the pyramid bears the year 1776 in Roman numerals. Below is the motto *novus ordo seclorum*, meaning "a new order of the ages."

The next time you write a check, take a close look at the electronic codes that appear on the face of the check. Do you know what these numbers stand for? Figure 14.2 gives you the answer.

Special Types of Checks

For most personal financial transactions, a check drawn on a personal checking account is an acceptable form of payment. In certain situations, though, a special type of check that carries a greater guarantee of payment may be needed.

A **certified check** is usually used when it is called for by a legal contract, such as a real estate or automobile sale agreement. Certified checks are considered less risky than personal checks because the bank on which they are drawn certifies that the funds are available to the payee. To certify a check, a bank uses the following procedure: First, a bank officer or other authorized employee verifies the check writer's signature and determines that there are sufficient funds in the checking account to pay

Figure 14.1   The Dollar Bill

the check. Then, the authorized employee signs the check and certifies it by marking, stamping, or perforating it so that it is less likely to be altered. By certifying the check, the bank guarantees payment and becomes liable for the amount certified, and the check writer no longer has access to the funds.

A less expensive alternative to a certified check is a **cashier's check.** The purchaser of a cashier's check does not need to have a checking account. He or she merely goes to the bank, requests a cashier's check for a certain amount, and pays the bank that amount plus a service charge. For some financial transactions, the payee may prefer a cashier's check to a personal check. A cashier's check has a better guarantee of payment because it is drawn by a bank against itself.

For people who do not maintain a checking account or prefer not to make payments with cash, a **money order** often serves the same function as a personal check. Money orders can be purchased at banks, some retail establishments, and the U.S. Postal Service. They are usually issued in smaller amounts and are cheaper than cashier's checks. Often, only the amount is filled in at the time the money order is issued. Until the blanks for the payee's name, the date, and the purchaser's signatures

Figure 14.2   Electronic Codes on a Check

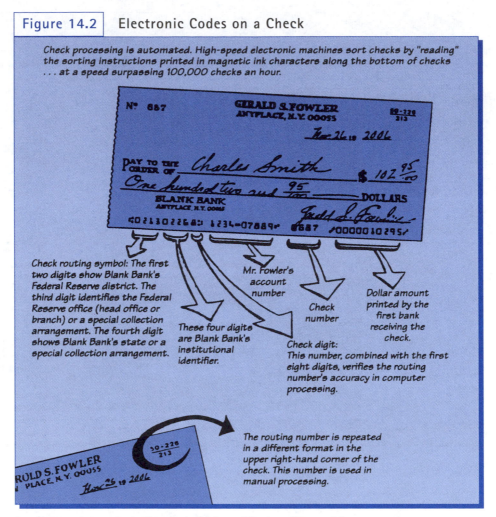

Source: Federal Reserve Bank of New York, *The Story of Checks and Electronic Payment*, 1983, p. 15.

are filled in, the money order is as risky as cash to the purchaser. For this reason, some banks require that the blank spaces be filled in when the money order is issued.

Travelers who want to protect their money against loss or theft can purchase **traveler's checks** through banks and travel companies. Traveler's checks are usually issued in $20, $50, $100, and $500 denominations. The usual cost is the check's face value plus a small percentage. Widely accepted both in the United States and abroad, traveler's checks are nearly as convenient to use as cash. The purchaser of a traveler's check signs the check at the time of purchase and again when it is cashed. This practice protects both the user and the cashing party. The issuing company will replace lost or stolen traveler's checks.

Check Processing and Collection

Each year more than 270 billion checks are processed in the United States. This means that more than 270 million checks are processed every business day. As seen in Figure 14.3, assume that Mrs. Henderson lives in Albany, New York, and conducts her banking with an Albany bank. Suppose that she buys a painting from a Sacramento, California, art dealer. The first place the check goes is to the art dealer's bank, where it is deposited. But the funds may not be immediately available to the art dealer unless Mrs. Henderson and the art dealer use the same bank in which the processing (clearing) of the check is handled internally. In practice, about 30 percent of checks are drawn on and deposited into the same bank.

However, an internally cleared check does not apply to our example. Instead, the art dealer's Sacramento bank will likely desire to verify the check with Mrs. Henderson's Albany bank, the paying bank, before it converts the check value to cash. However, banks do not generally conduct business with each other directly; instead, they go through an "intermediary bank" which serves as a middleman. There are three types of intermediary banks:

- The **Federal Reserve** is the central bank of the United States. Regional branches of the Federal Reserve handle check processing for banks that hold accounts with them, and they charge a fee for their services. Such services include check collection, air transportation of checks to the Federal Reserve Bank, and delivery of checks to paying banks. All financial institutions that

| Figure 14.3 | How the Payments System Works |

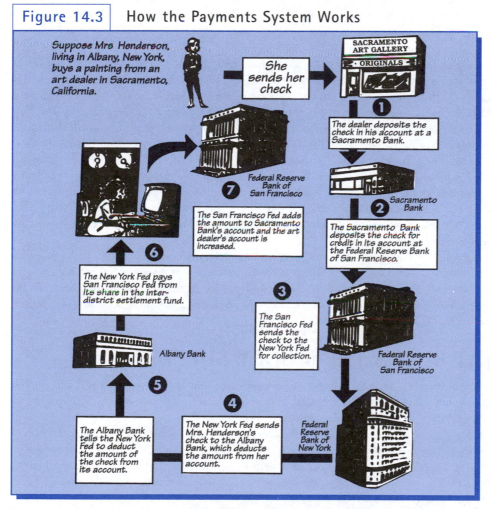

Suppose Mrs. Henderson, living in Albany, New York, buys a painting from an art dealer in Sacramento, California.

She sends her check

SACRAMENTO ART GALLERY • ORIGINALS •

1. The dealer deposits the check in his account at a Sacramento Bank.

Sacramento Bank

2. The Sacramento Bank deposits the check for credit in its account at the Federal Reserve Bank of San Francisco.

Federal Reserve Bank of San Francisco

3. The San Francisco Fed sends the check to the New York Fed for collection.

Federal Reserve Bank of San Francisco

4. The New York Fed sends Mrs. Henderson's check to the Albany Bank, which deducts the amount from her account.

Federal Reserve Bank of New York

5. The Albany Bank tells the New York Fed to deduct the amount of the check from its account.

Albany Bank

6. The New York Fed pays San Francisco Fed from its share in the inter-district settlement fund.

7. The San Francisco Fed adds the amount to Sacramento Bank's account and the art dealer's account is increased.

Federal Reserve Bank of San Francisco

People and organizations move money among themselves by using depository institutions, such as commercial banks, as their transfer mechanism. Depository institutions, in turn, use clearinghouses, correspondent banks, or Federal Reserve Banks as their transfer mechanism. Federal Reserve Banks use the Interdistrict Settlement Fund in Washington, DC, as their transfer mechanism. The fund settles net amounts due between Federal Reserve Banks daily. Let's trace a check through the Federal Reserve System's clearing and collection facilities to see how the Fed links the payments system.

Source: Federal Reserve Bank of New York, *The Story of Checks and Electronic Payment,* 1983, p. 13.

accept deposits can purchase Federal Reserve check collection and payment services. Federal Reserve Banks handle about 27 percent of all checks processed in the United States.

- **Correspondent banks** are banks that form partnerships with other banks in order to exchange checks and payments directly, bypassing the Federal Reserve and its check-processing fee. Outside banks may go through a correspondent bank to exchange checks and payments with one of its partners. For example, Mrs. Henderson's Albany bank and the art dealer's Sacramento bank may form partnerships with Citibank of New York which serves as the correspondent bank.

- Correspondent banks form a **clearinghouse corporation**, in which members exchange checks and payments in bulk, instead of on a check-by-check basis, which can be inefficient when each bank might receive thousands of checks in a day. The clearinghouse banks save up the checks drawn on other members and exchange them on a daily basis. The net payments for these checks are generally settled through Fedwire, an electronic funds transfer system that handles large-scale check settlement between U.S. banks. Correspondent banks and clearinghouse corporations make up the private sector of check clearing, and together they handle about 43 percent of U.S. checks.[3]

Returning to our check-clearing example, suppose that the Sacramento art dealer's bank uses the check-clearing services of the Federal Reserve. Assume that the Sacramento bank deposits Mrs. Henderson's check in its account at the Federal Reserve Bank of San Francisco. The San Francisco Federal Reserve Bank sends the check to the New York Federal Reserve Bank for collection. The New York Federal Reserve Bank then sends Mrs. Henderson's check to the Albany Bank, which deducts the amount from her account. The Albany bank then tells the New York Federal Reserve Bank to deduct the amount of the check from its account. The New York Federal Reserve Bank then pays the San Francisco Federal Reserve Bank from its share in the Interdistrict Settlement Fund of the Federal Reserve which is located in Washington, D.C. The San Francisco Federal Reserve Bank then adds the amount to the Sacramento bank's account and the art dealer's account is increased. These are the steps in the settlement process of a check that is cleared through the Federal Reserve System and are summarized in Figure 14.3.

Although the Federal Reserve is a major processor of checks, the number of checks that it processes has been declining since the mid-1990s. This is because of the use of ATMs and electronic payment methods, such as funds transfers and debit cards, which reduce the need to write paper checks. In the future, the use of checks will likely decrease as electronic payment methods become less expensive and more accessible and familiar to consumers.

WHAT BACKS THE MONEY SUPPLY?

If you ask your friends "What backs our money supply?" you may get answers such as "Gold or silver backs our money." No! Gold and silver were removed from our monetary system decades ago. We must look elsewhere to see what backs our money supply.

Recall that the major components of our money supply—paper currency and checking deposits—are promises to pay, or debts. Paper currency is the circulating debt of the Federal Reserve System, and checking deposits represent the debt of depository institutions. These items have no intrinsic value. A $20 bill is simply a piece of paper; a checking account is an accounting entry; and a 25-cent piece has less value as metal than its face value.

What underlies the value of a $10 bill or a $500 balance in a checking account? Currency and checking accounts are considered money because we widely accept them in return for goods and services. We accept money in exchange because we are confident that others will be willing to accept our money when we spend it. Put simply, money is anything that we generally accept as a medium of exchange.

---

3. Drawn from *When I pay for My Groceries by Check, Where Does That Check Go?* How Stuff Works, Inc., 2001, available at http://www.money.howstuffworks.com.

The law reinforces our confidence in the acceptability of currency. All U.S. currency, including paper money and coins, is designated as **legal tender**—that is, the federal government mandates its acceptance in transactions and requires that dollars be used in the payment of taxes. However, this does not mean that a particular type of currency must always be accepted. For example, a convenience store may legally refuse to accept bills in denominations of more than $20, or an automobile dealer may refuse to be paid only in pennies.

Although the legal tender pledge reinforces the general acceptability of currency, it does not apply to other types of money. For example, the government does not mandate that checks be legal tender. Nevertheless, checking accounts are an important component of the basic money supply. Although checks are a generally accepted medium of exchange, we may legally turn them down as payments for goods and services. Perhaps you have attempted to buy gasoline from an establishment that has a sign next to the cash register saying, "No out-of-town checks!"

MEASURING THE MONEY SUPPLY: THE M1 MONEY SUPPLY

So far in this chapter, we have discussed many forms of money. Let us now consider how the money supply is measured in the United States.

There are two approaches to defining and measuring money: the *narrow* definition of the money supply, which emphasizes the role of money as a *medium of exchange,* and the *broader* definitions of the money supply, which emphasize the role of money as a *temporary store of value.*

Table 14.2 lists the components of the U.S. money supply according to its narrowest definition, the **M1 money supply.** This measure of the money supply includes currency in the hands of the public, demand deposits, other checkable deposits (NOW and share draft accounts), and traveler's checks. M1 is expressed by the following formula:

M1 = Currency in the hands of the public + Demand deposits
+ Other checkable deposits + Traveler's checks

In our definition of money, we include currency only if it is *in the hands of the public.* Some cash is kept in bank vaults and released only when customers withdraw cash from their vaults. Other cash is kept on deposit at a Federal Reserve Bank, which stores the funds for future use. Until this cash is released by banks or a Federal Reserve Bank, it is not considered part of the money supply.

Notice that the components of M1 are highly *liquid* (immediately spendable) money that can be used to finance transactions. Coins and paper currency are as liquid as money can be. Checking

| Table 14.2 | The M1 Measure of the U.S. Money Supply, 2009 |

Component	In Billions of Dollars ($)	Percent of Total
Currency	824.1	51
Demand deposits	435.6	28
Other checkable deposits	309.8	20
Traveler's checks	5.5	1
Total	1,575.0	100

Source: Federal Reserve Board, *Money Stock Measures*, January 26, 2009, available at http://www.federalreserve.gov.

accounts? Banks are legally obligated to make the money in your checking account available to you upon demand. Traveler's checks, too, are immediately spendable money that we widely accept as payment for goods and services.[4]

As seen in Table 14.2, the M1 money supply equaled $1575 billion in 2009. Of this amount, 51 percent was issued by the U.S. Treasury and the Federal Reserve Banks as coins and paper currency; 48 percent was issued by our banking system as checking account money (demand deposits and other checkable deposits), and 1 percent came from traveler's checks. Put simply, checking accounts are a significant component of the M1 money supply.

Why are checking accounts a widely used type of money? First, making large payments by check is convenient. Imagine how much paper money—say, $20 bills—you would need to purchase a new house! Second, checks provide a record of payment, thus making it unnecessary to keep receipts for purchases of goods and services. Finally, checking accounts provide an element of safety. If you lose your checkbook, you can instruct your bank to stop payment on any future checks that are written on your account.

CHECK POINT

1. In the United States, who issues coin? How about paper currency?

2. How do checks clear from one bank to another?

3. What "backs" the U.S. money supply?

4. Identify the components of the U.S. money supply according to the M1 money supply.

HOW YOUR MONEY GROWS OVER TIME: COMPOUND INTEREST

In 1624, Native Americans sold Manhattan Island to Peter Minuit, governor of the Dutch West India Co. He paid for it with beads, cloth, and trinkets worth $24. If, at the end of 1624, the Native Americans had invested their $24 at 8-percent interest and reinvested the principal and accumulated interest, it would have been worth more than $89 trillion by 2000, 376 years later. With $89 trillion in the bank, the Native Americans could have repurchased all of Manhattan for $85 billion to $90 billion and still would have had plenty left over. This example illustrates the incredible power of **compound interest.**

When you add to your savings account at a bank, you receive repayment of the principal amount saved, as well as interest payments. By not spending a dollar today and saving it, you obtain more than a dollar to spend in the future. The interest rate is the percentage of your money that is added to your account each time you are paid interest. Simply put, the interest rate is the reward for saving. To a saver, the key is whether the interest is compounded and how it is compounded.

Suppose that you have just won $10,000 in a lottery. You would like to save the winnings so that you can eventually purchase a house. You place the money in a savings account at your bank, which offers you 5-percent interest each year. After 1 year, you will have a total of $10,500: your original $10,000 plus interest of $500 ($10,000 × 1.05 = $10,500).

---

4. Economists use broader measures of the money supply to account for other financial assets. The M2 measure of the money supply includes all of the components of M1, as well as (small-denomination) time deposits, money market deposit accounts, and money market mutual funds. M3, an even broader measure of the money supply, includes all of the components of M2, plus large time deposits, which are less easily converted into spendable money.

| Figure 14.4 | The Future Value of $10,000 Compounded Annually at an Interest Rate of 5 Percent |

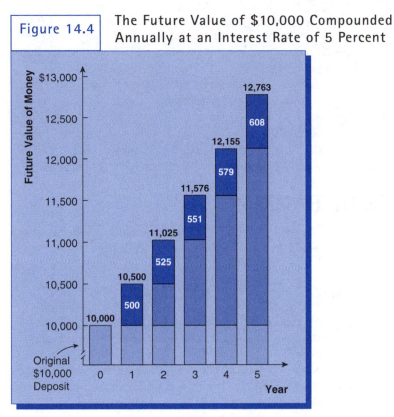

According to the concept of compound interest, a savings deposit earns "interest on interest." This means that interest earned in earlier periods is reinvested so that it earns interest in future periods. In this manner, the amount of interest you earn grows, or compounds. As seen in the figure, a $10,000 savings deposit compounded annually at an interest rate of 5 percent will have a future value of $12,763 at the end of the fifth year.

What happens if you hold your savings deposit for 2 years? If the interest rate remains constant at 5 percent and you reinvest your principal and accumulated interest, you will earn 5-percent interest on your accumulated savings each year. This process of earning interest on the interest, as well as on the principal, is known as *compounding*. At the end of 2 years, you will have $11,025 ($10,500 × 1.05 = $11,025). Notice that your interest increases to $525 in the second year ($11,025 − $10,500 = $525), which is $25 more than the $500 interest that you earned during the first year. Why do you earn more interest during the second year than in the first? Simply because you can now earn interest on the sum of the original principal and the interest you earned in the first year. You are now earning interest on interest, which is the concept of compound interest.

It is easy to use the concept of compound interest to calculate the value of your savings for any number of years. As seen in Figure 14.4, at the end of 3 years, the value of your savings will have grown to $11,576; at the end of 4 years, the value of your savings will have grown to $12,155; and at the end of 5 years, the value of your savings will have grown to $12,763. Indeed, compound interest really does make a difference.

Until now, we have assumed that the compounding period is always annual. However, banks sometimes compound interest on a quarterly or daily basis. What happens to the future value of your money when the compounding period is less than a year? You earn more money faster. The sooner your interest is paid, the sooner you start earning interest on it, and the sooner you realize the benefits of compound interest. For example, if a bank decided to switch from paying interest annually to paying interest daily, the number of compounding periods per year increases from 1 period to 365 periods. Your money grows faster as the number of compounding periods increases. For a given interest rate and identical saving period, the more frequent the compounding, the larger the future value of money. This explains why banks like to advertise daily compounding rather than annual or quarterly compounding. Also, it's not just time that adds to the future value of money—it's also the interest rate. Obviously, a higher interest rate will earn you more money.

Let's reconsider the Native Americans' sale of Manhattan Island to Peter Minuit. If the Native Americans had invested their $24 at 10-percent interest compounded annually at the end of 1624, they would have had about $129 quadrillion by the end of 2004. If they had invested the $24 at a slightly lower interest rate—say, 8 percent—they would have had only $121 trillion by the end of 2004.

THE BUSINESS OF BANKING

A commercial bank is a corporation that seeks to make a profit for its stockholders. How does a bank operate? To understand the business of banking more clearly, we can look at a bank's balance sheet, a tool that is used by accountants.

A Bank's Balance Sheet

A **balance sheet** is a two-column list that shows the financial position of a bank at a specific date. It shows everything of value that the bank owns (assets), the debts that it owes (liabilities), and the amount of the owners' investment (net worth) in the bank. The difference between a bank's assets and liabilities is its net worth. When a bank is established, its owners must place their own funds into the bank. These funds are the bank's initial net worth. If a bank makes profits, its net worth will rise. Conversely, the bank's net worth will fall if it incurs losses.

Table 14.3 shows the consolidated balance sheet for all commercial banks in the United States as of 2008. We will use this picture of the entire banking system to get an idea of what a commercial bank does and the importance of the assets and liabilities to an average or typical commercial bank in this country.

Let us consider the assets of the commercial banking system, which we see on the left side of Table 14.3. First are banks' reserves, which total $872 billion. **Reserves** are deposits that banks have received but have not lent out. Reserves can be kept either in vault cash or as deposits at a Federal Reserve Bank, neither of which earn interest for banks.

Because banks do not earn any interest on their reserves, why do they maintain holdings of reserves? Wouldn't a profit-seeking bank want to hold most of its assets in loans and securities that generate interest income? One reason to hold reserves is that on a particular day, some of a bank's customers might want to withdraw more cash than other customers are depositing. The bank must be able to fulfill its obligation for withdrawals, so it must have cash on hand to meet this commitment. Also, banks are required by law to hold a fraction of their checking deposits as reserves, as will be discussed later.

Next come the $7,204 billion of loans and $2,710 billion of securities owned by the commercial banking system. Loans are IOUs signed by households and businesses. Examples include commercial and industrial loans, real estate loans, and consumer loans for automobiles and other durable goods. Securities are IOUs issued by a government agency or a corporation when it borrows money. Both loans and securities provide interest income for banks. Finally, banks have "other" assets, such as the value of their office buildings and equipment.

On the right side of the balance sheet are banks' liabilities. The major liability is deposits, which equal $7,112 billion and include both checking deposits and a variety of savings deposits and time deposits. Why are deposits considered liabilities? Because bank customers have the right to withdraw funds from their deposit accounts at any time. Until they do, the banks owe them these funds. Another liability is bank borrowings. At a particular point in time, a bank may find that its reserves are inadequate to fulfill the withdrawal of deposits by its customers,

Table 14.3	Consolidated Balance Sheet for All U.S. Commercial Banks, September 2008 (billions of dollars)

Assets		Liabilities and Net Worth	
Cash assets (reserves)	872	Deposits:	7,112
Loans:	7,204	Checking deposits	695
Commercial/ industrial	1,600	Savings/time deposits	6,417
Real estate	3,822	Borrowings	2,624
Consumer	878	All other liabilities	1,204
Other	904	Total liabilities	10,940
Securities:	2,710	Net worth (assets − liabilities)	1,193
All other assets	1,347		
Total assets	12,133		

Source: Federal Reserve, *Assets and Liabilities of Commercial Banks in the U.S.*, March 13, 2009, available at http://www.federalreserve.gov.

and thus they may borrow reserves. A bank may borrow reserves from another bank or from a Federal Reserve Bank.

Also on the right side of the balance sheet is the banks' net worth, $1,193 billion, which represents the difference between assets ($12,133 billion) and liabilities ($10,940 billion). If a bank were to go out of business, selling all of its assets and using the proceeds to pay off all of its liabilities, the excess would go to the bank's stockholders—its owners.

The Reserve Requirement

By law, all banks are required to hold a certain percentage of their checking deposits on reserve either in the form of vault cash or as deposits at the Federal Reserve. Banks are not pleased to make such holdings because vault cash and deposits at the Federal Reserve do not pay interest.

Required reserves represent the minimum amount of vault cash and deposits at the Federal Reserve that a bank must maintain. **Actual reserves** are the amount that a bank is actually holding. If a bank is holding more than the law requires, it has **excess reserves,** which can be used to make loans or purchase government securities. Therefore, actual reserves are the sum of a bank's required and excess reserves, calculated as follows:

$$\text{Actual reserves} = \text{Required reserves} + \text{Excess reserves}$$

For example, U.S. Bank may have $80 million of actual reserves, of which $8 million must be held in required reserves. The remainder, $72 million, is the bank's excess reserves.

The **required reserve ratio** is a specific percentage of checking deposits that must be kept either as vault cash or as deposits at the Federal Reserve. It is established by the Federal Reserve System and directly limits the ability of banks to grant new loans. For example, a required reserve ratio of 10 percent on checking deposits means that a bank must have an amount on reserve equal to 10 percent of the value of the checking deposits it is holding. For example, if Chase Manhattan Bank has $50 million in checking accounts and a 10-percent required reserve ratio, it must maintain at least $5 million in actual reserves ($50,000,000 × 0.10 = $5,000,000).

Figure 14.5	The Process of Money Creation

(a) Wells Fargo Bank

Assets	Liabilities
Required Reserves = $100 Loans = $900	Checking Deposits = $1,000

(b) U.S. Bank

Assets	Liabilities
Required Reserves = $90 Loans = $810	Checking Deposits = $900

(c) Rainier Bank

Assets	Liabilities
Required Reserves = $81 Loans = $729	Checking Deposits = $810

THE PROCESS OF MONEY CREATION

If you were to ask your friends where money comes from, they might have a simple answer: "The government prints it." They might even have toured the U.S. Mint in Philadelphia or Denver and seen pennies and nickels being stamped, or they may have visited the Bureau of Engraving and Printing in Washington, D.C., and seen dollar bills being printed. As we have learned, however, most of our money comes from checking accounts issued by banks rather than from the government. Let us examine how banks create money.

Suppose that you walk into Wells Fargo Bank and deposit $1,000 cash into your checking account. The deposit of cash, which the bank keeps in its vault, results in a $1,000 decrease in the money supply (recall that the currency held by a bank is not part of the economy's money supply). However, the checking account component of the money supply rises by $1,000 because of the deposit. Thus, the total supply of money does not change. However, Wells Fargo Bank will not earn a profit by keeping all of the cash that it receives in its vault. It wants to make loans to the public.

Let's suppose that the required reserve ratio is 10 percent, indicating that a bank must keep 10 percent of its checking deposits as required reserves. Thus, Wells Fargo Bank will keep $100 in required reserves ($1,000 × 0.10 = $100) and make loans of $900. When Wells Fargo Bank makes these loans, the supply of money increases. Why? As a depositor, you still have your checking account of $1,000, but now borrowers hold $900 in their checking accounts. Therefore, the money supply equals $1,900. Figure 14.5(a) shows the change in the balance sheet of Wells Fargo Bank after it has made the loan.

Suppose that Wells Fargo Bank makes a loan to a computer software company that wants to purchase some equipment. The company buys $900 of equipment from another firm, which deposits the check in its account at U.S. Bank. Figure 14.5(b) shows what happens to the balance sheet of U.S. Bank. Its checking deposits increase by $900 as a result of the deposit. The bank must maintain $90 of required reserves ($900 × 0.10 = $90), and it can lend out $810. Suppose that the bank lends $810 to the owner of an espresso stand and opens a checking account for him. In this way, U.S. Bank creates an additional $810 of money. The espresso stand owner then purchases supplies from a wholesaler, who deposits the check in her account at Rainier Bank, which keeps $81 in reserve ($810 × .010 = $81) and makes $729 in loans. Figure 14.5(c) shows what happens to the balance sheet of Rainier Bank.

The process goes on and on. Each time we deposit a check and a bank makes a loan, more money is created. We can determine how much money is eventually created by the banking system by adding the money created by each bank:

Original checking deposit	=	$1,000
Wells Fargo Bank loan	=	900
U.S. Bank loan	=	810
Rainier Bank loan	=	729
	•	
	•	
	•	
Total money supply	=	$10,000

The process of money creation can continue forever. If we add the infinite sequence of numbers in our example, we find that the initial checking deposit of $1,000 results in a total money supply of $10,000. Put simply, the money supply of the banking system can be increased by a *multiple* of the initial checking deposit.[5]

We call the maximum amount of money that the banking system can generate with each dollar of reserves the **money multiplier.** In our example, the initial $1,000 of reserves leads to a money supply totaling $10,000, so the money multiplier is 10.

What determines the size of the money multiplier? The money multiplier is the reciprocal of the required reserve ratio, calculated as follows:

$$\text{Money multiplier} = 1 / \text{Required reserve ratio}$$

In our example, the required reserve ratio is 10 percent, so the money multiplier is 10 (1 / 0.10 = 10). If the required reserve ratio is 20 percent, the money multiplier is 5 (1 / 0.20 = 5).

Notice that the formula tells us the *maximum* amount of money that the banking system can generate with each dollar of reserves. In the real world, however, the ability of the banking system to create money is smaller than the formula suggests. The main reason is that the formula assumes that all loans make their way directly into checking accounts. In reality, people may hold part of their loans as currency. The currency kept in a person's wallet or safe-deposit box remains outside the banking system and cannot be held by banks as reserves from which to make loans. The greater the currency holdings, the smaller the money multiplier.

Using M1 as our measure of the money supply, the actual money multiplier in the United States is about 1.9. This is much smaller than the money multiplier of 5 as described in the example above. The reason the actual money multiplier has such a small value is because people hold sizable amounts of cash: A dollar of currency in circulation, unlike a dollar in bank reserves, does not support multiple dollars of the money supply.

THE FEDERAL DEPOSIT INSURANCE CORPORATION

Indeed, banks can affect the economy through their ability to create money. Therefore, there is much concern about the stability of our banking system. If many depositors lose confidence in a bank's financial position, they may attempt to rapidly withdraw funds from the bank. One source of confidence in our banking system is the Federal Deposit Insurance Corporation.

The **Federal Deposit Insurance Corporation (FDIC)** has been insuring deposits and promoting safe and sound banking practices since 1933. The FDIC sign, posted at insured financial institutions across the country, has become a symbol of confidence. Let us first consider the circumstances that led to the creation of the FDIC.

---

5. The basic money supply (M1) is the sum of currency held by the public plus checking accounts issued by banks. Thus, the *change* in the money supply equals the change in currency held by the public plus the change in checking accounts. Although, in our example of money creation, checking accounts increased by $10,000, the public now has $1,000 less currency because they deposited the currency in the bank. The money supply thus *increased* by $9,000 ($10,000 − $1,000 = $9,000).

The Great Depression of the 1930s caused financial chaos in the United States. More than 9,000 banks closed between the stock market crash of October 1929 and March 1933, when President Franklin D. Roosevelt took office. For all practical purposes, the nation's banking system had shut down completely even before Roosevelt (less than 48 hours after his inauguration) declared a "banking holiday," suspending all banking activities until stability could be restored. Among the actions taken by Congress to bring order to the system was the creation of the FDIC in June 1933. The intent was to provide a federal government guarantee of deposits so that customers' funds, within certain limits, would be safe and available to them on demand. After the introduction of federal deposit insurance, the number of bank failures declined sharply. Since the formation of the FDIC, not one depositor has lost a cent of insured funds because of bank failure.

Bank examinations are the front line of the FDIC's efforts to promote and maintain the safety and soundness of banks. Through bank examinations, the FDIC determines the condition of each bank and obtains a better understanding of the risks that it assumes in insuring the bank's deposits.

The FDIC also provides for a system of national deposit insurance. Until 2008, all types of bank deposits received were insured up to a limit of $100,000; this limit was temporarily increased until December 31, 2013, to $250,000 during the financial crisis of 2008–2010. To protect depositors when an insured bank fails, the FDIC pays depositors up to the 250,000 insurance limit and recovers as much money as possible from the failed institution's assets—primarily loans, real estate, and securities. To help prevent bank failure, the FDIC sometimes arranges a merger between a sound bank and a failing bank; this allows the failing bank to keep its doors open, thus preserving the confidence of the banking public.

This chapter has examined the nature of money and the operation of our banking system. The next chapter will broaden our understanding of these topics by considering the Federal Reserve and monetary policy.

CHECK POINT

1. Identify the major assets and liabilities of a typical commercial bank.

2. How do banks create money? Why does the banking system have a money multiplier?

3. How does the Federal Deposit Insurance Corporation promote stability in the nation's banking system?

Chapter Summary

1. Money is the set of assets in the economy that people use regularly to purchase goods and services from others. Money has three functions in the economy: It is a medium of exchange, a unit of account, and a store of value. These functions distinguish money from other assets such as stocks, bonds, and real estate.

2. Are credit cards money? Not at all! When you use a credit card to make a purchase, you obtain a short-term loan from the financial institution that issued the card. Credit cards are thus a method of postponing payment for a brief period. In shopping for a credit card, it is important to consider features such as the card's annual percentage rate, the grace period, fees such as an over-limit fee or late payment fee, and the annual cost of the card.

3. The basic money supply (M1) in the United States consists of coins, paper money, checking accounts, and traveler's checks. Under federal law, only the Federal Reserve System can issue paper currency, and only the U.S. Treasury can issue coins. Checking account money is created by the banking system.

4. The check collection system in the Untied States is efficient, but the collection process that a check goes through may be complicated. The check processing system is conducted by local clearinghouses, correspondent banks, and the Federal Reserve System's check collection network.

5. The U.S. economy has an array of banks, including commercial banks, savings and loan associations, mutual savings banks, and credit unions. We call these *depository institutions* because they accept deposits from people and provide checking accounts that are part of the money supply.

6. If you save money in a bank, you have alternatives to checking accounts, such as money market deposit accounts, savings accounts, and certificates of deposit. In shopping for an account, it is important to look at features such as the interest rate, the method of interest compounding, the annual percentage yield, the timing of interest payments, and fees.

7. A commercial bank is a corporation that seeks to make a profit for its stockholders. Among the most important assets of a bank are its reserves, loans, and government securities. Deposits and borrowings are a bank's major liabilities.

8. Most of our money comes from checking accounts issued by banks rather than currency. Through the process of lending reserves, banks create money. The money multiplier is used to calculate the maximum amount of money that the banking system can generate with each dollar of reserves. The money multiplier is the reciprocal of the required reserve ratio.

9. The FDIC has been insuring deposits and promoting safe and sound banking practices since 1933. The FDIC insures deposits up to $250,000 at virtually all U.S. banks. Since the formation of the FDIC, not one depositor has lost a cent of insured funds because of bank failure.

Key Terms and Concepts

money (322)

currency (323)

medium of exchange (323)

unit of account (323)

store of value (323)

demand deposit account (327)

negotiable order of withdrawal (NOW) account (327)

certified check (328)

cashier's check (329)

money order (329)

traveler's checks (330)

Federal Reserve (331)

correspondent bank (332)

clearinghouse corporation (332)

legal tender (333)

M1 money supply (333)

compound interest (334)

balance sheet (336)

reserves (336)

required reserves (337)

actual reserves (337)

excess reserves (337)

required reserve ratio (337)

money multiplier (339)

Federal Deposit Insurance Corporation (FDIC) (339)

Self-Test: Multiple-Choice Questions

1. The functions of money include all of the following *except*

   a. medium of exchange.
   b. store of value.
   c. unit of account.
   d. measure of productivity.

2. All of the following are components of the basic (M1) money supply *except*

   a. coins.
   b. paper currency.
   c. demand deposits.
   d. savings deposits.

3. Which type of checking account provides interest income to its holders?

   a. Negotiable order of withdrawal.
   b. Time deposit.
   c. Certificate of deposit.
   d. Demand deposit.

4. A _____ is generally considered to have the *least* guarantee of payment.

   a. personal check
   b. certified check
   c. cashier's check
   d. traveler's check

5. A commercial bank's balance sheet includes all of the following assets *except*

   a. government securities.
   b. loans to business and households.
   c. vault cash and deposits at the Federal Reserve.
   d. checking accounts and savings deposits.

6. Your savings account provides you the most interest income if interest is compounded on a _____ basis.

   a. daily
   b. weekly
   c. monthly
   d. yearly

7. If Tom and Barb Jacobs have individual savings accounts and a joint savings account at Wells Fargo Bank, the maximum amount of FDIC insurance coverage that they can have is

   a. $300,000.
   b. $500,000.
   c. $750,000.
   d. $950,000.

8. If the Federal Reserve sets the required reserve ratio at 20 percent, the money multiplier will be

   a. 0.2.
   b. 5.
   c. 10.
   d. 20.

9. The M1 money supply places primary emphasis on money as a

   a. medium of exchange.
   b. store of value.
   c. standard of debt.
   d. measure of price deflation.

10. The U.S. banking system includes all of the following *except* the

    a. Yakima Federal Savings and Loan Association.
    b. Central Washington University Credit Union.
    c. American National Bank.
    d. New York Stock Exchange.

Answers to Multiple-Choice Questions

1. d   2. d   3. a   4. a   5. d   6. a   7. c   8. b   9. a   10. d

Study Questions and Problems

1. Analyze each of the following assets in terms of their potential use as a medium of exchange, a unit of account, and a store of value. Which use is most appropriate for each asset?

    a. A Visa credit card
    b. A $20 Federal Reserve note
    c. 10 shares of Microsoft stock
    d. A 90-day Treasury bill
    e. A certificate of deposit at a commercial bank
    f. A checking account at a savings and loan association
    g. $20 worth of dimes

2. Table 14.4 shows hypothetical money supply data for the United States. Compute the basic (M1) money supply.

Table 14.4	Hypothetical Money Supply Data (billions of dollars)	
Money market deposit accounts		20
Checking deposits		150
Coin		10
Paper currency		90
Certificates of deposit		25
Traveler's checks		5
Mutual funds		15

3. For a commercial bank, which of the following items represent assets and which represent liabilities?

    a. Certificates of deposit
    b. Borrowings from a Federal Reserve Bank
    c. Bank office equipment
    d. Loans to businesses and households
    e. Holdings of government securities
    f. Checking deposits
    g. Deposits with a Federal Reserve Bank

4. If borrowers take a portion of their loans as cash rather than checkable deposits, what happens to the money multiplier of the commercial banking system?

5. If Jennifer Gray deposits a $100 bill into her checking account, and her bank has a required reserve ratio of 5 percent, how much will the bank's required reserves increase? What happens to excess reserves?

6. Suppose that the Federal Reserve sets the required reserve ratio at 15 percent. If the banking system has $10 million in excess reserves, what amount of checkable deposits can be created?

7. American National Bank has reserves of $100,000 and checking deposits of $500,000. The required reserve ratio is 20 percent. Suppose that households deposit $50,000 cash into their checking deposits at American National Bank, which then adds this amount to its reserves. How much excess reserves does the bank now have?

8. Suppose that the banking system has reserves totaling $50 billion. Also assume that required reserves are 25 percent of checking deposits, banks hold no excess reserves, and households hold no cash. What is the money multiplier?

9. Assume that you take $2,000 cash and deposit it in your bank checking account. If this $2,000 remains in the banking system as reserves and banks hold reserves equal to 20 percent of checking deposits, how much will the total amount of checking deposits in the banking system increase?

10. Table 14.5 shows the hypothetical balance sheet of the Bank of Ohio. Assuming that the required reserve ratio on checkable deposits is 10 percent, complete the following statements:

   a. The Bank of Ohio must maintain required reserves of _____.
   b. The Bank of Ohio has excess reserves in the amount of _____.
   c. The maximum that the Bank of Ohio can increase the money supply by lending is _____. If the Bank of Ohio actually lends the maximum amount that it is able to lend, what will happen to its excess reserves?
   d. Instead, suppose that the balance sheet pertains to the entire commercial banking system. The maximum that the banking system can increase the money supply by lending is _____.

Table 14.5   Balance Sheet of the Bank of Ohio

Assets		Liabilities	
Reserves	$55,000	Checkable deposits	$110,000
Loans	90,000	Savings deposits	75,000
Securities	28,000	Borrowings from other banks	8,000
Other	20,000		

The Federal Reserve and Monetary Policy

Chapter objectives

After reading this chapter, you should be able to:

1. Describe the structure and operation of the Federal Reserve System.

2. Identify the services that the Federal Reserve System provides for the U.S. economy.

3. Explain the purpose and operation of monetary policy.

4. Assess the advantages and disadvantages of monetary policy.

5. Evaluate whether Congress should reduce the independence of the Federal Reserve.

economics IN CONTEXT

In 2008 and 2009, developing gloom lay heavy and thick on the U.S. economy like smog in the air. Consumers, who account for about 70 percent of all economic activity, had lost a significant amount of their wealth as the value of their stocks fell in a sagging market. Increasingly, consumers put off their purchases, causing sales to fall and business profitability to decline. Economists feared that eroding profit expectations would dampen capital spending. Add in slower growth in much of the world economy, and the prospects for U.S. exporters were also looking grim.

To bolster the weakening economy, the Federal Reserve cut its interest rates. Its actions were aimed at Americans like Jim Riley, who owns a small construction firm in Fort Collins, Colorado. Mr. Riley was contemplating starting a new business that wouldn't experience the winter downturns that construction does. He thought about manufacturing new homes using an indoor facility; these homes could then be transported to a building site in any season. By 2009, however, his enthusiasm for the project had dwindled as the economy waned.

Indeed, few issues in economics evoke more emotion than the conduct of monetary policy. Critics maintain that the Federal Reserve System—also known as the Fed—has sometimes destabilized the economy by causing inflation or recession. However, proponents of the Fed argue that it has done a credible job of promoting economic stability. They maintain that severe economic shocks—such as stock market crashes, wars, rising oil prices, and foreign competition—have unsettled the economy, and the Fed has done its best to maintain a stable economy.

In this chapter, we will examine the nature and operation of the Fed. We will begin by considering its structure and how it attempts to control the money supply and interest rates in order to stabilize the economy.

THE FEDERAL RESERVE SYSTEM

The **Federal Reserve System (Fed),** is the central bank of the United States. It was legislated by Congress and signed into law by President Woodrow Wilson in 1913 to provide the nation with a safer, more flexible, and more stable monetary and financial system. All major countries have a central bank whose functions are broadly similar to those of the Fed. These central banks include the Bank of England, the Bank of Canada, and the Bank of Japan.

Before Congress created the Fed, periodic financial panics had plagued the nation. These panics contributed to many bank failures, business bankruptcies, and economic downturns. A particularly severe crisis in 1907 prompted the eventual passage of the Federal Reserve Act in 1913.

Structure of the Federal Reserve System

The Fed's structure was designed by Congress to give it a broad perspective on the economy and on economic activity in all parts of the nation. At the head of its formal organization is the Board of Governors, located in Washington, D.C. The 12 regional Federal Reserve Banks make up the next level. The organization of the Fed also includes the Federal Open Market Committee and three advisory councils. These bodies and other policy-making committees provide additional avenues for regional and private-sector participation in the Fed's activities.

Board of Governors.   The **Board of Governors** administers the Fed. The board consists of seven members who are appointed by the president and confirmed by the Senate to serve 14-year terms of office. Members may serve only one full term, but a member who has been appointed to complete an unexpired term may later be reappointed to a full term. These long terms help insulate the decisions of the board from day-to-day political pressures. The president designates, and the Senate confirms, two members of the Board of Governors to serve as chair and vice chair for 4-year terms. Only one member of the board may be selected from any one of the 12 Federal Reserve districts. In making appointments, the president is directed by law to select a fair representation of the financial, agricultural, industrial, and commercial interests and geographic divisions of the country.

As head of the nation's central bank, the chair appears before Congress to report on Federal Reserve policies, the Federal Reserve System's views about the economy, financial developments, and other matters. The chair also meets from time to time with the president of the United States and regularly confers with the secretary of the Treasury and the chair of the Council of Economic Advisers.

Board members usually meet several times a week. As they carry out their duties, members of the board routinely confer with officials of other government agencies, representatives of banking industry groups, officials of the central banks of other countries, members of Congress, and academicians.

Federal Open Market Committee.   The **Federal Open Market Committee (FOMC)** is the Fed's most important policy-making body for controlling the growth of the money supply. To do so, the FOMC oversees the purchase and sale of U.S. government securities. These operations are conducted by the Federal Reserve Bank of New York, which serves as the agent for the FOMC. The FOMC members include the seven members of the Board of Governors, the president of the Federal Reserve Bank of New York, and four other Reserve Bank presidents who serve 1-year terms on a rotating basis.

The Reserve Banks.   The day-to-day operations of the Fed are carried out by the 12 Federal Reserve Banks. As seen in Figure 15.1, each of the Federal Reserve Banks serves a certain region of

| Figure 15.1 | The 12 Federal Reserve Districts |

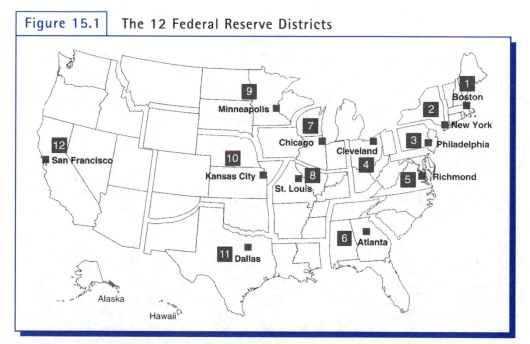

The day-to-day operations of the Federal Reserve System are carried out by the 12 Federal Reserve Banks, which are located throughout the United States.

the country and is named for the location of its headquarters—Atlanta, Boston, Chicago, Cleveland, Dallas, Kansas City, Minneapolis, New York, Philadelphia, Richmond, San Francisco, and St. Louis. Also, there are 25 Federal Reserve branch banks located throughout the country.

Although the Federal Reserve Banks are not motivated by profit, they do earn substantial revenues on the Fed's large holdings of income-producing government securities acquired in the process of implementing monetary policy. Also, the Federal Reserve Banks charge financial institutions for their check collection and other services. Almost all of these revenues are turned over to the U.S. Treasury. Moreover, the Fed receives no funding from the government.

The Federal Reserve Banks are owned by the banks that are members of the Federal Reserve System. That is, member banks are the stockholders of the Fed. Each Federal Reserve Bank has its own board of nine directors chosen from outside the Bank.

Finally, at the bottom of the Fed's organizational structure is the U.S. banking system, which consists of commercial banks, mutual savings banks, savings and loan associations, and credit unions.

The Independence of the Fed

Congress structured the Fed so that it would be independent within the government—that is, although the Fed is accountable to Congress, it is insulated from day-to-day political pressures. This reflects the conviction that the people who control the country's money supply should be independent of the people who make the government's spending decisions. Most studies of central bank independence rank the Fed among the most independent in the world. Three structural features make the Fed independent: the appointment procedure for governors, the appointment procedure for Reserve Bank presidents, and funding.

economics
IN ACTION

Ben Bernanke: Chairman of the Federal Reserve

In 2006, Ben Bernanke (pronounced ber-NAN-kee) succeeded Alan Greenspan as chairman of the Board of Governors of the Federal Reserve System. The son of a pharmacist and a schoolteacher, Bernanke was born in Augusta, Georgia, in 1953 and became an academic star. In the sixth grade, he won the state spelling bee but missed higher acclaim when he misspelled the word "edelweiss," a flower. While in high school, Bernanke taught himself calculus and scored 1590 out of a possible 1600 on his SAT exam.

Bernanke worked his way through college as a waiter at South of the Border restaurant during his summer breaks. After graduating summa cum laude in economic history from Harvard University, he continued his studies at the Massachusetts Institute of Technology, where he received his doctorate in economics in 1979. He went on to become an economics professor at Stanford University and chaired the economics department at Princeton University. Bernanke eventually became a member of the Fed's Board of Governors, chairman of the Council of Economic Advisers, and chairman of the Fed's Board of Governors.

Bernanke has written numerous books and articles on macroeconomics and monetary policy. He is a proponent of inflation targeting—the idea that central banks should set a target for inflation, around 2 percent, and stick with it. Bernanke also believes that it is difficult for central banks to prevent asset bubbles, such as house price booms, from occurring.

Bernanke is considered to be a quiet person with a quick wit. He was a Boston Red Sox fan until he adopted the Washington Nationals as his hometown baseball team. He is married to Spanish instructor Anna Bernanke, with whom he has 2 children.

The 7 members of the Board of Governors are appointed by the president of the United States and confirmed by the Senate. The Fed's independence derives from several factors. First, the appointments are staggered to reduce the chance that a single U.S. president could "stack" the board with appointees. Second, their terms of office are 14 years—much longer than elected officials' terms.

Also, each Reserve Bank president is appointed to a 5-year term by that Bank's board of directors, subject to final approval by the Board of Governors. This procedure adds to the Fed's independence because the directors of each Reserve Bank are not chosen by politicians but are selected to represent a cross-section of interests within the region—including banks, businesses, labor, and the public.

Finally, the Fed is structured to be self-sufficient in the sense that it meets its operating expenses primarily from the interest earnings on its holdings of government securities. Thus, it is independent of congressional decisions about appropriations.

Although the Fed is independent of congressional funding and administrative control, it is ultimately accountable to Congress and comes under government audit and review. The chair, other governors, and Reserve Bank presidents report regularly to Congress on monetary policy and regulatory policy, and they meet with government officials to discuss the economic programs of the Federal Reserve and the federal government.

The Functions of the Federal Reserve System

The Federal Reserve, as the overseer of the nation's monetary system, has a variety of important duties. Some of the important functions of the Fed include:

- Controlling the money supply through policies that affect the quantity of reserves that banks use to make loans.

- Acting as lender of last resort to banks in order to forestall financial panics.

- Regulating and supervising banks in order to maintain financial responsibility.

- Supplying services to banks such as check processing and electronic transfers of funds.

- Supplying services to the government, such as the transportation of currency, the issuance and redemption of Treasury securities, and the maintenance of the Treasury's checking account.

Although some of these functions are routine activities or have a service aspect, the major task of the Fed is to manage the nation's money supply in order to stabilize the economy. Let us consider the nature and operation of monetary policy.

C H E C K   P O I N T

1. What is the Fed, and why was it established?

2. Describe the organizational structure of the Fed.

3. Which committee is the Fed's most important policy-making body for controlling the growth of the money supply?

4. What are the major functions of the Fed?

MONETARY POLICY

Monetary policy consists of changing the economy's money supply in order to help the economy achieve maximum output and employment, as well as stable prices. To carry out monetary policy, the

Fed acts as the economy's "money manager." It tries to balance the flow of money and credit with the needs of the economy. Too much money in the economy can result in inflation; too little can stifle economic activity. The Fed seeks to strike a balance between these two extremes.

To balance the flow of money, the Fed influences the ability of banks to create checking account money through loans. This is accomplished by increasing or decreasing the volume of bank reserves. As we will see, by adding to bank reserves, the Fed can stimulate an increase in the money supply; by letting bank reserves fall, the Fed can induce a reduction in the money supply.

The Fed uses several important policy instruments to influence bank reserves and the money supply: open market operations, the discount rate, and the reserve requirement. Let us examine each of these policy tools.

Open Market Operations

Open market operations are the most useful and important of the Fed's policy tools. They refer to the purchase or sale of securities by the Fed. When the Fed conducts an open market operation, it makes a transaction with a bank or some other business or individual, but it does not effect a transaction directly with the federal government.

Each purchase or sale of securities by the Fed directly affects the volume of reserves in the banking system and, in the process, the economy as a whole. When the Fed wants to *increase* the flow of money and credit, it *buys* government securities from banks and businesses; when it wants to *restrict* the flow of money and credit, it *sells* government securities.

Open market operations occur largely through auctions in which security dealers are asked to submit bids to buy or offers to sell securities of the type and maturity that the Fed has elected to sell or to buy. The dealers' bids or offers are arranged according to price, and the Fed accepts amounts bid or offered in sequence, taking the highest prices bid for its sales and the lowest prices offered for its purchases, until the desired size of the whole transaction is reached.

The Fed's purchase of government securities can be illustrated by using balance sheets. Referring to Figure 15.2, suppose the Fed buys $10 million of securities from U.S. Bank. The Fed pays for the securities by increasing U.S. Bank's deposits at the Fed—its reserves—by $10 million. U.S. Bank's excess reserves increase by the full amount of the transaction.[1] With more excess reserves, it can make more loans and increase its checking deposits.

The process does not stop here. As deposit holders spend their newly acquired funds, the deposits move to other banks. These institutions set aside part of their new funds as reserves to back their new deposits, but they can lend the remainder. The resulting loans create additional new deposits, which

| Figure 15.2 | Fed Open Market Purchases of Securities Directly from a Commercial Bank |

Federal Reserve		**U.S. Bank**	
Assets	**Liabilities**	**Assets**	**Liabilities**
Government Securities + $10 million	Deposits of U.S. Bank + $10 million	Reserves with Fed + $10 million	
		Government Securities − $10 million	

When the Fed buys securities from a bank, it pays for the securities by increasing the bank's deposits at the Fed (its reserves). The bank's excess reserves increase by the full amount of the transaction. With more excess reserves, the bank can make more loans and increase its checking deposits.

---

1. Because this transaction does not affect U.S. Bank's checking deposits, against which the reserve requirement applies, its required reserves do not change. As a result, the bank's total reserves and excess reserves change by the same amount.

move, in part, to other depository institutions, expanding loans and deposits in the same manner. By the time the process ends, checking deposits usually will have risen by several times the amount of reserves created by the Fed's original action. Put simply, a purchase of securities by the Fed results in a multiple expansion of the money supply.

We saw in Chapter 14 that a change in bank reserves results in a multiplied change in the money supply. If the required reserve ratio is 20 percent, the $10 million purchase of securities from banks will result in a $50 million increase in the economy's money supply. Virtually the same result can be achieved if the Fed purchases securities from businesses or individuals, as these sellers generally deposit the money received from the sale of securities in banks. Conversely, if the Fed wanted to decrease the money supply, it would sell securities to banks, businesses, or individuals.

The main advantage of open market operations is flexibility: The Fed can purchase or sell government securities in large or small amounts. Also, open market operations have a speedy effect on bank reserves. As a result, open market operations are the main instrument of monetary policy.

As we have learned, the Federal Open Market Committee oversees the purchase and sale of U.S. government securities. The FOMC meets about every 6 weeks, more often if necessary, to establish policy. The FOMC meetings generally are divided into four parts: a review of recent actions by the managers of the Fed accounts, a discussion of general economic conditions, a discussion of financial conditions and monetary policy alternatives, and finally, a vote on monetary policy by FOMC members. Discussion is quite free, and often there is considerable diversity of opinion. Twice each year, in accordance with the law, the FOMC establishes its long-term goals for monetary policy and reports them to Congress.

Between meetings, the various members of the FOMC stay in touch through written and electronic correspondence. Moreover, an FOMC member talks daily with the Federal Reserve Bank of New York, which carries out the buying and selling of government securities. Telephone meetings of the entire FOMC may be called on very short notice, if necessary, and any member is free to object at any time to the manner in which the New York Bank is carrying out the instructions of the FOMC.

economics
IN ACTION

The Federal Funds Rate

Banks such as Bank of America actively trade reserves held at the Federal Reserve among themselves. This market for reserves is called the federal funds market. Banks with surplus balances in their accounts transfer reserves to those needing to boost their balances.

Typically, a federal funds transaction takes the form of an overnight loan. Arrangements are agreed upon by telephone between the lending bank and the borrowing bank and confirmed later by mail. The actual transfer of the reserves is normally accomplished by a phone call from the lending bank to the Federal Reserve Bank, instructing the latter to transfer the agreed-upon amount from its reserve account to that of the borrower. Generally, the Federal Reserve Bank will reverse the transaction on the following day.

The Federal Reserve focuses monetary policy on the interest rate that it can best influence: the federal funds rate. The Federal Reserve targets the federal funds rate by controlling the supply of reserves supplied to the federal funds market. For example, an increase in the amount of reserves supplied to the federal funds market causes the funds rate to fall; a decrease in the supply of reserves raises that rate. Indeed, the federal funds rate closely reflects the basic supply and demand conditions in the market for bank reserves that are influenced by the Fed's monetary policies. Therefore, analysts pay close attention to the federal funds rate for signals of changes in monetary policy.

The Discount Rate

Another policy tool of the Fed is the **discount rate**—the rate that Federal Reserve Banks charge for loans to banks. An important purpose of the Fed is to serve as a "lender of last resort" to banks that are in need. By lending funds to banks through its **discount window,** the Fed can help protect the safety and soundness of the nation's financial system.[2]

Financially sound banks can borrow from the Fed with few restrictions. Such loans are often made to banks that experience unexpected withdrawals of deposits or spikes in loan demand. However, the Fed expects that banks will not rely on the discount window as a regular source of funding. Discount window loans can also be made to help troubled banks that are on the verge of bankruptcy. The Fed closely monitors such loans, and troubled banks must demonstrate that they are conforming to the Fed's regulatory requirements.

Changes in the discount rate are initiated by the individual Federal Reserve Banks and must be approved by the Board of Governors. This coordination generally results in almost simultaneous changes at all 12 Federal Reserve Banks.

Discount rate changes have important effects on bank credit conditions. An increase in the discount rate, for example, makes it more costly for banks to borrow from Federal Reserve Banks. The higher cost may encourage banks to obtain funds by selling government securities rather than using the discount window. Also, it may force banks to screen their customers' loan applications more carefully and slow the growth of their loans. Thus, if the Fed raises the discount rate, banks are discouraged from borrowing reserves because borrowing becomes more costly. Conversely, lowering the discount rate induces banks to borrow additional reserves.

In principle, the Fed can use the discount rate as a tool of monetary policy, *reducing* the discount rate to *increase* bank reserves and the money supply and *increasing* the discount rate to *decrease* bank reserves and the money supply. In practice, changes in the discount rate have only minor effects on bank borrowing and the money supply. This is because the Fed expects that banks will not rely on the discount window as a regular source of funding.

The Reserve Requirement

Changing reserve requirements can also affect bank lending and the money supply. Recall that banks are required to maintain a fraction of their checking deposits in reserve, either as cash in their vaults or as deposits at the Federal Reserve. This fraction is known as the *required reserve ratio,* and it is applied to a bank's total checking deposit liabilities to determine the dollar amount of reserve assets that must be held. For example, a bank whose depositors own checking accounts equal to $100 million would need to have cash plus reserve accounts at the Fed equal to $10 million if the required reserve ratio were 10 percent.

Table 15.1 shows the required reserve ratios of banks as of 2009. Notice that required reserve ratios are structured to bear relatively less heavily on smaller banks than on larger banks. To provide banks with flexibility in meeting their reserve requirements, the Federal Reserve stipulates that banks must hold an average amount of reserves over a period of only 2 weeks rather than a specific amount on each day. Also, required reserve ratios pertain only to checking deposits rather than to savings time deposits.

As we learned in Chapter 14, the ability of the banking system to create checking deposit money is dependent on the required reserve ratio. A required reserve ratio of 10 percent requires a bank that receives a $100 deposit to maintain $10 in required reserves and thus lend out only $90 of that deposit. If the borrower then writes a check to someone who deposits the $90, the bank receiving that deposit

---

2. Banks once borrowed from Federal Reserve Banks by bringing securities and other asset documents to a teller's cage, or "window." The amount loaned was equal to the face value of the security, minus a "discount." Today, banks still borrow from Federal Reserve Banks. However, the term "discount window" is simply an expression for Fed loans that are repaid with interest at maturity, arranged by telephone, and recorded along with pledged collateral such as U.S. government securities.

Table 15.1	Required Reserve Ratios of the Fed

Type of Deposit	Required Reserve Ratio (percent)
Checking deposit	
$0 million–$10.3 million	0
$7.8 million–$44.4 million	3
More than $44.4 million	10
Savings and time deposits	No required reserve ratio

Source: Federal Reserve Board, Reserve Requirements, January 2009, available at http://www.federalreserve.gov.

will receive $90 when the check clears through the system. It can then lend $81 and must keep $9 in reserve. As the process continues, the banking system expands the initial deposit of $100 to a maximum of $1,000 ($100 + $90 + $81 + $72.90 + . . . = $1,000). If the required reserve ratio were 20 percent, the banking system would be able to expand the initial $100 deposit into a maximum of $500 ($100 + $80 + $64 + $51.20 +... = $500). Therefore, a *lower* required reserve ratio should result in an *increase* in the money supply; a *higher* required reserve ratio should result in a *decrease* in the money supply.

In principle, changes in required reserve ratios can be a useful tool of monetary policy. However, required reserve ratios currently play a relatively limited role in money creation in the United States. Why? Because even small changes in the required reserve ratio can substantially affect required reserves; adjustments to required reserve ratios are not well suited to the day-to-day implementation of monetary policy. Also, because required reserve ratios are an important factor in banks' business calculations, frequent changes in them would unnecessarily complicate these institutions' financial planning. Therefore, the Fed changes required reserve ratios only infrequently.

Term Auction Facility

Another Fed tool for changing bank reserves is its **term auction facility** (**TAF**). This tool was introduced in December 2007 in response to the global financial crisis. The inability of traditional monetary tools to calm financial markets resulted in the Fed adopting its TAF, and several other tools, to fill perceived gaps between open market operations and the discount window.

During normal market conditions, the Fed has discouraged banks from borrowing at the discount window on a routine basis, believing that banks should be able to meet their normal reserve needs through borrowing from other banks in the **federal funds market**. Borrowing from the Fed is therefore seen by a bank's stockholders and lenders as a sign of financial weakness. This perception of weakness could be very damaging to the reputation of a bank and could spark a crisis of confidence that would result in a run on the bank's deposits. During the financial crisis of 2007–2009, the Fed found the discount window a relatively ineffective way to deal with liquidity problems because many banks were reluctant to borrow from the Fed.

Under the TAF, the Fed auctions reserves off twice a month at which generally financially sound banks can bid for the right to borrow reserves for a period of 28 days. In contrast to the Fed's discount window, the total amount of reserves available at any TAF auction is determined and announced in advance by the Fed, and the rate is set in a competitive process among the eligible banks, so those banks with the highest bid rates receive the funds. Thus, the rate charged for borrowing can vary from auction to auction depending on overall demand for reserves relative to the amount being auctioned. Bids at each auction are subject to a minimum bid rate that is equal to the market's expectation of the average **federal funds rate** over that month. Also, limits are imposed on how much of the available reserves a particular bank can bid for in the auction in order to ensure that the reserves are be distributed across a number of institutions.

One advantage of an auction format is that banks can approach the Fed collectively rather than individually and obtain funds. Because banks generally attach less of a stigma of financial weakness to auctions than to traditional discount window borrowing, they have been more willing to come to the Fed for assistance during financial emergency. In this manner, the TAF is designed to improve liquidity by making it easier for sound banks to borrow when economic downturn occurs.

The TAF program was announced as a temporary program, with no fixed expiration date, that could be made permanent after assessment. It remains to be seen if it will become a permanent program of the Fed.

SHIFTING AGGREGATE DEMAND

Let us now examine the economic effects of monetary policy. In the short run, when prices are temporarily fixed, the Fed has the ability to affect the level of interest rates in the economy. When the Fed increases the money supply to reduce interest rates, aggregate demand increases, which results in an increase in output and employment. Conversely, a decrease in the money supply that increases interest rates will reduce aggregate demand, output, and employment. In the long run, however, a change in the money supply by the Fed affects only prices and not the level of output and employment. Using Figure 15.3, we will examine the sequence of events that occurs when the Fed conducts monetary policy.

| Figure 15.3 | The Effects of Monetary Policy on the Economy |

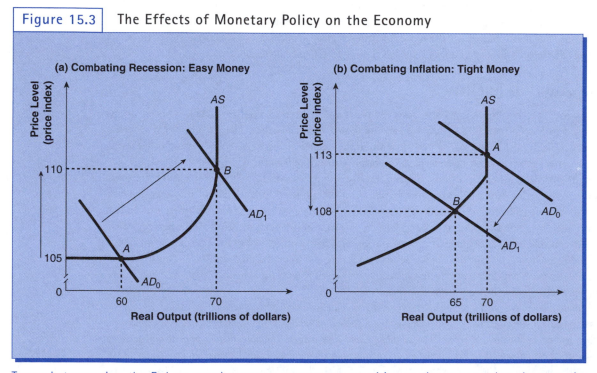

To combat recession, the Fed can purchase more government securities on the open market, decrease the discount rate, or reduce reserve requirements. This results in an increase in bank reserves. Banks will attempt to use the extra reserves to make more loans to businesses and households, thus increasing aggregate demand and the level of economic activity.

Expansionary Policy

Suppose that the economy is in recession, producing less than its full-employment potential. This situation is seen in Figure 15.3(a), where the equilibrium level of output is $60 trillion. The goal of the Fed in this situation is to stimulate the economy, increasing the level of output to $70 trillion.

We learned in Chapter 13 that fiscal policy can help promote the desired expansion. If the government were to reduce taxes, households would have more income to spend on consumption, and the aggregate demand would shift to the right. Similarly, an increase in government expenditures would also shift the aggregate demand curve to the right.

Monetary policy may also be used to shift aggregate demand. To combat recession, the Fed would adopt an *expansionary* (easy) monetary policy by *purchasing* more government securities on the open market, *decreasing* the discount rate, or *reducing* reserve requirements. As a result, bank reserves will increase. In turn, banks will attempt to use the extra reserves to make more loans. By offering lower interest rates, banks can encourage people to borrow additional money to purchase goods that are sensitive to interest cost, such as residential housing, automobiles, and large household appliances. Lower interest rates will also stimulate the demand for business investment in equipment and factories. In this manner, the expansionary monetary policy causes a rightward shift in the aggregate demand curve. In Figure 15.3(a), as aggregate demand increases from AD_0 to AD_1, the economy moves to the full-employment level of output. Table 15.2 shows the strategy for using the Fed's monetary tools for combating recession (inflation).

Although the short-run effect of the expansionary monetary policy will be to stimulate output and employment, the action also has important long-term effects. In the long run, an expansionary monetary policy may result in increased expectations of inflation, which cause higher long-term interest rates, as well as higher rates of inflation caused by an acceleration in the growth of the money supply. These effects may persist for many years and may have a greater effect on the economy than the initial effects of the Fed's action.

Restrictive Policy

Monetary policy can also be used to combat demand-pull inflation. Recall that demand-pull inflation occurs when buyers' demand for goods and services outpace sellers' capacity to supply them, thus forcing up prices on the goods and services that are available.

The objective of monetary policy in this situation is to decrease aggregate demand. Thus, the Fed will initiate a *restrictive* (tight) monetary policy by *selling* government securities on the open market, *raising* the discount rate, or *increasing* reserve requirements. All of these actions will decrease bank reserves, thereby driving interest rates upward. The combination of a smaller supply of loanable funds and higher interest rates will reduce consumption and investment spending. As seen in Figure 15.3(b), the aggregate demand curve will shift to the left, eliminating the excess spending and demand-pull inflation.[3]

When the Fed lowers the rate of growth in the money supply, the intended outcome is price stability, a long-run objective. Yet what are the short-term consequences of this action? In the

Table 15.2	Using Monetary Policy to Combat Recession or Inflation		
Economic Problem/Policy	Open Market Operations	Discount Rate	Reserve Requirement
Recession (easy money)	Buy securities	Decrease	Decrease
Inflation (tight money)	Sell securities	Increase	Increase

3. In the real world, the objective of tight money is to prevent inflation—that is, to halt further increases in the price level.

economics
IN ACTION

What Does a Quarter-Point Decrease in Interest Mean?

In 2001–2002, the Fed reduced interest rates 12 times in order to bolster the weakening economy. These reductions ranged from one-quarter of a percentage point to one-half of a percentage point at a time. How would a measly quarter of a percentage point decrease in interest rates bolster the economy?

In an economy built on credit, a decrease in borrowing costs can have an immediate and pronounced economic effect. Housing provides an illustration, as it is quickly affected by changes in interest rates. Homes are generally built with borrowed money; they are purchased with mortgages. Their sale, therefore, depends on the availability and price of borrowed money.

About two-thirds of American households own their homes. Those with fixed-rate mortgages, about 70 percent of households in 2002, are not affected by interest-rate decreases. However, the remaining 30 percent of households with adjustable-rate mortgages are affected. That small decrease in interest rates by the Fed could translate into one-quarter of a percentage point reduction on many mortgages with adjustable rates. For some, the lower rates could begin within weeks following a rate change by the Fed.

A quarter-point decrease on a $100,000 adjustable-rate mortgage might reduce the interest rate from 6.5 percent to 6.25 percent, reducing the monthly payment by $25, or $300 a year out of pocket. On a $150,000 mortgage, the cost reduction would be about $450 a year. This money could be spent on other goods, such as electronics, clothing, and transportation.

The effect on housing construction could also be immediate, prompting builders to increase their

commitments because of money costs or availability. Also, homeowners might increase their remodeling and repairs, a $115 billion per year business in 2002. Because of the lower rates, the National Association of Realtors estimates that perhaps 50,000 additional home sales could occur within 18 months of the Fed's action. At an average 2002 price of $145,000, that's about $7 billion. The impact on new single-family sales could be equal or greater. Assuming that it is equal—50,000 units—it would mean another $12 billion or so in additional transactions, as the average new-home price in 2002 was about $260,000.

Besides increasing single-family sales, a reduction in interest rates stimulates business in several sectors of the economy. For example, housing construction is a $275 billion per year industry, one the National Association of Home Builders describes as "a vital sector of local, state and national economies, creating jobs and generating taxes and wages." Based on its estimates, the construction of 50,000 single-family houses would generate 122,400 jobs in construction and construction-related industries; $4 billion in wages; and $800 million in federal, state, and local tax revenues and fees. Moreover, the association says, in the first 12 months after buying a newly built home, owners spend an average of $7,500 on furnishings, decorations, and improvements. Buyers of existing homes spend $2,500.

The effects spread widely, from local masons, plumbers, and carpenters to retailers, distributors, manufacturers, and suppliers of raw materials—to distant lumber producers and paint makers and to producers of electrical wiring, carpeting, and shingles. Indeed, a modest decrease in interest rates can have a pronounced effect on the economy.

Sources: National Association of Home Builders, *Economic and Housing Data,* available at http://www.nahb.com/facts/. See also National Association of Realtors, available at httjp://www.realtor.org.

short run, a decrease in the growth rate of the money supply causes a decline in aggregate demand and thus a fall in output and employment. This is why the Fed may be severely criticized when it attempts to combat inflation: Nobody wants to have his business shut down or be thrown out of work as a result of a restrictive monetary policy. Over time, however, price stability contributes to low interest rates and increases the confidence of consumers, savers, and investors, and thus it tends to promote economic expansion. Therefore, the Fed must consider whether the short-run side effects of combating inflation, which are adverse, are outweighed by the long-run benefits of price stability.

For example, in the early 1980s, the Fed successfully used a restrictive monetary policy to fight double-digit inflation. The Fed sold securities on the open market to reduce reserves in the banking system so as to increase the interest rate and slow the growth of borrowing and spending. As a result, short-term interest rates spiked to about 16 percent. Tight monetary policy helped bring inflation down from 13.5 percent in 1980 to 3.2 percent 3 years later, thus building the Fed's credibility as an inflation fighter. Lowering the inflation rate, however, was not painless. By decreasing the money supply, the Fed contributed to the 1981–1982 recession, during which the unemployment rate rose to 9.7 percent, the highest level since the Great Depression. Indeed, millions of unemployed Americans suffered as the economy moved toward price stability.

THE FEDERAL RESERVE AND ECONOMIC STABILIZATION

Economists generally view monetary policy as the first line of defense against economic instability, be it recession or inflation. This is because the Federal Reserve can alter monetary policy quickly in response to changes in the economy. Because most recessions last for only a few quarters, the timeliness of the response of monetary policy is crucial. In some cases, however, monetary policy may be insufficient to stabilize the economy, and thus exists the need for fiscal policy. Let us consider some examples of how the Federal Reserve has attempted to stabilize the economy.

The Recession of 2007–2009

Following six years of continuous expansion, the U.S. economy entered a recession at the end of 2007. The immediate cause of the recession was a collapse of the financial system due to the downward turn of the housing cycle and the rise in delinquencies on mortgages which resulted in substantial losses for many banks. Breakdowns in lending regulations and oversight, increased reliance on complex financial instruments that proved fragile under stress, and excessive risk taking by home buyers and bank lenders contributed to the financial crisis. Also, the Fed may have nurtured this problem. Beginning in 2001, the Fed cut interest rates to stimulate growth. With interest rates so low, many people felt mortgages were affordable and rushed to purchase homes that they could not afford. The Fed never saw the housing market as an overvalued asset bubble and thus did nothing to prevent it. Because many banks also made risky gambles on the values of mortgages, many lost enough money to be close to failure, so people no longer trusted banks. This further harmed the economy because it reduced the credit available, and the expectation of a severe recession and declining profits caused the stock market to crash. Loss of confidence in the economy caused decreases in consumption and investment which resulted in declining aggregate demand and economic contraction. Simply put, policy makers were confronted by two major economic problems: a collapse of the financial system and a downturn in the economy at large.

As the crisis worsened throughout 2008 and 2009, the Fed took extraordinary steps to stabilize the economy. For example, the Fed injected hundreds of billions of dollars in new liquidity into the banking system to prevent the failure of several large, interconnected banks. To provide liquidity to businesses and households, the Fed initiated measures to reduce interest rates so as to make loans for mortgages and business investment more affordable. Moreover, the Federal Deposit Insurance Corporation temporarily increased the deposit insurance limit from $100,000 to $250,000 to provide greater confidence in the banking system.

Figure 15.4 illustrates this situation. Initially, the economy was at point A, with output equaling, say, $92 trillion in 2008. The Fed worried that if it refrained from action, decreases in consumption and investment would cause the aggregate demand curve to decrease from AD_0 to AD_2; this would

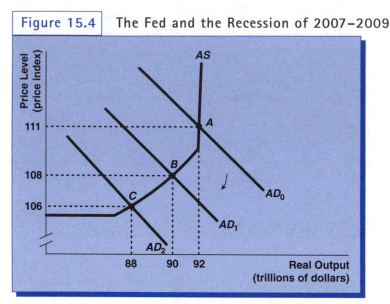

Figure 15.4   The Fed and the Recession of 2007–2009

To combat the recession, the Fed initiated an expansionary monetary policy. Although the policy could not eliminate the recession, it made it less severe. Because of the expansionary policy, the economy moved from *A* to *B* rather than from *A* to *C*, and the decline in output was smaller.

move the economy to equilibrium point *C*, where output equals, say, $88 trillion. When the Fed enacted an expansionary monetary policy, aggregate demand instead fell to AD_1, and the decline in output was smaller. Although the Fed's aggressive monetary policy could not completely offset the recession, it reduced its depth. However, policy makers felt that monetary policy by itself was insufficient to prevent the economy from undergoing sizable contraction. Therefore, expansionary fiscal policies, consisting of increased government expenditures and tax cuts, were initiated to supplement monetary policy's effort to bolster aggregate demand.

But what about the effect of the Fed's actions on the price level? Here, we must realize that there is a discrepancy between what Figure 15.4 shows, and what actually occurred. According to the figure, the price level should decline following a decrease in aggregate demand. During the 2007–2009 recession, however, prices actually rose. The reason is that inflation tends to have momentum: When inflation has been increasing at some rate for a period of time then, left alone, it will proceed at that same rate. Although prices rose during that period, the decrease in aggregate demand moderated their rate of increase, as the model of aggregate demand and aggregate supply would suggest.

2001 Attack on America

Besides combating recession and inflation, the Fed also attempts to stabilize the economy during times of national emergency. Consider how the Fed defended the U.S. financial system following the terrorist attacks on the United States in 2001.

It was a day like no other in U.S. history. September 11, 2001, marked the end of American global innocence, the onset of recession, and perhaps even the demise of the country's anything-is-possible economic exuberance. A devastating terrorist attack hit at the heart of the nation's economic and military power: the World Trade Center near Wall Street in New York City and the Pentagon in Washington, D.C., just miles from the White House.

In addition to causing thousands of lives to be lost, the attacks forced immediate changes in the way the nation conducted business. Following the attack, travel was suspended, sporting events were canceled, business offices were closed, and financial markets were shut down. Corporations, such as United Airlines and Boeing, announced layoffs of thousands of employees as sales plummeted.

Indeed, the attack seriously shook the nation's confidence, and economists feared that it could throw the United States into despair and recession.

Officials at the Fed realized that the future economic outlook depended on the behavior of U.S. consumers and businesses. Typically, consumers respond to a crisis by freezing—spending stops, and decisions about the future are put on hold. If fear and uncertainty prevail, how can people be expected to spend and invest for the future? If hijackers can steal commercial jets and crash them into high-profile buildings, how can people feel safe flying or working in ordinary skyscrapers?

While efforts were being made to rescue the victims of the attack, the immediate job ahead for the Federal Reserve was clear: It must address this national crisis and restore confidence as quickly as possible. As news spread about the nation's catastrophe, banks faced soaring demand for cash as nervous depositors began to pull money out of their accounts. The Fed quickly announced that it would keep its discount window open to any bank that needed it.

The provision of liquidity following September 11 was unprecedented in Federal Reserve history. On September 12, discount window borrowing by financial institutions peaked at more than $45 billion, compared with around $100 million on a typical day. On the same day, the Federal Reserve injected $38 billion in liquidity through open market operations, as opposed to a typical daily action of $3.5 billion. The Federal Reserve also extended swap lines of credit with the European Central Bank, the Bank of England, and the Bank of Canada in an attempt to provide liquidity to international markets. Simply put, the Fed sent a clear message to financial markets that it would provide sufficient liquidity to keep them operating in an orderly fashion.

Having restored confidence in the financial system, the Fed turned its attention to the disaster's impact on the economy. The Fed quickly cut the federal funds rate, its target for short-term interest rates, by a half a percentage point. Several large U.S. commercial banks responded to the Fed rate by reducing their lending rates to business and household customers.

As the situation eased, the Fed kept the financial system flush with cash, but at much lower levels than in previous days. Although the United States had suffered a major blow, the financial system proved to be quite resilient, with markets and companies functioning better than one might expect.

CHECK POINT

1. Describe the nature and operation of monetary policy.

2. Identify the instruments that the Fed uses to control the money supply.

3. Discuss how changes in the money supply by the Fed can result in changes in output, employment, and prices.

4. How would the Fed combat recession in the economy? How about inflation?

MONETARY POLICY: ADVANTAGES AND DISADVANTAGES

Most economists consider monetary policy to be an important tool for stabilizing the economy. Let us evaluate how well monetary policy works.

Advantages of Monetary Policy

One strength of monetary policy is that it interferes very little with the freedom of the market, although market imperfections sometimes intensify the effects of policy on particular sectors of the economy. A restrictive monetary policy cuts down the rate at which total spending can increase, but it does not dictate which particular expenditures must be slowed or reduced. If a restrictive monetary policy forces interest rates up from 6 percent to 8 percent, for example, you, the typical consumer, still have the option of borrowing money to purchase a new home, a car, or a major appliance. The expenditures that you cut in response to higher borrowing costs are the ones to which you attach the lowest priorities. Similarly, an expansionary monetary policy stimulates total spending, but the market also dictates its form.

Another strength is that monetary policy is flexible. The FOMC usually meets about every 6 weeks, reaches a decision, and acts on that decision immediately. Moreover, the FOMC can call extraordinary meetings if economic events require it. In contrast, the application of fiscal policy may be postponed for many months by congressional deliberations.

Finally, and perhaps most important, Congress has carefully insulated the Fed from day-to-day political pressures so that it may act in the best interests of the economy. As a result, the Fed can base its policy actions almost entirely on economic considerations rather than political ones. This allows the Fed to engage in policies that might be unpopular but necessary for the long-term health of the economy. Of course, it also empowers the Fed to pursue correct policies in spite of pressures to do otherwise.

Disadvantages of Monetary Policy

Formulating monetary policy is a difficult task, and policies have definite limitations. Promoting economic stability requires not only wise monetary policy but sound fiscal policy as well. It also requires

economics
IN ACTION

Economists Urge Congress to Leave the Fed Alone

During the economic downturn of 2007–2009, members of the U.S. Congress increasingly criticized the monetary policies of the Federal Reserve, characterizing them as inadequate to cope with a deteriorating economy. Some members of Congress proposed to expand the authority of the Government Accountability Office, the watchdog of Congress, to audit Fed monetary policy. Others disputed the appropriateness of the governance of the 12 regional Federal Reserve banks, which are overseen by private-sector boards of directors largely selected by commercial bankers.

In response to this criticism, more than 250 prominent economists signed a petition in 2009, noting that critics of the Fed were placing the independence of monetary policy at risk. They exhorted Congress to refrain from attacking the Fed because such attacks thwart its ability to combat recession or inflation.

The petition reflected increasing concern among economics professors, former Fed officials, and some investors that the intensity of the criticism from Congress of the Fed's managing of the economic crisis implied a preparedness to diminish the freedom the Fed has to change interest rates as it sees necessary. The petition pointed out that successful monetary policy needs to be forward looking so the Fed can adjust policy before the economy booms or falls into recession. Simply put, if the flexibility of monetary policy is stifled for political reasons, it could be very costly.

Arguing that the independence of the Fed is necessary for combating recession or inflation, the economists urged Congress not to interfere when the Fed decides to enact monetary policy. When the Fed decides it's time to begin changing monetary conditions, it must be permitted to do so without meddling, the economists noted.

Source: David Wessell, "Experts Tell Congress to Lay Off the Fed," *The Wall Street Journal*, July 16, 2009, p. A-3.

sufficient competition throughout the economy so that individual prices are free to move up and down. Obviously, trouble can develop in all three areas, so it is difficult to achieve perfect stability.

Policy trade-offs present another problem for the Fed. Basically, the Fed has one policy instrument: the money supply. Does this mean that the Fed can pursue only one goal? Consider the goals of price stability and full employment. As we have learned, combating inflation requires the Fed to decrease the money supply. However, a decrease in the money supply also results in declining economic activity and rising unemployment. Conversely, combating unemployment calls for an increase in the money supply, which may intensify inflation. Indeed, the short-run trade-offs between price stability and full employment make it difficult for the Fed to formulate policy.[4]

Finally, the extent to which monetary policy can revive a sagging economy has long been debated. Some economists argue that monetary policy is largely powerless to revive economic activity after a downturn. Recall that during a downturn, the Fed will adopt an expansionary monetary policy by increasing banks' excess reserves. However, this does not guarantee that banks will actually make loans. If businesses are pessimistic about future profits, they may be unwilling to borrow excess reserves, thus frustrating the expansionary monetary policy.[5]

Discretion or Rules: Fixed–Money Rule or Inflation Targeting?

The weaknesses of monetary policy highlight a debate concerning the conduct of monetary policy. Should the Fed be free to use its own discretion to stabilize the economy, or should it be limited to following rules? And if the Fed should follow rules, what kind of rules?

The case for discretionary monetary policy is founded on the notion that the economy is constantly affected by recessionary or expansionary forces. Without an active monetary policy based on the judgments of the Fed about the current needs of the economy, it is feared, the economy would oscillate in unacceptably wide swings. To decrease such instability, proponents maintain that the Fed can stimulate the economy when it becomes sluggish or restrain the economy when it overheats.

However, critics say that discretionary changes in the money supply may actually destabilize the economy. They note that the Fed does not have up-to-the-minute, reliable information about the state of the economy and prices. Information is limited because of lags in the publication of data. Also, the Fed has a less-than-perfect understanding of the way the economy works, including when and to what extent policy actions will affect aggregate demand. These limitations add to uncertainties in the policy process and make determining the appropriate setting of monetary policy instruments more difficult.

Rather than using its own discretion to conduct monetary policy, the Fed might adopt a fixed-rule policy independent of the state of the economy. One fixed-rule policy would be for the Fed to keep the quantity of money growing at a constant annual rate that is consistent with the average growth in the economy's productivity. The Fed's only purpose would be to use its monetary tools to make sure that the money supply increased steadily by, say, 3 percent per year. Proponents maintain that this approach would eliminate inappropriate monetary policy as a source of macroeconomic instability. However, critics contend that such a policy would limit the Fed's flexibility in responding to extraordinary circumstances, such as the September 11 terrorist attacks. They also note that the quantity of money in the economy is difficult to measure, and its relationship to overall spending—which drives prices up or down—tends to shift.

Some economists who favor a fixed-rule policy for the Fed call for *inflation targeting*, a policy that is used by Canada, Australia, New Zealand, and the United Kingdom. According to this policy,

---

4. The U.S. government faces similar policy conflicts when it formulates fiscal policy.

5. Economists at the Fed have examined the effects of monetary policy by estimating the cumulative response in output in the 2 years following a 1-percent change in the federal funds rate. They found that a 1-percentage point increase in the federal funds rate decreases quarterly output growth over the following 2 years by 1.2 percentage points. However, only a 0.5-percentage point increase in output occurs in response to a 1-percentage point decline in interest rates. Apparently, monetary policy tightening has more effect on output than monetary easing. See "Pushing on a String," *Monetary Trends*, Federal Reserve Bank of St. Louis, March 2003, available at http://www.stlouisfed.org.

the Fed would be required to announce a target range of inflation rates for, say, the next 2 years. It would then be expected to use its monetary tools to keep inflation within that range. If the Fed failed to achieve its target, it would have to explain what went wrong. Thus, inflation targeting would make monetary policy more predictable and accountable to the public. Proponents say that this policy would allow the Fed to focus on its major responsibility, controlling inflation. They also note that an optimal inflation rate would not only promise stable prices but also set the foundation for a healthy economy, including full employment and economic growth. However, critics say that inflation targeting would limit the Fed's flexibility in moderating fluctuations in economic activity and responding to unusual situations, such as the stock market crash of 1987.

SHOULD CONGRESS REDUCE THE INDEPENDENCE OF THE FEDERAL RESERVE?

Recall that when the Federal Reserve was created, Congress carefully insulated it from day-to-day political pressures so that it could act in the best interest of the country. Congress made the Fed responsible to itself rather than to the president or the political party in power. The Fed is governmental, but it is independent within government.

The primary argument for Fed independence is that monetary policy—which affects inflation, employment, and economic growth—is too important to be determined by politicians. Because elections occur frequently, politicians may be more concerned with the short-run benefits rather than the long-run costs of their economic policies. Put simply, politicians may put reelection, rather than the long-run health of the economy, first in their decision making.

The most sensitive aspect of the economy over which short- and long-run interests clash is inflation. Supporters of the Fed's independence maintain that monetary policy tends to become too expansionary if it is left to policy makers with short-run horizons, thus intensifying inflationary pressures. However, the Fed cannot assume that the goals of politicians reflect public sentiment. The public may prefer that officials at the Fed, rather than politicians, formulate monetary policy.

However, critics of the Fed's independence contend that, in a democracy, elected officials should formulate public policy. Because the voting public holds elected officials responsible for their economic policies, the president and Congress should exercise more control over monetary policy. Moreover, critics maintain that placing the Fed under the control of elected officials could reap benefits by coordinating monetary policy with the government's fiscal policy. Finally, critics argue that the Fed has not always used its independence well. For example, they note that monetary policy was too expansionary during the inflationary era of the 1970s and too restrictive during the recessionary era of the early 1990s.

This chapter has considered the Federal Reserve and monetary policy as a possible solution to macroeconomic instability. The next chapter will broaden our focus by discussing the United States in the global economy.

CHECK POINT

1. Identify the major strengths and weaknesses of monetary policy.

2. Why do some economists argue that the Fed should keep the money supply growing at a steady rate rather than actively manage the money supply in order to fine-tune the economy?

3. Why was the Fed structured so as to have a high degree of independence from the federal government? Discuss the advantages and disadvantages of the Fed's independence.

Chapter Summary

1. The Federal Reserve System, often simply called the Fed, is the central bank of the United States. It was legislated by Congress and signed into law by President Woodrow Wilson in 1913 to provide the nation with a safer, more flexible, and more stable monetary and financial system.

2. The Fed's structure was designed by Congress to give it a broad perspective on the economy. At the head of the Fed's formal organization is the Board of Governors. The 12 regional Federal Reserve Banks make up the next level. The organization of the Fed also includes the Federal Open Market Committee and three advisory councils. The Federal Reserve's stockholders are commercial banks that are members of the Fed.

3. The Fed, as the overseer of the nation's monetary system, has many important duties: acting as the lender of last resort, regulating and supervising banks, supplying services to banks and to the government, conducting foreign exchange operations, and controlling the money supply and interest rates.

4. The Fed's main responsibility is to formulate and implement monetary policy, which consists of manipulating the economy's money supply in order to help the economy achieve maximum output and employment, as well as stable prices. The Fed uses three policy instruments to influence the money supply: open market operations, the discount rate, and the reserve requirement.

5. In the short run, when prices are temporarily fixed, the Fed has the ability to affect the level of interest rates in the economy. When the Fed increases the money supply to reduce interest rates, aggregate demand increases, which results in an increase in output and employment. Conversely, a decrease in the money supply that increases interest rates will reduce aggregate demand, output, and employment. In the long run, a change in the money supply by the Fed affects only prices and not the level output and employment.

6. One strength of monetary policy is that it interferes very little with the freedom of the market. Monetary policy is also flexible and can be implemented quickly in response to changing economic circumstances. Finally, the Fed is insulated from day-to-day political pressures, so it can act in the best interests of the economy. This allows the Fed to engage in policies that might be unpopular but necessary for the long-run health of the economy.

7. Critics of the Fed argue that active changes in the money supply can and do destabilize the economy. They note that the Fed does not have up-to-the-minute, reliable information about the state of the economy and prices. Timing lags also limit the effectiveness of monetary policy. As a result, critics call for the elimination of activism in monetary policy in favor of a law requiring a fixed rate of increase in money each year.

Key Terms and Concepts

Federal Reserve System (Fed) (346)

Board of Governors (347)

Federal Open Market Committee (FOMC) (347)

monetary policy (349)

open market operations (350)

discount rate (352)

discount window (352)

term auction facility (TAF) (353)

federal funds market (353)

federal funds rate (353)

Self-Test: Multiple-Choice Questions

1. The main policy-making body of the Federal Reserve System is the

   a. Federal Advisory Council.
   b. Council of Economic Advisers.
   c. Board of Governors.
   d. Federal Open Market Committee.

2. The functions of the Federal Reserve System include all of the following *except*

   a. controlling the money supply.
   b. regulating and supervising banks.
   c. supplying check-processing services to banks.
   d. issuing deposit insurance to banks.

3. The most important monetary tool of the Fed is

   a. open market operations.
   b. the reserve requirement.
   c. the discount rate.
   d. the margin requirement.

4. It is common for commercial banks with surplus balances in their accounts to lend reserves overnight to banks with deficiencies of reserves. The interest rate that pertains to these loans is the

   a. discount rate.
   b. prime rate.
   c. federal funds rate.
   d. commercial loan rate.

5. To combat recession, the Fed would adopt a(n)

   a. contractionary monetary policy that shifts the aggregate demand curve to the right.
   b. contractionary monetary policy that shifts the aggregate demand curve to the left.
   c. expansionary monetary policy that shifts the aggregate demand curve to the right.
   d. expansionary monetary policy that shifts the aggregate demand curve to the left.

6. To counteract demand-pull inflation, the Fed would

   a. decrease the discount rate, decrease the required reserve ratio, and buy securities in the open market.
   b. decrease the discount rate, decrease the required reserve ratio, and sell securities in the open market.
   c. increase the discount rate, increase the required reserve ratio, and buy securities in the open market.
   d. increase the discount rate, increase the required reserve ratio, and sell securities in the open market.

7. If the Fed decreases the required reserve ratio, all of the following will be true *except*

   a. total reserves will remain unchanged.
   b. required reserves will decline and excess reserves will rise.
   c. the money multiplier will increase.
   d. the federal funds rate will increase.

8. If the Fed reduces the required reserve ratio from 25 percent to 20 percent, the value of the money multiplier

   a. will increase from 4 to 5.
   b. will increase from 5 to 6.
   c. will decrease from 5 to 4.
   d will decrease from 6 to 5.

9. To shield the Federal Reserve from political pressure, members of the Board of Governors

   a. serve lifetime appointments.
   b. are elected by the stockholders of the Fed.
   c. are appointed to 14-year terms.
   d. are elected by the voting public.

10. Concerning the short-run effects of monetary policy, an increase in the money supply works mainly through decreases in

   a. interest rates that result in additional investment and an increase in aggregate supply.
   b. interest rates that result in additional investment and an increase in aggregate demand.
   c. the purchasing power of money that result in declining consumption and a decrease in aggregate demand.
   d. the purchasing power of money that result in declining consumption and a decrease in aggregate supply.

Answers to Multiple-Choice Questions

1. c   2. d   3. a   4. c   5. c   6. d   7. d   8. a   9. c   10. b

Study Questions and Problems

1. Who is the current chair of the Board of Governors of the Federal Reserve System? Why has the chair of the Board of Governors been characterized as the second most powerful person in Washington, D.C., after the president?

2. If the Fed's independence were restricted so that it became subordinate to the president and Congress, would this affect the ability of monetary policy to combat recession or inflation?

3. When the Fed purchases government securities from commercial banks, businesses, or individuals, the nation's money supply increases. Explain how this works.

4. What is the discount rate, and how can the Fed use it to influence the nation's supply of money?

5. How can a decrease in the reserve requirement by the Fed result in an increase in the money supply?

6. Which is the Fed's most frequently used monetary instrument? Why?

7. If the Fed wants to increase the value of the dollar in terms of other currencies, what should it do? What should the Fed do if it wants to decrease the foreign exchange value of the dollar?

8. Suppose that the economy is suffering from a prolonged and deep recession. What changes in open market operations, the discount rate, and the reserve requirement would the Fed likely

enact? Explain how each change would affect bank reserves, the money supply, interest rates, and aggregate demand.

9. Suppose that the Fed adopts a restrictive monetary policy in order to combat demand-pull inflation. Assuming that the economy is closed to international trade, use the model of aggregate demand and aggregate supply to show the effects of the Fed's policy. Assume that the economy is open to international trade. How will changes in the international value of the dollar affect the performance of the economy? Now, answer the same set of questions by assuming that the Fed adopts an expansionary monetary policy to combat recession.

10. Why do some economists maintain that an active monetary policy by the Fed is counterproductive?

11. Explain how the Fed is structured to have certain checks and balances that limit the power of any one group inside or outside the Fed.

12. Why do critics argue that the Fed has exacerbated the income gap between the rich and the poor?

13. Suppose that the required reserve ratio on checking deposits is 15 percent and the Fed purchases $10 million in U.S. securities from the commercial banking system. What is the maximum amount of new money that the banking system could create?

14. Pioneer Bank has checking deposits of $10 million and total reserves of $7.5 million; the required reserve ratio is 10 percent. If the Fed sells $1.5 million in government securities to the bank, what will happen to its total reserves and excess reserves?

15. Figure 15.5 shows the balance sheet for the commercial banking system. Answer the following questions on the basis of this information.

    a. If the Fed set the required reserve ratio at 10 percent, banks would have required reserves of _____ and excess reserves of _____; the money multiplier would equal _____ , and the maximum amount of new money that the banking system could create would equal _____.

    b. If the Fed decreased the required reserve ratio to 5 percent, banks would have _____ of excess reserves; the money multiplier would equal _____ , and the maximum amount of new money that the banking system could create would equal_____.

Figure 15.5	Combined Balance Sheet of All Commercial Banks (billions of dollars)

Assets		Liabilities	
Cash in vault	$ 300	Checking deposits	$3,600
Reserves with	150	Due to other	850
Federal Reserve		banks and Fed	
Banks			
Loans	3,000		
Government	1,000		
securities			

Figure 15.6	Wisconsin National Bank's Balance Sheet (millions of dollars)

Assets		Liabilities	
Reserves with Fed	$90	Checking deposits	$120
Loans	10		
Government securities	20		

16. Figure 15.6 shows the balance sheet of Wisconsin National Bank. Assume that the Fed has set the required reserve ratio at 10 percent.

   a. Wisconsin National Bank would have required reserves of _____ and excess reserves of _____. The maximum amount of new money that the bank could create would equal _____.

   b. Suppose that the Fed sells $10 million in government securities to Wisconsin National Bank. After the sale, the bank would have _____ of required reserves and _____ of excess reserves. As a result of this transaction, Wisconsin National Bank's ability to create additional money would increase/decrease by _____.

   c. Instead, suppose that the Fed buys $10 million in government securities from Wisconsin National Bank. As a result of this transaction, Wisconsin National Bank's ability to create additional money would increase/decrease by _____.

the
International
Economy

16

The United States and the Global Economy

Chapter objectives

After reading this chapter, you should be able to:

1. Explain in what respects the United States is an open economy.

2. Discuss the advantages of specialization and trade.

3. Explain why free trade is controversial.

4. Identify the effects of import tariffs and summarize the arguments for trade restrictions.

5. Assess the advantages and disadvantages of the World Trade Organization and the North American Free Trade Agreement.

economics IN CONTEXT

U.S. sheep producers have long been dependent on the government. Burdened with high costs and inefficiencies and facing domestic competition from beef, chicken, and pork at the beginning of the new millennium, sheep producers attempted to limit foreign competition by petitioning the U.S. government for import restrictions.

Almost all U.S. lamb imports come from producers in New Zealand and Australia, who provide strong competition for U.S. producers. These producers have invested substantial resources in new technology and effective marketing, making them among the most efficient producers in the world. These cost savings were passed on to American consumers in the form of low-priced lamb.

In response to increasing imports of lamb, the American Sheep Industry Association complained that domestic producers were being seriously injured by foreign competition. As a result, the U.S. government imposed restrictions on lamb imports. This policy outraged farmers in Australia and New Zealand, who relied on exports to the United States for their livelihood. Moreover, American consumers complained that the trade restrictions prevented them from purchasing low-priced foreign lamb.

Simply put, consumers felt that they were being "fleeced" by the import restrictions on lamb.

The United States has generally recognized that open domestic markets and an open global trading system are superior to trade protection and isolationism when it comes to promoting broad-based growth and prosperity. For decades, our open economy has generated important benefits for the American people in the form of stronger growth and improved employment opportunities. The opportunity to acquire goods and services from abroad both encourages us as producers to stay competitive and allows us as consumers to raise our standard of living.

Although most people benefit from an open global trading system, some are hurt. To mitigate the unequal distribution of benefits and burdens in an open global system, some nations impose restrictions on international trade.

In this chapter, we will examine the benefits and costs of an open trading system. In particular, we will consider the effects on consumers, producers in exporting industries, and producers in import-competing industries.

THE UNITED STATES AS AN OPEN ECONOMY

In recent decades, the U.S. economy has become increasingly integrated into the world economy—that is, it has become an open economy. This integration has involved trade in goods and services, financial markets, the labor force, ownership of production facilities, and dependence on imported materials.

As a rough measure of the importance of international trade in a nation's economy, we can look at the nation's exports plus imports as a share of its gross domestic product (GDP). In 2006, the United States exported 10 percent of its GDP, while imports were 16 percent of GDP; the U.S. economy's openness to trade thus equaled 26 percent. The relative importance of international trade in the U.S. economy has increased by about 50 percent during the past century.

The United States exports a variety of goods, including grain, chemicals, scientific equipment, machinery, automobiles, computers, and commercial aircraft. It also imports many goods, such as steel, oil, automobiles, textiles, shoes, rubber, and foodstuffs such as bananas, tea, and coffee.

Table 16.1	The Fruits of Free Trade: A Global Fruit Basket

On a trip to the grocery store, consumers can find goods from all over the globe			
Apples	New Zealand	Limes	El Salvador
Apricots	China	Oranges	Australia
Bananas	Ecuador	Pears	South Korea
Blackberries	Canada	Pineapples	Costa Rica
Blueberries	Chile	Plums	Guatemala
Coconuts	Philippines	Raspberries	Mexico
Grapefruit	Bahamas	Strawberries	Poland
Grapes	Peru	Tangerines	South Africa

Source: Federal Reserve Bank of Dallas, *The Fruits of Free Trade,* 2002 Annual Report, p. 3, available at http://www
.dallasfed.org.

The biggest trade partners of the United States are Canada, Japan, Mexico, and China. Other leading trading partners include Germany, the United Kingdom, South Korea, Singapore, Belgium, and Luxembourg.

The significance of international trade for the U.S. economy is even more evident when we consider specific products. For example, we would have fewer personal computers without imported components, little aluminum if we did not import bauxite, no tin cans without imported tin, and no chrome bumpers if we did not import chromium. Students taking an 8 A.M. course in economics might sleep through the class if we did not import coffee and tea. Moreover, many of the products that we buy from foreigners would be much more costly if we depended on our own domestic production. Imagine the cost of greenhouse coffee! Table 16.1 provides examples of fruits that the United States imports.

THE ADVANTAGES
OF SPECIALIZATION AND TRADE

The idea of being self-sufficient might be appealing. You might even desire to live by yourself in an isolated area, such as northern Idaho or British Columbia. Living by your own means, you could only consume items that you produce. The food that you eat, the shirts and pants that you sew, and the house that you construct would be nothing like the items that you are currently able to purchase. You would not be able to obtain many products, such as computers, telephones, televisions, automobiles, and medicines. Because of the limitations of self-sufficiency, most people choose to specialize and trade with others.

Specialization and trade pertain not only to individuals but also to groups of individuals. Imagine what would happen if the people of your state desired to be self-sufficient and refused to trade with people in other regions of the country. Residents of Idaho, for example, could produce their own apples and wheat, but where would they get oranges and oil? Conceivably, they could grow oranges in greenhouses and drill for oil, but these items would come at a great cost. Therefore, it is not practical for each of the 50 states to be self-sufficient. The founders of the United States realized this, and thus they prohibited the imposition of trade barriers on interstate commerce. What is true for states is also true for countries. National specialization and trade can result in a more efficient use of the world's resources.

Specialization increases productivity in several ways. First, specialization saves time because workers focus exclusively on one task rather than switching from one job to another. Also, specialization allows production processes to be divided so that workers can practice and perfect a particular skill; this process is called the **division of labor.** People who practice a particular activity, such as hitting a baseball or keyboarding, tend to become much better at that activity than those who do not practice. Likewise, a country that specializes in the production of, say, machine tools tends to become highly productive in this activity. Finally, the division of labor fosters invention and innovation. As a worker learns a task very well, she might figure out ways to perform it better—perhaps by inventing a new machine or a routine to do it. Specialization and invention thus reinforce each other. However, the nature of specialization can also limit its benefits because repetitive jobs might cause workers to become bored and unproductive.

Indeed, the degree to which specialization can be practiced is limited by the size of the market. For many mass-produced items, producing for the world market provides a greater scope for specialization than producing for the domestic market. Boeing is an example: It has sold about 70 percent of its jetliners overseas in recent years. Without exports, Boeing would have found it difficult to cover the large design and tooling costs of its jetliners, and the jets might not have been produced at all.

The production of a Hewlett Packard (HP) laptop computer illustrates the process of specialization. When an American customer places an order online for an HP laptop, the order is transmitted to Quanta Computer Co. in Taiwan. To decrease labor costs, the company outsources the production of the computer to workers in Shanghai, China. They combine components from all over the globe to assemble the laptop, which is flown as freight to the United States and then sent to the customer. About 95 percent of the production of an HP laptop is outsourced to other countries. Other U.S. computer producers, including Gateway, Apple, and Dell, have similar rates of outsourcing. Table 16.2 shows what components go into the production of an HP laptop and where they come from.

Proponents of free trade contend that if each country does what it does best and allows trade, over the long run, all countries will enjoy lower costs and prices, as well as higher levels of output, income, and consumption, than they could achieve in isolation. In a dynamic world, market forces are constantly changing because of shifts in technologies, input productivities, and wages, as well as consumer tastes and preferences. A free market compels companies to make adjustments. For example, if the efficiency of the aluminum industry cannot keep pace with other sectors of the economy, resources will flow to other industries in which productivity is higher.

Table 16.2	Manufacturing a HP Pavilion, ZD8000 Laptop Computer

Component	Major Manufacturing Country
Microprocessor	United States
Graphics processor	Designed in the United States and Canada; produced in Taiwan
Magnesium casing	China
Hard-disk drives	Singapore, China, Japan, United States
Power supply	China
Memory chip	Germany, Taiwan, South Korea, United States
Liquid-crystal display	Japan, Taiwan, South Korea, China

Sources: Christopher Koch, "Outsourcing: Innovation Ships Out," *CIO Magazine*, January 15, 2005, pp. 18–21; and "The Laptop Trail," *The Wall Street Journal*, June 9, 2005, pp. B-1 and B-8.

economics
IN ACTION

Babe Ruth and the Principle of Comparative Advantage

Babe Ruth was the first great home-run hitter in baseball history. His batting talent and vivacious personality attracted huge crowds wherever he played. He made baseball more exciting by establishing homers as a common part of the game. Ruth set many major league records, achieving 2,056 career bases on balls and hitting two or more home runs in 72 games. He had a .342 lifetime batting average and 714 career home runs.

George Herman Ruth, Jr. (1895–1948), was born in Baltimore, Maryland. After playing baseball in the minor leagues, Ruth started his major league career as a left-handed pitcher with the Boston Red Sox in 1914. In 158 games with Boston, he compiled a pitching record of 89 wins and 46 losses, including two 20-win seasons—23 victories in 1916 and 24 in 1917. He eventually added five more wins as a hurler for the New York Yankees and ended his pitching career with a 2.28 earned run average. Ruth also had a 3–0 record in World Series competition, including one stretch of 29-2/3 consecutive scoreless innings. Ruth became the best left-handed pitcher in the American League.

Although Ruth had an absolute advantage in pitching, he had even greater talent at the plate. Simply put, Ruth's comparative advantage was in hitting. As a pitcher, Ruth had to rest his arm between appearances, and thus he could not bat in every game. To ensure his daily presence in the lineup, Ruth gave up pitching to play exclusively in the outfield.

In Ruth's 15 years with the Yankees, he dominated professional baseball. He teamed up with Lou Gehrig to form what became the greatest one-two hitting punch in baseball. Ruth was the heart of the 1927 Yankees, a team regarded by some baseball experts as the best in baseball history. That year, Ruth set a record of 60 home runs; at that time, a season comprised only 154 games, compared to 162 games today. He attracted so many fans that Yankee Stadium, which opened in 1923, was nicknamed "The House That Ruth Built." The Yankees released Ruth after the 1934 season, and he ended his playing career in 1935 with the Boston Braves. In his final game with Boston, Ruth hit three home runs.

The advantages to having Ruth switch from pitching to batting were enormous. Not only did the Yankees win four World Series during Ruth's tenure, but they also became baseball's most renowned franchise. Ruth was elected to the Baseball Hall of Fame in Cooperstown, New York, in 1936.

Sources: Edward Scahill, "Did Babe Ruth Have a Comparative Advantage as a Pitcher?" *Journal of Economic Education*, Vol. 21, 1990. See also Paul Rosenthal, *America at Bat: Baseball Stuff and Stories* (Washington, DC: National Geographic, 2002); Geoffrey C. Ward and Ken Burns, *Baseball: An Illustrated History* (New York: Alfred A. Knopf, 1994); and Keith Brandt, *Babe Ruth: Home Run Hero* (Mahwah, NJ: Troll, 1986).

COMPARATIVE ADVANTAGE AND INTERNATIONAL TRADE

To illustrate the advantages of specialization and trade, let us consider a world of only two countries—the United States and France—that each produce only two goods—automobiles and computers. Also assume that the resources in each country are equally suited to producing autos or computers. As a result, the production possibilities schedule of each country appears as a straight line in Figure 16.1.[1]

---

1. This implies that the law of increasing costs, discussed in Chapter 1, is replaced by the assumption of constant costs.

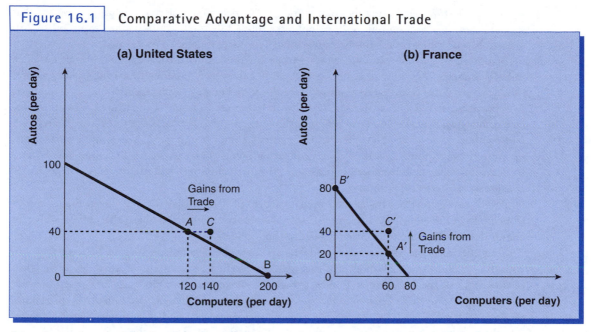

Figure 16.1 | Comparative Advantage and International Trade

(a) United States   **(b) France**

According to the principle of comparative advantage, countries should specialize in producing those goods in which they are relatively more efficient. Such specialization allows countries to realize gains in production and consumption.

Comparing the production possibilities schedules of the two countries, we see that the United States can produce more autos and more computers than France. If the United States devotes all its resources to auto production, it can produce 100 autos a day. France, on the other hand, can produce a maximum of 80 autos a day because it has less-efficient production skills than the United States does. Similarly, by devoting all its resources to producing a single good, the United States can produce a maximum of 200 computers a day, whereas France can produce only 80 computers a day. Again, the United States can outproduce France in computers because of its superior production skills.

Production and Consumption without Specialization and Trade

Without trade, the production possibilities schedule of each country defines the maximum amounts of two goods that are available for consumption. In other words, when there is no trade a country can consume only what it produces. Without trade, suppose that the United States decides to produce and consume 120 computers and 40 autos, shown by point A in Figure 16.1(a). Also suppose that France decides to produce and consume 60 computers and 20 autos, shown by point A' in Figure 16.1(b). Because we assume that the United States and France are the only two countries in the world, the world output of these goods totals 180 computers (120 + 60 = 180) and 60 autos (40 + 20 = 60).

Production and Consumption with Specialization and Trade

Now assume that the United States specializes in the production of computers and France specializes in the production of autos. As seen in Figure 16.1(a), the United States moves down its production possibilities schedule until it produces 200 computers, shown by point B. Similarly, France slides upward along its production possibilities schedule until it produces 80 autos, shown by point B' in Figure 16.1(*b*). Comparing the total world output before and after specialization, we see that specialization increases output by 20 computers (200 − 180 = 20) and 20 autos (80 − 60 = 20). Clearly, specialization is desirable because it allows resources to be used more efficiently.

Because specialization entails more efficient production, larger quantities of output are available to both countries. Referring to Figure 16.1(*a*), assume that the United States specializes in computer production at point *B* and agrees to import 40 autos from France in exchange for 60 of its computers. Are consumers in the United States better off with trade? Yes. At point *B*, the United States produces 200 computers. Subtracting the 60 computers that it exports to France leaves the United States with 140 computers; however, the United States imports 40 autos from France. The United States winds up consuming at point *C* in the figure. Comparing points *A* and *C*, we see that the United States can consume the same number of autos and 20 more computers because of trade. Clearly, U.S. consumers are better off with trade.

France also gains from trade. After exchanging 40 of its autos for 60 computers, France moves from point *A'* to point *C'* in Figure 16.1(*b*). French consumers thus have the same number of computers but 20 more autos than they had without trade.

Trade between the United States and France allows both countries to gain because they can consume a combination of goods that exceeds their production possibilities schedules.[2] The effect of international specialization and trade is thus equivalent to having more and better resources or discovering improved production techniques. By reallocating production assignments so that France produces 60 more autos at the expense of only 60 computers, and the United States produces 80 additional computers in exchange for only 40 autos, total auto production rises by 20 units (60 − 40 = 20) and total computer output rises by 20 units (80 − 60 = 20)—a win-win outcome for both countries.

Comparative Advantage

In our trading example, we assume that the United States is more efficient than France at producing both computers and autos. The possession of superior production skills is called having an *absolute advantage*. If the United States has an absolute advantage in the production of both goods, why does it specialize in the production of computers? Why does France, with absolute disadvantages in both goods, specialize in auto production? The answer lies in the principle of **comparative advantage,** which states that individuals and countries should specialize in producing goods in which they are *relatively*, not absolutely, more efficient. In other words, comparative advantage is the relative ability of one country to produce a good at a lower opportunity cost than some other country.

Let us return to our trading example in Figure 16.1 to determine the opportunity costs of producing computers and autos for the United States and France. Because workers in the United States can produce 200 computers or 100 autos, the opportunity cost of one computer is 0.5 auto (100/200 = 0.5). In France, because workers can produce 80 computers or 80 autos, the opportunity cost of one computer is one auto (80/80 = 1). Thus, the opportunity cost of computers is lower in the United States than in France. Therefore, the United States has a comparative advantage in the production of computers because it has a lower opportunity cost—that is, producing computers "costs" fewer autos. Similarly, France has a comparative advantage in the production of autos because its opportunity cost in that industry is lower.

According to the principle of comparative advantage, mutually beneficial trade between any two countries is possible whenever one country is relatively better at producing an item than the

---

2. How much each country gains from trade depends on the rate at which autos exchange for computers. The United States gains more from trade when a given quantity of its computers exchanges for larger quantities of French autos. In contrast, France gains more from trade when a given quantity of its autos trades for larger quantities of U.S. computers. Demand and supply conditions in the two countries determine the rate of exchange and thus the distribution of the gains from trade.

Table 16.3	**Examples of Comparative Advantage in International Trade**

Country	Product
Canada	Lumber
Israel	Citrus fruit
Italy	Wine
Mexico	Tomatoes
Saudi Arabia	Oil
China	Textiles
Japan	Automobiles
South Korea	Steel, ships
United Kingdom	Financial services

other country. Being "relatively better" suggests that one country can produce an item at a lower opportunity cost—that is, at a lower sacrifice of other items foregone.

There are many examples of comparative advantage. Brazil, for instance, is a major exporter of coffee because its soil and climate are relatively better suited to the cultivation of coffee. China, with its abundance of low-skilled labor, has a comparative advantage in the production of shirts that require much handiwork. Saudi Arabia has a comparative advantage in the production of oil because its vast oil reserves can be harvested at low cost. Canada is a major exporter of lumber because its forested land is relatively unproductive in nonforest crops. Table 16.3 provides other examples of comparative advantage.

But endowments of natural resources are not the only source of comparative advantage. For example, Japan has few natural resources, yet it is a major exporter of autos, steel, and electronics. The basic ingredients of auto production, such as iron ore, are imported by the Japanese. Japan's auto industry highlights the importance of acquiring comparative advantage by saving and accumulating capital and by constructing efficient factories. Moreover, countries can develop comparative advantages in goods that require a skilled labor force, such as scientific instruments, by channeling resources into education.

Superior knowledge also results in comparative advantage. Many years ago, Switzerland developed a comparative advantage in watches because the people of that country have superior knowledge and expertise in manufacturing watches. Similarly, semiconductor equipment is an export product of the United States because of the technical expertise of firms such as Intel Corp.

CHECK POINT

1. How does specialization promote increases in productivity?

2. How does the principle of comparative advantage explain the pattern of world trade?

3. What determines comparative advantage?

4. Discuss the argument for free trade.

WHY ARE FREE TRADE AND GLOBALIZATION CONTROVERSIAL?

Although all nations can benefit from specialization and trade, why do some people object to free trade? The answer is not hard to find. Despite the gains to the overall economy, some groups within the economy are likely to lose from free trade, whereas others gain much more. Opening up trade thus creates both winners and losers across the economy, as seen in Table 16.4.

Clearly, industries that produce goods in which the home country has a comparative advantage gain from free trade. For example, Boeing's production of jetliners expands when orders increase from foreign airline companies. Also, Boeing's workers find that the demand for their labor increases along with the level of production. Moreover, firms that supply engines, landing gear, and other inputs used to produce Boeing jetliners realize increased sales and employment. Indeed, people in the state of Washington, who account for a significant amount of the labor that goes into producing Boeing jetliners, benefit from international trade.

The consumer is another beneficiary of free trade. We have learned that competition among firms leads to increased output and lower prices. This also pertains to competition between domestic and foreign firms. Because international trade prevents markets from being dominated by one or a few domestic firms, there is more competition. This forces domestic firms to charge lower prices and to produce higher-quality goods—factors that consumers value. Clearly, American Airlines and its passengers are better off when Boeing and Airbus compete for its jetliner purchases. Also, trade can increase the diversity of products available to consumers. U.S. auto buyers, for example, can purchase Ford, Chevy, and Chrysler models, as well as Toyotas, Hondas, and Mitsubishis.

Reducing restrictions on trade, however, does not benefit everyone. Firms and workers in import-competing industries face declining sales, profits, and employment levels as foreign-produced goods displace domestic goods. Many workers who lose their jobs in import-competing industries do not have the skills they need to be easily reemployed at a comparable wage level. Also, firms and workers who supply inputs to these industries suffer because of foreign competition. Both management

Table 16.4	Advantages and Disadvantages of Globalization and Free Trade	
Advantages	**Disadvantages**
Productivity increases faster when countries produce goods and services in which they have a comparative advantage. Living standards can increase more rapidly.	Millions of Americans have lost jobs because of imports of shifts in production abroad. Most find new jobs that pay less.
Global competition and cheap imports constrain prices, so inflation is less likely to disrupt economic growth.	Millions of other Americans fear getting laid off, especially those in import-competing industries.
An open economy promotes technological development and innovation by bringing in fresh ideas from abroad.	Workers face demands for wage concessions from employers, which often threaten to export jobs abroad.
Jobs in export industries tend to pay about 15 percent more than jobs in import-competing industries.	Besides blue-collar jobs, service and white-collar jobs are increasingly at risk of being sent overseas.
Unfettered capital movements provide the United States with access to foreign investment and help maintain low interest rates.	American employees can lose their competitiveness when companies build state-of-the-art factories in low-wage countries, making them as productive as those in the United States.

and labor in these industries are likely to oppose free trade and seek government protection against imports. Seekers of protectionism are often established firms in aging industries that have lost their comparative advantage. High costs may be due to a lack of modern technology, inefficient management procedures, outmoded work rules, or high wages paid to domestic workers. In the United States, industries that have sought protectionism include shoes, textiles, steel, oil, and automobiles.

Government officials must balance the opposing interests of consumers and firms and workers in exporting industries against firms and workers in import-competing industries when setting a course for international trade policy.

LIMITING FOREIGN COMPETITION: TARIFFS

For centuries, governments have used tariffs to raise revenues and protect domestic producers from foreign competition. A **tariff** is a tax that is imposed on imports. For example, the United States imposes a tariff of 2.9 percent on autos. If a foreign car costs $30,000, the amount of the tariff will equal $870 ($30,000 × 0.029 = $870), and the domestic price including the tariff will be $30,870.[3]

We can use supply and demand analysis to understand the economic effects of tariffs. Figure 16.2 shows the steel market of the United States. The domestic supply and demand curves for steel are denoted by $S_{U.S.}$ and $D_{U.S.}$, respectively. In the absence of international trade, the equilibrium price of steel is $500 per ton, the quantity of steel supplied by U.S. producers is 10 million tons, and the quantity of steel demanded by U.S. consumers is 10 million tons.

| Figure 16.2 | The Economic Effects of Tariffs |

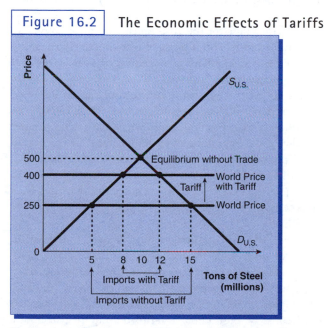

The cost of a tariff on an imported good is shifted to the domestic consumer through a higher product price. As a result, imports of the product decrease from their pretariff level. This reduction can be attributed to falling domestic consumption and rising domestic production. The effect of a tariff is to protect domestic producers from foreign competition.

---

3. Another way to restrict foreign competition is to impose a quota. A **quota** is a physical restriction on the quantity of goods traded each year. For example, a quota might state that no more than 1 million kilograms of cheese or 2 million kilograms of ice cream can be imported during a year.

Suppose that the U.S. economy is opened to international trade, and the rest of the world has a comparative advantage in steel. Assume that the world price of steel is $250 per ton. For simplicity, we will also assume that the United States takes the world price of steel as given.[4] At a price of $250, domestic consumption is 15 million tons and domestic production is 5 million tons. The quantity of imported steel, 10 million tons, reflects the horizontal difference between the U.S. demand curve and U.S. supply curve at a price of $250.

Free trade causes the domestic price of steel to fall from $500 to $250. As a result, consumers increase their purchases from 10 million tons to 15 million tons. Clearly, domestic consumers are better off because they can buy more steel at a lower price. However, domestic producers now sell less steel at a lower price than they did before trade. As production falls from 10 million tons to 5 million tons for domestic steel firms, profits decline and unemployment rises for domestic steelworkers.

In response to the domestic steel industry's pleas for protection against imports, assume that the U.S. government imposes a tariff of $150 per ton on steel that is imported into the United States. This increases the price of steel from $250 to $400 per ton. Therefore, domestic consumption declines from 15 million tons in the free-trade equilibrium to 12 million tons after the tariff is imposed. Also, domestic production increases from 5 million tons to 8 million tons, and the quantity of imports falls from 10 million tons to 4 million tons. Thus, a tariff tends to raise the price, lower the amounts consumed and imported, and increase domestic production.

Clearly, the tariff benefits domestic steel firms and their workers at the expense of domestic consumers. Because of the tariff, consumers pay more for farm equipment, refrigerators, and other steel-using products. Steel-using firms such as Ford (autos) and Caterpillar (tractors) will realize higher costs and lower sales because of the tariff on steel. As production declines for these firms, they will lay off some of their workers.

Another effect of tariffs is the revenue that they raise for the government. In our example, we assume that the tariff equals $150 per ton of steel imported. Multiplying this amount by the quantity of imports—4 million tons—yields tariff revenues of $600 million. This tariff revenue is a transfer of income from U.S. steel consumers to the U.S. government.

U.S. exporters are also indirectly impeded by a tariff. Because a tariff causes sales of imported steel to decline in the United States, the rest of the world has fewer dollars with which to purchase U.S. exports of computers, chemicals, and wheat. U.S. export industries, which have a comparative advantage, will thus decrease production. Also, if the imposition of an import tariff by the United States causes foreign nations to retaliate and impose tariffs on imports from the United States, U.S. export industries will suffer. Simply put, tariffs foster the growth of inefficient industries that do not have a comparative advantage and promote the decline of efficient industries that do have a comparative advantage. By causing resources to move from high-efficiency industries to low-efficiency industries, tariffs reduce people's standard of living.

For example, the U.S. government has imposed tariffs to limit imports of steel. In the 1950s, U.S. steelmakers dominated the world market, accounting for half of global steel output. Since the 1960s, however, foreign steelmakers have made significant inroads into the American market, turning the United States into a net importer of steel. To protect domestic producers, the U.S. government has consistently limited steel imports by imposing tariffs, quotas, and other barriers to trade. For example, in 2002, President George W. Bush imposed tariffs on imported steel for a 2-year period. The tariffs ranged from 8 percent to 30 percent on a variety of steel products. Bush hoped that the tariff relief would buy time for steel companies to reduce their labor costs and upgrade equipment so as to become competitive with producers in other nations. However, critics noted that protecting steel placed a heavy burden on American steel-using industries such as automobiles and earth-moving equipment. Although the tariffs would temporarily save roughly 6,000 jobs, the cost to U.S. consumers and steel-using firms of saving these jobs was between $800,000 and $1.1 million

---

4. This assumption implies that the United States is a small economy compared to the rest of the world. Although the small-economy assumption is not necessary to analyze the effects of international trade, it greatly simplifies the analysis.

economics
IN ACTION

The Regressive Nature of U.S. Tariffs

Does the burden of U.S. tariffs fall on all consumers in the same manner? No. Economists have shown that, on balance, U.S. tariffs are regressive because they disproportionately increase the relative price of goods consumed by lower-income Americans. Some of the most restrictive tariffs are levied on everyday consumer products such as footwear, textiles, and apparel.

Tariffs disproportionately affect the poor in two ways. First, many tariffs are highest on products that represent higher shares of income expenditures for lower-income households. Staple consumer products such as shoes and clothing face import taxes of more than 30 percent, some of the highest tariffs in the

U.S. tariff schedule. Footwear represents 1.3 percent of income expenditures for lower-income households, compared to just 0.5 percent for higher-income households. Second, products that are more commonly purchased by lower-income consumers are subject to higher import taxes than those commonly purchased by upper-income consumers. For example, lower-priced sneakers ($3–$6 per pair) are marked up with a 32-percent tariff, whereas higher-priced sneakers, such as $100 track shoes, are subject to a 20-percent tariff.

For government officials, a legitimate concern is whether the costs of a tax are shared uniformly by all people in a country or whether some income groups bear a disproportionate share of the cost. For tariffs, the cost tends to be disproportionately absorbed by the poor.

Source: Economic Report of the President, 2006, p. 157, available at http://www.gpoaccess.gov/eop/index.html.

per job. Moreover, the steel tariffs would cost as many as 13 jobs in steel-using industries for every steel job protected.[5]

ARGUMENTS FOR TRADE RESTRICTIONS

Although the free-trade argument is very persuasive, virtually all nations have imposed restrictions on international trade. Let us examine the main arguments for trade restrictions.

Job Protection

The issue of jobs has been a dominant factor in motivating government officials to levy trade restrictions on imported goods. During periods of economic recession, workers are especially eager to point out that cheap foreign goods undercut domestic production, resulting in a loss of domestic jobs to foreign labor. Alleged job losses to foreign competition have historically been a major force behind the desire of most U.S. labor leaders to reject free-trade policies.

This view, however, has a serious flaw: It fails to acknowledge the dual nature of international trade. Changes in a nation's imports of goods and services are closely related to changes in its exports. Nations export goods because they desire to import products from other nations. When the United States imports goods from abroad, foreigners gain purchasing power in dollars that will eventually be spent on U.S. goods, services, or financial assets. U.S. export industries then enjoy gains in sales

5. Robert Carbaugh and John Olienyk, "U.S. Steelmakers in Continuing Crisis," *Challenge*, 47, no. 1 (January–February 2004), pp. 86–106.

and employment, whereas the opposite occurs in U.S. import-competing industries. Rather than promoting overall unemployment, imports tend to generate job opportunities in some industries as part of the process by which they decrease employment in other industries. However, the job gains due to open trade policies tend to be less visible to the public than the readily observable job losses stemming from foreign competition. The more conspicuous losses have enabled many U.S. business and labor leaders in import-competing industries to combine forces in their opposition to free trade.

Protection against Cheap Foreign Labor

One of the most common arguments used to justify trade restrictions is that tariffs are needed to defend domestic jobs against cheap foreign labor. As indicated in Table 16.5, production workers in Austria and the United States are paid much higher wages, in terms of the U.S. dollar, than workers in countries such as Mexico and the Czech Republic. Thus, it could be argued that low wages abroad make it difficult for U.S. producers to compete with producers using cheap foreign labor, and unless U.S. producers are protected from imports, domestic output and employment levels will decrease.

Indeed, a widely held view maintains that competition from goods produced in low-wage countries is unfair and harmful to American workers. Moreover, companies that produce goods in foreign countries in order to take advantage of cheap labor should not be allowed to dictate the wages paid to American workers. A solution: Impose a tariff on goods imported to the United States to make up for the wage differential between foreign workers and U.S. workers in the same industry. That way, competition would be based on who makes the best product, not who works for the lowest wages. Therefore, if Calvin Klein wants to manufacture sweatshirts in Pakistan, the firm would be charged a tariff equal to the difference between the earnings of a Pakistani worker and that of a U.S. apparel worker.

Although this viewpoint may have widespread appeal, it fails to recognize the links among efficiency, wages, and labor. Labor cost per unit of output reflects not only the wage rate but also the productivity of labor. Even if domestic wages are, say, twice as high as foreign wages, if the productivity of domestic labor is more than twice that of foreign labor, domestic unit labor costs will be lower.

Table 16.5	Hourly Compensation Costs in U.S. Dollars for All Employees in Manufacturing, 2007	
Country		**Hourly Compensation (dollars/hour)**
Austria		43.17
Australia		34.75
Canada		31.91
United States		30.56
Japan		23.95
Czech Republic		9.67
Brazil		7.13
Mexico		3.91

Source: U.S. Department of Labor, Bureau of Labor Statistics, International Comparisons of Hourly Compensation Costs for All Employees in Manufacturing in 2007, March 26, 2009, available at http://www.bls.gov/.

For example, in 2000, wages in Malaysia were about 10 percent of wages in the United States. But Malaysian labor productivity was also about 10 percent of the U.S. level in 2000. This means that unit labor costs were approximately the same in Malaysia and the United States because the difference in productivity almost exactly offset the difference in wages between the two countries.

Fairness in Trade: A Level Playing Field

Fairness in trade is another reason given for protectionism. Business firms and workers often argue that foreign governments play by a different set of rules than the home government, giving foreign firms an unfair competitive advantage. Domestic producers contend that import restrictions should be enacted to offset these foreign advantages, thus creating a **level playing field** on which all producers could compete on equal terms.

U.S. companies often allege that foreign firms are not subject to the same government regulations as U.S. companies regarding pollution control and worker safety; this is especially true in many developing nations (such as Mexico and South Korea), where pollution enforcement has been lax. Moreover, foreign firms might not pay as much in corporate taxes or have to comply with employment regulations in areas such as affirmative action, minimum wage, and overtime pay. Also, foreign governments might erect high trade barriers that effectively close their markets to imports, or they might subsidize their producers so as to enhance their competitiveness in world markets.

Infant Industry

One commonly accepted case for tariff protection is the **infant industry argument.** This argument does not deny the validity of the case for free trade. However, it contends that in order for free trade to be meaningful, trading nations should temporarily shield their newly developing industries from foreign competition. Otherwise, mature foreign businesses, which are more efficient, could drive young domestic businesses out of the market. Only after the young companies have had time to become efficient producers should the tariff barriers be lifted and free trade take place.

Although there is some truth to the infant industry argument, it must be qualified in several respects. First, once a protective tariff is imposed, it is very difficult to remove, even after an industry has achieved maturity. Special-interest groups can often convince policy makers that further protection is justified. Second, it is very difficult to determine which industries will be capable of realizing their comparative advantage and thus merit protection. Third, the infant industry argument generally is not valid for mature, industrialized nations such as the United States, Germany, and Japan.

Noneconomic Arguments

Noneconomic considerations also enter into the arguments for protectionism. One such consideration is national security. The national security argument contends that a country might be put in jeopardy in the event of an international crisis or war if it depends heavily on foreign suppliers. Even though domestic producers might not be as efficient, tariff protections should be granted to ensure their continued existence. This argument has been applied to the major oil-importing nations, since several Arab nations imposed oil boycotts on the West in order to win support for the Arab position against Israel during the 1973 Middle East conflict. The problem, however, is deciding what constitutes an "essential industry." If the term is defined broadly, many industries may be able to win import protection, and the argument loses its meaning.

Another noneconomic argument is based on cultural considerations. New England may desire to preserve small-scale fishing; West Virginia may argue for tariffs on hand-blown glassware, on the grounds that these skills enrich the fabric of life; certain products such as narcotics may be considered socially undesirable, and restrictions or prohibitions may be placed on their importation. These arguments constitute legitimate reasons and cannot be ignored.

PURSUING TRADE LIBERALIZATION

Since World War II, advanced nations have significantly lowered their trade restrictions. Such trade liberalization has stemmed from two approaches.

The first is a reciprocal reduction of trade barriers on a nondiscriminatory basis. The 153 members of the **World Trade Organization (WTO)** acknowledge that tariff reductions agreed to by any two nations will be extended to all other members. Such an international approach encourages a gradual relaxation of tariffs throughout the world.

A second approach to trade liberalization occurs when a small group of nations, typically those in a geographic region, forms a regional trading arrangement. Under this system, member nations agree to impose lower trade barriers on nations within the group than on nonmember nations. The **North American Free Trade Agreement (NAFTA)** is an example of a regional trading arrangement.

Proponents of regional trading arrangements maintain that small blocs of nations with many similar interests are more likely than the vast number of dissimilar nations to liberalize trade dramatically. Critics, however, maintain that the members of a regional trading arrangement may not be greatly interested in global liberalization, only in liberalization among themselves. Let us examine two trading arrangements—the World Trade Organization and the North American Free Trade Agreement.

World Trade Organization

Established in 1995, the World Trade Organization is headquartered in Geneva, Switzerland. The main purpose of the WTO is to promote freer international trade. It does this by administering international trade agreements, facilitating trade negotiations of lower tariffs and quotas, resolving trade disputes, and providing technical assistance and training to developing countries. The WTO is not a government; individual nations are free to set their own appropriate levels of environmental, labor, health, and safety protections.

One of the most useful roles of the WTO is the adjudication of trade disputes. The dispute-settlement mechanism of the WTO provides for the formation of a dispute panel once a case is brought and sets time limits for each stage of the process. The decision of the panel may be taken to an appellate body, but the accused party cannot block the final decision.

For example, during the 1990s, the United States complained that governments in Europe were preventing U.S. producers from selling their beef in Europe. After consulting with experts, the WTO found that Europe had engaged in unfair trade. The European nations, therefore, had the choice of halting this practice or facing retaliation from the United States. Subsequently, the United States imposed 100-percent tariffs on imports of selected European goods in order to pressure Europe to open its markets to U.S. beef.

Although the WTO attempts to promote freer international trade, it has become a magnet for resistance to globalization by protectionists and critics of free trade. Protectionists include American steelworkers who complain that the free-trade policies of the WTO allow cheap Russian steel to flood the U.S. market, with the result that Russian workers have taken away their jobs. Also, critics of free trade are incensed that, as economies become more closely intertwined, trade policy increasingly impinges on such sensitive issues as social justice, product safety, and the environment.

For example, American environmentalists were outraged during the 1990s when the WTO ruled against a U.S. ban on imports of Malaysian shrimp from countries using nets that trap turtles and a ban on imports of Mexican tuna caught in ways that drown dolphins. Also, U.S. labor unions insist that Indonesian firms must pay livable wages to their workers and improve the working conditions in their "sweatshop" factories if they are to sell their goods in the United States. Finally, some church leaders have declared that the international debts of poor nations should be forgiven.

In spite of pressure for reform, the WTO has remained a centerpiece of the world trading system. Its policies are based on the notion that when countries can trade freely with each other, without import tariffs or other measures aimed at protecting the domestic market from competition, the world economy grows and everyone in general benefits. However, free trade can impose costs on firms and workers in import-competing industries. The protesters of the WTO are a reminder that the policies of the WTO must be weighed in a broader context of the world community and social justice, not just increased economic growth.

From NAFTA to CAFTA

The notion of a free-trade area among the United States, Canada, and Mexico has a long tradition. During the 1900s, the three nations considered the free-trade issue several times. However, because of the urgency of nation building and apprehensions concerning political sovereignty, the nations maintained restrictionist stances.

This outlook had changed by the 1990s. In 1993, the North American Free Trade Agreement was approved by the governments of the United States, Mexico, and Canada. The pact went into effect in 1994. By removing trade restrictions among themselves, the members hoped to gain better access to one another's markets, technology, labor, and expertise. In many respects, there were remarkable fits between the nations: The United States would benefit from Mexico's pool of cheap and increasingly skilled labor, while Mexico would benefit from U.S. investment and expertise. Moreover, trade between the United States and Canada was also expected to increase because of free trade.

Since NAFTA was established, proponents have maintained that the agreement has benefited the United States by expanding trade opportunities, reducing prices, increasing competition, and enhancing the ability of U.S. firms to attain economies of large-scale production. The United States produces more goods that benefit from large amounts of physical capital and a highly skilled workforce, including chemicals, plastics, cement, and sophisticated electronics. Moreover, NAFTA has allowed the United States and Mexico to form closer political ties.

But most analysts acknowledge that NAFTA has had a harmful effect on some segments of the U.S. economy. On the business side, the losers have been industries such as citrus growing and sugar, which rely on trade barriers to limit imports of low-priced Mexican goods. Other major losers have been unskilled workers, such as those in the apparel industry, whose jobs are most vulnerable to competition from low-paid workers abroad. Moreover, critics are especially concerned that Mexico's low wage scale and lax environmental regulations have encouraged U.S. companies to locate in Mexico, resulting in job losses in the United States. Simply put, although NAFTA has provided economic benefits to the participating countries, it has also raised some legitimate concerns.

The success of NAFTA inspired the United States to pursue additional trade agreements. In 2003, the United States and Chile signed a free-trade agreement, and in 2005, the United States and five nations in Central America signed the Central American Free Trade Agreement (CAFTA). The United States maintained that strengthening economic ties with its neighbors to the south would help encourage progress in political and social reform. It remains to be seen whether North and South America will ever agree to form a free-trade area of the Americas, as has been proposed.

CHECK POINT

1. Why do tariffs result in benefits for domestic producers but costs for domestic consumers?

2. What are the major arguments for trade restrictions? Explain the flaw in each argument.

3. How does the World Trade Organization attempt to improve the efficiency of the world trading system?

4. Is the North American Free Trade Agreement good for people in the United States? How about people in Mexico or Canada?

This chapter has considered the United States as an open economy and the importance of international trade. The next chapter will discuss the U.S. balance of payments and the markets in which Americans exchange dollars for other currencies.

Chapter Summary

1. In recent decades, the U.S. economy has become increasingly integrated into the world economy. This integration has involved trade in goods and services, financial markets, the labor force, ownership of production facilities, and dependence on imported materials.

2. Specialization and trade pertain not only to individuals but also to groups of individuals. By increasing productivity, specialization can result in a more efficient use of resources and an increase in output. However, the nature of specialization can limit its benefits because repetitive jobs might cause workers to become bored and unproductive.

3. Proponents of free trade contend that if each country does what it does best and allows trade, over the long run, all countries will enjoy lower costs and prices, as well as higher levels of output, income, and consumption, than they could achieve in isolation. A free market compels firms and their workers to adjust to forces such as shifts in technologies, input productivities, and consumer tastes and preferences.

4. The principle of comparative advantage underlies patterns of world trade. This principle states that countries should specialize in producing goods in which they are relatively, not absolutely, more efficient. In other words, comparative advantage is the relative ability of one country to produce a good at a lower opportunity cost than some other country. Among the sources of comparative advantage are natural endowments of resources, a skilled labor force, and superior knowledge.

5. Although economies can benefit from specialization and free trade, some people object to free trade. This is because some groups in the economy lose from free trade, while others gain. Consumers and firms and workers that produce goods in which the home country has a comparative advantage gain from free trade. However, firms and workers in import-competing industries suffer. Government officials must consider the opposing interests of these groups when setting a course for international trade policy.

6. To protect firms and workers from foreign competition, governments can impose tariffs and other trade restrictions. These devices, however, tend to foster the growth of inefficient industries that do not have a comparative advantage and promote the decline of efficient industries that do have a comparative advantage, thus reducing the standard of living for the nation.

7. Among the arguments for trade restrictions are job protection, protection against cheap foreign labor, fairness in trade, infant industry, national security, and preservation of culture.

8. Since World War II, advanced nations have significantly lowered their trade barriers. Such trade liberalization has stemmed from the World Trade Organization and regional trading arrangements such as the North American Free Trade Agreement.

Key Terms and Concepts

division of labor (373)

comparative advantage (376)

tariff (379)

quota (379)

level playing field (383)

infant industry argument (383)

World Trade Organization (WTO) (384)

North American Free Trade Agreement (NAFTA) (384)

Self-Test: Multiple-Choice Questions

1. Countries that trade on the basis of comparative advantage have _____ than countries that don't.

   a. more goods and services available to them
   b. higher production costs and transportation costs
   c. lower levels of product quality from which to choose
   d. lower levels of labor productivity

2. The major determinants of comparative advantage include all of the following *except*

   a. national income.
   b. climate.
   c. labor force skills.
   d. capital per worker.

3. Free trade and specialization tend to result in

   a. higher wages for workers in import-competing industries.
   b. higher product prices for domestic consumers.
   c. a smaller range of product availability for domestic consumers.
   d. increased profits for firms in export industries.

4. Trade between countries results in

   a. lower living standards.
   b. higher product prices.
   c. increased specialization.
   d. greater self-sufficiency.

5. Which of the following is *not* cited as a justification for trade restrictions?

   a. Permitting infant industries to mature and become competitive.
   b. Increasing jobs for workers in import-competing industries.
   c. Maintaining self-sufficiency for the nation's military.
   d. Fostering specialization based on the principle of comparative advantage.

6. Protectionist pressures in the United States have been caused by all of the following *except*

   a. deficits in the U.S. balance of trade.
   b. unemployment of U.S. workers.
   c. rising national income in developing nations.
   d. falling profits of U.S. manufacturers.

7. The imposition of a tariff on steel imports is *least* likely to result in a(n)

   a. increase in the production cost of steel-using industries.
   b. decrease in the quantity of steel imports.
   c. increase in the price of domestic steel.
   d. increase in productivity in the domestic steel industry.

8. Free traders maintain that an open economy is advantageous because it provides all of the following benefits *except*

   a. increased competition for world producers.
   b. a wider selection of products for consumers.
   c. utilization of the most efficient production methods.
   d. relatively high wages for all domestic workers.

9. A sudden shift from import tariffs to free trade may induce short-term unemployment in

a. import-competing industries.
b. industries that only export to foreign countries.
c. industries that sell domestically as well as export.
d. industries that neither import nor export.

10. Recent economic research supports the notion that productivity performance in industries is

a. directly related to the globalization of industries.
b. inversely related to the globalization of industries.
c. not related to the globalization of industries.
d. none of the above.

Answers to Multiple-Choice Questions

1. a   2. a   3. d   4. c   5. d   6. c   7. d   8. d   9. a   10. a

Study Questions and Problems

1. Table 16.6 shows the hypothetical production possibilities tables of Japan and South Korea. Use this information to answer the following questions.

a. What is the opportunity cost of producing a TV for Japan and for South Korea?
b. Which country has a comparative advantage in the production of TVs?
c. In the absence of trade and specialization, suppose that Japan produces and consumes at combination *B* and South Korea produces and consumes at combination *E'*. If these countries specialize according to the principle of comparative advantage, how much will total output increase?
d. Show how consumers in each country can share the gains in total output that result from specialization.

Table 16.6	Production Possibilities Schedules for Japan and South Korea					

	Japan			South Korea		
	TVs	DVD Players		TVs	DVD Players	
A	0	80	A'	0	120	
B	8	64	B'	6	96	
C	16	48	C'	12	72	
D	24	32	D'	18	48	
E	32	16	E'	24	24	
F	40	0	F'	30	0	

2. The United States tends to have a comparative advantage over other nations in the production of high-technology goods. What are the likely sources of this advantage?

3. Which individuals might gain from a tariff placed on imported textiles? Who might lose?

4. Why do economists maintain that trade barriers lead to a misallocation of resources in the world economy?

5. Although people may grow grapefruit in Idaho, why do they purchase most of their grapefruit from California and Florida?

6. Suppose that the U.S. government imposes a quota on cheese imported from Europe. Who would likely be helped and hurt?

7. What is NAFTA, and what have been its effects to date?

8. Explain how trade with low-wage countries affects jobs in the United States. How can the United States pay its workers higher wages than foreign nations and still be competitive in foreign markets?

9. Suppose that Canada can produce 160 machine tools by using all of its resources to produce machine tools and 120 calculators by devoting all of its resources to calculators. Comparative figures for Brazil are 120 machine tools and 120 calculators. According to the principle of comparative advantage, in which product should each country specialize?

10. Draw a demand and supply diagram for autos in the United States, a product in which the United States has a comparative disadvantage. Show the effect of Japanese imports on the domestic price and quantity. Now show a tariff that cuts the level of auto imports in half. Show the effects of the tariff on U.S. producers and consumers.

11. Table 16.7 shows the demand and supply schedules for computers in Australia. On the basis of this information, answer the following questions:

    a. In the absence of trade, what are the equilibrium price and quantity of computers for Australia?
    b. Suppose that the world price of computers is $1,500 per unit and Australia takes this price as given. How many computers will Australia produce, consume, and import?
    c. To protect its producers from world competition, suppose that the Australian government imposes a tariff of $500 per unit on computer imports. What effect will the tariff have on the price of computers in Australia, the quantity of computers supplied by Australian producers, the quantity of computers demanded by Australian consumers, and the quantity of imports? How much revenue will the Australian government gain because of the tariff?

Table 16.7	Australia's Computer Market

Price of Computers (in dollars)	Quantity Demanded	Quantity Supplied
4,000	10	40
3,500	15	35
3,000	20	30
2,500	25	25
2,000	30	20
1,500	35	15
1,000	40	10

International Finance

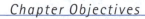

Chapter Objectives

After reading this chapter, you should be able to:

1. Explain what a current account deficit or surplus means.

2. Understand the foreign exchange quotations presented in major newspapers.

3. Identify the factors that determine the dollar's exchange rate.

4. Discuss the features of the major exchange rate systems of the world.

economics IN CONTEXT

During the early 2000s, the U.S. balance of payments (current account) reached record deficits, sparking fears of a flight from the dollar with wrenching consequences for U.S. economic prosperity. Nothing is intrinsically wrong with a country running such a deficit. But the United States has run a string of deficits for the past 20 years, and foreigners now hold unprecedented financial claims on the United States. At some point, foreigners might become reluctant to hold these dollars and set in motion a series of corrective economic adjustments that would result in sharply rising interest rates and recession for the U.S. economy.

Although international trade is an important component of the global economy, it is just one part of the picture. International finance is another part. The balance of payments is an important dimension of international finance, as is the financing of international trade.

In this chapter, we will examine the U.S. balance of payments and the markets in which Americans exchange dollars for other currencies. We will also expand our understanding of foreign currency markets by analyzing the advantages and disadvantages of various exchange rate systems.

THE BALANCE OF PAYMENTS

Every year, Americans conduct many transactions with foreigners. Some examples include the following:

- Sears imports shirts from Hong Kong.
- General Motors exports minivans to Brazil.
- Holiday Inn supplies rooms to German tourists visiting San Francisco.
- Ayako Ozawa, a student at Stanford University, receives gifts from her family in Japan.
- American investors receive dividends from their investments in Germany.
- Edgar Valdez, a resident of Mexico, purchases U.S. Treasury bills.
- George Thomas, who lives in Philadelphia, purchases stock in Sony Corp. of Japan.

The U.S. government compiles a statistical record of these and other transactions. This record is called the balance of payments. The **balance of payments** is a record of a country's international trading, borrowing, and lending. In the balance of payments, *inflows* of funds from foreigners to the United States are noted as *receipts,* with a plus sign. *Outflows* of funds from the United States to foreigners are noted as *payments,* with a minus sign. The balance of payments has two components, the current account and the capital and financial account, which we will now examine.

The Current Account

The first component of the balance of payments is the **current account,** which represents the dollar value of U.S. transactions in currently produced goods and services, investment income, and unilateral transfers.

The most widely reported component of the current account is the **balance of trade,** also known as the **trade balance.** This balance includes all the goods (merchandise) that the United States exports or imports: agricultural products, machinery, autos, petroleum, electronics, computer software, jetliners, textiles, and the like. Combining the exports and imports of goods gives the balance of trade. When exports exceed imports, the trade balance is a *surplus;* when imports exceed exports, the trade balance is a *deficit.*

Another component of the current account is exports and imports of **services.** Examples of internationally traded services include tourism, airline and shipping transportation, construction, architecture, engineering, consulting, information management, banking, insurance, medical, and legal. When exports exceed imports, the services balance is a *surplus;* when imports exceed exports, the services balance is a *deficit.*

Broadening the current account, we also include flows of **income.** This item consists of the net earnings (dividends and interest) on U.S. investments abroad—that is, earnings on U.S. investments abroad less payments on foreign investments in the United States. It also includes the net compensation of employees.

Finally, the current account includes **unilateral transfers.** These items—gifts—include transfers of goods and services or money between the United States and the rest of the world for which nothing is given in exchange—hence, they are unilateral. Examples of private transfers are gifts that Americans make to their families in Europe or living allowances that Japanese families send to their sons and daughters who attend college in the United States. The economic and military aid that the U.S. government provides to other governments is an example of a governmental unilateral transfer.

The **current account balance** is the sum of the trade balance, the services balance, net investment income, and net unilateral transfers. If the monetary inflows on these accounts exceed the monetary outflows, the current account balance is a *surplus.* But if the monetary outflows on these accounts exceeds the monetary inflows, the current account balance is a *deficit.*

The Capital and Financial Account

The second component of the balance of payments is the **capital and financial account.** Capital and financial transactions in the balance of payments represent all international purchases or sales of assets such as real estate, corporate stocks and bonds, and government securities. Changes in the foreign asset holdings of governments and central banks are also included in the capital and financial account.

When an American sells an asset (such as a golf course, a share of stock, or a bond) to a Japanese investor, the transaction is recorded in the capital and financial account as an inflow because funds flow into the United States to purchase the asset. When an American purchases a skyscraper in Switzerland, the transaction is recorded in the capital and financial account as an outflow because funds flow from the United States to purchase the asset.

The **capital and financial account balance** is the amount of inflows minus outflows. The capital and financial account balance is a *surplus* if those in the United States sell more assets to foreigners than they purchase from foreigners. The capital and financial account balance is a *deficit* if those in the United States buy more assets from foreigners than they sell to foreigners.

What Does a Current Account Deficit (Surplus) Mean?

The current account and the capital and financial account are not unrelated; they are essentially reflections of one another. Recall that each international transaction represents an exchange of goods, services, or assets among households, businesses, or governments. Thus, the two sides of the exchange must always balance. This means that, sign ignored, the current account balance equals the capital and financial account balance, as shown in the following equation:

Current account balance = Capital and financial account balance

It follows that any current account *deficit* must be balanced by a capital and financial account *surplus.* Conversely, any current account *surplus* must be balanced by a capital and financial account *deficit.*

To better understand this notion, assume that in a particular year, your spending is greater than your income. How will you finance your deficit? By borrowing or by selling some of your assets. You might liquidate some real assets (for example, sell your personal computer) or perhaps some financial assets (sell a U.S. government security that you own). In like manner, when a nation experiences a current account deficit, its expenditures for foreign goods and services are greater than the income that it receives from the international sales of its own goods and services, after making allowances for investment income flows and gifts to and from foreigners. The nation must somehow finance its current account deficit. But how? By borrowing or by selling assets. In other words, a nation's current account *deficit* is financed essentially by a net *inflow* of capital in its capital and financial account. Conversely, a nation's current account *surplus* is financed by a net *outflow* of capital in its capital and financial account.

Although the current account balance always equals the capital and financial account balance, the figures gathered on international transactions are not 100 percent accurate or complete. Consequently, an adjustment for measurement errors, the **statistical discrepancy,** is reported in the capital and financial account component of the balance of payments. Economists generally believe that the statistical discrepancy is primarily the result of large hidden capital and financial flows (for example, unidentified borrowing from the rest of the world or tax evasion), and so the item is placed in the capital and financial account component of the balance of payments.

THE U.S. BALANCE OF PAYMENTS

Table 17.1 shows the balance of payments for the United States between 1980 and 2008. Items in the current account and capital and financial account that provide inflows of funds from foreigners to the United States are positive; items that result in flows of funds from the United States to other nations have a minus sign.

Let us consider the U.S. balance of payments for 2008. As seen in the table, the United States had a merchandise trade balance of –$820.8 billion resulting from the difference between U.S. merchandise exports and merchandise imports. The United States was thus a net importer of merchandise. The

| Table 17.1 | U.S. Balance of Payments, 1980–2008 (billions of dollars) |

Year	Merchandise Trade Balance	Services Balance	Net Income Flows	Net Unilateral Transfers	Current Account Balance	Capital and Financial Account Balance
1980	−25.5	6.1	30.1	−8.3	2.4	−2.4
1984	−112.5	3.3	30.0	−20.6	−99.8	99.8
1988	−127.0	12.2	11.6	−25.0	−128.2	128.2
1992	−96.1	55.7	4.5	−32.0	−67.9	67.9
1996	−191.4	82.8	14.2	−40.5	−134.9	134.9
2000	−449.9	81.0	−13.3	−53.2	−435.5	435.4
2004	−665.5	48.4	24.1	−72.9	−665.9	665.9
2008	−820.8	139.7	127.5	−119.7	−673.3	673.3

Sources: U.S. Department of Commerce, *Survey of Current Business,* various issues. See also U.S. Department of Commerce, Bureau of Economic Analysis, available at http://www.bea.doc.gov.

table also shows that the United States has consistently realized merchandise trade deficits since 1980.

Discussions of U.S. competitiveness in merchandise trade often give the impression that the United States has consistently performed poorly relative to other nations. However, the merchandise trade deficit is a narrow concept because goods are only part of what the world trades. Another part of trade is services. Table 17.1 shows that in 2008, the United States realized a surplus of $139.7 billion on services transactions with foreigners. In recent decades, the United States has consistently generated a surplus in its services account, as seen in the table. The United States has been especially competitive in transportation, construction, engineering, finance, and certain health care services.

Next, we adjust the merchandise trade balance and the services balance for net income flows ($127.5 billion) and net unilateral transfers (–$119.7 billion). This gives the current account balance. As Table 17.1 shows, the United States had a current account deficit of –$673.3 billion in 2008. Because our exports were insufficient to pay for our imports, we either borrowed from foreigners or sold assets such as corporate stock, golf courses, real estate, and skyscrapers to make up the difference. The capital and financial account tells us how much was borrowed and sold. In 2008, the net borrowing and sale of assets by the United States was $673.3 billion. Since 1982, the United States has realized continuous current account deficits.

Indeed, we buy much more from foreigners than they buy from us. Therefore, foreigners lend or give us the funds to make up the difference between our imports and our exports. It would not be an overstatement to say that we borrow so much from foreigners to finance our current account deficits that we sell them pieces of America, so to speak. Those pieces consist primarily of real estate and corporate stock. However, foreigners also lend us billions of dollars each year in the form of purchases of government and corporate securities and other debt instruments.

Are U.S. Current Account Deficits Bad?

In both the media and popular opinion, current account deficits are often portrayed negatively, blamed on either the unfair practices of our trading partners or a lack of U.S. competitiveness in world markets. Some have even suggested that growing current account deficits will eventually interfere with the expansion of the U.S. economy.

When a nation realizes a current account deficit, it becomes a net borrower of funds from the rest of the world. Is this a problem? Not necessarily. The benefit of a current account deficit is the ability to push current spending beyond current production. However, the cost is the debt service that must be paid on the associated borrowing from the rest of the world.

Is it good or bad for a country to get into debt? Obviously, the answer depends on what the country does with the money. What matters for future income and living standards is whether the deficit is being used to finance more consumption or more investment. If it is being used exclusively to finance an increase in domestic investment, the burden could be slight. We know that investment spending increases a nation's stock of capital and expands an economy's capacity to produce goods and services. The value of this extra output may be sufficient to pay foreign creditors and to augment domestic spending. In this case, because future consumption need not be reduced, there is no true economic burden. If, on the other hand, foreign borrowing is used to finance or increase domestic consumption (private or public), there is no boost to future productive capacity. Therefore, to meet debt-service expense, future consumption must be reduced. Such a reduction represents the burden of borrowing. This is not necessarily bad; it all depends on how one values current versus future consumption.

In the past two decades, the United States has run continuous deficits in its current account. Can the United States run deficits indefinitely? Because the current account deficit arises mainly because foreigners desire to purchase American assets, there is no economic reason why the deficits cannot continue indefinitely. As long as the investment opportunities are large enough to provide foreign investors with competitive rates of return, they will be happy to continue supplying funds to the United States.

However, the consequence of a current account deficit is growing foreign ownership of the capital stock of the United States and a rising fraction of U.S. income that must be diverted overseas in the form of interest and dividends to foreigners. Whether the United States can sustain its current account deficit over the foreseeable future depends on whether foreigners are willing to increase their investments in U.S. assets. The current account deficit puts the economic fortunes of the United States partially in the hands of foreign investors.

Finally, do current account deficits cost Americans jobs? According to economists at the Federal Reserve Bank of New York, the U.S. current account deficit is not a threat to employment for the economy as a whole.[1] A high current account deficit may indeed hurt employment in particular firms and industries as workers are displaced by increased imports or by the relocation of production abroad. At the economy-wide level, however, the current account deficit is matched by an equal inflow of foreign capital, which finances employment-sustaining investment spending that would not otherwise occur. When viewed as the net inflow of foreign investment capital, the current account deficit produces jobs for the economy as a whole, both from the direct effects of higher employment in investment-oriented industries and from the indirect effects of higher investment spending on economy-wide employment. Viewing the current account deficit as a capital inflow thus helps dispel misconceptions about the adverse consequences of economic globalization on the domestic job market.

CHECK POINT

1. What is the balance of payments?

2. The balance of payments includes the current account and the capital and financial account. Identify the components of each.

3. What does a current account deficit mean? How about a current account surplus?

4. What are the advantages and disadvantages of a current account deficit for the United States?

THE FOREIGN EXCHANGE MARKET

Now that we have learned about international flows of exports, imports, investment, and income, let us consider how these transactions are financed. Financing these transactions involves the purchase and sale of foreign currencies, such as the Mexican peso and Japanese yen.

In most cases, the buying and selling of currencies takes place in the **foreign exchange market.** The currencies of most advanced and many developing economies are traded in this market. The foreign exchange market does not involve sending large loads of currency from one country to another. Typically, it involves electronic balances. Dollar-denominated balances in computers in the United States or other countries are traded for computer-housed balances around the world that are denominated in Japanese yen, British pounds, Swiss francs, or any of dozens of other commonly traded monies. In short, when "currency" is traded, paper and metal are not the usual media of exchange. Foreign exchange exists mainly in the world of cyberspace.

Most daily newspapers publish foreign exchange rates for major currencies. The **exchange rate** is the price of one currency in terms of another—for example, the number of dollars required to purchase one British pound. The dollar price of the pound may be, say, $2 = 1 pound. It is also

1. Matthew Higgins and Thomas Klitgaard, "Viewing the Current Account Deficit as a Capital Inflow," *Current Issues in Economics and Finance*, Federal Reserve Bank of New York, December 1999, pp. 1–6, available at http://www.by.frb.org.

possible to define the exchange rate as the number of units of foreign currency required to purchase 1 unit of domestic currency. For example, the pound price of the dollar may be 0.5 pound = $1. Of course, the pound price of the dollar is the reciprocal of the dollar price of the pound, calculated as shown:

$$\text{Pound price of the dollar} = 1/\text{Dollar price of the pound}$$
$$0.5 = 1/2$$

Therefore, if $2 is required to buy 1 pound, 0.5 pound is required to buy $1.

Table 17.2 shows examples of exchange rates for Wednesday, March 11, 2009. In columns 2 and 3 ("In U.S. Dollars") of the table, the selling prices of foreign currencies are listed in dollars. The columns state how many dollars are required to purchase one unit of a given foreign currency. For example, the quote for the European Union's euro for Wednesday was 1.2848. This means that $1.2848 (about $1.28) was required to purchase 1 euro. Columns 4 and 5 ("Currency per U.S. Dollar") show the foreign exchange rates from the opposite perspective, telling how many units of a foreign currency are required to buy a U.S. dollar. Again referring to Wednesday, it would take 0.7783 euros to purchase 1 U.S. dollar.

In a free market, exchange rates can and do change frequently, usually within a very narrow range. When the dollar price of the pound increases—for example, from $2 = 1 pound to $2.01 = 1 pound—the dollar has depreciated (weakened) relative to the pound. Currency **depreciation** means that it takes *more* units of a nation's currency to purchase a unit of some foreign currency. As a result, the prices of foreign goods increase for domestic consumers and imports decline. Conversely, when the dollar price of the pound decreases—say, from $2 = 1 pound to $1.99 = 1 pound—the value of the dollar has appreciated (strengthened) relative to the pound. Currency **appreciation** means that it takes *fewer* units of a nation's currency to purchase a unit of some foreign currency. Because foreign goods become more attractive to domestic consumers, imports tend to increase.

Referring to Table 17.2, look at columns 2 and 3 ("In U.S. Dollars"). Going forward in time from Tuesday (March 10) to Wednesday (March 11), we see that the dollar cost of the Mexican peso

Table 17.2	Foreign Exchange Quotations				
	Exchange Rates (Wednesday, March 11, 2009)				
		In U.S. Dollars		Currency per U.S. Dollars	
Country		Wednesday	Tuesday	Wednesday	Tuesday
Canada (dollar)		.7766	.7780	1.2860	1.2853
China (yuan)		.1462	.1462	6.8404	6.8404
Japan (yen)		.010289	.010130	97.19	98.72
Mexico (peso)		.0663	.0656	15.0807	15.2486
Russia (ruble)		.02859	.02852	34.977	35.063
United Kingdom (pound)		1.3869	1.3747	.7210	.7274
European Union (euro)		1.2848	1.2675	.7783	.7890

Sources: Reuters, *Currency Calculator*, available at http://www.reuters.com. See also Federal Reserve Bank of New York, "Foreign Exchange Rates," available at http://www.newyorkfed.org/markets/fxrates/ten.Am.cfm.

increased from \$0.0656 to \$0.0663; the dollar thus depreciated against the peso. This means that the peso appreciated against the dollar. To verify this conclusion, refer to columns 4 and 5 of the table ("Currency per U.S. Dollar"). Going forward in time from Tuesday to Wednesday, we see that the peso cost of the dollar decreased from 15.2486 pesos = \$1 to 15.0807 pesos = \$1. In similar fashion, we see that from Tuesday to Wednesday the U.S. dollar appreciated against the Canadian dollar from \$0.7780 = \$1 Canadian to \$0.7766 = \$1 Canadian; the Canadian dollar thus depreciated against the U.S. dollar from \$1.2853 Canadian = \$1 U.S. to \$1.2860 Canadian = \$1 U.S.

A Weak Dollar Is a Bonanza for European Tourists

Not only do changing currency values affect exporters, importers, and investors, they also affect tourists. Consider the impact of a depreciating dollar on European tourists.

Jackie Murphy held up a white pair of jogging shoes for her husband, Edward, to examine in a Nike store aisle piled high with boxes of shoes. She smiled when she saw the price tag.

"They're only \$55!" said Murphy, a tourist from London, England. "Do you like them? Try them on."

Although Murphy is an experienced shopper—it is one of her favorite pastimes back home—she was shocked at her purchasing power on a vacation to Orlando in 2005. The power came primarily from a currency exchange rate that had the British pound approaching twice the value of the U.S. dollar. "The exchange rate is fantastic," said Edward Murphy, who sells electronics in London. "We couldn't have timed it better to come over on our vacation." In 2005, the dollar reached a record low against the euro and an 11-year low against the pound.

Many European and Canadian visitors followed the Murphy's example, in part because of the inexpensive U.S. dollar. The American tourist industry was delighted with this situation. Because of the cheaper dollar, tourists could afford to stay longer, stay at nicer and more expensive hotels, take more tours, eat at more restaurants, and shop with bargain-basement enthusiasm. Adding to the bonanza for Europeans, airfares to and from the United States declined.

For example, the cheap dollar encouraged 15-year-old Molly Sanders of Liverpool, England, to purchase six heavy-metal T-shirts during a visit to Orlando, and her parents decided that they could afford a road trip to Miami. The family booked hotel reservations and purchased theme park tickets in the United States rather than in Britain. By obtaining the tickets in dollars instead of pounds, they saved about \$21 each day they went to the parks. The weaker dollar also allowed Molly to buy a large cup of Starbucks coffee in Miami for \$1.80 rather than paying \$2.80 in London. Similarly, an Apple iPod sold for \$300 in Miami but \$425 in London.

The exchange rate also led the British travel firm Virgin Holidays to renegotiate prices with the U.S. car rental companies and hotels that it uses. The new prices permitted the firm to offer a package of airfare to Orlando, seven nights' accommodations, and rental car for 399 pounds—130 pounds less than what it had previously offered. At the prevailing exchange rate, the discounted price was equal to \$718, for about \$234 in savings.[2]

EXCHANGE RATE DETERMINATION

What determines the equilibrium exchange value of a currency? Let us consider the exchange rate from the perspective of the United States—in dollars per unit of foreign currency. Like other prices, the exchange rate in a free market is determined by both demand and supply conditions.

---

2. "Coming to America: Exchange Rate Attracts Foreign Visitors," *Yakima Herald Republic,* March 18, 2004, p. 6-A; and "As Dollar Declines, Europeans See U.S. as Big Half-Off Sale," *The Wall Street Journal,* December 6, 2004, p. A1.

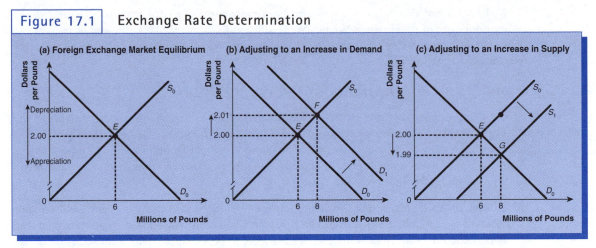

Figure 17.1   Exchange Rate Determination

(a) Foreign Exchange Market Equilibrium   (b) Adjusting to an Increase in Demand   (c) Adjusting to an Increase in Supply

In a free market, the equilibrium exchange rate is determined by the market forces of demand and supply. In the figure, market equilibrium occurs at point *E*, where S_0 and D_0 intersect. All else being equal, an increase in the demand for foreign currency results in a depreciation of the dollar; an increase in the supply of foreign currency causes the dollar to appreciate.

Figure 17.1 shows the market for the British pound. The demand curve for pounds, denoted by D_0, stems from the desire of Americans to purchase British goods, services, and assets. Like most demand schedules, the U.S. demand for pounds varies inversely with price. As the dollar price of the pound rises, British goods become more expensive for Americans, who thus purchase smaller quantities. Therefore, fewer pounds are demanded in the foreign exchange market.

The supply curve for pounds, denoted by S_0 in the figure, shows the quantity of pounds that will be offered to the market at various exchange rates. The British supply pounds to the market in order to purchase American goods, services, and assets. As the dollar price of the pound rises—hence, the pound price of the dollar falls—American goods become cheaper to the British, who are induced to purchase additional quantities. Therefore, more pounds are offered in the foreign exchange market to buy dollars with which to pay U.S. exporters.

As long as central bankers do not attempt to influence exchange rates, the **equilibrium exchange rate** is determined by the market forces of demand and supply. In Figure 17.1(*a*), exchange market equilibrium occurs at point *E*, where S_0 and D_0 intersect. A total of 6 million pounds will be traded at a price of $2 per pound. The foreign exchange market is precisely cleared, leaving neither an excess supply of nor an excess demand for pounds.

With given demand and supply schedules for pounds, there is no reason for the pound's exchange rate to deviate from the equilibrium level. In reality, it is unlikely that the equilibrium exchange rate will remain at the existing level for long. This is because the forces that underlie the location of the demand and supply schedules tend to change frequently, causing shifts in the schedules.

Referring to Figure 17.1(*b*), suppose that an increase in the quantity of British goods demanded by Americans causes the demand for pounds to increase. Therefore, the dollar price of the pound increases, meaning that the dollar *depreciates* against the pound. Conversely, a *decrease* in the demand for pounds causes the dollar to *appreciate*.

Now we will consider the effect of a change in the supply of pounds on the equilibrium exchange rate. Referring to Figure 17.1(*c*), suppose that expanding U.S. exports to the United Kingdom result in an *increase* in the supply of pounds on the foreign exchange market. This causes the dollar price of the pound to decrease, suggesting that the dollar *appreciates* against the pound. Conversely, a *decrease* in the supply of pounds causes the dollar to *depreciate*.

We have learned that a shift in the demand or supply curve of a currency causes changes in the equilibrium price of the currency. What factors induce shifts in these curves, causing the currency to depreciate or appreciate? We can analyze the behavior of exchange rates over two time periods, the long run and the short run.

Long-Run Determinants of Exchange Rates

Changes in the long-run value (1, 2, or even 5 years) of the exchange rate are attributable to the reactions of traders in the foreign exchange market to changes in four key factors: relative price levels, relative productivity levels, consumer preferences for domestic or foreign goods, and trade barriers. Note that these factors underlie trade in domestic and foreign goods and thus changes in the demand for exports and imports.

- **Relative prices.** Suppose that the domestic price level increases rapidly in Mexico but remains constant in the United States. Mexican consumers will desire low-priced computers produced by Dell and Gateway, thereby increasing the supply of pesos. At the same time, U.S. consumers will buy fewer tomatoes from Mexico, reducing the demand for pesos. The combination of an increase in the supply of pesos and a decrease in the demand for pesos will cause the dollar price of the peso to fall—that is, the dollar will appreciate.

- **Relative productivity levels.** If German CD manufacturers become more productive than Canadian manufacturers, they can produce CDs more cheaply than their Canadian competitors. Thus, Germany's exports of CDs to Canada will increase and its imports from Canada will decrease. This results in an appreciation of Germany's euro against Canada's dollar.

- **Consumer preferences.** If the preferences of Americans change in favor of Swiss watches, the demand for the Swiss franc will increase as Americans import more watches, causing a depreciation of the dollar against the franc.

- **Trade barriers.** Suppose that the U.S. government imposes tariffs on Toyota automobiles. By making Toyotas more expensive, the tariff will discourage Americans from purchasing them. This results in a decrease in the demand for Japanese yen and an appreciation of the dollar against the yen.

Short-Run Determinants of Exchange Rates

Economists believe that the determinants of exchange rate fluctuations are rather different in the short run (a few weeks or even days) than in the long run (a year or more). Thus, we will consider the short-run time frame when analyzing exchange rates. In the short run, foreign exchange transactions are dominated by transfers of investment funds (bank deposits and Treasury securities), which respond to differences in interest rates and to shifting expectations of future exchange rates; such transactions have a major influence on short-run exchange rates.

- **Relative interest rates.** A country with relatively *high* interest rates tends to find its currency's exchange value *appreciating*. You've already learned that a rise in interest rates makes an asset, such as a Treasury bill, more attractive to investors. Suppose that a tight monetary policy causes interest rates to be high in the United States, while an easy monetary policy causes interest rates to be low in Switzerland. Therefore, Swiss investors will find the United States an attractive place to purchase Treasury bills. The increase in the demand for U.S. Treasury bills results in an increase in the supply of Swiss francs and thus a decrease in the dollar price of the franc. The dollar therefore appreciates against the franc.

- **Expectations of future exchange rates.** Suppose that an unanticipated rise in the growth rate of the U.S. money supply is interpreted as a signal that the U.S. inflation rate will rise, which, in turn, signals a possible depreciation in the dollar's exchange rate. This set of expectations causes

Americans who intend to make purchases in Sweden to obtain kronor prior to the anticipated depreciation of the dollar (when the krona would become more expensive in dollars). Accordingly, the demand for kronor increases in the foreign exchange market. The increased demand for kronor results in a depreciation of the dollar.[3]

EXCHANGE RATE SYSTEMS

We have learned that exchange rates are determined by the actions of the investors, exporters, tourists, and importers who participate in the foreign exchange market. However, governments can also affect exchange rates. The extent and nature of government participation in foreign exchange markets define the various exchange rate systems. These systems include floating exchange rates and fixed exchange rates.

Floating Exchange Rates

In a **floating exchange rate system,** governments and central banks do not participate in the foreign exchange market. Instead, currency values are established daily in the foreign exchange market by demand and supply conditions. With floating exchange rates, an equilibrium exchange rate equates the demand for and supply of the home currency. Ideally, changes in the exchange rate will correct any imbalance in payments by inducing shifts in imports and exports of goods, services, and capital. The exchange rate depends on relative income levels among nations, relative interest rates, relative prices, and the like.

One advantage of floating exchange rates is their adjustment efficiency. Floating exchange rates respond quickly to changing demand and supply conditions, clearing the market of shortages or surpluses of a given currency. Thus, governments do not have to restore balance in international payments through painful adjustments in fiscal policy or monetary policy. Instead, they can use these policies to combat domestic unemployment and inflation.

Although there are strong arguments in favor of floating exchange rates, this system is often considered to be of limited usefulness to bankers and business people. Critics of floating exchange rates maintain that an unregulated market may lead to wide fluctuations in currency values, discouraging foreign trade and investment. Moreover, the greater freedom that floating exchange rates provide domestic policy makers may cause them to be more inclined to overspend, which contributes to inflation.

Fixed Exchange Rates

Rather than allowing exchange rates to be determined by market forces, governments sometimes attempt to maintain completely fixed exchange rates.[4] Today, **fixed exchange rates** are used primarily by developing nations that maintain ties to a key currency, such as the U.S. dollar. A key currency is one that is widely traded on world money markets, demonstrates a relatively stable value over time,

---

3. Concurrently, the Swedes, who hold the same set of expectations, will be less willing to give up kronor in exchange for dollars that will soon decrease in value. The supply of kronor offered in the foreign exchange market decreases. The increased demand for kronor and the decreased supply of kronor thus result in a depreciation of the dollar. In this way, future expectations of a currency's depreciation can be self-fulfilling.

4. How do central banks attempt to maintain fixed exchange rates? For example, to prevent the dollar from depreciating against the euro, the Federal Reserve could purchase dollars on the foreign exchange market, drawing on its holdings of euros. The increase in the demand for the dollar thus promotes an increase in the exchange value of the dollar against the euro. Instead, the Fed could adopt a contractionary monetary policy that will increase domestic interest rates and attract European purchases of American securities. As more dollars are demanded by Europeans, the value of the dollar will rise against the euro.

and is accepted as a means of international settlement. Fixed exchange rates are also used when a group of countries form an economic bloc, such as the European Monetary Union, discussed later in this chapter.

One reason why nations choose to tie their currencies to a key currency is that it is used as a means of international settlement. Consider a Venezuelan importer who wants to purchase beef from Argentina over the next year. If the Argentine exporter is unsure of what the Venezuelan bolivar will purchase in one year, he might reject the bolivar in settlement. Similarly, the Venezuelan importer might doubt the value of Argentina's peso. One solution is for the contract to be written in terms of a key currency, such as the U.S. dollar.

Maintaining ties to a key currency provides several benefits for developing nations. First, the prices of many developing nations' traded products are determined primarily in the markets of industrialized nations such as the United States. By linking their currencies to, say, the dollar, these nations can stabilize the domestic currency prices of their imports and exports. Second, many developing nations with high inflation link to the dollar (the United States has relatively low inflation) in order to exert restraint on domestic prices and reduce inflation. By making the commitment to stabilize their exchange rates against the dollar, governments hope to convince their citizens that they are willing to adopt the responsible monetary policies that are necessary to achieve low inflation.

The exchange rate system used by the United States is a combination of fixed and floating exchange rates. Known as **managed floating exchange rates,** the system allows the dollar to generally float in the foreign exchange market according to the market forces of demand and supply. However, governmental intervention may be used to stabilize the dollar's value when the foreign exchange market becomes disorderly and disruptive to international trade and investment.

MONETARY INTEGRATION IN EUROPE AND THE UNITED STATES

The globalization of economies has promoted opportunities and challenges for the international monetary system. Let us consider two challenges that are important for the new century.

The Euro: A Common Currency for Europe

One important challenge for the international monetary system is the development of the European Union. The **European Union (EU)** is a regional economic bloc consisting of 25 European nations. The primary objective of the EU has been to create an economic bloc in which trade and other transactions take place freely among member nations. From the 1950s to the 1990s, the EU succeeded in eliminating trade restrictions among member countries, allowing for the free movement of labor and capital within the union, and adopting common policies toward competition and agriculture.

In 1991, the EU agreed to achieve monetary unification in 1999 for those nations eligible to participate. Participation in the monetary unification would require nations to fulfill economic goals concerning inflation, public finances, interest rates, and exchange rates. The nations participating in the EU would have a common currency, a single exchange rate, a single monetary policy, and a single central bank to oversee the monetary policy.

In 2002, 11 European countries united to form the **European Monetary Union (EMU)** and replaced their individual currencies, such as the German mark and the French franc, with a single currency, the **euro.** At that point, the euro became the single currency in circulation throughout the monetary union. If the monetary union expands according to plans, in 2 or 3 decades, the euro will be in use throughout most of Western and Central Europe. The euro could prove a strong alternative to the U.S. dollar as a key currency for the global financial system. Financial markets will conduct transactions in euros, and central banks will want to hold some of their reserves in these currencies.

The EMU also created a new **European Central Bank** to take control of monetary policy and exchange rate policy for member countries. This central bank alone controls the supply of euros, sets the euro interest rate, and maintains permanently fixed exchange rates for the member countries. With a common central bank, the central bank of each participating nation performs operations similar to those of the 12 regional Federal Reserve Banks in the United States.

For Americans, the benefits of a common currency are easy to understand. Americans know that they can walk into a McDonald's or Burger King anywhere in the United States and purchase a hamburger with the dollar bills in their purses and wallets. Before the adoption of the euro, this was not the case in European countries. Because each nation had its own currency, a French person could not buy an item at a German store without first exchanging French francs for German marks. This would be like someone from St. Louis having to exchange Missouri currency for Illinois currency every time she visits Chicago. To make matters worse, because marks and francs floated against each other within a range, the number of marks a French traveler received one day differed from the number he would have received the day before or would receive the next. On top of the exchange rate uncertainty, travelers also paid a fee to exchange their currency, making a trip across the border a costly proposition indeed. Although the costs to individuals were limited because of the small quantities of money involved, firms incurred much larger costs. By replacing the various European currencies with a single currency—the euro—the EMU has avoided such costs.

On the downside, a lack of exchange rate flexibility and a loss of national monetary policy may prolong regional economic downturns. A country cannot lower interest rates when it goes into recession unless all of the other countries agree that this is a good policy, perhaps prolonging a localized recession. For example, the fact that Texas could not lower interest rates when a collapse in oil prices sent its economy into recession in 1986 may have extended that state's recession.

Indeed, the EMU is a groundbreaking monetary experiment. Never before have politically independent nations with a history of monetary independence and long-standing central banks given up that independence to form a common central bank and adopt a single currency. The success of the EMU remains an open question.

The Dollar: A Common Currency for the Americas?

Another challenge for the international monetary system is the integration of the U.S. dollar into the monetary systems of other countries in North and South America.

Many developing economies, such as Ecuador, experience high and unstable inflation rates when their governments increase the money supply to finance higher levels of government spending. High and unstable inflation rates result in a more unstable investment climate and a lower rate of economic growth. When people lose faith in the domestic currency, it is not uncommon for another currency to be used as a medium of exchange in the domestic economy. Because of its relative stability and use as an international currency, the U.S. dollar is frequently used for this purpose. **Dollarization** is said to occur when the U.S. dollar replaces the domestic currency as the official medium of exchange.

Advocates of dollarization argue that developing economies that replace their less-stable domestic currency with the U.S. dollar experience a lower and more stable inflation rate. A lower and more stable inflation rate, in turn, is expected to lead to a higher level of investment and a faster rate of economic growth. This benefit is larger when the domestic monetary authorities have a poor track record of maintaining a stable domestic money supply.

Opponents of dollarization note that the domestic monetary authorities have no control over the domestic money supply under this policy. The government of a dollarized economy cannot use discretionary monetary policy to deal with domestic macroeconomic problems. If the domestic economy experiences a business cycle that closely corresponds to the U.S. economy's business cycle, this may present less of a problem because the U.S. Federal Reserve might engage in appropriate monetary policy responses. Even if the Federal Reserve can be trusted to engage in "appropriate" policy responses, many countries are still reluctant to cede their control over domestic macroeconomic policy to a foreign agency. Countries that replace their national currencies with the dollar also lose the profit made by governments that issue money (profit exists because the purchasing power of coin and paper money exceeds the cost of producing the money).

Many U.S. policy makers argue that dollarization is an indication of the relatively high rate of success that the Federal Reserve has achieved in maintaining a stable currency in recent years. There is some concern, though, that foreign governments will attempt to exert political pressure to encourage the Federal Reserve to pursue monetary policies that are not consistent with U.S. monetary policy objectives. In the future, the dollarization debate is likely to be a major policy issue in the United States and in countries experiencing currency instability.

This chapter has examined the U.S. balance of payments and the markets in which Americans exchange dollars for other currencies. The next chapter will broaden our understanding of globalization by considering alternative economic systems and the economic problems of developing countries.

CHECK POINT

1. What is the foreign exchange rate? What does it mean when a currency depreciates (appreciates) in the foreign exchange market?

2. Identify the major factors that determine the exchange value of the dollar in the long run and in the short run.

3. Discuss the major features of floating exchange rates and fixed exchange rates.

4. What are the advantages and disadvantages of the European Monetary Union's adoption of the euro?

Chapter Summary

1. The balance of payments is a record of a country's international trading, borrowing, and lending. In the balance of payments, inflows of funds from foreigners to the United States are noted as receipts; outflows of funds from the United States to foreigners are noted as payments.

2. The balance of payments has two components, the current account and the capital and financial account. The current account represents the dollar value of transactions in currently produced goods and services, investment income, and unilateral transfers. If the monetary inflows on these accounts are greater (less) than monetary outflows, the current account balance is a surplus (deficit). The second component of the balance of payments is the capital and financial account, which represents international purchases or sales of assets such as real estate, corporate stocks and bonds, and government securities. The capital and financial account balance is a surplus (deficit) if domestic residents sell more (fewer) assets to foreigners than they purchase from them. Because the current account balance and capital and financial account balance always equal each other, any current account deficit (surplus) must be balanced by a capital and financial account surplus (deficit).

3. In the past two decades, the United States has run continuous deficits in its current account. Thus, foreigners lend or give us the funds to make up the difference between our imports and

our exports. It would not be an overstatement to say that we borrow so much from foreigners to finance our current account deficits that we sell them pieces of America. Those pieces consist primarily of real estate and corporate stock. However, foreigners also lend us billions of dollars each year in the form of purchases of government and corporate securities and other debt instruments.

4. The buying and selling of currencies generally takes place in the foreign exchange market. This market does not involve sending large loads of currency from one country to another. Typically, it involves electronic balances. Dollar-denominated balances in computers in the United States or other countries are traded for computer-housed balances around the world that are denominated in yen, pounds, francs, and the like. In short, when currency is traded, paper and metal are not the usual media of exchange.

5. Most daily newspapers publish foreign exchange rates for major currencies. The exchange rate is the price of one currency in terms of another. Currency depreciation (appreciation) means that it takes more (fewer) units of a nation's currency to purchase a unit of some foreign currency. The major factors that determine the equilibrium exchange rate in a free market are relative prices, relative productivity levels, consumer preferences, trade barriers, relative interest rates, and expectations of future exchange rates.

6. Although exchange rates are determined by demand and supply, governments can also affect exchange rates. The extent and nature of government participation in foreign exchange markets define the various exchange rate systems. These systems include floating exchange rates and fixed exchange rates.

7. As part of its strategy for forming a regional economic bloc, the European Union has pursued monetary integration. For participating nations, monetary integration implies a common currency, a single exchange rate, a single monetary policy, and a single central bank to oversee the monetary policy.

Key Terms and Concepts

balance of payments (392)

current account (392)

balance of trade (trade balance) (393)

services (393)

income (393)

unilateral transfers (393)

current account balance (393)

capital and financial account (393)

capital and financial account balance (393)

statistical discrepancy (394)

foreign exchange market (396)

exchange rate (396)

depreciation (397)

appreciation (397)

equilibrium exchange rate (399)

floating exchange rate system (401)

fixed exchange rates (401)

managed floating exchange rates (402)

European Union (EU) (402)

European Monetary Union (EMU) (402)

euro (402)

European Central Bank (403)

dollarization (403)

Self-Test: Multiple-Choice Questions

1. The current account of the balance of payments includes all of the following *except*

   a. flows of international investment.
   b. unilateral transfers.
   c. trade in merchandise.
   d. trade in services.

2. A surplus in the current account

   a. results in a surplus in the capital and financial account.
   b. results in a deficit in the capital and financial account.
   c. has no relation to the capital and financial account.
   d. none of the above.

3. Which of the following will *not* increase the demand for dollars in the foreign exchange market?

   a. Exports of Boeing jetliners to China.
   b. Travel by Swiss tourists in the United States.
   c. The desire of German investors to purchase U.S. Treasury bills.
   d. Imports of Honda Accords from Japan.

4. If the United States sells more assets to foreigners than it purchases from foreigners, the U.S.

   a. capital and financial account balance will show a surplus.
   b. services balance will show a deficit.
   c. current account balance will show a surplus.
   d. unilateral transfers balance will show a deficit.

5. American tourists in Mexico would prefer

   a. a depreciation of the dollar against the peso.
   b. an appreciation of the dollar against the peso.
   c. no change in the value of the dollar against the peso.
   d. none of the above.

6. Under a system of floating exchange rates, the exchange value of the dollar will depreciate if

   a. the U.S. economy grows more slowly than the rest of the world.
   b. U.S. consumer preferences worsen for goods of the foreign country.
   c. the United States has a higher inflation rate than the rest of the world.
   d. the United States has higher interest rates than the rest of the world.

7. The broadest account in the balance of payments is the

   a. unilateral transfers account.
   b. current account.
   c. merchandise trade account.
   d. investment income account.

8. Which of the following would induce a flow of funds from foreigners to the United States?

   a. Sears purchases shirts from a manufacturer in Taiwan.
   b. French investors collect interest on their holdings of U.S. Treasury bills.
   c. A German student spends a year studying at Boston University.
   d. Tom Sullivan makes a remittance to his relatives in Ireland.

9. If a Toyota automobile costs 4 million yen in Japan and the yen price of the dollar is 133.33 yen = $1, the dollar cost of the Toyota is

a. $25,000.
b. $30,000.
c. $35,000.
d. $40,000.

10. In the short run, the dollar's exchange value is determined by

a. tariffs and quotas.
b. productivity levels.
c. consumer preferences for domestic and foreign goods.
d. relative interest rates.

Answers to Multiple–Choice Questions

1. a   2. b   3. d   4. a   5. b   6. c   7. b   8. c   9. b   10. d

Study Questions and Problems

1. Indicate whether each of the following items represents a monetary inflow or outflow on the U.S. balance of payments:

a. A U.S. importer purchases a shipload of French wine.
b. A Japanese automobile firm builds an assembly plant in Kentucky.
c. A British manufacturer exports machinery to Taiwan on a U.S. vessel.
d. A U.S. college student spends a year studying in Switzerland.
e. U.S. charities donate food to people in drought-plagued Africa.
f. Japanese investors collect interest income on their holdings of U.S. government securities.
g. A German resident sends money to her relatives in the United States.
h. Lloyd's of London sells an insurance policy to a U.S. firm.
i. A Swiss resident receives dividends on his IBM stock.

2. Concerning a country's balance of payments, when would its current account be in surplus (deficit)? What would a current account surplus (deficit) imply for the capital and financial account? Is a current account deficit necessarily bad?

3. Why are some economists concerned that the United States borrows too much from abroad?

4. Table 17.3 summarizes hypothetical transactions, in billions of U.S. dollars, that took place during a given year.

a. Calculate the U.S. merchandise trade and current account balances.
b. Which of these balances pertains to the net borrowing (lending) position of the United States? How would you describe that position?

5. Table 17.4 shows supply and demand schedules for the British pound. Assume that exchange rates are flexible.

a. The equilibrium exchange rate equals _____. At this exchange rate, how many pounds will be purchased, and at what cost in terms of dollars?
b. Suppose that the exchange rate is $2 per pound. At this exchange rate, there is an excess (supply/demand) of pounds. This imbalance causes (an increase/a decrease) in the dollar price of the pound, which leads to (a/an) _____ in the quantity of pounds supplied and (a/an) _____ in the quantity of pounds demanded.

Table 17.3	International Transactions of the United States (billions of dollars)

U.S. capital inflows	100
Merchandise exports	375
Services imports	−20
Income receipts from abroad	35
Statistical discrepancy	30
Merchandise imports	−450
Net unilateral transfers	−45
Services exports	55
Income payments abroad	−25
U.S. capital outflows	−55

Table 17.4	Demand and Supply Schedules for the British Pound

Quantity of Pounds Supplied	Dollars per Pound	Quantity of Pounds Demanded
50	2.50	10
40	2.00	20
30	1.50	30
20	1.00	40
10	0.50	50

c. Suppose that the exchange rate is $1 per pound. At this exchange rate, there is an excess (supply/demand) for pounds. This imbalance causes (an increase/a decrease) in the price of the pound, which leads to (a/an) _____ in the quantity of pounds supplied and (a/an) _____ in the quantity of pounds demanded.

6. If the exchange rate changes from $1.70 = £1 to $1.68 = £1, what does this mean for the dollar? For the pound? What if the exchange rate changes from $1.70 = £1 to $1.72 = £1?

7. Table 17.5 gives hypothetical dollar/franc exchange values for Wednesday, May 1, 2003.

   a. Fill in the last two columns of the table with the reciprocal price of the dollar in terms of the franc.
   b. On Wednesday, the price of the two currencies was _____ dollars per franc, or _____ francs per dollar.
   c. From Tuesday to Wednesday, the dollar (appreciated/depreciated) against the franc; the franc (appreciated/depreciated) against the dollar.
   d. On Wednesday, the cost of buying 100 francs was _____ dollars; the cost of buying 100 dollars was _____ francs.

8. Assuming market-determined exchange rates, use demand and supply schedules for pounds to analyze the effect on the exchange rate (dollars per pound) between the U.S. dollar and the British pound under each of the following circumstances:

| Table 17.5 | Dollar/Franc Exchange Values |

	U.S. Dollar Equivalent		Currency per U.S. Dollar	
	Wed.	Tue.	Wed.	Tue.
Switzerland (franc)	0.7207	0.7225		

a. Voter polls suggest that Britain's Conservative government will be replaced by radicals who pledge to nationalize all foreign-owned assets.
b. The British economy and U.S. economy slide into recession, but the British recession is less severe than the U.S. recession.
c. The Federal Reserve adopts a tight monetary policy that dramatically increases U.S. interest rates.
d. The United Kingdom encounters severe inflation, while the United States experiences price stability.
e. Fears of terrorism reduce U.S. tourism in the United Kingdom.
f. The British government invites U.S. firms to invest in British oil fields.
g. The rate of productivity growth in the United Kingdom decreases sharply.
h. An economic boom occurs in the United Kingdom, which induces the British to purchase more U.S.-made autos, trucks, and computers.
i. Both the United Kingdom and the United States experience 10-percent inflation.

9. Explain why you agree or disagree with each of the following statements:

a. A nation's currency will depreciate if its inflation rate is less than that of its trading partners.
b. A nation whose interest rate falls more rapidly than that of other nations can expect the exchange value of its currency to depreciate.
c. A nation whose economy grows more slowly than its major trading partners can expect the exchange value of its currency to appreciate.
d. A nation's currency will appreciate if its interest rate rises relative to that of its trading partners and its income level falls relative to that of its trading partners.

10. Suppose that the United States has a system of managed floating exchange rates. What policies could the Federal Reserve implement to prevent the dollar from depreciating below acceptable levels? How about appreciating beyond acceptable levels? What are the weaknesses of these policies?

CHAPTER 18

Economic Systems and Developing Countries

Chapter objectives

After reading this chapter, you should be able to:

1. Discuss how a market economy, command economy, and mixed economy answer the so-called fundamental economic questions.

2. Explain why transition economies began moving toward capitalism in the 1990s.

3. Discuss the obstacles to economic growth faced by developing nations.

4. Identify sources of aid for developing countries.

economics IN CONTEXT

If Rip Van Winkle were to wake up in 2007 after a 30-year sleep, he would be surprised by the world. In 1974, at the beginning of his slumber, about one-third of the world's population lived under Chinese- or Soviet-style central planning dictated by Communist Party leadership. Although these economies were not wealthy, they muddled along without any immediate fear of disintegration.

Imagine Rip Van Winkle's shock upon waking in 2007. The Soviet empire has collapsed. Germany has reunited. China has embraced capitalism and has realized phenomenal growth. Many developing countries in Latin America, Eastern Europe, and East Asia are attracting large sums of investment. In spite of these changes, however, about 3 billion people—nearly half the world's population—live on $2 or less per day.

In this chapter, we will discuss the economic systems that nations prefer to implement and what underlies their choices. We will also examine why some nations are rich and others are poor, consider obstacles that have prevented poor nations from developing, and identify policies that might help them increase their growth rates.

ECONOMIC SYSTEMS AND THE FUNDAMENTAL ECONOMIC QUESTIONS

Every society, regardless of its wealth and power, must make certain decisions about the production and distribution of its goods and services: (1) *What* goods will be produced, and in what quantities? (2) *How* will these goods be produced? (3) *For whom* will these goods be produced? These questions are known as the **fundamental economic questions**.

The first economic decision—what goods to produce—is influenced by the problem of scarcity, which means that a society cannot have all the goods that it would like to have. Producing more of one good requires producing less of another good. In the United States, most production is geared toward consumer goods, whereas less effort is devoted to the production of military goods. In the former Soviet Union, a relatively large share of national output went to military goods, causing Soviet consumers to become frustrated. Japan has emphasized investment in plants and equipment to produce goods such as autos and consumer electronics while allocating a negligible share of national output to military equipment.

After deciding what goods to produce, a society must determine how to combine scarce resources and technology to produce these goods. For example, a shoe can be manufactured primarily by hand (labor), primarily by machine (capital), or partially by hand and partially by machine. Which production method uses society's scarce resources most efficiently? Should college students be taught in large classes by professors (highly skilled labor) or in small sections by graduate teaching assistants (less-skilled labor)?

Another business decision involves the location of production. The growth of the global economy, coupled with technological advancement, has enabled many companies to move production easily around the world. For example, Toyota Inc. shifts the assembly of its autos between its plants in Japan and the United States in response to changing market conditions. Kellogg Company of Battle Creek, Michigan, produces breakfast cereals in more than 20 countries and sells them in more than 150 countries. U.S. companies haven't made televisions for years. The last U.S. producer, Zenith

Inc., shifted its television assembly to Mexico in the 1980s to cut labor costs. By deciding to close its U.S. factories, Zenith admitted that its U.S.-made televisions could not compete against lower-cost foreign competitors.

The final decision—for whom goods will be produced—refers to the distribution of output among different groups within society. Who should receive the computers, VCRs, automobiles, and other goods produced by the economy? Should the distribution of goods and services among households be based on their ability to buy them? For example, students majoring in engineering generally find jobs that pay much higher incomes than students majoring in education or sociology. Thus, engineers are able to buy more goods and services than teachers, who earn less. Although there are significant exceptions, whites tend to earn more than minorities; men tend to earn more than women; and college graduates tend to earn more than high school graduates. Moreover, Americans generally earn more than Africans and Asians. The income inequality around the world contributes to greatly different standards of living. Instead of distributing goods on the basis of ability to pay, would need be a better criterion?

The manner in which these decisions are made depends on a society's economic system. There are three broad types of economies: the market economy, the command economy, and the mixed economy. Let us consider the main features of each type of economy.

The Market Economy

A **market economy**, also called **capitalism**, is a free-enterprise system that is rooted in private property and markets. Individuals and businesses have the freedom to possess and dispose of goods, services, and resources as they choose. Buyers and sellers are brought together in markets. Buyers come to markets expressing their desire to purchase property in the form of goods, services, and resources at various prices. Sellers come to markets expressing their desire to supply property in the form of goods, services, and resources at various prices. In this manner, property is exchanged at freely negotiated prices.

Because the market system leads to production efficiency, high employment, and economic growth, proponents contend, the need for governmental control is small. The extreme case of a market economy—one in which the government has almost no economic role—is called a **laissez-faire economy**; in this case, the main purpose of the government is to protect private property and provide a legal system that allows free markets.

In a market economy, goods and services are produced and resources are supplied in competitive markets consisting of many sellers and buyers. This means that economic power is decentralized because it is widely distributed. A system of prices and markets, with profits and losses, determines *what, how,* and *for whom* goods will be produced. Because suppliers are self-interested and attempt to maximize profits, they tend to combine resources in such a manner as to produce a good or service at the lowest cost. Suppliers also make production decisions according to the dollar expenditures of consumers who decide what goods will be produced. Goods and services are distributed to consumers who have the income to purchase them. Households that have more income—because they possess more valuable resources—can afford to purchase more goods and services.

Although a market economy recognizes economic freedom and human initiative, it is not without problems. For example, the motivation to manufacture goods at the lowest cost could cause business firms to make production decisions with little regard for the safety of workers or the quality of the environment. Firms might be able to cut costs by adopting unsafe working procedures for employees or by dumping hazardous wastes into the environment. Also, the ability of individual consumers to determine what goods and services should be produced is weakened if a small number of firms dominate a market. Furthermore, the operation of a market economy does not guarantee full employment for workers or the absence of poverty; it also does not ensure that firms will produce goods that are safe for use by consumers.

economics
IN ACTION

Who's Free, Who's Not

Which nations of the world have the most economic freedom? Each year, the Heritage Foundation publishes its *Index of Economic Freedom,* which ranks the world's economies according to 10 categories: banking and finance, investment flows, monetary policy, financial burden of government, trade policy, wages and prices, government intervention in the economy, property rights, regulation, and black markets. Table 18.1 gives examples from the 2008 *Index of Economic Freedom.* Hong Kong and Singapore had the highest degree of economic freedom, and economic freedom was strong throughout North America and Europe. Economic freedom was lowest in Iran and North Korea.

A good way to understand the implications of the index is to compare average per-capita incomes. The average person living in a mostly unfree or repressed economy in 2009 lived a life of poverty on only about $3,000 a year. Compare this with the prosperous residents of the world's free economies, where the average per-capita income was about $28,000—more than nine times greater. Simply put, economic freedom has a major impact on the difference between poverty and prosperity, according to the Heritage Foundation.

Table 18.1   Index of Economic Freedom

Free	Mostly Free	Mostly Unfree	Repressed
Hong Kong	Czech Republic	Lebanon	Nigeria
Singapore	Belgium	Nicaragua	Laos
Ireland	Lithuania	Brazil	Cuba
Luxembourg	Japan	China	Venezuela
United Kingdom	Greece	Russia	Libya
Iceland	Mexico	Indonesia	Zimbabwe
Denmark	Peru	Egypt	Iran
United States	Malaysia	Sierra Leone	North Korea

Source: The Heritage Foundation, *2008 Index of Economic Freedom,* available at http://www.index.heritage.org.

The Command Economy

By contrast, a **command economy** (also called a planned economy or communism) is one in which government makes all the decisions concerning production and distribution. In a command economy, the government owns virtually all the means of production, including land and capital. Business firms are also government owned. Economic decisions regarding the organization of production, the use of resources, and the prices of goods and services are made by government planners. Individual production units receive detailed plans and orders that carry the weight of law. The government also establishes the composition and distribution of output, as well as wage levels for workers. In short, in a command economy, the government answers the fundamental questions of *what, how,* and *for whom* goods will be produced through its control of resources and its power to enforce decisions.

Central planning was the primary method of organization in the Soviet Union, in other countries in Eastern Europe, and in China prior to their movement toward market economics in the late 1980s.

By the 1990s, command economies were disappearing rapidly. Cuba and North Korea, however, still make extensive use of central planning.

Advocates of a command economy contend that the system is superior to a market economy in achieving a fair distribution of income. Because the government owns the means of production, small groups of people are prevented from acquiring a disproportionate fraction of a nation's wealth. It is also argued that central planning can help decrease unemployment by channeling additional labor into production processes. For example, farming can be carried out by labor using hand tools or capital equipment such as tractors. If planners desire to keep agricultural workers employed, they will mandate that less equipment and more labor be used in farming. Finally, it is maintained that national goals can be easily formulated and pursued by a small number of central planners.

Central planning, however, can be criticized on the grounds that it is inconsistent with economic freedom and that it creates an elite class of government bureaucrats. Central planning can also suffer from the problem of overproduction of some goods and underproduction of other goods. This is because the decisions of planners regarding the types and amounts of output produced may not coincide with the preferences of consumers. Moreover, the absence of a profit motive for innovation and entrepreneurship may lead to inferior product quality, production inefficiencies, and reduced economic growth. Finally, in an economy in which central planners are distant from the actual production operations, long-term environmental damage may occur. As witnessed in Eastern Europe, serious water and air pollution have been a consequence of the failure of central planners to include environmental quality in many of their decisions.

The Mixed Economy

No modern economy exactly fits the description of the polar categories of market economy and command economy. Instead, all economies are **mixed economies,** with elements of both market and command economies.

In a mixed economy, the most important decision mechanism is the market that provides answers to *what, how,* and *for whom* goods will be produced. However, the government plays an important role in modifying the operation of the market. The government establishes laws and rules that regulate economic behavior, provides public services such as education and national defense, regulates pollution and product safety, initiates policies to combat unemployment and inflation, modifies the distribution of income, and the like. In short, the objective of a mixed economy is to leave economic decisions to the market when it is operating well, but to intervene in the economy when market outcomes become unacceptable.

Indeed, the blend of market and command varies among mixed economies. Today, most economic decisions in the United States are made in the marketplace, although the government often modifies the operation of the market. However, governments are more heavily involved in the economy in Sweden and Denmark than in the United States. These nations embrace **socialism** as an economic system.

Socialists believe that a country's resources should be used according to an overall economic plan that is formulated by manufacturers, farmers, workers, and government officials working together. Through such planning, socialists hope to adjust production to the needs of the people. Although the forces of demand and supply may influence production and prices under the socialist economic plan, many decisions regarding how much to produce and what to charge are made by political authorities. Many socialists also call for the redistribution of wealth through taxation. They favor laws to help the aged, the unemployed, the disabled, and other people in need. Moreover, many socialists believe that the government should provide free education and medical services to everyone and should help all citizens obtain safe and sanitary housing at rents that they can afford. Indeed, implementing socialist goals calls for a relatively large amount of government activity in a mixed economy.

TRANSITION ECONOMIES

By the 1990s, the centrally planned economies of the Soviet Union and Eastern Europe had collapsed and began switching to capitalism. Also, the Chinese and Indian economies were embracing capitalism. Let us consider some of the reforms that these countries have undertaken to introduce capitalism into their economic systems.

Eastern Europe

In 1989, the world witnessed unprecedented developments in Eastern Europe as many countries moved toward democracy and economic reform. Countries such as Hungary, Poland, Czechoslovakia, and the Soviet Union discarded their centrally controlled state economies and moved toward systems in which private ownership of property predominated and most resources were allocated through markets. These transitions reflected the failure of central planning systems to provide either political freedom or a decent standard of living.

In 1990, for example, per-capita real income in the Soviet Union was less than one-tenth that of the United States. Another example is the case of the two Germanys. Starting from the same point at the end of World War II and sharing a common culture, East Germany and West Germany followed two different paths. East Germany became an industrial wasteland with rundown, outmoded factories and a polluted environment, whereas West Germany achieved one of the highest living standards in the world.

The fundamental motivation for change in Eastern Europe was the failure of the economies there to generate a high standard of living for their people. The economic policies pursued in these countries failed because they were unable to provide adequate incentives for producers to supply the goods and services that consumers wanted to purchase in an efficient manner. The widespread use of price controls, reliance on inefficient public enterprises, extensive barriers to competition with the rest of the world, and government regulation of production and investment all obstructed the normal operation of markets. The lack of enforceable property rights severely restricted incentives for entrepreneurs. Over time, the weaknesses of the political and economic systems of Eastern Europe and the contrasting success of market-oriented systems became obvious. This created pressure that led to the collapse of Eastern Europe's communist governments.

Economists generally agree that Eastern Europe's transition toward a healthy market economy requires major restructuring of their economies: Sound fiscal and monetary policies must be established; domestic price controls must be removed; economies must be opened to international market forces; private property rights must be established, along with a legal system to protect these rights; domestic competition must be promoted; and the government's involvement in the economy must be reduced.

China

For more than 2,000 years, China maintained a policy of self-reliance that caused its economy to lag far behind advanced countries. In 1978, China initiated new economic reforms that have transformed one of the poorest economies in the world into one of the fastest-growing. What underlies this transformation?

Modern China began in 1949, when a revolutionary communist movement captured control of the government. Soon after the communist takeover, China instituted Soviet-style central planning, with an emphasis on rapid economic growth, particularly industrial growth. The state took over urban manufacturing industry, collectivized agriculture, eliminated household farming, and established compulsory production quotas.

By the 1970s, China could see its once-poor neighbors—Japan, Singapore, Taiwan, South Korea, and Hong Kong—enjoying extraordinary growth and prosperity. This led China to "marketize" its economy through small, step-by-step changes to minimize economic disruption and political opposition. In agriculture and industry, reforms were made to increase the role of the producing unit, to increase individual incentives, and to reduce the role of state planners. Most goods were sold for market-determined—not state-controlled—prices. Greater competition was allowed, both among new firms and between new firms and state firms; by 2000, nonstate firms manufactured about 75 percent of China's industrial output. Moreover, China opened its economy to foreign investment and joint ventures. The Chinese government's monopoly over foreign trade was also disbanded; in its place, special economic zones were established in which firms could keep foreign exchange earnings and hire and fire workers.

By the early 2000s, China had made all the easy economic adjustments in its transition toward capitalism: letting farmers sell their own produce and opening its doors to foreign investors and salespeople. Other reforms, however, still needed to be addressed: (1) the massive restructuring of state-owned industries, which were losing money; (2) the cleanup of bankrupt state banks; (3) the creation of a social security system in a society that once guaranteed a job for life; and (4) the establishment of a monetary system with a central bank free of Communist Party or government control. If China were to shut down its money-losing enterprises, millions of workers would be laid off with no benefits; their addition to the 100-million-plus workers already adrift in China could be volatile. In addition, banks that had lent state companies cash would require cash infusions if bankruptcies increased in the state sector. Such loans could render a central bank monetary policy ineffective and fuel inflation.

Although China has dismantled much of its centrally planned economy and has permitted free enterprise to replace it, political freedoms have not increased. Recall the Chinese government's use of military force to end a pro-democracy demonstration in Beijing's Tiananmen Square in 1989, which led to loss of life and demonstrated the Communist Party's determination to maintain its political power. China's evolution toward capitalism has thus consisted of expanded use of market forces under a communist political system. Today, China describes itself as a *socialist market economy.*

India

India is another example of an economy that has improved its economic performance following the enactment of more open markets. The economy of India is broad, including manufacturing, agriculture, handicrafts, and many services. The advent of the digital age and the large number of young and educated Indians fluent in English have transformed India into a major destination for global outsourcing of customer services and technical support.

India and China have followed different avenues of development. China has traveled the traditional development route of countries like South Korea and Japan, becoming a center for low-wage manufacturing of goods. Knowing that it could not compete with China in manufacturing, India decided that its best opportunity was in exporting services which embodied its abundance of highly educated workers.

After gaining independence from Britain in 1947, India engaged in socialism and adopted tariffs and quotas to protect its infant industries. It also enacted prohibitions on foreign investment to restrict competition, tight regulations over private business and financial markets, a large governmental sector, and state planning. This resulted in India's shutting itself off from the mainstream world from the 1950s to 1980s. During this period, India's economy achieved only a modest rate of growth and poverty was widespread. Increasingly, people in India realized that public sector policy had failed India.

By 1991, government officials in India knew that their system of regulation and protectionism hampered economic growth, and that change was needed. The result was a movement toward a market-based economy. The policy that government must approve industrial investment expenditures was eliminated, quotas on imports were abolished, export subsidies were slashed, and import tariffs were reduced from an average of 88 percent in 1989 to 32 percent in 1995. Also, Indian firms were allowed to borrow funds from global markets. These reforms helped India evolve from an agriculture-based and closed economy into a more open and progressive one that promotes foreign investment and emphasizes industry and services. The result has been a notable decrease in India's poverty rate.

Despite these gains, much of India's economy is still subject to restrictions on trade and foreign investment. In food retailing, for example, foreign investment is prohibited. As of 2007, labor productivity in this industry was only 5 percent of the U.S. level. Much of this discrepancy was due to most of India's food retailers being mom-and-pop counter stores instead of modern supermarkets. India is expected to become the world's most populous country in the near future. A high rate of population growth provides India the advantage of an abundant labor supply and strong consumer demand. However, it also points out the necessity of investing in education and health care and creating adequate opportunities for employment. It remains to be seen whether India's government, private sector, and society at large will demonstrate the political will needed to work together and help the people of India achieve a higher standard of living.

CHECK POINT

1. Identify the fundamental economic questions that all economies must answer.

2. How do a market economy, a command economy, and a mixed economy answer the fundamental economic questions?

3. Why are all contemporary economies of the world best classified as mixed economies?

4. In the 1990s, why did the transition economies begin to move away from central planning and toward capitalism?

THE ECONOMICS OF DEVELOPING COUNTRIES

We have learned that no one economic system can fulfill the objectives of all nations. As a result, nations embrace a variety of economic systems that embody elements of capitalism and central planning. Similarly, not all nations use the same strategy for promoting economic development. Thus, some nations, such as the United States, have advanced economies and high standards of living. Yet other developing nations, such as Bangladesh and Ethiopia, remain poor. What accounts for these differences?

It is a commonly accepted practice to array all nations according to real income and then to draw a dividing line between advanced and developing ones. Included in the category of **advanced nations** are those of North America and Western Europe, plus Australia, New Zealand, and Japan. Most nations of the world are classified as developing, or less developed, nations. **Developing nations** include most of those in Africa, Asia, Latin America, and the Middle East. Table 18.2 provides economic and social indicators for selected nations as of 2005. In general, advanced nations are characterized by relatively high levels of gross domestic product per capita, longer life expectancies, and high levels of adult literacy. Today, the richest 20 percent of the world's population receives more than 80 percent of the world's income, suggesting that there is considerable income inequality among nations.

OBSTACLES TO ECONOMIC DEVELOPMENT

The economic development criteria are identical for developing countries and for advanced economies. Both must use their existing supplies of resources more efficiently and increase their available supplies of resources. Although all developing countries are aware of these criteria for economic development, why have some experienced economic growth, while others have lagged far behind? The economic, institutional, and cultural conditions in these nations are the reasons they experience different rates of economic growth. Consider the following obstacles to economic development:

Table 18.2	Basic Economic and Social Indicators for Selected Nations, 2005		
	Gross National Income per Capita (in dollars)*	Life Expectancy (years)	Adult Illiteracy (percent)
United States	41,950	78	< 5
Switzerland	37,080	70	< 5
Japan	31,410	80	< 5
Mexico	10,030	72	10
India	3,460	65	21
Guinea	2,240	46	76
Chad	1,470	48	52
Mozambique	1,270	46	59

*At purchasing power parity.

Source: World Bank Group, Country Data, available at http://www.worldbank.org/data/. Click on "Data," "Quick Reference Tables," and "GNI Per Capita (PPP)."

- Many developing countries possess inadequate natural resources, such as mineral deposits, arable land, and sources of power.

- There are problems with human resources in developing countries. Developing countries tend to be overpopulated and have high rates of population growth. These growing populations decrease developing countries' capacities to save, invest, and increase productivity. Developing countries often experience high levels of both unemployment and underemployment.

- Developing countries generally have shortages of capital goods such as public utilities, machinery, and factories. These shortages stem from a lack of saving and investment because the nations are too poor to save. Insufficient amounts of capital goods contribute to low levels of labor productivity. Moreover, technological advancement is slow in developing countries, which retards economic development.

- The economies of many developing countries are nondiversified and emphasize the production of primary products such as bauxite, copper, and agricultural goods. Developing countries would generally prefer to diversify their economies by fostering manufacturing industries.

- Besides economic factors, institutional and cultural factors can hinder economic development. For example, political corruption and bribery are common in many developing countries. Also, economic growth depends in part on the desire to develop. Are people in developing countries willing to make the necessary changes in their ways of doing things to promote growth?

Another problem of developing countries is limited access to foreign markets. If we examine the characteristics of trade among developing nations, we find that developing nations are highly dependent on advanced nations. A majority of developing-nation exports go to advanced nations, and most developing-nation imports originate in advanced nations. Trade among developing nations is relatively minor.

Although developing countries as a whole have improved their penetration of world markets during the past 2 decades, global protectionism has been a hindrance to their market access. This is especially true for agricultural products and labor-intensive manufactured products such as clothing and textiles. These products are important to the world's poor because they represent more than half of low-income countries' exports and about 70 percent of the least developed countries' export revenues.

economics
IN ACTION

Does the Fair-Trade Movement Help Poor Coffee Farmers?

The next time you drink a cup of coffee, you might consider whether it is "fair trade" coffee. Started in Europe during the 1990s, and now infiltrating the United States, the fair-trade coffee movement aims to increase the incomes of poor farmers in developing countries by implementing a system whereby farmers can sell their beans directly to roasters and retailers, bypassing the traditional practice of selling to middlemen in their own countries. This arrangement allows farmers to earn as much as $1.26 per pound for their beans, compared with the $0.40 per pound they would receive from the middlemen. Fair-trade coffee carries a logo identifying it as such.

Under the fair-trade system, farmers organize in cooperatives of as many as 2,500 members that set prices and arrange for export directly to brokerage firms and other distributors. Middlemen—known as "coyotes" in Nicaragua—previously handled this role. However, the movement has led to incidents of violence in some places in Latin America, mostly involving middlemen who have been bypassed.

Fair trade has achieved much success in Europe, where fair-trade coffee sells in 35,000 stores and has sales of $250 million a year. In some countries, such as the Netherlands and Switzerland, fair-trade coffee accounts for as much as 5 percent of total coffee sales. But fair-trade activists admit that selling Americans on the idea of buying coffee with a social theme is more challenging than it is in Europe. Americans, they note, tend to be less aware of social problems in the developing world than Europeans. Nevertheless, some grocery chains, such as Safeway, sell fair-trade coffee to their American customers.

Yet critics question the extent to which fair-trade coffee actually helps. They note that the biggest winners are not the farmers but rather the retailers, which sometimes charge huge markups on fair-trade coffee while promoting themselves as corporate citizens. They can get away with it because consumers generally are given little or no information about how much of a product's price goes to farmers.

Sources: "A Global Effort for Poor Coffee Farmers," *The Wall Street Journal,* November 23, 1999, pp. A2 and A4; and "At Some Retailers, Fair Trade Carries a Very High Cost," *The Wall Street Journal,* June 8, 2004, pp. A-1 and A-10.

However, developing countries themselves contribute to the problem. As seen in Table 18.3, developing countries generally impose tariffs that are much higher than those imposed by advanced countries.

Besides using tariffs to protect their producers from import-competing goods, advanced countries support developing countries with subsidies, especially in agriculture. Subsidies are often rationalized on the noneconomic benefits of agriculture, such as food security and maintenance of rural communities. By encouraging the production of agricultural commodities, subsidies discourage agricultural imports, thus displacing developing-country exports in advanced-country markets. The case of U.S. subsidies to sugar producers illustrates the adverse effects of support on developing countries' exporters. Moreover, the unwanted surpluses of agricultural commodities that result from government support are often dumped into world markets with the aid of export subsidies. This depresses prices for many agricultural commodities and reduces the export revenues of developing countries.

Simply put, developing countries experience a **vicious circle of poverty.** They save little and thus invest little in physical and human capital because they are poor, and because they do not invest, their outputs per capita remain low and they remain poor. Even if the vicious circle were to be broken, a rapid increase in population would leave the standard of living unchanged.

Table 18.3	Tariffs of Selected Developing Countries and Advanced Countries	
		Average Tariff Rate (percent)
Developing Countries		
Egypt		36.8
Argentina		31.9
Congo		27.3
Malaysia		24.5
Mongolia		17.6
China		10.0
Advanced Countries		
Canada		6.5
European Union		5.4
Japan		5.1
United States		3.5

Source: World Trade Organization, *World Tariff Profiles*, 2008, available at http://www.intracen.org.

TENSIONS BETWEEN DEVELOPING COUNTRIES AND ADVANCED COUNTRIES

In spite of the economic frustrations of developing countries, most scholars and policy makers today agree that the best strategy for poor countries to develop is to take advantage of international trade. In the past two decades, many developing countries have seen the wisdom of this strategy and opened their markets to international trade and foreign investment. And yet, ironically, in spite of the support that scholars from advanced countries have given to this change, the advanced world has sometimes increased its own barriers to imports from these developing countries. Why is this so?

Think of the world economy as a ladder. On the bottom rungs are the developing countries, which produce mainly textiles and other low-tech goods. Toward the top are the United States, Japan, and other industrial countries, which manufacture sophisticated software, electronics, and pharmaceuticals. Up and down the middle rungs are all the other nations, producing everything from memory chips to autos to steel. From this perspective, economic development is simple: Everyone attempts to climb to the next rung. This works well if the topmost countries can create new industries and products, thus adding another rung to the ladder. Such invention permits older industries to move overseas, while new jobs are generated at home. But if innovation stalls at the highest rung, that's bad news for Americans who must compete with lower-wage workers in developing countries.

Developing countries face a predicament: In order to make progress, they must displace producers of the least advanced goods that are still being produced in the advanced countries. For example, if Zambia produces textiles and apparel, it must compete against American and European producers of these goods. As producers in advanced countries suffer from import competition, they tend to seek trade protection in order to avoid it. However, this protection denies critical market access to developing countries, thwarting their attempts to grow. Thus, there is a bias against their catching up to the advanced countries.

Those in advanced countries who are protected from competition with developing countries tend to include those who are already near the bottom of the advanced countries' income distributions. Many of these people work in labor-intensive industries and have limited skills and low wages. These are the people whom income redistribution programs ought to aid, not hinder. To some extent, advanced countries face a trade-off between helping their own poor and helping the world's poor. But critics note that the world as a whole needs to treat all the poor as its own, and the purpose of international institutions is to ensure that this occurs. For example, it is the responsibility of the World Trade Organization (WTO) to prevent advanced countries' trade policies from tilting too far in favor of their own people and against the rest of the world. This is why recent meetings of the WTO have been filled with tensions between poor and rich countries.

However, providing developing countries with greater access to the markets of advanced countries will not solve all of their problems. Developing countries also face structural weaknesses in their economies that are compounded by nonexistent or inadequate institutions and policies in the fields of law and order, sustainable macroeconomic management, and public services.

ECONOMIC GROWTH STRATEGIES

In attempting to achieve economic development, poor countries have pursued two competing strategies. Let us examine these strategies.

During the 1950s and 1960s, the growth strategy of **import substitution** became popular in many developing nations such as Argentina, Brazil, and Mexico; some countries still use it today. Import substitution involves the extensive use of trade barriers to protect domestic industries from import competition. For example, if a nation imports fertilizer, import substitution would call for the establishment of a domestic fertilizer industry to produce replacements for the imports. In the extreme, import-substitution policies could lead to complete self-sufficiency.

The rationale for import substitution arises from developing countries' perspective on trade. Many developing countries feel that they cannot export manufactured goods because they cannot compete with established firms in industrialized countries, especially in view of the high trade barriers maintained by those countries. Given the need for economic growth and development, developing countries have no choice but to manufacture for themselves some of the goods they now import. The use of tariffs and quotas restricts imports, and the domestic market is reserved for domestic manufacturers. The protection of start-up industries is intended to allow them to grow to a size at which they can compete with the industries of developed countries.

Another development strategy is **export-led growth.** The strategy is outward oriented because it links the domestic economy to the world economy. Instead of pursuing growth by protecting domestic industries that are suffering from a comparative disadvantage, this strategy promotes growth through the export of manufactured goods. Trade controls are either nonexistent or very low, in the sense that any disincentives to export resulting from import barriers are counterbalanced by export subsidies. Industrialization is viewed as a natural outcome of development instead of an objective that is pursued at the expense of an economy's efficiency. By the 1970s, many developing countries were abandoning their import-substitution strategies and shifting to export-led growth. Among the countries that have benefited from export-led growth are South Korea, Malaysia, and China.

What is the evidence concerning these growth strategies? Generally, researchers have found that nations implementing export-led growth policies have superior economic performance compared to those using import-substitution policies.[1] This is because export-led growth policies introduce international competition to domestic markets, which encourages efficient firms and discourages inefficient ones. By creating a more competitive environment, such policies also promote higher productivity and hence faster economic growth. Conversely, import-substitution policies that rely on trade protection switch the demand to products that are produced domestically. Exporting is then discouraged by both the increased cost of imported inputs and the increased cost of domestic inputs relative to the price received by exporters.

---

1. David Dollar and Art Kraay, *Trade, Growth, and Poverty* (Washington, DC: World Bank Development Research Group, 2001).

AID TO DEVELOPING COUNTRIES

Dissatisfied with their economic performance and convinced that many of their problems are the result of shortcomings in the existing international trading system, developing nations have pressed their collective demands on advanced nations for institutions and policies to improve the climate for economic development in the international trading system. Among the institutions and policies that have been created to support developing countries are the World Bank, the International Monetary Fund, and the Generalized System of Preferences.

World Bank

During the 1940s, two international institutions were established to ease the transition from a wartime to a peacetime environment and to help prevent a recurrence of the turbulent economic conditions of the Great Depression era. The World Bank and the International Monetary Fund were established at the United Nations Monetary and Financial Conference held at Bretton Woods, New Hampshire, in July 1944. Developing nations view these institutions as sources of funds to promote economic development and financial stability.

The **World Bank** is an international organization that provides loans to developing countries aimed toward poverty reduction and economic development. Headquartered in Washington, D.C., it lends money to member governments and their agencies and to private firms in the member nations. The World Bank is not a "bank" in the common sense. It is one of the United Nations' specialized agencies, made up of 184 member countries. These countries are jointly responsible for financing the institution and deciding how its money is spent.

The World Bank makes loans to developing members that cannot obtain money from other sources at reasonable terms. These loans are given for specific development projects, such as hospitals, schools, highways, and dams. The World Bank is involved in projects as diverse as raising AIDS awareness in Guinea, supporting the education of girls in Bangladesh, improving health care delivery in Mexico, and helping India rebuild after a devastating earthquake. The World Bank provides low-interest-rate loans, and in some cases interest-free loans, to developing countries that have little or no capacity to borrow on market terms.

In recent years, the World Bank has funded the debt-refinancing activities of some of the most heavily indebted developing nations. The bank encourages private investment in member countries. The World Bank receives its funds from contributions by wealthy developed countries.

Some 10,000 development professionals from nearly every country in the world work in the World Bank's headquarters in Washington, D.C., or in its 109 country offices. They provide many technical assistance services for members.

International Monetary Fund

Another source of aid to developing countries (as well as advanced countries) is the **International Monetary Fund (IMF),** which is also headquartered in Washington, D.C. With a membership of 184 nations, the IMF can be thought of as a bank for the central banks of member nations. Over a given time period, some nations will face balance-of-payments surpluses, and others will face deficits. A nation with a deficit initially draws on its stock of foreign currencies, such as the dollar, that are accepted in payment by other nations. However, the deficit nation will sometimes have insufficient amounts of currency. That is when other nations, through the IMF, can provide assistance. By making currencies available to the IMF, the surplus nations channel funds to nations with temporary deficits. Over the long run, the deficits must be corrected, and the IMF attempts to ensure that this adjustment is as prompt and orderly as possible.

The funds of the IMF come from two major sources: quotas and loans. Subscriptions, which are pooled funds of member nations, generate most of the IMF's funds. The size of a member's subscription depends on its economic and financial importance in the world; nations with larger economic importance have larger subscriptions. The subscriptions are increased periodically as a means of boosting the IMF's resources. The IMF also obtains funds through loans from member nations. The IMF has lines of credit with major industrial nations, as well as with Saudi Arabia.

All IMF loans are subject to some degree of *conditionality.* This means that in order to obtain a loan, the deficit nation must agree to implement economic and financial policies stipulated by the IMF. These policies are intended to correct the member's balance-of-payments deficit and to promote noninflationary economic growth. However, the conditionality attachment to IMF lending has often met strong resistance from deficit nations. The IMF has sometimes demanded that deficit nations undergo austerity programs that involve severe reductions in public spending, private consumption, and imports in order to live within their means.

Critics of the IMF note that its bailouts may contribute to the so-called *moral-hazard problem,* in which nations realize the benefits of their decisions when things go well but are protected when things go poorly. If nations do not suffer the costs of bad decisions, won't they be encouraged to make other bad decisions in the future? Another area of concern is the contractionary effect of the IMF's restrictive monetary and fiscal policy conditions. Won't such conditions cause business and bank failures, induce deeper recession, and limit government spending to help the poor? Many analysts believe the answer is yes.

Generalized System of Preferences

Given inadequate access to the markets of industrial countries, developing countries have pressed industrial countries to reduce their tariff walls. To help developing nations strengthen their international competitiveness and expand their industrial base, many industrialized nations have extended nonreciprocal tariff preferences to the exports of developing nations. Under this **Generalized System of Preferences (GSP),** major industrial nations temporarily reduce tariffs on designated manufactured imports from developing nations below the levels applied to imports from other industrial nations. The GSP is not a uniform system, however, because it consists of many individual schemes that differ in the types of products covered and the extent of tariff reduction. Simply put, the GSP attempts to promote economic development in developing countries through increased trade rather than foreign aid.

The trade preferences granted by industrial countries are voluntary. They are not WTO obligations. Donor countries determine the eligibility criteria, the product coverage, the size of preference margins, and the duration of the preference. In practice, industrial-country governments rarely grant deep preferences in sectors in which developing countries have a large export potential. Thus, developing countries often obtain only limited preferences in sectors in which they have a comparative advantage. The main reason for these limited preferences is that, in some sectors, there is strong domestic opposition to liberalization in industrial countries.

CHECK POINT

1. Identify the obstacles to development that poor countries face.

2. Describe the "ladder of economic development."

3. Concerning economic growth strategies, what is meant by import substitution and export-led growth?

4. What policies and institutions have been created to aid developing countries?

Chapter Summary

1. Every society must make certain decisions regarding the production and distribution of goods and services: (1) *What* goods will be produced, and in what quantities? (2) *How* will these goods be produced? (3) *For whom* will these goods be produced? These questions are known as the fundamental economic questions.

2. The manner in which the fundamental economic questions are answered depends on a society's economic system. There are three broad types of economies: the market economy, the command economy, and the mixed economy. The United States has a mixed economy.

3. By the 1990s, the centrally planned economies in the Soviet Union and Eastern Europe had collapsed and began switching to capitalism. Also, the Chinese economy started embracing capitalism. These nations are known as transition economies.

4. The advanced nations are those of North America and Western Europe, plus Australia, New Zealand, and Japan. Most nations of the world are classified as developing nations. These nations include most of those in Africa, Asia, Latin America, and the Middle East. Compared to advanced countries, developing countries generally have lower levels of real GDP per capita, shorter life expectancies, and lower levels of adult literacy.

5. For developing nations, obstacles to economic growth include inadequate natural resources, low rates of saving and investment, shortages of capital goods, low productivity levels, modest technological advancement, and lack of access to the markets of advanced countries. Many developing nations experience a vicious circle of poverty: They save little and thus invest little in physical and human capital because they are poor, and because they do not invest, their outputs per capita remain low and they remain poor.

6. In attempting to achieve economic development, poor countries have pursued two competing strategies: import substitution and export-led growth. Researchers have generally found that developing countries have benefited the most from export-led growth strategies.

7. Among the institutions and policies that have been created to support developing countries are the World Bank, the International Monetary Fund, and the Generalized System of Preferences.

Key Terms and Concepts

fundamental economic questions (412)

market economy (413)

capitalism (413)

laissez-faire economy (413)

command economy (414)

mixed economies (415)

socialism (415)

advanced nations (418)

developing nations (418)

vicious circle of poverty (420)

import substitution (422)

export-led growth (422)

World Bank (423)

International Monetary Fund (IMF) (423)

Generalized System of Preferences (GSP) (424)

Self-Test: Multiple-Choice Questions

1. Before China and the Soviet Union switched to a market economy, the institution that was most prevalent in their economies was

    a. central planning by the government.

    b. private ownership of property.

    c. goods rationed according to the ability to pay.

    d. flexible prices and wages.

2. For most developing countries, _____ constitute the largest share of domestic output.

    a. steel and automobiles

    b. banking and financial services

    c. oil and natural gas

    d. agricultural goods and raw materials

3. In a capitalist economy, the role of government is best described as

    a. limited.

    b. unlimited.

    c. nonexistent.

    d. significant.

4. Economic growth in developing countries is hindered by all of the following *except*

    a. a low supply of capital goods.

    b. a low birth rate.

    c. the development of strong labor unions.

    d. high productivity of workers.

5. Which institution's main purpose is to provide low-interest-rate loans to developing countries to help them build hospitals, schools, roads, and bridges?

    a. World Bank.

    b. Organization of Petroleum Exporting Countries.

    c. Bank of America.

    d. European Union.

6. For most developing countries,

    a. productivity is high among domestic workers.

    b. adult literacy rates are high.

    c. saving and investment rates are low.

    d. technological advances are widespread.

7. Advanced countries include all of the following *except*

    a. Japan.

    b. Sweden.

    c. United States.

    d. Mozambique.

8. Capitalist economies include all of the following *except*

    a. a pricing system based on supply and demand.

    b. a system of private property.

    c. self-interest among households and entrepreneurs.

    d. separation of the economy from the business sector.

9. The economic system that best describes the U.S. economy is a

    a. command economy.

    b. socialist economy.

c. capitalist economy.

d. mixed market economy.

10. The sources of aid to developing countries include all of the following *except*

a. the Generalized System of Preferences.

b. import tariffs of advanced countries.

c. the World Bank.

d. the International Monetary Fund.

Answers to Multiple-Choice Questions

1. a   2. d   3. a   4. d   5. a   6. c   7. d   8. d   9. d   10. b

Study Questions and Problems

1. Why do incentive and coordination problems arise in economies that embrace central planning? How are those problems dealt with in a market economy?

2. Why do nations such as Sweden and Norway prefer socialism to capitalism?

3. Evaluate the prospects for the transformation of the Chinese and Eastern European economies into market economies.

4. Why are some nations rich and other nations poor?

5. In what ways do advanced nations help developing nations?

6. Suppose that you are the manager of an automobile assembly plant. Explain how you might attain production goals under a communist system and under a capitalist system.

7. Describe the merits of import substitution versus export-led growth as strategies for economic development.

Glossary

a

ability-to-pay principle   The principle that people with greater income and wealth should be taxed at a higher rate because their ability to pay is presumably greater. (*Chapter 9*)

accounting profit   Total revenue minus explicit costs; costs that are payable to others, such as wages, materials, and interest. (*Chapter 4*)

actual reserves   The amount of vault cash and Federal Reserve deposits that a bank is actually holding; the sum of a bank's required and excess reserves. (*Chapter 14*)

administrative lag   The inability to get quick action on fiscal policy because of the way Congress operates. (*Chapter 13*)

advanced nations   Nations with relatively high per-capita income and standards of living, such as those in North America and Western Europe, as well as Australia, New Zealand, and Japan. (*Chapter 18*)

advertising   An attempt at product differentiation by imperfectly competitive firms; the goal is to make buyers aware of the unique features of their products, to convince buyers that their product is different from those of their competitors, or both. (*Chapter 6*)

aggregate demand curve   A graphical representation of the total demand of all people for all final goods and services produced in an economy. (*Chapter 12*)

aggregate quantity demanded   The quantity of final output that buyers will purchase at a given price level. (*Chapter 12*)

aggregate quantity supplied   The quantity of final output that will be supplied by producers at a particular price level. (*Chapter 12*)

aggregate supply curve   A graphical representation of the total supply of all final goods and services in an economy. (*Chapter 12*)

antitrust policy   The attempt to foster a market structure that will lead to increased competition and curb anticompetitive behavior that harms consumers; laws designed to prevent unfair business practices. (*Chapter 8*)

appreciation   The strengthening of a currency; fewer units of a nation's currency are needed to purchase a unit of some foreign currency. (*Chapter 17*)

arbitration   A process whereby a person called an arbitrator listens to both sides of a labor dispute and makes a decision that is binding on both sides. (*Chapter 7*)

automatic stabilizers   Changes in government spending and tax revenues that occur automatically as the economy fluctuates; they prevent aggregate demand from decreasing too much in bad times and rising too much in good times, thus stabilizing the economy. (*Chapter 13*)

average fixed cost   The total fixed cost per unit of output; total fixed cost divided by output. (*Chapter 4*)

average tax rate   Total taxes due divided by total income. (*Chapter 9*)

average total cost   The total cost per unit of output; total cost divided by output. (*Chapter 4*)

average variable cost   The total variable cost per unit of output; total variable cost divided by output. (*Chapter 4*)

b

balance of payments   A record of a country's international trading, borrowing, and lending. (*Chapter 17*)

balance of trade (trade balance)   A component of the current account that includes all the goods (merchandise) that a country exports or imports. (*Chapter 17*)

balance sheet   A two-column list that shows the financial position of a bank at a specific date. (*Chapter 14*)

barriers to entry   Impediments created by the government or by the firm or firms already in the market that protect an established firm from potential competition. (*Chapter 5*)

benefits-received principle   The principle that taxes should be paid in proportion to the benefits that taxpayers derive from public expenditures. (*Chapter 9*)

Board of Governors   A seven-member board appointed by the president and confirmed by the Senate to serve 14-year terms of office; administers the Federal Reserve System. (*Chapter 15*)

business cycle   Recurrent ups and downs in the level of economic activity extending over several years. (*Chapter 11*)

c

capacity utilization rate   The ratio of an industry's production to its capacity. (*Chapter 1*)

capital and financial account   A component of the balance of payments that includes all international purchases or sales of assets such as real estate, corporate stocks and bonds, and government securities. (*Chapter 17*)

capital and financial account balance   The amount of capital and financial inflows minus capital and financial outflows. (*Chapter 17*)

capital goods   Goods used to produce other goods and services in the future, such as factories and machines; a source of economic growth potential. (*Chapter 1*)

capitalism   A free-enterprise system that is rooted in private property and markets; also called a market economy. (*Chapter 18*)

cartel   A formal organization of firms that attempts to act as if there were only one firm in the industry (monopoly); the purpose of a cartel is to reduce output and increase price in order to increase the joint profits of its members. (*Chapter 6*)

cashier's check   A type of check purchased by someone who does not necessarily have a checking account; issued by a bank for a fee plus the amount of the check. (*Chapter 14*)

certified check   A type of check that may be called for by a legal contract, such as a real estate or automobile sale agreement; considered less risky than a personal check because the bank on which it is drawn certifies that the funds are available. (*Chapter 14*)

change in demand   A shift in a demand curve caused by a demand shifter. (*Chapter 2*)

change in quantity demanded   A movement along a demand curve caused by a change in the price of the good under consideration. (*Chapter 2*)

change in supply   A shift in a supply curve induced by a supply shifter. (*Chapter 2*)

classical economists   A group of economists who dominated economic thinking prior to the Great Depression; they believed that the market economy automatically adjusts to ensure the full employment of its resources and that economic downturns are temporary, so government should not interfere in economic affairs. (*Chapter 12*)

Clayton Act of 1914   Federal legislation enacted to make explicit the intent of the Sherman Act of 1890; broadened federal antitrust powers to outlaw price discrimination, some mergers, exclusive contracts between supplier and buyer and to prohibit interlocking boards of directors among competing firms. (*Chapter 8*)

collective bargaining   A process whereby unions act on behalf of workers to bargain with employers on matters relating to employment; allows one negotiator to act as the workers' agent rather than having each worker negotiate his or her own labor contract. (*Chapter 7*)

command-and-control regulations   Government-imposed restrictions or mandates on the spillover costs of production. (*Chapter 8*)

command economy   An economy in which the government makes all decisions concerning production and distribution; also called planned economy or communism. (*Chapter 18*)

comparative advantage   The principle that individuals and countries should specialize in producing goods in which they are relatively—not absolutely—more efficient. (*Chapter 16*)

complementary goods   Goods that are used in conjunction with one another. A decrease in the price of one good will increase the demand for another good; conversely, an increase in the price of one good will decrease the demand for another good. (*Chapter 2*)

compound interest   The increase in the value of savings that is the result of earning interest on interest. (*Chapter 14*)

concentration ratio   The percentage of an industry's sales that are accounted for by the four largest firms in an industry; a low concentration ratio suggests a high degree of competition, whereas a high concentration ratio implies an absence of competition. (*Chapter 6*)

conglomerate merger   A merger that brings together two firms producing in different industries. (*Chapter 6*)

constant returns to scale   A situation that occurs when a firm's output changes by the same percentage as that of all inputs. (*Chapter 4*)

consumer goods   Goods that are available for immediate use by households and do not contribute to future production in the economy, such as food, electricity, and clothing. (*Chapter 1*)

consumer price index (CPI)   An indicator of inflation that is calculated by the U.S. Bureau of Labor Statistics by sampling households and businesses; a monitoring of consumer expenditures on specified goods and services. (*Chapter 11*)

corporate average fuel economy (CAFÉ)   Government-enacted standards that apply to all cars and light trucks sold in the United States; originally enacted in 1975, CAFÉ represents the foundation of U.S. energy conservation policy. (*Chapter 8*)

corporation   A "legal person" that conducts business just as an individual does; corporations are owned by stockholders, who receive profits in the form of dividends. (*Chapter 9*)

correspondent bank   Banks that form partnerships with other banks in order to exchange checks and payments directly, bypassing the Federal Reserve and its check-processing fee. (*Chapter 14*)

cost-of-living adjustment (COLA)   The annual adjustment of Social Security benefits to reflect inflation. (*Chapter 9*)

cost-push inflation   Inflation caused by upward pressure on the sellers' side of the market. (*Chapter 11*)

creative destruction   According to economist Joseph Schumpeter, in a dynamic economy, the drive to temporarily capture monopoly profits results in old technologies, goods, and livelihoods being replaced by new ones; ideas and creativity are the prime sources of growth in a capitalist economy, and profits are the fuel. (*Chapter 10*)

crowding-out effect A situation that occurs when private spending (consumption or investment) falls as a result of increased government expenditures and subsequent budget deficits. (*Chapter 13*)

currency The money in use in a country. (*Chapter 14*)

current account A component of the balance of payments; the value of transactions in currently produced goods and services, income flows, and unilateral transfers. (*Chapter 17*)

current account balance The sum of the trade balance, the services balance, net income, and net unilateral transfers. (*Chapter 17*)

cyclical unemployment Fluctuating unemployment that coincides with the business cycle and is a repeating short-run problem. (*Chapter 11*)

d

deflation A continuing fall in the average price level that occurs when price reductions on some goods and services outweigh price increases on all others. (*Chapter 11*)

demand A schedule showing the amount of a good or service that a buyer is willing and able to purchase at each possible price during a particular period. (*Chapter 2*)

demand curve A graphical representation of a market demand schedule. (*Chapter 2*)

demand curve for labor The value of the marginal product of labor curve; on a graph, a representation of the wage rate and the amount of labor that a firm is willing to hire at each rate. (*Chapter 7*)

demand deposit account A regular checking account that does not pay interest; the money in the account is available to the account holder "on demand" by writing a check, making a withdrawal, or transferring funds. (*Chapter 14*)

demand-pull inflation Inflation originating from upward pressure on the buyers' side of the market; a situation in which "too much money chases too few goods." (*Chapter 11*)

demand shifter A change in a variable that causes a shift in a demand curve. (*Chapter 2*)

dependent variable A variable that is functionally dependent on another variable. (*Chapter 1*)

depreciation The weakening of a currency; more units of one nation's currency are needed to purchase a unit of another's currency. (*Chapter 17*)

depression A very deep and prolonged recession. (*Chapter 11*)

deregulation The federal dismantling of regulations in industries (such as airlines, trucking, and railroads) in which the existing regulations have outlived their usefulness; an attempt by the government to increase price competition and provide incentives for companies to introduce new products and services. (*Chapter 8*)

derived demand Demand for an input that arises from, and varies with, the demand for the product it helps produce. (*Chapter 7*)

developing nations Nations with relatively low levels of industrialization and low standards of living; these include most of the nations of Africa, Asia, Latin America, and the Middle East. (*Chapter 18*)

diminishing marginal returns The addition of more workers continues to increase output, but by successfully smaller increments. (*Chapter 4*)

diminishing marginal utility As a person consumes additional units of a particular good, each additional unit provides less and less additional utility (satisfaction). (*Chapter 2*)

direct relationship A relationship in which two variables show a positive relationship to each other—that is, as one variable increases (decreases), the other also increases (decreases). (*Chapter 1*)

discount rate The rate that Federal Reserve Banks charge for loans to banks. (*Chapter 15*)

discount window An expression for Federal Reserve loans that are repaid with interest at maturity, arranged by telephone, and recorded along with pledged collateral such as U.S. government securities. (*Chapter 15*)

discouraged worker A person who is out of work, would like to work, and is available for work but has stopped looking for work because of lack of success in finding a job. (*Chapter 11*)

discretionary fiscal policy The deliberate use of changes in government expenditures and taxation to affect aggregate demand and to influence the economy's performance in the short run. (*Chapter 13*)

diseconomies of scale A situation in which a firm's unit cost increases and its long-run average total cost curve turns upward. (*Chapter 4*)

distribution of income The way income is divided among members of society; reflects the manner in which people share in the rewards from the production of goods and services. (*Chapter 9*)

division of labor The process of dividing production processes so that workers can practice and perfect a particular skill. (*Chapter 16*)

dollarization The process of replacing a local currency with the U.S. dollar as a medium of exchange; by replacing their less stable currencies with the dollar, developing countries hope to experience a lower and more stable inflation rate. (*Chapter 17*)

e

economic growth The increased productive capabilities of an economy that are made possible by either an increasing resource base or technological advancement. (*Chapter 1 and Chapter 10*)

economic profit   Total revenue minus the sum of explicit and implicit costs. (*Chapter 4*)

economic regulation   Federal legislation enacted to control the prices, wages, conditions of entry, standards of service, or other important economic characteristics of particular industries. (*Chapter 8*)

economic sanctions   Government-imposed limitations, or complete bans, placed on customary trade or financial relations between nations. (*Chapter 1*)

economics   The study of choice under conditions of scarcity. (*Chapter 1*)

economies of scale   A situation in which a firm's long-run average total cost curve slopes downward, showing an increase in scale and production, which results in a decline in cost per unit. (*Chapter 4*)

efficiency   The point at which an economy is operating along its production possibilities curve, thereby realizing its output potential. (*Chapter 1*)

elastic demand   The percentage change in quantity demanded is greater than the percentage change in price. (*Chapter 3*)

equilibrium exchange rate   The rate determined by the market forces of demand and supply; central bankers do not attempt to influence the exchange rate. (*Chapter 17*)

equilibrium price   The price at which buyers' intentions are equal to sellers' intentions. (*Chapter 2*)

euro   The common currency that was introduced by the European Monetary Union in 2002. (*Chapter 17*)

European Central Bank   Central bank created by the European Monetary Union to take control of monetary policy and exchange rate policy for member countries; the bank controls the supply of euros, sets the euro interest rate, and maintains permanently fixed exchange rates for member countries. (*Chapter 17*)

European Monetary Union (EMU)   A system in which European countries united to replace their individual currencies with a single currency, the euro. (*Chapter 17*)

European Union (EU)   A regional economic bloc consisting of 25 European nations; its primary objective has been to create an economic bloc in which trade and other transactions take place freely among member nations. (*Chapter 17*)

excess capacity   The difference between the output corresponding to minimum average total cost and the output produced by a monopolistically competitive firm in the long run. (*Chapter 6*)

excess reserves   Extra reserves that a bank is holding; can be used to make loans or purchase government securities. (*Chapter 14*)

exchange rate   The price of one currency in terms of another. (*Chapter 17*)

expenditure approach   A method of calculating GDP by totaling the expenditures on goods and services produced during the current year. (*Chapter 10*)

explicit costs   Payments made to others as a cost of running a business. (*Chapter 4*)

export-led growth   Growth based on exporting in foreign markets. (*Chapter 18*)

externality   A cost or benefit imposed on people other than the producers and consumers of a good or service; also called a spillover. (*Chapter 8*)

factors of production   Inputs used in the production of goods and services. (*Chapter 1*)

fair-return price   A price that is just high enough to cover a regulated firm's average total cost. (*Chapter 8*)

federal debt   The cumulative amount of outstanding borrowing from the public over the nation's history. (*Chapter 13*)

federal deficit   The difference between total federal spending and revenues in a given year; the annual amount of government borrowing. (*Chapter 13*)

Federal Deposit Insurance Corporation (FDIC)   The organization that insures deposits and promotes safe and sound banking practices; conducts examinations and audits, insures deposits up to $100,000 at U.S. banks, and arranges for the disposition of assets and deposit liabilities of insured banks that fail; established by Congress in 1933. (*Chapter 14*)

federal funds market   Trading market for reserves held at the Federal Reserve; banks with surplus balances in their accounts transfer reserves to those needing to boost their balances. (*Chapter 15*)

federal funds rate   The benchmark rate of interest charged for the short-term use of reserve funds; a market-determined rate. (*Chapter 15*)

Federal Open Market Committee (FOMC)   The policy-making body of the Federal Reserve that oversees the purchase and sale of U.S. government securities. (*Chapter 15*)

Federal Reserve System (Fed)   The central bank of the United States; legislated by Congress and signed into law by President Wilson in 1913 to provide the nation with a safe, flexible, and stable monetary and financial system. (*Chapter 15*)

fiscal policy   The use of government expenditures and taxes to promote particular macroeconomic goals, such as full employment, stable prices, and economic growth. (*Chapter 13*)

fixed exchange rates   Rates that are used primarily by small, developing nations to maintain ties to a key currency, such as the U.S. dollar. (*Chapter 17*)

fixed input   Any resource for which the quantity cannot be varied during the period under consideration. (*Chapter 4*)

flat-rate income tax   A proposed substitute for the current federal tax system; such a system would do away with the existing tax rates on personal income and replace them with a single tax rate; exemptions, deductions, and credits would be abolished. (*Chapter 9*)

floating exchange rate system A system in which governments and central banks do not participate in the foreign exchange market; an equilibrium exchange rate equates the demand for and supply of the home currency. (*Chapter 17*)

foreign exchange market A market in which currencies are bought and sold. (*Chapter 17*)

free-rider problem A situation that exists when it is impossible to exclude a consumer from the consumption of a public good, regardless of whether the consumer pays for it; others pay for the consumer's use of a good. (*Chapter 8*)

frictional unemployment Unemployment that arises from normal labor turnover. (*Chapter 11*)

full employment To an economist, the natural rate of unemployment; something less than 100 percent employment of the labor force. (*Chapter 11*)

functional distribution of income Distribution showing the shares of a nation's income that accrue to the factors of production (land, labor, capital, and entrepreneurship) as rent, wages, interest, and profits. (*Chapter 9*)

fundamental economic questions All societies must answer the following questions: What goods will be produced? How will these goods be produced? For whom will these goods be produced? (*Chapter 18*)

g

game theory A method of studying oligopolistic behavior by analyzing a series of strategies and payoffs among rival firms. (*Chapter 6*)

GDP deflator The broadest price index used to calculate real GDP; the ratio of the cost of buying all final goods and services in the current year to the cost of buying the identical goods at base-year prices. (*Chapter 10*)

Generalized System of Preferences (GSP) A system in which the major industrial nations temporarily reduce tariffs on designated manufactured imports from developing nations below the levels applied to imports from other industrial nations. (*Chapter 18*)

government expenditures Federal, state, and local government outlays of funds. (*Chapter 9*)

government purchases Expenditures by federal, state, and local governments on goods and services such as street lighting, sewage systems, national parks, fire trucks, engineers, teachers, and the like. (*Chapter 9*)

government purchases of goods and services Spending on final output by federal, state, and local governments, including the entire payroll of all governments. (*Chapter 10*)

gross domestic product (GDP) The market value of all final goods and services produced within a country in a given year. (*Chapter 10*)

gross private domestic investment All private-sector spending on investment; also known as gross investment. (*Chapter 10*)

h

horizontal merger A merger in which one firm combines with another firm that sells similar products in the same market. (*Chapter 6*)

human capital The knowledge, experience, and skills of the labor force. (*Chapter 9 and Chapter 10*)

hyperinflation A rapid and uncontrolled inflation that destroys an economy. (*Chapter 11*)

i

imperfect competition A market in which more than one seller competes for sales with many other sellers, each of which has some price-making ability. (*Chapter 6*)

implicit costs Costs that represent the value of resources used in production for which no monetary payment is made. (*Chapter 4*)

import substitution A strategy in which countries protect their import-competing industries by imposing tariffs on imported goods. (*Chapter 18*)

incentive-based regulations Government attempts to control the spillover costs of production; these regulations are flexible because they allow producers to find ways to achieve the objective. (*Chapter 8*)

income Earnings on U.S. investments abroad less payments on foreign investments in the United States; also includes the net compensation of employees. (*Chapter 17*)

income effect A decrease in the price of a good creates an increase in the purchasing power of consumers' money incomes. (*Chapter 2*)

increasing marginal returns The marginal product of an added worker increases the marginal product of the first worker, thereby increasing returns to the firm. (*Chapter 4*)

independent variable A variable that initiates change in other variables. (*Chapter 1*)

inefficiency The failure of an economy to realize the output potential of its production possibilities curve. (*Chapter 1*)

inelastic demand The percentage change in quantity demanded is smaller than the percentage change in price. (*Chapter 3*)

infant industry argument An argument for tariff protection contending that in order for free trade to be meaningful, trading nations should temporarily shield their newly developing industries from foreign competition. (*Chapter 16*)

inferior good A good for which demand falls as consumer income rises, such as secondhand appliances or inexpensive cuts of meat. (*Chapter 2*)

inflation A sustained or continuous rise in the general price level. (*Chapter 11*)

infrastructure   Public capital, including roads, bridges, airports, and utilities. (*Chapter 10*)

International Monetary Fund (IMF)   A source of aid to developing countries; a bank for the central banks of member nations. (*Chapter 18*)

inverse relationship   A relationship in which two variables show a negative relationship to each other—that is, as one variable increases (decreases), the other decreases (increases). (*Chapter 1*)

k

Keynes, John Maynard   British economist who theorized that the market economy is inherently unstable; the level of economic activity depends on the total spending of consumers, businesses, and government; the government must intervene to protect jobs and income. (*Chapter 12*)

l

Laffer curve   Named after Arthur Laffer, a graphical representation of the relationship between the income tax rate that a government imposes and the total tax revenues that the government collects. (*Chapter 13*)

laissez-faire economy   The extreme case of a market economy in which the government has almost no economic role except to protect private property and provide a legal system that allows free markets. (*Chapter 18*)

law of demand   The principle that price and quantity demanded are inversely (negatively) related, assuming that all other factors affecting the quantity demanded remain the same. (*Chapter 2*)

law of diminishing marginal returns   The principle that explains the decline in the marginal product curve; after some point, the marginal product diminishes as additional units of a variable resource are added to a fixed resource. (*Chapter 4*)

law of increasing opportunity cost   The principle that opportunity costs increase as more of a good is produced. (*Chapter 1*)

law of supply   The principle that, in general, sellers are willing and able to make more of their product available at a higher price than at a lower price, all other determinants of supply being constant. (*Chapter 2*)

legal tender   All U.S. currency, including paper money and coins; the federal government mandates its acceptance in transactions and requires that dollars be used in the payment of taxes. (*Chapter 14*)

level playing field   The contention of domestic producers that import restrictions should be enacted to offset foreign advantages; all producers should compete on equal terms. (*Chapter 16*)

long run   Period during which all inputs are considered to be variable in amount; there are no fixed inputs. (*Chapter 4*)

long-run average total cost curve   A curve that shows the minimum cost per unit of producing each output level when any desired size of factory can be constructed. (*Chapter 4*)

losses   Negative profit, achieved when costs are greater than revenues. (*Chapter 4*)

m

M1 money supply   Money supply consisting of currency in the hands of the public, demand deposits, other checkable deposits, and traveler's checks; the narrowest definition of the U.S. money supply. (*Chapter 14*)

macroeconomics   The branch of economics that is concerned with the overall performance of the economy. (*Chapter 1*)

managed floating exchange rates   A system that allows the dollar to float in the foreign exchange market according to the market forces of demand and supply; central banks may try to stabilize exchange rates in the short run to provide financial security. (*Chapter 17*)

marginal cost   The change in total cost when one more unit of output is produced. (*Chapter 4*)

marginal product   The change in output that results from increasing the amount of labor by one unit, holding all other inputs fixed. (*Chapter 4*)

marginal product of labor   The additional output produced by hiring one more unit of labor. (*Chapter 7*)

marginal propensity to consume   The fraction of additional income that people spend. (*Chapter 12*)

marginal propensity to save   The fraction of additional income that is saved. (*Chapter 12*)

marginal revenue   The increase in total revenue resulting from the sale of another unit of output, calculated as total revenue divided by the change in quantity between any two points on the total revenue schedule. (*Chapter 5*)

marginal revenue = marginal cost rule   Total profit is maximized when marginal revenue is equal to marginal cost. (*Chapter 5*)

marginal tax rate   The fraction of additional income paid in taxes, calculated as the change in taxes due divided by the change in income. (*Chapter 9*)

market   Mechanism through which buyers (demanders) and sellers (suppliers) communicate in order to trade goods and services. (*Chapter 2*)

market economy   A free-enterprise system that is rooted in private property and markets; also called capitalism. (*Chapter 18*)

market equilibrium   A situation that occurs when the price of a product adjusts so that the quantity consumers will purchase at that price is identical to the quantity suppliers will sell; the point at which the forces of demand and supply are balanced. (*Chapter 2*)

market failure   A situation that occurs when a market fails to allocate resources efficiently. (*Chapter 8*)

mediation   A process whereby an outside party is called in to help resolve disagreements between labor and management. (*Chapter 7*)

Medicare   A federal government health insurance program whose objective is to reduce the financial burden of illness on the elderly. (*Chapter 9*)

medium of exchange   A function of money; something that people are willing to accept in payment for goods and services. (*Chapter 14*)

merger   A practice in which firms combine under a single ownership or control; the merged firm is larger, and therefore it may realize economies of scale as output expands and usually has a greater ability to control the market price of its product. (*Chapter 6*)

microeconomics   The branch of economics that focuses on the choices made by households and firms and the effects those choices have on particular markets. (*Chapter 1*)

minimum wage   The smallest amount of money per hour that an employer can legally pay a worker. (*Chapter 7*)

mixed economy   An economy that has elements of both market and command economies. (*Chapter 9 and Chapter 18*)

models   Simplified representations of the real world that we use to help us understand, explain, and predict economic phenomena in the real world; also called theories. (*Chapter 1*)

monetary policy   Changing the economy's money supply in order to help the economy achieve maximum output and employment and stable prices; carried out by the Federal Reserve. (*Chapter 15*)

money   The set of assets in the economy that people use regularly to purchase goods and services from other people; functions as a medium of exchange, a unit of account, and a store of value. (*Chapter 14*)

money multiplier   The maximum amount of money that the banking system can generate with each dollar of reserves; the reciprocal of the required reserve ratio. (*Chapter 14*)

money order   A form of payment that serves the same function as a personal check; can be issued by businesses other than banks; usually issued in smaller amounts and at a lower cost than cashier's checks. (*Chapter 14*)

monopolistic competition   The market structure that is closest to perfect competition; this structure is based on a large number of firms, each firm having a relatively small share of the total market. (*Chapter 6*)

monopoly   A market structure characterized by a single supplier of a good or service for which there is no close substitute. (*Chapter 5*)

multiplier   The ratio of the change in national output to the change in aggregate demand; indicates the extent to which the change in aggregate demand is "multiplied" into changes in larger output and income. (*Chapter 12*)

multiplier effect   The result of changes in aggregate demand caused by the multiplier; an improvement in economic activity in one sector of the economy multiplies as it flows through the economy. (*Chapter 12*)

n

national sales tax   A proposed alternative to the current federal income tax system; this system would entail a federal consumption tax collected at the retail level by businesses. (*Chapter 9*)

natural monopoly   A market structure in which one firm can supply a product to the entire market at a lower cost per unit than could be achieved by two or more firms each supplying only some of it. (*Chapter 5*)

natural rate of unemployment   The level of unemployment at which there is no cyclical unemployment; the sum of frictional unemployment and structural unemployment. (*Chapter 11*)

negotiable order of withdrawal (NOW) account   A type of checking account that pays interest but typically requires a larger minimum balance. (*Chapter 14*)

net exports   Sales of a country's goods and services to foreigners during a particular time period minus purchases of foreign-produced goods and services by that country's residents—in other words, exports minus imports. (*Chapter 10*)

nominal GDP   Gross domestic product expressed in terms of the prices existing in the year in which the goods and services were produced; also known as current-dollar GDP. (*Chapter 10*)

nominal income   The actual number of dollars of income received during a year. (*Chapter 11*)

nominal interest rate   The interest rate that a bank pays. (*Chapter 11*)

normal good   A good that is purchased more often as consumer income rises, such as a ski trip or a new car. (*Chapter 2*)

normal profit   The minimum profit necessary to keep a firm in operation; normal profit occurs when total revenue just covers the sum of explicit and implicit costs; zero economic profit. (*Chapter 4*)

normative economics   A term used to describe economic value judgments that cannot be tested empirically. (*Chapter 1*)

North American Free Trade Agreement (NAFTA)   A pact approved in 1993 by the governments of the United States, Canada, and Mexico to remove trade restrictions among them. (*Chapter 16*)

o

oligopoly   A form of imperfect competition in which a small number of firms compete with one another, and each firm has significant price-making ability. (*Chapter 6*)

open market operations   The purchase or sale of securities by the Federal Reserve; transactions made with a bank or some other business or individual but not directly with the federal government; the most useful and important policy tool of the Fed. (*Chapter 15*)

operational lag   The time it takes for a fiscal policy, once enacted, to be put into operation. (*Chapter 13*)

opportunity cost   The value of the best alternative sacrificed; the cost of any particular economic choice. (*Chapter 1*)

Organization of Petroleum Exporting Countries (OPEC)   A group of nations that sells oil on the world market; the best-known cartel. (*Chapter 6*)

outsourcing   Contracting out functions that once were done in-house. (*Chapter 7*)

p

partnership   A form of business organization in which two or more owners pool their financial resources and business skills. (*Chapter 9*)

peak   The phase of a business cycle when real GDP is at a temporary high and employment and profits are strong. (*Chapter 11*)

peak-load pricing   A pricing strategy whereby consumers pay more for electricity used during periods of peak energy demand and less for electricity used during off-peak periods. (*Chapter 8*)

perfect competition   A market characterized by insignificant barriers to entry or exit, many sellers and buyers, a standardized product produced by firms in the industry, and perfect information; the most competitive market structure. (*Chapter 5*)

personal consumption expenditures   Purchases of final goods and services by households and individuals. (*Chapter 10*)

personal distribution of income   Distribution showing how the nation's income is shared by households; it indicates the share of before-tax annual money income received. (*Chapter 9*)

positive economics   A term used to describe the facts of the economy, dealing with the way in which the economy works. (*Chapter 1*)

price ceiling   The government-imposed maximum legal price that a seller may charge for a product. (*Chapter 3*)

price discrimination   The practice of charging some customers a lower price than others for an identical good, even though there is no difference in the cost to the firm for supplying these consumers. (*Chapter 6*)

price elasticity of demand   A formula that measures how responsive, or sensitive, buyers are to a change in price. (*Chapter 3*)

price floor   A government-imposed price that prevents prices from falling below a legally mandated level. (*Chapter 3*)

price index   A mechanism used to adjust GDP figures so that the figures only show changes in actual output. (*Chapter 10*)

price taker   A firm that has to "take," or accept, the price established by the market; a perfectly competitive firm. (*Chapter 5*)

private goods   Goods that are produced through the market system; private goods are divisible subject to the exclusion principle and to the principle of rival consumption. (*Chapter 8*)

privatization   The process of turning public firms or enterprises into private ones in order to promote competition. (*Chapter 5*)

product differentiation   The fundamental characteristic of monopolistic competition; the assumption that the product of each firm is not a perfect substitute for the products of competing firms. (*Chapter 6*)

production   The use of resources to make outputs of goods and services available for human wants. (*Chapter 4*)

production function   The relationship between physical output and the quantity of resources used in the production process. (*Chapter 4*)

production possibilities curve   A graphical illustration of the maximum combinations of two goods that an economy can produce, given its available resources and technology. (*Chapter 1*)

productivity   A ratio that measures the quantity of output produced relative to the amount of work required to produce it; total output divided by hours worked. (*Chapter 10*)

profit   The difference between the amount of revenues a firm takes in (total revenue) and the amount it spends for wages, materials, electricity, and so on (total cost). (*Chapter 4*)

public goods   Goods such as national defense, highways, lighthouses, and air-traffic control; goods that are indivisible and are not subject to the exclusion principle. (*Chapter 8*)

q

quantity supplied   The quantity of a good that is available at any given time or price, assuming that all of the other determinants of supply remain unchanged; a single point on a supply schedule. (*Chapter 2*)

quota   A physical restriction on the quantity of goods traded each year. (*Chapter 16*)

r

rate of economic growth   The percentage change in the level of economic activity from one year to the next. (*Chapter 10*)

real GDP   Nominal GDP adjusted to reflect only changes in output, not changes in prices; real GDP measures actual (real) production and shows how actual production—rather than the prices of what is produced—has changed; also known as constant-dollar GDP. (*Chapter 10*)

real income   The actual number of dollars received (nominal income) adjusted for any change in price; measures real purchasing power—that is, the amount of goods and services that can be purchased with nominal income. (*Chapter 11*)

real interest rate   The interest rate that is adjusted for inflation, calculated as the nominal interest rate minus the inflation rate. (*Chapter 11*)

recession   A period of significant decline in total output, income, employment, and trade that lasts from 6 months to a year and is marked by widespread contraction in many sectors in the economy; the phase of the business cycle that begins at a peak and ends at a trough. (*Chapter 11*)

recognition lag   The time between the beginning of inflation or recession and the recognition that it is actually occurring. (*Chapter 13*)

recovery   The phase of the business cycle when real GDP rises, industrial output expands, profits increase, and employment moves toward full employment; also called expansion. (*Chapter 11*)

rent controls   A mechanism used to protect low-income households from escalating rents caused by perceived housing shortages and to make housing more affordable to the poor. (*Chapter 3*)

required reserve ratio   A specific percentage of checking deposits that must be kept either as vault cash or as deposits at the Federal Reserve; directly limits the ability of banks to grant new loans; established by the Federal Reserve System. (*Chapter 14*)

required reserves   The minimum amount of vault cash and deposits at the Federal Reserve that a bank must maintain. (*Chapter 14*)

reserves   Deposits that banks have received but have not lent out; can be kept either in vault cash or as deposits at a Federal Reserve Bank. (*Chapter 14*)

rule of 70   An indicator of the power of growth rates, determined by dividing 70 by the growth rate; indicates the number of years it will take for the level of real GDP to double. (*Chapter 10*)

S

Say's Law   A law attributed to 19th-century economist Jean-Baptiste Say according to which supply creates its own demand; whatever is produced (supplied) will create the income necessary to purchase the product; therefore, overproduction is not possible. (*Chapter 12*)

scarcity   The principle that there are not enough—nor can there ever be enough—goods and services to satisfy the wants and needs of everyone. (*Chapter 1*)

services   Work done by doctors, dentists, lawyers, engineers, accountants, and the like for consumers. (*Chapter 17*)

Sherman Act of 1890   The cornerstone of federal antitrust law; the act prohibits contracts and conspiracies in the restraint of trade, as well as monopolization and the threat of monopolization of an industry. (*Chapter 8*)

shock effect   An assumption whereby the minimum wage leads to an increase in the demand for labor, thus moderating some unemployment. (*Chapter 7*)

short run   Period during which the quantity of at least one input is fixed and the quantities of other inputs can be varied. (*Chapter 4*)

shortage   The amount by which the quantity demanded exceeds the quantity supplied; excess demand. (*Chapter 2*)

shut-down rule   In the short run, a firm should continue to produce if total revenue exceeds total variable cost; otherwise, it should shut down. (*Chapter 5*)

slope   On a graph, the vertical distance between two points (the "rise") divided by the horizontal distance between the two points (the "run"). (*Chapter 1*)

social regulation   Government regulation that is intended to correct a variety of undesirable side effects in a market economy that relate to health, safety, and the environment; examples include the regulations imposed by the Environmental Protection Agency, the Food and Drug Administration, and the Occupational Safety and Health Administration. (*Chapter 8*)

Social Security   The largest retirement and disability program in the United States, created as a means of providing income security upon retirement to people who would not otherwise have that form of security; also known as Old-Age, Survivors, and Disability Insurance. (*Chapter 9*)

socialism   An economic system in which the government is actively involved in the economy and an overall economic plan is formulated by manufacturers, farmers, workers, and government officials working together. (*Chapter 18*)

sole proprietorship   A firm that is owned and operated by one individual. (*Chapter 9*)

spillover   A cost or benefit imposed on people other than the producers and consumers of a good or service; also called an externality. (*Chapter 8*)

spillover benefit   A desirable spillover or externality; a benefit imposed on people other than the producers and consumers of a good. (*Chapter 8*)

spillover cost   An undesirable spillover or externality; a cost imposed on people other than the producers and consumers of a good. (*Chapter 8*)

stagflation   A decline in aggregate supply that results in falling output, increased unemployment, and rising prices; recession (stagnation) with inflation. (*Chapter 12*)

statistical discrepancy   An adjustment for measurement errors that is reported in the capital account component of the balance of payments. (*Chapter 17*)

store of value   A function of money; the ability to save money and then use it to make future purchases. (*Chapter 14*)

strikes   Work stoppages called by a majority of the voting members of a union; strikes occur when workers feel that stopping work is the best way to pressure their employer into granting their demands. (*Chapter 7*)

structural unemployment   Unemployment that occurs when individuals' skills do not match what employers require or when job seekers are geographically separated from job opportunities. (*Chapter 11*)

substitute goods   Goods for which a reduction in the price of one good will decrease the demand for the other good; conversely, an increase in the price of one good will increase the demand for the other good. (*Chapter 2*)

substitution effect   When the price of a good falls—and all other determinants of demand remain the same—the price falls relative to the prices of all other similar goods. (*Chapter 2*)

supply   A schedule that shows the amount of a good or service that a firm or household is willing and able to sell at each possible price during a particular period. (*Chapter 2*)

supply curve   A graphical representation of a market supply schedule; a line showing the quantities of a good or service that are supplied at various prices. (*Chapter 2*)

supply shifter   A change in a variable that causes a shift in a supply curve. (*Chapter 2*)

surplus   The amount by which the quantity supplied exceeds the quantity demanded; excess supply. (*Chapter 2*)

t

tariff   A tax imposed on imports. (*Chapter 16*)

taxable income   Gross income minus exemptions, deductions, and credits. (*Chapter 9*)

theories   Simplified representations of the real world that we use to help us understand, explain, and predict economic phenomena in the real world; also called models. (*Chapter 1*)

total cost   The sum of the value of all resources used over a given period to manufacture a good; the sum of total fixed cost and total variable cost. (*Chapter 4*)

total fixed cost   The sum of all costs that do not vary with output; also called overhead cost. (*Chapter 4*)

total product   The maximum quantity of output that can be produced from a given amount of inputs. (*Chapter 4*)

total revenue Dollars earned by sellers of a product, calculated by multiplying the quantity sold over a period by the price. (*Chapter 3 and Chapter 5*)

total variable cost   The sum of all costs that change as the rate of output varies; total variable cost depends on weekly or monthly output. (*Chapter 4*)

transfer payments   Payments of income (such as unemployment compensation or Medicaid) from taxpayers to individuals who make no contribution to current output for these payments. (*Chapter 9*)

traveler's checks   Checks that are usually issued in $20, $50, $100, and $500 denominations; they are used by travelers to protect against loss or theft and are widely accepted both in the United States and abroad. (*Chapter 14*)

trough   The phase of the business cycle when real GDP is at a low point, just before it begins to turn upward, and unemployment and idle productive capacity are at their highest levels. (*Chapter 11*)

u

underground economy   Unreported barter and cash transactions that take place outside recorded market channels. (*Chapter 10*)

unemployed   Individuals who do not have jobs but are actively seeking work. (*Chapter 11*)

unemployment insurance   The system that helps support consumer spending during periods of job loss and provides economic security to workers through income maintenance; established as part of the Social Security Act of 1935. (*Chapter 11*)

unemployment rate   The number of people unemployed divided by the labor force (the number of people holding or seeking jobs). (*Chapter 11*)

unilateral transfers   A component of the current account; gifts that include transfers of goods and services or money between the United States and the rest of the world for which nothing is given in exchange. (*Chapter 17*)

union shop   A workplace in which employees are required to join the recognized union within a specified length of time after their employment with the firm begins; each state may accept or reject union shops. (*Chapter 7*)

unions   Organizations that allow their members to sell their services collectively, thus giving the members more bargaining power than they would have if they acted individually. (*Chapter 7*)

unit elastic demand   The percentage change in quantity demanded equals the percentage change in price. (*Chapter 3*)

unit of account   A function of money; allows consumers to compare the relative values of goods; a measure that specifies price. (*Chapter 14*)

V

value of the marginal product of a worker   The increase in revenue that results from hiring an additional worker; the dollar value of a worker's contribution to production. (*Chapter 7*)

value–added tax (VAT)   A proposed substitute for the current federal tax system; a tax that would be collected at the various stages of production of goods and services. (*Chapter 9*)

variable input   Resources (such as labor and materials) whose quantities can be altered in the short run. (*Chapter 4*)

vertical merger   A merger between firms that are in the same industry but at different stages in the production process. (*Chapter 6*)

vicious circle of poverty   A cycle in which developing nations cannot break out of low standards of living. (*Chapter 18*)

W

World Bank   An international organization that provides loans to developing countries aimed toward poverty reduction and economic development. (*Chapter 18*)

World Trade Organization (WTO)   An organization whose 148 members acknowledge that tariff reductions agreed to by any two nations will be extended to all other members; encourages a gradual relaxation of tariffs throughout the world. (*Chapter 16*)

Index

Page numbers in *italics* indicate illustrations